ERP Baan IV Documentation Common Module

by

G. John Sagmiller

* * * * *

PUBLISHED BY:

Freedom of Speech Publishing, Inc.

* * * * *

ERP Baan IV Document

ERP Baan IV Document   By G. John Sagmiller. Certified in Baan. My Documents and notes I used as a Baan and LN consultant for over 15 years Infor and BAAN ERP system information.

* * * * *

ERP Baan IV Document -Baan 4 documentation

How to and how it works. My notes from over 15 Years.

By G. John Sagmiller. Certified in Baan. My Documents and notes I used as a Baan and LN consultant for over 15 years.   Infor and BAAN ERP system information.

Common
BAAN Common
MCS - Tables
COM - Common Data
COV - Conversion to BAAN IV
EDI - Electronic Data Interchange
GLO - Global Localization
QMS - Quality Management System

```
***********************************************************************
Module Descriptions

Common
COM - Common Data
EDI - Electronic Data Interchange
MCS - Master Data and System Tables
QMS - Quality Management System
Constraint Planning
CLP - Cyclic Planning
RMP - Resource Master Planning
RPU - Resource Plan Units
RPD - Resource Planning Data
Distribution
CMS - Commission and Rebate Control System
INV - Inventory Control
ILC - Location Control
LTC - Lot Control
PUR - Purchase Control
PSC - Supply Chain Purchase Schedule Control
PST - Purchase Statistics
RPL - Replenishment Order Control
SMI - Sales and Marketing Information
SLS - Sales Control
SSC - Supply Chain Sales Schedule Control
SST - Sales Statistics
Finance
ACP - Accounts Payable
ACR - Accounts Receivable
CMG - Cash Management
CAL - Cost Allocation
FBS - Financial Budget System
Financial Integration
FST -Financial Statements
FAS - Fixed Assets
GLD - General Ledger
SBI -Supply Chain Self - Billed Invoicing
Manufacturing
BOM - Bill of Material Control
CRP -Capacity Requirements Planning
CPR - Cost Accounting
EDM - Engineering Data Management
HRA - Hours Accounting
ITM - Item Control
MPS - Master Production Scheduling
MRP - Material Requirements Planning
PCS Budgets
PCS Projects
GRT - Product Classification
PCF - Product Configuration
RPT - Repetitive Manufacturing
ROU -Routing
SFC - Shop Floor Control
Orgware
BRG - BAAN IV b Enterprise Modeler
BRG - BAAN IV c Enterprise Modeler
Target User Manual
Workflow Management System
Process
FRM -Formula Management
PMG - Production Management
ROU - Process Routing
Project
```

PTC - Project Budget
PDM - Project Data Management
BOP - Project Estimating
HRS - Project Hours Accounting
PIN - Project Invoicing
PPC-2 - Project Monitoring
PSS-1 - Project Planning
PPC - Project Progress
PSS - Project Requirements
Service
SMA - Service & Maintenance - Service Analysis
Service with ILC
Tools
Administration
CHM - Chart Manager
CMT - Component Merge Tool
Customization and development - general data
Forms
Graphical User Interface (GUI)
Graphical User Interface Reference
Installation Concepts
Menus
Programming
Queries
Reports
User Interface
Transportation
ACS - Address Control
CDE - Central Data Entry
DRP - Distribution Requirements Planning
ECS - Employee Control System
ICS - Invoice Control System
PAC - Packing Control
TCD - Transport Common Data
TCO - Transport Costing
TFM -Transport Fleet Management
TFC - Transport Fuel Control
TOC - Transport Order Control
TOD - Transport Order Documents
TOH - Transport Order History
TOP - Transport Order Planning
TRC - Transport Rate Control
Utilities
XCH - Exchange BAAN IVc

Common

BAAN Common

1   General
OBJECTIVE OF THIS PACKAGE
The BAAN Common package allows you to maintain the common master data. This data
is used by all the BAAN IV packages.
2   Related B-Objects

Seq. No.	B-Object	Description	B-Object Usage
1	tc tc-proc	Common Procedures	Mandatory child
1	tc mcs10010	Tables (MCS)	Mandatory child
2	tc com10010	Common Data (COM)	Mandatory child
3	tc par00010	TRITON Common Parameters	Mandatory child
4	tc tc-00090	BAAN Common Error Recovery	Mandatory child
5	tc mcs00090	System Performance	Mandatory child

MCS - Tables

1   **Tables (MCS)**
1.1 General
OBJECTIVE OF THIS MODULE
This module allows you to initialize the package and control the 30 or so
tables. You initialize the package by setting a number of parameters. The tables
contain one or more (alphanumeric) codes to which data is linked consisting of
descriptions and values. As this information is frequently used in the system it
must be fully and carefully defined.
1.2 Related B-Objects

Seq. No.	B-Object	Description	B-Object Usage
1	tc mcs00010	Logistic Tables	Optional child
2	tc mcs00020	Financial Tables	Optional child
3	tc mcs00090	System Performance	Optional child

2   Introduction to Logistic Tables
2.1 General
OBJECTIVE OF BUSINESS OBJECT
This b-object allows you to control all sorts of data relating to the logistical
functions in the BAAN IV packages.
SEE ALSO METHOD(S)
•   Table Coding
2.2 Session Overview

Seq.	Session	Description	Session Usage
1	tcmcs0145m000	Maintain Areas	Mandatory
2	tcmcs0128m000	Maintain Commodity Codes	Mandatory
3	tcmcs0110m000	Maintain Countries	Mandatory
4	tcmcs0147m000	Maintain First Free Numbers	Mandatory
5	tcmcs0180m000	Maintain Forwarding Agents	Mandatory
6	tcmcs0123m000	Maintain Item Groups	Mandatory
7	tcmcs0146m000	Maintain Languages	Mandatory
8	tcmcs0131m000	Maintain Lines of Business	Mandatory
9	tcmcs0124m000	Maintain Price Groups	Mandatory
10	tcmcs0134m000	Maintain Price Lists	Mandatory
11	tcmcs0105m000	Maintain Reasons for Rejection	Mandatory

12	tcmcs0115m000	Maintain Product Types	Mandatory
13	tcmcs0104m000	Maintain Routes	Mandatory
14	tcmcs0116m000	Maintain Seasonal Patterns	Mandatory
15	tcmcs0122m000	Maintain Selection Codes	Mandatory
16	tcmcs0118m000	Maintain Signal Codes	Mandatory
17	tcmcs0144m000	Maintain Statistics Groups	Mandatory
18	tcmcs0141m000	Maintain Terms of Delivery	Mandatory
19	tcmcs0119m000	Maintain Titles	Mandatory
20	tcmcs0101m000	Maintain Units	Mandatory
21	tcmcs0107m000	Maintain Units by Language	Mandatory
22	tcmcs0106m000	Maintain Unit Sets	Mandatory
23	tcmcs0112m000	Maintain Units by Unit Set	Mandatory
24	tcmcs0103m000	Maintain Warehouses	Mandatory
26	tcmcs0197m000	Maintain Use of Performance Boosters	Mandatory
27	tcmcs0129m000	Maintain Quality Groups	Mandatory
28	tcmcs0130m000	Maintain Skills	Mandatory
101	tcmcs0445m000	Print Areas	Print
102	tcmcs0428m000	Print Commodity Codes	Print
103	tcmcs0410m000	Print Countries	Print
104	tcmcs0447m000	Print First Free Numbers	Print
105	tcmcs0480m000	Print Forwarding Agents	Print
106	tcmcs0423m000	Print Item Groups	Print
107	tcmcs0446m000	Print Languages	Print
108	tcmcs0431m000	Print Lines of Business	Print
109	tcmcs0424m000	Print Price Groups	Print
110	tcmcs0434m000	Print Price Lists	Print
111	tcmcs0405m000	Print Reasons for Rejection	Print
112	tcmcs0415m000	Print Product Types	Print
113	tcmcs0404m000	Print Routes	Print
114	tcmcs0416m000	Print Seasonal Patterns	Print
115	tcmcs0422m000	Print Selection Codes	Print

```
| 116 | tcmcs0418m000 | Print Signal Codes              | Print
|
| 117 | tcmcs0444m000 | Print Statistics Groups         | Print
|
| 118 | tcmcs0441m000 | Print Terms of Delivery         | Print
|
| 119 | tcmcs0419m000 | Print Titles                    | Print
|
| 120 | tcmcs0401m000 | Print Units                     | Print
|
| 121 | tcmcs0407m000 | Print Units by Language         | Print
|
| 122 | tcmcs0406m000 | Print Unit Sets                 | Print
|
| 123 | tcmcs0412m000 | Print Units by Unit Set         | Print
|
| 124 | tcmcs0403m000 | Print Warehouses                | Print
|
| 125 | tcmcs0429m000 | Print Quality Groups            | Print
|
| 126 | tcmcs0430m000 | Print Skills                    | Print
|
| 201 | tcmcs0545m000 | Display Areas                   | Display
|
| 202 | tcmcs0528m000 | Display Commodity Codes         | Display
|
| 203 | tcmcs0510m000 | Display Countries               | Display
|
| 204 | tcmcs0547m000 | Display First Free Numbers      | Display
|
| 205 | tcmcs0580m000 | Display Forwarding Agents       | Display
|
| 206 | tcmcs0523m000 | Display Item Groups             | Display
|
| 207 | tcmcs0546m000 | Display Languages               | Display
|
| 208 | tcmcs0531m000 | Display Lines of Business       | Display
|
| 209 | tcmcs0524m000 | Display Price Groups            | Display
|
| 210 | tcmcs0534m000 | Display Price Lists             | Display
|
| 211 | tcmcs0505m000 | Display Reasons for Rejection   | Display
|
| 212 | tcmcs0515m000 | Display Product Types           | Display
|
| 213 | tcmcs0504m000 | Display Routes                  | Display
|
| 214 | tcmcs0516m000 | Display Seasonal Patterns       | Display
|
| 215 | tcmcs0522m000 | Display Selection Codes         | Display
|
| 216 | tcmcs0518m000 | Display Signal Codes            | Display
|
| 217 | tcmcs0544m000 | Display Statistics Groups       | Display
|
| 218 | tcmcs0541m000 | Display Terms of Delivery       | Display
|
| 219 | tcmcs0519m000 | Display Titles                  | Display
|
| 220 | tcmcs0501m000 | Display Units                   | Display
|
```

221	tcmcs0507m000	Display Units by Language	Display
222	tcmcs0506m000	Display Unit Sets	Display
223	tcmcs0512m000	Display Units by Unit Set	Display
224	tcmcs0503m000	Display Warehouses	Display
225	tcmcs0529m000	Display Quality Groups	Display
226	tcmcs0530m000	Display Skills	Display
999	tcmcs0119s000	Maintain Titles	Optional
999	tcmcs0503s000	Display Warehouse List	Display
999	tcmcs0539s000	Display Order Steps	Display
999	tcmcs0542s000	Display Order Types	Display
999	tcmcs0642s000	Display Order Steps (Procedure)	Display

---

3 Mandatory Sessions

3.1 Maintain Areas (tcmcs0145m000)

SESSION OBJECTIVE
To define the geographical areas used in other sessions.
SEE ALSO KEYWORD(S)
• Areas

```
tcmcs0145m000                          multi-occ (2)    Form 1-1
+----------------------------------------------------------------------+
| Maintain Areas                                      Company: 000 |
|----------------------------------------------------------------------|
|                                                                      |
| Area  Description                                                    |
|                                                                      |
|   1.. 2............................                                  |
|                                                                      |
+----------------------------------------------------------------------+
```

1. Area
For further information, see keyword(s)
"Areas".
2. Description
Enter a clear description here.

3.2 Maintain Commodity Codes (tcmcs0128m000)

SESSION OBJECTIVE
To define the commodity codes used in other sessions.
SEE ALSO KEYWORD(S)
• Commodity Codes

```
tcmcs0128m000                          multi-occ (2)    Form 1-1
+----------------------------------------------------------------------+
| Maintain Commodity Codes                            Company: 000 |
|----------------------------------------------------------------------|
|                                                                      |
| Commodity Code  Description                                          |
|                                                                      |
|      1....... 2............................                          |
|                                                                      |
+----------------------------------------------------------------------+
```

1. Commodity Code
For further information, see keyword(s)
"Commodity Codes".
2. Description

Enter a clear description here.
3.3   Maintain Countries (tcmcs0110m000)
SESSION OBJECTIVE
To maintain countries.
SEE ALSO KEYWORD(S)
• Countries

```
+----------------------------------------------------------------------+
| Maintain Countries                                    Company: 000 |
|----------------------------------------------------------------------|
|                                                                      |
| Code Description                 ICC Telephone Telex  Fax    EU Member |
|                                                                      |
|                                                                      |
| 1.. 2............................ 3.. 4.....   5..... 6..... 7....   |
|                                                                      |
+----------------------------------------------------------------------+
```
1.   Country
The code by which the country is recognized in BAAN IV.
2.   Description
Enter a clear description here.
3.   ICC
The international country code is an informative field.
4.   Telephone
The international access number for the telephone of the country.
5.   Telex
The international access number for the telex of the country.
6.   Fax
The international access number for the fax of the country.
7.   EU Member State
Here you can indicate if the country is an EU member state.

```
+----------------------------------------------------------------------+
| Maintain Countries                                    Company: 000 |
|----------------------------------------------------------------------|
|                                                                      |
| Code  GEO Country Code   Print      Print Tax       Print Tax       |
|                          Line Tax   by Tax Authority Exemption      |
|                                                                      |
| 1..  2..               3....    4....           5....           |
|                                                                      |
+----------------------------------------------------------------------+
```
1.   Country
The code by which the country is recognized in BAAN IV.
2.   GEO Country Code
The GEO Country Code is used in the European Intrastat tax statement. If no GEO
country code is entered, the normal country code will be used.
3.   Print Line Tax
Using this parameter, you can determine how tax amounts are printed on order
documents.
Yes
If using a tax provider, tax amounts are printed by line on the order document,
in addition to the total tax amounts printed on the footer of the document.
No
Only the total tax amounts are printed on the footer of the order document.
See also help about Global Localisation (Tax Provider).
4.   Print Tax by Tax Authority
Using this parameter, you can determine how tax amounts are printed on order
documents.
Yes
In addition to the total tax amounts printed in the footer of the document, tax
amounts by tax authority are printed on the order document.
No

Only the total tax amounts are printed on the footer of the order document.
See also help about Global Localisation (Tax Provider).
5.   Print Tax Exemption
Yes
If not using the tax provider, tax exemption certificate numbers are printed on
the order document.
No
Tax exemption certificate numbers are not printed on the order document.
See also help about Global Localisation (Tax Provider).
3.4   Maintain First Free Numbers (tcmcs0147m000)
SESSION OBJECTIVE
To define the first free number for each number type. This allows orders to be
arranged in groups.
SEE ALSO KEYWORD(S)
•   First Free Numbers

```
tcmcs0147m000                            multi/group (3     Form 1-1
+----------------------------------------------------------------------+
|  Maintain First Free Numbers                          Company: 000   |
|----------------------------------------------------------------------|
|                                                                      |
|  Type of Number: 1.......................                            |
|                                                                      |
|   Se-           Description              First Free Blocked for Def.Fin. |
|   ries                                   Number Input      Company   |
|                                                                      |
|        2..  3.......................     4....... 5....         6..  |
|                                                                      |
+----------------------------------------------------------------------+
```

1.   Type of Number
The following values are possible:
Purchase Order *
•   Confirm Planned INV Purchase Orders (tdinv3220m000)
•   Maintain Purchase Orders (tdpur4101m000)
Production Order *
•   Maintain Production Orders (tisfc0101m000)
Sales Order *
•   Maintain Sales Orders (tdsls4101m000)
•   Process Quotations (tdsls1202s000)
Sales Quotation *
•   Maintain Quotations (tdsls1101m000)
Purchase Invoice *
•   Print Purchase Invoices (tdpur4404m000)
Sales Invoice *
•   Print Sales Invoices (tdsls4404m000)
Picking List (SLS Order)
•   Print Picking Lists (tdsls4402m000)
Packing Slip Sales Order
•   Print Packing Slips (tdsls4403m000)
Project
•   Maintain Projects (tipcs2101m000)
Product Variant
•   Maintain Product Variants (tipcf5101m000)
•   Product Configurator (tipcf5120s000)
Financial Document
Warehouse order
•   Enter Inventory Transactions (tdilc1120m000)
•   Generate Cycle Counting Orders (tdilc5210m000)
•   Enter Inventory Transactions by Item (tdinv1101m000)
•   Generate Cycle Counting Orders (tdinv1220m000)
Purchase Contract *
•   Maintain Purchase Contracts (tdpur3101m000)
•   Copy Purchase Contracts (tdpur3801m000)
Sales Contract *

- Maintain Sales Contracts (tdsls3101m000)
- Copy Sales Contracts (tdsls3801m000)

Purchase Inquiry *
- Maintain Inquiry Lines (tdpur1102s000)

Lot *
- Maintain Lots (tdltc0101m000)
- Copy Ranges of Lots (tdltc0103s000)
- Maintain Lot ID Structure (tdltc0105m000)
- Convert Non-Lot Item to Lot Item (tdltc0130m000)

Receipt *
- Maintain Receipts (tdpur4120m000)

Service Order *
- Maintain Service Orders (tssma3101m000)

Bill of Lading (Sales)
- Print Bills of Lading (tdsls4421m000)

Budget
- Maintain Budgets (tipcs0101m000)

Replenishment Order
- Maintain Replenishment Orders (tdrpl0110m000)

Picking List (RPL)
- Print Replenishment Order Picking Lists (tdrpl0412m000)

Packing Slip (RPL)
- Print Replenishment Order Packing Slips (tdrpl0416m000)

Bill of Lading (RPL)
- Maintain Replenishment Order Bills of Lading (tdrpl0118s000)

Transport Invoice
- Print Invoices (trics2400m000)

Transport Order
- Maintain Order Procedures (trtoc0130m000)
- Copy Sales Orders to Transport Orders (trtoc2200m000)

Inbound Order
Outbound Order
Assembly Order
Storage Order
Transhipment Order
ECO Order

For the options marked "*" you can define number series.

2. Series

A wide range of documents/orders etc. are numbered on the basis of the concept of predefined series (ranges) and first free numbers within those series. The series number can be used to distinguish between various types of orders, e.g.: national and international sales orders.

Length of series number (recorded in e.g. Maintain Sales Order Parameters (tdsls4100m000)): 2 digits. By reserving the first 2 digits of the order number for the series number, you can distinguish up to 99 different order types. The system automatically assigns the sequence number within every series (e.g. 10 0001 = sequence number 1 within series 10). A number of types of first free numbers have a predetermined series numbering. You cannot change these or add a new series number to it. You can only change the description and the first free number.

You can enter the first free number for each series number. Using series numbers depends on initializing with the following parameters.

Adjusted in session:
- Parameter Description:

Maintain PCS Parameters (tipcs0100m000)
- Budget Series
- Project Series

Maintain Inquiry Parameters (tdpur1100m000)
- Series in Inquiry Numbering

Maintain Purchase Contract Parameters (tdpur3100m000)
- Series in Contract Numbering

Maintain Purchase Order Parameters (tdpur4100m000)
- Series in Order Numbering

- Series in Invoice Numbering
- Series in Receipt Numbering

Maintain SFC Parameters (tisfc0100m000)
- Series in Production Order Numbers

Maintain Quotation Parameters (tdsls1100m000)
- Series in Quotation Numbering

Maintain Sales Contract Parameters (tdsls3100m000)
- Series in Contract Numbering

Maintain Sales Order Parameters (tdsls4100m000)
- Series in Invoice Numbering
- Series in Sales Order Numbering

For these parameters, you may choose from the following:

No Series

The first free number indicates with which number the first order, quotation, or contract number must start. This number consists of six positions. When entering an order (for example), the system consults the table with numbers and assigns the first free number to the new order. As soon as a number has been used, the first free number is automatically raised by one.

One Digit

You can choose from the series numbers 0 through 9 and indicate the first free number for each series number. The series number is the first digit of the order, quotation, or contract number. When entering an order (for example), enter this series number first. For the remaining five positions of the number, the system consults the table with numbers and copies the first free number.

Two Digits

You can choose from series numbers 0 through 99 and indicate the first free number for each series number. The series number is the first two digits of the order, quotation or order number. When entering an order (for example), enter the series number first. For the remaining four positions, the system consults the table with numbers and copies the first free number to the series.

3.   Description

Enter a clear description here.

4.   First Free Number

For further information, see keyword(s) "First Free Numbers".

5.   Series Blocked   for Input   This field indicates if an order series must be blocked for
input. This may be of interest to reserve series for orders to be generated (e.g. EDI orders). Yes

The series is blocked for input.

No

The series is not blocked for input.

6.   Company

The default financial company number belonging to this series.

3.5   Maintain Forwarding Agents (tcmcs0180m000)

SESSION OBJECTIVE

To record the forwarding agents that can be selected in other sessions.

SEE ALSO KEYWORD(S)
- Forwarding Agents

tcmcs0180m000   multi-occ (2)   Form 1-1

```
+-------------------------------------------------------------------------+
| Maintain Forwarding Agents                               Company: 000   |
|-------------------------------------------------------------------------|
|                                                                         |
| Code     Description                      Supplier                      |
|                                                                         |
|    1..   2............................    3.....   4_____   |
|                                                                         |
+-------------------------------------------------------------------------+
```

1.   Forwarding Agent

For further information, see keyword(s) "Forwarding Agents".

2.   Description

Enter a clear description here.

3.   Supplier

The number uniquely identifying the supplier.

This supplier is used when copying Sales and Purchase Orders to Transport Orders.

When the forwarding agent has been filled in the Sales or Purchase order the supplier code is taken to create a subcontracting record for the generated transport order. The data to be entered must be defined in the session "Maintain Suppliers (tccom2101m000)".

4.   Name

The first part of the supplier's name.

3.6   Maintain Item Groups (tcmcs0123m000)

SESSION OBJECTIVE

To define the item groups used in other sessions.

SEE ALSO KEYWORD(S)

- Item Groups

```
tcmcs0123m000                                       multi-occ (2)    Form 1-1
+--------------------------------------------------------------------------+
| Maintain Item Groups                                       Company: 000  |
|--------------------------------------------------------------------------|
|                                                                          |
| Code     Description                                                     |
|                                                                          |
| 1.....   2............................                                   |
|                                                                          |
+--------------------------------------------------------------------------+
```

1.   Item Group

For further information, see keyword(s)
"Item Groups".

2.   Description

Enter a clear description here.

3.7   Maintain Languages (tcmcs0146m000)

SESSION OBJECTIVE

To record the languages used in other sessions.

SEE ALSO KEYWORD(S)

- Languages

```
tcmcs0146m000                                       multi-occ (2)    Form 1-1
+--------------------------------------------------------------------------+
| Maintain Languages                                         Company: 000  |
|--------------------------------------------------------------------------|
|                                                                          |
| Lang  Description                    System Language                     |
|                                                                          |
| 1..   2............................  3  4_____  |
|                                                                          |
+--------------------------------------------------------------------------+
```

1.   Language

For further information, see keyword(s)
"Languages".

2.   Description

Enter a clear description here.

3.   System Language

The system language of BAAN IV. On the basis of this system language, external documents are printed in another language.

The data to be entered must be defined in the session "Maintain Languages (ttaad1110m000)".

Some of the system languages are: 1   Dutch
                                     2   English
                                     3   German
                                     4   French

4.   Language Description

The description of the system language.

3.8   Maintain Lines of Business (tcmcs0131m000)

SESSION OBJECTIVE
To maintain lines of business.
SEE ALSO KEYWORD(S)
•   Lines of Business
tcmcs0131m000   multi-occ (2)   Form 1-1
+---+
Maintain Lines of Business   Company: 000
Line of Business   Description
1.....   2...........................
+---+
1.   Line of Business
For further information, see keyword(s)
"Lines of Business".
2.   Description
Enter a clear description here.
3.9   Maintain Price Groups (tcmcs0124m000)
SESSION OBJECTIVE
To define the price groups used in other sessions.
SEE ALSO KEYWORD(S)
•   Price Groups
tcmcs0124m000   multi-occ (2)   Form 1-1
+---+
Maintain Price Groups   Company: 000
Code   Description   Price Unit
1.....   2...........................   3..   4_____
+---+
1.   Price Group
For further information, see keyword(s)
"Price Groups".
2.   Description
Enter a clear description here.
3.   Price Unit
The unit of the discount grades for each price group. This unit appears as
information in sessions where you define discounts by price group.
The data to be entered must be defined in the session "Maintain Units
(tcmcs0101m000)".
4.   Description
3.10 Maintain Price Lists (tcmcs0134m000)
SESSION OBJECTIVE
To maintain price lists.
SEE ALSO KEYWORD(S)
•   Price Lists
tcmcs0134m000   multi-occ (2)   Form 1-1
+---+
Maintain Price Lists   Company: 000
Code   Description   Currency Description
1.. 2...........................   3.. 4_____
+---+
1.   Price List
For further information, see keyword(s)
"Price Lists".

2.   Description
Enter a clear description here.
3.   Currency
The code of the currency belonging to the price list code. A currency must be
recorded in each price list as prices can be stored by price list, item and item
group. Wherever prices are recorded, the associated currency should be
available.
The data to be entered must be defined in the session "Maintain Currencies
(tcmcs0102m000)".
4.   Description
3.11 Maintain Reasons for Rejection (tcmcs0105m000)
SESSION OBJECTIVE
To maintain reasons for rejection.
SEE ALSO KEYWORD(S)
•   Reasons for Rejection
tcmcs0105m000   multi-occ (2)   Form 1-1
+---+
Maintain Reasons for Rejection   Company: 000
Code   Description
1.. 2.............................
+---+
1.   Reason
For further information, see keyword(s)
"Reasons for Rejection".
2.   Description
Enter a clear description here.
3.12 Maintain Product Types (tcmcs0115m000)
SESSION OBJECTIVE
To maintain product types.
SEE ALSO KEYWORD(S)
•   Product Types
tcmcs0115m000   multi-occ (2)   Form 1-1
+---+
Maintain Product Types   Company: 000
Code   Description
1.. 2............................
+---+
1.   Product Type
For further information, see keyword(s)
"Product Types".
2.   Description
Enter a clear description here.
3.13 Maintain Routes (tcmcs0104m000)
SESSION OBJECTIVE
To maintain routes.
SEE ALSO KEYWORD(S)
•   Routes
tcmcs0104m000   multi-occ (2)   Form 1-1
+---+
Maintain Routes   Company: 000
Code   Description   Day
1.... 2................................ 3.............
+---+

```
|                                                                          |
+--------------------------------------------------------------------------+
1.      Route
For further information, see keyword(s)
"Routes".
2.      Description
Enter a clear description here.
3.      Day
The day on which the items must be delivered. This day is printed on picking
lists that are printed for sales orders using the session "Print Picking Lists
(tdsls4402m000)".
3.14  Maintain Seasonal Patterns (tcmcs0116m000)
SESSION OBJECTIVE
To maintain seasonal patterns.
HOW TO USE THE SESSION
The parameter "Period Length for Item History" (in the session "Maintain INV
Parameters (tdinv0100m000)") determines the number of seasonal factors.
SEE ALSO KEYWORD(S)
•       Seasonal Patterns
tcmcs0116m000                                   single-occ (1)    Form 1-1
+--------------------------------------------------------------------------+
|   Maintain Seasonal Patterns                            Company: 000   |
|--------------------------------------------------------------------------|
|                                                                          |
|    Seasonal Pattern    :   1..                                           |
|    Description         :   2...........................                  |
|                                                                          |
|    Seasonal Factor  (1): 3.                                              |
|                     (2): 3.                                              |
|                     (3): 3.                                              |
|                     (4): 3.                                              |
|                     (5): 3.                                              |
|                     (6): 3.                                              |
|                     (7): 3.                                              |
|                     (8): 3.                                              |
|                     (9): 3.                                              |
|                    (10): 3.                                              |
|                    (11): 3.                                              |
|                    (12): 3.                                              |
|                    (13): 3.                                              |
|                                                                          |
+--------------------------------------------------------------------------+
1.      Seasonal Pattern
For further information, see keyword(s)
"Seasonal Patterns".
2.      Description
Enter a clear description here.
3.      Seasonal Factor
The seasonal factors are the coefficients for each seasonal period. These
factors determine the increase and decrease of the safety stock or the expected
demand in a certain period.
3.15  Maintain Selection Codes (tcmcs0122m000)
SESSION OBJECTIVE
To define the selection criteria used in other sessions.
SEE ALSO KEYWORD(S)
•       Selection Codes
tcmcs0122m000                                   multi-occ (2)    Form 1-1
+--------------------------------------------------------------------------+
|   Maintain Selection Codes                              Company: 000   |
|--------------------------------------------------------------------------|
|                                                                          |
|    Code     Description                                                  |
|                                                                          |
```

```
|     1..  2........................                                      |
|                                                                         |
+-------------------------------------------------------------------------+
```
1.   Selection Code
For further information, see keyword(s)
"Selection Codes".
2.   Description
Enter a clear description here.
3.16 Maintain Signal Codes (tcmcs0118m000)
SESSION OBJECTIVE
To define define the signal codes used in other sessions.
SEE ALSO KEYWORD(S)
•   Signals
tcmcs0118m000   single-occ (1)   Form 1-1

```
+-------------------------------------------------------------------------+
| Maintain Signal Codes                              Company: 000 |
|-------------------------------------------------------------------------|
|                                                                         |
| Signal Code                 : 1..                                       |
|                                                                         |
| Description                 : 2...........................              |
|                                                                         |
| Blocking Status                                                         |
|                                                                         |
| Purchase                    : 3...........................              |
| Sales                       : 4...........................              |
| Requisition through Production: 5...........................            |
| Production Issue            : 6...........................              |
| Process Issue               : 7...........................              |
|                                                                         |
+-------------------------------------------------------------------------+
```

1.   Signal Code
For further information, see keyword(s)
"Signals".
2.   Description
Enter a clear description here.
3.   Purchase
This blocking status indicates if the item to which this signal code is linked
is free or blocked for purchase. Free
The item can be freely used in the module "Purchase Control (PUR)".
Blocked
As soon as you enter this item in e.g. the sessions "Maintain Purchase Contract
Lines (tdpur3102s000)" and "Maintain Purchase Order Lines (tdpur4102s000)", the
system will reject it.
4.   Sales
This blocking status indicates whether the item to which the concerned signal
code is linked is free of blocked for sales. Free
The item can be freely used in the module "Sales Control (SLS)".
Blocked
As soon as you enter this item in e.g. the sessions "Maintain Sales Contract
Lines (tdsls3102s000)" and "Maintain Sales Order Lines (tdsls4102s000)", the
system will reject it.
5.   Requisition through Production
This blocking status indicates whether the main item to which the concerned
signal code is linked is free or blocked for production orders.
Free
The item can be freely used in the module "Shop Floor Control (SFC)".
Blocked
As soon as you try to use this item in the session "Maintain Production Orders
(tisfc0101m000)", the system will refuse this. The modules generating
purchase/production advice (INV, MPS, MRP) likewise react to the signal code and
hence will not generate production orders for the item. By consulting the

exception messages in the module "Material Requirements Planning (MRP)" you can find out which signal code causes the item to be blocked.

6. Production Issue

This blocking status indicates whether the item to which the concerned signal code is linked is free or blocked for issue from a warehouse to a production order or to a project in BAAN Project.

Free

The item can be freely issued for production orders in the module "Shop Floor Control (SFC)", provided that acquisition via production is not blocked. The system also consults the blocking status when issuing materials from the warehouse to a project in the module "Planned Warehouse Orders".

Blocked

As soon as you try to use this item in the sessions, "Enter Material Issue for Production Orders (ticst0101m000)" and "Issue Inventory (tisfc0207m000)", the system will refuse this. The system will also refuse to issue materials in the sessions "Confirm Planned Warehouse Orders (tppss6225m000)" and "Transfer Planned Warehouse Orders (tppss6235m000)".

7. Process Issue

This blocking status indicates whether the item to which the concerned signal code is linked is free or blocked for issue from a warehouse to a production batch. Free

The item can be freely issued for production batches in the module "Production Management (PMG)", provided that acquisition via production is not blocked.

Blocked

As soon as you try to use this item in the session "Enter Material Issue for Production Batches (pspmg0111m000)", the system will refuse this.

3.17 Maintain Statistics Groups (tcmcs0144m000)

SESSION OBJECTIVE

To define the statistics groups used in other sessions.

SEE ALSO KEYWORD(S)

• Statistics Groups

tcmcs0144m000   multi-occ (2)   Form 1-1

```
+----------------------------------------------------------------------+
| Maintain Statistics Groups                            Company: 000   |
|----------------------------------------------------------------------|
| Code     Description                                                  |
|                                                                      |
| 1.....   2............................                                |
|                                                                      |
+----------------------------------------------------------------------+
```

1. Statistics Group

For further information, see keyword(s) "Statistics Groups".

2. Description

Enter a clear description here.

3.18 Maintain Terms of Delivery (tcmcs0141m000)

SESSION OBJECTIVE

To define the terms of delivery used in other sessions.

SEE ALSO KEYWORD(S)

• Terms of Delivery

tcmcs0141m000   single-occ (1)   Form 1-1

```
+----------------------------------------------------------------------+
| Maintain Terms of Delivery                            Company: 000   |
|----------------------------------------------------------------------|
|                                                                      |
| Code                 : 1..                                           |
|                                                                      |
| Description          : 2............................                 |
| Cash on Delivery     : 3....                                         |
| Carriage Paid        : 4....                                         |
| Point of Title PaBaange: 5..................                         |
| Text                 : 6____                                         |
|                                                                      |
```

```
+--------------------------------------------------------------------------+
```
1.   Terms of Delivery
For further information, see keyword(s)
"Terms of Delivery".
2.   Description
Enter a clear description here.
3.   Cash on Delivery
Cash on delivery means that goods are delivered on the condition that they are
paid for immediately on receipt. When purchase orders or sales orders are copied
to transport orders via the session "Copy Orders to BAAN Transportation
(trtoc2999m000)", the corresponding field on the transport order is filled with
the value selected here.
4.   Carriage Paid
Carriage paid means that the carriage or postage has been paid by the consignor.
When you copy purchase and sales orders to transport orders in the session "Copy
Orders to BAAN Transportation (trtoc2999m000)", the corresponding field on the
transport order is filled with the value selected here. This field also
determines who is to pay for the transport order line.
This field also determines who is to be billed for the transport order line.
Yes
The customer is the customer or supplier of the purchasing/sales department.
No
The customer is the customer or supplier of the purchase/sales order.
5.   Point of Title PaBaange
The point at which title passes, either origin or destination, is used by the
tax provider TAXWARE's Master Tax System to determine the taxing jurisdiction.
SEE ALSO METHOD(S)
•   Global Localisation (Tax Provider)
6.   Text

3.19 Maintain Titles (tcmcs0119m000)

SESSION OBJECTIVE
To maintain titles.
SEE ALSO KEYWORD(S)
•   Titles

tcmcs0119m000   multi-occ (2)   Form 1-1
```
+--------------------------------------------------------------------------+
|  Maintain Titles                                        Company: 000  |
|--------------------------------------------------------------------------|
|                                                                          |
|  Title    Description                                                     |
|                                                                          |
|     1..   2..........................                                     |
|                                                                          |
+--------------------------------------------------------------------------+
```
1.   Title
For further information, see keyword(s)
"Titles".
2.   Description
Enter a clear description here.

3.20 Maintain Units (tcmcs0101m000)

SESSION OBJECTIVE
To maintain units.
SEE ALSO KEYWORD(S)
•   Units

tcmcs0101m000   multi-occ (2)   Form 1-1
```
+--------------------------------------------------------------------------+
|  Maintain Units                                         Company: 000  |
|--------------------------------------------------------------------------|
|                                                                          |
|  Char    Description                   Physical        Rounding Factor   |
|  Unit                                  Quantity                          |
|                                                                          |
|  1..     2.............................  3.............    4...          |
```

```
|                                                                      |
+----------------------------------------------------------------------+
```
1.   Unit
For further information, see keyword(s)
"Units".
2.   Description
Enter a clear description here. For further information, see keyword(s)
"Units by Language".
3.   Physical Quantity
The physical quantity the unit belongs to.
4.   Rounding Factor
The rounding method indicates how quantities in this unit must be rounded. If
the system is to round to whole numbers, for instance, it will not accept the
input of fractions.
As long as a unit is used in the application, the rounding method can only be
modified to a limited extent: a change to a higher degree of precision will be
accepted, one to a lower degree of precision will not.
3.21 Maintain Units by Language (tcmcs0107m000)
SESSION OBJECTIVE
To maintain short language-dependent unit descriptions.
SEE ALSO KEYWORD(S)
•   Units by Language
tcmcs0107m000   multi/group (3   Form 1-1
```
+-----------------------------------------------------------------------+
|  Maintain Units by Language                           Company: 000  |
|---------------------------------------------------------------------|
|  Unit  : 1..   2_____                    |
|                                                                     |
|  Lang Description              Language-Specific      Short Unit     |
|                                Unit Description       Description    |
|                                                                     |
|   3.. 4_____    5........................... 6....    |
|                                                                     |
+-----------------------------------------------------------------------+
```
1.   Unit
The unit for which foreign language descriptions must be recorded.
2.   Description
3.   Language
The language of the unit description. These language codes should have already
been defined in the session "Maintain Languages (tcmcs0146m000)".
4.   Description
5.   Language-Specif- ic Unit Description
Enter a clear description here.
6.   Sh. Unit Descr.
The short language-dependent description of the unit which is printed on
external documents.
3.22 Maintain Unit Sets (tcmcs0106m000)
SESSION OBJECTIVE
To maintain unit sets.
SEE ALSO KEYWORD(S)
•   Unit Sets
tcmcs0106m000   zoom   multi-occ (2)   Form 1-1
```
+-----------------------------------------------------------------------+
|  Maintain Unit Sets                                   Company: 000  |
|---------------------------------------------------------------------|
|                                                                     |
|  Unit Set       Description                                          |
|                                                                     |
|        1.....   2...........................                         |
|                                                                     |
+-----------------------------------------------------------------------+
```
1.   Unit Set
For further information, see keyword(s)

"Unit Sets".
2.   Description
Enter a clear description here.
3.23 Maintain Units by Unit Set (tcmcs0112m000)
SESSION OBJECTIVE
To maintain units by unit set.
SEE ALSO KEYWORD(S):
•   Units By Unit Set, Unit Sets (tcmcs006), Units (tcmcs001)
tcmcs0112m000   multi/group (3   Form 1-1
+--+
Maintain Units by Unit Set   Company: 000
Unit Set   : 1..... 2_____
Char   Description   INV   Distr. Mfg.   Price Stor. Con-
Unit   tainer
3..   4_____ 5..... 6..... 7..... 8..... 9..... 10....
+--+
1.   Unit Set
For further information, see keyword(s)
"Unit Sets".
2.   Description
3.   Unit
For further information, see keyword(s)
"Units".
4.   Description
5.   Inventory
Yes
This unit can be used as an inventory unit.
No
This unit cannot be used as an inventory unit.
Stop
In new situations, this unit can no longer be used as an inventory unit.
Existing actions using this unit can be continued and finished as normal.
6.   Distribution
Yes
This unit can be used as a quantity unit.
No
This unit cannot be used as a quantity unit.
Stop
In new situations, this unit can no longer be used as a quantity unit. Existing
actions using this unit can be continued and finished as normal.
7.   Manufacturing
Yes
This unit can be used as a production unit.
No
This unit cannot be used as a production unit.
Stop
In new situations, this unit can no longer be used as a production unit.
Existing actions using this unit can be continued and finished as normal.
For further information, see method(s):
•   Blocking Units of Measure in BAAN Process
8.   Price
Yes
This unit can be used as a price unit.
No
This unit cannot be used as a price unit.
Stop
In new situations, this unit can no longer be used as a price unit. Existing
actions using this unit can be continued and finished as normal.

9.   Storage
Yes
This unit can be used as a storage unit.
No
This unit cannot be used as a storage unit.
Stop
In new situations, this unit can no longer be used as a storage unit. Existing actions using this unit can be continued and finished as normal.
10.   Container
Yes
This unit can be used as a container in (containerized) container/item combinations in the session "Maintain Item Data by Item and Container (tiitm0130m000)".
Container/item combinations are automatically generated when:
•   an item with the following features is maintained in the session "Maintain Item Data (tiitm0101m000)":
•   Process Item = Yes and
•   Containerized = Yes
•   the session "Update Containerized Items (tiitm0230m000)" is executed
No
This unit cannot be used as a container.
Stop
This unit may no longer be used as a container in new situations. Ongoing actions using this unit can be continued and finished as normal.
After setting this field to "Stop" it is advised to run the session "Update Containerized Items (tiitm0230m000)" to ensure that all container/item combinations are updated according to the "Signal Code Expired Container Items" parameter.

3.24 Maintain Warehouses (tcmcs0103m000)

SESSION OBJECTIVE
To define data about the warehouses used in other sessions.
Companies with a single warehouse must define at least one warehouse, otherwise orders cannot be processed.
SEE ALSO KEYWORD(S)
•   Warehouses
SEE ALSO METHOD(S)
•   Address Verification for Tax Provider
INFORMATION ABOUT DISPLAY FIELDS:
•   Locations

```
tcmcs0103m000                              single-occ (1)   Form 1-2 >
+--------------------------------------------------------------------+
| Maintain Warehouses                                    Company: 000 |
|--------------------------------------------------------------------|
|                                                                    |
| Warehouse                        : 1..                              |
|                                                                    |
| Description                      : 2..............................  |
| Country                          : 3.. 4_____   |
| Name                             : 5..............................  |
|                                  : 6..............................  |
| Address                          : 7..............................  |
|                                  : 8..............................  |
| 9_____: 10.............................  |
| 11_____: 12.............................  |
| 13_____1415.......                       |
| 16_____1718...                           |
| ZIP Code                         : 19........                       |
| Transportation Address           : 20____                          |
| Finance Company                  : 21. 22_____  |
|                                                                    |
+--------------------------------------------------------------------+
```

1.   Warehouse
For further information, see keyword(s)

"Warehouses".
2.   Description
Enter a clear description here.
3.   Country
The code of the country where the warehouse has been established. Enter the country code. It should have already been defined in the session "Maintain Countries (tcmcs0110m000)".
4.   Description
5.   Name
The first part of the warehouse name.
6.   Name 2
The second part of the warehouse name. If the previous field is not long enough to show the full name, you can use this field as well.
7.   Address
The first part of the address of the warehouse.
8.   Address 2
The second part of the address of the warehouse. If the previous field is too short for the full address, you can also use this field.
9.   Program domain string
10.   City
The place where the warehouse has been established. It appears on documents under the delivery address in the module "Purchase Control (PUR)".
For tax provider users, the city and state or province where the warehouse has been established. The city and state or province should be separated by a comma ",", such as "Menlo Park, CA".
For further information, see method(s)
•   Address Verification for Tax Provider
If a post code is used, it is assumed that it is also entered in one of the address fields as the format for international ZIP codes differs from one country to another.
11.   Program domain string
12.   City 2
The second part of the place where the warehouse has been established. It appears on documents under the delivery address in the module "Purchase Control (PUR)".
For tax provider users, the ZIP Code or Postal Code where the warehouse has been established.
For further information, see method(s)
•   Address Verification for Tax Provider
13.   Program domain string
14.   Program domain of string length 1
15.   GEO Code
A GEO code is a code used together or in lieu of address information such as city, state/province, and ZIP/postal code to uniquely identify a taxing jurisdiction. The tax provider determines the GEO code based upon the address information entered and the county and city limits selected.
The format of the GEO code varies by tax provider. AVP uses a two-digit GEO code; the GEO code together with the city, state, and ZIP code, identifies the taxing jurisdiction. Vertex uses a nine-digit GEO code comprised of a two digit state code, three-digit county code, and a four-digit city code. A tenth digit is used to identify if the jurisdiction is inside or outside of the city limits.
16.   Program domain string
17.   Program domain of string length 1
18.   Answer on question y/n
19.   ZIP Code
The ZIP code of the address where the warehouse is situated. It is used in places (for instance on documents, in sorts) where only the ZIP code is required.
20.   Address Code
The address if the package is run in association with the package BAAN Transportation. The address refers to an address in the b-object "Address Control (ACS)" in the package BAAN Transportation.
21.   Company

The number of the Finance company associated with this warehouse. All transaction for this warehouse result in financial transactions for the above company.

22.   Company Name
The company's name.

```
+-------------------------------------------------------------------------+
|  Maintain Warehouses                                    Company: 000  |
|-------------------------------------------------------------------------|
|                                                                         |
|   Warehouse                          : 1..                              |
|                                                                         |
|   Warehouse Type                     : 2...............                 |
|   Nettable Warehouse                 : 3....                            |
|   Locations                          : 4____                            |
|   Receipt Location                   : 5.......                         |
|   Inspection Receipt Location        : 6.......                         |
|   Multi-Item Locations               : 7....                            |
|   Multi-Lot by Item Locations        : 8....                            |
|   Min. % Free for Inbound Advice     : 9..                              |
|                                                                         |
+-------------------------------------------------------------------------+
```

1.   Warehouse
For further information, see keyword(s)
"Warehouses".

2.   Warehouse Type
The type of warehouse. Normal
Normal warehouses with or without a location system used for storing goods.
Work-in-Process
Warehouses used to store intermediate inventory used to supply production lines/work centers.
Transit
Warehouses for registering inventory in transit. These warehouses are used in the module "Replenishment Order Control (RPL)" to trace inventory during transportation.

3.   Nettable Warehouse
No
This warehouse is a so-called "non-nettable" warehouse. Non-nettable warehouses are ignored by the MRP and MPS algorithm. The resupply of such warehouses is planned with DRP in the module "Distribution Requirements Planning (DRP)". In addition, direct purchases can be written to non-nettable warehouses or they can be stocked via the SIC principle.
Yes
This warehouse is a so-called "nettable" warehouse. Nettable warehouses are ignored by the DRP algorithm. The replenishment of the inventory of these warehouses is planned using MRP, MPS and SIC in the modules "Material Requirements Planning (MRP)", "Master Production Scheduling (MPS)" and "Inventory Control (INV)" or takes place through manual purchases. An exception is a "nettable" "Work-in-Process" warehouse, because it can also be resupplied by DRP.

4.   Locations
A warehouse may comprise multiple inventory locations. These may be free or fixed locations. Inventory is then registered by location in the module "Location Control (ILC)".
The session "Change Location System by Warehouse (tdilc0231m000)" loads the receipt and inspection locations. Subsequently, the system sets the field "Locations" to "Yes". Yes
The warehouse has either multiple fixed locations or free locations. You must define the locations in the session "Maintain Locations (tdilc0110m000)".
No
The warehouse has no locations or at most one fixed location per item. You can record this in the session "Maintain Items by Warehouse (tdinv0101m000)".

5.   Receipt Location

If you use locations, in each warehouse a location may be available in which items may be placed which are not subject to inspection when they are received. With the help of inbound advice, the items from this location are assigned to other inventory locations which have not been defined as inspection locations in the module "Location Control (ILC)".

If you have chosen for a location system, you can maintain this field. By default, the inspection location is shown which has been defined via the following session:

•   Maintain Warehouses (tcmcs0103m000)

6.   Inspection Receipt Location

Aside from the "normal" locations, there may also be inspection locations present in a warehouse. An inspection location is exclusively designated for storing purchased items which have been marked for inspection in the module "Purchase Control (PUR)". After the items have been approved in the session "Maintain Approvals (tdpur4121m000)", they are transferred to a "normal" location. Inventories stored in an inspection location are always registered as inventory on hold.

If you have chosen for a location system, you can maintain this field. By default, the inspection location is shown which has been defined via the following session:

•   Maintain Warehouses (tcmcs0103m000)

7.   Multi-Item Locations

For each warehouse, you can indicate which items may be stored at a location: either items with the same item code or items with different item codes. You can select:

Yes

Different items may be stored at one location.

No

At each location, only one item may be stored.

8.   Multi-Lot by Item Locations

For items subject to lot control, you must indicate whether many lots of the same items may be stored at a location. Yes

Different lots of one item may be stored at one location.

No

At each location, only one lot of a specific item may be stored.

In combination with the field "Multi-Item Locations", four variant are possible:

•   Different items and different lots of each item are allowed.
•   Different items are allowed, but only one lot of each item.
•   Only one item is allowed at the location, but of this item, more than one lot may be stored.
•   Only one lot of one item is allowed at the location.

9.   Min. % Free for Inbound Advice

The minimum percentage of free capacity that a location must have before inbound advice can be generated.

When the calculated capacity occupation of a location reaches a certain upper limit, inbound advice for the location would no longer be advisable. If the available capacity for each location is small, too many locations are approached when receiving items for storage. In order to avoid wasting time, the capacity occupation is recorded as a percentage for each location in this field. The capacity occupation is calculated as follows:

$$\frac{\text{Total Capacity} - \text{Available Capacity}}{\text{Total Capacity}} \times 100\%$$

If a location is filled in with a percentage greater or equal to the value entered in this field, the system will report that the location is occupied for x%, "x" being the calculated percentage.

3.25 Maintain Use of Performance Boosters (tcmcs0197m000)

SESSION OBJECTIVE

To link performance boosters to sessions, to users, or to a combination of these.

NOTE: Wherever in an application a booster can be applied, but that booster has not been set in this session, the following will occur: table Use of Performance Boosters (tcmcs097) will be inserted with the booster concerned for the user and

the session that is running and the validation in the field "Booster Valid" will
be "Not Active"
HOW TO USE THE SESSION
Performance Boosters can be used at three levels, each starting with another
identifier. The following combinations may therefore be made:

```
+------------------------------------------------------------------+
| Session            | Performance Booster | User                 |
|--------------------+---------------------+----------------------|
| Performance Booster | Session            | Performance Booster  |
| User               | User               | Session              |
+------------------------------------------------------------------+
```

It is necessary to always fill in the performance booster which should be used
and the session for which the booster is valid.
SEE ALSO KEYWORD(S)
•   Use of Performance Boosters

tcmcs0197m000   multi/group (3   Form 1-3 >

```
+------------------------------------------------------------------------+
|  Maintain Use of Performance Boosters                  Company: 000    |
|------------------------------------------------------------------------|
|                                                                        |
|  Session                 :  1........... 2_____    |
|                                                                        |
|  Performance Booster        User          Value        Booster Valid   |
|                                                                        |
|  3.....................     4..........    5.........   6.............  |
|                                                                        |
+------------------------------------------------------------------------+
```

1.   Session
Entering the session will make the system employ the performance booster in this
session, if applicable. If it is not applicable, entering the session will have
no effect at all.
See the field "Performance Booster" for a list of sessions to which the
performance booster is relevant.
2.   Description
3.   Performance Booster
For further information, see keyword(s)
"Use of Performance Boosters".
Available performance boosters: * [GO1] Display Interval * [G02] Number of
Servers
* [G03] Maximum Invoice Lines * [G04] Embedded Financial Int.
Display Interval With this option you can influence the time between two refresh
actions. Decreasing the frequency with which the program refreshes the screen
will have a positive effect on the speed of large processing sessions.
Use is recommended in the sessions:
•   Generate Planned (MPS)/MRP Orders/Batches (timrp1210m000)
•   Generate Master Production Schedule (timps3201m000)
•   Generate Planned PRP Orders (tipcs5201m000)
•   Transfer Planned PRP Purchase Orders (tipcs5260m000)
•   Generate Inbound Advice (tdilc4203m000)
•   Generate Outbound Advice (tdilc4201m000)
Numbers of Servers This option allows you to set the extra number of bshells to
be started parallel to the session concerned, which you should fill in the field
"Session". It is also possible to join the Number of Servers to one "User".
Use is recommended in the sessions:
•   Update Sales Statistics (tdsst0201m000)
•   Print Sales Invoices (tdsls4404m000)
If booster has been set for this session, the session "Process Delivered Sales
Orders (tdsls4223m000)" will run parallel to printing the invoices.
•   Process Delivered Sales Orders (tdsls4223m000)
•   Process Delivered Purchase Orders (tdpur4223m000)
•   Select Invoices for Payment (tfcmg1220m000)
•   Audit Batches (tfgld1211s000)
•   Generate Planned (MPS)/MRP Orders/Batches (timrp1210m000)

- Generate Master Production Schedule (timps3201m000)
- Execute Single Site Master Production Scheduling (timps3202s000)
- Print Cost Control (tpppc4411m000)

Maximum Invoice Lines Whenever the possibility to collect several orders on one invoice is used, invoices can contain a great number of lines. The transaction to book these lines to BAAN Finance can become too large, depending on e.g. the size of the rollback-segments of your database. This option limits the maximum number of lines on one invoice, thus reducing the size of the transaction mentioned.

Use is only possible in:
- Print Sales Invoices (tdsls4404m000)

The check on maximum invoice lines will not be performed if the field "Invoicing by Installments" for the current order is set to "Yes". Printing will continue untill the end of this order.
- Print Invoices (trics2400m000)
- Print Contract Installment Invoices (tssma2472m000)
- Print Service Order Invoices (tssma3473m000)
- Print Invoices (tppin4474m000)

Embedded Financial Integration With this option a financial integration will be processed using a Dynamic Link Library instead of the parallel running session "Update Integr Trans and Real Time Post to Finance (backgrd.) (tfgld4200s000)". This will speed up the sessions in which a financial integration is involved.

4. User
The user for whom the booster is valid. If this field is left empty the booster is valid for all users that start the session.

5. Value

6. Booster Valid

```
tcmcs0197m000                                    multi/group (3  < Form 2-3 >
+------------------------------------------------------------------------------+
|  Maintain Use of Performance Boosters                        Company: 000  |
|------------------------------------------------------------------------------|
|                                                                            |
|  Performance Booster     : 1......................                          |
|                                                                            |
|  Session       Description           User        Value       Booster Valid  |
|                                                                            |
|  2........... 3_____  4.......... 5........ 6...........  |
|                                                                            |
+------------------------------------------------------------------------------+
```

1. Performance Booster
For further information, see keyword(s)
"Use of Performance Boosters".
Available performance boosters: * [GO1] Display Interval * [G02] Number of Servers
* [G03] Maximum Invoice Lines * [G04] Embedded Financial Int.
Display Interval With this option you can influence the time between two refresh actions. Decreasing the frequency with which the program refreshes the screen will have a positive effect on the speed of large processing sessions.
Use is recommended in the sessions:
- Generate Planned (MPS)/MRP Orders/Batches (timrp1210m000)
- Generate Master Production Schedule (timps3201m000)
- Generate Planned PRP Orders (tipcs5201m000)
- Transfer Planned PRP Purchase Orders (tipcs5260m000)
- Generate Inbound Advice (tdilc4203m000)
- Generate Outbound Advice (tdilc4201m000)

Numbers of Servers This option allows you to set the extra number of bshells to be started parallel to the session concerned, which you should fill in the field "Session". It is also possible to join the Number of Servers to one "User".
Use is recommended in the sessions:
- Update Sales Statistics (tdsst0201m000)
- Print Sales Invoices (tdsls4404m000)

If booster has been set for this session, the session "Process Delivered Sales Orders (tdsls4223m000)" will run parallel to printing the invoices.

- Process Delivered Sales Orders (tdsls4223m000)
- Process Delivered Purchase Orders (tdpur4223m000)
- Select Invoices for Payment (tfcmg1220m000)
- Audit Batches (tfgld1211s000)
- Generate Planned (MPS)/MRP Orders/Batches (timrp1210m000)
- Generate Master Production Schedule (timps3201m000)
- Execute Single Site Master Production Scheduling (timps3202s000)
- Print Cost Control (tpppc4411m000)

Maximum Invoice Lines Whenever the possibility to collect several orders on one invoice is used, invoices can contain a great number of lines. The transaction to book these lines to BAAN Finance can become too large, depending on e.g. the size of the rollback-segments of your database. This option limits the maximum number of lines on one invoice, thus reducing the size of the transaction mentioned.

Use is only possible in:
- Print Sales Invoices (tdsls4404m000)

The check on maximum invoice lines will not be performed if the field "Invoicing by Installments" for the current order is set to "Yes". Printing will continue untill the end of this order.
- Print Invoices (trics2400m000)
- Print Contract Installment Invoices (tssma2472m000)
- Print Service Order Invoices (tssma3473m000)
- Print Invoices (tppin4474m000)

Embedded Financial Integration With this option a financial integration will be processed using a Dynamic Link Library instead of the parallel running session "Update Integr Trans and Real Time Post to Finance (backgrd.) (tfgld4200s000)". This will speed up the sessions in which a financial integration is involved.

2.   Session
Entering the session will make the system employ the performance booster in this session, if applicable. If it is not applicable, entering the session will have no effect at all.
See the field "Performance Booster" for a list of sessions to which the performance booster is relevant.

3.   Description
4.   User
The user for whom the booster is valid. If this field is left empty the booster is valid for all users that start the session.

5.   Value
6.   Booster Valid

tcmcs0197m000   multi/group (3 < Form 3-3

```
+-----------------------------------------------------------------------+
| Maintain Use of Performance Boosters                     Company: 000 |
|-----------------------------------------------------------------------|
|                                                                       |
| User                      : 1..........  2_____   |
|                                                                       |
| Performance Booster         Session        Value       Booster Valid  |
|                                                                       |
| 3.......................   4..........  5........   6.............    |
|                                                                       |
+-----------------------------------------------------------------------+
```

1.   User
The user for whom the booster is valid. If this field is left empty the booster is valid for all users that start the session.

2.   Description
3.   Performance Booster
For further information, see keyword(s)
"Use of Performance Boosters".
Available performance boosters: * [GO1] Display Interval * [G02] Number of Servers
* [G03] Maximum Invoice Lines * [G04] Embedded Financial Int.

Display Interval With this option you can influence the time between two refresh actions. Decreasing the frequency with which the program refreshes the screen will have a positive effect on the speed of large processing sessions.
Use is recommended in the sessions:
• Generate Planned (MPS)/MRP Orders/Batches (timrp1210m000)
• Generate Master Production Schedule (timps3201m000)
• Generate Planned PRP Orders (tipcs5201m000)
• Transfer Planned PRP Purchase Orders (tipcs5260m000)
• Generate Inbound Advice (tdilc4203m000)
• Generate Outbound Advice (tdilc4201m000)
Numbers of Servers This option allows you to set the extra number of bshells to be started parallel to the session concerned, which you should fill in the field "Session". It is also possible to join the Number of Servers to one "User".
Use is recommended in the sessions:
• Update Sales Statistics (tdsst0201m000)
• Print Sales Invoices (tdsls4404m000)
If booster has been set for this session, the session "Process Delivered Sales Orders (tdsls4223m000)" will run parallel to printing the invoices.
• Process Delivered Sales Orders (tdsls4223m000)
• Process Delivered Purchase Orders (tdpur4223m000)
• Select Invoices for Payment (tfcmg1220m000)
• Audit Batches (tfgld1211s000)
• Generate Planned (MPS)/MRP Orders/Batches (timrp1210m000)
• Generate Master Production Schedule (timps3201m000)
• Execute Single Site Master Production Scheduling (timps3202s000)
• Print Cost Control (tpppc4411m000)
Maximum Invoice Lines Whenever the possibility to collect several orders on one invoice is used, invoices can contain a great number of lines. The transaction to book these lines to BAAN Finance can become too large, depending on e.g. the size of the rollback-segments of your database. This option limits the maximum number of lines on one invoice, thus reducing the size of the transaction mentioned.
Use is only possible in:
• Print Sales Invoices (tdsls4404m000)
The check on maximum invoice lines will not be performed if the field "Invoicing by Installments" for the current order is set to "Yes". Printing will continue untill the end of this order.
• Print Invoices (trics2400m000)
• Print Contract Installment Invoices (tssma2472m000)
• Print Service Order Invoices (tssma3473m000)
• Print Invoices (tppin4474m000)
Embedded Financial Integration With this option a financial integration will be processed using a Dynamic Link Library instead of the parallel running session "Update Integr Trans and Real Time Post to Finance (backgrd.) (tfgld4200s000)". This will speed up the sessions in which a financial integration is involved.
4.   Session
Entering the session will make the system employ the performance booster in this session, if applicable. If it is not applicable, entering the session will have no effect at all.
See the field "Performance Booster" for a list of sessions to which the performance booster is relevant.
5.   Value
6.   Booster Valid
3.26 Maintain Quality Groups (tcmcs0129m000)
SESSION OBJECTIVE
To maintain quality groups.
SEE ALSO KEYWORD(S)
• Quality Groups
tcmcs0129m000   zoom   multi-occ (2)   Form 1-1
+---+
Maintain Quality Groups   Company: 000

```
|  Quality Group  Description                                                |
|                                                                            |
|          1.....  2...........................                              |
|                                                                            |
+----------------------------------------------------------------------------+
```

1.   Quality Group
For further information, see keyword(s)
"Quality Groups".
2.   Description
Enter a clear description here.
3.27 Maintain Skills (tcmcs0130m000)
SESSION OBJECTIVE
To define the various skills required to use the different instruments for the
quality tests in the Quality Management System (QMS) module.
SEE ALSO KEYWORD(S)
•   Skills
tcmcs0130m000   multi-occ (2)   Form 1-1

```
+----------------------------------------------------------------------------+
| Maintain Skills                                       Company: 000  |
|----------------------------------------------------------------------------|
|                                                                            |
| Skill        Description                                                   |
|                                                                            |
|          1...  2...........................                               |
|                                                                            |
+----------------------------------------------------------------------------+
```

1.   Skill
For further information, see keyword(s)
"Skills".
2.   Description
Enter a clear description here.
4   Optional Sessions
4.1   Maintain Titles (tcmcs0119s000)
SESSION OBJECTIVE
To maintain titles.
SEE ALSO KEYWORD(S)
•   Titles
tcmcs0119s000   multi-occ (2)   Form 1-1

```
+--Maintain Titles-------------------------------------------------+
|                                                                  |
| Title   Description                                              |
|                                                                  |
|    1..  2...........................                            |
|                                                                  |
+------------------------------------------------------------------+
```

1.   Title
For further information, see keyword(s)
"Titles".
2.   Description
Enter a clear description here.
5   Other Print Sessions
5.1   Print Areas (tcmcs0445m000)
tcmcs0445m000   single-occ (4)   Form 1-1

```
+----------------------------------------------------------------------------+
| Print Areas                                           Company: 000  |
|----------------------------------------------------------------------------|
|                                                                            |
| Area        from : 1..                                                     |
|             to   : 2..                                                      |
|                                                                            |
+----------------------------------------------------------------------------+
```

1.   Area from
2.   Area to

5.2   Print Commodity Codes (tcmcs0428m000)

tcmcs0428m000   single-occ (4)   Form 1-1
+---+
Print Commodity Codes   Company: 000
Commodity Code from : 1.......
to   : 2.......
+---+
1.   Commodity Code from
2.   Commodity Code to

5.3   Print Countries (tcmcs0410m000)

tcmcs0410m000   single-occ (4)   Form 1-1
+---+
Print Countries   Company: 000
Country   from : 1..
to   : 2..
+---+
1.   Country from
2.   Country to

5.4   Print First Free Numbers (tcmcs0447m000)

tcmcs0447m000   single-occ (4)   Form 1-1
+---+
Print First Free Numbers   Company: 000
Type of Number   from : 1........................
to   : 2........................
Series   from : 3..
to   : 4..
+---+
1.   Type of Number from
2.   Type of Number to
3.   Series from
4.   Series to

5.5   Print Forwarding Agents (tcmcs0480m000)

tcmcs0480m000   single-occ (4)   Form 1-1
+---+
Print Forwarding Agents   Company: 000
Forwarding Agent   from :   1..
to   :   2..
Supplier   from : 3.....
to   : 4.....
+---+
1.   Forwarding Agent from
2.   Forwarding Agent to
3.   Supplier from
4.   Supplier to

5.6   Print Item Groups (tcmcs0423m000)

tcmcs0423m000   single-occ (4)   Form 1-1
+---+
Print Item Groups   Company: 000
Item Group   from : 1.....
+---+

```
|                    to   : 2.....                                           |
|                                                                            |
+----------------------------------------------------------------------------+
1.     Item Group from
2.     Item Group to
5.7    Print Languages (tcmcs0446m000)
tcmcs0446m000                                single-occ (4)    Form 1-1
+----------------------------------------------------------------------------+
|  Print Languages                                          Company: 000  |
|----------------------------------------------------------------------------|
|                                                                            |
|  Language        from : 1..                                                |
|                  to   : 2..                                                |
|                                                                            |
+----------------------------------------------------------------------------+
1.     Language from
2.     Language to
5.8    Print Lines of Business (tcmcs0431m000)
tcmcs0431m000                                single-occ (4)    Form 1-1
+----------------------------------------------------------------------------+
|  Print Lines of Business                                  Company: 000  |
|----------------------------------------------------------------------------|
|                                                                            |
|  Line of Business       from : 1.....                                      |
|                         to   : 2.....                                      |
|                                                                            |
+----------------------------------------------------------------------------+
1.     Line of Business from
2.     Line of Business to
5.9    Print Price Groups (tcmcs0424m000)
tcmcs0424m000                                single-occ (4)    Form 1-1
+----------------------------------------------------------------------------+
|  Print Price Groups                                       Company: 000  |
|----------------------------------------------------------------------------|
|                                                                            |
|  Price Group       from : 1.....                                           |
|                    to   : 2.....                                           |
|                                                                            |
+----------------------------------------------------------------------------+
1.     Price Group from
2.     Price Group to
5.10   Print Price Lists (tcmcs0434m000)
tcmcs0434m000                                single-occ (4)    Form 1-1
+----------------------------------------------------------------------------+
|  Print Price Lists                                        Company: 000  |
|----------------------------------------------------------------------------|
|                                                                            |
|  Price List        from : 1..                                             |
|                    to   : 2..                                             |
|                                                                            |
+----------------------------------------------------------------------------+
1.     Price List from
2.     Price List to
5.11   Print Reasons for Rejection (tcmcs0405m000)
tcmcs0405m000                                single-occ (4)    Form 1-1
+----------------------------------------------------------------------------+
|  Print Reasons for Rejection                              Company: 000  |
|----------------------------------------------------------------------------|
|                                                                            |
|  Reason                 from : 1..                                         |
|                         to   : 2..                                         |
|                                                                            |
+----------------------------------------------------------------------------+
```

```
1.    Reason from
2.    Reason to
5.12  Print Product Types (tcmcs0415m000)
tcmcs0415m000                               single-occ (4)   Form 1-1
+----------------------------------------------------------------------+
|  Print Product Types                              Company: 000  |
|----------------------------------------------------------------------|
|                                                                      |
|  Product Type        from : 1..                                 |
|                      to   : 2..                                 |
|                                                                      |
+----------------------------------------------------------------------+
1.    Product Type from
2.    Product Type to
5.13  Print Routes (tcmcs0404m000)
tcmcs0404m000                               single-occ (4)   Form 1-1
+----------------------------------------------------------------------+
|  Print Routes                                     Company: 000  |
|----------------------------------------------------------------------|
|                                                                      |
|  Route      from : 1....                                        |
|             to   : 2....                                        |
|                                                                      |
+----------------------------------------------------------------------+
1.    Route from
2.    Route to
5.14  Print Seasonal Patterns (tcmcs0416m000)
tcmcs0416m000                               single-occ (4)   Form 1-1
+----------------------------------------------------------------------+
|  Print Seasonal Patterns                          Company: 000  |
|----------------------------------------------------------------------|
|                                                                      |
|  Seasonal Pattern        from : 1..                             |
|                          to   : 2..                             |
|                                                                      |
+----------------------------------------------------------------------+
1.    Seasonal Pattern from
2.    Seasonal Pattern to
5.15  Print Selection Codes (tcmcs0422m000)
tcmcs0422m000                               single-occ (4)   Form 1-1
+----------------------------------------------------------------------+
|  Print Selection Codes                            Company: 000  |
|----------------------------------------------------------------------|
|                                                                      |
|  Selection Code        from : 1..                               |
|                        to   : 2..                               |
|                                                                      |
+----------------------------------------------------------------------+
1.    Selection Code from
2.    Selection Code to
5.16  Print Signal Codes (tcmcs0418m000)
tcmcs0418m000                               single-occ (4)   Form 1-1
+----------------------------------------------------------------------+
|  Print Signal Codes                               Company: 000  |
|----------------------------------------------------------------------|
|                                                                      |
|  Signal Code        from : 1..                                  |
|                     to   : 2..                                  |
|                                                                      |
+----------------------------------------------------------------------+
1.    Signal Code from
2.    Signal Code to
5.17  Print Statistics Groups (tcmcs0444m000)
```

```
tcmcs0444m000                          single-occ (4)    Form 1-1
+----------------------------------------------------------------------+
|  Print Statistics Groups                           Company: 000      |
|----------------------------------------------------------------------|
|                                                                      |
|  Statistics Group        from : 1.....                               |
|                          to   : 2.....                               |
|                                                                      |
+----------------------------------------------------------------------+
1.    Statistics Group from
2.    Statistics Group to
5.18  Print Terms of Delivery (tcmcs0441m000)
tcmcs0441m000                          single-occ (4)    Form 1-1
+----------------------------------------------------------------------+
|  Print Terms of Delivery                           Company: 000      |
|----------------------------------------------------------------------|
|                                                                      |
|  Terms of Delivery       from : 1..                                  |
|                          to   : 2..                                  |
|                                                                      |
|  Print Language              : 3..  4_____             |
|                                                                      |
+----------------------------------------------------------------------+
1.    Terms of Delivery from
2.    Terms of Delivery to
3.    Print Language
The language in which you want to print the texts linked to the code.
4.    Description
5.19  Print Titles (tcmcs0419m000)
tcmcs0419m000                          single-occ (4)    Form 1-1
+----------------------------------------------------------------------+
|  Print Titles                                      Company: 000      |
|----------------------------------------------------------------------|
|                                                                      |
|  Title        from : 1..                                             |
|               to   : 2..                                             |
|                                                                      |
+----------------------------------------------------------------------+
1.    Title from
2.    Title to
5.20  Print Units (tcmcs0401m000)
tcmcs0401m000                          single-occ (4)    Form 1-1
+----------------------------------------------------------------------+
|  Print Units                                       Company: 000      |
|----------------------------------------------------------------------|
|                                                                      |
|  Unit        from : 1..                                              |
|              to   : 2..                                              |
|                                                                      |
+----------------------------------------------------------------------+
1.    Unit from
2.    Unit to
5.21  Print Units by Language (tcmcs0407m000)
tcmcs0407m000                          single-occ (4)    Form 1-1
+----------------------------------------------------------------------+
|  Print Units by Language                           Company: 000      |
|----------------------------------------------------------------------|
|                                                                      |
|  Code          from : 1..                                            |
|                to   : 2..                                            |
|                                                                      |
|  Language      from : 3..                                            |
|                to   : 4..                                            |
```

```
|                                                                              |
+------------------------------------------------------------------------------+
1.     Code from
2.     Code to
3.     Language from
4.     Language to
5.22  Print Unit Sets (tcmcs0406m000)
tcmcs0406m000                              single-occ (4)    Form 1-1
+------------------------------------------------------------------------------+
| Print Unit Sets                                         Company: 000 |
|------------------------------------------------------------------------------|
|                                                                      |
| Unit Set          from    1.....                                     |
|                   to       2.....                                     |
|                                                                      |
+------------------------------------------------------------------------------+
1.     Unit Set from
2.     Unit Set to
5.23  Print Units by Unit Set (tcmcs0412m000)
tcmcs0412m000                              single-occ (4)    Form 1-1
+------------------------------------------------------------------------------+
| Print Units by Unit Set                                 Company: 000 |
|------------------------------------------------------------------------------|
|                                                                      |
| Unit Set          from : 1.....                                      |
|                   to   : 2.....                                      |
|                                                                      |
| Unit              from : 3..                                        |
|                   to   : 4..                                        |
|                                                                      |
+------------------------------------------------------------------------------+
1.     Unitset
2.     Unitset
3.     Unit
4.     Unit
5.24  Print Warehouses (tcmcs0403m000)
tcmcs0403m000                              single-occ (4)    Form 1-1
+------------------------------------------------------------------------------+
| Print Warehouses                                        Company: 000 |
|------------------------------------------------------------------------------|
|                                                                      |
| Warehouse         from : 1..                                        |
|                   to   : 2..                                        |
|                                                                      |
+------------------------------------------------------------------------------+
1.     Warehouse from
2.     Warehouse to
5.25  Print Quality Groups (tcmcs0429m000)
tcmcs0429m000                              single-occ (4)    Form 1-1
+------------------------------------------------------------------------------+
| Print Quality Groups                                    Company: 000 |
|------------------------------------------------------------------------------|
|                                                                      |
| Quality Group        from : 1.....                                   |
|                      to   : 2.....                                   |
|                                                                      |
+------------------------------------------------------------------------------+
1.     Quality Group
2.     Quality Group
5.26  Print Skills (tcmcs0430m000)
tcmcs0430m000                              single-occ (4)    Form 1-1
+------------------------------------------------------------------------------+
| Print Skills                                            Company: 000 |
```

```
|-------------------------------------------------------------------------|
|  Skill          From : 1...                                             |
|                 To   : 2...                                             |
|                                                                         |
+-------------------------------------------------------------------------+
```

1.   Skill
2.   Skill
6   Introduction to Financial Tables
6.1   General
OBJECTIVE OF BUSINESS OBJECT
This b-object allows you to control all sorts of data relating to the financial
functions in the BAAN IV packages.
SEE ALSO METHOD(S)
•   Table Coding
6.2   Session Overview

Seq.	Session	Description	Session Usage
1	tcmcs0120m000	Maintain Bank Addresses	Mandatory
2	tcmcs0102m000	Maintain Currencies	Mandatory
3	tcmcs0108m000	Maintain Currency Rates	Mandatory
4	tcmcs0125m000	Maintain Factoring Companies	Mandatory
5	tcmcs0126m000	Maintain Banks by Factoring Company	Mandatory
7	tcmcs0155m000	Maintain Invoicing Methods	Mandatory
8	tcmcs0111m000	Maintain Late Payment Surcharges	Mandatory
9	tcmcs0153m000	Maintain Rounding Codes	Mandatory
10	tcmcs0137m000	Maintain Tax Codes	Mandatory
11	tcmcs0136m000	Maintain Tax Codes by Country	Mandatory
12	tcmcs0113m000	Maintain Terms of Payment	Mandatory
13	tcmcs0114m000	Maintain Payment Schedules	Mandatory
14	tcmcs0109m000	Maintain Credit Insurance Companies	Mandatory
15	tcmcs0132s000	Maintain Single Tax Rates	Mandatory
16	tcmcs0133s000	Maintain Multiple Tax Rates	Mandatory
17	tcmcs0135s000	Maintain Tax Rates by Tax Code	Mandatory
101	tcmcs0420m000	Print Bank Addresses	Print
102	tcmcs0402m000	Print Currencies	Print
103	tcmcs0408m000	Print Currency Rates	Print
104	tcmcs0425m000	Print Factoring Companies	Print
105	tcmcs0426m000	Print Banks by Factoring Company	Print
106	tcmcs0447m000	Print First Free Numbers	Print

107	tcmcs0455m000	Print Invoicing Methods	Print
108	tcmcs0411m000	Print Late Payment Surcharges	Print
109	tcmcs0453m000	Print Rounding Codes	Print
110	tcmcs0437m000	Print Tax Codes	Print
111	tcmcs0436m000	Print Tax Codes by Country	Print
112	tcmcs0413m000	Print Terms of Payment	Print
113	tcmcs0414m000	Print Payment Schedules	Print
114	tcmcs0409m000	Print Credit Insurance Companies	Print
201	tcmcs0520m000	Display Bank Addresses	Display
202	tcmcs0502m000	Display Currencies	Display
203	tcmcs0508m000	Display Currency Rates	Display
204	tcmcs0525m000	Display Factoring Companies	Display
205	tcmcs0526m000	Display Banks by Factoring Company	Display
206	tcmcs0547m000	Display First Free Numbers	Display
207	tcmcs0555m000	Display Invoicing Methods	Display
208	tcmcs0511m000	Display Late Payment Surcharges	Display
209	tcmcs0553m000	Display Rounding Codes	Display
210	tcmcs0537m000	Display Tax Codes	Display
211	tcmcs0536m000	Display Tax Codes by Country	Display
212	tcmcs0513m000	Display Terms of Payment	Display
213	tcmcs0514m000	Display Payment Schedules	Display
214	tcmcs0509m000	Display Credit Insurance Companies	Display
999	tcmcs0532s000	Display Single Tax Rates	Display
999	tcmcs0533s000	Display Multiple Tax Rates	Display
999	tcmcs0535s000	Display Tax Rates by Tax Code	Display

7   Mandatory Sessions
7.1   Maintain Bank Addresses (tcmcs0120m000)
SESSION OBJECTIVE
To record the addresses of banks used in other sessions.
SEE ALSO KEYWORD(S)
•   Bank Addresses
SEE ALSO METHOD(S)
•   Address Verification for Tax Provider
tcmcs0120m000   single-occ (1)   Form 1-1
+--+
Maintain Bank Addresses   Company: 000

```
|                                                                          |
| Bank Address              : 1..........                                  |
|                                                                          |
| Country                   : 2..  3_____       |
| Name                      : 4.....................................       |
|                           : 5...........................                 |
| Address                   : 6...........................                 |
|                           : 7...........................                 |
| 8_____    : 9...........................                 |
| 10_____    : 11..........................                 |
| 12_____    1314.......                                    |
| 15_____    1617...                                        |
|                                                                          |
+--------------------------------------------------------------------------+
```

1.   Bank Address
For further information, see keyword(s)
"Bank Addresses".
2.   Country
The code of the country where the bank is based. Select the concerned country
code. This code should have been defined in the session "Maintain Countries
(tcmcs0110m000)".
3.   Description
4.   Name
The first part of the bank name.
5.   Name 2
The second part of the bank name.
6.   Address
The first part of the bank address.
7.   Address 2
The second part of the bank address.
8.   Program domain string
9.   City
The first part of the city where the bank is based.
For tax provider users, the city and state or province where the bank is based.
The city and state or province should be separated by a comma ",", such as
"Menlo Park, CA".
For further information, see method(s)
•   Address Verification for Tax Provider
10.   Program domain string
11.   City 2
The second part of the city where the bank is based.
For tax provider users, the ZIP Code or Postal Code where the bank is based.
For further information, see method(s)
•   Address Verification for Tax Provider
12.   Program domain string
13.   Program domain of string length 1
14.   GEO Code
A GEO code is a code used together or in lieu of address information such as
city, state/province, and ZIP/postal code to uniquely identify a taxing
jurisdiction. The tax provider determines the GEO code based upon the address
information entered and the county and city limits selected.
The format of the GEO code varies by tax provider. AVP uses a two-digit GEO
code; the GEO code together with the city, state, and ZIP code, identifies the
taxing jurisdiction. Vertex uses a nine-digit GEO code comprised of a two digit
state code, three-digit county code, and a four-digit city code. A tenth digit
is used to identify if the jurisdiction is inside or outside of the city limits.
15.   Program domain string
16.   Program domain of string length 1
17.   Answer on question y/n
7.2   Maintain Currencies (tcmcs0102m000)
SESSION OBJECTIVE
To maintain currencies.
HOW TO USE THE SESSION

Choose option "Zoom [zoom]" to start session "Maintain Currency Rates
(tcmcs0108s000)".
SEE ALSO KEYWORD(S)
•   Currencies
tcmcs0102m000   zoom   single-occ (1)   Form 1-1

```
+----------------------------------------------------------------------+
|  Maintain Currencies                                   Company: 000  |
|----------------------------------------------------------------------|
|                                                                      |
|  Currency           :      1..                                       |
|                                                                      |
|  Description        : 2............................                  |
|  Short Description  :      3..                                       |
|                                                                      |
|  Rounding Factor    : 4...                                           |
|                                                                      |
+----------------------------------------------------------------------+
```

1.   Currency
For further information, see keyword(s)
"Currencies".
SEE ALSO METHOD(S)
•   Currency Formats
2.   Description
Enter a clear description here.
3.   Short Description
The short description in the international currency indication for the monetary
unit.
4.   Rounding Factor
The rounding method indicates how the system rounds off amounts in the currency
concerned.
SEE ALSO METHOD(S)
•   Currency Formats
7.3   Maintain Currency Rates (tcmcs0108m000)
SESSION OBJECTIVE
To maintain currency rates.
SEE ALSO METHOD(S)
•   Currency Differences
SEE ALSO KEYWORD(S)
•   Currency Rates
tcmcs0108m000   multi/group (3   Form 1-1

```
+----------------------------------------------------------------------+
|  Maintain Currency Rates                               Company: 000  |
|----------------------------------------------------------------------|
|                                                                      |
|  Currency     :    1..   2_____                 |
|                                                                      |
|  Effective Date   Purchase Rate   Sales Rate     EU Rate      Rate Factor |
|                                                                      |
|     3.........   4.....        5.....         6.....            7..... |
|                                                                      |
+----------------------------------------------------------------------+
```

1.   Currency
For further information, see keyword(s)
"Currencies".
SEE ALSO METHOD(S)
•   Currency Formats
2.   Description
3.   Effective Date
The date as from which the currency rate is valid.
4.   Purchase Rate
The purchase rate is the factor by which purchase transaction amounts in a
foreign currency are multiplied to produce the amounts in the home currency.

```
+----------------------------------------------------------------+
```

```
| Amount in foreign currency x Purchase Rate = Amount in home curr.|
+-----------------------------------------------------------------+
```
The purchase rate is valid as from the date recorded in the field "Effective
Date" in this session. When printing invoices the system always consults the
purchase and sales rate, whatever the invoice date.

5.   Sales Rate

The sales rate is the factor by which sales transaction amounts in a foreign
currency are multiplied to produce the amounts in the home currency.
```
+-----------------------------------------------------------------+
| Amount in foreign currency x Sales Rate = Amount in home currency |
+-----------------------------------------------------------------+
```
The sales rate is valid as from the date recorded in the field "Effective Date"
in this session.

6.   EU Rate

The rate used in the European Union when import and export data is processed for
intra-EU transaction reporting.

7.   Rate Factor

The unit to which the purchase and sales rate applies. (standard value = 1).
Example:

Factor = 1   : the rate applies to 1 x currency
Factor = 10,000   : the rate applies to 10,000 x currency

Italian lira, rate =0.0512   factor = 10,000

$$200,000 \text{ lire} = \frac{200,000 \times 0.0512}{10,000} = 1.02 \text{ in home currency}$$

7.4   Maintain Factoring Companies (tcmcs0125m000)

SESSION OBJECTIVE

To define data about the factoring companies used in other sessions.

SEE ALSO KEYWORD(S)

•   Factoring Companies

SEE ALSO METHOD(S)

•   Address Verification for Tax Provider

tcmcs0125m000   single-occ (1)   Form 1-1
```
+------------------------------------------------------------------------+
|  Maintain Factoring Companies                          Company: 000    |
|------------------------------------------------------------------------|
|                                                                        |
|  Code                    : 1..                                         |
|                                                                        |
|  Country                 : 2..  3_____             |
|  Name                    : 4.................................          |
|                           : 5...............................           |
|  Address                 : 6...............................            |
|                           : 7...............................           |
|  8_____  : 9...............................            |
|  10_____  : 11..............................            |
|  12_____  1314.......                                   |
|  15_____  1617...                                       |
|  Bank                    : 18.  19_____  20_____   |
|                                                                        |
+------------------------------------------------------------------------+
```
1.   Factoring Company

For further information, see keyword(s)
"Factoring Companies".

2.   Country

The code of the country where the factoring company is based.

3.   Description

4.   Name

The first part of the name of the factoring company.

5.   Name 2

The second part of the name of the factoring company.

6.   Address
The first part of the address of the factoring company.
7.   Address 2
The second part of the address of the factoring company.
8.   Program domain string
9.   City
The third part of the address of the factoring company.
For tax provider users, the city and state or province where the factoring
company is based. The city and state or province should be separated by a comma
",", such as "Menlo Park, CA".
For further information, see method(s)
•   Address Verification for Tax Provider
10.   Program domain string
11.   City 2
The second part of the city where the factoring company is based.
For tax provider users, the ZIP Code or Postal Code where the factoring company
is based.
For further information, see method(s)
•   Address Verification for Tax Provider
12.   Program domain string
13.   Program domain of string length 1
14.   GEO Code
A GEO code is a code used together or in lieu of address information such as
city, state/province, and ZIP/postal code to uniquely identify a taxing
jurisdiction. The tax provider determines the GEO code based upon the address
information entered and the county and city limits selected.
The format of the GEO code varies by tax provider. AVP uses a two-digit GEO
code; the GEO code together with the city, state, and ZIP code, identifies the
taxing jurisdiction. Vertex uses a nine-digit GEO code comprised of a two digit
state code, three-digit county code, and a four-digit city code. A tenth digit
is used to identify if the jurisdiction is inside or outside of the city limits.
15.   Program domain string
16.   Program domain of string length 1
17.   Answer on question y/n
18.   Bank
The default bank relation of this factoring company. The data to be entered must
be defined in the session "Maintain Banks by Factoring Company (tcmcs0126m000)".
19.   Name
The first part of the bank name.
20.   Bank Account
The account number of the factoring company.
7.5   Maintain Banks by Factoring Company (tcmcs0126m000)
SESSION OBJECTIVE
To maintain banks per factoring company.
SEE ALSO KEYWORD(S)
•   Bank Addresses, Factoring Companies (tcmcs025)

```
tcmcs0126m000                              multi/group (3    Form 1-1
+--------------------------------------------------------------------------+
|  Maintain Banks by Factoring Company                    Company: 000  |
|--------------------------------------------------------------------------|
|                                                                          |
|  Factoring Company: 1..   2_____             |
|                                                                          |
|  Bank       Bank Type      Bank Addresses   Bank Account    Account Type |
|                                                                          |
|       3..  4........       5..........      6..............  7...........|
|                                                                          |
+--------------------------------------------------------------------------+
```

1.   Factoring Company
For further information, see keyword(s)
"Factoring Companies".
2.   Name
The first part of the name of the factoring company.

3.   Bank
The code by which the bank is known at the factoring company.
4.   Bank Type
In this field you can select the type of bank.
Bank
The account number of the factoring company is a bank account. This is the default value.
Giro
The account number of the factoring company is a giro account.
5.   Bank Addresses
For further information, see keyword(s)
"Bank Addresses".
6.   Bank Account
The account number of the factoring company. In the session "Maintain COM Parameters (tccom0000m000)" in the field "Check on Bank Account No." you can indicate if this bank account number must be checked.
7.   Account Type
The type of account. Normal Account
The account of the factoring company is a normal current account. This is the default value.
Blocked Account
The account of the factoring company is a blocked account. This is used for payments against invoices with blocked account amounts from subcontractors.

7.6   Maintain Invoicing Methods (tcmcs0155m000)

SESSION OBJECTIVE
To define the invoicing methods used in other sessions.
SEE ALSO KEYWORD(S)
•   Invoicing Methods

tcmcs0155m000   multi-occ (2)   Form 1-1
+---+
Maintain Invoicing Methods   Company: 000
Code   Description   Collect   Gross/Net
1.. 2............................ 3....   4.......
+---+

1.   Invoicing Method
For further information, see keyword(s)
"Invoicing Methods".
2.   Description
Enter a clear description here.
3.   Collect
You may either print a summary invoice or not. The combination of the fields, "Collect" and "Gross/Net" allows you to define four invoice methods:
•   Collective and Net Invoices
•   Non-Collective and Net Invoices
•   Collective and Gross Invoices
•   Non-Collective and Gross Invoices
Yes
Collective Invoices means that deliveries appear on one invoice when delivering several orders to customers. The orders, however, are individually specified.
No
With Non-Collective invoices, an invoice is made for each order.
4.   Gross/Net
You may either print the discount on the invoice or not. Net
The line item discount is not printed on the invoice.
Gross
The line item discount is printed on the invoice.

7.7   Maintain Late Payment Surcharges (tcmcs0111m000)

SESSION OBJECTIVE
To maintain late payment surcharges.
SEE ALSO KEYWORD(S)
•   Late Payment Surcharges

```
+-----------------------------------------------------------------------+
| Maintain Late Payment Surcharges                      Company: 000    |
|-----------------------------------------------------------------------|
|                                                                       |
|  Code    Description                  Number of Days   Percentage     |
|                                                                       |
|   1..   2.............................   3..           4.             |
|                                                                       |
+-----------------------------------------------------------------------+
```

1.   Late Payment Surcharge
For further information, see keyword(s)
"Late Payment Surcharges".
2.   Description
Enter a clear description here.
3.   Number of Days
A period of a number of days after the invoice date in which payment can take
place without the late payment surcharge. After this period, a late payment
surcharge applies and the customer has to pay the goods amount + late payment
surcharge + Tax over both.
4.   Percentage
As soon as the number of days of the late payment surcharge has lapsed, a
percentage above the net goods amount must be paid as a surcharge. This
percentage is subject to Tax (see example). If the receiver of the invoice pays
within the stated period, he/she may deduct the percentage from the invoice
amount. In BAAN IV late payment surcharges are calculated as follows:
Example:
Net Goods Amount: 1000.00
Late Payment Surcharge 2%:   20.00
                           ------- +
                           1020.00
Tax 18,5 %   188.70
                           ------- +
                           1208.70
The late payment surcharge is calculated over the net goods amount; the Tax is
then calculated over the net goods amount + late payment surcharge.
In case of several Tax percentages applying to one order, the late payment
surcharge is distributed proportionally over the Tax percentages.
7.8   Maintain Rounding Codes (tcmcs0153m000)
SESSION OBJECTIVE
To maintain rounding data.
SEE ALSO KEYWORD(S)
•   Rounding Codes

```
+-----------------------------------------------------------------------+
| Maintain Rounding Codes                               Company: 000    |
|-----------------------------------------------------------------------|
|                                                                       |
|  Code        : 1..                                                    |
|                                                                       |
|  Description : 2...........................                           |
|                                                                       |
|                                                                       |
|    To Amount      Round to                                            |
|                                                                       |
|    3              4..                                                 |
|    5......        6..                                                 |
|    7......        8..                                                 |
|    9......        10.                                                 |
|    11.....        12.                                                 |
|    13.....        14.                                                 |
|                                                                       |
+-----------------------------------------------------------------------+
```

1.   Rounding Code
For further information, see keyword(s)
"Rounding Codes".
2.   Description
Enter a clear description here.
3.   To Amount
The first upper limit of the rounding method.
4.   Round to
The first rounding line.
5.   To Amount
The second upper limit of the rounding method.
6.   Round to
The second rounding line.
7.   To Amount
The third upper limit of the rounding method.
8.   Round to
The third rounding line.
9.   To Amount
The fourth upper limit of the rounding method.
10.   Round to
The fourth rounding line.
11.   To Amount
The fifth upper limit of the rounding method.
12.   Round to
The fifth rounding line.
13.   To Amount
The sixth upper limit of the rounding method.
14.   Round to
The sixth rounding line.

7.9   Maintain Tax Codes (tcmcs0137m000)
SESSION OBJECTIVE
To maintain tax codes.
SEE ALSO KEYWORD(S)
•   Tax Codes

```
tcmcs0137m000                                 multi-occ (2)   Form 1-1
+------------------------------------------------------------------------------+
| Maintain Tax Codes                                          Company: 000 |
|------------------------------------------------------------------------------|
|                                                                              |
| Code        Description                                                      |
|                                                                              |
| 1........   2.............................                                    |
|                                                                              |
+------------------------------------------------------------------------------+
```

1.   Tax Code
For further information, see keyword(s)
"Tax Codes".
2.   Description
Enter a clear description here.

7.10 Maintain Tax Codes by Country (tcmcs0136m000)
SESSION OBJECTIVE
To maintain tax codes per country.
SEE ALSO KEYWORD(S) ·
•   Countries, Tax Codes (tcmcs037)

```
tcmcs0136m000                     zoom      single-occ (1)  Form 1-2 >
+------------------------------------------------------------------------------+
| Maintain Tax Codes by Country                               Company: 000 |
|------------------------------------------------------------------------------|
|                                                                              |
| Country                          :      1.. 2_____ |
| Tax Code                         : 3........ 4_____ |
|                                                                              |
| Description                      : 5.............................          |
```

```
| Tax Type                          : 6...........                           |
| Round up Tax amounts              : 7....                                   |
| Singular Tax                      : 8....                                   |
| Expense Purchase Tax              : 9....                                   |
| 10_____ : 11.......... 12_____ |
| Sales Tax Account                 : 13.......... 12_____ |
| Account for Tax on Advance Payments: 14.......... 12_____ |
| Account for Tax on Advance Receipts: 15.......... 12_____ |
| Contra Account Shifted Tax Purchase: 16.......... 12_____ |
| Contra Account Shifted Tax Sales  : 17.......... 12_____ |
| Interim Account for Tax on Payments: 18.......... 12_____ |
| Interim Account for Tax on Receipts: 19.......... 12_____ |
|                                                                             |
+-----------------------------------------------------------------------------+
```

1.   Country
For further information, see keyword(s)
"Countries".
The data to be entered must be defined in the session "Maintain Countries
(tcmcs0110m000)".
2.   Description
3.   Tax Code
For further information, see keyword(s)
"Tax Codes".
The data to be entered must be defined in the session "Maintain Tax Codes
(tcmcs0137m000)".
4.   Description
5.   Description
Enter a clear description here.
6.   Tax Type
Normal
The Tax amount is added to the net amount (to become the gross amount) and
directly included in the Tax analysis as chargeable or payable Tax amount in the
package BAAN Finance.
Shifted
The amount is not added to the net amount, but posted to a Tax account.
Simultaneously, a reverse entry is generated on a Tax contra-account in the
package BAAN Finance. In the Tax analysis in the package BAAN Finance the amount
is included twice, once as an entry on the Tax account, and once as a reverse
entry on the Tax contra-account. In the Netherlands, "shifted Tax" is used in
relation to legislation concerning the ultimate responsibility for payment of
taxes and social security contributions (invoices from subcontractors to main
contractor). In the European Union it may be used for purchase invoices from
other EU countries: such invoices do not state any Tax, but when posting them
you have to calculate a fictitious Tax amount (against the national Tax rate)
which is included on the Tax report as both chargeable and payable.
On Payments
This Tax is paid in the same way as normal Tax, but only becomes reclaimable or
payable after the invoice has been paid. The Tax will be posted to an interim
account, and will be transferred to the "real" Tax account only when the invoice
is paid. If this type of Tax is used in another type of transaction it is
directly posted to the Tax account.
7.   Round up Tax amounts
This field allows you to indicate whether the Tax amount for this Tax code
should be rounded up or not. In some countries the Tax amounts must always be
rounded up.
8.   Singular Tax
Yes
The Tax code refers to a single Tax percentage. One Tax amount is calculated on
the basis of one percentage and posted to one Tax ledger account in the package
BAAN Finance.
No
The Tax code refers to a multiple Tax percentage. Several lines can be defined
which together constitute the total Tax amount. Each Tax line can be posted to a

separate Tax ledger account in the package BAAN Finance. The Tax lines can be defined in the session "Maintain Tax Rates by Tax Code (tcmcs0135s000)".

9.   Expense Purchase Tax

The expense purchase tax indicator is used to identify tax codes or tax code levels which require that tax amounts be "expensed" to the purchase account rather than accrued as a deduction of sales tax payable. It is not necessary that the ledger account actually be an expense type account, "expense" is being used as a generic term to describe any purchase for internal use.

The setting of this field will also determine whether the label of the purchase tax account field in the Maintain Tax Codes by Country (tcmcs0136m000) and Maintain Tax Rates by Tax Code (tcmcs0135s000) sessions will be displayed as "Purchase Tax Account" or "Interim Purchase Tax Account"

Yes

Tax amounts for purchases recorded in the Accounts Payable module will be posted to the purchase ledger account and dimensions of the goods.

For matched purchase invoices, the "Interim Purchase Tax Account" specified will be used when the purchase invoice is registered and then the tax amount will be reclassed to the ledger account and dimensions of the purchase during the invoice approval process. The ledger account and dimensions of the purchase will be taken from the integration tables for the purchase receipt transaction.

For non-matched purchase invoices with taxes calculated at the transaction line level, tax amounts will be posted directly to the ledger account and dimensions of the purchased goods and the "Interim Purchase Tax Account" will not be used at all.

No

Tax amounts for purchases recorded in the Accounts Payable module will be posted to the account specified in the "Purchase Tax Account" field.

10.   Expense Purchase Tax

11.   Purchase Tax Account

The Tax account in the package BAAN Finance to which the Tax amount will be posted if the Tax type is not "On Payments" and the Tax is linked to a purchase invoice transaction or a ledger transaction with the Tax type "Purchase". This Tax account is also used for posting paid purchase invoices with the Tax type "On Payments"

12.   Ledger Account Description

13.   Sales Tax Account

The Tax account in the package BAAN Finance to which the Tax amount will be posted if the Tax type is not "On Payments" and the Tax is linked to a sales invoice transaction or a ledger transaction with the Tax type "Sales". This Tax account is also used for posting paid sales invoices with the Tax type "On Payments".

14.   Account for Tax on Advance Payments

The Tax account, in the package BAAN Finance, to which the Tax amount is to be posted if it was calculated over advance payments to a supplier. When, later, the purchase invoice is posted and the advance payment is allocated to a purchase invoice, a reverse entry is posted on the Tax account for this amount.

15.   Account for Tax on Advance Receipts

The Tax account, in the package BAAN Finance, to which the Tax amount is to be posted if it was calculated over an advance payment from a supplier. When, later, the sales invoice is posted and the advance payment is allocated to a sales invoice, a reverse entry is posted on the Tax account for this amount.

16.   Contra Account Shifted Tax Purchase

The Tax account in the package BAAN Finance account to which the reverse entry for the Tax amount will be posted if the Tax type is "Shifted" and the Tax is linked to a purchase invoice transaction or to a ledger account transaction with the Tax type "Purchase".

17.   Contra Account Shifted Tax Sales

The Tax account in the package BAAN Finance account to which the reverse entry for the Tax amount will be posted if the Tax type is "Shifted" and the Tax is linked to a sales invoice transaction or to a ledger account transaction with the Tax type "Sales".

18.   Interim Account for Tax on Payments

The interim account in the package BAAN Finance to which the Tax amount is
posted if the Tax type is "On Payments" and the Tax is linked to a purchase
invoice transaction. As soon as a purchase invoice with the Tax type "On
Payments" is paid, a reverse entry is generated for the amount on this account.
19.   Interim Account for Tax on Receipts
The interim account in the package BAAN Finance to which the Tax amount is
posted if the Tax type is "On Payments" and the Tax is linked to sales purchase
invoice transaction. As soon as a sales invoice with the Tax type "On Payments"
is paid, a reverse entry is generated for the amount on this account.

```
tcmcs0136m000                      zoom        single-occ (1) < Form 2-2
+--------------------------------------------------------------------------+
| Maintain Tax Codes by Country                          Company: 000   |
|--------------------------------------------------------------------------|
|  Country                            :      11.  12_____      |
|  Tax Code                           : 13.......  14_____      |
|                                                                          |
|  Sales Ledger Account               : 15.........   16_____   |
|  Amounts Entered in BAAN Finance    : 17...............                  |
|  1...........................        2 18....  19_____        |
|  3...........................        4 20....  19_____        |
|  5...........................        6 21....  19_____        |
|  7...........................        8 22....  19_____        |
|  9...........................       1023....  19_____         |
|  Tax Authority Code                 : 24........  25_____      |
+--------------------------------------------------------------------------+
```

1.   Dimension Description
2.   Separator
3.   Dimension Description
4.   Separator
5.   Dimension Description
6.   Separator
7.   Dimension Description
8.   Separator
9.   Dimension Description
10.   Separator
11.   Country
For further information, see keyword(s)
"Countries".
The data to be entered must be defined in the session "Maintain Countries
(tcmcs0110m000)".
12.   Description
13.   Tax Code
For further information, see keyword(s)
"Tax Codes".
The data to be entered must be defined in the session "Maintain Tax Codes
(tcmcs0137m000)".
14.   Description
15.   Sales Ledger Account
The sales account is needed to post sales invoice totals to package BAAN
Finance. The net turnover amounts of the invoices entered with this Tax code are
posted to this account.
16.   Ledger Account Description
17.   Amounts Entered in BAAN Finance
The way in which amounts with this Tax code must be entered into the package
BAAN Finance.
Gross
In the package BAAN Finance each amount is entered as a gross amount, after
which the system calculates the Tax amount and the net amount.
Example:
Tax rate is 16 (Gross) amount entered is 232
The system calculates the Tax amount as 232 x 16/116 = 32
The net amount is 232 - 32 = 200.
Net

In the package BAAN Finance, each amount is entered as net amount, after which the system calculates the Tax amount and the gross amount.
Example: Tax rate is 16 (Net) amount entered is 200
The system calculates the Tax amount as 200 x 16/100 = 32
The gross amount is then 200 + 32 = 232
Gross over Hundred
In the package BAAN Finance each amount is entered as a gross amount, after which the system calculates the Tax amount and the net amount. However, the Tax rate is calculated as a percentage of the gross rather than the net amount.
Example: Tax rate is 16 (Gross) amount entered is 232
The system calculates the Tax amount as 232 x 16/100 = 37.12 !
The net amount is 232 - 37.12 = 194.88 !
In some countries this method is used for travel and accommodation costs.
18.   Dimension 1
Dimensions can be classified into different dimension types which can be freely defined by the user in the session "Maintain Dimensions (tfgld0110m000)".
19.   Dimension Description
The description of the dimension entered.
20.   Dimension 2
Dimensions can be classified into different dimension types which can be freely defined by the user in the session "Maintain Dimensions (tfgld0110m000)".
21.   Dimension 3
Dimensions can be classified into different dimension types which can be freely defined by the user in the session "Maintain Dimensions (tfgld0110m000)".
22.   Dimension 4
Dimensions can be classified into different dimension types which can be freely defined by the user in the session "Maintain Dimensions (tfgld0110m000)".
23.   Dimension 5
Dimensions can be classified into different dimension types which can be freely defined by the user in the session "Maintain Dimensions (tfgld0110m000)".
24.   Tax Authority Code
A Tax Authority is a Government Body with jurisdiction over the sales taxes in a specific area. The state of California, the province of Ontario, the county of Dade, and the city of Atlanta are all examples of Tax Authorities.
25.   Description
Description of the Tax Authority Code is maintained here.
7.11 Maintain Terms of Payment (tcmcs0113m000)
SESSION OBJECTIVE
To define the terms of payment used in other sessions.
SEE ALSO KEYWORD(S)
•   Terms of Payment

```
tcmcs0113m000                      zoom       single-occ (1)   Form 1-2 >
+---------------------------------------------------------------------+
| Maintain Terms of Payment                           Company: 000    |
|---------------------------------------------------------------------|
|                                                                     |
|   Terms of Payment              :    1..                            |
|                                                                     |
|   Description                   : 2............................     |
|                                                                     |
|   Payment Period                :    3..  4........................ |
|                                                                     |
|   Discount Period 1    [days] :    5..                              |
|   Discount Period 2    [days] :    6..                              |
|   Discount Period 3    [days] :    7..                              |
|   Discount Percentage 1         : 8..     [%]                       |
|   Discount Percentage 2         : 9..     [%]                       |
|   Discount Percentage 3         : 10.     [%]                       |
|   Discount Including Tax         : 11...                             |
|   Discount on Invoices           : 12...                            |
|   Text                           : 13___                            |
|                                                                     |
+---------------------------------------------------------------------+
```

1.   Terms of Payment
For further information, see keyword(s)
"Terms of Payment".
2.   Description
Enter a clear description here.
3.   Payment Period
The payment period is the period which is added to the invoice date to calculate
the due date. It may be expressed in days or months.
4.   Payment Period Type
The unit of the payment period.
Days
The payment period is expressed in days.
Months
The payment period is expressed in calendar months.
If you select the value "Months", the field "Due Date Calculation Method" is
automatically filled with the value "End of Month" and the field "Priority for
Due Date Calc." with the value "Not Applicable". You cannot maintain these
fields.
5.   Discount Period 1
The number of days after the invoice date during which the discount recorded in
the field "Discount Percentage 1" may be subtracted.
You can enter up to 3 discount periods with the corresponding discount
percentages. During the number of days in this field, the first discount
percentage is valid.
6.   Discount Period 2
The number of days after the invoice date during which the discount recorded in
the field "Discount Percentage 2" may be subtracted.
You can only maintain this field if the field "Discount Period 1" has a value
unequal to zero.
The number of days must be greater than the number of days in the field
"Discount Period 1", or zero (if there is no second discount period).
7.   Discount Period 3
The number of days after the invoice date during which the discount recorded in
the field "Discount Percentage 3" may be subtracted.
You can only maintain this field if the field "Discount Period 2" has a value
unequal to zero.
The number of days must be greater than the number of days in the field
"Discount Period 2", or zero (if there is no third discount period).
8.   Discount Percentage 1
The discount percentage that may be subtracted in the first discount period as
recorded in the field "Discount Period 1" in the session "Maintain Terms of
Payment (tcmcs0113m000)".
You can enter up to 3 discount periods with the associated percentages. The
percentage in this field is valid during the first period. You can only maintain
this field if the field "Discount Period 1" has a value unequal to zero.
9.   Discount Percentage 2
The discount percentage that may be subtracted in the second discount period as
recorded in the field "Discount Period 2" in the session "Maintain Terms of
Payment (tcmcs0113m000)".
You can only maintain this field if the field "Discount Period 2" has a value
unequal to zero.
The percentage must be less than the percentage in the field "Discount Period
1", or zero (if there is no second discount percentage).
10.   Discount Percentage 3
The discount percentage that may be subtracted in the third discount period as
recorded in the field "Discount Period 3" in the session "Maintain Terms of
Payment (tcmcs0113m000)".
You can only maintain this field if the field "Discount Period 3" has a value
unequal to zero.
The percentage must be less than the percentage in the field "Discount Period
2", or zero (if there is no third discount percentage).
11.   Discount Including Tax

Depending on your choice, the discount off the invoice amount can be calculated with or without Tax. Yes
The discount is calculated over the full invoice amount including Tax. This is standard procedure in, for instance, Germany and South Africa.
No
The discount is calculated over the invoice amount after subtracting the Tax amount. This is standard in the Netherlands and the UK.
12.   Discount on Invoices
The Tax can be calculated on the basis of the net amount or the net amount after subtraction of the allowed cash discount. The latter is calculated with the discount percentage recorded in the field "Discount Percentage 1". Yes
The Tax is calculated over the net amount after subtracting the allowed payment discount as calculated with the percentage in the field "Discount Percentage 1". This is the usual practice in, for instance, Great Britain.
No
The Tax is calculated over the net amount. This is the usual procedure in most of the other countries.
13.   Text

```
tcmcs0113m000                    zoom        single-occ (1) < Form 2-2
+--------------------------------------------------------------------+
| Maintain Terms of Payment                          Company: 000    |
|--------------------------------------------------------------------|
|                                                                    |
|  Terms of Payment            :          1.. 2_____  |
|                                                                    |
|  Due Date Calculation Method :      3...........                   |
|  Priority for Due Date Calc. :    4..............                  |
|  Discount Date Calc. Method  :      5...........                   |
|  Discount Date Calc. Priority :  6..............                   |
|  Fence for Due Date    [days] :         7..                        |
|  Fence for Disc. Date  [days] :         8..                        |
|  Tolerance for Disc. Percentage:        9..   [%]                  |
|  Tolerance for Disc. Amount  : 10.............                     |
|  Tolerance Disc. Period [days] :        11.                        |
|  Payment Days          [Day 1]:         12                         |
|                        [Day 2]:         13                         |
|                        [Day 3]:         14                         |
|  Use Pmt. Days for Disc. Calc. :        15...                      |
|                                                                    |
+--------------------------------------------------------------------+
```

1.   Terms of Payment
For further information, see keyword(s)
"Terms of Payment".
2.   Description
3.   Due Date Calculation Method
This fields determines how the due date will be calculated.
Immediately
The due date is the invoice date + payment period.
End of Month
The due date depends on the value of the field "Priority for Due Date Calc.":
Month End
The due date is the end of the month + payment period (end of the month is the last day of the month of the invoice date).
Payment Period
The due date is the invoice date + payment period; the resulting date is then shifted to the end of the month. You cannot maintain this field if the field "Payment Period Type" has the value "Months".
4.   Priority for Due Date Calc.
If you have selected the value "End of Month" in the field "Due Date Calculation Method" you must indicate here when the date is to be shifted to the end of the month.
Not Applicable

This value is assigned automatically if the field "Due Date Calculation Method" has the value "Immediately".
Month End
The invoice date is first shifted to the end of the month, after which the payment period is added.
Payment Period
The payment period is first added to the invoice date, after which the resulting date is shifted to the end of the month. You cannot maintain this field if the field "Payment Period Type" has the value "Months".
5.   Discount Date Calc. Method
This field determines how the discount date will be calculated.
Immediately
The discount date is the invoice date + the discount period.
End of Month
The calculation of the discount date depends on the field "Discount Date Calculation Priority":
Month End
The discount date is the end of the month + discount period (end of the month is the last day of the month of the invoice date).
Payment Period
The discount date is the invoice date + discount period; the resulting date is then shifted to the end of the month.
6.   Discount Date Calculation Priority
If you have selected the value "End of Month" in the field "Discount Date Calc. Method" you must indicate here when the date is to be
shifted to the end of the month.
Not Applicable
This value is assigned automatically if the field "Discount Date Calc. Method" has the value "Immediately".
Month End
The invoice date is first shifted to the end of the month, after which the discount period is added.
Payment Period
The discount period is first added to the invoice date, after which the resulting date is shifted to the end of the month.
7.   Fence for Due Date
If the field "Due Date Calculation Method" has the value "End of Month", the due date will be shifted from this day to the end of the next month (not the current month). This does not happen if the field has the value 0.
You can only maintain this field if the field "Due Date Calculation Method" has the value "End of Month"; otherwise, it is automatically set to zero.
8.   Fence for Disc. Date
If the field "Discount Date Calc. Method" has the value "End of Month", the discount date will be shifted from this day to the end of the next month (not the current month). This does not happen if the field has the value 0.
You can only maintain this field if the field "Discount Date Calc. Method" has the value "End of Month"; otherwise, it is automatically set to zero.
9.   Tolerance for Disc. Percentage
The maximum percentage by which the customer may exceed the discount stated in the terms of payment.
If a customer subtracts a larger discount from the payment than is stated in the terms of payment, the system will issue a warning unless:
•   the difference between allowed and actual discount is less than the amount in the field "Tolerance for Disc. Amount"
•   the difference between allowed and actual discount in percentages is less than the percentage in the field "Tolerance for Disc. Percentage"
If one or both of these values is exceeded, the system will issue a warning.
10.   Tolerance for Disc. Amount
The maximum amount by which the customer may exceed the discount stated in the terms of payment.
If a customer subtracts a larger discount from the payment than is stated in the terms of payment, the system will issue a warning unless:

- the difference between allowed and actual discount is less than the amount in the field "Tolerance for Disc. Amount"
- the difference between allowed and actual discount in percentages is less than the percentage in the field "Tolerance for Disc. Percentage"

If one or both of the above values is exceeded, the system will issue a warning.

SEE ALSO METHOD(S)
- Currency Formats

11.   Tolerance for Disc. Period

The maximum number of days by which the customer is allowed to exceed the discount date.

If a customer exceeds the discount period the system will issue a warning, unless:
- the allowed discount period is exceeded with fewer days than are recorded in the field "Tolerance for Disc. Period"

12.   Payment Day 1

The first fixed payment date according to the terms of payment. The due date of an invoice is shifted to the first available fixed payment date (if the fixed payment dates are unequal to zero).

You may include up to 3 fixed payment days in the terms of payment. A fixed payment day is recorded as a day number in the month.

Example: The fixed payment days entered are 10, 20 and 30. The due date of 5 February 1994 is changed into 10 February 1994. The due date of 26 February 1994 is changed into 28 February 1994 (as 30 February does not exist).

13.   Payment Day 2

The second fixed payment date according to the terms of payment. The due date of an invoice is shifted to the first available fixed payment date (if the fixed payment dates are unequal to zero).

You can only maintain this field if the field "Payment Day 1" has a value unequal to zero.

14.   Payment Day 3

The third fixed payment date according to the terms of payment. The due date of an invoice is shifted to the first available fixed payment date (if the fixed payment dates are unequal to zero).

You can only maintain this field if the field "Payment Day 2" has a value unequal to zero.

15.   Use Payment Days for Disc. Calc

Fixed payment dates may be used to determine the due date or to also determine discount dates.

Yes

Both the due date and the discount dates are shifted to the first available payment date.

No

Only the due date is shifted to the first available payment date.

7.12 Maintain Payment Schedules (tcmcs0114m000)

SESSION OBJECTIVE

To maintain payment schedules.

SEE ALSO KEYWORD(S)
- Payment Schedules, Terms of Payment (tcmcs013)

```
tcmcs0114m000                                  multi/group (3    Form 1-1
+------------------------------------------------------------------------+
| Maintain Payment Schedules                               Company: 000  |
|------------------------------------------------------------------------|
|                                                                        |
|  Terms of Payment    : 1..  2_____            |
|                                                                        |
|  Payment Period          Perc. of Inv. Amount                          |
|                                                                        |
|          4... 3_____              5..                              |
|                                                                        |
+------------------------------------------------------------------------+
```

1.   Terms of Payment

For further information, see keyword(s) "Payment Schedules".

2.	Description
3.	Payment Period Type
The unit for the payment period as recorded for these terms of payment in the
field "Payment Period Type" in the session "Maintain Terms of Payment
(tcmcs0113m000)".
4.	Number of Days after Invoice Date
The period within which part of the amount is to be paid. The field "Payment
Period Type" in the session "Maintain Terms of Payment (tcmcs0113m000)"
contains the time unit in which this period is recorded.
5.	Percentage of Invoice Amount
The percentage of the total amount to be paid within the period specified. The
total of all percentages must be 100.
7.13 Maintain Credit Insurance Companies (tcmcs0109m000)
SESSION OBJECTIVE
To record the credit insurance companies used in other sessions.
SEE ALSO KEYWORD(S)
•	Credit Insurance Companies
SEE ALSO METHOD(S)
•	Address Verification for Tax Provider
tcmcs0109m000   single-occ (1)   Form 1-1

```
+-------------------------------------------------------------------------+
| Maintain Credit Insurance Companies                      Company: 000   |
|-------------------------------------------------------------------------|
|                                                                         |
| Credit Insurance Company: 1..                                           |
|                                                                         |
| Country              : 2..  3_____           |
| Name                 : 4...............................                 |
|                       : 5...............................                 |
| Address              : 6...............................                 |
|                       : 7...............................                 |
| 8_____     : 9...............................                |
| 10_____     : 11..............................                |
| 12_____     1314.......                                       |
| 15_____     1617...                                           |
|                                                                         |
+-------------------------------------------------------------------------+
```

1.	Credit Insurance Company
For further information, see keyword(s)
"Credit Insurance Companies".
2.	Country
The country where the credit insurance company is based. The data to be entered
must be defined in the session "Maintain Countries (tcmcs0110m000)".
3.	Description
4.	Name
The first part of the name of the credit insurance company.
5.	Name 2
The second part of the name of the credit insurance company.
6.	Address
The first part of the address of the credit insurance company.
7.	Address 2
The second part of the name of the credit insurance company.
8.	Program domain string
9.	City
The city where the credit insurance company is based.
For tax provider users, the city and state or province where the credit
insurance company is based. The city and state or province should be separated
by a comma ",", such as "Menlo Park, CA".
For further information, see method(s)
•	Address Verification for Tax Provider
10.	Program domain string
11.	City 2
The second part of the city where the credit insurance company is based.

For tax provider users, the ZIP Code or Postal Code where the credit insurance company is based.
For further information, see method(s)
*   Address Verification for Tax Provider
12.   Program domain string
13.   Program domain of string length 1
14.   GEO Code
A GEO code is a code used together or in lieu of address information such as city, state/province, and ZIP/postal code to uniquely identify a taxing jurisdiction. The tax provider determines the GEO code based upon the address information entered and the county and city limits selected.
The format of the GEO code varies by tax provider. AVP uses a two-digit GEO code; the GEO code together with the city, state, and ZIP code, identifies the taxing jurisdiction. Vertex uses a nine-digit GEO code comprised of a two digit state code, three-digit county code, and a four-digit city code. A tenth digit is used to identify if the jurisdiction is inside or outside of the city limits.
15.   Program domain string
16.   Program domain of string length 1
17.   Answer on question y/n
7.14   Maintain Single Tax Rates (tcmcs0132s000)
SESSION OBJECTIVE
To record the Tax rate for each Tax code.
SEE ALSO KEYWORD(S)
*   Tax Rates by Tax Code

```
tcmcs0132s000                                    multi/group (3     Form 1-1
+--Maintain Single Tax Rates-----------------------------------------------+
|                                                                          |
|  Country      :       1.. 2_____                |
|  Tax Code     : 3........ 4.............................                  |
|                                                                          |
|  Effective Date Tax Rate   Max.Tax Amount  Tax Base Amount  Rate for Excess |
|                               in HC            in HC                      |
|                                                                          |
|     5........ 6..         7.............  8.............        9..       |
|                                                                          |
+--------------------------------------------------------------------------+
```

1.   Country
For further information, see keyword(s)
"Countries".
The data to be entered must be defined in the session "Maintain Countries (tcmcs0110m000)".
2.   Description
3.   Tax Code
For further information, see keyword(s)
"Tax Codes".
The data to be entered must be defined in the session "Maintain Tax Codes (tcmcs0137m000)".
4.   Language-Specif- ic Unit Description
Enter a clear description here.
5.   Effective Date
The effective date for the relevant Tax rate. Tax rates can be defined per date.
6.   Tax Rate
The Tax rate depending on the country and the Tax code.
7.   Maximum Tax Amount
This is an amount in home currency which is defined at the individual tax level for a single or multi level tax structure. A maximum amount can be defined for each level of tax. A tax level might be a state, county, province, etc.
When tax is calculated for that tax level, it's home currency amount is compared with this amount. If it is greater, the tax amount is set to this maximum in home currency and the foreign currency amount is recalculated.
SEE ALSO METHOD(S)
*   Currency Formats
8.   Tax Base Amount

In certain jurisdictions, tax is charged progressively. Tax is applied to a certain tax base amount at one rate and applied to any excess amount at a different rate. This is the tax base amount is defined in home currency.
SEE ALSO METHOD(S)
•   Currency Formats
9.   Rate for Excess Amount
According to rules of some states the tax rate is to be applied upto a certain tax amount and anything above that tax base amount should be taxes at a different rate. This field defines the rate of tax for excess amount.
7.15 Maintain Multiple Tax Rates (tcmcs0133s000)
SESSION OBJECTIVE
To record the Tax rate for each Tax code.
SEE ALSO KEYWORD(S)
•   Tax Rates by Tax Code

```
tcmcs0133s000                                 multi/group (3    Form 1-1
+--Maintain Multiple Tax Rates------------------------------------------------+
|                                                                             |
| Country       :      1.. 2_____                  |
| Tax Code      : 3........ 4............................                      |
| Sequence No. :       5                                                      |
|                                                                             |
| Effective Date Tax Rate     Max.Tax Amount  Tax Base Amount  Rate for Excess|
|                                  in HC           in HC                      |
|                                                                             |
|    6........ 7..          8.............  9.............        10.          |
|                                                                             |
+-----------------------------------------------------------------------------+
```

1.   Country
For further information, see keyword(s)
"Countries".
The data to be entered must be defined in the session "Maintain Countries (tcmcs0110m000)".
2.   Description
3.   Tax Code
For further information, see keyword(s)
"Tax Codes".
The data to be entered must be defined in the session "Maintain Tax Codes (tcmcs0137m000)".
4.   Language-Specif- ic Unit Description
Enter a clear description here.
5.   Sequence No.
The Tax sequence number pertains to non-EU turnover tax, the Tax rate being composed of several rates, for instance a regional and a national one, as in the US.
6.   Effective Date
The effective date for the relevant Tax rate. Tax rates can be defined per date.
7.   Tax Rate
The Tax rate depending on the country and the Tax code.
8.   Maximum Tax Amount
This is an amount in home currency which is defined at the individual tax level for a single or multi level tax structure. A maximum amount can be defined for each level of tax. A tax level might be a state, county, province, etc.
When tax is calculated for that tax level, it's home currency amount is compared with this amount. If it is greater, the tax amount is set to this maximum in home currency and the foreign currency amount is recalculated.
SEE ALSO METHOD(S)
•   Currency Formats
9.   Tax Base Amount
In certain jurisdictions, tax is charged progressively. Tax is applied to a certain tax base amount at one rate and applied to any excess amount at a different rate. This is the tax base amount is defined in home currency.
SEE ALSO METHOD(S)
•   Currency Formats

10.   Rate for Excess Amount
According to rules of some states the tax rate is to be applied upto a certain tax amount and anything above that tax base amount should be taxes at a different rate. This field defines the rate of tax for excess amount.

7.16 Maintain Tax Rates by Tax Code (tcmcs0135s000)

SESSION OBJECTIVE
To record the Tax rate for each Tax code.
SEE ALSO KEYWORD(S)
•   Tax Rates by Tax Code

```
tcmcs0135s000                        zoom      single-occ (1)   Form 1-2 >
+--Maintain Tax Rates by Tax Code-------------------------------------------+
|                                                                           |
|   Country                              :      1.. 2_____   |
|   Tax Code                             :  3........ 4_____    |
|   Sequence No.                         :      5..                          |
|                                                                           |
|   Description                          :  6......                          |
|   Calculation Method                   :  7.............                   |
|   Expense Purchase Tax                 :  8....                            |
|   9_____ : 10........  11_____   |
|   Sales Tax Account                    : 12..........  11_____   |
|   Account for Tax on Advance Payments: 13..........  11_____     |
|   Account for Tax on Advance Receipts: 14..........  11_____     |
|   Interim Account for Tax on Payments: 15..........  11_____     |
|   Interim Account for Tax on Receipts: 16..........  11_____     |
|   Contra Account Shifted Tax Purchase: 17..........  11_____     |
|   Contra Account Shifted Tax Sales  : 18..........  11_____      |
|                                                                           |
+---------------------------------------------------------------------------+
```

1.   Country
The country where the Tax code is applicable.
2.   Description
3.   Tax Code
The code for recording tax rates (Value Added Tax (Tax) in EU countries or other types of turnover tax).
4.   Description
5.   Sequence No.
The Tax sequence number pertains to non-EU turnover tax, the Tax rate being composed of several rates, for instance a regional and a national one, as in the US.
6.   Description
Enter a clear description here.
7.   Calculation Method
Parallel
Parallel tax calculation means that e.g. the combination of tax rates 5% and 15% result in an eventual tax rate of 20%.
Cumulative
Cumulative tax calculation means that the second tax rate is applied over the first tax rate. The combination of tax rates 10% and 5% will result in an eventual tax rate of 15.5% (= 10% + 5% + (10% / 100% * 5%)).
8.   Expense Purchase Tax
The expense purchase tax indicator is used to identify tax codes or tax code levels which require that tax amounts be "expensed" to the purchase account rather than accrued as a deduction of sales tax payable. It is not necessary that the ledger account actually be an expense type account, "expense" is being used as a generic term to describe any purchase for internal use.
The setting of this field will also determine whether the label of the purchase tax account field in the Maintain Tax Codes by Country (tcmcs0136m000) and Maintain Tax Rates by Tax Code (tcmcs0135s000) sessions will be displayed as "Purchase Tax Account" or "Interim Purchase Tax Account"
Yes
Tax amounts for purchases recorded in the Accounts Payable module will be posted to the purchase ledger account and dimensions of the goods.

For matched purchase invoices, the "Interim Purchase Tax Account" specified will be used when the purchase invoice is registered and then the tax amount will be reclassed to the ledger account and dimensions of the purchase during the invoice approval process. The ledger account and dimensions of the purchase will be taken from the integration tables for the purchase receipt transaction. For non-matched purchase invoices with taxes calculated at the transaction line level, tax amounts will be posted directly to the ledger account and dimensions of the purchased goods and the "Interim Purchase Tax Account" will not be used at all.
No
Tax amounts for purchases recorded in the Accounts Payable module will be posted to the account specified in the "Purchase Tax Account" field.

9.   Expense Purchase Tax
10.   Purchase Tax Account
The Tax account in the package BAAN Finance to which the Tax amount will be posted if the Tax type is not "On Payments" and the Tax is linked to a purchase invoice transaction or a ledger transaction with the Tax type "Purchase". This Tax account is also used for posting paid purchase invoices with the Tax type "On Payments"

11.   Ledger Account Description
12.   Sales Tax Account
The Tax account in the package BAAN Finance to which the Tax amount will be posted if the Tax type is not "On Payments" and the Tax is linked to a sales invoice transaction or a ledger transaction with the Tax type "Sales". This Tax account is also used for posting paid sales invoices with the Tax type "On Payments".

13.   Account for Tax on Advance Payments
The Tax account, in the package BAAN Finance, to which the Tax amount is to be posted if it was calculated over advance payments to a supplier. When, later, the purchase
invoice is posted and the advance payment is allocated to a purchase invoice, a reverse entry is posted on the Tax account for this amount.

14.   Account for Tax on Advance Receipts
The Tax account, in the package BAAN Finance, to which the Tax amount is to be posted if it was calculated over an advance payment from a supplier. When, later, the sales invoice
is posted and the advance payment is allocated to a sales invoice, a reverse entry is posted on the Tax account for this amount.

15.   Interim Account for Tax on Payments
The interim account in the package BAAN Finance to which the Tax amount is posted if the Tax type is "On Payments" and the Tax is linked to a purchase invoice transaction. As soon as a purchase invoice with the Tax type "On Payments" is paid, a reverse entry is generated for the amount on this account.

16.   Interim Account for Tax on Receipts
The interim account in the package BAAN Finance to which the Tax amount is posted if the Tax type is "On Payments" and the Tax is linked to sales purchase invoice transaction. As soon as a sales invoice with the Tax type "On Payments" is paid, a reverse entry is generated for the amount on this account.

17.   Contra Account Shifted Tax Purchase
The Tax account in the package BAAN Finance account to which the reverse entry for the Tax amount will be posted if the Tax type is "Shifted" and the Tax is linked to a purchase invoice transaction or to a ledger account transaction with the Tax type "Purchase".

18.   Contra Account Shifted Tax Sales
The Tax account in the package BAAN Finance account to which the reverse entry for the Tax amount will be posted if the Tax type is "Shifted" and the Tax is linked to a sales invoice transaction or to a ledger account transaction with the Tax type "Sales".

```
tcmcs0135s000                    zoom        single-occ (1) < Form 2-2
+--Maintain Tax Rates by Tax Code-------------------------------------------+
|                                                                           |
| Country                     :      1.. 12_____    |
| Tax Code                    : 13....... 14_____    |
```

```
|  Sequence No.                          :         15.                              |
|                                                                                   |
|  2.............................   3 16....  17_____             |
|  4.............................   5 18....  17_____             |
|  6.............................   7 19....  17_____             |
|  8.............................   9 20....  17_____             |
|  10............................  1121....  17_____             |
|  Tax Authority Code                    : 22........ 23_____     |
|                                                                                   |
+-----------------------------------------------------------------------------------+
```

1.   Country
The country where the Tax code is applicable.
2.   Label Dimension
3.   Separator
4.   Label Dimension
5.   Separator
6.   Label Dimension
7.   Separator
8.   Label Dimension
9.   Separator
10.   Label Dimension
11.   Separator
12.   Description
13.   Tax Code
The code for recording tax rates (Value Added Tax (Tax) in EU countries or other
types of turnover tax).
14.   Description
15.   Sequence No.
The Tax sequence number pertains to non-EU turnover tax, the Tax rate being
composed of several rates, for instance a regional and a national one, as in the
US.
16.   Dimension 1
Dimensions can be classified into different dimension types which can be freely
defined by the user in the session "Maintain Dimensions (tfgld0110m000)".
17.   Dimension Description
The description of the dimension entered.
18.   Dimension 2
Dimensions can be classified into different dimension types which can be freely
defined by the user in the session "Maintain Dimensions (tfgld0110m000)".
19.   Dimension 3
Dimensions can be classified into different dimension types which can be freely
defined by the user in the session "Maintain Dimensions (tfgld0110m000)".
20.   Dimension 4
Dimensions can be classified into different dimension types which can be freely
defined by the user in the session "Maintain Dimensions (tfgld0110m000)".
21.   Dimension 5
Dimensions can be classified into different dimension types which can be freely
defined by the user in the session "Maintain Dimensions (tfgld0110m000)".
22.   Tax Authority Code
23.   Description
Description of the Tax Authority Code is maintained here.
8   Other Print Sessions
8.1   Print Bank Addresses (tcmcs0420m000)

tcmcs0420m000   single-occ (4)   Form 1-1

```
+-----------------------------------------------------------------------------------+
|  Print Bank Addresses                                          Company: 000  |
|-----------------------------------------------------------------------------------|
|                                                                                   |
|  Bank Address    from : 1..........                                               |
|                  to   : 2..........                                               |
+-----------------------------------------------------------------------------------+
```

1.   Bank Address from
2.   Bank Address to

8.2 Print Currencies (tcmcs0402m000)

tcmcs0402m000   single-occ (4)   Form 1-1

```
+----------------------------------------------------------------------+
|  Print Currencies                                     Company: 000    |
|----------------------------------------------------------------------|
|                                                                      |
|  Currency       from : 1..                                           |
|                 to   : 2..                                           |
|                                                                      |
+----------------------------------------------------------------------+
```

1.   Currency from
2.   Currency to

8.3 Print Currency Rates (tcmcs0408m000)

tcmcs0408m000   single-occ (4)   Form 1-1

```
+----------------------------------------------------------------------+
|  Print Currency Rates                                 Company: 000    |
|----------------------------------------------------------------------|
|                                                                      |
|  Currency        from :         1..                                  |
|                  to   :         2..                                  |
|                                                                      |
|  Effective Date from : 3........                                     |
|                  to   : 4........                                    |
|                                                                      |
+----------------------------------------------------------------------+
```

1.   Currency From
2.   Currency to
3.   Effective Date From
4.   Effective Date to

8.4 Print Factoring Companies (tcmcs0425m000)

tcmcs0425m000   single-occ (4)   Form 1-1

```
+----------------------------------------------------------------------+
|  Print Factoring Companies                            Company: 000    |
|----------------------------------------------------------------------|
|                                                                      |
|  Factoring Company from : 1..                                        |
|                    to   : 2..                                        |
|                                                                      |
+----------------------------------------------------------------------+
```

1.   Factoring Company From
2.   Factoring Company to

8.5 Print Banks by Factoring Company (tcmcs0426m000)

tcmcs0426m000   single-occ (4)   Form 1-1

```
+----------------------------------------------------------------------+
|  Print Banks by Factoring Company                     Company: 000    |
|----------------------------------------------------------------------|
|                                                                      |
|  Factoring Company from : 1..                                        |
|                    to   : 2..                                        |
|                                                                      |
|  Bank            from : 3..                                          |
|                  to   : 4..                                          |
|                                                                      |
+----------------------------------------------------------------------+
```

1.   Factoring Company From
2.   Factoring Company to
3.   Bank From
4.   Bank to

8.6 Print First Free Numbers (tcmcs0447m000)

tcmcs0447m000   single-occ (4)   Form 1-1

```
+----------------------------------------------------------------------+
|  Print First Free Numbers                          Company: 000  |
|----------------------------------------------------------------------|
|                                                                      |
|  Type of Number        from : 1.......................                |
|                        to   : 2.......................                |
|                                                                      |
|  Series                from : 3..                                     |
|                        to   : 4..                                     |
+----------------------------------------------------------------------+
```

1.   Type of Number from
2.   Type of Number to
3.   Series from
4.   Series to
8.7   Print Invoicing Methods (tcmcs0455m000)

tcmcs0455m000   single-occ (4)   Form 1-1

```
+----------------------------------------------------------------------+
|  Print Invoicing Methods                           Company: 000  |
|----------------------------------------------------------------------|
|                                                                      |
|  Invoicing Method      from : 1..                                     |
|                        to   : 2..                                     |
|                                                                      |
+----------------------------------------------------------------------+
```

1.   Invoicing Method from
2.   Invoicing Method to
8.8   Print Late Payment Surcharges (tcmcs0411m000)

tcmcs0411m000   single-occ (4)   Form 1-1

```
+----------------------------------------------------------------------+
|  Print Late Payment Surcharges                     Company: 000  |
|----------------------------------------------------------------------|
|                                                                      |
|  Late Payment Surcharge    from : 1..                                 |
|                            to   : 2..                                 |
|                                                                      |
+----------------------------------------------------------------------+
```

1.   Late Payment Surcharge from
2.   Late Payment Surcharge to
8.9   Print Rounding Codes (tcmcs0453m000)

tcmcs0453m000   single-occ (4)   Form 1-1

```
+----------------------------------------------------------------------+
|  Print Rounding Codes                              Company: 000  |
|----------------------------------------------------------------------|
|                                                                      |
|  Rounding Code         from : 1..                                     |
|                        to   : 2..                                     |
|                                                                      |
+----------------------------------------------------------------------+
```

1.   Rounding Code from
2.   Rounding Code to
8.10 Print Tax Codes (tcmcs0437m000)

tcmcs0437m000   single-occ (4)   Form 1-1

```
+----------------------------------------------------------------------+
|  Print Tax Codes                                   Company: 000  |
|----------------------------------------------------------------------|
|                                                                      |
|  Tax Code          from : 1........                                   |
|                    to   : 2........                                   |
|                                                                      |
+----------------------------------------------------------------------+
```

1.   Tax Code from
2.   Tax Code to
8.11 Print Tax Codes by Country (tcmcs0436m000)

```
tcmcs0436m000                            single-occ (4)    Form 1-1
+----------------------------------------------------------------------+
|  Print Tax Codes by Country                         Company: 000  |
|----------------------------------------------------------------------|
|                                                                    |
|   Country        from : 1..                                        |
|                  to   : 2..                                        |
|                                                                    |
|   Tax Code       from : 3.......                                   |
|                  to   : 4.......                                   |
|                                                                    |
+----------------------------------------------------------------------+
1.     Country from
2.     Country to
3.     Tax Code from
4.     Tax Code to
8.12   Print Terms of Payment (tcmcs0413m000)
tcmcs0413m000                            single-occ (4)    Form 1-1
+----------------------------------------------------------------------+
|  Print Terms of Payment                             Company: 000  |
|----------------------------------------------------------------------|
|                                                                    |
|   Terms of Payment        from : 1..                               |
|                           to   : 2..                               |
|                                                                    |
|   Print Language          : 3..   4_____        |
|                                                                    |
+----------------------------------------------------------------------+
1.     Terms of Payment From
2.     Terms of Payment to
3.     Print Language
The language in which you want to print the texts linked to the code.
4.     Description
8.13   Print Payment Schedules (tcmcs0414m000)
tcmcs0414m000                            single-occ (4)    Form 1-1
+----------------------------------------------------------------------+
|  Print Payment Schedules                            Company: 000  |
|----------------------------------------------------------------------|
|                                                                    |
|   Terms of Payment        from :  1..                              |
|                           to   :  2..                              |
|                                                                    |
|   Days after Inv. Date    from : 3...                              |
|                           to   : 4...                              |
|                                                                    |
+----------------------------------------------------------------------+
1.     Terms of Payment From
2.     Terms of Payment to
3.     Number of Days after Invoice Date From
4.     Number of Days after Invoice Date to
8.14   Print Credit Insurance Companies (tcmcs0409m000)
tcmcs0409m000                            single-occ (4)    Form 1-1
+----------------------------------------------------------------------+
|  Print Credit Insurance Companies                   Company: 000  |
|----------------------------------------------------------------------|
|                                                                    |
|   Credit Insurance Company from : 1..                              |
|                           to   : 2..                               |
|                                                                    |
+----------------------------------------------------------------------+
1.     Credit Insurance Company From
2.     Credit Insurance Company to
9      Introduction to System Performance
```

9.1 Session Overview

Seq.	Session	Description	Session Usage
1	tcmcs0197m000	Maintain Use of Performance Boosters	Mandatory
2	tcmcs0198m000	Maintain Table Boosters	Mandatory
3	tcmcs0497m000	Print Use of Performance Boosters	Print
4	tcmcs0498m000	Print Table Boosters	Print
5	tcmcs0597m000	Display Use of Performance Boosters	Display
6	tcmcs0598m000	Display Table Boosters	Display

10   Mandatory Sessions

10.1   Maintain Use of Performance Boosters (tcmcs0197m000)

SESSION OBJECTIVE

To link performance boosters to sessions, to users, or to a combination of these.

NOTE: Wherever in an application a booster can be applied, but that booster has not been set in this session, the following will occur: table Use of Performance Boosters (tcmcs097) will be inserted with the booster concerned for the user and the session that is running and the validation in the field "Booster Valid" will be "Not Active"

HOW TO USE THE SESSION

Performance Boosters can be used at three levels, each starting with another identifier. The following combinations may therefore be made:

Session	Performance Booster	User
Performance Booster User	Session User	Performance Booster Session

It is necessary to always fill in the performance booster which should be used and the session for which the booster is valid.

SEE ALSO KEYWORD(S)

• Use of Performance Boosters

```
tcmcs0197m000                              multi/group (3     Form 1-3 >
+--------------------------------------------------------------------+
|  Maintain Use of Performance Boosters               Company: 000   |
|--------------------------------------------------------------------|
|                                                                    |
|  Session                   : 1........... 2_____   |
|                                                                    |
|  Performance Booster         User          Value       Booster Valid |
|                                                                    |
|  3........................   4..........   5.........  6...........  |
|                                                                    |
+--------------------------------------------------------------------+
```

1.   Session

Entering the session will make the system employ the performance booster in this session, if applicable. If it is not applicable, entering the session will have no effect at all.

See the field "Performance Booster" for a list of sessions to which the performance booster is relevant.

2.   Description

3.   Performance Booster

For further information, see keyword(s) "Use of Performance Boosters".

Available performance boosters: * [GO1] Display Interval * [G02] Number of Servers
* [G03] Maximum Invoice Lines * [G04] Embedded Financial Int.
Display Interval With this option you can influence the time between two refresh actions. Decreasing the frequency with which the program refreshes the screen will have a positive effect on the speed of large processing sessions.
Use is recommended in the sessions:
- Generate Planned (MPS)/MRP Orders/Batches (timrp1210m000)
- Generate Master Production Schedule (timps3201m000)
- Generate Planned PRP Orders (tipcs5201m000)
- Transfer Planned PRP Purchase Orders (tipcs5260m000)
- Generate Inbound Advice (tdilc4203m000)
- Generate Outbound Advice (tdilc4201m000)

Numbers of Servers This option allows you to set the extra number of bshells to be started parallel to the session concerned, which you should fill in the field "Session". It is also possible to join the Number of Servers to one "User".
Use is recommended in the sessions:
- Update Sales Statistics (tdsst0201m000)
- Print Sales Invoices (tdsls4404m000)

If booster has been set for this session, the session "Process Delivered Sales Orders (tdsls4223m000)" will run parallel to printing the invoices.
- Process Delivered Sales Orders (tdsls4223m000)
- Process Delivered Purchase Orders (tdpur4223m000)
- Select Invoices for Payment (tfcmg1220m000)
- Audit Batches (tfgld1211s000)
- Generate Planned (MPS)/MRP Orders/Batches (timrp1210m000)
- Generate Master Production Schedule (timps3201m000)
- Execute Single Site Master Production Scheduling (timps3202s000)
- Print Cost Control (tpppc4411m000)

Maximum Invoice Lines Whenever the possibility to collect several orders on one invoice is used, invoices can contain a great number of lines. The transaction to book these lines to BAAN Finance can become too large, depending on e.g. the size of the rollback-segments of your database. This option limits the maximum number of lines on one invoice, thus reducing the size of the transaction mentioned.
Use is only possible in:
- Print Sales Invoices (tdsls4404m000)

The check on maximum invoice lines will not be performed if the field "Invoicing by Installments" for the current order is set to "Yes". Printing will continue untill the end of this order.
- Print Invoices (trics2400m000)
- Print Contract Installment Invoices (tssma2472m000)
- Print Service Order Invoices (tssma3473m000)
- Print Invoices (tppin4474m000)

Embedded Financial Integration With this option a financial integration will be processed using a Dynamic Link Library instead of the parallel running session "Update Integr Trans and Real Time Post to Finance (backgrd.) (tfgld4200s000)". This will speed up the sessions in which a financial integration is involved.
4.   User
The user for whom the booster is valid. If this field is left empty the booster is valid for all users that start the session.
5.   Value
6.   Booster Valid

tcmcs0197m000   multi/group (3 < Form 2-3 >
+---+
Maintain Use of Performance Boosters   Company: 000
Performance Booster   : 1........................
Session   Description   User   Value   Booster Valid
2........... 3_____   4........... 5........ 6............

```
|                                                                            |
+----------------------------------------------------------------------------+
```
1.   Performance Booster
For further information, see keyword(s)
"Use of Performance Boosters".
Available performance boosters: * [GO1] Display Interval * [G02] Number of
Servers
* [G03] Maximum Invoice Lines * [G04] Embedded Financial Int.
Display Interval With this option you can influence the time between two refresh
actions. Decreasing the frequency with which the program refreshes the screen
will have a positive effect on the speed of large processing sessions.
Use is recommended in the sessions:
•   Generate Planned (MPS)/MRP Orders/Batches (timrp1210m000)
•   Generate Master Production Schedule (timps3201m000)
•   Generate Planned PRP Orders (tipcs5201m000)
•   Transfer Planned PRP Purchase Orders (tipcs5260m000)
•   Generate Inbound Advice (tdilc4203m000)
•   Generate Outbound Advice (tdilc4201m000)
Numbers of Servers This option allows you to set the extra number of bshells to
be started parallel to the session concerned, which you should fill in the field
"Session". It is also possible to join the Number of Servers to one "User".
Use is recommended in the sessions:
•   Update Sales Statistics (tdsst0201m000)
•   Print Sales Invoices (tdsls4404m000)
If booster has been set for this session, the session "Process Delivered Sales
Orders (tdsls4223m000)" will run parallel to printing the invoices.
•   Process Delivered Sales Orders (tdsls4223m000)
•   Process Delivered Purchase Orders (tdpur4223m000)
•   Select Invoices for Payment (tfcmg1220m000)
•   Audit Batches (tfgld1211s000)
•   Generate Planned (MPS)/MRP Orders/Batches (timrp1210m000)
•   Generate Master Production Schedule (timps3201m000)
•   Execute Single Site Master Production Scheduling (timps3202s000)
•   Print Cost Control (tpppc4411m000)
Maximum Invoice Lines Whenever the possibility to collect several orders on one
invoice is used, invoices can contain a great number of lines. The transaction
to book these lines to BAAN Finance can become too large, depending on e.g. the
size of the rollback-segments of your database. This option limits the maximum
number of lines on one invoice, thus reducing the size of the transaction
mentioned.
Use is only possible in:
•   Print Sales Invoices (tdsls4404m000)
The check on maximum invoice lines will not be performed if the field "Invoicing
by Installments" for the current order is set to "Yes". Printing will continue
untill the end of this order.
•   Print Invoices (trics2400m000)
•   Print Contract Installment Invoices (tssma2472m000)
•   Print Service Order Invoices (tssma3473m000)
•   Print Invoices (tppin4474m000)
Embedded Financial Integration With this option a financial integration will be
processed using a Dynamic Link Library instead of the parallel running session
"Update Integr Trans and Real Time Post to Finance (backgrd.) (tfgld4200s000)".
This will speed up the sessions in which a financial integration is involved.
2.   Session
Entering the session will make the system employ the performance booster in this
session, if applicable. If it is not applicable, entering the session will have
no effect at all.
See the field "Performance Booster" for a list of sessions to which the
performance booster is relevant.
3.   Description
4.   User
The user for whom the booster is valid. If this field is left empty the booster
is valid for all users that start the session.

5.   Value
6.   Booster Valid

tcmcs0197m000   multi/group (3 < Form 3-3

+--+
Maintain Use of Performance Boosters   Company: 000
User   : 1.......... 2_____
Performance Booster   Session   Value   Booster Valid
3...................... 4........... 5......... 6.............
+--+

1.   User
The user for whom the booster is valid. If this field is left empty the booster
is valid for all users that start the session.
2.   Description
3.   Performance Booster
For further information, see keyword(s)
"Use of Performance Boosters".
Available performance boosters: * [GO1] Display Interval * [G02] Number of
Servers
* [G03] Maximum Invoice Lines * [G04] Embedded Financial Int.
Display Interval With this option you can influence the time between two refresh
actions. Decreasing the frequency with which the program refreshes the screen
will have a positive effect on the speed of large processing sessions.
Use is recommended in the sessions:
•   Generate Planned (MPS)/MRP Orders/Batches (timrp1210m000)
•   Generate Master Production Schedule (timps3201m000)
•   Generate Planned PRP Orders (tipcs5201m000)
•   Transfer Planned PRP Purchase Orders (tipcs5260m000)
•   Generate Inbound Advice (tdilc4203m000)
•   Generate Outbound Advice (tdilc4201m000)
Numbers of Servers This option allows you to set the extra number of bshells to
be started parallel to the session concerned, which you should fill in the field
"Session". It is also possible to join the Number of Servers to one "User".
Use is recommended in the sessions:
•   Update Sales Statistics (tdsst0201m000)
•   Print Sales Invoices (tdsls4404m000)
If booster has been set for this session, the session "Process Delivered Sales
Orders (tdsls4223m000)" will run parallel to printing the invoices.
•   Process Delivered Sales Orders (tdsls4223m000)
•   Process Delivered Purchase Orders (tdpur4223m000)
•   Select Invoices for Payment (tfcmg1220m000)
•   Audit Batches (tfgld1211s000)
•   Generate Planned (MPS)/MRP Orders/Batches (timrp1210m000)
•   Generate Master Production Schedule (timps3201m000)
•   Execute Single Site Master Production Scheduling (timps3202s000)
•   Print Cost Control (tpppc4411m000)
Maximum Invoice Lines Whenever the possibility to collect several orders on one
invoice is used, invoices can contain a great number of lines. The transaction
to book these lines to BAAN Finance can become too large, depending on e.g. the
size of the rollback-segments of your database. This option limits the maximum
number of lines on one invoice, thus reducing the size of the transaction
mentioned.
Use is only possible in:
•   Print Sales Invoices (tdsls4404m000)
The check on maximum invoice lines will not be performed if the field "Invoicing
by Installments" for the current order is set to "Yes". Printing will continue
untill the end of this order.
•   Print Invoices (trics2400m000)
•   Print Contract Installment Invoices (tssma2472m000)

- Print Service Order Invoices (tssma3473m000)
- Print Invoices (tppin4474m000)

Embedded Financial Integration With this option a financial integration will be processed using a Dynamic Link Library instead of the parallel running session "Update Integr Trans and Real Time Post to Finance (backgrd.) (tfgld4200s000)". This will speed up the sessions in which a financial integration is involved.

4. Session
Entering the session will make the system employ the performance booster in this session, if applicable. If it is not applicable, entering the session will have no effect at all.
See the field "Performance Booster" for a list of sessions to which the performance booster is relevant.

5. Value
6. Booster Valid

10.2 Maintain Table Boosters (tcmcs0198m000)

SESSION OBJECTIVE
This session can be used to link table boosters to sessions or users.

HOW TO USE THE SESSION
Table boosters can be defined at three levels. These levels are explained in figure below:

Start input on:

```
   1st form      2nd form      3rd form
+-------------------------------------+
| Session     | Table name | User      |
|-------------+------------+-----------|
| User        | Session    | Session   |
| Table name  | User       | Table name |
+-------------------------------------+
```

Filling in the table name is mandatory in all situations.

SEE ALSO KEYWORD(S)
- Table Boosters

```
tcmcs0198m000                              multi/group (3    Form 1-3 >
+-----------------------------------------------------------------------------+
|  Maintain Table Boosters                                 Company: 000  |
|-----------------------------------------------------------------------------|
|                                                                             |
|  Session        : 1...........  2_____             |
|                                                                             |
|  User           Name            Table    Load Option Max No    Booster      |
|                                 Name                 of Rows   Valid        |
|                                                                             |
|  3..........  4_____  5...... 6......... 7........ 8..........  |
|                                                                             |
+-----------------------------------------------------------------------------+
```

1. Session
Entering the session will make the system employ the performance booster in this session, if applicable. If it is not applicable, entering the session will have no effect at all.
See the field "Performance Booster" for a list of sessions to which the performance booster is relevant.

2. Description
3. User
The user for whom the booster is valid. If this field is left empty the booster is valid for all users that access the table.

4. Description
5. Table Name
The table which should be loaded in internal memory. The tables can be loaded in two ways: Full or Incremental. Choose one of these options in the field "Load Option".
Table codes and descriptions can be found by session "Display Table Definitions (ttadv4520m000)".

6. Load Option

This field indicates how tables will be kept in internal memory. The options are:
Full: The table in the field "Table Name" will be loaded for all rows in the table, unless the number of rows is greater than the number of rows mentioned in the field "Maximum Number of Rows".
Incremental: Each new accessed row of the table will be kept in the internal memory. In this way any searches for the same row will be faster.
7.   Maximum Number of Rows
The maximum number of rows which can be loaded into internal memory for the table specified in "Table Name".
8.   Booster Valid

```
tcmcs0198m000                                  multi/group (3  < Form 2-3 >
+--------------------------------------------------------------------------+
|  Maintain Table Boosters                              Company: 000  |
|--------------------------------------------------------------------------|
|                                                                          |
|  Table Name    : 1.......  2_____           |
|                                                                          |
|  Session        Description      User         Load Option Max No   Booster   |
|                                                           of Rows  Valid     |
|                                                                          |
|  3..........  4_____  5..........  6..........  7........  8......... |
|                                                                          |
+--------------------------------------------------------------------------+
```

1.   Table Name
The table which should be loaded in internal memory. The tables can be loaded in two ways: Full or Incremental. Choose one of these options in the field "Load Option".
Table codes and descriptions can be found by session "Display Table Definitions (ttadv4520m000)".
2.   Description
3.   Session
Entering the session will make the system employ the performance booster in this session, if applicable. If it is not applicable, entering the session will have no effect at all.
See the field "Performance Booster" for a list of sessions to which the performance booster is relevant.
4.   Description
5.   User
The user for whom the booster is valid. If this field is left empty the booster is valid for all users that access the table.
6.   Load Option
This field indicates how tables will be kept in internal memory. The options are:
Full: The table in the field "Table Name" will be loaded for all rows in the table, unless the number of rows is greater than the number of rows mentioned in the field "Maximum Number of Rows".
Incremental: Each new accessed row of the table will be kept in the internal memory. In this way any searches for the same row will be faster.
7.   Maximum Number of Rows
The maximum number of rows which can be loaded into internal memory for the table specified in "Table Name".
8.   Booster Valid

```
tcmcs0198m000                                  multi/group (3  < Form 3-3
+--------------------------------------------------------------------------+
|  Maintain Table Boosters                              Company: 000  |
|--------------------------------------------------------------------------|
|                                                                          |
|  User: 1..........  2_____                     |
|                                                                          |
|  Session        Description      Table        Load Option Max No   Booster   |
|                                  Name                     of Rows  Valid     |
|                                                                          |
```

```
|    3............. 4_____ 5....... 6.......... 7........ 8......... |
|                                                                               |
+-------------------------------------------------------------------------------+
```

1.   User
The user for whom the booster is valid. If this field is left empty the booster
is valid for all users that access the table.
2.   Description
3.   Session
Entering the session will make the system employ the performance booster in this
session, if applicable. If it is not applicable, entering the session will have
no effect at all.
See the field "Performance Booster" for a list of sessions to which the
performance booster is relevant.
4.   Description
5.   Table Name
The table which should be loaded in internal memory. The tables can be loaded in
two ways: Full or Incremental. Choose one of these options in the field "Load
Option".
Table codes and descriptions can be found by session "Display Table Definitions
(ttadv4520m000)".
6.   Load Option
This field indicates how tables will be kept in internal memory. The options
are:
Full: The table in the field "Table Name" will be loaded for all rows in the
table, unless the number of rows is greater than the number of rows mentioned in
the field "Maximum Number of Rows".
Incremental: Each new accessed row of the table will be kept in the internal
memory. In this way any searches for the same row will be faster.
7.   Maximum Number of Rows
The maximum number of rows which can be loaded into internal memory for the
table specified in "Table Name".
8.   Booster Valid
11   Other Print Sessions
11.1 Print Use of Performance Boosters (tcmcs0497m000)

```
tcmcs0497m000                                    single-occ (4)    Form 1-1
+-------------------------------------------------------------------------------+
| Print Use of Performance Boosters                          Company: 000  |
|-------------------------------------------------------------------------------|
|                                                                               |
| Session              From : 1............                                     |
|                      To   : 2............                                     |
|                                                                               |
| Performance Booster From : 3.......................                           |
|                      To   : 4.......................                          |
|                                                                               |
| User                 From : 5............                                     |
|                      To   : 6..........                                       |
|                                                                               |
+-------------------------------------------------------------------------------+
```

1.   Session Code
2.   Session Code
3.   Performance Facility
4.   Performance Facility
5.   User
6.   User
11.2 Print Table Boosters (tcmcs0498m000)

```
tcmcs0498m000                                    single-occ (4)    Form 1-1
+-------------------------------------------------------------------------------+
| Print Table Boosters                                       Company: 000  |
|-------------------------------------------------------------------------------|
|                                                                               |
| Session     From : 1............                                              |
|             To   : 2............                                              |
```

```
|                                                                        |
| User         From : 3..........                                        |
|              To   : 4..........                                        |
|                                                                        |
| Table Name From : 5.......                                             |
|              To   : 6.......                                           |
|                                                                        |
+------------------------------------------------------------------------+
1.    Session Code
2.    Session Code
3.    User
4.    User
5.    Table Name
6.    Table Name
```

1 Common Data (COM)

1.1 General

OBJECTIVE OF THIS MODULE

This module allows you to maintain data about:

- Companies
- Employees
- Customers
- Suppliers
- Concern Structure
- Planning Board Groups 1
- Default Charts per User per Session
- Sales Listing Data

The BAAN IV applications make frequent use of this information.

1.2 Related B-Objects

Seq. No.	B-Object	Description	B-Object Usage
1	tc com00010	Company Data	Optional child
2	tc com00020	Employee Data	Optional child
3	tc com00030	Customer Data	Optional child
4	tc com00040	Supplier Data	Optional child
5	tc com00050	Trade Relation	Optional child
6	tc com00060	Intra EU Transactions	Optional child
7	tc com00070	Chart and Planning Board Data	Optional child

2 Introduction to Company Data

2.1 General

OBJECTIVE OF BUSINESS OBJECT

This b-object allows you to control such data as the address, language and currency of your company as well as any subsidiaries using the software package.

SEE ALSO KEYWORD(S)

- Companies

2.2 Session Overview

Seq.	Session	Description	Session Usage

1	tccom0100m000	Maintain Company Data	Mandatory
101	tccom0400m000	Print Company Data	Print
201	tccom0500m000	Display Company Data	Display

3 Mandatory Sessions

3.1 Maintain Company Data (tccom0100m000)

SESSION OBJECTIVE

To maintain company data. These are used in a number of other sessions.

SEE ALSO KEYWORD(S)

• Companies

```
tccom0100m000                          single-occ (1)   Form 1-2 >
+----------------------------------------------------------------------+
|  Maintain Company Data                              Company: 000  |
|----------------------------------------------------------------------|
|                                                                  |
|  Company                      :     1..  2_____    |
|                                                                  |
|  Country                      :     3..  4_____    |
|  Name                         : 5...................................  |
|                               : 6..............................  |
|  Address                      : 7..............................  |
|                               : 8..............................  |
|  9_____       : 10.............................  |
|  11_____       : 12.............................  |
|  13_____14 15.......                               |
|  16_____17 18...                                   |
|  ZIP Code                     : 19........                       |
|                                                                  |
|  Transportation Address       : 20____                           |
|                                                                  |
+----------------------------------------------------------------------+
```

1. Company

For further information, see keyword(s)
"Companies".
When installing the BAAN IV applications on the system, the data about your own company are usually recorded under company number 100. If the company has subsidiaries using the software, each subsidiary should be assigned its own company number.

2. Name

This field displays the name of the company.

3. Country

The country code of the country where the company is established. You should have defined the country code to be entered in the session "Maintain Countries (tcmcs0110m000)".

4. Description

5. Company Name

The company's name. The data on the 7 fields from "Name" to "Country" are printed on the packing list (module "Sales Control (SLS)").

6. Name 2

The second part of the company name. If the length of the previous field is insufficient for a full description of the name of the company, you may also use this field.

7. Address

The first part of the company address.

8. Address 2

The second part of the company address. If the length of the previous field is too small, you may also use this field for the address description of the company.

9. Program domain string

10.   City
The city where the company is established.
For tax provider users, the city and state or province where the company is
established. The city and state or province should be separated by a comma ","
such as "Menlo Park, CA".
For further information, see method(s)
•   Address Verification for Tax Provider
11.   Program domain string
12.   City 2
The second part of the name of the city where the company is established.
For tax provider users, the ZIP code or Postal code where the company is
established.
For further information, see method(s)
•   Address Verification for Tax Provider
If you are not a tax provider user and the previous field provides insufficient
room for entering the city of residence, you may also use this field.
13.   Program domain string
14.   Program domain of string length 1
15.   GEO Code
A GEO code is a code used together or in lieu of address information such as
city, state/province, and ZIP/postal code to uniquely identify a taxing
jurisdiction. The tax provider determines the GEO code based upon the address
information entered and the county and city limits selected.
The format of the GEO code varies by tax provider. AVP uses a two-digit GEO
code; the GEO code together with the city, state, and ZIP code, identifies the
taxing jurisdiction. Vertex uses a nine-digit GEO code comprised of a two digit
state code, three-digit county code, and a four-digit city code. A tenth digit
is used to identify if the jurisdiction is inside or outside of the city limits.
A GEO code is a code used together or in lieu of address information such as
city, state/province, and ZIP/postal code to uniquely identify a taxing
jurisdiction. The tax provider determines the GEO code based upon the address
information entered and the county and city limits selected.
The format of the GEO code varies by tax provider. AVP uses a two-digit GEO
code; the GEO code together with the city, state, and ZIP code, identifies the
taxing jurisdiction. Vertex uses a nine-digit GEO code comprised of a two digit
state code, three-digit county code, and a four-digit city code. A tenth digit
is used to identify if the jurisdiction is inside or outside of the city limits.
16.   Program domain string
17.   Program domain of string length 1
18.   Answer on question y/n
19.   ZIP Code
The ZIP code of the city where the company is established. On the two fields
reserved for "City", you can record the post code which must appear as address
data on order documents.
20.   Address Code
The address if the package is run in association with the package BAAN
Transportation. The address refers to an address in the b-object "Address
Control (ACS)" in the package BAAN Transportation.
tccom0100m000   single-occ (1) < Form 2-2
+---+
Maintain Company Data   Company: 000
Company   :   1__   2_____
Language   :   3..   4_____
Currency   :   5..   6_____
City (letterhead)   :   7............................
Mailing Number   :   8......
Tax ID of Own Company   :   9..................
Tax ID of Fiscal Unit   :   10.................

```
+-------------------------------------------------------------------------+
1.      Company
For further information, see keyword(s)
"Companies".
2.      Name
3.      Language
The language in which the company communicates. Internal documents are printed
in this language. This language code also serves as default in the sessions:
•       Maintain Customers (tccom1101m000)
•       Maintain Suppliers (tccom2101m000)
You should have already defined the language code to be entered via the session
"Maintain Languages (tcmcs0146m000)".
4.      Description
5.      Currency
Indicates the currency in which, for example, the financial accounts as well as
the purchase and sales statistics of the company are maintained.
6.      Description
7.      City (letterhead)
The city of the consignor is printed in the letterhead on trade documents (e.g.
an order acknowledgement).
It is also printed on the transport order acknowledgement (BAAN Transportation).
You can record the name of the city on this field.
8.      Mailing Number
The consignor's number is printed on the packing list (sales) and is the member
number or customer number assigned to your company by the forwarding agent.
This field is not used in the package BAAN Transportation.
9.      Tax ID of Own Company
As from 1993, companies trading within the EU are legally required to report
their import/export activities. Reporting is based on the Tax number. If you do
not fill the Tax number the system will issue a message.
You can only enter this number if the country in the company data is an EU
country. After entering a Tax number, BAAN IV will support the reporting of
import/export data.
10.     Tax ID of Fiscal Unit
The Tax number applying if the import and export data are reported by third
parties.
4       Other Print Sessions
4.1     Print Company Data (tccom0400m000)
tccom0400m000                                    single-occ (4)    Form 1-1
+-------------------------------------------------------------------------+
|  Print Company Data                                       Company: 000  |
|-------------------------------------------------------------------------|
|                                                                         |
|  Company         from : 1..                                             |
|                  to   : 2..                                             |
|                                                                         |
+-------------------------------------------------------------------------+
1.      Company from
2.      Company to
5       Introduction to Employee Data
5.1     General
OBJECTIVE OF BUSINESS OBJECT
This b-object allows you to control all required employee data.
SEE ALSO KEYWORD(S)
•       Employees
5.2     Session Overview
```

Seq.	Session	Description	Session Usage
1	tccom0101m000	Maintain Employees	Mandatory

```
|  101 | tccom0401m000 | Print Employees              | Print
|
|  201 | tccom0501m000 | Display Employees            | Display
|
|  203 | tccom0502s000 | Display Employee All Data    | Display
|
```

---

6 Mandatory Sessions
6.1 Maintain Employees (tccom0101m000)
SESSION OBJECTIVE
To maintain employee data. These are used in a number of other sessions.
SEE ALSO KEYWORD(S)
• Employees

```
tccom0101m000                          single-occ (1)   Form 1-2 >
+-----------------------------------------------------------------------+
| Maintain Employees                                    Company: 000    |
|-----------------------------------------------------------------------|
|                                                                       |
| Employee               :     1.....                                   |
|                                                                       |
| Name                   : 2.................................           |
| Name 2                 : 3.............................               |
| Address                : 4.............................               |
| Address 2              : 5.............................               |
| City                   : 6.............................               |
| City 2                 : 7.............................               |
| ZIP Code               : 8........                                    |
| Country                : 9..  10_____         |
| Language               : 11.  12_____        |
| Telephone              : 13.............                              |
| Telephone 2            : 14.............                              |
| Telephone 3            : 15.............                              |
| Fax                    : 16.............                              |
| E-mail                 : 17.........................................  |
|                                                                       |
+-----------------------------------------------------------------------+
```

1.   Employee
For further information, see keyword(s)
"Employees".
2.   Name
The employee's name. On several places in the BAAN IV applications, you can
search for employees by entering the name as search key. You should therefore
always enter names in the same way - for instance first the surname, then the
initials.
3.   Name 2
The second part of the employee's name.
4.   Address
The first part of the employee's address.
5.   Address 2
The second part of the employee's address.
6.   City
The employee's city.
7.   City 2
The second part of the employee's city.
8.   ZIP code
The employee's ZIP code.
9.   Country
The country where the employee lives.
10.   Description
11.   Language
The language code indicates the language in which the work instructions are
printed. The language code should have already been defined in the session
"Maintain Languages (tcmcs0146m000)".

12.   Description
13.   Telephone
The employee's full telephone number.
14.   Telephone 2
The employee's second telephone number (if any).
15.   Telephone 3
The employee's third telephone number (if any).
16.   Fax
The employee's fax number.
17.   E-mail
Additional information, e.g. the employee's e-mail address.

tccom0101m000   single-occ (1) < Form 2-2
+--+
Maintain Employees   Company: 000
Employee   :   1.....
First Date of Employment   : 2.........
Last Date of Employment   : 3.........
Work Center   :   4.. 5_____
Hourly Labor Rate   [6__]: 7....
Employment   [h/wk] :   8.
Working Time Table   :   9.. 10_____
Trade Group   :   11. 12_____
Days by week   :   13
Hours by day   :   14.
Billing Rate   :   15
+--+

1.   Employee
For further information, see keyword(s)
"Employees".
2.   First Date of Employment
The date on which the employee was hired. This field is checked when you are
entering hours. Spent production hours cannot be entered on a date which is
earlier than the date when the employee was hired.
3.   Last Date of Employment
The date on which an employee left the company. Spent production hours after
this date cannot be posted to the employee.
4.   Work Center
The work center to which the employee has been assigned.
5.   Description
The description of the work center.
6.   Currency
Indicates the currency in which, for example, the financial accounts as well as
the purchase and sales statistics of the company are maintained.
7.   Hourly Labor Rate
The labor rate per employee. This is the total labor costs per employee divided
by the number of productive hours on an annual basis. Together with the machine
rate in the machine file, the labor rate forms the basis for the actual costs.
SEE ALSO METHOD(S)
•   Currency Formats
8.   Employment
The available hours per week are the number of hours that the employee is
present per week, based on normal work hours. This value is used in order to
check the weekly list of hours per employee in the hours accounting.
9.   Working Time Table
The working time table is used in the hours accounting in order to calculate the
work hours spent. In the hours accounting by employee, the start time and end
time of an employee's activity are registered. The hours spent on the activity

are calculated from the working hours and breaks entered in the working time table.
The code of the work time table should have already been defined via the session "Maintain Working Time Tables (tihra1110m000)".
10. Description
The description of the working time table.
11. Trade Group
The trade group to which the employee is attached.
12. Description
13. Days by week
The number of days a week the employee normally works.
14. Hours by day
The number of hours a day the employee normally works.
15. Sales Rate
The sales rate that can be charged in case of prime cost work.
7 Other Print Sessions
7.1 Print Employees (tccom0401m000)

```
tccom0401m000                          single-occ (4)    Form 1-1
+------------------------------------------------------------------+
| Print Employees                               Company: 000  |
|------------------------------------------------------------------|
|                                                              |
| Employee            from :      1.....                       |
|                     to   :      2.....                       |
|                                                              |
| Work Center         from :        3..                        |
|                     to   :        4..                        |
|                                                              |
| Select by Date           : 5....                             |
|                                                              |
| Reference Date           : 6........                         |
|                                                              |
+------------------------------------------------------------------+
```

1. Employee from
2. Employee to
3. Work Center from
4. Work Center to
5. Select by Date
Yes
You only want to print employees currently employed. Record the "Reference Date" on the following field.
No
You want to print all employee data.
6. Reference Date
When you choose to select by date, you can enter the "Reference Date" on this field. The program prints data of only those employees for whom the first date of employment is after the "Reference Date".
8 Introduction to Customer Data
8.1 General
OBJECTIVE OF BUSINESS OBJECT
This b-object allows you to control data about customers and prospects.
SEE ALSO KEYWORD(S)
• Customers
• Customer Postal Addresses
• Delivery Addresses
• Banks by Customer
8.2 Session Overview

Seq.	Session	Description	Session Usage
1	tccom1101m000	Maintain Customers	Mandatory

2	tccom1103m000	Maintain Customer Postal Addresses	Optional
3	tccom1102m000	Maintain Delivery Addresses	Optional
4	tccom1105m000	Maintain Banks by Customer	Optional
5	tccom1110m000	Maintain Prospects	Optional
6	tccom1110s000	Maintain Prospects	Optional
101	tccom1401m000	Print Customers	Print
102	tccom1403m000	Print Customer Postal Addresses	Print
103	tccom1402m000	Print Delivery Addresses	Print
104	tccom1405m000	Print Banks by Customer	Print
105	tccom1404m000	Print Customer Credit Limit Data	Print
201	tccom1501m000	Display Customers	Display
202	tccom1503m000	Display Customer Postal Addresses	Display
203	tccom1502m000	Display Delivery Addresses	Display
204	tccom1505m000	Display Banks by Customer	Display
999	tccom1510s000	Display Customer List	Display

9 Mandatory Sessions

9.1 Maintain Customers (tccom1101m000)

SESSION OBJECTIVE
To maintain customer data.
SEE ALSO KEYWORD(S)
• Customers
SEE ALSO METHOD(S)
• Address Verification for Tax Provider

```
tccom1101m000                     zoom      single-occ (1)   Form 1-6 >
+--------------------------------------------------------------------+
| Maintain Customers                                  Company: 000   |
|--------------------------------------------------------------------|
|                                                                    |
| Customer              : 1..... 2...................                |
|                                                                    |
| Title                 : 3.. 4_____               |
| Country               : 5.. 6_____              |
| Name                  : 7.............................             |
|                         8.............................             |
| Address               : 9.............................             |
|                        10.............................             |
| 11_____: 12.............................            |
| 13_____: 14.............................            |
| 15_____ 1617.......                                 |
| 18_____ 1920...                                     |
| ZIP Code              : 21........                                 |
| Transportation Address: 22____                                     |
| Search Key            : 23.............                            |
| Text                  : 24___                                      |
|                                                                    |
+--------------------------------------------------------------------+
```

1.   Customer

For further information, see keyword(s)
"Customers".
2.   Customer Status
Normal Customer
The customer pays his invoices on time.
Doubtful Customer
For this customer, each sales order is blocked in the order procedure if the
parameter "Block if Customer is Doubtful" in session "Maintain Sales Order
Parameters (tdsls4100m000)" is on "Yes".
Blocked Customer
No sales order may be entered for a blocked customer.
Prospect
This relation type allows you to record the general data of a prospective
customer. Invoicing is not possible.
3.   Title
By using a title code, you may assign a prefix to a customer, e.g. engineering
works or subcontractor. The title code is printed on the correspondence with the
customer. The title code must first be recorded in the session "Maintain Titles
(tcmcs0119m000)".
4.   Description
5.   Country
The code of the country where the customer is established.
6.   Description
7.   Name
The first part of the customer's name. The "search key" field is filled by the
system with the first 16 positions of the customer's name behind the last
period. Therefore you should enter, for example, "J. Jansen Ltd", not "J. Jansen
L.t.d.".
8.   Name 2
The second part of the customer's name. If the previous field has insufficient
length for the customer's name, you may also use this field.
9.   Address
The first part of the customer's address.
10.   Address 2
The second part of the customer's address. If the previous field has
insufficient length for the description of the address, you may also use this
field.
11.   Program domain string
12.   City
The city where the customer is established.
For tax provider users, the city and state or province where the customer is
established. The city and state or province should be separated by a comma ","
such as "Menlo Park, CA".
For further information, see method(s)
•   Address Verification for Tax Provider
If a ZIP code is used, it is assumed that this code is also entered on one of
the address fields. The "ZIP code" in "Maintain Customers (tccom1101m000)", is
not printed on order documents, but is exclusively used for sorting purposes, as
the format and position of international ZIP codes on such documents differ from
country to country.
13.   Program domain string
14.   City 2
The second part of the place where the customer is established.
For tax provider users, the ZIP Code or Postal Code where the customer is
established.
For further information, see method(s)
•   Address Verification for Tax Provider
15.   Program domain string
16.   Program domain of string length 1
17.   GEO Code
A GEO code is a code used together or in lieu of address information such as
city, state/province, and ZIP/postal code to uniquely identify a taxing

jurisdiction. The tax provider determines the GEO code based upon the address information entered and the county and city limits selected.

The format of the GEO code varies by tax provider. AVP uses a two-digit GEO code; the GEO code together with the city, state, and ZIP code, identifies the taxing jurisdiction. Vertex uses a nine-digit GEO code comprised of a two digit state code, three-digit county code, and a four-digit city code. A tenth digit is used to identify if the jurisdiction is inside or outside of the city limits.

18.   Program domain string
19.   Program domain of string length 1
20.   Answer on question y/n
21.   ZIP Code

The ZIP code serves two purposes:

•   It is used for sorting customers.
•   It appears only on forwarding documents on which no other address data is printed than the ZIP code to be entered in this field.

This ZIP code does not appear as address data in order documents! On the two fields reserved for "City", you can record the post code which must appear as address data on order documents.

22.   Address Code

The address if the package is run in association with the package BAAN Transportation. The address refers to an address in the b-object "Address Control (ACS)" in the package BAAN Transportation.

23.   Search Key

The search key is used to search for customers. The system fills in the search key on the basis of customer's name. It does so by filling in the first 16 positions of the customer's name behind the last period and converting them to capital letters.

Example: J. Jansen becomes JANSEN Attention!: Do not fill in "J. Jansen L.t.d.", but "J. Jansen Ltd".

24.   Text
Yes
A text has been assigned to the customer.
No
No text has been assigned to the customer.

```
tccom1101m000                            single-occ (1) < Form 2-6 >
+----------------------------------------------------------------------+
| Maintain Customers                                    Company: 000   |
|----------------------------------------------------------------------|
|                                                                      |
| Customer                      : 1..... 2_____  |
|                                                                      |
| Postal Address                : 3..    4_____  |
| Delivery Address              : 5..    6_____  |
|                                                                      |
| Default Financial Company     : 7..    8_____  |
| One-Time Customer             : 9....                                |
| Customer for Statistics Update: 10.... 11_____  |
| Customer for Prices/Discounts : 12.... 13_____  |
| Customer for Texts            : 14.... 15_____  |
| Parent Customer (Finance)     : 16.... 17_____  |
| Purchasing Reference          : 18...........................        |
| Accounting Reference          : 19...........................        |
| Our Supplier Number           : 20............                       |
| Language                      : 21.    22_____    |
|                                                                      |
+----------------------------------------------------------------------+
```

1.   Customer
For further information, see keyword(s) "Customers".
2.   Name
The first part of the customer's name.
3.   Postal Address

The postal address is the address the trade document (e.g. order acknowledgement, invoice etc.) is sent to. You should have already defined this address in the fields "Name", "Address" and "City" in the session "Maintain Customers (tccom1101m000)". However, you can also record other postal addresses for a customer via the session "Maintain Customer Postal Addresses (tccom1103m000)". In this way, you can record the normal and post box address of a customer.

NOTE: You can also record a specific postal address for each order.

4.   Name
The first part of the customer name.

5.   Delivery Address
The delivery address is the address at which the goods are normally delivered. This address appears as default in the session "Maintain Sales Orders (tdsls4101m000)". You can overwrite this default when entering a sales order as you may record more than one address for a customer with the session "Maintain Delivery Addresses (tccom1102m000)". When the delivery address is not filled in, the system assumes that the postal address is also the delivery address.

NOTE: You may also record a specific delivery address on the order level.

6.   Name
The first part of the customer name.

7.   Default Financial Company
The number of the financial company. This is the default value for the financial company as used in the session "Maintain Sales Orders (tdsls4101m000)".

8.   Name
The description associated with the selected code.

9.   One-Time Customer
A one-time customer can be used as general code for incidental customers. The invoice address of such customers is recorded in the package BAAN Finance whenever an invoice for such a customer is transferred from the module "Sales Control (SLS)" to BAAN Finance or is created directly in BAAN Finance. When the invoice is removed, the invoice address is removed as well.

10.   Customer Code for Statistics Update
The customer number if the turnover statistics must be registered under a customer number different from the one on the order.

Skip this field if the turnover should be written to the number of the customer on the order.

11.   Name
The description associated with the selected code.

12.   Customer for Prices/Discounts
The terms and conditions associated with this customer number will be the basis for calculating the price and discount. This field is relevant if the customer is another than the customer on the order.

Skip this field if the system is to retrieve the price and discount recorded under the customer number on the order.

13.   Name
The description associated with the selected code.

14.   Customer for Texts
The customer number under which the customer-specific texts (item descriptions) are stored. Skip this field if the system is to retrieve the texts recorded under the customer number on the order.

15.   Name
The description associated with the selected code.

16.   Parent Customer (Finance)
The reminder and the statement of account produced in the package BAAN Finance can be sent to another customer than the one receiving the invoice. In the package BAAN Finance, various sessions are available to call displays by "Parent" customer.

17.   Name
The description associated with the selected code.

18.   Purchasing Reference
The name of the contact person in the purchasing department of the customer.

19.   Accounting Reference

The name of the contact person at the "Accounting" dept. of the customer. This name appears on various external documents behind "Ref.:".
20.   Our Supplier Number
The supplier number by which the customer identifies you.
21.   Language
The language in which external documents must be printed for this customer. The data to be entered must be defined in the session "Maintain Languages (tcmcs0146m000)".
22.   Description

```
tccom1101m000                              single-occ (1) < Form 3-6 >
+------------------------------------------------------------------------+
|  Maintain Customers                                  Company: 000  |
|------------------------------------------------------------------------|
|                                                                        |
|   Customer                         : 1.....  2_____   |
|                                                                        |
|   Telephone               3__: 4_____  5.............                |
|   Telex                       : 6_____  7.............                |
|   Fax                         : 8_____  9.............                |
|   Line of Business            :    10.  11_____        |
|   Currency                    :    12.  13_____        |
|   Area                        :    14.  15_____        |
|   Route                       : 16...   17_____        |
|   Sales Rep                   : 18....  19_____       |
|   Sales Price List            :    20.  21_____        |
|   Price List for Direct Delivery:  22.  21_____        |
|   Terms of Payment            :    23.  24_____        |
|   Terms of Delivery           :    25.  26_____        |
|   Late Payment Surcharge      :    27.  28_____        |
|                                                                        |
+------------------------------------------------------------------------+
```

1.   Customer
For further information, see keyword(s) "Customers".
2.   Name
The first part of the customer's name.
3.   Country
The code of the country where the customer is established.
4.   Telephone
The international access number for the telephone of the country.
5.   Telephone
The telephone number (dialing code and subscription number) of the customer.
6.   Telex
The international access number for the telex of the country.
7.   Telex
The telex number of the customer.
8.   Fax
The international access number for the fax of the country.
9.   Fax
The fax number of the customer.
10.   Line of Business
The line of business to which the customer belongs. The code is used as a sorting criterion for the sales statistics.
11.   Description
12.   Currency
The currency in which the customer is invoiced, unless it has been changed on the order level. The currency code should already have been defined in the session "Maintain Currencies (tcmcs0102m000)".
13.   Description
14.   Area
The code of the area in which the customer is established. The area code is used as sorting criteria for the sales statistics.
15.   Description

16.   Route
On the order level, you can overwrite the route code which you have assigned to a customer. When printing picking lists and packing slips, you can select by route code.
17.   Description
18.   Sales Rep
The sales rep is the employee of your company who maintains contact with the customer. The employee number of the sales rep is also used as a sorting criterion in the sales statistics. When the module "Sales and Marketing Information (SMI)" is implemented, you can retrieve the default sales rep by choosing option "<Ctrl>[R]" (see the parameter "Employee per ZIP Code/Area/Line of Business").
The employee number must first be defined in the session "Maintain Employees (tccom0101m000)".
19.   Name
The employee's name.
20.   Sales Price List
By assigning a price list code, you can link the price and/or discount agreements to a group of customers.

BAAN Distribution

In the module "Sales Control (SLS)", a number of sessions is available for recording prices and/or discounts for each price list code:
•   Maintain Prices by Price List and Item (tdsls0104m000)
•   Maintain Discounts by Price List and Price Group (tdsls0105m000)
•   Maintain Discounts by Price List (tdsls0106m000)
BAAN Transportation
In the package BAAN Transportation rates for transport and storage services can be stated by price list code. This allows you to use the same rate structure for a group of customers (with the same price list). This can be done in the sessions:
•   Maintain Transport Rate Codes by Price List (trtrc1130m000)
•   Maintain Warehousing Rate Codes by Price List (trwrc1120m000)
The code should have already been defined in the session "Maintain Price Lists (tcmcs0134m000)".
21.   Description
22.   Price List for Direct Delivery
By using a price list for direct deliveries, you can link the price and discount agreements to a group of customers. The system consults these agreements whenever an order line refers to a direct delivery.
BAAN Distribution
In the module "Sales Control (SLS)" the following sessions are available to state prices and/or discounts for each price list:
•   Maintain Prices by Price List and Item (tdsls0104m000)
•   Maintain Discounts by Price List and Price Group (tdsls0105m000)
•   Maintain Discounts by Price List (tdsls0106m000)
BAAN Transportation
In BAAN Transportation you can state rates for transport and storage by price list. This allows you to use the same rate structure for a group of customers (with the same price list).
This is possible in the sessions:
•   Maintain Transport Rate Codes by Price List (trtrc1130m000)
•   Maintain Warehousing Rate Codes by Price List (trwrc1120m000)
23.   Terms of Payment
The terms of payment comprise the following data:
•   the payment term
•   the discount term
•   the discount percentage to be considered if the amount debited is paid within the discount term.

The above data are defaults which can be adjusted for each invoice in the package BAAN Finance.
The description of the terms of payment appears on various documents.
24.   Description
25.   Terms of Delivery
The terms of delivery contain the agreement which has been made with the customer about the way in which goods will be delivered or services rendered. The terms of delivery are printed on various documents.
26.   Description
27.   Late Payment Surcharge
The late payment surcharge indicates the percentage which is charged over the goods amount or over any rendered services. This surcharge may be deducted by the customer who receives the invoice if he pays within the term indicated. The description of the late payment surcharge code is printed on external documents. This code is a default which can be changed on each individual invoice in the package BAAN Finance.
28.   Description

```
tccom1101m000                   zoom        single-occ (1) < Form 4-6 >
+--------------------------------------------------------------------------+
| Maintain Customers                                       Company: 000    |
|--------------------------------------------------------------------------|
|                                                                          |
|   Customer                    :      1.....  2_____ |
|                                                                          |
|   Forwarding Agent            :        3..  4_____ |
|   Order Discount              :      5..    [%]                          |
|   Supplier                    :      6..... 7_____ |
|   Order Type                  :        8..  9_____ |
|   Gross Item Prices in Service :     10...                               |
|   Invoicing Method            :       11. 12_____  |
|   Number of Extra Invoice Copies:        13                              |
|   Invoice Interval            :       14. [days]                         |
|   Date Invoiced               : 15_____                               |
|   Reminder Method             :       16. 17_____  |
|   Statement Method            :       18. 19_____  |
|   Payment Method              :       20. 21_____  |
|   Extra Days after Due Date   :      22..                                |
|                                                                          |
+--------------------------------------------------------------------------+
```

1.   Customer
For further information, see keyword(s)
"Customers".
2.   Name
The first part of the customer's name.
3.   Forwarding Agent
The forwarding agent is responsible for shippinging goods to a customer. This forwarding agent appears as a default on sales contracts and sales orders, but may be changed later. Sales orders may be printed on a packing list by agent.
4.   Description
5.   Order Discount
The order discount percentage that appears as a default on a sales order for the customer. For BAAN Transportation, this is the default on a transport order or inventory order.
6.   Supplier
The customer's supplier number. If a customer is also supplier, you can record the supplier number.
7.   Name
The first part of the supplier's name.
8.   Order Type
The default sales order type for the session "Maintain Sales Orders (tdsls4101m000)". If left blank, the default will be taken from the session "Maintain Defaults by User (Sales) (tdsls4123m000)".
9.   Description

10.   Gross Item Prices in
This field is used in the package BAAN Service.   Service   Yes
When you enter the actual cost of service orders in the session "Maintain Actual
Service Order Costs and Revenues (tssma3110m000)", the price and discount lists
recorded in the module "Sales Control (SLS)" are not consulted. The default for
the price on the line item is the sales price recorded in the session "Maintain
Item Data (tiitm0101m000)". Generally speaking, no discount is deducted from the
price of items used in service and maintenance; consequently, the default for
the discount on the order line of the service order is 0.
No
When entering the actual costs of service orders in the session, "Maintain
Actual Service Order Costs and Revenues (tssma3110m000)", the price and discount
lists recorded in the module "Sales Control (SLS)" are consulted when
determining the default for the price and discount on the order line of the
service order.
11.   Invoicing Method
Invoicing methods can be recorded by customer by means of an invoicing method
code. The invoice method indicates whether a separate invoice is to be printed
for each order or several orders may be printed on a summary invoice. You can
also indicate whether gross or net invoicing will take place. When a gross
amount is invoiced, the order line discount is not printed on the invoice. The
invoicing method is not used in the package BAAN Transportation. Instead, a
customer be assigned his/her own "Invoicing Type" in the session "Maintain
Defaults by Customer (trtcd2120m000)".
12.   Description
13.   Number of Extra Invoice Copies
The number of invoice copies to be printed in addition to the original.
Enter the number of extra copies (default value 0, maximum value 9).
14.   Invoice Interval
The minimal number of days between two sales invoices to be sent. In this way,
you can ensure that a customer is invoiced (e.g.) once every two weeks.
15.   Date Invoiced
The last invoice date is updated in the session "Print Sales Invoices
(tdsls4404m000)". The last invoice date and the invoice interval determine the
date on which the customer may be invoiced next.
16.   Reminder Method
The way in which the customer is reminded. The data to be entered must be
defined in the session "Maintain Reminder Methods (tfacr3120m000)".
17.   Description
The description of the reminding method.
18.   Statement Method
The statement method specifies to whom, and how frequently a statement of
account is to be sent. For further information, see keyword(s)
"Statement of Account Methods".
19.   Description
The description of the statement method.
20.   Payment Method
The default payment method to convert a sales invoice into cash - e.g. direct
debit, check, bank order. The data to be entered must be defined in the session
"Maintain Payment Methods (tfcmg0140m000)".
21.   Description
The description of the payment method.
22.   Extra Days after Due Date
The average number of days the customer pays before or after the due date of the
invoice.
Example: If the value of this field is 10, and the due date of the invoice is 10
July 1994, the expected payment date is 20 July 1994.
This field is relevant to the b-object "Cash Flow Forecast" in the package BAAN
Finance where it is used for:
•   calculating the expected payment date in the session "Maintain Sales
Invoices (tfacr1110s000)";
•   maintaining the expected payment date in the session "Maintain Customer
Invoice Cash Date (tfcmg3110m000)".

- calculating a cash flow forecast on the basis of the expected payment date in the session "Update Cash Forecast (tfcmg3210m000)".

```
+------------------------------------------------------------------------+
| Maintain Customers                                     Company: 000    |
|------------------------------------------------------------------------|
|                                                                        |
| Customer                            :        1.....  2_____   |
|                                                                        |
| Bank                                : 3..  4_____  5_____   |
| Tax                                 : 6....                            |
| Tax Number                          : 7...................             |
| Verification Date                   : 8........                        |
| Financial Customer Group            : 9.. 10_____   |
| Affiliated Company                  : 11...                            |
| Affiliated Company No.              : 12.            13_____   |
| Credit Limit                        : 14............                   |
| Credit Limit Insured                : 15............                   |
| Credit Insurance Company            :          16. 17_____   |
| Reference Credit Insurance Company : 18.............                   |
| Expiry Date of Insured Credit Limit:    19........                     |
|                                                                        |
+------------------------------------------------------------------------+
```

1.   Customer
For further information, see keyword(s)
"Customers".
2.   Name
The first part of the customer's name.
3.   Bank
The code of the bank through which the financial transactions with the customer take place. This is only used as a default value, since multiple bank relations may be used for each customer.
4.   Name
The first part of the bank name.
5.   Bank Account
The customer's bank account number.
6.   Tax
Yes
Tax is charged over the sales invoice amount.
No
No Tax is charged over the sales invoice amount. Enter the amount, e.g. 10000000
7.   Tax Number
The Tax number used for reporting transactions between EU countries. The system will issue a warning if you leave the field empty.
8.   Verification Date
The last verification date of the Tax number. To ensure that the information contained in the import/export reports be reliable, you should check Tax numbers on a regular basis. The last verification date is stored here.
9.   Financial Customer Group
Financial groups are used to classify customers for administrative reasons. In the package BAAN Finance, various ledger accounts can be recorded for each financial customer group.
10.   Description
The description of the selected financial customer group.
11.   Affiliated Company
An affiliated company is a customer working with the BAAN IV applications within the same concern as your own company (Multi-Site). The affiliated company is used in :
- (multiplant) MPS to distinguish the dependent from the independent demand when analyzing the order file.
- (multicompany) EDI to determine the company for which an internal EDI message is meant.
12.   Affiliated Company No.

The company number of the affiliated company.
13.   Company Name
The company's name.
14.   Credit Limit
The credit limit is the maximum financial risk that you accept or have insured
for this customer. When you create orders, the system continually checks whether
the amount of created and invoiced orders does not exceed the credit limit. The
system warns you if this is the case.
BAAN Distribution
By setting the parameter "Block if Credit Limit is Exceeded" in the session
"Maintain Sales Order Parameters (tdsls4100m000)" to "Yes", you can also block
the "Process Sales Orders" procedure.
BAAN Transportation
In the sessions "Maintain TOC Parameters (trtoc0100m000)" and "Maintain WOC
Parameters (trwoc0100m000)" you can indicate if the order entered is to be
blocked if the credit limit is exceeded, or if only a warning is to be given.
In the session "Maintain Defaults by Customer (trtcd2120m000)" you can specify
by customer whether the system has to block the procedure or not. To determine
whether the credit limit is exceeded, both the outstanding order balance and the
outstanding invoice balance are relevant.
SEE ALSO METHOD(S)
•   Currency Formats
15.   Credit Limit Insured
The credit limit which has been insured with the credit insurance company
specified.
SEE ALSO METHOD(S)
•   Currency Formats
16.   Credit Insurance Company
The credit insurance company where (part of) the customer's credit limit is
insured.
17.   Name
The first part of the name of the credit insurance company.
18.   Reference Credit Insurance Company
The reference number under which the credit insurance company knows the
customer.
19.   Expiry Date of Insured Credit Limit
The expiry date of the credit limit insurance.

```
tccom1101m000                         zoom         single-occ (1) < Form 6-6
+--------------------------------------------------------------------------+
|  Maintain Customers                                       Company: 000   |
|--------------------------------------------------------------------------|
|                                                                          |
|   Customer                          : 1.....   2_____ |
|                                                                          |
|   Back Order                        : 3....                              |
|   Ship Complete                     : 4....                              |
|   Customer Priority                 : 5.                                 |
|                                                                          |
|   Acknowledge by Exception          : 6....                             |
|                                                                          |
|   Order Balance                     : 7_____                    |
|   Invoice Balance                   : 8_____                    |
|                                                                          |
+--------------------------------------------------------------------------+
```

1.   Customer
For further information, see keyword(s)
"Customers".
2.   Name
The first part of the customer's name.
3.   Back Order
Yes

Back orders are allowed. The value in the column "Back Order" (in the session "Maintain Deliveries (tdsls4120m000)") is set to "Ordered - Delivered" by the system. You can still change this value.
No
Back orders are not allowed. The value in the column "Back Order" (in the session "Maintain Deliveries (tdsls4120m000)") is always 0.
4.   Ship Complete
This field provides the default for the field "Ship Complete" in the session "Maintain Sales Orders (tdsls4101m000)". The default value can still be changed in that session.
Yes
Orders for this customer must always be shipped in their entirety (all order lines at the same time). This means that backorders or partial deliveries are not allowed. The field "Back Order" must therefore read "No".
No
Orders for this customer do not neceBaanrily have to be shipped complete.
5.   Customer Priority
A customer can be provided with a priority number. A low number signifies a high priority; a high number signifies a low priority. Priority codes can be used when supplying good to customers.
6.   Acknowledge by Exception
Indicates if the customer is to be acknowledged by exception. If set to "Yes", the customer will receive sales order acknowledgments for only those sales order lines for which an "Acknowledgment Code" has been assigned.
This allows you to govern which changes to the sales order line consistute a change to be picked up during the next sales order acknowledgment print. This accomodates those customers who wish to only receive order acknowledgments on a exceptional basis, who wish to receive order acknowledgments only under certain conditions, such as only when specific, pertinent data has changed. For example, a customer may prefer to receive an acknowledgment for his order ONLY if you (the supplier) make changes to the delivery date, item and/or price.
Yes
Sales order acknowledgments for this customer are only generated for sales order lines for which an "Acknowledgment Code" has been assigned. Specifically, new lines and changed lines are included on the order acknowledgment only if an "Acknowledgment Code" has been assigned to that line.
No
Sales order acknowledgments for this customer are generated for sales order lines regardless of the existance of an "Acknowledgment Code".
For further information, see keyword(s)
"Sales Order Acknowledgments Codes"
7.   Amount (11+2)
SEE ALSO METHOD(S)
•   Currency Formats
8.   Amount (11+2)
SEE ALSO METHOD(S)
•   Currency Formats
10   Optional Sessions
10.1 Maintain Customer Postal Addresses (tccom1103m000)
SESSION OBJECTIVE
To maintain addresses by customer.
SEE ALSO KEYWORD(S)
•   Customer Postal Addresses
SEE ALSO METHOD(S)
•   Address Verification for Tax Provider

```
tccom1103m000                                    single-occ (1)    Form 1-1
+------------------------------------------------------------------------------+
| Maintain Customer Postal Addresses                            Company: 000   |
|------------------------------------------------------------------------------|
|                                                                              |
| Customer            :      1.....  2_____    |
| Postal Address      :         3..                                            |
|                                                                              |
```

```
| Country                    :        4..  5_____ |
| Name                       : 6.................................... |
|                            : 7.............................. |
| Address                    : 8.............................. |
|                            : 9.............................. |
| 10_____    : 11............................ |
| 12_____    : 13............................ |
| 14_____    1516...... |
| 17_____    1819... |
| ZIP Code                   : 20........ |
| Transportation Address     :      21____ |
| Tax Number                 : 22................. |
| Verification Date          : 23........ |
|                            | |
+-------------------------------------------------------------------------+
```

1.   Customer
The number identifying the customer. Enter the code of the customer for which
you want to display the data.
2.   Name
The first part of the customer's name.
3.   Postal Address
For further information, see keyword(s)
"Customer Postal Addresses".
4.   Country
The code of the country where the customer is established. By default the system
shows the information recorded for the customer in the session "Maintain
Customers (tccom1101m000)".
5.   Description
6.   Name
The first part of the customer name. By default the system shows the information
recorded for the customer in the session "Maintain Customers (tccom1101m000)".
7.   Name 2
The second part of the customer's name. By default the system shows the
information recorded for the customer in the session "Maintain Customers
(tccom1101m000)".
8.   Address
The first part of the customer's address. By default the system shows the
information recorded for the customer in the session "Maintain Customers
(tccom1101m000)".
9.   Address 2
The second part of the customer's address. By default the system shows the
information recorded for the customer in the session "Maintain Customers
(tccom1101m000)".
10.   Program domain string
11.   City
The city where the customer is established.
For tax provider users, the city and state or province where the customer is
established. The city and state or province should be separated by a comma ","
such as "Menlo Park, CA".
For further information, see method(s)
•   Address Verification for Tax Provider
By default the system shows the information recorded for the customer in the
session "Maintain Customers (tccom1101m000)".
12.   Program domain string
13.   City 2
The second part of the place where the customer is established.
For tax provider users, the ZIP Code or Postal Code where the customer is
established.
For further information, see method(s)
•   Address Verification for Tax Provider
By default the system shows the information recorded for the customer in the
session "Maintain Customers (tccom1101m000)".
14.   Program domain string

15. Program domain of string length 1
16. GEO Code

A GEO code is a code used together or in lieu of address information such as city, state/province, and ZIP/postal code to uniquely identify a taxing jurisdiction. The tax provider determines the GEO code based upon the address information entered and the county and city limits selected.

The format of the GEO code varies by tax provider. AVP uses a two-digit GEO code; the GEO code together with the city, state, and ZIP code, identifies the taxing jurisdiction. Vertex uses a nine-digit GEO code comprised of a two digit state code, three-digit county code, and a four-digit city code. A tenth digit is used to identify if the jurisdiction is inside or outside of the city limits.

17. Program domain string
18. Program domain of string length 1
19. Answer on question y/n
20. ZIP Code

The ZIP code appears only on forwarding documents on which no other address data is printed. By default the system shows the information recorded for the customer in the session "Maintain Customers (tccom1101m000)".

21. Address Code

The address if the package is run in association with the package BAAN Transportation. The address refers to an address in the b-object "Address Control (ACS)" in the package BAAN Transportation.

22. Tax Number

The Tax number of your own company. As from 1993, companies trading within the EU are legally required to report their import/export activities. Reporting is based on the Tax number.

23. Verification Date

The last verification date of the Tax number. To ensure that the information contained in import/export reports be reliable, you should check Tax numbers on a regular basis. The last verification date is stored here.

10.2 Maintain Delivery Addresses (tccom1102m000)

SESSION OBJECTIVE
To maintain delivery addresses by customer.

SEE ALSO KEYWORD(S)
• Delivery Addresses

SEE ALSO METHOD(S)
• Address Verification for Tax Provider

```
tccom1102m000                                  single-occ (1)    Form 1-1
+-------------------------------------------------------------------------+
| Maintain Delivery Addresses                              Company: 000   |
|-------------------------------------------------------------------------|
|                                                                         |
|  Customer              :     1.....  2_____   |
|  Delivery Address      :      3..                                        |
|  Country               :      4..  5_____        |
|  Name                  : 6...................................            |
|                        : 7...............................               |
|  Address               : 8...............................               |
|                        : 9...............................               |
|  10_____: 11...............................            |
|  12_____: 13...............................            |
|  14_____1516.......                                    |
|  17_____1819...                                        |
|  ZIP Code              : 20........                                      |
|  Transportation Address:     21____                                     |
|  Route                 :     22...  23_____       |
|  Tax Number            : 24..................                           |
|  Verification Date     : 25........                                      |
|                                                                         |
+-------------------------------------------------------------------------+
```

1. Customer
The number identifying the customer. Enter the code of the customer for which you want to display the data.

2.   Name
The first part of the customer's name.
3.   Delivery Address
For further information, see keyword(s)
"Delivery Addresses".
4.   Country
The code of the country where the customer is established. By default the system shows the information recorded for the customer in the session "Maintain Customers (tccom1101m000)".
5.   Description
6.   Name
The first part of the customer name. By default the system shows the information recorded for the customer in the session "Maintain Customers (tccom1101m000)".
7.   Name 2
The second part of the customer name. It is printed on external documents. By default the system shows the information recorded for the customer in the session "Maintain Customers (tccom1101m000)".
8.   Address
The first part of the customer's address. By default the system shows the information recorded for the customer in the session "Maintain Customers (tccom1101m000)".
9.   Address 2
The second part of the customer's address. By default the system shows the information recorded for the customer in the session "Maintain Customers (tccom1101m000)".
10.   Program domain string
11.   City
The city where the customer is established.
For tax provider users, the city and state or province where the customer is established. The city and state or province should be separated by a comma ","
such as "Menlo Park, CA".
For further information, see method(s)
•   Address Verification for Tax Provider
By default the system shows the information recorded for the customer in the session "Maintain Customers (tccom1101m000)".
12.   Program domain string
13.   City 2
The second part of the place where the customer is established.
For tax provider users, the ZIP Code or Postal Code where the customer is established.
For further information, see method(s)
•   Address Verification for Tax Provider
By default the system shows the information recorded for the customer in the session "Maintain Customers (tccom1101m000)".
14.   Program domain string
15.   Program domain of string length 1
16.   GEO Code
A GEO code is a code used together or in lieu of address information such as city, state/province, and ZIP/postal code to uniquely identify a taxing jurisdiction. The tax provider determines the GEO code based upon the address information entered and the county and city limits selected.
The format of the GEO code varies by tax provider. AVP uses a two-digit GEO code; the GEO code together with the city, state, and ZIP code, identifies the taxing jurisdiction. Vertex uses a nine-digit GEO code comprised of a two digit state code, three-digit county code, and a four-digit city code. A tenth digit is used to identify if the jurisdiction is inside or outside of the city limits.
17.   Program domain string
18.   Program domain of string length 1
19.   Answer on question y/n
20.   ZIP Code
The ZIP code appears only on forwarding documents on which no other address data is printed. By default the system shows the information recorded for the customer in the session "Maintain Customers (tccom1101m000)".

21.   Address Code
The address if the package is run in association with the package BAAN
Transportation. The address refers to an address in the b-object "Address
Control (ACS)" in the package BAAN Transportation.
22.   Route
On the order level, you can overwrite the route code which you have assigned to
a customer. When printing picking lists and packing slips, you can select by
route code.
23.   Description
24.   Tax Number
The Tax number of your own company. As from 1993, companies trading within the
EU are legally required to report their import/export activities. Reporting is
based on the Tax number.
25.   Verification Date
The last verification date of the Tax number. To ensure that the information
contained in import/export reports be reliable, you should check Tax numbers on
a regular basis. The last verification date is stored here.
10.3 Maintain Banks by Customer (tccom1105m000)
SESSION OBJECTIVE
To maintain banks by customer. This information is required for processing in
the package BAAN Finance.
SEE ALSO KEYWORD(S)
•   Banks by Customer

```
tccom1105m000                              multi/group (3      Form 1-1
+-------------------------------------------------------------------------+
| Maintain Banks by Customer                            Company: 000  |
|-------------------------------------------------------------------------|
|                                                                     |
| Customer    : 1.....   2_____   |
|                                                                     |
| Bank         Bank Type     Bank Address   Name  Bank Account  Account Type |
|                                                                     |
|     3..  4.........     5...........  6___  7...........  8.............. |
|                                                                     |
+-------------------------------------------------------------------------+
```

1.   Customer
The number uniquely identifying the customer. The data to be entered must be
defined in the session "Maintain Customers (tccom1101m000)".
2.   Name
The first part of the customer's name.
3.   Bank
The code of the bank through which the financial transactions with the customer
take place.
4.   Bank Type
The bank type indicates if the account is giro account or a normal bank account.
Bank
The customer's account is a bank account. This value is offered as default
value.
Giro
The account is a giro account. No checks are carried out on this number.
5.   Bank Address
The address of the bank. The data to be entered must be defined in the session
"Maintain Bank Addresses (tcmcs0120m000)".
6.   Name
The first part of the bank name.
7.   Bank Account
The customer's bank account number.
8.   Account Type
The account type is relevant to the processing of financial data in the package
BAAN Finance. Normal Account
The bank account is a normal bank account. This value is offered as default
value.
Blocked Account

The bank account is a blocked account. Such accounts are used for payments on invoices from subcontractors in the b-object "Supplier Payments".
See also information in the b-object "Subcontracting".
10.4 Maintain Prospects (tccom1110m000)
SESSION OBJECTIVE
To maintain prospects. Prospects are potential customers.
HOW TO USE THE SESSION
Choose option "Continue [cont.process]" to record additional information by means of 'Features' (additional user-definable fields). The 'zoom' option allows you to call a menu from which you can convert the prospect into a customer.
SEE ALSO KEYWORD(S)
•   Customers
SEE ALSO METHOD(S)
•   Address Verification for Tax Provider

```
tccom1110m000                        zoom       single-occ (1)   Form 1-2 >
+------------------------------------------------------------------------+
|  Maintain Prospects                                    Company: 000   |
|------------------------------------------------------------------------|
|                                                                        |
|  Prospect                     : 1.....                                 |
|                                                                        |
|  Title                        :   2..  3_____ |
|  Country                      :   4..  5_____ |
|  Name                         : 6...................................... |
|                               : 7................................       |
|  Address                      : 8................................       |
|                               : 9................................       |
|  10_____   : 11...............................       |
|  12_____   : 13...............................       |
|  14_____   1516.......                              |
|  17_____   1819...                                  |
|  ZIP Code                     : 20........                             |
|  Postal Address               :   21.  22_____  |
|  Search Key                   : 23.............                        |
|  Text                         : 24___                                  |
|                                                                        |
+------------------------------------------------------------------------+
```

1.   Customer
For further information, see keyword(s) "Customers".
2.   Title
By using a title code, you may assign a prefix to a customer, e.g. engineering works or subcontractor. The title code is printed on the correspondence with the customer. The title code must first be recorded in the session "Maintain Titles (tcmcs0119m000)".
3.   Description
4.   Country
The code of the country where the customer is established.
5.   Description
6.   Name
The first part of the customer's name. The "search key" field is filled by the system with the first 16 positions of the customer's name behind the last period. Therefore you should enter, for example, "J. Jansen Ltd", not "J. Jansen L.t.d.".
7.   Name 2
The second part of the customer's name. If the previous field has insufficient length for the customer's name, you may also use this field.
8.   Address
The first part of the customer's address.
9.   Address 2

The second part of the customer's address. If the previous field has insufficient length for the description of the address, you may also use this field.

10.   Program domain string
11.   City

The city where the customer is established.

For tax provider users, the city and state or province where the customer is established. The city and state or province should be separated by a comma "," such as "Menlo Park, CA".

For further information, see method(s)

•   Address Verification for Tax Provider

If a ZIP code is used, it is assumed that this code is also entered on one of the address fields. The "ZIP code" in "Maintain Customers (tccom1101m000)", is not printed on order documents, but is exclusively used for sorting purposes, as the format and position of international ZIP codes on such documents differ from country to country.

12.   Program domain string
13.   City 2

The second part of the place where the customer is established.

For tax provider users, the ZIP Code or Postal Code where the customer is established.

For further information, see method(s)

•   Address Verification for Tax Provider

14.   Program domain string
15.   Program domain of string length 1
16.   GEO Code

A GEO code is a code used together or in lieu of address information such as city, state/province, and ZIP/postal code to uniquely identify a taxing jurisdiction. The tax provider determines the GEO code based upon the address information entered and the county and city limits selected.

The format of the GEO code varies by tax provider. AVP uses a two-digit GEO code; the GEO code together with the city, state, and ZIP code, identifies the taxing jurisdiction. Vertex uses a nine-digit GEO code comprised of a two digit state code, three-digit county code, and a four-digit city code. A tenth digit is used to identify if the jurisdiction is inside or outside of the city limits.

17.   Program domain string
18.   Program domain of string length 1
19.   Answer on question y/n
20.   ZIP Code

The ZIP code serves two purposes:

•   It is used for sorting customers.
•   It appears only on forwarding documents on which no other address data is printed than the ZIP code to be entered in this field.

This ZIP code does not appear as address data in order documents! On the two fields reserved for "City", you can record the post code which must appear as address data on order documents.

21.   Postal Address

The postal address is the address the trade document (e.g. order acknowledgement, invoice etc.) is sent to. You should have already defined this address in the fields "Name", "Address" and "City" in the session "Maintain Customers (tccom1101m000)". However, you can also record other postal addresses for a customer via the session "Maintain Customer Postal Addresses (tccom1103m000)". In this way, you can record the normal and post box address of a customer.

NOTE: You can also record a specific postal address for each order.

22.   Name

The first part of the customer name.

23.   Search Key

The search key is used to search for customers. The system fills in the search key on the basis of customer's name. It does so by filling in the first 16 positions of the customer's name behind the last period and converting them to capital letters.

Example: J. Jansen becomes JANSEN Attention!: Do not fill in "J. Jansen L.t.d.", but "J. Jansen Ltd".

24.   Text

tccom1110m000   zoom   single-occ (1) < Form 2-2

```
+-----------------------------------------------------------------------+
| Maintain Prospects                                     Company: 000   |
|-----------------------------------------------------------------------|
|                                                                       |
| Prospect                      : 1.....  2_____      |
|                                                                       |
| Telephone                     : 3_____ 4.............                |
| Telex                         : 3_____ 5.............                |
| Fax                           : 3_____ 6.............                |
| Area                          :    7..  8_____       |
| Language                      :    9..  10_____       |
| Currency                      :   11.   12_____       |
| Line of Business              :   13.   14_____       |
| Sales Rep                     : 15....  16_____     |
| Terms of Payment              :   17.   18_____       |
| Financial Customer Group      :   19.   20_____       |
|                                                                       |
+-----------------------------------------------------------------------+
```

1.   Customer
For further information, see keyword(s) "Customers".
2.   Name
The first part of the customer's name.
3.   Fax
The international access number for the fax of the country.
4.   Telephone
The telephone number (dialing code and subscription number) of the customer.
5.   Telex
The telex number of the customer.
6.   Fax
The fax number of the customer.
7.   Area
The code of the area in which the customer is established. The area code is used as sorting criteria for the sales statistics.
8.   Description
9.   Language
The language in which external documents must be printed for this customer. The data to be entered must be defined in the session "Maintain Languages (tcmcs0146m000)".
10.   Description
11.   Currency
The currency in which the customer is invoiced, unless it has been changed on the order level.
12.   Description
13.   Line of Business
The line of business to which the customer belongs. The code is used as a sorting criterion for the sales statistics.
14.   Description
15.   Sales Rep
The sales rep is the employee of your company who maintains contact with the customer. The employee number of the sales rep is also used as a sorting criterion in the sales statistics. When the module "Sales and Marketing Information (SMI)" is implemented, you can retrieve the default sales rep by choosing option "<Ctrl>[R]" (see the parameter "Employee per ZIP Code/Area/Line of Business").
16.   Name
The employee's name.
17.   Terms of Payment
The terms of payment comprise the following data:

- the payment term
- the discount term
- the discount percentage to be considered if the amount debited is paid within the discount term.

The above data are defaults which can be adjusted for each invoice in the package BAAN Finance.

The description of the terms of payment appears on various documents.

18. Description
19. Financial Customer Group

Financial groups are used to classify customers for administrative reasons. In the package BAAN Finance, various ledger accounts can be recorded for each financial customer group.

20. Description

The description of the selected financial customer group.

10.5 Maintain Prospects (tccom1110s000)

SESSION OBJECTIVE

To maintain prospects. Prospects are potential customers.

HOW TO USE THE SESSION

Choose option "Continue [cont.process]" to record additional information by means of 'Features' (additional user-definable fields). The 'zoom' option allows you to call a menu from which you can convert the prospect into a customer.

SEE ALSO KEYWORD(S)

- Customers

SEE ALSO METHOD(S)

- Address Verification for Tax Provider

```
tccom1110s000                        zoom      single-occ (1)   Form 1-2 >
+-Maintain Prospects-----------------------------------------------------------+
|                                                                              |
|  Prospect                      : 1.....                                      |
|                                                                              |
|  Title                         :   2.. 3_____        |
|  Country                       :   4.. 5_____      |
|  Name                          : 6..................................         |
|                                : 7.............................              |
|  Address                       : 8.............................              |
|                                : 9.............................              |
|  10_____   : 11.............................             |
|  12_____   : 13.............................             |
|  14_____   1516.......                                   |
|  17_____   1819...                                       |
|  ZIP Code                      : 20........                                  |
|  Postal Address                :   21. 22_____      |
|  Search Key                    : 23.............                             |
|  Text                          : 24___                                       |
|                                                                              |
+------------------------------------------------------------------------------+
```

1. Customer

For further information, see keyword(s)
"Customers".

2. Title

By using a title code, you may assign a prefix to a customer, e.g. engineering works or subcontractor. The title code is printed on the correspondence with the customer. The title code must first be recorded in the session "Maintain Titles (tcmcs0119m000)".

3. Description
4. Country

The code of the country where the customer is established.

5. Description
6. Name

The first part of the customer's name. The "search key" field is filled by the system with the first 16 positions of the customer's name behind the last period. Therefore you should enter, for example, "J. Jansen Ltd", not "J. Jansen L.t.d.".

7.   Name 2
The second part of the customer's name. If the previous field has insufficient length for the customer's name, you may also use this field.

8.   Address
The first part of the customer's address.

9.   Address 2
The second part of the customer's address. If the previous field has insufficient length for the description of the address, you may also use this field.

10.   Program domain string

11.   City
The city where the customer is established.
For tax provider users, the city and state or province where the customer is established. The city and state or province should be separated by a comma "," such as "Menlo Park, CA".
For further information, see method(s)
•   Address Verification for Tax Provider
If a ZIP code is used, it is assumed that this code is also entered on one of the address fields. The "ZIP code" in "Maintain Customers (tccom1101m000)", is not printed on order documents, but is exclusively used for sorting purposes, as the format and position of international ZIP codes on such documents differ from country to country.

12.   Program domain string

13.   City 2
The second part of the place where the customer is established.
For tax provider users, the ZIP Code or Postal Code where the customer is established.
For further information, see method(s)
•   Address Verification for Tax Provider

14.   Program domain string

15.   Program domain of string length 1

16.   GEO Code
A GEO code is a code used together or in lieu of address information such as city, state/province, and ZIP/postal code to uniquely identify a taxing jurisdiction. The tax provider determines the GEO code based upon the address information entered and the county and city limits selected.
The format of the GEO code varies by tax provider. AVP uses a two-digit GEO code; the GEO code together with the city, state, and ZIP code, identifies the taxing jurisdiction. Vertex uses a nine-digit GEO code comprised of a two digit state code, three-digit county code, and a four-digit city code. A tenth digit is used to identify if the jurisdiction is inside or outside of the city limits.

17.   Program domain string

18.   Program domain of string length 1

19.   Answer on question y/n

20.   ZIP Code
The ZIP code serves two purposes:
•   It is used for sorting customers.
•   It appears only on forwarding documents on which no other address data is printed than the ZIP code to be entered in this field.
This ZIP code does not appear as address data in order documents! On the two fields reserved for "City", you can record the post code which must appear as address data on order documents.

21.   Postal Address
The postal address is the address the trade document (e.g. order acknowledgement, invoice etc.) is sent to. You should have already defined this address in the fields "Name", "Address" and "City" in the session "Maintain Customers (tccom1101m000)". However, you can also record other postal addresses for a customer via the session "Maintain Customer Postal Addresses (tccom1103m000)". In this way, you can record the normal and post box address of a customer.
NOTE: You can also record a specific postal address for each order.

22.   Name
The first part of the customer name.
23.   Search Key
The search key is used to search for customers. The system fills in the search
key on the basis of customer's name. It does so by filling in the first 16
positions of the customer's name behind the last period and converting them to
capital letters.
Example: J. Jansen becomes JANSEN Attention!: Do not fill in "J. Jansen L.t.d.",
but "J. Jansen Ltd".
24.   Text

```
tccom1110s000                    zoom        single-occ (1) < Form 2-2
+--Maintain Prospects--------------------------------------------------------+
|                                                                            |
|  Prospect                      : 1.....  2_____  |
|                                                                            |
|  Telephone                     : 3_____  4..............                   |
|  Telex                         : 3_____  5..............                   |
|  Fax                           : 3_____  6..............                   |
|  Area                          :    7..  8_____            |
|  Language                      :    9..  10_____            |
|  Currency                      :    11.  12_____            |
|  Line of Business              :    13.  14_____            |
|  Sales Rep                     : 15....  16_____       |
|  Terms of Payment              :    17.  18_____              |
|  Financial Customer Group      :    19.  20_____              |
|                                                                            |
+----------------------------------------------------------------------------+
```

1.   Customer
For further information, see keyword(s)
"Customers".
2.   Name
The first part of the customer's name.
3.   Fax
The international access number for the fax of the country.
4.   Telephone
The telephone number (dialing code and subscription number) of the customer.
5.   Telex
The telex number of the customer.
6.   Fax
The fax number of the customer.
7.   Area
The code of the area in which the customer is established. The area code is used
as sorting criteria for the sales statistics.
8.   Description
9.   Language
The language in which external documents must be printed for this customer. The
data to be entered must be defined in the session "Maintain Languages
(tcmcs0146m000)".
10.   Description
11.   Currency
The currency in which the customer is invoiced, unless it has been changed on
the order level.
12.   Description
13.   Line of Business
The line of business to which the customer belongs. The code is used as a
sorting criterion for the sales statistics.
14.   Description
15.   Sales Rep
The sales rep is the employee of your company who maintains contact with the
customer. The employee number of the sales rep is also used as a sorting
criterion in the sales statistics. When the module "Sales and Marketing
Information (SMI)" is implemented, you can retrieve the default sales rep by

choosing option "<Ctrl>[R]" (see the parameter "Employee per ZIP Code/Area/Line of Business").

16.   Name
The employee's name.

17.   Terms of Payment
The terms of payment comprise the following data:
•   the payment term
•   the discount term
•   the discount percentage to be considered if the amount debited is paid within the discount term.
The above data are defaults which can be adjusted for each invoice in the package BAAN Finance.
The description of the terms of payment appears on various documents.

18.   Description

19.   Financial Customer Group
Financial groups are used to classify customers for administrative reasons. In the package BAAN Finance, various ledger accounts can be recorded for each financial customer group.

20.   Description
The description of the selected financial customer group.

11   Other Print Sessions
11.1 Print Customers (tccom1401m000)

tccom1401m000   single-occ (4)   Form 1-1
+---+
Print Customers   Company: 000
Sort by   : 1..................
Customer   from : 2.....
to   : 3.....
Search Key   from : 4..............
to   : 5..............
Country   from :   6..
to   :   7..
ZIP Code   from : 8........
to   : 9........
Cust. Status   from : 10............
to   : 11............
Including Features : 12...
+---+

1.   Sort by
Indicate the sequence in which customers must be printed:
1.   Customer
2.   Search Key
3.   ZIP Code
2.   Customer from
3.   Customer to
4.   Search Key from
5.   Search Key to
6.   Country from
7.   Country to
8.   ZIP Code from
9.   ZIP Code to
10.   Customer Status from
11.   Customer Status to
12.   Including Features
Yes
If features have been added to a customer or prospect, they are printed.
No

No features are printed.

11.2 Print Customer Postal Addresses (tccom1403m000)

tccom1403m000   single-occ (4)   Form 1-1

```
+-------------------------------------------------------------------------+
|  Print Customer Postal Addresses                       Company: 000  |
|-------------------------------------------------------------------------|
|                                                                         |
|  Customer                    from : 1.....                              |
|                              to   : 2.....                              |
|                                                                         |
|  Postal Address              from :    3..                              |
|                              to   :    4..                              |
|                                                                         |
+-------------------------------------------------------------------------+
```

1.   Customer from
2.   Customer to
3.   Postal Address from
4.   Postal Address to

11.3 Print Delivery Addresses (tccom1402m000)

tccom1402m000   single-occ (4)   Form 1-1

```
+-------------------------------------------------------------------------+
|  Print Delivery Addresses                              Company: 000  |
|-------------------------------------------------------------------------|
|                                                                         |
|  Customer                    from : 1.....                              |
|                              to   : 2.....                              |
|                                                                         |
|  Delivery Address            from :    3..                              |
|                              to   :    4..                              |
|                                                                         |
+-------------------------------------------------------------------------+
```

1.   Customer from
2.   Customer to
3.   Delivery Address from
4.   Delivery Address to

11.4 Print Banks by Customer (tccom1405m000)

tccom1405m000   single-occ (4)   Form 1-1

```
+-------------------------------------------------------------------------+
|  Print Banks by Customer                               Company: 000  |
|-------------------------------------------------------------------------|
|                                                                         |
|  Customer   From : 1.....                                               |
|             To   : 2.....                                               |
|                                                                         |
|  Bank       From :    3..                                               |
|             To   :    4..                                               |
|                                                                         |
+-------------------------------------------------------------------------+
```

1.   Customer from
2.   Customer to
3.   Bank from
4.   Bank to

11.5 Print Customer Credit Limit Data (tccom1404m000)

tccom1404m000   single-occ (4)   Form 1-1

```
+-------------------------------------------------------------------------+
|  Print Customer Credit Limit Data                      Company: 000  |
|-------------------------------------------------------------------------|
|                                                                         |
|  Customer                     From :    1.....                          |
|                               To   :    2.....                          |
|                                                                         |
|  Credit Insurance Company From :        3..                             |
|                               To   :        4..                         |
```

```
|                                                                   |    |
| Expiry Date            From : 5........                           |    |
|                        To   : 6........                           |    |
|                                                                   |    |
+-------------------------------------------------------------------+
```

1.   Customer from
2.   Customer to
3.   Credit Insurance Company from
4.   Credit Insurance Company to
5.   Expiry Date of Insured Credit Limit from
6.   Expiry Date of Insured Credit Limit to
12   Introduction to Supplier Data
12.1 General
OBJECTIVE OF BUSINESS OBJECT
This b-object allows you to control data about suppliers and potential
suppliers.
SEE ALSO KEYWORD(S)
•   Suppliers
•   Supplier Postal Addresses
•   Banks by Supplier
12.2 Session Overview

Seq.	Session	Description	Session Usage
1	tccom2101m000	Maintain Suppliers	Mandatory
2	tccom2103m000	Maintain Supplier Postal Addresses	Optional
3	tccom2105m000	Maintain Banks by Supplier	Optional
101	tccom2401m000	Print Suppliers	Print
102	tccom2403m000	Print Supplier Postal Addresses	Print
103	tccom2405m000	Print Banks by Supplier	Print
201	tccom2501m000	Display Suppliers	Display
202	tccom2503m000	Display Supplier Postal Addresses	Display
203	tccom2505m000	Display Banks by Supplier	Display
1013	tccom2510s000	Display Supplier List	Display

13   Mandatory Sessions
13.1 Maintain Suppliers (tccom2101m000)
SESSION OBJECTIVE
To maintain supplier data.
SEE ALSO KEYWORD(S)
•   Suppliers
SEE ALSO METHOD(S)
•   Address Verification for Tax Provider

```
tccom2101m000                    zoom      single-occ (1)  Form 1-5 >
+-------------------------------------------------------------------+
| Maintain Suppliers                                 Company: 000   |
|-------------------------------------------------------------------|
|                                                                   |
| Supplier               : 1.....        2...................       |
|                                                                   |
| Title                  :   3.. 4_____   |
| Country                :   5.. 6_____   |
```

```
+------------------------------------------------------------------------------+
| Name                         : 7....................................          |
|                              : 8.............................                 |
| Address                      : 9.............................                 |
|                              : 10............................                 |
| 11_____      : 12...........................                 |
| 13_____      : 14...........................                 |
| 15_____      1617.......                                      |
| 18_____      1920...                                          |
| ZIP Code                     : 21........                                     |
| Transportation Address       : 22____                                         |
| Search Key                   : 23.............                                |
| Text                         : 24___                                          |
|                              :                                                |
+------------------------------------------------------------------------------+
```

1.   Supplier
For further information, see keyword(s)
"Suppliers".
2.   Supplier Status
Actual
Purchase inquiries, contracts and orders can be created without limitations.
Potential
Purchase orders cannot be created; Purchase inquiries can be created.
Purchase Entry Blocked
New orders cannot be created; existing orders can be processed.
Payments Blocked
Payments cannot be processed.
Paym. & Purch. Entr. Bl.
Combination of the statuses "Purchase Entry Blocked" and "Payments Blocked".
3.   Title
With the title code, a supplier may be furnished with a prefix: e.g. Wholesaler.
The title code is printed on the correspondence with the supplier. The title
code must first be recorded in the session "Maintain Titles (tcmcs0119m000)".
4.   Description
5.   Country
The country where the supplier is established. The country code is:
•   printed on documents;
•   used in combination with the Tax code of the item in order to retrieve the
correct Tax percentage;
•   used as sorting criterion for the purchase statistics.
6.   Description
7.   Name
The first part of the supplier's name. On several places in the BAAN IV
applications, you can search for suppliers by entering the name as search key.
You should therefore always enter names in the same way - for instance first the
surname, then the initials.
8.   Name 2
The second part of the supplier's name.
9.   Address
The supplier's address.
10.   Address 2
The second part of the supplier's address.
11.   Program domain string
12.   City
The city of the supplier.
For tax provider users, the city and state or province where the supplier is
established. The city and state or province should be separated by a comma ","
such as "Menlo Park, CA".
For further information, see method(s)
•   Address Verification for Tax Provider
If a ZIP code is used, it is assumed that this code is also entered on one of
the address fields. The "ZIP code" in session "Maintain Customers
(tccom1101m000)", is not printed on order documents, but is exclusively used for

sorting purposes, as the format and position of international ZIP codes on such documents differ from country to country.

13.   Program domain string
14.   City 2
The second part of the description of the city where the supplier is established.
For tax provider users, the ZIP Code or Postal Code where the supplier is established.
For further information, see method(s)
•   Address Verification for Tax Provider
15.   Program domain string
16.   Program domain of string length 1
17.   GEO Code
A GEO code is a code used together or in lieu of address information such as city, state/province, and ZIP/postal code to uniquely identify a taxing jurisdiction. The tax provider determines the GEO code based upon the address information entered and the county and city limits selected.
The format of the GEO code varies by tax provider. AVP uses a two-digit GEO code; the GEO code together with the city, state, and ZIP code, identifies the taxing jurisdiction. Vertex uses a nine-digit GEO code comprised of a two digit state code, three-digit county code, and a four-digit city code. A tenth digit is used to identify if the jurisdiction is inside or outside of the city limits.
18.   Program domain string
19.   Program domain of string length 1
20.   Answer on question y/n
21.   ZIP Code
This ZIP code:
•   is used for sorting suppliers.
•   appears only on forwarding documents on which no address data is printed other than the ZIP code which is to be entered.
This ZIP code does not appear as address data on order documents! You must record the post code which has to appear as address data on order documents on one of the two fields reserved for "City".
22.   Address Code
The address if the package is run in association with the package BAAN Transportation. The address refers to an address in the b-object "Address Control (ACS)" in the package BAAN Transportation.
23.   Search Key
The search key is used in order to search for suppliers by their name. The system fills in the search key by filling in the first 16 positions of the supplier's name behind the last period and converting them to capital letters.
Example : J. Jansen becomes JANSEN Attention!: Do not fill in "J. Jansen L.t.d.", but "J. Jansen Ltd".
The search argument is used to search for suppliers by name.
24.   Text
Yes
A text has been assigned to the supplier.
No
No text has been assigned to the supplier.

```
tccom2101m000                          single-occ (1) < Form 2-5 >
+----------------------------------------------------------------------+
|  Maintain Suppliers                                 Company: 000  |
|----------------------------------------------------------------------|
|                                                                      |
|  Supplier                        : 1.....  2_____  |
|                                                                      |
|  Postal Address                  :   3.. 4_____  |
|  Warehouse                       :   5.. 6_____    |
|                                                                      |
|  Default Financial Company       :   7.. 8_____  |
|  One-Time Supplier               : 9....                             |
|  Supplier for Prices/Discounts   : 10.... 11_____  |
|  Supplier for Texts              : 12.... 13_____  |
```

```
| Sales Reference              : 14..............................          |
| Accounting Reference         : 15..............................          |
| Our Customer Number          : 16..............                          |
| Telephone                    : 17____  18..............                  |
| Telex                        : 19____  20..............                  |
| Fax                          : 21____  22..............                  |
|                                                                          |
+--------------------------------------------------------------------------+
```

1.   Supplier
For further information, see keyword(s)
"Suppliers".
2.   Name
The first part of the supplier's name.
3.   Postal Address
The postal address is the address the trade documents (such as the purchase
order) are sent to. You should have defined this address in the session
"Maintain Suppliers (tccom2101m000)" on the fields "Name", "Address" and "City".
However, you can also record other postal addresses per supplier via the session
"Maintain Supplier Postal Addresses (tccom2103m000)". In this way, you can
record the normal address of a supplier, as well as the P.O. box address if
applicable.
4.   Name
The first part of the supplier's name.
5.   Warehouse
The warehouse is the place where the supplier must deliver his goods.
6.   Description
7.   Company
The number of the financial company. This company number is the default value
for the financial number as used in the session "Maintain Purchase Orders
(tdpur4101m000)".
8.   Name
The description associated with the selected code.
9.   One-Time Supplier
A one-time supplier can be used as general code for incidental suppliers. The
invoice address of such suppliers is recorded in the package BAAN Finance when
the order is removed from the module Purchase Control (PUR).
NOTE: The combination of one-time supplier and subcontracting is not allowed.
10.   Supplier for Prices/Discounts
The terms and conditions associated with this supplier number will be the basis
for calculating the price and discount. This field is relevant if the supplier
is another than the supplier on the order.
11.   Name
The description associated with the selected code.
12.   Supplier for Texts
The supplier number under which the supplier-specific texts (item descriptions)
are stored. Skip this field if the system has to retrieve the texts stored under
the supplier on the order.
13.   Name
The description associated with the selected code.
14.   Sales Reference
The name of the sales person at the supplier's with whom you can confer on the
items to be purchased.
15.   Accounting Reference
The name of the contact person at the supplier's with whom you can discuss
administrative matters. This name appears on external documents behind "Ref.":.
16.   Our Customer Number
The customer number by which the supplier identifies you.
17.   Telephone
The international access number for the telephone of the country. This code must
first be defined in the session "Maintain Countries (tcmcs0110m000)".
18.   Telephone
The telephone number (dialing code and supplier's subscription number).
19.   Telex

The international access number for the telex of the country. This code must first be defined in the session "Maintain Countries (tcmcs0110m000)".
20.   Telex
The supplier's telex number.
21.   Fax
The international access number for the fax of the country. This code must first be defined in the session "Maintain Countries (tcmcs0110m000)".
22.   Fax
The supplier's fax number.

```
tccom2101m000                              single-occ (1) < Form 3-5 >
+--------------------------------------------------------------------------+
|  Maintain Suppliers                                      Company: 000  |
|--------------------------------------------------------------------------|
|                                                                          |
|  Supplier                     : 1.....  2_____ |
|                                                                          |
|  Language                     :   3..  4_____  |
|  Line of Business             : 5.....  6_____  |
|  Currency                     :   7..  8_____  |
|  Order Type                   :   9..  10_____  |
|  Affiliated Company           :  11...                                   |
|  Affiliated Company No.        :  12.  13_____  |
|  Area                         :  14.  15_____  |
|  Contact (Purchase)           : 16....  17_____ |
|  Factoring Company            :  18.  19_____ |
|  Customer Number at Factor. Co.: 20........                               |
|  Purchase Price List          :  21.  22_____  |
|  Terms of Payment             :  23.  24_____  |
|  Terms of Delivery            :  25.  26_____  |
|  Late Payment Surcharge       :  27.  28_____  |
|                                                                          |
+--------------------------------------------------------------------------+
```

1.   Supplier
For further information, see keyword(s)
"Suppliers".
2.   Name
The first part of the supplier's name.
3.   Language
The language in which external documents for this supplier must be printed. This code must first be defined in the session "Maintain Languages (tcmcs0146m000)".
4.   Description
5.   Line of Business
The line of business is the type of industry to which the supplier belongs.
6.   Description
7.   Currency
The currency used by the supplier for invoicing.
8.   Description
9.   Order Type
The default purchase order type for the session "Maintain Purchase Orders (tdpur4101m000)". If left blank, the default will be taken from "Maintain Defaults by User (Purchase) (tdpur4123m000)".
10.   Description
11.   Affiliated Company
An affiliated company is a supplier working with BAAN IV within the same concern as your own company (Multi-Site). The affiliated company is used in:
•   (multiplant) MPS to distinguish inter-plant and normal deliveries.
•   (multicompany) EDI to determine the company for which an internal EDI message is meant.
12.   Affiliated Company No.
The company number of the affiliated company.
13.   Company Name
The company's name.
14.   Area

The code of the area where the supplier is established.
15.   Description
16.   Contact (Purchase)
The employee number of the employee responsible within your company for the
purchase activities at this supplier's.
17.   Name
The employee's name.
18.   Factoring Company
The factoring company is responsible for collecting payments for this supplier.
All payments must be directed to this factoring company and not to the company
itself.
19.   Name
The first part of the name of the factoring company.
20.   Customer Number at Factor. Co.
The supplier number with which the supplier is registered at the factoring
company.
21.   Purchase Price List
The purchase price list can be linked to various suppliers. Special prices
and/or discounts for goods can be recorded by price list. One price agreement
can be recorded for one supplier group as well.
22.   Description
23.   Terms of Payment
With the terms of payment:
•   the date can be calculated on which the payment term and the discount term
expire.
•   the discount amount can be calculated.
This is default data that can be adjusted in the package BAAN Finance for each
invoice.
24.   Description
25.   Terms of Delivery
The terms of delivery contain the agreement which has been made with the
supplier about how the goods will be delivered. The terms of delivery are
printed on external documents (among other places).
26.   Description
27.   Late Payment Surcharge
The late payment surcharge is an amount added to the goods amount. It may be
deducted from the supplier's invoice when payment is made within the time period
set. The description of the late payment surcharge code is printed on the
purchase order and the purchase invoice.
This is a default value that can be changed for each individual invoice in the
package BAAN Finance.
28.   Description

```
tccom2101m000                    zoom        single-occ (1) < Form 4-5 >
+-----------------------------------------------------------------------------+
|  Maintain Suppliers                                        Company: 000  |
|-----------------------------------------------------------------------------|
|                                                                             |
|   Supplier                   : 1.....   2_____  |
|                                                                             |
|   Payment Method             :    3.. 4_____   |
|   Extra Days after Due Date  :    5...                                    |
|   Financial Supplier Group   :    6.. 7_____   |
|   Order Discount             : 8..    [%]                                 |
|                                                                             |
|   Customer                   : 9.....   10_____  |
|   Subcontracting             : 11...                                      |
|   Inspection                 : 12...                                      |
|   Tax                        : 13...                                      |
|   Tax Number                 : 14................                         |
|   Bank                       : 15.  16_____  17_____  |
|                                                                             |
+-----------------------------------------------------------------------------+
```

1.   Supplier

For further information, see keyword(s)
"Suppliers".
2.   Name
The first part of the supplier's name.
3.   Payment Method
The default payment method for paying the purchase invoice. It can be changed in
the package BAAN Finance for each invoice.
The data to be entered must be defined in the session "Maintain Payment Methods
(tfcmg0140m000)".
4.   Description
The description of the payment method.
5.   Extra Days after Due Date
The average number of days you pay the supplier before or after the due date of
the invoice.
Example: If the value of this field is 10, and the due date of the invoice is 10
July 1994, the expected payment date is 20 July 1994.
This field is relevant to the b-object "Cash Flow Forecast" in the package BAAN
Finance where it is used for:
•   calculating the expected payment date in the session "Maintain Purchase
Invoices (tfacp1110s000)";
•   maintaining the expected payment date in the session "Maintain Supplier
Invoice Cash Date (tfcmg3111m000)".
•   calculating a cash flow forecast on the basis of the expected payment date
in the session "Update Cash Forecast (tfcmg3210m000)".
6.   Financial Supplier Group
Financial supplier groups are used to classify suppliers for administrative
reasons. In the package BAAN Finance, various ledger accounts can be recorded
for each financial supplier group.
You need not fill in this field if the parameter "FINANCE implemented" in the
session "Maintain COM Parameters (tccom0000m000)" is on "No".
The data to be entered must be defined in the session "Maintain Financial
Supplier Groups (tfacp0110m000)".
7.   Description
The description of the financial supplier group.
8.   Order Discount
The order discount percentage. This value is used as default for each purchase
order.
9.   Customer
The corresponding customer number of the supplier. When preparing payments for a
supplier, you can consult the unpaid items of the corresponding customer number.
10.   Name
The first part of the customer's name.
11.   Subcontracting
The supplier can be a subcontractor. Yes
You can record extra supplier data relating to subcontracting in the module
"Accounts Payable (ACP)" of the package BAAN Finance.
No
You cannot record any extra subcontracting data for this supplier.
NOTE: The combination of one-time supplier and subcontracting is not allowed.
12.   Inspection
Yes
The goods delivered by this supplier must be inspected on arrival. However, this
is done only for items which have the value "Yes" on the field "Inspection" in
the session "Maintain Item Data (tiitm0101m000)".
No
The goods delivered by this supplier must not be inspected on arrival.
13.   Tax
On this field, you can indicate whether Tax must be paid to this supplier.
Yes
Tax is charged over the purchase invoice amount.
No
No Tax is charged over the purchase invoice amount.
14.   Tax Number

The Tax number used for reporting transactions between EU countries. Reporting such transactions is mandatory.

15. Bank

The code of the bank through which financial transactions between your company and the supplier take place.

16. Name

The first part of the bank name.

17. Bank Account

The number of a payment and/or receipt account at the bank.

```
tccom2101m000                      zoom       single-occ (1) < Form 5-5
+----------------------------------------------------------------------+
| Maintain Suppliers                                    Company: 000   |
|----------------------------------------------------------------------|
|                                                                      |
|  Supplier                    : 1.....  2_____  |
|                                                                      |
|  Order Balance               : 3_____                       |
|  Invoice Balance             : 4_____                       |
|  Supplier Status             : 5_____                           |
|                                                                      |
+----------------------------------------------------------------------+
```

1. Supplier

For further information, see keyword(s)
"Suppliers".

2. Name

The first part of the supplier's name.

3. Amount (11+2)

SEE ALSO METHOD(S)

• Currency Formats

4. Amount (11+2)

SEE ALSO METHOD(S)

• Currency Formats

5. Supplier Status

Actual

Purchase inquiries, contracts and orders can be created without limitations.

Potential

Purchase orders cannot be created; Purchase inquiries can be created.

Purchase Entry Blocked

New orders cannot be created; existing orders can be processed.

Payments Blocked

Payments cannot be processed.

Paym. & Purch. Entr. Bl.

Combination of the statuses "Purchase Entry Blocked" and "Payments Blocked".

14 Optional Sessions

14.1 Maintain Supplier Postal Addresses (tccom2103m000)

SESSION OBJECTIVE

To maintain addresses by supplier. These addresses are used to send correspondence to.

SEE ALSO KEYWORD(S)

• Supplier Postal Addresses

SEE ALSO METHOD(S)

• Address Verification for Tax Provider

```
tccom2103m000                             single-occ (1)   Form 1-1
+----------------------------------------------------------------------+
| Maintain Supplier Postal Addresses                    Company: 000   |
|----------------------------------------------------------------------|
|                                                                      |
|  Supplier                    : 1.....  2_____    |
|  Postal Address              :   3..                                 |
|                                                                      |
|  Country                     :   4..  5_____    |
|  Name                        : 6..............................       |
|                              : 7..............................       |
```

```
| Address                      : 8...........................        |
|                              : 9...........................        |
| 10_____  : 11..........................        |
| 12_____  : 13..........................        |
| 14_____  1516.......                           |
| 17_____  1819...                               |
| ZIP Code                     : 20........                          |
| Transportation Address       : 21____                              |
|                                                                    |
+--------------------------------------------------------------------+
```

1.   Supplier
The supplier number by which the supplier is identified. Enter the code of the
customer for which you want to display the data.
2.   Name
The first part of the supplier's name. This name has been assigned to the
supplier in the session "Maintain Suppliers (tccom2101m000)".
3.   Postal Address
For further information, see keyword(s)
"Supplier Postal Addresses".
4.   Country
The country where the supplier is established. The country code is:
•   printed on documents;
•   used in combination with the Tax code of the item in order to retrieve the
correct Tax percentage;
•   used as sorting criterion for the purchase statistics. The default is the
country code assigned to the supplier in the session "Maintain Suppliers
(tccom2101m000)". The country code should have been already recorded via the
session "Maintain Countries (tcmcs0110m000)".
5.   Description
6.   Name
The first part of the supplier's name. The default is the name assigned to the
supplier in the session "Maintain Suppliers (tccom2101m000)".
7.   Name 2
The second part of the supplier's name. The default is the second name assigned
to the supplier in "Maintain Suppliers (tccom2101m000)".
8.   Address
The supplier's address. The default is the address assigned to the supplier in
"Maintain Suppliers (tccom2101m000)".
9.   Address 2
The second part of the supplier's address. The default is the second address
assigned to the supplier in "Maintain Suppliers (tccom2101m000)".
10.   Program domain string
11.   City
The city of the supplier.
For tax provider users, the city and state or province where the supplier is
established. The city and state or province should be separated by a comma ","
such as "Menlo Park, CA".
For further information, see method(s)
•   Address Verification for Tax Provider
The default is the city assigned to the supplier in "Maintain Suppliers
(tccom2101m000)".
12.   Program domain string
13.   City 2
The second part of the description of the city where the supplier is
established.
For tax provider users, the ZIP Code or Postal Code where the supplier is
established.
For further information, see method(s)
•   Address Verification for Tax Provider
The default is the description assigned to the supplier on the second field of
"City" in "Maintain Suppliers (tccom2101m000)".
14.   Program domain string
15.   Program domain of string length 1

16. GEO Code

A GEO code is a code used together or in lieu of address information such as city, state/province, and ZIP/postal code to uniquely identify a taxing jurisdiction. The tax provider determines the GEO code based upon the address information entered and the county and city limits selected.

The format of the GEO code varies by tax provider. AVP uses a two-digit GEO code; the GEO code together with the city, state, and ZIP code, identifies the taxing jurisdiction. Vertex uses a nine-digit GEO code comprised of a two digit state code, three-digit county code, and a four-digit city code. A tenth digit is used to identify if the jurisdiction is inside or outside of the city limits.

17. Program domain string

18. Program domain of string length 1

19. Answer on question y/n

20. ZIP Code

The ZIP code only appears on forwarding documents on which no other address data is printed. The default is the post code assigned to the supplier in "Maintain Suppliers (tccom2101m000)".

21. Address Code

The address if the package is run in association with the package BAAN Transportation. The address refers to an address in the b-object "Address Control (ACS)" in the package BAAN Transportation.

14.2 Maintain Banks by Supplier (tccom2105m000)

SESSION OBJECTIVE

To maintain banks by supplier.

SEE ALSO KEYWORD(S)

•   Banks by Supplier

```
tccom2105m000                              multi/group (3    Form 1-1
+-------------------------------------------------------------------------+
|  Maintain Banks by Supplier                             Company: 000  |
|-------------------------------------------------------------------------|
|                                                                         |
|  Supplier    : 1.....   2_____             |
|                                                                         |
|  Bank         Bank Type     Bank Address  Bank Account     Account Type |
|                                                                         |
|     3.. 4........      5..........  6.................  7............. |
|                                                                         |
+-------------------------------------------------------------------------+
```

1.   Supplier
The number uniquely identifying the supplier. The data to be entered must be defined in the session "Maintain Customers (tccom1101m000)".
2.   Name
The first part of the supplier's name.
3.   Bank
The code of the bank through which the financial transactions with the supplier take place.
4.   Bank Type
The type of bank indicates if the account is a giro or a bank account.
Bank
The supplier's account is a bank account. This value is offered as default value.
Giro
The account is a giro account. No checks are carried out on this number.
5.   Bank Address
The address of the bank. The data to be entered must be defined in the session "Maintain Bank Addresses (tcmcs0120m000)".
6.   Bank Account
The number of a payment and/or receipt account at the bank.
7.   Account Type
The account type is relevant to the processing of financial data in the BAAN Finance package. Normal Account
The bank account is a normal bank account. This value is offered as default value.

Blocked Account
The bank account is a blocked account. Such accounts are used for payments on
invoices from subcontractors in the b-object "Supplier Payments".
See also the information in the b-object "Subcontracting".

15 Other Print Sessions

15.1 Print Suppliers (tccom2401m000)

tccom2401m000   single-occ (4)   Form 1-1

```
+-------------------------------------------------------------------------+
| Print Suppliers                                          Company: 000 |
|-------------------------------------------------------------------------|
|                                                                         |
| Sort by             : 1.................                                |
|                                                                         |
| Supplier      from : 2.....                                             |
|               to   : 3.....                                             |
|                                                                         |
| Search Key    from : 4..............                                    |
|               to   : 5..............                                    |
|                                                                         |
| Country       from :   6..                                             |
|               to   :   7..                                             |
|                                                                         |
| ZIP Code      from : 8........                                          |
|               to   : 9........                                          |
|                                                                         |
| Suppl. Status from : 10.....................                            |
|               to   : 11.....................                            |
|                                                                         |
+-------------------------------------------------------------------------+
```

1.   Sort by
Enter the sequence in which the suppliers must be printed.
1 The selected suppliers are printed in order of supplier number.
2 The selected suppliers are printed in order of search key.
3 The selected suppliers are printed in order of post code.
2.   Supplier from
3.   Supplier to
4.   Search Key from
5.   Search Key to
6.   Country from
7.   Country to
8.   ZIP Code from
9.   ZIP Code to
10.   Supplier Status from
11.   Supplier Status to

15.2 Print Supplier Postal Addresses (tccom2403m000)

tccom2403m000   single-occ (4)   Form 1-1

```
+-------------------------------------------------------------------------+
| Print Supplier Postal Addresses                          Company: 000 |
|-------------------------------------------------------------------------|
|                                                                         |
| Supplier                        from : 1.....                          |
|                                 to   : 2.....                          |
|                                                                         |
| Postal Address                  from :   3..                           |
|                                 to   :   4..                           |
|                                                                         |
+-------------------------------------------------------------------------+
```

1.   Supplier from
2.   Supplier to
3.   Postal Address from
4.   Postal Address to

15.3 Print Banks by Supplier (tccom2405m000)

tccom2405m000   single-occ (4)   Form 1-1

```
+--------------------------------------------------------------------------+
| Print Banks by Supplier                                  Company: 000    |
|--------------------------------------------------------------------------|
|                                                                          |
|  Supplier        From : 1.....                                           |
|                  To   : 2.....                                           |
|                                                                          |
|  Bank            From :   3..                                            |
|                  To   :   4..                                            |
|                                                                          |
+--------------------------------------------------------------------------+
```

1.   Supplier from
2.   Supplier to
3.   Bank from
4.   Bank to
16   Introduction to Trade Relations
16.1 General
OBJECTIVE OF BUSINESS OBJECT
This b-object allows you to record the relationships between parent companies
and their subsidiaries for trade relations in the module "Sales and Marketing
Information (SMI)".
16.2 Session Overview

Seq.	Session	Description	Session Usage
1	tccom3101m000	Maintain Concern Structure of Trade Relations	Mandatory
101	tccom3401m000	Print Concern Structure of Trade Relations	Print

17   Mandatory Sessions
17.1 Maintain Concern Structure of Trade Relations (tccom3101m000)
SESSION OBJECTIVE
To maintain the concern structure of trade relations.
SEE ALSO KEYWORD(S)
•   Concern Structure
tccom3101m000   multi/group (3   Form 1-1

```
+--------------------------------------------------------------------------+
| Maintain Concern Structure of Trade Relations            Company: 000    |
|--------------------------------------------------------------------------|
|                                                                          |
|  Parent Customer: 1.....  2_____               |
|  Parent Supplier: 3.....  4_____               |
|                                                                          |
|  Child Customer  Child Supplier  Participation  Contact  Name      Text  |
|                                                                          |
|      5.....          6.....          7..        8..... 9_____   10___ |
|                                                                          |
|  11_____                                       |
+--------------------------------------------------------------------------+
```

1.   Parent Customer
The number of the customer which is parent company to one or more subsidiaries.
The data to be entered must be defined in the session "Maintain Customers
(tccom1101m000)".
2.   Name
The first part of the customer's name.
3.   Parent Supplier
The number of the supplier which is parent company to one or more daughter
companies. The data to be entered must be defined in the session "Maintain
Suppliers (tccom2101m000)".
4.   Name
The first part of the supplier's name.

5.   Child Customer
The customer which is a subsidiary of the parent company recorded.
The data to be entered must be defined in the session "Maintain Customers
(tccom1101m000)".
6.   Child Supplier
The supplier which is a subsidiary of the parent company recorded.
The data to be entered must be defined in the session "Maintain Suppliers
(tccom2101m000)".
7.   Participation
The percentage with which the parent company takes part in the daughter company.
8.   Contact
Your company's contact person for this company. The data to be entered must be
defined in the session "Maintain Employees (tccom0101m000)".
9.   Name
The employee's name.
10.   Text
11.   Name
18   Other Print Sessions
18.1   Print Concern Structure of Trade Relations (tccom3401m000)
tccom3401m000   single-occ (4)   Form 1-1
+--+
Print Concern Structure of Trade Relations   Company: 000
Parent Customer   From : 1.....
To   : 2.....
Parent Supplier   From : 3.....
To   : 4.....
Print Text   : 5....
+--+
1.   Parent Customer from
2.   Parent Customer to
3.   Parent Supplier from
4.   Parent Supplier to
5.   Print Text
19   Introduction to Intra EU Transactions
19.1   General
OBJECTIVE OF BUSINESS OBJECT
To register and report the goods flow and the associated financial transactions
between the member countries of the European Union (EU).
SEE ALSO KEYWORD(S)
•   Sales Listing Data
•   Additional Statistical Information Sets
•   Import/Export Statistics
SEE ALSO METHOD(S)
•   Import/Export Reporting
Display the procedure and show the sessions in:
•   Procedure Intra EU Transactions
19.2   Session Overview

Seq.	Session	Description	Session Usage
1	tccom7105m000	Maintain Additional Statistical Info	Mandatory
2	tccom7170m000	Maintain Sales Listing	Mandatory
3	tccom7270m000	Process Sales Listing	Mandatory

4	tccom7171m000	Maintain Import/Export Statistics	Mandatory
5	tccom7271m000	Process Import/Export Statistics	Mandatory
101	tccom7405m000	Print Additional Statistical Informatio	Print
102	tccom7470m000	Print Sales Listing	Print
103	tccom7471m000	Print Import/Export Statistics	Print
201	tccom7505m000	Display Additional Statistical Informat	Display
202	tccom7570m000	Display Sales Listing	Display
203	tccom7571m000	Display Import/Export Statistics	Display

20   Mandatory Sessions

20.1 Maintain Additional Statistical Information Sets (tccom7105m000)

SESSION OBJECTIVE
To maintain additional statistical information sets.
SEE ALSO KEYWORD(S)
- Additional Statistical Information Sets

```
tccom7105m000                                    single-occ (1)    Form 1-1
+-------------------------------------------------------------------------+
| Maintain Additional Statistical Information Sets      Company: 000  |
|-------------------------------------------------------------------------|
|                                                                         |
| Code              : 1..                                                 |
| Description       : 2...........................                        |
|                                                                         |
| Additional Data for Import/Export Statistics                            |
|                                                                         |
| Field     Prompt              Length     Default Contents               |
|        1 3..............        4. 5........                            |
|        2 3..............        4. 5........                            |
|        3 3..............        4. 5........                            |
|        4 3..............        4. 5........                            |
|        5 3..............        4. 5........                            |
|        6 3..............        4. 5........                            |
|                                                                         |
+-------------------------------------------------------------------------+
```

1.   Additional Statistical Information Set
Code uniquely identifying each additional information set.
2.   Description
The description of the additional information set.
3.   Prompt Additional Info
Within the import/export reporting procedure you can use up to 6 user-defined
fields. Enter the required prompt for these fields.
4.   Length Additional Info
Within the import/export reporting procedure you can work use up to 6 user-
defined fields. Enter the required length for these fields.
5.   Default Contents
The default value for the user-defined field. The value will be adopted in all
statistical transactions.

20.2 Maintain Sales Listing (tccom7170m000)

SESSION OBJECTIVE
To maintain the data to be included in the sales listing.
HOW TO USE THE SESSION

Only data entered manually (field "Type" has the value "Manually" or "Corrected Manually") can be maintained without restriction: all invoice data can be modified. Of non-manually produced invoices only the Tax number (if empty) and the subcontracting indicator can be changed. Processed lines can no longer be changed.

SEE ALSO KEYWORD(S)
•   Sales Listing Data

```
tccom7170m000                          single-occ (1)    Form 1-1
+------------------------------------------------------------------------+
| Maintain Sales Listing                              Company: 000 |
|------------------------------------------------------------------------|
|                                                                        |
| Type              : 1......................  Processed     : 2____     |
| Comp/Tr.Type/Inv  : 3.. /4.. /5.......                                 |
| Invoice Date      : 6.........                                         |
|                                                                        |
| Customer          : 7.....  8_____        |
| Tax Number        : 9..................                               |
| Currency          : 10.  11_____Rate     : 12....    per 13.... |
| Goods Value        : 14............      [15_____16_]          |
| Subcontracting    : 17...                                              |
|                                                                        |
+------------------------------------------------------------------------+
```

1.   Type
The origin of the invoice. Invoices are produced within various BAAN IV modules. Invoices on the "Sales Listing" can also be created manually.
The following types of origin are available:
•   Sales Order
•   Purchase Order
•   Finance
•   Service Order
•   Manually
•   Corrected Manually
2.   Processed
This field indicates whether the transaction has already been processed.
3.   Company
The financial company number linked to the order.
4.   Comp/Tr.Type/Inv
The transaction type linked to the invoice.
5.   Invoice
The number of the invoice containing the transaction.
6.   Invoice Date
The date assigned to the invoice.
7.   Customer
The customer for whom the invoice was created.
8.   Name
The first part of the customer's name.
9.   Tax Number
The Tax number for which the invoice was created.
10.   Currency
The invoice currency.
11.   Description
12.   EU Rate
The currency rate of the transaction. It is adopted from the order of origin.
13.   Rate Factor
The rate factor of the currency. This factor is adopted from the related order.
14.   Goods Value
The total goods amount on the invoice. The goods amount consists of the net order line amount excluding Tax and late payment surcharge. It is expressed in the invoice currency.
SEE ALSO METHOD(S)
•   Currency Formats
15.   Amount (11+2)

SEE ALSO METHOD(S)
- Currency Formats

+---+
|Goods Value   Ftccom7/0.rate]actor |
+---+

16.   Currency
Indicates the currency in which, for example, the financial accounts as well as
the purchase and sales statistics of the company are maintained.
17.   Subcontracting
This field indicates if the invoice includes amounts resulting from deliveries
of subcontracting items.
20.3 Process Sales Listing (tccom7270m000)
SESSION OBJECTIVE
To create a final listing in the form of a printed report or a sequential file.
HOW TO USE THE SESSION
The layout of the sequential file looks like follows:

+--+
| Field |Start Position| Length |
|------------------------------+--------------+--------|
Tax number	1	20
Goods value (home currency)	21	14
Subcontracting indicator	35	1
+--+

During import/export reporting, the status of each invoice is set to
"Processed".
SEE ALSO KEYWORD(S)
- Sales Listing Data
tccom7270m000   single-occ (4)   Form 1-1

+--+
Process Sales Listing   Company: 000
From   To
Type   : 1....................   - 2....................
Comp/Tr.Type/Inv :   3.. /4.. /5.......   -   6.. /7.. /8.......
Invoice Date   :   9........   -   10........
Tax Number   : 11...................   - 12...................
Customer   :   13....   -   14....
Header Text   : 15...
Including Processed Lines   : 16...
Recalculate Amounts in Home Currency: 17...
Rounding Factor   : 18..
+--+

1.   Type from
2.   Type to
3.   Comp/Tr.Type/Inv
4.   Comp/Tr.Type/Inv
5.   Invoice from
6.   Comp/Tr.Type/Inv
7.   Comp/Tr.Type/Inv
8.   Invoice to
9.   Invoice Date from
10.   Invoice Date to
11.   Tax Number from
12.   Tax Number to
13.   Customer from
14.   Customer to
15.   Answer on question y/n
16.   Including Processed Lines
Indicate if transactions which have already been processed must be included in
the report.

17.   Recalculate Amounts in Home Currency
This field determines if the goods amount must be based on the current EU
currency rate.
Yes
The goods amount is calculated on the basis of the goods amount in the foreign
currency and the current EU rate. For nonprocessed lines the new rate is stored
in the table, so that the old rate is overwritten!
No
The goods amount is equal to the goods amount in your home currency at the time
of invoicing the order.
18.   Rounding Factor
The rounding factor for amounts in the sales listing.
20.4 Maintain Import/Export Statistics (tccom7171m000)
SESSION OBJECTIVE
To maintain the data to be included in the import and export statistics.
HOW TO USE THE SESSION
Only data entered manually (field "Type" has the value "Manually" or "Corrected
Manually") can be maintained without restriction: all transaction data can be
modified. Non-manually produced transactions can only be partly maintained.
Processed lines can no longer be changed.
SEE ALSO KEYWORD(S)
•   Import/Export Statistics
tccom7171m000   single-occ (1)   Form 1-2 >
+--+
Maintain Import/Export Statistics   Company: 000
Type   : 1...................... Processed   : 2____
Order   : 3.....
Transact.Type : 4.......................
Position   : 5...
Sequence No. : 6...
Item   : 7.............. 8_____
Commodity Code :   9....... 10_____
Transact.Date : 11........
Quantity   : 12.......   [13_]
Alt. Quantity : 14.......   [24_]
Weight   : 15.....   [kg]
Currency   : 16. 17_____ Rate   : 18....   per 19....
Goods Value   : 20............[16_]   [21_____22_]
Stat. Value   : 23............[22_]
+--+
1.   Type
This field indicates the origin (module) of the import/export transaction.
The following origins are available:
•   Sales Order
•   Purchase Order
•   Finance
•   Service Order
•   Manually
•   Corrected Manually
•   Projects
•   Replenishment Orders
2.   Processed
Status indicating if the transaction is included in a definitive report.
3.   Order
The number of the order causing the import/export transaction.
4.   Transaction Type
The transaction type. A transaction may be an issue or a receipt. The following
transaction types are available:
•   - (Mat.Requirement)

- + (Planned Receipt)
5. Position
The position number of the line item causing the import/export transaction.
6. Sequence No.
The sequence number identifying the transaction.
7. Item
The code of the standard item to which the transaction refers. Data about customized items is stored under the item of origin.
8. Description
9. Commodity Code
Commodity code of the item to be reported.
10. Description
11. Transaction Date
The date of the import/export transaction.
12. Quantity
The quantity of the import/export transaction in the inventory unit.
SEE ALSO METHOD(S)
- Quantity Formats
13. Inventory Unit
The item inventory is primarily recorded in the inventory unit or Stockkeeping Unit (SKU). The item's cost price (product cost) is also based on this unit.
14. Alternative Quantity
The alternative quantity of a delivery or a receipt.
SEE ALSO METHOD(S)
- Quantity Formats
15. Weight
The weight of the goods delivered or received. It is calculated on the basis of the transaction quantity (inventory unit) and the weight of the item as recorded in item file.
16. Currency
The transaction currency.
17. Description
18. Rate
The currency rate of the transaction. It is adopted from the order of origin.
19. Rate Factor
The currency rate factor of the transaction. It is adopted from the order of origin.
20. Goods Value
The net goods value of the import/export transaction.
SEE ALSO METHOD(S)
- Currency Formats
21. Amount (11+2)
SEE ALSO METHOD(S)
- Currency Formats

+--+
|Goods Value   Ftccom7/0.rate]actor |
+--+

22. Currency
Indicates the currency in which, for example, the financial accounts as well as the purchase and sales statistics of the company are maintained.
23. Statistical Value
The statistical value of the delivered or received goods. By default this field is filled with the invoice amount and can be adapted manually.
SEE ALSO METHOD(S)
- Currency Formats
24. Alternative Unit for EU Reporting
Apart from the quantity in the inventory unit, the tax reporting may also be submitted in an alternative unit. The unit used here will be used as alternative unit.
This unit must be defined as an alternative unit for the item in the session "Maintain Conversion Factors (tiitm0120m000)". If this parameter is not filled or if the unit is not defined as an alternative unit for the item, the

alternative quantity in the import/export statistics will be filled with the
normal quantity, expressed in the inventory unit.

```
+------------------------------------------------------------------------+
| Maintain Import/Export Statistics              Company: 000 |
|------------------------------------------------------------------------|
|                                                                        |
| Type          : 1_____ Processed    : 2____ |
| Order         : 3_____                                                 |
| Transact.Type : 4_____                              |
| Position      : 5___                                                   |
| Sequence No.  : 6___                                                   |
|                                                                        |
| Country       : 7..  8_____ |
| Country of Org.: 9.. 8_____ |
| Area          : 10.  11_____ |
| Terms of Del. : 12.  13_____ |
| Forw.Agent    : 14.  15_____ |
| Reference     : 16........                                             |
| Add. Info Set : 17.  18_____ |
| 19_____2021........   19_____2021........ |
| 19_____2021........   19_____2021........ |
| 19_____2021........   19_____2021........ |
|                                                                        |
+------------------------------------------------------------------------+
```

1.   Type
This field indicates the origin (module) of the import/export transaction.
The following origins are available:
•   Sales Order
•   Purchase Order
•   Finance
•   Service Order
•   Manually
•   Corrected Manually
•   Projects
•   Replenishment Orders
2.   Processed
Status indicating if the transaction is included in a definitive report.
3.   Order
The number of the order causing the import/export transaction.
4.   Transaction Type
The transaction type. A transaction may be an issue or a receipt. The following
transaction types are available:
•   - (Mat.Requirement)
•   + (Planned Receipt)
5.   Position
The position number of the line item causing the import/export transaction.
6.   Sequence No.
The sequence number identifying the transaction.
7.   Country
The country of origin/destination of the import/export transaction.
8.   Description
9.   Country of Origin
The country of origin of the item to be reported.
10.   Area
The area of origin/destination of the import/export transaction.
11.   Description
12.   Terms of Delivery
The terms of delivery linked to the import/export transaction.
13.   Description
14.   Forwarding Agent
The forwarding agent responsible for the import/export transaction.
15.   Description

16.   Reference
The reference/extra feature of the import/export transaction. This reference is automatically loaded with the corresponding invoice number.
17.   Additional Statistical Information Set
The additional information set used to fill in the user-defined fields.
18.   Description
The description of the additional information set.
19.   Prompt Additional Info
Within the import/export reporting procedure you can use up to 6 user-defined fields. Enter the required prompt for these fields.
20.   Colon
21.   Extra Information
Additional information about a delivery or a receipt.
20.5 Process Import/Export Statistics (tccom7271m000)
SESSION OBJECTIVE
To generate a final report in printed form or as a sequential file.
HOW TO USE THE SESSION
Enter the selection boundaries and select the desired report type before starting the process.
The layout of the sequential file looks like follows:

Field	Start Position	Length
Own Tax number	1	20
Year number for transaction	21	4
Month number for transaction	25	2
Day number for transaction	27	2
Date of transaction	29	10
Type	39	2
Transaction type	41	1
Order	42	6
Position	48	4
Position sequence number	52	4
Item	56	16
Commodity code	72	8
Qty (invent.unit, 2 decimals)	80	12
Qty (alternative unit, 2 dec.)	92	12
Weight (3 decimals)	104	11
Goods amount (home currency)	115	14
Statistical value	129	14
Country	143	3
Area	146	3
Terms of delivery	149	3
Forwarding Agent	152	3
Country of origin	155	3
Currency	158	3
Reference	162	10
Extra information 1	172	10
Extra information 2	182	10
Extra information 3	192	10
Extra information 4	202	10
Extra information 5	212	10
Extra information 6	222	10

The field "Type" may have one of the following values:
1 = Sales Order
2 = Purchase Order
3 = Finance
4 = Service Order
5 = Manually
6 = Corrected Manually
7 = Projects
8 = Replenishment Orders

The "Transaction type" may have the following values:
1 = + (Planned Receipt)
2 = - (Mat.Requirement)
During import/export reporting, the status of each transaction is set to "Processed".
SEE ALSO KEYWORD(S)
•   Import/Export Statistics

tccom7271m000   single-occ (4)   Form 1-1
+--+
Process Import/Export Statistics   Company: 000
From   To
Type   : 1...................... - 2......................
Order   :   3..... -   4.....
Transaction Type: 5...................... - 6......................
Position   :   7... -   8...
Transaction Date: 9......... -   10........
Item   From :   11..............
To   :   12..............
Country   :   13. -   14.
Including Processed Lines   : 15...
Recalculate Amounts in Home Currency: 16...
Rounding Factor   : 17..
+--+
1.   Type from
2.   Type to
3.   Order from
4.   Order to
5.   Transaction Type from
6.   Transaction Type to
7.   Position from
8.   Position to
9.   Transaction Date from
10.   Transaction Date to
11.   Item from
12.   Item to
13.   Country from
14.   Country to
15.   Including Processed Lines
Indicate if transactions which have already been processed must be included in the report.
16.   Recalculate Amounts in Home Currency
This field determines if the goods amount must be based on the current EU currency rate.
Yes
The goods amount is calculated on the basis of the goods amount in the foreign currency and the current EU rate. For nonprocessed lines the new rate is stored in the table, so that the old rate is overwritten!
No
The goods amount is equal to the goods amount in your home currency at the time of invoicing the order.
17.   Rounding Factor
The rounding factor for amounts in the sales statistics.
21   Other Print Sessions
21.1 Print Additional Statistical Information Sets (tccom7405m000)
tccom7405m000   single-occ (4)   Form 1-1
+--+
| Print Additional Statistical Information Sets   Company: 000 |

```
|-------------------------------------------------------------------------|
|                                                                         |
|  Sequence No.  from : 1..                                               |
|                to   : 2..                                               |
|                                                                         |
+-------------------------------------------------------------------------+
1.    Sequence No. from
2.    Sequence No. to
21.2  Print Sales Listing (tccom7470m000)
tccom7470m000                              single-occ (4)   Form 1-1
+-------------------------------------------------------------------------+
|  Print Sales Listing                                    Company: 000  |
|-------------------------------------------------------------------------|
|                                                                         |
|                            From                        To               |
|  Type             : 1...................  -  2...................       |
|  Comp/Tr.Type/Inv :  3.. /4.. /5.......   -    6.. /7.. /8.......        |
|  Invoice Date     :           9.........  -           10........        |
|  Tax Number       : 11..................  -  12..................       |
|  Customer         :            13....  -              14....            |
|                                                                         |
|                                                                         |
|  Including Processed Lines      : 15...                                 |
|                                                                         |
|  Delete Processed Lines         : 16...                                 |
|                                                                         |
|  Rounding Factor                : 17..                                  |
|                                                                         |
+-------------------------------------------------------------------------+
1.    Type from
2.    Type to
3.    Comp/Tr.Type/Inv
4.    Comp/Tr.Type/Inv
5.    Invoice from
6.    Comp/Tr.Type/Inv
7.    Comp/Tr.Type/Inv
8.    Invoice to
9.    Invoice Date from
10.   Invoice Date to
11.   Tax Number from
12.   Tax Number to
13.   Customer from
14.   Customer to
15.   Including Processed Lines
Indicate if transactions which have already been processed must be included in
the report. Data can be processed with the session "Process Sales Listing
(tccom7270m000)".
16.   Delete Processed Lines
Using this option you can remove processed data from the file. Data can be
processed with the session "Process Sales Listing (tccom7270m000)".
17.   Rounding Factor
Here you can define the rounding factor with which to round off amounts.
21.3  Print Import/Export Statistics (tccom7471m000)
tccom7471m000                              single-occ (4)   Form 1-1
+-------------------------------------------------------------------------+
|  Print Import/Export Statistics                         Company: 000  |
|-------------------------------------------------------------------------|
|                                                                         |
|                             From                         To             |
|  Type             : 1.....................  - 2.....................    |
|  Order            :            3.....   -             4.....            |
|  Transaction Type: 5.....................  - 6.....................     |
|  Position         :            7...   -              8...               |
```

```
| Transaction Date:             9........    -           10........  |
| Item      From :     11..............                              |
|           To   :     12..............                             |
| Country        :                   13.   -              14.       |
|                                                                   |
| Including Processed Lines        : 15...                          |
|                                                                   |
| Delete Processed Lines           : 16...                         |
|                                                                   |
| Rounding Factor                  : 17..                          |
|                                                                   |
+-------------------------------------------------------------------+
```

1.   Type from
2.   Type to
3.   Order from
4.   Order to
5.   Transaction Type from
6.   Transaction Type to
7.   Position from
8.   Position to
9.   Transaction Date from
10. Transaction Date to
11. Item from
12. Item to
13. Country from
14. Country to
15.   Including Processed Lines
Indicate if transactions which have already been processed must be included in
the report.
16.   Delete Processed Lines
Using this option you can remove processed data from the file. Data can be
processed with the session "Process Import/Export Statistics (tccom7271m000)".
17.   Rounding Factor
Here you can enter the rounding factor with which to round off amounts.
22   Introduction to Chart and Planning Board Data
22.1 General
OBJECTIVE OF BUSINESS OBJECT
This b-object allows you to control the default data and parameters required to
use charts and the graphical planning board.
Display the procedure and show the sessions in:
•   Chart and Planning Board Data Procedure
22.2 Session Overview

Seq.	Session	Description	Session Usage
1	tccom5101m000	Maintain Planning Board Groups	Mandatory
2	tccom5110m000	Maintain Default Charts by User and Ses	Mandatory
3	tccom5410m000	Print Default Charts by User and Sessio	Print
4	tccom5105m000	Maintain Planning Board Groups	Mandatory
201	tccom5501s000	Display Planning Board Groups	Display
202	tccom5510m000	Display Default Charts by User and Sess	Display
203	tccom5505s000	Display Planning Board Groups	Display

23   Mandatory Sessions
23.1 Maintain Planning Board Groups (tccom5101m000)

SESSION OBJECTIVE
To maintain planning board groups.
SEE ALSO KEYWORD(S)
• Planning Board Groups 1
tccom5101m000   single-occ (1)   Form 1-1
+--+
Maintain Planning Board Groups   Company: 000
Planning Board Group: 1.. 2.............................
Scale Factor
View :Zero Capacity: 3....   Scale :Year   : 17... 18.
Relations   : 4..............   Month   : 19... 20.
Relation Draw: 5..............   Week   : 21... 22.
Float Time   : 6....   Day   : 23...
Critical Path: 7....   Day Part   : 24...
Color:Background   : 8.........   Day Part Factor : 25
(9.. 10. 11.)   Horizon   [days]: 26..
Foreground   : 12........   Date Display   : 27.............
Activity   : 13........   Scale Unit Width: 28
Progress   : 14........
Relation   : 15........   Font :Font Height   : 29
Critical Path: 16........   Line Height   : 30
+--+
1.   Planning Board Group
For further information, see keyword(s)
"Planning Board Groups 1".
2.   Description
The description of a planning board group.
3.   Zero Capacity
This parameter indicates if zero-capacity is to be shown on the graphical
planning board.
4.   Relation
This parameter indicates if (network)relations are to be shown on the graphical
planning board.
5.   Relation Drawing Method
This parameter indicates how (network)relations are to be shown on the graphical
planning board. Straight Lines
A network relation is visible as a combination of a horizontal and a vertical
line.
Sloping Lines
A network relation is visible as the shortest line between two points.
6.   Delay
This parameter indicates if the (network)float times calculated are to be shown
on the graphical planning board.
7.   Critical Path
This parameter indicates if the critical path determined by the network
calculation is to be shown on the graphical planning board. The critical path is
shown by rendering the activities and relations in a special color.
8.   Background
The parameter specifying the background color of the graphical planning board.
9.   Color Number Background for Red
10.   Color Number Background for Green
11.   Color Number Background for Blue
12.   Foreground
The parameter specifying the foreground color.
13.   Activity
The parameter specifying the basic color of the activities.
14.   Progress
The parameter specifying the color of that part of the activity that has been
reported completed.

15. Relation
The parameter specifying the color of the (network)relations.
16. Critical Path
The parameter specifying the color of the activities and relations constituting the critical path.
17. Year
This parameter indicates if the time scale representing year numbers is to be shown on the graphical planning board.
18. Zoom Factor Timescale Year
This factor specifies the number of scale unit used to represent a calendar year on the graphical planning board. If the planning board shows other time scales in addition to the year scale, it is always the scale factor of the scale with the smallest time unit which determines how the time scale on the board is represented.
19. Month
This parameter indicates if the time scale representing calendar days is to be shown on the graphical planning board.
20. Zoom Factor Timescale Month
This factor specifies the number of scale units used to represent a calendar month on the graphical planning board. If the planning board shows other time scales in addition to the year scale, it is always the scale factor of the scale with the smallest time unit which determines how the time scale on the board is represented.
21. Week
This parameter indicates if the time scale representing week numbers is to be shown on the graphical planning board.
22. Zoom Factor Timescale Week
This factor specifies the number of scale units used to represent a calendar week on the graphical planning board. If the planning board shows other time scales in addition to the year scale, it is always the scale factor of the scale with the smallest time unit which determines how the time scale on the board is represented.
23. Day
This parameter indicates if the time scale representing day numbers is to be shown on the graphical planning board.
24. Day Part
This parameter indicates if the time scale representing day parts is to be shown on the graphical planning board.
25. Day Part Factor
This factor specifies the number of parts in which a day on the day scale is to be subdivided. It is relevant if the time scale represents day parts.
26. Planning Horizon
The planning horizon for the graphical planning board in days. It defines the work area within which you can manipulate the data.
27. Date Display
The method of numbering the days on the time scale. You can select from:
• Calendar Date
• Day Number by Week
28. Scale Unit Width
The smallest controllable unit on the planning board is called the "planning board unit". The physical length by which it is represented is limited by technical display possibilities. The base unit defined for time scales is the day. The scale unit width is the number of planning board units representing the scale unit on the planning board.
29. Font Height
The smallest controllable unit on the planning board is called the "planning board unit". The physical length by which it is represented is limited by technical display possibilities. The font height of the text on the planning board is specified in planning board units.
30. Line Height
The smallest controllable unit on the planning board is called the "planning board unit". The physical length by which it is represented is limited by

technical display possibilities. The line height of the text on the planning
board is specified in planning board units.
23.2 Maintain Default Charts by User and Session (tccom5110m000)
SESSION OBJECTIVE
To maintain default Charts by user and session.
SEE ALSO KEYWORD(S)
•   Default Charts per User per Session
tccom5110m000   multi/group (3   Form 1-1
+--+
Maintain Default Charts by User and Session   Company: 000
Login Code: 1.......
Session Code   Chart Manager   Chart Type
2............   3.............   4..............
+--+
1.   Login Code
The login code of the user for whom the default charts are defined.
2.   Session Code
The code of the session to which the default chart applies.
3.   Chart Manager
The code of the Chart Manager application used as default in the session.
4.   Chart Type
The default chart type shown if the user selected invokes the session.
23.3 Maintain Planning Board Groups (tccom5105m000)
tccom5105m000   single-occ (1)   Form 1-2 >
+--+
Maintain Planning Board Groups   Company: 000
Planning Board Group: 1.. 2............................
Scale Factor
View :Zero Capacity: 3....   Scale :Year   : 19... 20.
Relations   : 4..............   Month   : 21... 22.
Relation Draw: 5..............   Week   : 23... 24.
Float Time   : 6....   Day   : 25...
Markers   : 7....   Day Part   : 26...
Marker Desc. : 8....
Critical Path: 9....   Day Part Factor : 27
Horizon   [days]: 28..
Color:Background   : 10........   Date Display   : 29..............
(11. 12. 13.)   Scale Unit Width: 30
Foreground   : 14........
Activity   : 15........ Font :Font Height   : 31
Progress   : 16........   Line Height   : 32
Relation   : 17........
Critical Path: 18........
+--+
1.   Planning Board Group
For further information, see keyword(s)
"Planning Board Groups 1".
2.   Description
The description of a planning board group.
3.   Zero Capacity
This parameter indicates if zero-capacity is to be shown on the graphical
planning board.
4.   Relation
This parameter indicates if (network)relations are to be shown on the graphical
planning board.
5.   Relation Drawing Method

This parameter indicates how (network)relations are to be shown on the graphical planning board. Straight Lines
A network relation is visible as a combination of a horizontal and a vertical line.
Sloping Lines
A network relation is visible as the shortest line between two points.
6.   Delay
This parameter indicates if the (network)float times calculated are to be shown on the graphical planning board.
7.   Markers
This parameter indicates if any markers are to be shown on the graphical planning board.
8.   Show Marker Descriptions
This parameter indicates if the marker descriptions are to be shown on the graphical planning board.
9.   Critical Path
This parameter indicates if the critical path determined by the network calculation is to be shown on the graphical planning board. The critical path is shown by rendering the activities and relations in a special color.
10.   Background
The parameter specifying the background color of the graphical planning board.
11.   Color Number Background for Red
12.   Color Number Background for Green
13.   Color Number Background for Blue
14.   Foreground
The parameter specifying the foreground color.
15.   Activity
The parameter specifying the basic color of the activities.
16.   Progress
The parameter specifying the color of that part of the activity that has been reported completed.
17.   Relation
The parameter specifying the color of the (network)relations.
18.   Critical Path
The parameter specifying the color of the activities and relations constituting the critical path.
19.   Year
This parameter indicates if the time scale representing year numbers is to be shown on the graphical planning board.
20.   Zoom Factor Timescale Year
This factor specifies the number of scale unit used to represent a calendar year on the graphical planning board. If the planning board shows other time scales in addition to the year scale, it is always the scale factor of the scale with the smallest time unit which determines how the time scale on the board is represented.
21.   Month
This parameter indicates if the time scale representing calendar days is to be shown on the graphical planning board.
22.   Zoom Factor Timescale Month
This factor specifies the number of scale units used to represent a calendar month on the graphical planning board. If the planning board shows other time scales in addition to the year scale, it is always the scale factor of the scale with the smallest time unit which determines how the time scale on the board is represented.
23.   Week
This parameter indicates if the time scale representing week numbers is to be shown on the graphical planning board.
24.   Zoom Factor Timescale Week
This factor specifies the number of scale units used to represent a calendar week on the graphical planning board. If the planning board shows other time scales in addition to the year scale, it is always the scale factor of the scale with the smallest time unit which determines how the time scale on the board is represented.

25.   Day
This parameter indicates if the time scale representing day numbers is to be
shown on the graphical planning board.
26.   Day Part
This parameter indicates if the time scale representing day parts is to be shown
on the graphical planning board.
27.   Day Part Factor
This factor specifies the number of parts in which a day on the day scale is to
be subdivided. It is relevant if the time scale represents day parts.
28.   Planning Horizon
The planning horizon for the graphical planning board in days. It defines the
work area within which you can manipulate the data.
29.   Date Display
The method of numbering the days on the time scale. You can select from:
•   Calendar Date
•   Day Number by Week
30.   Scale Unit Width
The smallest controllable unit on the planning board is called the "planning
board unit". The physical length by which it is represented is limited by
technical display possibilities. The base unit defined for time scales is the
day. The scale unit width is the number of planning board units representing the
scale unit on the planning board.
31.   Font Height
The smallest controllable unit on the planning board is called the "planning
board unit". The physical length by which it is represented is limited by
technical display possibilities. The font height of the text on the planning
board is specified in planning board units.
32.   Line Height
The smallest controllable unit on the planning board is called the "planning
board unit". The physical length by which it is represented is limited by
technical display possibilities. The line height of the text on the planning
board is specified in planning board units.

```
tccom5105m000                               single-occ (1) < Form 2-2
+-------------------------------------------------------------------------+
|  Maintain Planning Board Groups                          Company: 000   |
|-------------------------------------------------------------------------|
|                                                                         |
|Planning Board Group: 1..  2_____            |
|                                                                         |
|PROJECT PLAN            Color        Expand   EXECUTION PLAN      Color   |
|Budget Labor Lines  : 3.........     4....    Labor Action       :17......|
|Material Lines      : 5.........     6....    Material Action     :18......|
|Equipment Lines     : 7.........     8....    Equipment Action    :19......|
|Subcontracting Lines: 9.........     10...    Subcontr. Action    :20......|
|Budget Sundry Lines : 11........     12...    Sundry Cost Action  :21......|
|                                                                         |
|Subactivity         : 13........                                         |
|Inactive Relation   : 14........             Milestones                  |
|                                             Milestone Symbol    :22......|
|                                             Milestone Color     :23....  |
|Default Relat. Delay          : 15...        Show on One Line     :24...  |
|Default Step Perc. Compl.     : 16.          Show on First Line  :25...   |
|                                                                         |
+-------------------------------------------------------------------------+
```

1.   Planning Board Group
For further information, see keyword(s)
"Planning Board Groups 1".
2.   Description
The description of a planning board group.
3.   Budget Labor Lines
The parameter specifying the color of the markers.
4.   Expand Budget Material Lines
5.   Budget Material Lines

The parameter specifying the color of the markers.
6.   Expand Budget Material Lines
7.   Budget Equipment Lines
The parameter specifying the color of the markers.
8.   Expand Budget Equipment Lines
9.   Budget Subcontracting Lines
The parameter specifying the color of the markers.
10.   Expand Budget Subcontracting Lines
11.   Budget Sundry Lines
The parameter specifying the color of the markers.
12.   Expand Budget Sundry Cost Lines
13.   Subactivity
The parameter specifying the basic color of the activities.
14.   Inactive Relation
The parameter specifying the color of the (network)relations.
15.   Default Relat. Delay
16.   Default Step Perc. Compl.
17.   Labor Action
The parameter specifying the color of the markers.
18.   Material Action
The parameter specifying the color of the markers.
19.   Equipment Action
The parameter specifying the color of the markers.
20.   Subcontr. Action
The parameter specifying the color of the markers.
21.   Sundry Cost Action
The parameter specifying the color of the markers.
22.   Milestone Symbol
23.   Milestone Color
24.   Show Milestones on One Line
25.   Show Milestones on First Line
24   Other Print Sessions
24.1 Print Default Charts by User and Session (tccom5410m000)

```
tccom5410m000                              single-occ (4)    Form 1-1
+--------------------------------------------------------------------------+
| Print Default Charts by User and Session              Company: 000 |
|--------------------------------------------------------------------------|
|                                                                          |
|                                                                          |
| Login Code    From : 1.......                                            |
|               To   : 2.......                                            |
|                                                                          |
| Session Code  From : 3............                                       |
|               To   : 4...........                                        |
|                                                                          |
+--------------------------------------------------------------------------+
```

1.   Login Code From
2.   Login Code to
3.   Session Code From
4.   Session Code to
25   Introduction to TRITON Common Parameters
25.1 General
OBJECTIVE OF BUSINESS OBJECT
The BAAN IV configuration is initialized by your software vendor. This involves
the setting of a number of parameters in order to tailor the system to your
company-specific requirements.
Please note that some parameters cannot be changed without MAJOR CONSEQUENCES
for data storage and data processing as soon as the system is operational!

```
+-------------------------------------------------+
| Therefore contact your software vendor before  |
| changing these parameters!                     |
+-------------------------------------------------+
```

All parameters in BAAN Common are listed below. The ones that will have far-reaching consequences when they are changed afterwards, are marked with the * sign.

Initialize Parameters (tcmcs0295m000)
- Compact Version Installed

Maintain System Configuration Parameters (tisfc0000m000)
- MPS Implemented
- PCF implemented
- PCS Implemented

Maintain COM Parameters (tccom0000m000)
- FINANCE implemented
- TRANSPORTATION implemented

Maintain Intra EU Transaction Parameters (tccom7100m000)
- EU Statistical Reporting Implemented
- Alternative Unit for EU Reporting
- Item Code for Customized Items in EU Reporting
- Method of Logging Cost/Service Items

Maintain EDI Parameters (tcedi0100m000)
- EDI Implemented
- Standard Path
- Make Use of Tracefile
- Name of Tracefile
- Our Identification
- Store All Received Messages
- Store All Sent Messages
- Fixed Part
- Date Format
- First Free Number
- Action on First Message on New Date
- Suppress Blank Text Lines on Generation
- Suppress Blank Generated Text Fields

Maintain API Parameters (tcapil136m000)
- API type
- Interface Provider
- Interface Used

Maintain Tax Provider Parameters (tccoml150m000)
- '%FFtccoml150m0001txpr'
- '%FFtccoml150m0001potp'
- '%FFtccoml150m0001txms'

25.2   Related B-Objects

Seq. No.	B-Object	Description	B-Object Usage
30	tc mcs00010	Logistic Tables	Mandatory before
40	ti itm00010	Item Master Data	Mandatory before

25.4   Session Overview

Seq.	Session	Description	Session Usage
1	tcmcs0295m000	Initialize Parameters	Mandatory
2	tccom0000m000	Maintain COM Parameters	Mandatory
3	tccom7100m000	Maintain Intra EU Transaction Parameter	Mandatory
4	tcapil136m000	Maintain API Parameters	Optional

26   Mandatory Sessions
26.1 Initialize Parameters (tcmcs0295m000)

SESSION OBJECTIVE

To set the default values of the parameters for the whole package. Do this when installing the software.

tcmcs0295m000   single-occ (4)   Form 1-1
```
+--------------------------------------------------------------------------+
| Initialize Parameters                                   Company: 000 |
|--------------------------------------------------------------------------|
|                                                                          |
|                                                                          |
|   +----------------------+                                               |
|   | Module   : 1_____ |                                               |
|   | Parameter: 2_____ |                                               |
|   +----------------------+                                               |
+--------------------------------------------------------------------------+
```

1.   Module
2.   Parameter

26.2 Maintain COM Parameters (tccom0000m000)

SESSION OBJECTIVE

To set the parameters that determine how the module "Common Data (COM)" will be operated.

SEE ALSO KEYWORD(S)
•   Parameters

tccom0000m000   single-occ (1)   Form 1-1
```
+--------------------------------------------------------------------------+
| Maintain COM Parameters                                 Company: 000 |
|--------------------------------------------------------------------------|
|                                                                          |
|                                                                          |
| FINANCE implemented                    : 1........................      |
|                                                                          |
| Check on Bank Account No.              : 2........................      |
|                                                                          |
| TRANSPORTATION implemented             : 3........................      |
|                                                                          |
| Determine Routes with TRANSPORTATION   : 4........................      |
|                                                                          |
| Destination Sales Tax Applicable       : 5........................      |
|                                                                          |
+--------------------------------------------------------------------------+
```

1.   FINANCE implemented

If the value of this field is switched from "No" to "Yes", the system will check for customer for whom no financial groups have been defined. In that case this field cannot be switched to "Yes". All customer must be assigned a financial group.

Yes

By assigning a financial group to the customer in the session "Maintain Customers (tccom1101m000)", you can select reports by financial group in the package BAAN Finance. You can also define a control account for each financial group.

No

The module Common Data (COM) is not integrated with BAAN Finance.

2.   Check on Bank Account No.

With this parameter, you indicate whether an 11 check, 97 modulo check or no check must be carried out when entering a bank account number.

11 Check

The 11 check is carried out on Dutch bank account numbers (among others):

$9p1 + 8p2 + 7p3 + 6p4 + 5p5 + 4p2 + 3p2 + 2p1$

in which: p1 = the position of the first number of the account number.
In order to enter a foreign bank number to which no 11 check applies, you must
enter the letter B on the first position of the field, followed by the bank
account number.
97 Check
Among others, the 97 check is applied to Belgian bank numbers.
In this method, the sum of the first 10 digits of the entered numbers is divided
by 97. The remainder must equal the number that is formed by the digits on
position 11 and 12 of the bank account number.
In order to enter a foreign bank number to which no 97 check applies, enter the
letter B, followed by the bank account number.
No Check
The system does not check whether the bank account number is valid.
3.   TRANSPORTATION implemented
Yes
The package BAAN Transportation is implemented.
No
The above package is not implemented.
4.   Determine Routes with TRANSPORTATION
Yes
In the field "Route" of session "Maintain Customers (tccom1101m000)" you have an
option
to calculate the route.
No
You cannot calculate the route.
5.   Destination Taxes Applicable
26.3 Maintain Intra EU Transaction Parameters (tccom7100m000)
SESSION OBJECTIVE
To set the parameters that determine how the b-object "Intra EU Transactions"
will be operated.
SEE ALSO KEYWORD(S)
•   Parameters
tccom7100m000   single-occ (1)   Form 1-1
+---+
Maintain Intra EU Transaction Parameters   Company: 000
EU Statistical Reporting Implemented   : 1........................
Alternative Unit for EU Reporting   : 2.. 3_____
Item Cd.for Custom.Items in EU Reporting: 4.............. 5_____
Method of Logging Cost/Service Items   : 6........................
+---+
1.   EU Statistical Reporting Implemented
Yes
The Sales Listing and Intrastat report can be printed in BAAN IV.
No
The Sales Listing and Intrastat report cannot be printed.
2.   Alternative Unit for EU Reporting
Apart from the quantity in the inventory unit, the tax reporting may also be
submitted in an alternative unit. The unit used here will be used as alternative
unit.
This unit must be defined as an alternative unit for the item in the session
"Maintain Conversion Factors (tiitm0120m000)". If this parameter is not filled
or if the unit is not defined as an alternative unit for the item, the
alternative quantity in the import/export statistics will be filled with the
normal quantity, expressed in the inventory unit.
3.   Description
4.   Item Code for Customized Items in EU Reporting

The treatment of customer-specific items in Tax reporting depends on the definition of the 'original item' they are derived from. The item of origin is specified in the session "Maintain
Customized Item Data (tipcs2121m000)".
There are two different procedures:
• if the item of origin field is filled with the code of a standard item, then the statistical record will refer to the standard item.
• if the item of origin field is not filled, then the Tax statistics will refer to the 'Item Code' as defined in the parameter. Standard items are defined in the session "Maintain Item Data (tiitm0101m000)".
5. Description
6. Method of Logging Cost/Service Items
Cost and service items can be treated in three different ways:
Always
Cost and service items are always included in sales listing and statistical reports.
If Commodity Code Filled
Cost and service items are only included in the sales listing and statistical reports if the commodity code is filled.
Never
Cost and service items will never be included.
27 Optional Sessions
27.1 Maintain API Parameters (tcapil136m000)

```
 tcapil136m000                               single-occ (1)    Form 1-1
 +----------------------------------------------------------------------+
 | Maintain API Parameters                              Company: 000 |
 |----------------------------------------------------------------------|
 |                                                                    |
 | API type              : 1...................                       |
 |                                                                    |
 | Interface Provider    : 2.............................             |
 | Interface Used        : 3....                                      |
 |                                                                    |
 +----------------------------------------------------------------------+
```

1. API type
The types of external applications that interface with BAAN IV's API.
Tax Provider
BAAN IV interface to an external tax provider.
2. Interface Provider
The available interface providers for the specified API type.
TAXWARE's Master Tax System
BAAN IV will interface to TAXWARE's Master Tax System.
Quantum for Sales/Use Tax
BAAN IV will interface to Quantum for Sales/Use Tax.
None
No external tax provider interface will be used.
3. Interface Used
Indicate whether or not the specified API interface is being used by BAAN IV.
Yes
BAAN IV will interface with the selected provider for the specified API type.
No
No interface for the specified API type is active.
27.2 Maintain Tax Provider Parameters (tccoml150m000)

```
 tccoml150m000                               single-occ (1)    Form 1-1
 +----------------------------------------------------------------------+
 | Maintain Tax Provider Parameters                     Company: 000 |
 |----------------------------------------------------------------------|
 |                                                                    |
 | Using Tax Provider                    : 1....                      |
 |                                                                    |
 | Point of Title PaBaange                : 2...................       |
 |                                                                    |
 | Warn if Tax on ACR Invoices           : 3....                      |
 |                                                                    |
```

```
|                                                                              |
+------------------------------------------------------------------------------+
1.     Tax Provider
2.     Point of Title PaBaange
3.     Warn if Tax on ACP invoices
28     Introduction to Logistic Tables
28.1  General
OBJECTIVE OF BUSINESS OBJECT
This b-object allows you to control all sorts of data relating to the logistical
functions in the BAAN IV packages.
SEE ALSO METHOD(S)
•      Table Coding
28.2  Session Overview
```

Seq.	Session	Description	Session Usage
1	tcmcs0145m000	Maintain Areas	Mandatory
2	tcmcs0128m000	Maintain Commodity Codes	Mandatory
3	tcmcs0110m000	Maintain Countries	Mandatory
4	tcmcs0147m000	Maintain First Free Numbers	Mandatory
5	tcmcs0180m000	Maintain Forwarding Agents	Mandatory
6	tcmcs0123m000	Maintain Item Groups	Mandatory
7	tcmcs0146m000	Maintain Languages	Mandatory
8	tcmcs0131m000	Maintain Lines of Business	Mandatory
9	tcmcs0124m000	Maintain Price Groups	Mandatory
10	tcmcs0134m000	Maintain Price Lists	Mandatory
11	tcmcs0105m000	Maintain Reasons for Rejection	Mandatory
12	tcmcs0115m000	Maintain Product Types	Mandatory
13	tcmcs0104m000	Maintain Routes	Mandatory
14	tcmcs0116m000	Maintain Seasonal Patterns	Mandatory
15	tcmcs0122m000	Maintain Selection Codes	Mandatory
16	tcmcs0118m000	Maintain Signal Codes	Mandatory
17	tcmcs0144m000	Maintain Statistics Groups	Mandatory
18	tcmcs0141m000	Maintain Terms of Delivery	Mandatory
19	tcmcs0119m000	Maintain Titles	Mandatory
20	tcmcs0101m000	Maintain Units	Mandatory
21	tcmcs0107m000	Maintain Units by Language	Mandatory
22	tcmcs0106m000	Maintain Unit Sets	Mandatory
23	tcmcs0112m000	Maintain Units by Unit Set	Mandatory

```
|   24 | tcmcs0103m000 | Maintain Warehouses                        | Mandatory
|
|   26 | tcmcs0197m000 | Maintain Use of Performance Boosters       | Mandatory
|
|   27 | tcmcs0129m000 | Maintain Quality Groups                    | Mandatory
|
|   28 | tcmcs0130m000 | Maintain Skills                            | Mandatory
|
|  101 | tcmcs0445m000 | Print Areas                                | Print
|
|  102 | tcmcs0428m000 | Print Commodity Codes                      | Print
|
|  103 | tcmcs0410m000 | Print Countries                            | Print
|
|  104 | tcmcs0447m000 | Print First Free Numbers                   | Print
|
|  105 | tcmcs0480m000 | Print Forwarding Agents                    | Print
|
|  106 | tcmcs0423m000 | Print Item Groups                          | Print
|
|  107 | tcmcs0446m000 | Print Languages                            | Print
|
|  108 | tcmcs0431m000 | Print Lines of Business                    | Print
|
|  109 | tcmcs0424m000 | Print Price Groups                         | Print
|
|  110 | tcmcs0434m000 | Print Price Lists                          | Print
|
|  111 | tcmcs0405m000 | Print Reasons for Rejection                | Print
|
|  112 | tcmcs0415m000 | Print Product Types                        | Print
|
|  113 | tcmcs0404m000 | Print Routes                               | Print
|
|  114 | tcmcs0416m000 | Print Seasonal Patterns                    | Print
|
|  115 | tcmcs0422m000 | Print Selection Codes                      | Print
|
|  116 | tcmcs0418m000 | Print Signal Codes                         | Print
|
|  117 | tcmcs0444m000 | Print Statistics Groups                    | Print
|
|  118 | tcmcs0441m000 | Print Terms of Delivery                    | Print
|
|  119 | tcmcs0419m000 | Print Titles                               | Print
|
|  120 | tcmcs0401m000 | Print Units                                | Print
|
|  121 | tcmcs0407m000 | Print Units by Language                    | Print
|
|  122 | tcmcs0406m000 | Print Unit Sets                            | Print
|
|  123 | tcmcs0412m000 | Print Units by Unit Set                    | Print
|
|  124 | tcmcs0403m000 | Print Warehouses                           | Print
|
|  125 | tcmcs0429m000 | Print Quality Groups                       | Print
|
|  126 | tcmcs0430m000 | Print Skills                               | Print
|
|  201 | tcmcs0545m000 | Display Areas                              | Display
|
```

202	tcmcs0528m000	Display Commodity Codes	Display
203	tcmcs0510m000	Display Countries	Display
204	tcmcs0547m000	Display First Free Numbers	Display
205	tcmcs0580m000	Display Forwarding Agents	Display
206	tcmcs0523m000	Display Item Groups	Display
207	tcmcs0546m000	Display Languages	Display
208	tcmcs0531m000	Display Lines of Business	Display
209	tcmcs0524m000	Display Price Groups	Display
210	tcmcs0534m000	Display Price Lists	Display
211	tcmcs0505m000	Display Reasons for Rejection	Display
212	tcmcs0515m000	Display Product Types	Display
213	tcmcs0504m000	Display Routes	Display
214	tcmcs0516m000	Display Seasonal Patterns	Display
215	tcmcs0522m000	Display Selection Codes	Display
216	tcmcs0518m000	Display Signal Codes	Display
217	tcmcs0544m000	Display Statistics Groups	Display
218	tcmcs0541m000	Display Terms of Delivery	Display
219	tcmcs0519m000	Display Titles	Display
220	tcmcs0501m000	Display Units	Display
221	tcmcs0507m000	Display Units by Language	Display
222	tcmcs0506m000	Display Unit Sets	Display
223	tcmcs0512m000	Display Units by Unit Set	Display
224	tcmcs0503m000	Display Warehouses	Display
225	tcmcs0529m000	Display Quality Groups	Display
226	tcmcs0530m000	Display Skills	Display
999	tcmcs0119s000	Maintain Titles	Optional
999	tcmcs0503s000	Display Warehouse List	Display
999	tcmcs0539s000	Display Order Steps	Display
999	tcmcs0542s000	Display Order Types	Display
999	tcmcs0642s000	Display Order Steps (Procedure)	Display

29   Mandatory Sessions

29.1   Maintain Areas (tcmcs0145m000)

SESSION OBJECTIVE
To define the geographical areas used in other sessions.
SEE ALSO KEYWORD(S)
• 	Areas
tcmcs0145m000   multi-occ (2)   Form 1-1
+--+
Maintain Areas   Company: 000
Area Description
1.. 2............................
+--+
1. 	Area
For further information, see keyword(s)
"Areas".
2. 	Description
Enter a clear description here.
29.2 Maintain Commodity Codes (tcmcs0128m000)
SESSION OBJECTIVE
To define the commodity codes used in other sessions.
SEE ALSO KEYWORD(S)
• 	Commodity Codes
tcmcs0128m000   multi-occ (2)   Form 1-1
+--+
Maintain Commodity Codes   Company: 000
Commodity Code Description
1....... 2............................
+--+
1. 	Commodity Code
For further information, see keyword(s)
"Commodity Codes".
2. 	Description
Enter a clear description here.
29.3 Maintain Countries (tcmcs0110m000)
SESSION OBJECTIVE
To maintain countries.
SEE ALSO KEYWORD(S)
• 	Countries
tcmcs0110m000   multi-occ (2)   Form 1-2 >
+--+
Maintain Countries   Company: 000
Code Description   ICC Telephone Telex Fax   EU Member
1.. 2............................ 3.. 4.....   5..... 6..... 7....
+--+
1. 	Country
The code by which the country is recognized in BAAN IV.
2. 	Description
Enter a clear description here.
3. 	ICC
The international country code is an informative field.
4. 	Telephone
The international access number for the telephone of the country.

5.   Telex
The international access number for the telex of the country.
6.   Fax
The international access number for the fax of the country.
7.   EU Member State
Here you can indicate if the country is an EU member state.

```
+---------------------------------------------------------------------------+
|  Maintain Countries                                     Company: 000  |
|---------------------------------------------------------------------------|
|   Code   GEO Country Code   Print       Print Tax          Print Tax       |
|                             Line Tax    by Tax Authority   Exemption       |
|                                                                            |
|   1..    2..                3....       4....              5....            |
|                                                                            |
+---------------------------------------------------------------------------+
```

1.   Country
The code by which the country is recognized in BAAN IV.
2.   GEO Country Code
The GEO Country Code is used in the European Intrastat tax statement. If no GEO
country code is entered, the normal country code will be used.
3.   Print Line Tax
Using this parameter, you can determine how tax amounts are printed on order
documents.
Yes
If using a tax provider, tax amounts are printed by line on the order document,
in addition to the total tax amounts printed on the footer of the document.
No
Only the total tax amounts are printed on the footer of the order document.
See also help about Global Localisation (Tax Provider).
4.   Print Tax by Tax Authority
Using this parameter, you can determine how tax amounts are printed on order
documents.
Yes
In addition to the total tax amounts printed in the footer of the document, tax
amounts by tax authority are printed on the order document.
No
Only the total tax amounts are printed on the footer of the order document.
See also help about Global Localisation (Tax Provider).
5.   Print Tax Exemption
Yes
If not using the tax provider, tax exemption certificate numbers are printed on
the order document.
No
Tax exemption certificate numbers are not printed on the order document.
See also help about Global Localisation (Tax Provider).

29.4 Maintain First Free Numbers (tcmcs0147m000)
SESSION OBJECTIVE
To define the first free number for each number type. This allows orders to be
arranged in groups.
SEE ALSO KEYWORD(S)
•   First Free Numbers

tcmcs0147m000   multi/group (3   Form 1-1

```
+---------------------------------------------------------------------------+
|  Maintain First Free Numbers                            Company: 000  |
|---------------------------------------------------------------------------|
|                                                                            |
|  Type of Number: 1.......................                                  |
|                                                                            |
|   Se-          Description                First Free  Blocked for  Def.Fin. |
|   ries                                    Number      Input        Company  |
|                                                                            |
|         2..   3...........................  4.......  5....              6.. |
```

1.   Type of Number
The following values are possible:
Purchase Order *
•   Confirm Planned INV Purchase Orders (tdinv3220m000)
•   Maintain Purchase Orders (tdpur4101m000)
Production Order *
•   Maintain Production Orders (tisfc0101m000)
Sales Order *
•   Maintain Sales Orders (tdsls4101m000)
•   Process Quotations (tdsls1202s000)
Sales Quotation *
•   Maintain Quotations (tdsls1101m000)
Purchase Invoice *
•   Print Purchase Invoices (tdpur4404m000)
Sales Invoice *
•   Print Sales Invoices (tdsls4404m000)
Picking List (SLS Order)
•   Print Picking Lists (tdsls4402m000)
Packing Slip Sales Order
•   Print Packing Slips (tdsls4403m000)
Project
•   Maintain Projects (tipcs2101m000)
Product Variant
•   Maintain Product Variants (tipcf5101m000)
•   Product Configurator (tipcf5120s000)
Financial Document
Warehouse order
•   Enter Inventory Transactions (tdilc1120m000)
•   Generate Cycle Counting Orders (tdilc5210m000)
•   Enter Inventory Transactions by Item (tdinv1101m000)
•   Generate Cycle Counting Orders (tdinv1220m000)
Purchase Contract *
•   Maintain Purchase Contracts (tdpur3101m000)
•   Copy Purchase Contracts (tdpur3801m000)
Sales Contract *
•   Maintain Sales Contracts (tdsls3101m000)
•   Copy Sales Contracts (tdsls3801m000)
Purchase Inquiry *
•   Maintain Inquiry Lines (tdpur1102s000)
Lot *
•   Maintain Lots (tdltc0101m000)
•   Copy Ranges of Lots (tdltc0103s000)
•   Maintain Lot ID Structure (tdltc0105m000)
•   Convert Non-Lot Item to Lot Item (tdltc0130m000)
Receipt *
•   Maintain Receipts (tdpur4120m000)
Service Order *
•   Maintain Service Orders (tssma3101m000)
Bill of Lading (Sales)
•   Print Bills of Lading (tdsls4421m000)
Budget
•   Maintain Budgets (tipcs0101m000)
Replenishment Order
•   Maintain Replenishment Orders (tdrpl0110m000)
Picking List (RPL)
•   Print Replenishment Order Picking Lists (tdrpl0412m000)
Packing Slip (RPL)
•   Print Replenishment Order Packing Slips (tdrpl0416m000)
Bill of Lading (RPL)
•   Maintain Replenishment Order Bills of Lading (tdrpl0118s000)
Transport Invoice

- Print Invoices (trics2400m000)

Transport Order
- Maintain Order Procedures (trtoc0130m000)
- Copy Sales Orders to Transport Orders (trtoc2200m000)

Inbound Order
Outbound Order
Assembly Order
Storage Order
Transhipment Order
ECO Order

For the options marked "*" you can define number series.

2.   Series

A wide range of documents/orders etc. are numbered on the basis of the concept of predefined series (ranges) and first free numbers within those series. The series number can be used to distinguish between various types of orders, e.g.: national and international sales orders.

Length of series number (recorded in e.g. Maintain Sales Order Parameters (tdsls4100m000)): 2 digits. By reserving the first 2 digits of the order number for the series number, you can distinguish up to 99 different order types. The system automatically assigns the sequence number within every series (e.g. 10 0001 = sequence number 1 within series 10). A number of types of first free numbers have a predetermined series numbering. You cannot change these or add a new series number to it. You can only change the description and the first free number.

You can enter the first free number for each series number. Using series numbers depends on initializing with the following parameters.

Adjusted in session:
- Parameter Description:

Maintain PCS Parameters (tipcs0100m000)
- Budget Series
- Project Series

Maintain Inquiry Parameters (tdpur1100m000)
- Series in Inquiry Numbering

Maintain Purchase Contract Parameters (tdpur3100m000)
- Series in Contract Numbering

Maintain Purchase Order Parameters (tdpur4100m000)
- Series in Order Numbering
- Series in Invoice Numbering
- Series in Receipt Numbering

Maintain SFC Parameters (tisfc0100m000)
- Series in Production Order Numbers

Maintain Quotation Parameters (tdsls1100m000)
- Series in Quotation Numbering

Maintain Sales Contract Parameters (tdsls3100m000)
- Series in Contract Numbering

Maintain Sales Order Parameters (tdsls4100m000)
- Series in Invoice Numbering
- Series in Sales Order Numbering

For these parameters, you may choose from the following:

No Series

The first free number indicates with which number the first order, quotation, or contract number must start. This number consists of six positions. When entering an order (for example), the system consults the table with numbers and assigns the first free number to the new order. As soon as a number has been used, the first free number is automatically raised by one.

One Digit

You can choose from the series numbers 0 through 9 and indicate the first free number for each series number. The series number is the first digit of the order, quotation, or contract number. When entering an order (for example), enter this series number first. For the remaining five positions of the number, the system consults the table with numbers and copies the first free number.

Two Digits

You can choose from series numbers 0 through 99 and indicate the first free number for each series number. The series number is the first two digits of the order, quotation or order number. When entering an order (for example), enter the series number first. For the remaining four positions, the system consults the table with numbers and copies the first free number to the series.

3.   Description
Enter a clear description here.

4.   First Free Number
For further information, see keyword(s)
"First Free Numbers".

5.   Series Blocked   for Input   This field indicates if an order series must be blocked for
input. This may be of interest to reserve series for orders to be generated (e.g. EDI orders). Yes
The series is blocked for input.
No
The series is not blocked for input.

6.   Company
The default financial company number belonging to this series.

29.5 Maintain Forwarding Agents (tcmcs0180m000)

SESSION OBJECTIVE
To record the forwarding agents that can be selected in other sessions.

SEE ALSO KEYWORD(S)
•   Forwarding Agents

tcmcs0180m000   multi-occ (2)   Form 1-1

```
+---------------------------------------------------------------------+
| Maintain Forwarding Agents                           Company: 000   |
|---------------------------------------------------------------------|
|                                                                     |
| Code    Description                    Supplier                     |
|                                                                     |
|   1..  2...........................  3.....  4_____      |
|                                                                     |
+---------------------------------------------------------------------+
```

1.   Forwarding Agent
For further information, see keyword(s)
"Forwarding Agents".

2.   Description
Enter a clear description here.

3.   Supplier
The number uniquely identifying the supplier.
This supplier is used when copying Sales and Purchase Orders to Transport Orders.
When the forwarding agent has been filled in the Sales or Purchase order the supplier code is taken to create a subcontracting record for the generated transport order. The data to be entered must be defined in the session "Maintain Suppliers (tccom2101m000)".

4.   Name
The first part of the supplier's name.

29.6 Maintain Item Groups (tcmcs0123m000)

SESSION OBJECTIVE
To define the item groups used in other sessions.

SEE ALSO KEYWORD(S)
•   Item Groups

tcmcs0123m000   multi-occ (2)   Form 1-1

```
+---------------------------------------------------------------------+
| Maintain Item Groups                                 Company: 000   |
|---------------------------------------------------------------------|
|                                                                     |
| Code     Description                                                |
|                                                                     |
| 1.....  2...........................                                |
|                                                                     |
```

```
+-----------------------------------------------------------------------+
```
1.   Item Group
For further information, see keyword(s)
"Item Groups".
2.   Description
Enter a clear description here.
29.7 Maintain Languages (tcmcs0146m000)
SESSION OBJECTIVE
To record the languages used in other sessions.
SEE ALSO KEYWORD(S)
•   Languages
tcmcs0146m000   multi-occ (2)   Form 1-1
```
+-----------------------------------------------------------------------+
| Maintain Languages                                   Company: 000 |
|-----------------------------------------------------------------------|
|                                                                       |
| Lang  Description                   System Language                   |
|                                                                       |
|  1.. 2..........................  3  4_____  |
|                                                                       |
+-----------------------------------------------------------------------+
```
1.   Language
For further information, see keyword(s)
"Languages".
2.   Description
Enter a clear description here.
3.   System Language
The system language of BAAN IV. On the basis of this system language, external
documents are printed in another language.
The data to be entered must be defined in the session "Maintain Languages
(ttaad1110m000)".
Some of the system languages are: 1 Dutch
                                     2 English
                                     3 German
                                     4 French
4.   Language Description
The description of the system language.
29.8 Maintain Lines of Business (tcmcs0131m000)
SESSION OBJECTIVE
To maintain lines of business.
SEE ALSO KEYWORD(S)
•   Lines of Business
tcmcs0131m000   multi-occ (2)   Form 1-1
```
+-----------------------------------------------------------------------+
| Maintain Lines of Business                           Company: 000 |
|-----------------------------------------------------------------------|
|                                                                       |
| Line of Business        Description                                   |
|                                                                       |
|            1..... 2...........................                        |
|                                                                       |
+-----------------------------------------------------------------------+
```
1.   Line of Business
For further information, see keyword(s)
"Lines of Business".
2.   Description
Enter a clear description here.
29.9 Maintain Price Groups (tcmcs0124m000)
SESSION OBJECTIVE
To define the price groups used in other sessions.
SEE ALSO KEYWORD(S)
•   Price Groups
tcmcs0124m000   multi-occ (2)   Form 1-1

```
+---------------------------------------------------------------------+
|  Maintain Price Groups                              Company: 000  |
|-------------------------------------------------------------------|
|                                                                   |
|  Code     Description                   Price Unit                |
|                                                                   |
|  1.....   2...........................  3..  4_____  |
|                                                                   |
+---------------------------------------------------------------------+
```

1.   Price Group
For further information, see keyword(s)
"Price Groups".
2.   Description
Enter a clear description here.
3.   Price Unit
The unit of the discount grades for each price group. This unit appears as
information in sessions where you define discounts by price group.
The data to be entered must be defined in the session "Maintain Units
(tcmcs0101m000)".
4.   Description
29.10 Maintain Price Lists (tcmcs0134m000)
SESSION OBJECTIVE
To maintain price lists.
SEE ALSO KEYWORD(S)
•   Price Lists
tcmcs0134m000   multi-occ (2)   Form 1-1

```
+---------------------------------------------------------------------+
|  Maintain Price Lists                               Company: 000  |
|-------------------------------------------------------------------|
|                                                                   |
|Code   Description               Currency Description              |
|                                                                   |
|  1..  2...........................   3..  4_____    |
|                                                                   |
+---------------------------------------------------------------------+
```

1.   Price List
For further information, see keyword(s)
"Price Lists".
2.   Description
Enter a clear description here.
3.   Currency
The code of the currency belonging to the price list code. A currency must be
recorded in each price list as prices can be stored by price list, item and item
group. Wherever prices are recorded, the associated currency should be
available.
The data to be entered must be defined in the session "Maintain Currencies
(tcmcs0102m000)".
4.   Description
29.11 Maintain Reasons for Rejection (tcmcs0105m000)
SESSION OBJECTIVE
To maintain reasons for rejection.
SEE ALSO KEYWORD(S)
•   Reasons for Rejection
tcmcs0105m000   multi-occ (2)   Form 1-1

```
+---------------------------------------------------------------------+
|  Maintain Reasons for Rejection                     Company: 000  |
|-------------------------------------------------------------------|
|                                                                   |
|  Code     Description                                             |
|                                                                   |
|  1..  2...........................                                |
|                                                                   |
+---------------------------------------------------------------------+
```

1.   Reason
For further information, see keyword(s)
"Reasons for Rejection".
2.   Description
Enter a clear description here.
29.12 Maintain Product Types (tcmcs0115m000)
SESSION OBJECTIVE
To maintain product types.
SEE ALSO KEYWORD(S)
•   Product Types
tcmcs0115m000   multi-occ (2)   Form 1-1
+--+
Maintain Product Types   Company: 000
Code   Description
1.. 2.............................
+--+
1.   Product Type
For further information, see keyword(s)
"Product Types".
2.   Description
Enter a clear description here.
29.13 Maintain Routes (tcmcs0104m000)
SESSION OBJECTIVE
To maintain routes.
SEE ALSO KEYWORD(S)
•   Routes
tcmcs0104m000   multi-occ (2)   Form 1-1
+--+
Maintain Routes   Company: 000
Code   Description   Day
1.... 2............................ 3.............
+--+
1.   Route
For further information, see keyword(s)
"Routes".
2.   Description
Enter a clear description here.
3.   Day
The day on which the items must be delivered. This day is printed on picking
lists that are printed for sales orders using the session "Print Picking Lists
(tdsls4402m000)".
29.14 Maintain Seasonal Patterns (tcmcs0116m000)
SESSION OBJECTIVE
To maintain seasonal patterns.
HOW TO USE THE SESSION
The parameter "Period Length for Item History" (in the session "Maintain INV
Parameters (tdinv0100m000)") determines the number of seasonal factors.
SEE ALSO KEYWORD(S)
•   Seasonal Patterns
tcmcs0116m000   single-occ (1)   Form 1-1
+--+
Maintain Seasonal Patterns   Company: 000
Seasonal Pattern   :   1..

```
| Description          : 2..........................         |
|                                                            |
| Seasonal Factor (1): 3.                                    |
|                  (2): 3.                                   |
|                  (3): 3.                                   |
|                  (4): 3.                                   |
|                  (5): 3.                                   |
|                  (6): 3.                                   |
|                  (7): 3.                                   |
|                  (8): 3.                                   |
|                  (9): 3.                                   |
|                 (10): 3.                                   |
|                 (11): 3.                                   |
|                 (12): 3.                                   |
|                 (13): 3.                                   |
|                                                            |
+------------------------------------------------------------+
```

1.   Seasonal Pattern
For further information, see keyword(s)
"Seasonal Patterns".
2.   Description
Enter a clear description here.
3.   Seasonal Factor
The seasonal factors are the coefficients for each seasonal period. These
factors determine the increase and decrease of the safety stock or the expected
demand in a certain period.
29.15 Maintain Selection Codes (tcmcs0122m000)
SESSION OBJECTIVE
To define the selection criteria used in other sessions.
SEE ALSO KEYWORD(S)
•   Selection Codes

```
tcmcs0122m000                          multi-occ (2)    Form 1-1
+------------------------------------------------------------+
| Maintain Selection Codes                   Company: 000 |
|------------------------------------------------------------|
|                                                            |
| Code    Description                                        |
|                                                            |
|    1..  2..........................                        |
|                                                            |
+------------------------------------------------------------+
```

1.   Selection Code
For further information, see keyword(s)
"Selection Codes".
2.   Description
Enter a clear description here.
29.16 Maintain Signal Codes (tcmcs0118m000)
SESSION OBJECTIVE
To define define the signal codes used in other sessions.
SEE ALSO KEYWORD(S)
•   Signals

```
tcmcs0118m000                          single-occ (1)    Form 1-1
+------------------------------------------------------------+
| Maintain Signal Codes                      Company: 000 |
|------------------------------------------------------------|
|                                                            |
| Signal Code                  : 1..                        |
|                                                            |
| Description                  : 2..........................  |
|                                                            |
| Blocking Status                                            |
|                                                            |
| Purchase                     : 3..........................  |
```

```
| Sales                      : 4............................ |
| Requisition through Production: 5............................ |
| Production Issue           : 6............................ |
| Process Issue              : 7............................ |
|                                                            |
+------------------------------------------------------------+
```

1.   Signal Code
For further information, see keyword(s)
"Signals".
2.   Description
Enter a clear description here.
3.   Purchase
This blocking status indicates if the item to which this signal code is linked
is free or blocked for purchase. Free
The item can be freely used in the module "Purchase Control (PUR)".
Blocked
As soon as you enter this item in e.g. the sessions "Maintain Purchase Contract
Lines (tdpur3102s000)" and "Maintain Purchase Order Lines (tdpur4102s000)", the
system will reject it.
4.   Sales
This blocking status indicates whether the item to which the concerned signal
code is linked is free of blocked for sales. Free
The item can be freely used in the module "Sales Control (SLS)".
Blocked
As soon as you enter this item in e.g. the sessions "Maintain Sales Contract
Lines (tdsls3102s000)" and "Maintain Sales Order Lines (tdsls4102s000)", the
system will reject it.
5.   Requisition through Production
This blocking status indicates whether the main item to which the concerned
signal code is linked is free or blocked for production orders.
Free
The item can be freely used in the module "Shop Floor Control (SFC)".
Blocked
As soon as you try to use this item in the session "Maintain Production Orders
(tisfc0101m000)", the system will refuse this. The modules generating
purchase/production advice (INV, MPS, MRP) likewise react to the signal code and
hence will not generate production orders for the item. By consulting the
exception messages in the module "Material Requirements Planning (MRP)" you can
find out which signal code causes the item to be blocked.
6.   Production Issue
This blocking status indicates whether the item to which the concerned signal
code is linked is free or blocked for issue from a warehouse to a production
order or to a project in BAAN Project.
Free
The item can be freely issued for production orders in the module "Shop Floor
Control (SFC)", provided that acquisition via production is not blocked. The
system also consults the blocking status when issuing materials from the
warehouse to a project in the module "Planned Warehouse Orders".
Blocked
As soon as you try to use this item in the sessions, "Enter Material Issue for
Production Orders (ticst0101m000)" and "Issue Inventory (tisfc0207m000)", the
system will refuse this. The system will also refuse to issue materials in the
sessions "Confirm Planned Warehouse Orders (tppss6225m000)" and "Transfer
Planned Warehouse Orders (tppss6235m000)".
7.   Process Issue
This blocking status indicates whether the item to which the concerned signal
code is linked is free or blocked for issue from a warehouse to a production
batch. Free
The item can be freely issued for production batches in the module "Production
Management (PMG)", provided that acquisition via production is not blocked.
Blocked
As soon as you try to use this item in the session "Enter Material Issue for
Production Batches (pspmg0111m000)", the system will refuse this.

29.17 Maintain Statistics Groups (tcmcs0144m000)
SESSION OBJECTIVE
To define the statistics groups used in other sessions.
SEE ALSO KEYWORD(S)
•   Statistics Groups
tcmcs0144m000   multi-occ (2)   Form 1-1
+--+
Maintain Statistics Groups   Company: 000
Code   Description
1..... 2.............................
+--+
1.   Statistics Group
For further information, see keyword(s)
"Statistics Groups".
2.   Description
Enter a clear description here.
29.18 Maintain Terms of Delivery (tcmcs0141m000)
SESSION OBJECTIVE
To define the terms of delivery used in other sessions.
SEE ALSO KEYWORD(S)
•   Terms of Delivery
tcmcs0141m000   single-occ (1)   Form 1-1
+--+
Maintain Terms of Delivery   Company: 000
Code   : 1..
Description   : 2.............................
Cash on Delivery   : 3....
Carriage Paid   : 4....
Point of Title PaBaange: 5..................
Text   : 6____
+--+
1.   Terms of Delivery
For further information, see keyword(s)
"Terms of Delivery".
2.   Description
Enter a clear description here.
3.   Cash on Delivery
Cash on delivery means that goods are delivered on the condition that they are
paid for immediately on receipt. When purchase orders or sales orders are copied
to transport orders via the session "Copy Orders to BAAN Transportation
(trtoc2999m000)", the corresponding field on the transport order is filled with
the value selected here.
4.   Carriage Paid
Carriage paid means that the carriage or postage has been paid by the consignor.
When you copy purchase and sales orders to transport orders in the session "Copy
Orders to BAAN Transportation (trtoc2999m000)", the corresponding field on the
transport order is filled with the value selected here. This field also
determines who is to pay for the transport order line.
This field also determines who is to be billed for the transport order line.
Yes
The customer is the customer or supplier of the purchasing/sales department.
No
The customer is the customer or supplier of the purchase/sales order.
5.   Point of Title PaBaange

The point at which title passes, either origin or destination, is used by the
tax provider TAXWARE's Master Tax System to determine the taxing jurisdiction.
SEE ALSO METHOD(S)
•   Global Localisation (Tax Provider)
6.   Text

29.19 Maintain Titles (tcmcs0119m000)

SESSION OBJECTIVE
To maintain titles.
SEE ALSO KEYWORD(S)
•   Titles

```
tcmcs0119m000                              multi-occ (2)    Form 1-1
+---------------------------------------------------------------------+
| Maintain Titles                                  Company: 000 |
|---------------------------------------------------------------------|
|                                                                     |
| Title   Description                                                 |
|                                                                     |
|    1..  2..............................                             |
|                                                                     |
+---------------------------------------------------------------------+
```

1.   Title
For further information, see keyword(s)
"Titles".
2.   Description
Enter a clear description here.

29.20 Maintain Units (tcmcs0101m000)

SESSION OBJECTIVE
To maintain units.
SEE ALSO KEYWORD(S)
•   Units

```
tcmcs0101m000                              multi-occ (2)    Form 1-1
+---------------------------------------------------------------------+
| Maintain Units                                   Company: 000 |
|---------------------------------------------------------------------|
|                                                                     |
| Char   Description              Physical        Rounding Factor |
| Unit                            Quantity                            |
|                                                                     |
| 1..    2.............................  3.............    4...    |
|                                                                     |
+---------------------------------------------------------------------+
```

1.   Unit
For further information, see keyword(s)
"Units".
2.   Description
Enter a clear description here. For further information, see keyword(s)
"Units by Language".
3.   Physical Quantity
The physical quantity the unit belongs to.
4.   Rounding Factor
The rounding method indicates how quantities in this unit must be rounded. If
the system is to round to whole numbers, for instance, it will not accept the
input of fractions.
As long as a unit is used in the application, the rounding method can only be
modified to a limited extent: a change to a higher degree of precision will be
accepted, one to a lower degree of precision will not.

29.21 Maintain Units by Language (tcmcs0107m000)

SESSION OBJECTIVE
To maintain short language-dependent unit descriptions.
SEE ALSO KEYWORD(S)
•   Units by Language

```
tcmcs0107m000                              multi/group (3   Form 1-1
+---------------------------------------------------------------------+
```

```
+-----------------------------------------------------------------------------+
| Maintain Units by Language                              Company: 000 |
|-----------------------------------------------------------------------------|
|                                                                             |
|  Unit  : 1.. 2_____                                 |
|                                                                             |
|  Lang Description          Language-Specific          Short Unit            |
|                            Unit Description           Description           |
|                                                                             |
|   3.. 4_____ 5...........................  6....             |
|                                                                             |
+-----------------------------------------------------------------------------+
```

1.   Unit
The unit for which foreign language descriptions must be recorded.
2.   Description
3.   Language
The language of the unit description. These language codes should have already
been defined in the session "Maintain Languages (tcmcs0146m000)".
4.   Description
5.   Language-Specif- ic Unit Description
Enter a clear description here.
6.   Sh. Unit Descr.
The short language-dependent description of the unit which is printed on
external documents.

29.22 Maintain Unit Sets (tcmcs0106m000)
SESSION OBJECTIVE
To maintain unit sets.
SEE ALSO KEYWORD(S)
•   Unit Sets
tcmcs0106m000   zoom   multi-occ (2)   Form 1-1

```
+-----------------------------------------------------------------------------+
| Maintain Unit Sets                                     Company: 000 |
|-----------------------------------------------------------------------------|
|                                                                             |
|  Unit Set       Description                                                 |
|                                                                             |
|        1.....   2...........................                                |
|                                                                             |
+-----------------------------------------------------------------------------+
```

1.   Unit Set
For further information, see keyword(s)
"Unit Sets".
2.   Description
Enter a clear description here.

29.23 Maintain Units by Unit Set (tcmcs0112m000)
SESSION OBJECTIVE
To maintain units by unit set.
SEE ALSO KEYWORD(S):
•   Units By Unit Set, Unit Sets (tcmcs006), Units (tcmcs001)
tcmcs0112m000   multi/group (3   Form 1-1

```
+-----------------------------------------------------------------------------+
| Maintain Units by Unit Set                             Company: 000 |
|-----------------------------------------------------------------------------|
|                                                                             |
|  Unit Set     : 1..... 2_____                       |
|                                                                             |
|  Char   Description        INV   Distr. Mfg.    Price Stor.  Con-           |
|  Unit                                                        tainer         |
|                                                                             |
|  3..     4_____ 5..... 6..... 7..... 8..... 9..... 10....       |
|                                                                             |
+-----------------------------------------------------------------------------+
```

1.   Unit Set
For further information, see keyword(s)

"Unit Sets".
2.   Description
3.   Unit
For further information, see keyword(s)
"Units".
4.   Description
5.   Inventory
Yes
This unit can be used as an inventory unit.
No
This unit cannot be used as an inventory unit.
Stop
In new situations, this unit can no longer be used as an inventory unit.
Existing actions using this unit can be continued and finished as normal.
6.   Distribution
Yes
This unit can be used as a quantity unit.
No
This unit cannot be used as a quantity unit.
Stop
In new situations, this unit can no longer be used as a quantity unit. Existing
actions using this unit can be continued and finished as normal.
7.   Manufacturing
Yes
This unit can be used as a production unit.
No
This unit cannot be used as a production unit.
Stop
In new situations, this unit can no longer be used as a production unit.
Existing actions using this unit can be continued and finished as normal.
For further information, see method(s):
•   Blocking Units of Measure in BAAN Process
8.   Price
Yes
This unit can be used as a price unit.
No
This unit cannot be used as a price unit.
Stop
In new situations, this unit can no longer be used as a price unit. Existing
actions using this unit can be continued and finished as normal.
9.   Storage
Yes
This unit can be used as a storage unit.
No
This unit cannot be used as a storage unit.
Stop
In new situations, this unit can no longer be used as a storage unit. Existing
actions using this unit can be continued and finished as normal.
10.   Container
Yes
This unit can be used as a container in (containerized) container/item
combinations in the session "Maintain Item Data by Item and Container
(tiitm0130m000)".
Container/item combinations are automatically generated when:
•   an item with the following features is maintained in the session "Maintain
Item Data (tiitm0101m000)":
•   Process Item = Yes and
•   Containerized = Yes
•   the session "Update Containerized Items (tiitm0230m000)" is executed
No
This unit cannot be used as a container.
Stop

This unit may no longer be used as a container in new situations. Ongoing actions using this unit can be continued and finished as normal.
After setting this field to "Stop" it is advised to run the session "Update Containerized Items (tiitm0230m000)" to ensure that all container/item combinations are updated according to the "Signal Code Expired Container Items" parameter.

29.24 Maintain Warehouses (tcmcs0103m000)

SESSION OBJECTIVE
To define data about the warehouses used in other sessions.
Companies with a single warehouse must define at least one warehouse, otherwise orders cannot be processed.
SEE ALSO KEYWORD(S)
• Warehouses
SEE ALSO METHOD(S)
• Address Verification for Tax Provider
INFORMATION ABOUT DISPLAY FIELDS:
• Locations

```
tcmcs0103m000                          single-occ (1)   Form 1-2 >
+-----------------------------------------------------------------------+
| Maintain Warehouses                                  Company: 000  |
|-----------------------------------------------------------------------|
|                                                                       |
| Warehouse                   : 1..                                     |
|                                                                       |
| Description                 : 2..............................         |
| Country                     : 3.. 4_____    |
| Name                        : 5................................       |
|                             : 6..............................         |
| Address                     : 7..............................         |
|                             : 8..............................         |
| 9_____   : 10.............................         |
| 11_____   : 12.............................         |
| 13_____   1415.......                              |
| 16_____   1718...                                  |
| ZIP Code                    : 19........                              |
| Transportation Address      : 20____                                 |
| Finance Company             : 21. 22_____  |
|                                                                       |
+-----------------------------------------------------------------------+
```

1.   Warehouse
For further information, see keyword(s) "Warehouses".
2.   Description
Enter a clear description here.
3.   Country
The code of the country where the warehouse has been established. Enter the country code. It should have already been defined in the session "Maintain Countries (tcmcs0110m000)".
4.   Description
5.   Name
The first part of the warehouse name.
6.   Name 2
The second part of the warehouse name. If the previous field is not long enough to show the full name, you can use this field as well.
7.   Address
The first part of the address of the warehouse.
8.   Address 2
The second part of the address of the warehouse. If the previous field is too short for the full address, you can also use this field.
9.   Program domain string
10.   City
The place where the warehouse has been established. It appears on documents under the delivery address in the module "Purchase Control (PUR)".

For tax provider users, the city and state or province where the warehouse has been established. The city and state or province should be separated by a comma ",", such as "Menlo Park, CA".

For further information, see method(s)

-     Address Verification for Tax Provider

If a post code is used, it is assumed that it is also entered in one of the address fields as the format for international ZIP codes differs from one country to another.

11.   Program domain string

12.   City 2

The second part of the place where the warehouse has been established. It appears on documents under the delivery address in the module "Purchase Control (PUR)".

For tax provider users, the ZIP Code or Postal Code where the warehouse has been established.

For further information, see method(s)

-     Address Verification for Tax Provider

13.   Program domain string

14.   Program domain of string length 1

15.   GEO Code

A GEO code is a code used together or in lieu of address information such as city, state/province, and ZIP/postal code to uniquely identify a taxing jurisdiction. The tax provider determines the GEO code based upon the address information entered and the county and city limits selected.

The format of the GEO code varies by tax provider. AVP uses a two-digit GEO code; the GEO code together with the city, state, and ZIP code, identifies the taxing jurisdiction. Vertex uses a nine-digit GEO code comprised of a two digit state code, three-digit county code, and a four-digit city code. A tenth digit is used to identify if the jurisdiction is inside or outside of the city limits.

16.   Program domain string

17.   Program domain of string length 1

18.   Answer on question y/n

19.   ZIP Code

The ZIP code of the address where the warehouse is situated. It is used in places (for instance on documents, in sorts) where only the ZIP code is required.

20.   Address Code

The address if the package is run in association with the package BAAN Transportation. The address refers to an address in the b-object "Address Control (ACS)" in the package BAAN Transportation.

21.   Company

The number of the Finance company associated with this warehouse. All transaction for this warehouse result in financial transactions for the above company.

22.   Company Name

The company's name.

```
tcmcs0103m000                                    single-occ (1) < Form 2-2
+-------------------------------------------------------------------------+
| Maintain Warehouses                                       Company: 000  |
|-------------------------------------------------------------------------|
|                                                                         |
|  Warehouse                            : 1..                             |
|                                                                         |
|  Warehouse Type                       : 2..............                 |
|  Nettable Warehouse                   : 3....                           |
|  Locations                            : 4____                           |
|  Receipt Location                     : 5.......                        |
|  Inspection Receipt Location          : 6.......                        |
|  Multi-Item Locations                 : 7....                           |
|  Multi-Lot by Item Locations          : 8....                           |
|  Min. % Free for Inbound Advice       : 9..                             |
|                                                                         |
+-------------------------------------------------------------------------+
```

1.   Warehouse
For further information, see keyword(s)
"Warehouses".
2.   Warehouse Type
The type of warehouse. Normal
Normal warehouses with or without a location system used for storing goods.
Work-in-Process
Warehouses used to store intermediate inventory used to supply production
lines/work centers.
Transit
Warehouses for registering inventory in transit. These warehouses are used in
the module "Replenishment Order Control (RPL)" to trace inventory during
transportation.
3.   Nettable Warehouse
No
This warehouse is a so-called "non-nettable" warehouse. Non-nettable warehouses
are ignored by the MRP and MPS algorithm. The resupply of such warehouses is
planned with DRP in the module "Distribution Requirements Planning (DRP)". In
addition, direct purchases can be written to non-nettable warehouses or they can
be stocked via the SIC principle.
Yes
This warehouse is a so-called "nettable" warehouse. Nettable warehouses are
ignored by the DRP algorithm. The replenishment of the inventory of these
warehouses is planned using MRP, MPS and SIC in the modules "Material
Requirements Planning (MRP)", "Master Production Scheduling (MPS)" and
"Inventory Control (INV)" or takes place through manual purchases. An exception
is a "nettable" "Work-in-Process" warehouse, because it can also be resupplied
by DRP.
4.   Locations
A warehouse may comprise multiple inventory locations. These may be free or
fixed locations. Inventory is then registered by location in the module
"Location Control (ILC)".
The session "Change Location System by Warehouse (tdilc0231m000)" loads the
receipt and inspection locations. Subsequently, the system sets the field
"Locations" to "Yes". Yes
The warehouse has either multiple fixed locations or free locations. You must
define the locations in the session "Maintain Locations (tdilc0110m000)".
No
The warehouse has no locations or at most one fixed location per item. You can
record this in the session "Maintain Items by Warehouse (tdinv0101m000)".
5.   Receipt Location
If you use locations, in each warehouse a location may be available in which
items may be placed which are not subject to inspection when they are received.
With the help of inbound advice, the items from this location are assigned to
other inventory locations which have not been defined as inspection locations in
the module "Location Control (ILC)".
If you have chosen for a location system, you can maintain this field. By
default, the inspection location is shown which has been defined via the
following session:
•   Maintain Warehouses (tcmcs0103m000)
6.   Inspection Receipt Location
Aside from the "normal" locations, there may also be inspection locations
present in a warehouse. An inspection location is exclusively designated for
storing purchased items which have been marked for inspection in the module
"Purchase Control (PUR)". After the items have been approved in the session
"Maintain Approvals (tdpur4121m000)", they are transferred to a "normal"
location. Inventories stored in an inspection location are always registered as
inventory on hold.
If you have chosen for a location system, you can maintain this field. By
default, the inspection location is shown which has been defined via the
following session:
•   Maintain Warehouses (tcmcs0103m000)
7.   Multi-Item Locations

For each warehouse, you can indicate which items may be stored at a location:
either items with the same item code or items with different item codes. You can
select:
Yes
Different items may be stored at one location.
No
At each location, only one item may be stored.
8.   Multi-Lot by Item Locations
For items subject to lot control, you must indicate whether many lots of the
same items may be stored at a location. Yes
Different lots of one item may be stored at one location.
No
At each location, only one lot of a specific item may be stored.
In combination with the field "Multi-Item Locations", four variant are possible:
•   Different items and different lots of each item are allowed.
•   Different items are allowed, but only one lot of each item.
•   Only one item is allowed at the location, but of this item, more than one
lot may be stored.
•   Only one lot of one item is allowed at the location.
9.   Min. % Free for Inbound Advice
The minimum percentage of free capacity that a location must have before inbound
advice can be generated.
When the calculated capacity occupation of a location reaches a certain upper
limit, inbound advice for the location would no longer be advisable. If the
available capacity for each location is small, too many locations are approached
when receiving items for storage. In order to avoid wasting time, the capacity
occupation is recorded as a percentage for each location in this field. The
capacity occupation is calculated as follows:

```
   Total Capacity - Available Capacity
   ------------------------------------------ x 100%
            Total Capacity
```

If a location is filled in with a percentage greater or equal tc the value
entered in this field, the system will report that the location is occupied for
x%, "x" being the calculated percentage.
29.25 Maintain Use of Performance Boosters (tcmcs0197m000)
SESSION OBJECTIVE
To link performance boosters to sessions, to users, or to a combination of
these.
NOTE: Wherever in an application a booster can be applied, but that booster has
not been set in this session, the following will occur: table Use of Performance
Boosters (tcmcs097) will be inserted with the booster concerned for the user and
the session that is running and the validation in the field "Booster Valid" will
be "Not Active"
HOW TO USE THE SESSION
Performance Boosters can be used at three levels, each starting with another
identifier. The following combinations may therefore be made:

Session	Performance Booster	User
Performance Booster	Session	Performance Booster
User	User	Session

It is necessary to always fill in the performance booster which should be used
and the session for which the booster is valid.
SEE ALSO KEYWORD(S)
•   Use of Performance Boosters

```
tcmcs0197m000                              multi/group (3    Form 1-3 >
+-----------------------------------------------------------------------+
|  Maintain Use of Performance Boosters                   Company: 000  |
|-----------------------------------------------------------------------|
|                                                                       |
| Session                 :  1........... 2_____      |
|                                                                       |
```

```
| Performance Booster        User        Value        Booster Valid       |
|                                                                         |
| 3.....................     4..........  5.........   6..............     |
|                                                                         |
+-------------------------------------------------------------------------+
```

1.   Session
Entering the session will make the system employ the performance booster in this
session, if applicable. If it is not applicable, entering the session will have
no effect at all.
See the field "Performance Booster" for a list of sessions to which the
performance booster is relevant.
2.   Description
3.   Performance Booster
For further information, see keyword(s)
"Use of Performance Boosters".
Available performance boosters: * [GO1] Display Interval * [G02] Number of
Servers
* [G03] Maximum Invoice Lines * [G04] Embedded Financial Int.
Display Interval With this option you can influence the time between two refresh
actions. Decreasing the frequency with which the program refreshes the screen
will have a positive effect on the speed of large processing sessions.
Use is recommended in the sessions:
•   Generate Planned (MPS)/MRP Orders/Batches (timrp1210m000)
•   Generate Master Production Schedule (timps3201m000)
•   Generate Planned PRP Orders (tipcs5201m000)
•   Transfer Planned PRP Purchase Orders (tipcs5260m000)
•   Generate Inbound Advice (tdilc4203m000)
•   Generate Outbound Advice (tdilc4201m000)
Numbers of Servers This option allows you to set the extra number of bshells to
be started parallel to the session concerned, which you should fill in the field
"Session". It is also possible to join the Number of Servers to one "User".
Use is recommended in the sessions:
•   Update Sales Statistics (tdsst0201m000)
•   Print Sales Invoices (tdsls4404m000)
If booster has been set for this session, the session "Process Delivered Sales
Orders (tdsls4223m000)" will run parallel to printing the invoices.
•   Process Delivered Sales Orders (tdsls4223m000)
•   Process Delivered Purchase Orders (tdpur4223m000)
•   Select Invoices for Payment (tfcmg1220m000)
•   Audit Batches (tfgld1211s000)
•   Generate Planned (MPS)/MRP Orders/Batches (timrp1210m000)
•   Generate Master Production Schedule (timps3201m000)
•   Execute Single Site Master Production Scheduling (timps3202s000)
•   Print Cost Control (tpppc4411m000)
Maximum Invoice Lines Whenever the possibility to collect several orders on one
invoice is used, invoices can contain a great number of lines. The transaction
to book these lines to BAAN Finance can become too large, depending on e.g. the
size of the rollback-segments of your database. This option limits the maximum
number of lines on one invoice, thus reducing the size of the transaction
mentioned.
Use is only possible in:
•   Print Sales Invoices (tdsls4404m000)
The check on maximum invoice lines will not be performed if the field "Invoicing
by Installments" for the current order is set to "Yes". Printing will continue
untill the end of this order.
•   Print Invoices (trics2400m000)
•   Print Contract Installment Invoices (tssma2472m000)
•   Print Service Order Invoices (tssma3473m000)
•   Print Invoices (tppin4474m000)
Embedded Financial Integration With this option a financial integration will be
processed using a Dynamic Link Library instead of the parallel running session
"Update Integr Trans and Real Time Post to Finance (backgrd.) (tfgld4200s000)".
This will speed up the sessions in which a financial integration is involved.

4.   User
The user for whom the booster is valid. If this field is left empty the booster
is valid for all users that start the session.
5.   Value
6.   Booster Valid

```
tcmcs0197m000                                      multi/group (3  < Form 2-3 >
+---------------------------------------------------------------------------+
| Maintain Use of Performance Boosters                      Company: 000  |
|---------------------------------------------------------------------------|
|                                                                           |
| Performance Booster      : 1.......................                       |
|                                                                           |
| Session        Description          User       Value      Booster Valid  |
|                                                                           |
| 2........... 3_____  4.......... 5........ 6.............  |
|                                                                           |
+---------------------------------------------------------------------------+
```

1.   Performance Booster
For further information, see keyword(s)
"Use of Performance Boosters".
Available performance boosters: * [GO1] Display Interval * [G02] Number of
Servers
* [G03] Maximum Invoice Lines * [G04] Embedded Financial Int.
Display Interval With this option you can influence the time between two refresh
actions. Decreasing the frequency with which the program refreshes the screen
will have a positive effect on the speed of large processing sessions.
Use is recommended in the sessions:
•   Generate Planned (MPS)/MRP Orders/Batches (timrp1210m000)
•   Generate Master Production Schedule (timps3201m000)
•   Generate Planned PRP Orders (tipcs5201m000)
•   Transfer Planned PRP Purchase Orders (tipcs5260m000)
•   Generate Inbound Advice (tdilc4203m000)
•   Generate Outbound Advice (tdilc4201m000)
Numbers of Servers This option allows you to set the extra number of bshells to
be started parallel to the session concerned, which you should fill in the field
"Session". It is also possible to join the Number of Servers to one "User".
Use is recommended in the sessions:
•   Update Sales Statistics (tdsst0201m000)
•   Print Sales Invoices (tdsls4404m000)
If booster has been set for this session, the session "Process Delivered Sales
Orders (tdsls4223m000)" will run parallel to printing the invoices.
•   Process Delivered Sales Orders (tdsls4223m000)
•   Process Delivered Purchase Orders (tdpur4223m000)
•   Select Invoices for Payment (tfcmg1220m000)
•   Audit Batches (tfgld1211s000)
•   Generate Planned (MPS)/MRP Orders/Batches (timrp1210m000)
•   Generate Master Production Schedule (timps3201m000)
•   Execute Single Site Master Production Scheduling (timps3202s000)
•   Print Cost Control (tpppc4411m000)
Maximum Invoice Lines Whenever the possibility to collect several orders on one
invoice is used, invoices can contain a great number of lines. The transaction
to book these lines to BAAN Finance can become too large, depending on e.g. the
size of the rollback-segments of your database. This option limits the maximum
number of lines on one invoice, thus reducing the size of the transaction
mentioned.
Use is only possible in:
•   Print Sales Invoices (tdsls4404m000)
The check on maximum invoice lines will not be performed if the field "Invoicing
by Installments" for the current order is set to "Yes". Printing will continue
untill the end of this order.
•   Print Invoices (trics2400m000)
•   Print Contract Installment Invoices (tssma2472m000)
•   Print Service Order Invoices (tssma3473m000)

- Print Invoices (tppin4474m000)

Embedded Financial Integration With this option a financial integration will be processed using a Dynamic Link Library instead of the parallel running session "Update Integr Trans and Real Time Post to Finance (backgrd.) (tfgld4200s000)". This will speed up the sessions in which a financial integration is involved.

2. Session

Entering the session will make the system employ the performance booster in this session, if applicable. If it is not applicable, entering the session will have no effect at all.

See the field "Performance Booster" for a list of sessions to which the performance booster is relevant.

3. Description

4. User

The user for whom the booster is valid. If this field is left empty the booster is valid for all users that start the session.

5. Value

6. Booster Valid

tcmcs0197m000   multi/group (3 < Form 3-3

```
+---------------------------------------------------------------------------+
| Maintain Use of Performance Boosters                        Company: 000  |
|---------------------------------------------------------------------------|
|                                                                           |
| User                      : 1...........  2_____|
|                                                                           |
| Performance Booster         Session         Value         Booster Valid   |
|                                                                           |
| 3........................  4............  5.........   6.............      |
|                                                                           |
+---------------------------------------------------------------------------+
```

1. User

The user for whom the booster is valid. If this field is left empty the booster is valid for all users that start the session.

2. Description

3. Performance Booster

For further information, see keyword(s)
"Use of Performance Boosters".

Available performance boosters: * [GO1] Display Interval * [G02] Number of Servers

* [G03] Maximum Invoice Lines * [G04] Embedded Financial Int.

Display Interval With this option you can influence the time between two refresh actions. Decreasing the frequency with which the program refreshes the screen will have a positive effect on the speed of large processing sessions.

Use is recommended in the sessions:
- Generate Planned (MPS)/MRP Orders/Batches (timrp1210m000)
- Generate Master Production Schedule (timps3201m000)
- Generate Planned PRP Orders (tipcs5201m000)
- Transfer Planned PRP Purchase Orders (tipcs5260m000)
- Generate Inbound Advice (tdilc4203m000)
- Generate Outbound Advice (tdilc4201m000)

Numbers of Servers This option allows you to set the extra number of bshells to be started parallel to the session concerned, which you should fill in the field "Session". It is also possible to join the Number of Servers to one "User".

Use is recommended in the sessions:
- Update Sales Statistics (tdsst0201m000)
- Print Sales Invoices (tdsls4404m000)

If booster has been set for this session, the session "Process Delivered Sales Orders (tdsls4223m000)" will run parallel to printing the invoices.
- Process Delivered Sales Orders (tdsls4223m000)
- Process Delivered Purchase Orders (tdpur4223m000)
- Select Invoices for Payment (tfcmg1220m000)
- Audit Batches (tfgld1211s000)
- Generate Planned (MPS)/MRP Orders/Batches (timrp1210m000)
- Generate Master Production Schedule (timps3201m000)

- Execute Single Site Master Production Scheduling (timps3202s000)
- Print Cost Control (tpppc4411m000)

Maximum Invoice Lines Whenever the possibility to collect several orders on one invoice is used, invoices can contain a great number of lines. The transaction to book these lines to BAAN Finance can become too large, depending on e.g. the size of the rollback-segments of your database. This option limits the maximum number of lines on one invoice, thus reducing the size of the transaction mentioned.

Use is only possible in:
- Print Sales Invoices (tdsls4404m000)

The check on maximum invoice lines will not be performed if the field "Invoicing by Installments" for the current order is set to "Yes". Printing will continue untill the end of this order.
- Print Invoices (trics2400m000)
- Print Contract Installment Invoices (tssma2472m000)
- Print Service Order Invoices (tssma3473m000)
- Print Invoices (tppin4474m000)

Embedded Financial Integration With this option a financial integration will be processed using a Dynamic Link Library instead of the parallel running session "Update Integr Trans and Real Time Post to Finance (backgrd.) (tfgld4200s000)". This will speed up the sessions in which a financial integration is involved.

4.   Session

Entering the session will make the system employ the performance booster in this session, if applicable. If it is not applicable, entering the session will have no effect at all.

See the field "Performance Booster" for a list of sessions to which the performance booster is relevant.

5.   Value

6.   Booster Valid

29.26 Maintain Quality Groups (tcmcs0129m000)

SESSION OBJECTIVE

To maintain quality groups.

SEE ALSO KEYWORD(S)
- Quality Groups

```
tcmcs0129m000                         zoom       multi-occ (2)    Form 1-1
+---------------------------------------------------------------------------+
| Maintain Quality Groups                                    Company: 000   |
|---------------------------------------------------------------------------|
|                                                                           |
| Quality Group   Description                                               |
|                                                                           |
|      1.....   2...........................                                 |
|                                                                           |
+---------------------------------------------------------------------------+
```

1.   Quality Group

For further information, see keyword(s) "Quality Groups".

2.   Description

Enter a clear description here.

29.27 Maintain Skills (tcmcs0130m000)

SESSION OBJECTIVE

To define the various skills required to use the different instruments for the quality tests in the Quality Management System (QMS) module.

SEE ALSO KEYWORD(S)
- Skills

```
tcmcs0130m000                                    multi-occ (2)    Form 1-1
+---------------------------------------------------------------------------+
| Maintain Skills                                            Company: 000   |
|---------------------------------------------------------------------------|
|                                                                           |
| Skill          Description                                                |
|                                                                           |
|      1...   2...........................                                   |
```

```
|                                                                          |
+--------------------------------------------------------------------------+
1.    Skill
For further information, see keyword(s)
"Skills".
2.    Description
Enter a clear description here.
30    Optional Sessions
30.1  Maintain Titles (tcmcs0119s000)
SESSION OBJECTIVE
To maintain titles.
SEE ALSO KEYWORD(S)
•     Titles
tcmcs0119s000                                multi-occ (2)    Form 1-1
+--Maintain Titles----------------------------------------------+
|                                                               |
| Title    Description                                          |
|                                                               |
|     1..  2............................                        |
|                                                               |
+---------------------------------------------------------------+
1.    Title
For further information, see keyword(s)
"Titles".
2.    Description
Enter a clear description here.
31    Other Print Sessions
31.1  Print Areas (tcmcs0445m000)
tcmcs0445m000                                single-occ (4)    Form 1-1
+--------------------------------------------------------------------------+
| Print Areas                                      Company: 000 |
|------------------------------------------------------------------------|
|                                                                        |
| Area        from : 1..                                                 |
|             to   : 2..                                                  |
|                                                                        |
+--------------------------------------------------------------------------+
1.    Area from
2.    Area to
31.2  Print Commodity Codes (tcmcs0428m000)
tcmcs0428m000                                single-occ (4)    Form 1-1
+--------------------------------------------------------------------------+
| Print Commodity Codes                            Company: 000 |
|------------------------------------------------------------------------|
|                                                                        |
| Commodity Code from : 1.......                                         |
|              to   : 2.......                                            |
|                                                                        |
+--------------------------------------------------------------------------+
1.    Commodity Code from
2.    Commodity Code to
31.3  Print Countries (tcmcs0410m000)
tcmcs0410m000                                single-occ (4)    Form 1-1
+--------------------------------------------------------------------------+
| Print Countries                                  Company: 000 |
|------------------------------------------------------------------------|
|                                                                        |
| Country      from : 1..                                                 |
|              to   : 2..                                                  |
|                                                                        |
+--------------------------------------------------------------------------+
1.    Country from
2.    Country to
```

31.4 Print First Free Numbers (tcmcs0447m000)

```
tcmcs0447m000                               single-occ (4)    Form 1-1
+--------------------------------------------------------------------------+
| Print First Free Numbers                            Company: 000 |
|--------------------------------------------------------------------------|
|                                                                          |
| Type of Number       from : 1.......................                     |
|                      to   : 2.......................                     |
|                                                                          |
| Series               from : 3..                                         |
|                      to   : 4..                                         |
|                                                                          |
+--------------------------------------------------------------------------+
```

1.   Type of Number from
2.   Type of Number to
3.   Series from
4.   Series to

31.5 Print Forwarding Agents (tcmcs0480m000)

```
tcmcs0480m000                               single-occ (4)    Form 1-1
+--------------------------------------------------------------------------+
| Print Forwarding Agents                             Company: 000 |
|--------------------------------------------------------------------------|
|                                                                          |
| Forwarding Agent     from :    1..                                      |
|                      to   :    2..                                      |
|                                                                          |
| Supplier             from : 3.....                                      |
|                      to   : 4.....                                      |
+--------------------------------------------------------------------------+
```

1.   Forwarding Agent from
2.   Forwarding Agent to
3.   Supplier from
4.   Supplier to

31.6 Print Item Groups (tcmcs0423m000)

```
tcmcs0423m000                               single-occ (4)    Form 1-1
+--------------------------------------------------------------------------+
| Print Item Groups                                   Company: 000 |
|--------------------------------------------------------------------------|
|                                                                          |
| Item Group      from : 1.....                                          |
|                 to   : 2.....                                          |
|                                                                          |
+--------------------------------------------------------------------------+
```

1.   Item Group from
2.   Item Group to

31.7 Print Languages (tcmcs0446m000)

```
tcmcs0446m000                               single-occ (4)    Form 1-1
+--------------------------------------------------------------------------+
| Print Languages                                     Company: 000 |
|--------------------------------------------------------------------------|
|                                                                          |
| Language      from : 1..                                              |
|               to   : 2..                                              |
|                                                                          |
+--------------------------------------------------------------------------+
```

1.   Language from
2.   Language to

31.8 Print Lines of Business (tcmcs0431m000)

```
tcmcs0431m000                               single-occ (4)    Form 1-1
+--------------------------------------------------------------------------+
| Print Lines of Business                             Company: 000 |
|--------------------------------------------------------------------------|
|                                                                          |
```

```
| Line of Business        from : 1.....                              |
|                         to   : 2.....                              |
|                                                                    |
+--------------------------------------------------------------------+
1.    Line of Business from
2.    Line of Business to
31.9  Print Price Groups (tcmcs0424m000)
tcmcs0424m000                          single-occ (4)    Form 1-1
+--------------------------------------------------------------------+
| Print Price Groups                              Company: 000 |
|--------------------------------------------------------------------|
|                                                                    |
| Price Group        from : 1.....                                   |
|                    to   : 2.....                                   |
|                                                                    |
+--------------------------------------------------------------------+
1.    Price Group from
2.    Price Group to
31.10 Print Price Lists (tcmcs0434m000)
tcmcs0434m000                          single-occ (4)    Form 1-1
+--------------------------------------------------------------------+
| Print Price Lists                               Company: 000 |
|--------------------------------------------------------------------|
|                                                                    |
| Price List        from : 1..                                       |
|                   to   : 2..                                       |
|                                                                    |
+--------------------------------------------------------------------+
1.    Price List from
2.    Price List to
31.11 Print Reasons for Rejection (tcmcs0405m000)
tcmcs0405m000                          single-occ (4)    Form 1-1
+--------------------------------------------------------------------+
| Print Reasons for Rejection                     Company: 000 |
|--------------------------------------------------------------------|
|                                                                    |
| Reason                  from : 1..                                 |
|                         to   : 2..                                 |
|                                                                    |
+--------------------------------------------------------------------+
1.    Reason from
2.    Reason to
31.12 Print Product Types (tcmcs0415m000)
tcmcs0415m000                          single-occ (4)    Form 1-1
+--------------------------------------------------------------------+
| Print Product Types                             Company: 000 |
|--------------------------------------------------------------------|
|                                                                    |
| Product Type        from : 1..                                     |
|                     to   : 2..                                     |
|                                                                    |
+--------------------------------------------------------------------+
1.    Product Type from
2.    Product Type to
31.13 Print Routes (tcmcs0404m000)
tcmcs0404m000                          single-occ (4)    Form 1-1
+--------------------------------------------------------------------+
| Print Routes                                    Company: 000 |
|--------------------------------------------------------------------|
|                                                                    |
| Route    from : 1....                                              |
|          to   : 2....                                              |
|                                                                    |
```

```
+----------------------------------------------------------------------+
1.    Route from
2.    Route to
31.14 Print Seasonal Patterns (tcmcs0416m000)
tcmcs0416m000                              single-occ (4)   Form 1-1
+----------------------------------------------------------------------+
| Print Seasonal Patterns                            Company: 000 |
|----------------------------------------------------------------------|
|                                                                      |
| Seasonal Pattern          from : 1..                                |
|                           to   : 2..                                |
|                                                                      |
+----------------------------------------------------------------------+
1.    Seasonal Pattern from
2.    Seasonal Pattern to
31.15 Print Selection Codes (tcmcs0422m000)
tcmcs0422m000                              single-occ (4)   Form 1-1
+----------------------------------------------------------------------+
| Print Selection Codes                              Company: 000 |
|----------------------------------------------------------------------|
|                                                                      |
| Selection Code          from : 1..                                  |
|                         to   : 2..                                  |
|                                                                      |
+----------------------------------------------------------------------+
1.    Selection Code from
2.    Selection Code to
31.16 Print Signal Codes (tcmcs0418m000)
tcmcs0418m000                              single-occ (4)   Form 1-1
+----------------------------------------------------------------------+
| Print Signal Codes                                 Company: 000 |
|----------------------------------------------------------------------|
|                                                                      |
| Signal Code          from : 1..                                     |
|                      to   : 2..                                     |
|                                                                      |
+----------------------------------------------------------------------+
1.    Signal Code from
2.    Signal Code to
31.17 Print Statistics Groups (tcmcs0444m000)
tcmcs0444m000                              single-occ (4)   Form 1-1
+----------------------------------------------------------------------+
| Print Statistics Groups                            Company: 000 |
|----------------------------------------------------------------------|
|                                                                      |
| Statistics Group          from : 1.....                             |
|                           to   : 2.....                             |
|                                                                      |
+----------------------------------------------------------------------+
1.    Statistics Group from
2.    Statistics Group to
31.18 Print Terms of Delivery (tcmcs0441m000)
tcmcs0441m000                              single-occ (4)   Form 1-1
+----------------------------------------------------------------------+
| Print Terms of Delivery                            Company: 000 |
|----------------------------------------------------------------------|
|                                                                      |
| Terms of Delivery          from : 1..                               |
|                            to   : 2..                               |
|                                                                      |
| Print Language                  : 3..   4_____      |
|                                                                      |
+----------------------------------------------------------------------+
```

1.   Terms of Delivery from
2.   Terms of Delivery to
3.   Print Language
The language in which you want to print the texts linked to the code.
4.   Description

31.19 Print Titles (tcmcs0419m000)

```
tcmcs0419m000                              single-occ (4)    Form 1-1
+----------------------------------------------------------------------+
| Print Titles                                        Company: 000 |
|----------------------------------------------------------------------|
|                                                                      |
| Title        from : 1..                                              |
|              to   : 2..                                              |
|                                                                      |
+----------------------------------------------------------------------+
```

1.   Title from
2.   Title to

31.20 Print Units (tcmcs0401m000)

```
tcmcs0401m000                              single-occ (4)    Form 1-1
+----------------------------------------------------------------------+
| Print Units                                         Company: 000 |
|----------------------------------------------------------------------|
|                                                                      |
| Unit        from : 1..                                               |
|             to   : 2..                                               |
|                                                                      |
+----------------------------------------------------------------------+
```

1.   Unit from
2.   Unit to

31.21 Print Units by Language (tcmcs0407m000)

```
tcmcs0407m000                              single-occ (4)    Form 1-1
+----------------------------------------------------------------------+
| Print Units by Language                             Company: 000 |
|----------------------------------------------------------------------|
|                                                                      |
| Code          from : 1..                                             |
|               to   : 2..                                             |
|                                                                      |
| Language      from : 3..                                             |
|               to   : 4..                                             |
|                                                                      |
+----------------------------------------------------------------------+
```

1.   Code from
2.   Code to
3.   Language from
4.   Language to

31.22 Print Unit Sets (tcmcs0406m000)

```
tcmcs0406m000                              single-occ (4)    Form 1-1
+----------------------------------------------------------------------+
| Print Unit Sets                                     Company: 000 |
|----------------------------------------------------------------------|
|                                                                      |
| Unit Set       from   1.....                                         |
|                to     2.....                                         |
|                                                                      |
```

```
+-----------------------------------------------------------------------+
1.    Unit Set from
2.    Unit Set to
31.23 Print Units by Unit Set (tcmcs0412m000)
tcmcs0412m000                           single-occ (4)    Form 1-1
+-----------------------------------------------------------------------+
| Print Units by Unit Set                            Company: 000 |
|-----------------------------------------------------------------------|
|                                                                       |
| Unit Set          from : 1.....                                       |
|                   to   : 2.....                                       |
|                                                                       |
| Unit              from : 3..                                          |
|                   to   : 4..                                          |
|                                                                       |
+-----------------------------------------------------------------------+
1.    Unitset
2.    Unitset
3.    Unit
4.    Unit
31.24 Print Warehouses (tcmcs0403m000)
tcmcs0403m000                           single-occ (4)    Form 1-1
+-----------------------------------------------------------------------+
| Print Warehouses                                   Company: 000 |
|-----------------------------------------------------------------------|
|                                                                       |
| Warehouse         from : 1..                                          |
|                   to   : 2..                                          |
|                                                                       |
+-----------------------------------------------------------------------+
1.    Warehouse from
2.    Warehouse to
31.25 Print Quality Groups (tcmcs0429m000)
tcmcs0429m000                           single-occ (4)    Form 1-1
+-----------------------------------------------------------------------+
| Print Quality Groups                               Company: 000 |
|-----------------------------------------------------------------------|
|                                                                       |
| Quality Group        from : 1.....                                    |
|                      to   : 2.....                                    |
|                                                                       |
+-----------------------------------------------------------------------+
1.    Quality Group
2.    Quality Group
31.26 Print Skills (tcmcs0430m000)
tcmcs0430m000                           single-occ (4)    Form 1-1
+-----------------------------------------------------------------------+
| Print Skills                                       Company: 000 |
|-----------------------------------------------------------------------|
|                                                                       |
| Skill            From : 1...                                          |
|                  To   : 2...                                          |
|                                                                       |
+-----------------------------------------------------------------------+
1.    Skill
2.    Skill
32    Item Master Data
32.1  General
```

OBJECTIVE OF BUSINESS OBJECT

This b-object makes it possible to maintain data of standard items in "BAAN IV".
These items are split into the following item types:

- Cost
- Generic

Manufactured
- Purchased
- Service
- Subcontracting

Standard item data is part of the complete product structure. This structure generally consists of data relating to:
- items, such as inventory, delivery time, and cost price;
- the structure of items, such as production bills of material;
- operations to be carried out, routing data.

Data of customized items is recorded in the module Project Control (PCS).
Data of generic items is recorded in the module Product Configuration (PCF).
A variety of item data is adjusted from other modules and sessions.
An important aspect of item control is the integral control of the flow of goods. This is partly based on forecasts and partly based on customer-specific orders. The point where these two control methods converge is often a stock point.
The subfunctions belonging to this b-object will give more detailed information on:
- Order Policy
- Order System
- Order Method

Combination of fields in the item file determine how data is processed in "BAAN IV". One of these data processing methods is the generation of recommended orders for items.
Some of the criteria for generating recommended orders is determined via the session "Maintain Item Data (tiitm0101m000)" by setting item data, such as:
- Order System
- Order Method
- Fixed Order Quantity
- Economic Order Quantity
- Re-Order Point
- Order Interval
- First Allowed Order Date
- Maximum Inventory
- Inventory Carrying Costs
- Expected Annual Issue
- Order Costs

Display the procedure and show the sessions in:
- Item Master Data Procedure

In this b-object only the session "Maintain Item Data (tiitm0101m000)" must be run. You are advised to start with the session "Maintain Item Default Data (tiitm0110m000)".

33   Introduction to BAAN Common Error Recovery
33.1 General
OBJECTIVE OF BUSINESS OBJECT
This b-object contains auxiliary programs for checking and eliminating inconsistencies in the database. This may be useful when the customer balances in the customer file (outstanding orders/invoices) are incorrect. The programs in this business object allow you to rebuild those customer balances.

33.2 Session Overview

Seq.	Session	Description	Session Usage
3	tccom2210m000	Rebuild Customer Order Balance	Optional
4	tccom2220m000	Rebuild Supplier Order Balance	Optional

34   Optional Sessions
34.1 Rebuild Customer Order Balance (tccom2210m000)
SESSION OBJECTIVE
To rebuild the order balance for customers.

SEE ALSO KEYWORD(S)
* Customers

```
tccom2210m000                        single-occ (4)    Form 1-1
+---------------------------------------------------------------------+
|  Rebuild Customer Order Balance                   Company: 000  |
|-----------------------------------------------------------------|
|                                                                 |
|  Customer             from : 1.....                             |
|                       to   : 2.....                             |
|                                                                 |
|  Test                      : 3....                              |
|                                                                 |
|  +------------------------------------------+                   |
|  | Customer    : 4_____                    |                   |
|  | Order Type  : 5_____  |                   |
|  | Order       : 6_____                   |                   |
|  +------------------------------------------+                   |
|                                                                 |
+---------------------------------------------------------------------+
```

1.   from Customer
2.   to Customer
3.   [y/n]
4.   Customer
5.   Number Type
6.   orno.p

34.2 Rebuild Supplier Order Balance (tccom2220m000)

SESSION OBJECTIVE
To rebuild the order balance for suppliers.

SEE ALSO KEYWORD(S)
* Suppliers

```
tccom2220m000                        single-occ (4)    Form 1-1
+---------------------------------------------------------------------+
|  Rebuild Supplier Order Balance                   Company: 000  |
|-----------------------------------------------------------------|
|                                                                 |
|  Supplier             from : 1.....                             |
|                       to   : 2.....                             |
|                                                                 |
|  Test                      : 3....                              |
|                                                                 |
|  +----------------------+                                       |
|  | Supplier    : 4_____ |                                       |
|  | Order       : 5_____ |                                       |
|  +----------------------+                                       |
|                                                                 |
+---------------------------------------------------------------------+
```

1.   from Supplier
2.   to Supplier
3.   [y/n] Test
4.   Supplier
The number identifying the supplier for whom the purchase order is intended.
5.   Purchase Order
The order number identifying the purchase order.

35   Introduction to System Performance
35.1 Session Overview

Seq.	Session	Description	Session Usage
1	tcmcs0197m000	Maintain Use of Performance Boosters	Mandatory
2	tcmcs0198m000	Maintain Table Boosters	Mandatory

```
|   3 | tcmcs0497m000 | Print Use of Performance Boosters    | Print
|
|   4 | tcmcs0498m000 | Print Table Boosters                 | Print
|
|   5 | tcmcs0597m000 | Display Use of Performance Boosters  | Display
|
|   6 | tcmcs0598m000 | Display Table Boosters               | Display
|
```

---

36   Mandatory Sessions

36.1 Maintain Use of Performance Boosters (tcmcs0197m000)

SESSION OBJECTIVE

To link performance boosters to sessions, to users, or to a combination of
these.

NOTE: Wherever in an application a booster can be applied, but that booster has
not been set in this session, the following will occur: table Use of Performance
Boosters (tcmcs097) will be inserted with the booster concerned for the user and
the session that is running and the validation in the field "Booster Valid" will
be "Not Active"

HOW TO USE THE SESSION

Performance Boosters can be used at three levels, each starting with another
identifier. The following combinations may therefore be made:

+---+
| Session | Performance Booster | User |
|---------------------+---------------------+-------------------|
| Performance Booster | Session | Performance Booster |
| User | User | Session |
+---+

It is necessary to always fill in the performance booster which should be used
and the session for which the booster is valid.

SEE ALSO KEYWORD(S)

•   Use of Performance Boosters

tcmcs0197m000   multi/group (3   Form 1-3 >

+--+
Maintain Use of Performance Boosters   Company: 000
Session   : 1........... 2_____
Performance Booster   User   Value   Booster Valid
3.....................   4..........   5........   6.............
+--+

1.   Session

Entering the session will make the system employ the performance booster in this
session, if applicable. If it is not applicable, entering the session will have
no effect at all.

See the field "Performance Booster" for a list of sessions to which the
performance booster is relevant.

2.   Description

3.   Performance Booster

For further information, see keyword(s)
"Use of Performance Boosters".

Available performance boosters: * [GO1] Display Interval * [G02] Number of
Servers
* [G03] Maximum Invoice Lines * [G04] Embedded Financial Int.

Display Interval With this option you can influence the time between two refresh
actions. Decreasing the frequency with which the program refreshes the screen
will have a positive effect on the speed of large processing sessions.

Use is recommended in the sessions:

•   Generate Planned (MPS)/MRP Orders/Batches (timrp1210m000)
•   Generate Master Production Schedule (timps3201m000)

- Generate Planned PRP Orders (tipcs5201m000)
- Transfer Planned PRP Purchase Orders (tipcs5260m000)
- Generate Inbound Advice (tdilc4203m000)
- Generate Outbound Advice (tdilc4201m000)

Numbers of Servers This option allows you to set the extra number of bshells to be started parallel to the session concerned, which you should fill in the field "Session". It is also possible to join the Number of Servers to one "User".
Use is recommended in the sessions:
- Update Sales Statistics (tdsst0201m000)
- Print Sales Invoices (tdsls4404m000)

If booster has been set for this session, the session "Process Delivered Sales Orders (tdsls4223m000)" will run parallel to printing the invoices.
- Process Delivered Sales Orders (tdsls4223m000)
- Process Delivered Purchase Orders (tdpur4223m000)
- Select Invoices for Payment (tfcmg1220m000)
- Audit Batches (tfgld1211s000)
- Generate Planned (MPS)/MRP Orders/Batches (timrp1210m000)
- Generate Master Production Schedule (timps3201m000)
- Execute Single Site Master Production Scheduling (timps3202s000)
- Print Cost Control (tpppc4411m000)

Maximum Invoice Lines Whenever the possibility to collect several orders on one invoice is used, invoices can contain a great number of lines. The transaction to book these lines to BAAN Finance can become too large, depending on e.g. the size of the rollback-segments of your database. This option limits the maximum number of lines on one invoice, thus reducing the size of the transaction mentioned.
Use is only possible in:
- Print Sales Invoices (tdsls4404m000)

The check on maximum invoice lines will not be performed if the field "Invoicing by Installments" for the current order is set to "Yes". Printing will continue untill the end of this order.
- Print Invoices (trics2400m000)
- Print Contract Installment Invoices (tssma2472m000)
- Print Service Order Invoices (tssma3473m000)
- Print Invoices (tppin4474m000)

Embedded Financial Integration With this option a financial integration will be processed using a Dynamic Link Library instead of the parallel running session "Update Integr Trans and Real Time Post to Finance (backgrd.) (tfgld4200s000)". This will speed up the sessions in which a financial integration is involved.
4.   User
The user for whom the booster is valid. If this field is left empty the booster is valid for all users that start the session.
5.   Value
6.   Booster Valid

tcmcs0197m000   multi/group (3 < Form 2-3 >
+--+
Maintain Use of Performance Boosters   Company: 000
Performance Booster   : 1.......................
Session   Description   User   Value   Booster Valid
2........... 3_____ 4.......... 5......... 6..............
+--+

1.   Performance Booster
For further information, see keyword(s)
"Use of Performance Boosters".
Available performance boosters: * [GO1] Display Interval * [G02] Number of Servers
* [G03] Maximum Invoice Lines * [G04] Embedded Financial Int.

Display Interval With this option you can influence the time between two refresh actions. Decreasing the frequency with which the program refreshes the screen will have a positive effect on the speed of large processing sessions.
Use is recommended in the sessions:
• Generate Planned (MPS)/MRP Orders/Batches (timrp1210m000)
• Generate Master Production Schedule (timps3201m000)
• Generate Planned PRP Orders (tipcs5201m000)
• Transfer Planned PRP Purchase Orders (tipcs5260m000)
• Generate Inbound Advice (tdilc4203m000)
• Generate Outbound Advice (tdilc4201m000)
Numbers of Servers This option allows you to set the extra number of bshells to be started parallel to the session concerned, which you should fill in the field "Session". It is also possible to join the Number of Servers to one "User".
Use is recommended in the sessions:
• Update Sales Statistics (tdsst0201m000)
• Print Sales Invoices (tdsls4404m000)
If booster has been set for this session, the session "Process Delivered Sales Orders (tdsls4223m000)" will run parallel to printing the invoices.
• Process Delivered Sales Orders (tdsls4223m000)
• Process Delivered Purchase Orders (tdpur4223m000)
• Select Invoices for Payment (tfcmg1220m000)
• Audit Batches (tfgld1211s000)
• Generate Planned (MPS)/MRP Orders/Batches (timrp1210m000)
• Generate Master Production Schedule (timps3201m000)
• Execute Single Site Master Production Scheduling (timps3202s000)
• Print Cost Control (tpppc4411m000)
Maximum Invoice Lines Whenever the possibility to collect several orders on one invoice is used, invoices can contain a great number of lines. The transaction to book these lines to BAAN Finance can become too large, depending on e.g. the size of the rollback-segments of your database. This option limits the maximum number of lines on one invoice, thus reducing the size of the transaction mentioned.
Use is only possible in:
• Print Sales Invoices (tdsls4404m000)
The check on maximum invoice lines will not be performed if the field "Invoicing by Installments" for the current order is set to "Yes". Printing will continue untill the end of this order.
• Print Invoices (trics2400m000)
• Print Contract Installment Invoices (tssma2472m000)
• Print Service Order Invoices (tssma3473m000)
• Print Invoices (tppin4474m000)
Embedded Financial Integration With this option a financial integration will be processed using a Dynamic Link Library instead of the parallel running session "Update Integr Trans and Real Time Post to Finance (backgrd.) (tfgld4200s000)". This will speed up the sessions in which a financial integration is involved.
2. Session
Entering the session will make the system employ the performance booster in this session, if applicable. If it is not applicable, entering the session will have no effect at all.
See the field "Performance Booster" for a list of sessions to which the performance booster is relevant.
3. Description
4. User
The user for whom the booster is valid. If this field is left empty the booster is valid for all users that start the session.
5. Value
6. Booster Valid

```
tcmcs0197m000                                          multi/group (3  < Form 3-3
+----------------------------------------------------------------------------+
| Maintain Use of Performance Boosters                        Company: 000   |
|----------------------------------------------------------------------------|
|                                                                            |
| User                       : 1.......... 2_____     |
```

```
|                                                                            |
|   Performance Booster          Session        Value        Booster Valid   |
|                                                                            |
|   3...................         4............   5.........   6.............  |
|                                                                            |
+----------------------------------------------------------------------------+
```

1.   User
The user for whom the booster is valid. If this field is left empty the booster
is valid for all users that start the session.
2.   Description
3.   Performance Booster
For further information, see keyword(s)
"Use of Performance Boosters".
Available performance boosters: * [GO1] Display Interval * [G02] Number of
Servers
* [G03] Maximum Invoice Lines * [G04] Embedded Financial Int.
Display Interval With this option you can influence the time between two refresh
actions. Decreasing the frequency with which the program refreshes the screen
will have a positive effect on the speed of large processing sessions.
Use is recommended in the sessions:
•   Generate Planned (MPS)/MRP Orders/Batches (timrp1210m000)
•   Generate Master Production Schedule (timps3201m000)
•   Generate Planned PRP Orders (tipcs5201m000)
•   Transfer Planned PRP Purchase Orders (tipcs5260m000)
•   Generate Inbound Advice (tdilc4203m000)
•   Generate Outbound Advice (tdilc4201m000)
Numbers of Servers This option allows you to set the extra number of bshells to
be started parallel to the session concerned, which you should fill in the field
"Session". It is also possible to join the Number of Servers to one "User".
Use is recommended in the sessions:
•   Update Sales Statistics (tdsst0201m000)
•   Print Sales Invoices (tdsls4404m000)
If booster has been set for this session, the session "Process Delivered Sales
Orders (tdsls4223m000)" will run parallel to printing the invoices.
•   Process Delivered Sales Orders (tdsls4223m000)
•   Process Delivered Purchase Orders (tdpur4223m000)
•   Select Invoices for Payment (tfcmg1220m000)
•   Audit Batches (tfgld1211s000)
•   Generate Planned (MPS)/MRP Orders/Batches (timrp1210m000)
•   Generate Master Production Schedule (timps3201m000)
•   Execute Single Site Master Production Scheduling (timps3202s000)
•   Print Cost Control (tpppc4411m000)
Maximum Invoice Lines Whenever the possibility to collect several orders on one
invoice is used, invoices can contain a great number of lines. The transaction
to book these lines to BAAN Finance can become too large, depending on e.g. the
size of the rollback-segments of your database. This option limits the maximum
number of lines on one invoice, thus reducing the size of the transaction
mentioned.
Use is only possible in:
•   Print Sales Invoices (tdsls4404m000)
The check on maximum invoice lines will not be performed if the field "Invoicing
by Installments" for the current order is set to "Yes". Printing will continue
untill the end of this order.
•   Print Invoices (trics2400m000)
•   Print Contract Installment Invoices (tssma2472m000)
•   Print Service Order Invoices (tssma3473m000)
•   Print Invoices (tppin4474m000)
Embedded Financial Integration With this option a financial integration will be
processed using a Dynamic Link Library instead of the parallel running session
"Update Integr Trans and Real Time Post to Finance (backgrd.) (tfgld4200s000)".
This will speed up the sessions in which a financial integration is involved.
4.   Session

Entering the session will make the system employ the performance booster in this session, if applicable. If it is not applicable, entering the session will have no effect at all.
See the field "Performance Booster" for a list of sessions to which the performance booster is relevant.
5.   Value
6.   Booster Valid
36.2 Maintain Table Boosters (tcmcs0198m000)
SESSION OBJECTIVE
This session can be used to link table boosters to sessions or users.
HOW TO USE THE SESSION
Table boosters can be defined at three levels. These levels are explained in figure below:
Start input on:

```
    1st form      2nd form      3rd form
+-----------------------------------+
| Session    | Table name | User        |
|-----------+-----------+-----------|
| User       | Session    | Session     |
| Table name | User       | Table name  |
+-----------------------------------+
```

Filling in the table name is mandatory in all situations.
SEE ALSO KEYWORD(S)
•   Table Boosters

```
tcmcs0198m000                              multi/group (3    Form 1-3 >
+-------------------------------------------------------------------------+
| Maintain Table Boosters                                Company: 000  |
|-------------------------------------------------------------------------|
|                                                                         |
| Session      : 1.......... 2_____           |
|                                                                         |
| User         Name            Table   Load Option Max No  Booster      |
|                              Name                of Rows Valid         |
|                                                                         |
| 3.......... 4_____ 5....... 6.......... 7........ 8...........  |
|                                                                         |
+-------------------------------------------------------------------------+
```

1.   Session
Entering the session will make the system employ the performance booster in this session, if applicable. If it is not applicable, entering the session will have no effect at all.
See the field "Performance Booster" for a list of sessions to which the performance booster is relevant.
2.   Description
3.   User
The user for whom the booster is valid. If this field is left empty the booster is valid for all users that access the table.
4.   Description
5.   Table Name
The table which should be loaded in internal memory. The tables can be loaded in two ways: Full or Incremental. Choose one of these options in the field "Load Option".
Table codes and descriptions can be found by session "Display Table Definitions (ttadv4520m000)".
6.   Load Option
This field indicates how tables will be kept in internal memory. The options are:
Full: The table in the field "Table Name" will be loaded for all rows in the table, unless the number of rows is greater than the number of rows mentioned in the field "Maximum Number of Rows".
Incremental: Each new accessed row of the table will be kept in the internal memory. In this way any searches for the same row will be faster.
7.   Maximum Number of Rows

The maximum number of rows which can be loaded into internal memory for the table specified in "Table Name".

8.   Booster Valid

```
+--------------------------------------------------------------------------+
| Maintain Table Boosters                              Company: 000 |
|--------------------------------------------------------------------------|
|                                                                          |
| Table Name      : 1.......  2_____            |
|                                                                          |
| Session        Description    User        Load Option Max No   Booster   |
|                                                        of Rows  Valid     |
|                                                                          |
| 3............ 4_____  5.......... 6.......... 7........ 8........ |
|                                                                          |
+--------------------------------------------------------------------------+
```

1.   Table Name
The table which should be loaded in internal memory. The tables can be loaded in two ways: Full or Incremental. Choose one of these options in the field "Load Option".
Table codes and descriptions can be found by session "Display Table Definitions (ttadv4520m000)".

2.   Description

3.   Session
Entering the session will make the system employ the performance booster in this session, if applicable. If it is not applicable, entering the session will have no effect at all.
See the field "Performance Booster" for a list of sessions to which the performance booster is relevant.

4.   Description

5.   User
The user for whom the booster is valid. If this field is left empty the booster is valid for all users that access the table.

6.   Load Option
This field indicates how tables will be kept in internal memory. The options are:
Full: The table in the field "Table Name" will be loaded for all rows in the table, unless the number of rows is greater than the number of rows mentioned in the field "Maximum Number of Rows".
Incremental: Each new accessed row of the table will be kept in the internal memory. In this way any searches for the same row will be faster.

7.   Maximum Number of Rows
The maximum number of rows which can be loaded into internal memory for the table specified in "Table Name".

8.   Booster Valid

```
+--------------------------------------------------------------------------+
| Maintain Table Boosters                              Company: 000 |
|--------------------------------------------------------------------------|
|                                                                          |
| User: 1..........  2_____                      |
|                                                                          |
| Session        Description    Table      Load Option Max No   Booster    |
|                               Name                    of Rows  Valid      |
|                                                                          |
| 3............ 4_____  5....... 6.......... 7........ 8........    |
|                                                                          |
+--------------------------------------------------------------------------+
```

1.   User
The user for whom the booster is valid. If this field is left empty the booster is valid for all users that access the table.

2.   Description

3.   Session

Entering the session will make the system employ the performance booster in this session, if applicable. If it is not applicable, entering the session will have no effect at all.
See the field "Performance Booster" for a list of sessions to which the performance booster is relevant.

4.   Description
5.   Table Name
The table which should be loaded in internal memory. The tables can be loaded in two ways: Full or Incremental. Choose one of these options in the field "Load Option".
Table codes and descriptions can be found by session "Display Table Definitions (ttadv4520m000)".

6.   Load Option
This field indicates how tables will be kept in internal memory. The options are:
Full: The table in the field "Table Name" will be loaded for all rows in the table, unless the number of rows is greater than the number of rows mentioned in the field "Maximum Number of Rows".
Incremental: Each new accessed row of the table will be kept in the internal memory. In this way any searches for the same row will be faster.

7.   Maximum Number of Rows
The maximum number of rows which can be loaded into internal memory for the table specified in "Table Name".

8.   Booster Valid

37   Other Print Sessions

37.1 Print Use of Performance Boosters (tcmcs0497m000)

tcmcs0497m000   single-occ (4)   Form 1-1

```
+----------------------------------------------------------------------+
| Print Use of Performance Boosters                     Company: 000   |
|----------------------------------------------------------------------|
|                                                                      |
| Session              From : 1............                            |
|                      To   : 2............                            |
|                                                                      |
| Performance Booster  From : 3......................                  |
|                      To   : 4......................                  |
|                                                                      |
| User                 From : 5..........                             |
|                      To   : 6..........                             |
|                                                                      |
+----------------------------------------------------------------------+
```

1.   Session Code
2.   Session Code
3.   Performance Facility
4.   Performance Facility
5.   User
6.   User

37.2 Print Table Boosters (tcmcs0498m000)

tcmcs0498m000   single-occ (4)   Form 1-1

```
+----------------------------------------------------------------------+
| Print Table Boosters                                  Company: 000   |
|----------------------------------------------------------------------|
|                                                                      |
| Session      From : 1............                                    |
|              To   : 2............                                    |
|                                                                      |
| User         From : 3..........                                     |
|              To   : 4..........                                     |
|                                                                      |
| Table Name   From : 5.......                                         |
|              To   : 6.......                                         |
|                                                                      |
+----------------------------------------------------------------------+
```

```
1.     Session Code
2.     Session Code
3.     User
4.     User
5.     Table Name
6.     Table Name
COV - Conversion to BAAN IV
```

1   Introduction to Conversion to BAAN IV
1.1   Session Overview

Seq.	Session	Description	Session Usage
1	tccov0000m000	Conversion of TRITON 3.x -> BAAN IV	Mandatory
101	tccov1001m000	Conversion of Distribution 3.x -> 3.1B	Optional
102	tccov1002m000	Conv of Distribution 3.1B -> BAAN IV	Optional
201	tccov2001m000	Chng Sign in Open Item Table (tfacp200)	Optional
202	tccov2002m000	Change Step for Antic. Unalloc/Adv Paym	Optional
203	tccov2003m000	Check Standing Order (tfcmg114)	Optional
204	tccov2004m000	Check AnticipatedDoc (facp200/tfacr200)	Optional
205	tccov2005m000	Change Enumerated Field (tfcmg108)	Optional
301	tccov3001m000	Conv of Manufacturing 3.1A -> BAAN IV	Optional
302	tccov3002m000	Conversion Units to Units by Unit Sets	Optional
303	tccov3003m000	Conversion Unit Conversion Factors	Optional
304	tccov3004m000	Fill Auxiliary Item Table (tiitm100)	Optional
501	tccov5001m000	Conv of Transportation -> BAAN IV (TCO)	Optional

2   Mandatory Sessions
2.1   Conversion of TRITON 3.x -> BAAN IV (tccov0000m000)
SESSION OBJECTIVE
This session will convert your tables to BAAN IV. Depending on the indicated
package-conversions the following sessions will automatically be started:
BAAN Distribution: Conversion of Distribution 3.x -> 3.1B (tccov1001m000)
Conversion of Distribution 3.1B -> BAAN IV (tccov1002m000)
BAAN Manufacturing: Conversion of Manufacturing 3.1A -> BAAN IV (tccov3001m000)
Conversion Units to Units by Unit Sets (tccov3002m000) Conversion Unit
Conversion Factors (tccov3003m000) Fill Auxiliary Item Table (tiitm100)
(tccov3004m000)
BAAN Finance: Change Sign in Open Item Table (tfacp200) (tccov2001m000) Change
Step for Antic. Unalloc/Adv Payments (tccov2002m000) Check Standing Order
(tfcmg114) (tccov2003m000) Check Anticipated Document (facp200/tfacr200)
(tccov2004m000) Change Enumerated Field (tfcmg108) (tccov2005m000)
BAAN Transportation: Conversion of Transportation 3.x -> BAAN IV (TCO)
(tccov5001m000)

```
tccov0000m000                              single-occ (1)    Form 1-3 >
+----------------------------------------------------------------------+
| Conversion of TRITON 3.x -> BAAN IV                     Company: 000 |
|----------------------------------------------------------------------|
|                                                                      |
```

```
| Original TRITON Version       : 1.........                          |
|                                                                     |
| USED PACKAGES FOR CONVERSION                                        |
| BAAN Distribution             : 2....                               |
| BAAN Manufacturing            : 3....                               |
| BAAN Finance                  : 4....                               |
| BAAN Project                  : 5....                               |
| BAAN Transportation           : 6....                               |
|                                                                     |
| Real Conversion               : 7....                               |
|                                                                     |
|                                                                     |
| Version           : 1_____                                      |
| User              : 8_____                                |
| Date              : 9_____                                      |
| Time              : 10___                                           |
| Number of Retries : 11_                                             |
+---------------------------------------------------------------------+
```

1.   Original TRITON Version
The original version of Triton which must be converted.
2.   BAAN Distribution
Indicate if Distribution is used in the to be converted version.
3.   BAAN Manufacturing
Indicate if Manufacturing is used in the to be converted version.
4.   BAAN Finance
Indicate if Finance is used in the to be converted version.
5.   BAAN Project
Indicate if Project is used in the to be converted version.
6.   BAAN Transportation
Indicate if Transportation is used in the to be converted version.
7.   Real Conversion
Yes
The system does a real conversion and tables will be updated.
No
The system does no real conversion and table won't be updated.
For every real and no real conversion, a log-file will be made which you can
find in the directory $BSE\log. The name of the log-file depends on the session
which has been run and has the format log.covxxxx.
8.   User
The logincode of the user who has run the conversion.
9.   Date
The date you entered the session and a conversion has been run.
10.   Time
The time you entered the session and a conversion has been run.
11.   Number of Retries
Number of times the conversion program has been started.

tccov0000m000   single-occ (1) < Form 2-3 >

```
+---------------------------------------------------------------------+
| Conversion of TRITON 3.x -> BAAN IV                  Company: 000   |
|---------------------------------------------------------------------|
| BAAN Distribution                                                   |
| Conv. of Distribution 3.x -> 3.1B       : 1_____  |
| Conv. of Distribution 3.1B -> BAAN 4.0  : 2_____  |
| BAAN Manufacturing                                                  |
| Conv. of Manufacturing 3.1A -> BAAN IV  : 3_____  |
| Conv. units to units/unit sets          : 4_____  |
| Conv. units conv. factors               : 5_____  |
| Fill auxiliary Item table (tiitm100)    : 6_____  |
| BAAN Finance                                                        |
| Change sign in Open Item Table (tfacp200) : 7_____  |
| Change step for antic. unall./adv. paym. : 8_____  |
| Check standing order (tfcmg114)         : 9_____  |
| Check adv./unall. paym.rec.             : 10_____  |
```

```
|   Change enumerated Field (tfcmg108)        : 11_____           |
|   Update payment difference (ant.)          : 12_____           |
|                                                                               |
+-------------------------------------------------------------------------------+
```

1.   Conv. of Distribution 3.x -> 3.1B
The status of the specified session of the conversion. The possible options are:
•   Status not defined : The initial value.
•   Execution not necessary : For the conversion it is not necessary to run
this session.
•   Not executed : For the conversion it is necessary to run this session, but
the session is not executed yet.
•   Execution aborted : During running the session an error occurred.
•   In process : The session is running.
•   Execution completed : The session is executed and no error occurred

2.   Conv. of Distribution 3.1B -> BAAN 4.0
The status of the specified session of the conversion. The possible options are:
•   Status not defined : The initial value.
•   Execution not necessary : For the conversion it is not necessary to run
this session.
•   Not executed : For the conversion it is necessary to run this session, but
the session is not executed yet.
•   Execution aborted : During running the session an error occurred.
•   In process : The session is running.
•   Execution completed : The session is executed and no error occurred

3.   Conv. of Manufacturing 3.1A -> BAAN IV
The status of the specified session of the conversion. The possible options are:
•   Status not defined : The initial value.
•   Execution not necessary : For the conversion it is not necessary to run
this session.
•   Not executed : For the conversion it is necessary to run this session, but
the session is not executed yet.
•   Execution aborted : During running the session an error occurred.
•   In process : The session is running.
•   Execution completed : The session is executed and no error occurred

4.   Conv. units to units/unit sets
The status of the specified session of the conversion. The possible options are:
•   Status not defined : The initial value.
•   Execution not necessary : For the conversion it is not necessary to run
this session.
•   Not executed : For the conversion it is necessary to run this session, but
the session is not executed yet.
•   Execution aborted : During running the session an error occurred.
•   In process : The session is running.
•   Execution completed : The session is executed and no error occurred

5.   Conv. units conv. factors
The status of the specified session of the conversion. The possible options are:
•   Status not defined : The initial value.
•   Execution not necessary : For the conversion it is not necessary to run
this session.
•   Not executed : For the conversion it is necessary to run this session, but
the session is not executed yet.
•   Execution aborted : During running the session an error occurred.
•   In process : The session is running.
•   Execution completed : The session is executed and no error occurred

6.   Fill auxiliary Item table (tiitm100)
The status of the specified session of the conversion. The possible options are:
•   Status not defined : The initial value.
•   Execution not necessary : For the conversion it is not necessary to run
this session.
•   Not executed : For the conversion it is necessary to run this session, but
the session is not executed yet.
•   Execution aborted : During running the session an error occurred.
•   In process : The session is running.

- Execution completed : The session is executed and no error occurred
7. Change sign in Open Item Table (tfacp200)
The status of the specified session of the conversion. The possible options are:
- Status not defined : The initial value.
- Execution not necessary : For the conversion it is not necessary to run this session.
- Not executed : For the conversion it is necessary to run this session, but the session is not executed yet.
- Execution aborted : During running the session an error occurred.
- In process : The session is running.
- Execution completed : The session is executed and no error occurred
8. Change step for antic. unall./adv. paym.
The status of the specified session of the conversion. The possible options are:
- Status not defined : The initial value.
- Execution not necessary : For the conversion it is not necessary to run this session.
- Not executed : For the conversion it is necessary to run this session, but the session is not executed yet.
- Execution aborted : During running the session an error occurred.
- In process : The session is running.
- Execution completed : The session is executed and no error occurred
9. Check standing order (tfcmg114)
The status of the specified session of the conversion. The possible options are:
- Status not defined : The initial value.
- Execution not necessary : For the conversion it is not necessary to run this session.
- Not executed : For the conversion it is necessary to run this session, but the session is not executed yet.
- Execution aborted : During running the session an error occurred.
- In process : The session is running.
- Execution completed : The session is executed and no error occurred
10. Check adv./unall. paym.rec.
The status of the specified session of the conversion. The possible options are:
- Status not defined : The initial value.
- Execution not necessary : For the conversion it is not necessary to run this session.
- Not executed : For the conversion it is necessary to run this session, but the session is not executed yet.
- Execution aborted : During running the session an error occurred.
- In process : The session is running.
- Execution completed : The session is executed and no error occurred
11. Change enumerated Field (tfcmg108)
The status of the specified session of the conversion. The possible options are:
- Status not defined : The initial value.
- Execution not necessary : For the conversion it is not necessary to run this session.
- Not executed : For the conversion it is necessary to run this session, but the session is not executed yet.
- Execution aborted : During running the session an error occurred.
- In process : The session is running.
- Execution completed : The session is executed and no error occurred
12. Update payment difference (ant.)
The status of the specified session of the conversion. The possible options are:
- Status not defined : The initial value.
- Execution not necessary : For the conversion it is not necessary to run this session.
- Not executed : For the conversion it is necessary to run this session, but the session is not executed yet.
- Execution aborted : During running the session an error occurred.
- In process : The session is running.
- Execution completed : The session is executed and no error occurred

```
|-------------------------------------------------------------------|
|                                                                   |
| BAAN Transportation                                               |
| Trans. Conv 3.x -> BAAN IV (TCO) : 1_____       |
| BAAN Project                     : 2_____       |
|                                                                   |
+-------------------------------------------------------------------+
```

1.   Conversion of Transportation 3.x -> BAAN IV (TCO)
The status of the specified session of the conversion. The possible options are:
• Status not defined : The initial value.
• Execution not necessary : For the conversion it is not necessary to run this session.
• Not executed : For the conversion it is necessary to run this session, but the session is not executed yet.
• Execution aborted : During running the session an error occurred.
• In process : The session is running.
• Execution completed : The session is executed and no error occurred
2.   BAAN Project
The status of the specified session of the conversion. The possible options are:
• Status not defined : The initial value.
• Execution not necessary : For the conversion it is not necessary to run this session.
• Not executed : For the conversion it is necessary to run this session, but the session is not executed yet.
• Execution aborted : During running the session an error occurred.
• In process : The session is running.
• Execution completed : The session is executed and no error occurred
3   Optional Sessions
3.1   Conversion of Distribution 3.x -> 3.1B (tccov1001m000)
SESSION OBJECTIVE
This session will only be executed if the original version has to be upgraded to 3.1B. This session is an intermediate step for the conversion to BAAN IV.
This session will convert the following tables:
• Selections
• Selection Lines
• Letters
• Layouts by Letter
• Planned INV Purchase Orders
• Statuses
• Messages to be Generated
• Generated Messages
• Generated Batchnumbers
• Purchase Orders
• Receipts
• Sales Orders
• Customers
A textfile will be created for "Selections". This text will be filled with the Expressions of the "Selection Lines".
A textfile will be created for "Letters". This text will be filled with the Layouts of the "Layouts by Letter".
If the Company of "Planned INV Purchase Orders" is equal to 0 then there will be an update. The new company number will be derived from the Supplier of the "Planned INV Purchase Orders".
The field Parent Relation of table "Messages to be Generated" will be filled with the Relation of the same table.
The fields Network, Our Reference, Parent Relation, Date Sent, Time Sent, Send Status and Sequence No. of table "Generated Batchnumbers" will be filled with the fields Network, Our Reference, Relation, Date Sent, Time Sent, Send Status and Sequence No. of table "Generated Messages".
The field Finance Company of table "Receipts" will be updated with field Company of table "Purchase Orders".

If the field Financial Customer Group of table "Sales Orders" is empty then the field will be updated with the Financial Customer Group of the Customer.
If there is no record in table "Statuses" for the module INS, then a new record will be inserted with the current date.

```
tccov1001m000                                    single-occ (4)    Form 1-1
+------------------------------------------------------------------------+
| Conversion of Distribution 3.x -> 3.1B                  Company: 000   |
|------------------------------------------------------------------------|
|                                                                        |
| Real Conversion                    : 1....                             |
|                                                                        |
+------------------------------------------------------------------------+
```

1.   Real Conversion
Yes
The system does a real conversion and tables will be updated.
No
The system does no real conversion and table won't be updated.
For every real and no real conversion, a log-file will be made which you can find in the directory $BSE\log. The name of the log-file depends on the session which has been run and has the format log.covxxxx.

3.2   Conversion of Distribution 3.1B -> BAAN IV (tccov1002m000)
SESSION OBJECTIVE
If this session is a background process (started from tccov0000m000), then the length of all domains will be converted automatically. You can also start this session as a main process. Then you can specify the domain length of your current (customized) version.
This session will convert the following tables:
•   Parameter Tables
•   Purchase Statistics
•   Purchase Price List
•   Purchase Inquiries
•   Sales Statistics
•   Sales Price List
•   Sales (Success Percentage)
•   Distribution Ordertypes
•   Currency Rates
•   Inventory (Planner/Buyer)
In general, if there are new table fields then they will be filled with the initial values of the table definition.
All Type of Number with the value Production Batch which are in "First Free Numbers" are converted to the value Proforma Sales Invoice.
Within EDI, all EDI Messages which use incomming and outgoing sessions, are now converted to use dynamic link libraries (DLL's).
The Item Category of "Purchase Inquiry Lines (tdpur002) and "Purchase Inquiry Line History" are updated with Customized Item if Project is filled otherwise it will be filled with Standard Item.
The Unit of "Discount Parameters by Supplier and Price Group", "Discount Parameters by Price List and Price Group", "Price Parameters by Supplier and Item" and "Price Parameters by Price List by Item (tdpur037) will be update when the Grade by Quantity/Amount has value Quantity.
The Item Category of "Sales Quotation Lines (tdsls002) and "Sales Quotation Line History" are updated with Customized Item if Budget is filled. Also the Status of "Sales Quotation Line History" will be filled with Cancelled if Record Type (1-4) is equal to failed or with Processed if Record Type (1-4) is equal to copied to sales order.
The Unit of "Discount Parameters by Customer and Price Group", "Discount Parameters by Price List and Price Group", "Price Parameters by Customer per Item" and "Price Parameters by Price List by Item (tdsls037) will be update when the Grade by Quantity/Amount has value Quantity.
The Currency Rate Sales and Rate factor of "Sales Deliveries" will be updated from "Sales Orders". The Currency Rate Sales and Rate factor of "Sales Order Line History" will be updated from "Sales Order History".

The Planner of "Planned INV Production Orders" and "Planned INV Purchase Orders" will be updated from "Items".
In Replenishment Orders, the Order Procedure in "Replenishment Order Types" will be updated from the "TOC Parameters" and the Series from "Order Procedure (trtoc030).
In Common, the Order Procedure in "Order Types" will be updated from the "TOC Parameters" and the Series from "Order Procedure".
Parameter fields from table tcmcs095 (Parameters (tcmcs095)) will be put into various new parameter tables.
The Procedure Mask will be extended from 15 to 20 order steps. Therefor an update for the following tables will be done, Parameters (tcmcs095), Order Steps (tcmcs039), Order Types (tcmcs042), Replenishment Order Types (tdrpl004), Replenishment Order Lines (tdrpl100) and Receipts (tdpur045).
The Primary Key Fields of the purchase statistic tables "Purchase Statistics Master File (Turnover)", "Purchase Statistics Master File (Order Intake)", "Purchase Statistics Master File (Cancellations)", "Purchase Statistics Compression (Turnover)", "Purchase Statistics Compression (Order Intake)", "Purchase Statistics Compression (Cancellations)", "Purchase Statistics Sort File (Key File)" and "Purchase Budgets" will be upgraded due to increased field lengths.
The Primary Key Fields of the sales statistic tables "Sales Statistics Master File (Turnover)", "Sales Statistics Master File (Order Intake)", "Sales Statistics Master File (Cancellations)", "Sales Statistics Compression (Turnover)", "Sales Statistics Compression (Order Intake)", "Sales Statistics Compression (Cancellations)", "Sales Statistics Sort File (Key File)" and "Sales Budgets" will be upgraded due to increased field lengths.

tccov1002m000   single-occ (4)   Form 1-1

+---+
Conversion of Distribution 3.1B -> BAAN IV   Company: 000
Real Conversion   : 1....
Convert Statistics : 2....
Domain Length   3.1b Curr 4.0   3.1b Curr 4.0
3.1b   3.1b
tcccty   3_   4.   5_   tccwar   30   31   32
tccreg   6_   7.   8_   tccsgp   33   34   35
tccbrn   9_   10   11   tccitg   36   37   38
tccotp   12   13   14   tccprj   39   40   41
tfacr.ficu   15   16   17   tcitem   42   43   44
tccplt   18   19   20   tcncmp   45   46   47
tcemno   21   22   23   tfacp.fisu 48   49   50
tcsuno   24   25   26   tccuno   51   52   53
tccdel   27   28   29   tdsmi.cper 54   55   56
+---+

1.   Real Conversion
Yes
The system does a real conversion and tables will be updated.
No
The system does no real conversion and table won't be updated.
For every real and no real conversion, a log-file will be made which you can find in the directory $BSE\log. The name of the log-file depends on the session which has been run and has the format log.covxxxx.
2.   Convert Statistics
Indicate if statistics has to be updated.
3.   tcccty
Domain length of Country in standard 3.1b version.
4.   tcccty
Domain length of Country in current (customized) 3.1b version.
5.   tcccty

Domain length of Country in Baan 4.0 version.
6.   tccreg
Domain length of Area in standard 3.1b version.
7.   tccreg
Domain length of Area in current (customized) 3.1b version.
8.   tccreg
Domain length of Area in Baan 4.0 version.
9.   tccbrn
Domain length of Line of Business in standard 3.1b version.
10.   tccbrn
Domain length of Line of Business in current 3.1b version.
11.   tccbrn
Domain length of Line of Business in Baan 4.0 version.
12.   tccotp
Domain length of Order Type in standard 3.1b version.
13.   tccotp
Domain length of Order Type in current (customized) 3.1b version.
14.   tccotp
Domain length of Order Type in Baan 4.0 version.
15.   tfacr.ficu
Domain length of Financial Customer Group in standard 3.1b version.
16.   tfacr.ficu
Domain length of Financial Customer Group in current (customized) 3.1b version.
17.   tfacr.ficu
Domain length of Financial Customer Group in Baan 4.0 version.
18.   tccplt
Domain length of Price List in standard 3.1b version.
19.   tccplt
Domain length of Price List in current (customized) 3.1b version.
20.   tccplt
Domain length of Price List in Baan 4.0 version.
21.   tcemno
Domain length of Employee in standard 3.1b version.
22.   tcemno
Domain length of Employee in current (customized) 3.1b version.
23.   tcemno
Domain length of Employee in Baan 4.0 version.
24.   tcsuno
Domain length of Supplier in standard 3.1b version.
25.   tcsuno
Domain length of Supplier in current (customized) 3.1b version.
26.   tcsuno
Domain length of Supplier in Baan 4.0 version.
27.   tccdel
Domain length of Delivery Address in standard 3.1b version.
28.   tccdel
Domain length of Delivery Address in current (customized) 3.1b version.
29.   tccdel
Domain length of Delivery Address in Baan 4.0 version.
30.   tccwar
Domain length of Warehouse in standard 3.1b version.
31.   tccwar
Domain length of Warehouse in current (customized) 3.1b version.
32.   tccwar
Domain length of Warehouse in Baan 4.0 version.
33.   tccsgp
Domain length of Statistics Group in standard 3.1b version.
34.   tccsgp
Domain length of Statistics Group in current (customized) 3.1b version.
35.   tccsgp
Domain length of Statistics Group in Baan 4.0 version.
36.   tccitg
Domain length of Item Group in standard 3.1b version.

37.   tccitg
Domain length of Item Group in current (customized) 3.1b version.
38.   tccitg
Domain length of Item Group in Baan 4.0 version.
39.   tccprj
Domain length of Project in standard 3.1b version.
40.   tccprj
Domain length of Project in current (customized) 3.1b version.
41.   tccprj
Domain length of Project in Baan 4.0 version.
42.   tcitem
Domain length of Item in standard 3.1b version.
43.   tcitem
Domain length of Item in current (customized) 3.1b version.44. tcitem
Domain length of Item in Baan 4.0 version.
45.   tcncmp
Domain length of Company in standard 3.1b version.
46.   tcncmp
Domain length of Company in current (customized) 3.1b version.
47.   tcncmp
Domain length of Company in Baan 4.0 version.
48.   tfacp.fisu
Domain length of Financial Supplier Group in standard 3.1b version.
49.   tfacp.fisu
Domain length of Financial Supplier Group in current (customized) 3.1b version.
50.   tfacp.fisu
Domain length of Financial Supplier Group in Baan 4.0 version.
51.   tcsuno
Domain length of Customer in standard 3.1b version.
52.   tccuno
Domain length of Customer in current (customized) 3.1b version.
53.   tccuno
Domain length of Customer in Baan 4.0 version.
54.   tdsmi.cper
Domain length of Contact Person in standard 3.1b version.
55.   tdsmi.cper
Domain length of Contact Person in current (Customized) 3.1b version.
56.   tdsmi.cper
Domain length of Contact Person in Baan 4.0 version.

3.3   Change Sign in Open Item Table (tfacp200) (tccov2001m000)

SESSION OBJECTIVE

This program will update the purchase open items table.
When the reconciliation was done and the anticipated payment included a currency
difference, the amount was written with a wrong sign. This caused differences in
the checklist. With this program those currency differences are read and the
sign is changed. The tables are updated when the value of "Real Conversion" is
yes. An error log will be written to the disk.

```
tccov2001m000                              single-occ (4)    Form 1-1
+--------------------------------------------------------------------+
| Change Sign in Open Item Table (tfacp200)             Company: 000 |
|--------------------------------------------------------------------|
|                                                                    |
|                                                                    |
| Real Conversion   : 1....                                          |
|                                                                    |
+--------------------------------------------------------------------+
```

1.   Real Conversion
Yes
The system does a real conversion and tables will be updated.
No
The system does no real conversion and table won't be updated.

For every real and no real conversion, a log-file will be made which you can
find in the directory $BSE\log. The name of the log-file depends on the session
which has been run and has the format log.covxxxx.

3.4 Change Step for Antic. Unalloc/Adv Payments (tccov2002m000)

SESSION OBJECTIVE

This program will update the purchase open items table.
When the reconciliation was done and the anticipated payment included a currency
difference, the amount was written with a wrong sign. This caused differences in
the checklist. With this program those currency differences are read and the
sign is changed. The tables are updated when the value of "Real Conversion" is
yes. An error log will be written to the disk.

```
tccov2002m000                                  single-occ (4)    Form 1-1
+--------------------------------------------------------------------------+
|  Change Step for Antic. Unalloc/Adv Payments            Company: 000  |
|--------------------------------------------------------------------------|
|                                                                          |
|                                                                          |
|  Real Conversion    : 1....                                              |
|                                                                          |
+--------------------------------------------------------------------------+
```

1.   Real Conversion
Yes
The system does a real conversion and tables will be updated.
No
The system does no real conversion and table won't be updated.
For every real and no real conversion, a log-file will be made which you can
find in the directory $BSE\log. The name of the log-file depends on the session
which has been run and has the format log.covxxxx.

3.5 Check Standing Order (tfcmg114) (tccov2003m000)

SESSION OBJECTIVE

This program will update the standing order number in the table for posting data
for anticipated payments without invoice. The standing order number is a new
field which is added to table "Posting Data for Anticipated Payments without
Invoice". When the field "Real Conversion" is "Yes" then the table is updated.

SESSION OBJECTIVE

This program will update the standing order number in the table for posting data
for anticipated payments without invoice. The standing order number is a new
field which is added to table "Posting Data for Anticipated Payments without
Invoice". When the field "Real Conversion" is "Yes" then the table is updated.

```
tccov2003m000                                  single-occ (4)    Form 1-1
+--------------------------------------------------------------------------+
|  Check Standing Order (tfcmg114)                        Company: 000  |
|--------------------------------------------------------------------------|
|                                                                          |
|                                                                          |
|  Real Conversion    : 1....                                              |
|                                                                          |
+--------------------------------------------------------------------------+
```

1.   Real Conversion
Yes
The system does a real conversion and tables will be updated.
No
The system does no real conversion and table won't be updated.
For every real and no real conversion, a log-file will be made which you can
find in the directory $BSE\log. The name of the log-file depends on the session
which has been run and has the format log.covxxxx.

3.6 Check Anticipated Document (facp200/tfacr200) (tccov2004m000)

SESSION OBJECTIVE

This program reads the open items tables for unallocated/advance
receipts/payments. It will check if the anticipated document number is filled.
This is not allowed and will cause differences on the checklist for both
unallocated and anticipated documents. The total difference of those two
documents will be zero. The selected records are stored in a file and if "Real

Conversion" is set to "Yes", the anticipated document will be made empty. This is also done for the non-finalized transaction table and the finalized transaction table. When the field "Real Conversion" is "Yes", the tables will be updated.

SESSION OBJECTIVE
This program reads the open items tables for unallocated/advance receipts/payments. It will check if the anticipated document number is filled. This is not allowed and will cause differences on the checklist for both unallocated and anticipated documents. The total difference of those two documents will be zero. The selected records are stored in a file and if "Real Conversion" is set to "Yes", the anticipated document will be made empty. This is also done for the non-finalized transaction table and the finalized transaction table. When the field "Real Conversion" is "Yes", the tables will be updated.

```
tccov2004m000                           single-occ (4)    Form 1-1
+----------------------------------------------------------------------+
| Check Anticipated Document (facp200/tfacr200)        Company: 000   |
|----------------------------------------------------------------------|
|                                                                      |
|                                                                      |
| Real Conversion   : 1....                                            |
|                                                                      |
+----------------------------------------------------------------------+
```

1.   Real Conversion
Yes
The system does a real conversion and tables will be updated.
No
The system does no real conversion and table won't be updated.
For every real and no real conversion, a log-file will be made which you can find in the directory $BSE\log. The name of the log-file depends on the session which has been run and has the format log.covxxxx.

3.7   Change Enumerated Field (tfcmg108) (tccov2005m000)
SESSION OBJECTIVE
This program reads the table "One-Time Supplier Addresses".
An enumerated field is changed. The enum values are converted from two enum values to 8, of which only four are visible to the user. The enum values will be changed to the new values. When the field "Real Conversion" is "Yes", the table will be updated.

SESSION OBJECTIVE
This program reads the table "One-Time Supplier Addresses".
An enumerated field is changed. The enum values are converted from two enum values to 8, of which only four are visible to the user. The enum values will be changed to the new values. When the field "Real Conversion" is "Yes", the table will be updated.

```
tccov2005m000                           single-occ (4)    Form 1-1
+----------------------------------------------------------------------+
| Change Enumerated Field (tfcmg108)                   Company: 000   |
|----------------------------------------------------------------------|
|                                                                      |
|                                                                      |
| Real Conversion   : 1....                                            |
+----------------------------------------------------------------------+
```

1.   Real Conversion
Yes
The system does a real conversion and tables will be updated.
No
The system does no real conversion and table won't be updated.
For every real and no real conversion, a log-file will be made which you can find in the directory $BSE\log. The name of the log-file depends on the session which has been run and has the format log.covxxxx.

3.8   Conversion of Manufacturing 3.1A -> BAAN IV (tccov3001m000)
This session will convert the data in the current company as follows:
•   The surcharge history will be created based on the tables:

- Cost Price Surcharges by Item and Cost Price Component
- Cost Price Surcharge Bases by Item and Cost Price Component
- Cost Price Surcharges by Item and Effective Date
- Cost Price Surcharge Bases by Effective Date

by zooming to the subsession "Update Surcharges in Calculated Cost Price (ticpr2270s000)". This will only be done if the parameter 'CPR', '3101' is not present in "Statuses".
- Empty field tiedm100.cdrw
- Fill "ECO Lines" with initial value from data definition
- Fill fields timps000.edev/rsto with initial values from data definition
- Fill field timps320.indt with January 1, 1990 (if empty)
- Fill field timps510.ncmp as in script timps3201
- Fill field timps530.ncmp as in script timps3201
- Fill field timrp021.ncmp as in script timpr1210
- Empty fields tipcs700.stoc/logn
- Empty field tipcs850.cfsg
- Fill fields tirou000.futr/past with initial values from data definition

(This session is only necessary if the original/old version was 3.0B and will only work if the parameter 'CPR', '3101' is not present in tcmcs096).

```
tccov3001m000                                single-occ (4)    Form 1-1
+--------------------------------------------------------------------------+
| Conversion of Manufacturing 3.1A -> BAAN IV             Company: 000     |
|--------------------------------------------------------------------------|
|                                                                          |
| Real Conversion  : 1....                                                 |
|                                                                          |
+--------------------------------------------------------------------------+
```

1.   Real Conversion
Yes
The system does a real conversion and tables will be updated.
No
The system does no real conversion and table won't be updated.
For every real and no real conversion, a log-file will be made which you can find in the directory $BSE\log. The name of the log-file depends on the session which has been run and has the format log.covxxxx.

3.9   Conversion Units to Units by Unit Sets (tccov3002m000)

SESSION OBJECTIVE
As to dealing with (alternative) units, the BAAN IV version differs from previous versions considerably. That is why a conversion must be performed for the automatic generation of unit sets and units by unit set.
The scope of the session is:

TABLE	DESCRIPTION	FIELD	DESCRIPTION
tiedm010	Engineering Items		
		cuni	Unit
tiitm001	Items		
		cuni	Inventory Unit
	tiitm003		
	Alternative Units	cuni	
	Alternative Unit		
	tiitm002 Item Default Data		
		cuni	Inventory Unit
		stgu	Storage Unit
		cuqp	Purchase Unit
		cupp	Purchase Price Unit
		cuqs	Sales Unit
		cups	Sales Price Unit
	tipcs002		
	Calculation Parts	cuni	Unit
	tipcs021		
	Customized Items	cuni	Inventory Unit
		stgu	Storage Unit

The use of unit sets in BAAN IV is mandatory. This session is part of the conversion to BAAN IV once the new software is installed.

HOW TO USE THE SESSION

If the session is activated directly from a menu, two questions will be displayed on the screen:

• Real Conversion :

You can choose a simulation, in which unit sets and units by unit set will be created (in the session). However, they will not be stored in the database.

• Log Results :

You can generate results in a log file "unit.conv" in the $BSE/log directory. If the log file does not exist, it will be created. Otherwise, any results will be added to this file. If the session is started in background (e.g. from TRITON Exchange), the above questions will not be displayed, and the conversion will start right away. The conversion results will then automatically be stored in the log file "log.unit.conv" in the $BSE/log directory.

SPECIAL OPTIONS

First of all, the system tests whether parameters have been set in "MCS Parameters". If this is not the case (with Real Conversion = Yes), a record will be created in "MCS Parameters". That record will contain the basic units found in "Units". The contents of "MCS Parameters" and "Units" must match each other (e.g. there may not be two or more units with the same physical quantity and conversion factor = 1). If the basic units in this parameter table are filled properly, the session will be using these basic units.

The existing item group will be loaded in the internal memory.

Any existing unit sets will be loaded in the internal memory.

Based on the "Alternative Units" table, all alternative units will be collected by item. If these items do not yet belong to a unit set, a new unit set will be created in the "Unit Sets" table, and the corresponding units will be written in the "Units By Unit Set" table. (Only items for which the unit set has not yet been entered will be selected).

The same goes for the "Item Default Data" table. For each item group the system determines whether a unit set already exists, or whether a new unit set must be created.

In the same manner, the relevant unit sets will be defined for the tables "Customized Items", "Calculation Parts" and "Engineering Items".

tccov3002m000   single-occ (4)   Form 1-1

```
+---------------------------------------------------------------------+
| Conversion Units to Units by Unit Sets            Company: 000  |
|---------------------------------------------------------------------|
|                                                                     |
|  Real Conversion              : 1....                               |
|                                                                     |
|  Log Results                  : 2....                               |
|                                                                     |
|  3_____                    |
+---------------------------------------------------------------------+
```

1.   Real Conversion
Yes
The system does a real conversion and tables will be updated.
No
The system does no real conversion and table won't be updated.
For every real and no real conversion, a log-file will be made which you can find in the directory $BSE\log. The name of the log-file depends on the session which has been run and has the format log.covxxxx.

2.   Log Results
Indicate if logging of the unit conversion has to be done.

3.   Process information
The table code and description which is currently processing.

3.10 Conversion Unit Conversion Factors (tccov3003m000)

SESSION OBJECTIVE
As to dealing with (alternative) units, the BAAN IV version differs from
previous versions considerably. That is why a conversion must be performed for
the automatic generation of unit conversion factors.
The scope of the conversion is:

TABLE	DESCRIPTION	FIELD DESCRIPTION
tcmcs001	Units	
		conv Conversion Factor
		tiitm003
		Alternative Units
		conv Conversion Factor
		tipcs021
		Customized Items cvqp
		Conversion Factor Purchase Unit
		cvpp Conversion
		Factor Purchase Price Unit

As many conversion factors as possible are recorded at the general level
(without item/item group). This session is part of the conversion to BAAN IV
once the new software is installed.
The tables "Units", "Alternative Units" and "Customized Items" must remain
unchanged in the BAAN IV version, like in 3.1: This results in two advantages:
•   the conversion can be performed after the installation of BAAN IV
•   the conversion can be performed anew
The conversion of conversion factors may involve conflicting situations:
In versions 3.1 and lower it was possible to record any conversion factor. In
BAAN IV, however, it will not be possible to record a (customized) item-specific
conversion factor for conversion between two units (except for units with the
same physical quantities). The session will recognize these conflicting
situations and write them to the log file. However, if a final conversion is
performed, a different conversion factor will be generated.
HOW TO USE THE SESSION
If the session is activated directly from a menu, two questions will be
displayed on the screen:
•   Real Conversion :
You can choose a simulation, in conversion factors will be created (in the
session). However, they will not be stored in the database.
•   Log Results :
        You can generate results in a log file "unit.conv" in the $BSE/log
directory. If the log file does not exist, it will be created. Otherwise, any
results will be added to this file. If the session is started in background
(e.g. from TRITON Exchange), the above questions will not be displayed, and the
conversion will start right away. The conversion results will then automatically
be stored in the log file "log.unit.conv" in the $BSE/log directory.
SPECIAL OPTIONS
First of all, the system tests whether parameters have been set in "MCS
Parameters". If this is not the case (with Real Conversion = Yes), a record will
be created in "MCS Parameters". That record will contain the basic units found
in "Units". The contents of "MCS Parameters" and "Units" must match each other
(e.g. there may not be two or more units with the same physical quantity and
conversion factor = 1). If the basic units in this parameter table are filled
properly, the session will be using these basic units.
The first conversion step involves the definition of general conversion factors
based on the field "Conversion Factor" from the "Units" table. These conversion
factors will be retained in the internal memory.
The customized conversion factors ("Conversion Factor") from the "Alternative
Units" table are determined by item and also loaded in the internal memory. If
there is already a conversion factor with the same value at the general level, a
conversion factor will not be generated by item.
Next, the conversion factors for customized items from the "Customized Items"
table are determined and also loaded in the internal memory. Here two conversion
factors are relevant, i.e. "Conversion Factor Purchase Unit and Conversion
Factor Purchase Price Unit. If there is already a conversion factor with the

same value at the general level, a conversion factor will not be generated by item.

Following this conversion, the system will optimize: For each item group the system will check in the internal table containing conversion factors by item and by customized item, whether the same conversion factors are used per unit. If so, a conversion factor will be generated per item group, and the existing conversion factors by item / customized item will be deleted.

Finally, with "Real Conversion" the converted conversion factors will be written in "Conversion Factors".

```
tccov3003m000                              single-occ (4)    Form 1-1
+-------------------------------------------------------------------------+
| Conversion Unit Conversion Factors                     Company: 000 |
|-------------------------------------------------------------------------|
|                                                                         |
| Real Conversion               : 1....                                  |
|                                                                         |
| Log Results                   : 2....                                  |
|                                                                         |
| 3_____                       |
+-------------------------------------------------------------------------+
```

1.   Real Conversion
Yes
The system does a real conversion and tables will be updated.
No
The system does no real conversion and table won't be updated.
For every real and no real conversion, a log-file will be made which you can find in the directory $BSE\log. The name of the log-file depends on the session which has been run and has the format log.covxxxx.

2.   Log Results
Indicate if logging of the unit conversion has to be done.

3.   Process information

3.11 Fill Auxiliary Item Table (tiitm100) (tccov3004m000)
SESSION OBJECTIVE
This program will update tiitm100 from tiitm001.
Table tiitm100 has been defined for using the item containers. The number of records should be the same in tiitm001 and tiitm100.
If an item container is used in some applications e.g. in purchase orders, the program will read tiitm100 before it will read tiitm001.
Example:
```
tdpur041 item       tiitm100 reli
       cntr --->            cntr
                            item ---> tiitm001 item
```

```
tccov3004m000                              single-occ (4)    Form 1-1
+-------------------------------------------------------------------------+
| Fill Auxiliary Item Table (tiitm100)                   Company: 000 |
|-------------------------------------------------------------------------|
|                                                                         |
| Real Conversion               : 1....                                  |
|                                                                         |
|   +-----------------------------------+                                 |
|   |2_____   |                                |
|   |3_____|                                |
|   |4__                                 |                                |
|   |5_____|                                |
|   +-----------------------------------+                                 |
|                                                                         |
+-------------------------------------------------------------------------+
```

1.   Real Conversion
Yes
The system does a real conversion and tables will be updated.
No
The system does no real conversion and table won't be updated.

For every real and no real conversion, a log-file will be made which you can find in the directory $BSE\log. The name of the log-file depends on the session which has been run and has the format log.covxxxx.

2.   Action
Process information (Updating, Clearing or Filling).

3.   Item
For further information, see keyword(s)
"Items".
Display of Item which is currently processing.

4.   Container
A container is a unit belonging to a unit set and indicates how the item is sold to the customer. (See also the field "Containerized" in the session "Maintain Item Data (tiitm0101m000)")
For further information, see keyword(s)
•   Units
•   Units By Unit Set
For further information, see method(s)
•   Using Containers
•   Containerized Items
The Container which is currently processing.

5.   Item
For further information, see keyword(s)
"Items".
The Related Item which is currently processing.

3.12 Conversion of Transportation 3.x -> BAAN IV (TCO) (tccov5001m000)
SESSION OBJECTIVE
This session will convert table "Cost Lines".
If there is a link with Finance and the costing-record has status "Posted" then the cost-line field "Match Status" will get value "All Approved".

```
tccov5001m000                                    single-occ (4)    Form 1-1
+-------------------------------------------------------------------------------+
| Conversion of Transportation 3.x -> BAAN IV (TCO)         Company: 000    |
|-------------------------------------------------------------------------------|
|                                                                               |
| Real Conversion                      : 1....                                  |
|                                                                               |
+-------------------------------------------------------------------------------+
```

1.   Real Conversion
Yes
The system does a real conversion and tables will be updated.
No
The system does no real conversion and table won't be updated.
For every real and no real conversion, a log-file will be made which you can find in the directory $BSE\log. The name of the log-file depends on the session which has been run and has the format log.covxxxx.

EDI - Electronic Data Interchange

1   Electronic Data Interchange (EDI)
1.1   General
OBJECTIVE OF THIS MODULE
More and more companies exchange data - especially order and invoice data - by electronic means. The module Electronic Data Interchange (EDI) enables you to directly exchange information between computer systems and companies. This is especially useful in order to transfer information on such transactions as orders, invoices, allocations and calls on contracts. The module can also be used to exchange general information as product specifications, price lists and plans.
Working with the module Electronic Data Interchange (EDI) in an open environment requires agreements on the data to be exchanged and its structure. On the international level, the agreements are laid down in the EDIFACT (Europe) and

the ANSI X12 (USA) standards. Nationally, agreements have been made per line of business.
The module Electronic Data Interchange (EDI) allows you to create new messages. Codes, conversions and conversion setups are user-defined.

1.2   Related B-Objects

Seq. No.	B-Object	Description	B-Object Usage
1	tc edi00010	EDI Master Data	Optional child
2	tc edi00020	Networks	Optional child
3	tc edi00030	Coding and Conversion Data	Optional child
4	tc edi00031	Additional Conversion Data	Optional child
5	tc edi00032	Additional Coding Data	Optional child
6	tc edi00040	Conversion Parameters	Optional child
7	tc edi00050	Import/Export	Optional child
8	tc edi00060	Communication	Optional child
9	tc edi00070	EDI History	Optional child
10	tc edi00080	Message Data	Optional child

2   Introduction to EDI Master Data

2.1   General

OBJECTIVE OF BUSINESS OBJECT
This b-object allows you to manage a set of messages to be used in the module "Electronic Data Interchange (EDI)".
This b-object involved the following data:
•   Organizations
•   EDI Messages
•   Supported EDI Messages
•   Relations
•   EDI Messages Supported by Relations
•   Outgoing Messages by Session
Your can only use messages which are supported by BAAN IV. Your EDI partners can only exchanges message with you which are available in your company. Usually this is only a subset of the set of all messages which BAAN IV supports.
Display the procedure and show the sessions in:
•   EDI Master Data Procedure

2.2   Session Overview

Seq.	Session	Description	Session Usage
1	tcedi0103m000	Maintain Organizations	Mandatory
2	tcedi0105m000	Maintain EDI Messages	Mandatory
3	tcedi0101m000	Maintain Supported EDI Messages	Mandatory
4	tcedi0110m000	Maintain Relations	Mandatory
5	tcedi0111m000	Maintain EDI Messages Supported by Rela	Mandatory

```
|      6 | tcedi0130m000 | Maintain Relation Structure for Outgoin| Mandatory
|
|      7 | tcedi0115m000 | Maintain Outgoing Messages by Session  | Mandatory
|
|     10 | tcedi0100m000 | Maintain EDI Parameters                | Mandatory
|
|    101 | tcedi0403m000 | Print Organizations                    | Print
|
|    102 | tcedi0405m000 | Print EDI Messages                     | Print
|
|    103 | tcedi0401m000 | Print Supported EDI Messages           | Print
|
|    104 | tcedi0410m000 | Print Relations                        | Print
|
|    105 | tcedi0411m000 | Print EDI Messages Supported by Relati | Print
|
|    106 | tcedi0430m000 | Print Rel Structure Outgoing Messages  | Print
|
|    107 | tcedi0415m000 | Print Outgoing Messages by Session     | Print
|
|    201 | tcedi0503s000 | Display Organizations                  | Display
|
|    202 | tcedi0505s000 | Display EDI Messages                   | Display
|
|    203 | tcedi0501s000 | Display EDI Messages Supported by Appli| Display
|
|    204 | tcedi0510s000 | Display EDI Relations                  | Display
|
|    205 | tcedi0515s000 | Display Outgoing Messages by Session   | Display
|
```

---

3   Mandatory Sessions

3.1   Maintain Organizations (tcedi0103m000)

SESSION OBJECTIVE
To define the organizations that will be used in EDI.
SEE ALSO KEYWORD(S)
• 	Organizations

```
tcedi0103m000                               multi-occ (2)    Form 1-2 >
+---------------------------------------------------------------------------+
| Maintain Organizations                                     Company: 000   |
|---------------------------------------------------------------------------|
|                                                                           |
| Organization                    Code in      Derived   Association Root   |
|                                  Message                Assigned    Org.   |
|                                                                           |
| 1.. 2.........................  3.....       4....     5.....       6.. |
|                                                                           |
+---------------------------------------------------------------------------+
```

1.   Organization
The code which uniquely identifies the organization.
2.   Description
Enter a clear description here.
3.   Code in Message
The code used in the message to identify the organization. Each organization has
its own unique code.
Examples of organization codes:
• 	Odette 			OD
• 	United Nations 		UN
4.   Derived
Each organization can develop its own set of messages or use the message and
code set of another organization. In the former case the organization is called
a root organization, in the latter, a derived organization. Yes

The organization uses a message set and/or code set which is derived from another organization.
No
The organization is independent.
5.   Association Assigned
If the organization uses messages derived from those of other organizations, this is made clear by a code in the header of the EDI message.
The header will then contain the code of the derived organization as well as of the root organization. Enter the code of the derived organization as used in the EDI messages.
6.   Root-Organizati on
The root organization if the organization defined here is a derived organization. A derived organization may only refer to a root organization, not to another derived organization.

```
tcedi0103m000                              multi-occ (2)  < Form 2-2
+-----------------------------------------------------------------------+
| Maintain Organizations                              Company: 000  |
|-----------------------------------------------------------------------|
|                                                                       |
| Organization                  Test Indicator   Date Format        |
|                                                                       |
|                                                                       |
| 1.. 2......................  3.....          4...................... |
|                                                                       |
+-----------------------------------------------------------------------+
```

1.   Organization
The code which uniquely identifies the organization.
2.   Description
Enter a clear description here.
3.   Test Indicator
Indication identifying incoming messages for this organization as test messages. A test message is checked but not copied to the database.
4.   Date Format
The date format used in outgoing EDI messages.
3.2   Maintain EDI Messages (tcedi0105m000)
SESSION OBJECTIVE
To define the EDI messages that will be used in EDI.
SEE ALSO KEYWORD(S)
•   EDI Messages

```
tcedi0105m000                              single-occ (1)  Form 1-1
+-----------------------------------------------------------------------+
| Maintain EDI Messages                               Company: 000  |
|-----------------------------------------------------------------------|
|                                                                       |
| EDI Message                 : 1.....                              |
|                                                                       |
| Description                 : 2.............................      |
| Message Type                : 3..............                     |
| Change Order                : 4....                              |
| Library Incoming            : 5............  6_____ |
| Library Outgoing            : 7............  8_____ |
|                                                                       |
| Incoming Message Data---------------------+                       |
| Processing Type             : 9..........                        |
| File Layout                 : 10......                           |
| Level Identification Position : 11.                              |
| Level Identification Length  : 12.                              |
|                                                                       |
+-----------------------------------------------------------------------+
```

1.   EDI Message
This code uniquely identifies an EDI message. Depending on the direction, it identifies an incoming or outgoing message.
2.   Description

The description associated with the message code.

3.   Message Type

The message type. This field is for information purposes only.

EDIFACT

The message is an EDIFACT message.

Non-EDIFACT

The message is an EDI message, but not an EDIFACT message.

Single File

Not supported.

4.   Change Order

Indicates if the message represents, or is in reference to, an new order or an order change. This field is relevant for the order and order acknowledgment messages, specifically, the purchase order outbound, sales orders inbound, as well as order acknowledgment inbound and outbound.

Yes

The message represents, or is in reference to, an order change request. For example, if the message is an incoming order, an existing sales order will be updated with the data specified in the message. (Examples of this include the ANSI X12 860, and the UN/EDIFACT ORDCHG). On the other hand, if the message is an outbound order acknowledgment, this field may be used to indicate that the message is in response to a received order change message. (Examples of this include the ANSI X12 865).

No

The message represents, or is in reference to, a new order request. For example, if the message is an incoming order, a new sales order will be generated with the data specified in the message. (Examples of this include the ANSI X12 850, and the UN/EDIFACT ORDERS). On the other hand, if the message is an outbound order acknowledgment, this field may be used to indicate that the message is in response to a received new order request. (Examples of this include the ANSI X12 850, and the UN/EDIFACT ORDRSP).

5.   Library Incoming

The session used to convert incoming messages into data in the system database.

6.   Library Incoming

7.   Library Outgoing

The session used to read data from the system database and use it in messages.

8.   Library Outgoing

9.   Incoming Message Processing Type

Indicates the way in which the incoming EDI messages will be processed. The value defined here at the message level serves as the default for the value to be entered in session "Maintain EDI Messages Supported by Relations (tcedi0111m000)".

Interactive

The incoming EDI message is read from the ASCII file and saved in the "Saved Messages to be Received" table without any processing of the message. This provides the option to maintain and view incoming EDI message data for review and approval, prior to the validation and update into the BAAN IV application for which the message is destined.

Automatic

The validation and processing of the incoming EDI message will be done automatically when the message is read from the ASCII file(s).

10.   File Layout

Type of file layout to be used for the specific EDI message.

Single

Incoming EDI message data will be stored in one ASCII file. In this case, the field "Level Identification Position" must be specified. In addition, the field "Level Identification Length" must be specified if the field type defined in the session "Maintain Networks (tcedi0120m000)" is of a fixed length.

Multiple

Incoming EDI message data will be divided into multiple ASCII files.

11.   Level Identification Position

The position within the message (ASCII file) record of the Level Identification defined in session "Maintain Conversion Setups (Relationships) (tcedi5112s000)".

This is either the starting position of the field or the field number, depending on the field type specified in session "Maintain Networks (tcedi0120m000)". You will need to check the message's conversion setup definition to ensure that no other field is defined residing the same position(s).
This field only applies if the File Layout is "Single".
For further information, see keyword(s):
• 	Conversion Setups (Relationships)
• 	Networks
12. 	Level Identification Length
The length of the "Level Identification" defined in session "Maintain Conversion Setups (Relationships) (tcedi5112s000)". The maximum length is six.
This is only applicable if the "File Layout" is "Single" and the field "Field Type", specified in session "Maintain Networks (tcedi0120m000)", is "Fixed Length".
For further information, see keyword(s):
• 	Conversion Setups (Relationships)
• 	Networks
3.3 	Maintain Supported EDI Messages (tcedi0101m000)
SESSION OBJECTIVE
To define the supported EDI messages that will be used in EDI.
SEE ALSO KEYWORD(S)
• 	Supported EDI Messages


```
tcedi0101m000                                multi/group (3    Form 1-1
+----------------------------------------------------------------------------+
|  Maintain Supported EDI Messages                         Company: 000  |
|----------------------------------------------------------------------------|
|                                                                            |
|  Organization  : 1.. 2_____                       |
|                                                                            |
|  EDI Message      Direction  Active  Code in   Description                |
|                                      Message                               |
|                                                                            |
|      3.....  4..        5....  6.....    7............................ |
|                                                                            |
+----------------------------------------------------------------------------+
```

1. 	Organization
The organization within which the code is valid.
2. 	Description
3. 	EDI Message
This code uniquely identifies an EDI message. Depending on the direction, it identifies an incoming or outgoing message.
4. 	Direction
The message can be incoming or outgoing. In
The message is an incoming message.
Out
The message is an outgoing message.
5. 	Active
Indicates for this network if incoming EDI messages are to be processed.
Yes
Incoming messages are processed.
No
Incoming messages are not processed.
6. 	Code in Message
The code identifying the message.
7. 	Description
The description of the message. The description entered here refers to the combination of message and organization. It is displayed in various EDI sessions.
3.4 	Maintain Relations (tcedi0110m000)
SESSION OBJECTIVE
To record the (business) relations that you will communicate with through EDI.

```
+------------------------------------------------------------------------+
| Maintain Relations                                     Company: 000   |
|------------------------------------------------------------------------|
|                                                                        |
| Relation                      : 1.....                                 |
|                                                                        |
| Description                   : 2............................          |
|                                                                        |
| Customer                      : 3.....  4_____ |
| Supplier                      : 5.....  6_____ |
|                                                                        |
| Network                       : 7.....  8_____    |
|                                                                        |
| Incrementing Reference Numbers: 9....                                  |
| Check Duplicate Order Numbers : 10...                                  |
|                                                                        |
| Sales Order Change Response   : 11........................            |
|                                                                        |
+------------------------------------------------------------------------+
```

1. 	Relation

An outgoing message for this relation is sent to the network address of the parent relation. For both relations the field "Network Address" in the session "Maintain Relation Data by Network (tcedi0128m000)" must be filled.

When maintaining a relation which must be suitable for multicompany EDI applications, the following conditions have to be met:

• 	The field "Affiliated Company" for the customer entered and the field "Affiliated Company" for the supplier entered must be on "Yes".

• 	The field "Affiliated Company No." for the customer must be equal to the field "Affiliated Company No." for the supplier.

If these conditions are fulfilled, the relation can be linked to an internal multicompany network using the session "Maintain Relation Data by Network (tcedi0128m000)".

The affiliated company found for the customer and/or supplier is used in EDI to determine the company for which messages must be generated.

SEE ALSO METHOD(S)

• 	Communication for Multi-Company Networks

2. 	Description

Enter a clear description here.

3. 	Customer

The customer associated with the relation.

4. 	Name

The first part of the customer's name.

5. 	Supplier

The supplier linked to the relation.

6. 	Name

The first part of the supplier's name.

7. 	Network

The standard network for the relation. A multicompany network (the field "Multicompany" is on "Yes") is only allowed if the conditions described at the field "Relation" have been met.

8. 	Description

The description of the network.

9. 	Incrementing Reference Numbers

For each relation you can indicate whether the system is to check if the last reference number of incoming messages is the highest reference number.

Yes

The system checks if the new reference number is higher than the reference numbers of all previous messages of the same relation.

No

The sequence of reference numbers is not checked.

10. Check Duplicate Order Numbers
In addition to the (standard) check if a message reference has been received
earlier from the same relation, the system can also check if the document number
(order, invoice) has been received before.
For inbound sales order change messages, the system checks the sales order /
change order sequence number combination for uniqueness.
Yes
The system checks if a document with this number has been received earlier.
No
The document number is not checked.
11. Sales Order Change Response
Indicates the type of EDI Order Acknowledgment message to generate in response
to a received EDI Order Change message, for this relation.
'%ENtcedi.order.ack' Generate an Order Acknowledgment message in reponse to a
received Order Change message. The Order Acknowledgment message is the
acknowledgment message for which the "Change Order", defined for the message, is
set to "ENtcyesno.no". (eg. in ANSI X12 standards, this may correspond to the
865 message).
to No. (eg. in ANSI X12 standards, this may correspond to the 855 message).
'%ENtcedi.order.chg.ack' Generate an Order Change Acknowlegdment message in
response to a received Order Change message. The Order Change Acknowledgment
message is the acknowledgment message for which the "Change Order" is set to
Yes. (eg. in ANSI X12 standards, this may correspond to the 865 message).
3.5 Maintain EDI Messages Supported by Relations (tcedi0111m000)
SESSION OBJECTIVE
To define the messages supported by relations that will be used in EDI.
SEE ALSO KEYWORD(S)
• EDI Messages Supported by Relations

```
tcedi0111m000                                    single-occ (1)   Form 1-2 >
+--------------------------------------------------------------------------+
| Maintain EDI Messages Supported by Relations              Company: 000   |
|--------------------------------------------------------------------------|
|                                                                          |
|   Relation             : 1.....  2_____       |
|   Organization         :   3..   4_____        |
|   EDI Message          : 5.....  6_____        |
|   Direction            : 7..                                             |
|   Order Type           : 8.................................  9_____  |
|                                                                          |
|   Type of Number       : 10...............                               |
|   Network              : 11....  12_____         |
|   Conversion Setup     : 13....  14_____          |
|   Person Responsible   : 15..........  16_____        |
|   Block                : 17...                                           |
|   Print                : 18...                                           |
|                                                                          |
|   Incoming Message                                                       |
|   Processing Type      : 19........                                      |
|                                                                          |
+--------------------------------------------------------------------------+
```

1. Relation
An outgoing message for this relation is sent to the network address of the
parent relation. For both relations the field "Network Address" in the session
"Maintain Relation Data by Network (tcedi0128m000)" must be filled.
2. Description
3. Organization
The code which uniquely identifies the organization.
4. Description
5. EDI Message
This code uniquely identifies an EDI message. Depending on the direction, it
identifies an incoming or outgoing message.
6. Description
The description associated with the message code.

7. Direction
The message can be incoming or outgoing.
8. Order Type
The order type is used to make distinctions within a specific EDI message.
Example:
- A sales order may be a normal order or a return order.
- A transport order may be a collect or a distribution order.
9. Description
Indicates the type of received order.
Normal Order
The order is a normal order. The associated order type may not be of the category "return order".
Return Order
The order is a return order. The associated order type must be of the category "return order".
10. Type of Number
The number type to which the series applies.
11. Network
The network that is used for the combination of relation and message.
12. Description
The description of the network.
13. Conversion Setup
The conversion setup used for the combination of relation and message.
14. Description
The description of the conversion setup.
15. Person Responsible
The user assigned to the combination of relation and message.
16. Person Responsible
17. Block
Indicates whether the order is blocked for further processing after receipt. Yes
The order is blocked with reason "Telematics (EDI)". It must be released before it can processed any further.
No
The order is not blocked and will be included in the procedure.
18. Print
Here you can indicate if a document must be printed (this must be supported by the software). Yes
The system prints a report containing the data received (incoming message) or the document (outgoing message).
No
No document is printed.
19. Incoming Message Processing Type
Indicates the way in which the incoming EDI message will be processed for the relation.
Interactive
The incoming EDI message is read from the ASCII file and saved in the "Saved Messages to be Received" table without any processing of the message. This provides the option to maintain and view incoming EDI message data for review and approval, prior to the validation and update into the BAAN IV application for which the message is destined.
Automatic
The validation and processing of the incoming EDI message will be done automatically when the message is read from the ASCII file(s).

```
tcedi0111m000                              single-occ (1) < Form 2-2
+----------------------------------------------------------------------+
| Maintain EDI Messages Supported by Relations          Company: 000  |
|----------------------------------------------------------------------|
|                                                                      |
|  Relation            : 1_____  2_____             |
|  Organization        :    3__  4_____            |
|  EDI Message         : 5_____  6_____            |
|  Direction           : 7__                                          |
|  Order Type          : 8_____ 9_____   |
```

```
|                                                                              |
| Character Conversion: 10....  11_____            |
|                                                                              |
| SLS Order Type      :   12.  13_____            |
| Order Procedure     :   14.  15_____            |
| Series              :   16.  17_____            |
|                                                                              |
| Item Code System    :   18.  19_____            |
|                                                                              |
+------------------------------------------------------------------------------+
```

1.   Relation
An outgoing message for this relation is sent to the network address of the
parent relation. For both relations the field "Network Address" in the session
"Maintain Relation Data by Network (tcedi0128m000)" must be filled.

2.   Description

3.   Organization
The code which uniquely identifies the organization.

4.   Description

5.   EDI Message
This code uniquely identifies an EDI message. Depending on the direction, it
identifies an incoming or outgoing message.

6.   Description
The description associated with the message code.

7.   Direction
The message can be incoming or outgoing.

8.   Order Type
The order type is used to make distinctions within a specific EDI message.
Example:
•   A sales order may be a normal order or a return order.
•   A transport order may be a collect or a distribution order.

9.   Description
Indicates the type of received order.
Normal Order
The order is a normal order. The associated order type may not be of the
category "return order".
Return Order
The order is a return order. The associated order type must be of the category
"return order".

10.   Character Conversion
The character conversion code defines how characters from the application
environment should be transferred to the ASCII files. You can for instance state
that all characters should be converted to upper case or that specific
punctuation marks should be ignored in the EDI message.

11.   Description
The description of the character conversion code.

12.   SLS Order Type
The order type determines which sessions (in which sequence) will be part of the
order procedure. In addition, you can further predetermine the procedure by
assigning one of the following categories to the order type: cost order, collect
order, return order, subcontracting order.

13.   Description

14.   Order Procedure
The order procedure from the "BAAN Transportation" package to orders will be
copied to. For further information, see keyword(s) "Order Procedure".

15.   Description

16.   Order Series
The series in which the document is placed.

17.   Description

18.   Item Code System
The item code ID that can be used in outgoing messages to convert item codes on
the basis of the data recorded in the session "Maintain Item Codes by Item Code
System (tiitm0112m000)". The value entered overrules the default value of the
field "Default Qualifier" in the conversion setup.

19.   Description
3.6   Maintain Relation Structure for Outgoing Messages (tcedi0130m000)
SESSION OBJECTIVE
To maintain the relation structure for outgoing EDI messages.
SEE ALSO KEYWORD(S)
•   Relation Structure for Outgoing Messages
tcedi0130m000   multi/group (3   Form 1-1
+--+
Maintain Relation Structure for Outgoing Messages   Company: 000
Parent Relation: 1..... 2_____
Network   : 3..... 4_____
Organization : 5..   6_____
EDI Message   : 7..... 8_____
Child Relation Description   Network Address
9..... 2_____   10_____
+--+
1.   Parent Relation
The EDI relation to which outgoing messages for the underlying relations are
sent.
2.   Description
3.   Network
The code uniquely identifying the network.
4.   Description
The description of the network.
5.   Organization
The code which uniquely identifies the organization.
6.   Description
7.   EDI Message
This code uniquely identifies an EDI message. Depending on the direction, it
identifies an incoming or outgoing message.
8.   Description
The description associated with the message code.
9.   Child Relation
An outgoing message for this relation is sent to the network address of the
parent relation. For both relations the field "Network Address" in the session
"Maintain Relation Data by Network (tcedi0128m000)" must be filled.
10.   Network Address
3.7   Maintain Outgoing Messages by Session (tcedi0115m000)
SESSION OBJECTIVE
To define the outgoing messages that will be used in EDI by session.
SEE ALSO KEYWORD(S)
•   Outgoing Messages by Session
tcedi0115m000   multi/group (3   Form 1-1
+--+
Maintain Outgoing Messages by Session   Company: 000
Session   : 1........... 2_____
Organization Description   EDI Message   Description
3.. 4_____   5..... 6_____
+--+
1.   Session
EDI messages can be created within various sessions. Enter the session code.
Examples of sessions supporting EDI messages are:
•   Print Order Acknowledgements (tdsls4401m000)

- Print Packing Slips (tdsls4403m000)
- Print Sales Invoices (tdsls4404m000)
- Print Purchase Orders (tdpur4401m000)
- Print Order Acknowledgements (trtoc1400m000)

2. Session
3. Organization
The code which uniquely identifies the organization.
4. Description
5. EDI Message
This code uniquely identifies an EDI message. Depending on the direction, it identifies an incoming or outgoing message.
6. Description
The description associated with the message code.

3.8 Maintain EDI Parameters (tcedi0100m000)

SESSION OBJECTIVE
To set the parameters that determine how the module "Electronic Data Interchange (EDI)" will be operated.

SEE ALSO KEYWORD(S)
- EDI Parameters

```
tcedi0100m000                          single-occ (1)    Form 1-2 >
+----------------------------------------------------------------------+
| Maintain EDI Parameters                              Company: 000 |
|----------------------------------------------------------------------|
|                                                                      |
| EDI Implemented                      : 1....                         |
| Standard Path                        : 2................................  |
| Make Use of Tracefile                : 3....                         |
| Name of Tracefile                    : 4.......                      |
| Our Identification                   : 5...............              |
| Store All Received Messages          : 6....                         |
| Store All Sent Messages              : 7....                         |
|                                                                      |
| Reference Number                                                     |
| Fixed Part                           : 8........                     |
| Date Format                          : 9......................       |
| First Free Number                    : 10.......                     |
| Action on First Message on New Date  : 11............                |
|                                                                      |
| Suppress Blank Text Lines on Generation: 12...                       |
| Suppress Blank Generated Text Fields   : 13...                       |
|                                                                      |
+----------------------------------------------------------------------+
```

1. EDI Implemented
2. Standard Path
The standard directory is used as standard value in the field "Path" in the session "Maintain Networks (tcedi0120m000)" The directory is also used for exchanging data via the sessions "Export EDI Data (tcedi6221m000)" and "Import EDI Data (tcedi6220m000)". The directory you enter here must be present on your system.
3. Make Use of Tracefile
The session "Common Session for Incoming Messages (tcedi7220s000)" can generate a trace file. This session is a subprocess of the session "EDI Interchange Controller (tcedi7210m000)".
A trace file contains process data about read/created ASCII files.
Yes
Trace files are generated.
No
No trace files are generated.
4. Name of Tracefile
The name of the trace file. The field "Make Use of Tracefile" indicates whether or not it is used. The system will automatically generate new versions of the trace file. For instance, if the file name is "trace", the system will generate ASCII files with the names:

- trace.0001
- trace.0002
- etc.

Please make sure that the length of the name is five positions shorter than the maximum length of file names supported by your operation system.

5.   Our Identification

Network addresses are used to identify users in a network. Generally, such addresses are assigned by the network manager.

This field contains the standard value for the field "Our Identification" in the session "Maintain Networks (tcedi0120m000)".

Fill in your own network address.

6.   Store All Received Messages

Yes

All EDI messages received are logged in a separate directory.

No

Received EDI messages are not logged.

7.   Store All Sent Messages

Yes

All EDI messages sent are logged in a separate directory.

No

Sent EDI messages are not logged. Yes

All EDI messages to be sent are logged in a special directory.

No

EDI messages to be sent are not logged.

8.   Fixed Part

Outgoing messages should always have a reference. The structure of the reference number is defined in the following fields:

- Fixed Part
- Date Format
- First Free Number

The following possibilities are available:

- Fixed Part/Date/Sequence Number
- Fixed Part/Sequence Number
- Date/Sequence Number

Reference numbers are always fourteen positions long. This means that the sequence number occupies the positions which are not occupied by:

- Fixed Part and/or Date Enter the fixed part of your reference number.

9.   Date Format

The date format used as part of the reference number. When selecting the date format, you should take into account that the reference number has a length of 14 positions.

10.   First Free Number

The first free number used as reference number in the next outgoing message.

Example: Fixed Part   : COMPANY Date Format   : Without Century Number

First Free Number: 5

The first free reference number will be: COMPANY9401015

The first free number is automatically incremented whenever an outgoing message is created. You can adjust the first free number manually.

11.   Action on First Message on New Date

Start with 0

The first outgoing message on a day has sequence number 0.

Start with 1

The first outgoing message on a day has sequence number 1.

Last Number + 1

The first outgoing message has as sequence number the number of the last message to have been sent plus 1. Select one of the three options available.

12.   Suppress Blank Text Lines on Generation

In outgoing messages, blank lines in text blocks can be suppressed. This means that they are not included in the EDI message.

Yes

Empty lines are suppressed.

No

Empty lines are not suppressed.

13.   Suppress Blank Generated Text Fields
If the text fields for outgoing messages are not filled, they may be ignored in
the EDI message.
Yes
When generating EDI messages the system ignores empty text fields.
No
Empty text fields are not ignored.

```
tcedi0100m000                                single-occ (1) < Form 2-2
+-------------------------------------------------------------------------+
|  Maintain EDI Parameters                                 Company: 000   |
|-------------------------------------------------------------------------|
|                                                                         |
|   Interchange Message                       : 1.....                    |
|   Interchange Header Conversion Setup       : 2.....                    |
|   Message Overhead Conversion Setup         : 3.....                    |
|                                                                         |
+-------------------------------------------------------------------------+
```

1.   Interchange Message
The name of the dummy message used in the various organizations to describe the
layout of the interchange header and the joint message overhead. This dummy
message must be specified if you intend to use the option to collect all
messages for a relation (field "New Batch Number" in the session "Maintain
Relation Data by Network (tcedi0128m000)" has the value "By Recipient").
The file structure will then be:

```
+------------------+
| bano | neta | ... |                        1)
+------------------+

        +---------------------------+
        | bano | neta | INVOICE| ... |        2)
        +---------------------------+
                - invoice1                     3)
                - invoice2
                .
                .
                .
        +---------------------------+
        | bano | neta | ORDERS | ... |        2)
        +---------------------------+
                - order1                       3)
                - order2
                .
                .
```

1.   "Interchange Header Conversion Setup" :
described in the dummy message This record is created once for each relation.
2.   "Message Overhead Conversion Setup" :
described in the dummy message This record is created for each group of
messages. In order to prevent message overhead records with different layouts
being generated, the layout is retrieved from the dummy message.
3.   "Conversion Setup" :
the layout as specified for the message concerned.
2.   Interchange Header Conversion Setup
The name of the conversion setup in which the interchange-header layout is
described. This conversion setup should be included in the dummy message in the
field "Interchange Message".
3.   Message Overhead Conversion Setup
The name of the conversion setup containing the layout of the joint message
overhead. This conversion setup must be included in the dummy message in
"Interchange Message" and may be present as identification of the overhead in
all other messages.
4   Other Print Sessions
4.1   Print Organizations (tcedi0403m000)

```
tcedi0403m000                                single-occ (4)   Form 1-1
+-------------------------------------------------------------------------+
|  Print Organizations                                     Company: 000   |
```

```
|-------------------------------------------------------------------------|
|                                                                         |
|  Organization        from : 1..                                         |
|                      to   : 2..                                         |
|                                                                         |
+-------------------------------------------------------------------------+
1.    Organization from
2.    Organization to
4.2   Print EDI Messages (tcedi0405m000)
tcedi0405m000                              single-occ (4)    Form 1-1
+-------------------------------------------------------------------------+
|  Print EDI Messages                                   Company: 000  |
|-------------------------------------------------------------------------|
|                                                                         |
|  EDI Message      From : 1.....                                         |
|                   To   : 2.....                                         |
|                                                                         |
+-------------------------------------------------------------------------+
1.    EDI Message From
2.    EDI Message to
4.3   Print Supported EDI Messages (tcedi0401m000)
tcedi0401m000                              single-occ (4)    Form 1-1
+-------------------------------------------------------------------------+
|  Print Supported EDI Messages                         Company: 000  |
|-------------------------------------------------------------------------|
|                                                                         |
|  Organization     from :    1..                                        |
|                   to   :    2..                                        |
|                                                                         |
|  EDI Message      from : 3.....                                        |
|                   to   : 4.....                                        |
|                                                                         |
|  Direction        from : 5..                                           |
|                   to   : 6..                                           |
|                                                                         |
+-------------------------------------------------------------------------+
1.    Organization from
2.    Organization to
3.    EDI Message from
4.    EDI Message to
5.    Direction from
6.    Direction to
4.4   Print Relations (tcedi0410m000)
tcedi0410m000                              single-occ (4)    Form 1-1
+-------------------------------------------------------------------------+
|  Print Relations                                      Company: 000  |
|-------------------------------------------------------------------------|
|                                                                         |
|  Relation        from : 1.....                                         |
|                  to   : 2.....                                         |
|                                                                         |
+-------------------------------------------------------------------------+
1.    Relation from
2.    Relation to
4.5   Print EDI Messages Supported by Relations (tcedi0411m000)
tcedi0411m000                              single-occ (4)    Form 1-1
+-------------------------------------------------------------------------+
|  Print EDI Messages Supported by Relations            Company: 000  |
|-------------------------------------------------------------------------|
|                                                                         |
|  Relation        From : 1.....                                         |
|                  To   : 2.....                                         |
|                                                                         |
```

```
|  Organization      From :     3..                                          |
|                    To   :     4..                                          |
|                                                                            |
|  EDI Message       From : 5.....                                           |
|                    To   : 6.....                                           |
|                                                                            |
|  Direction         From : 7..                                              |
|                    To   : 8..                                              |
|                                                                            |
+----------------------------------------------------------------------------+
1.     Relation From
2.     Relation to
3.     Organization From
4.     Organization to
5.     EDI Message From
6.     EDI Message to
7.     Direction From
8.     Direction to
```

4.6 Print Relation Structure for Outgoing Messages (tcedi0430m000)

```
tcedi0430m000                                single-occ (4)    Form 1-1
+----------------------------------------------------------------------------+
|  Print Relation Structure for Outgoing Messages           Company: 000  |
|----------------------------------------------------------------------------|
|                                                                            |
|  Parent Relation From : 1.....                                             |
|                   To   : 2.....                                            |
|                                                                            |
+----------------------------------------------------------------------------+
1.     Relation
2.     Relation
```

4.7 Print Outgoing Messages by Session (tcedi0415m000)

```
tcedi0415m000                                single-occ (4)    Form 1-1
+----------------------------------------------------------------------------+
|  Print Outgoing Messages by Session                       Company: 000  |
|----------------------------------------------------------------------------|
|                                                                            |
|  Session          from : 1............                                     |
|                   to   : 2............                                     |
|                                                                            |
+----------------------------------------------------------------------------+
1.     Session from
2.     Session to
```

5 Introduction to Networks

5.1 General

OBJECTIVE OF BUSINESS OBJECT

To control the various data flows. Communication is possible via different networks, such as a Value Added Network (VAN)

In this business object the following data sets are used:
*   Networks
*   Connect Frequencies by Network
*   Connect Times by Network
*   Relations by Network

Display the procedure and show the sessions in:
*   Networking Procedure

5.2 Session Overview

Seq.	Session	Description	Session Usage
1	tcedi0120m000	Maintain Networks	Mandatory
2	tcedi0122m000	Maintain Connect Frequencies by Network	Mandatory

```
|   3 | tcedi0125m000 | Maintain Connect Times by Network       | Mandatory
|
|   4 | tcedi0225m000 | Generate Connect Times by Network       | Mandatory
|
|   5 | tcedi0128m000 | Maintain Relation Data by Network       | Mandatory
|
| 101 | tcedi0420m000 | Print Networks                          | Print
|
| 102 | tcedi0422m000 | Print Connect Frequencies by Network    | Print
|
| 103 | tcedi0425m000 | Print Connect Times by Network          | Print
|
| 104 | tcedi0428m000 | Print Relation Identification by Networ| Print
|
| 201 | tcedi0520s000 | Display Networks                        | Display
|
```

6   Mandatory Sessions
6.1   Maintain Networks (tcedi0120m000)
SESSION OBJECTIVE
To define the networks to be used in EDI.
SEE ALSO KEYWORD(S)
•   Networks
tcedi0120m000   single-occ (1)   Form 1-2 >
```
+----------------------------------------------------------------------+
| Maintain Networks                                       Company: 000 |
|----------------------------------------------------------------------|
|                                                                      |
| Network                 : 1.....                                     |
|                                                                      |
| Description             : 2.............................             |
| Path                    : 3......................................    |
| Our Identification      : 4...............                           |
|                                                                      |
| Multicompany            : 5....                                      |
| Start Read Batch                                                     |
| after Generating        : 6....                                      |
|                                                                      |
| General Reference       : 7....                                      |
| Fixed Part              : 8.........                                 |
| Date Format             : 9.......                                   |
| First Free Number       : 10........                                 |
| Action on New Date      : 11............                             |
|                                                                      |
+----------------------------------------------------------------------+
```
1.   Network
The code uniquely identifying the network.
2.   Description
The description of the network.
3.   Path
The base directory for the network.
SEE ALSO METHOD(S)
•   Network Directory Structure
The directory which you enter must already exist on your system. After entering
the directory, the system will generate the subdirectories.
4.   Our Identification
Your network address on this network.
5.   Multicompany
Indicates whether this network will be used for internal communication between
different BAAN IV companies.
SEE ALSO METHOD(S).
•   Multi-Company Network
Yes

The network will be used for internal communication.
No
The network will be used for communication with external EDI relations.
6.   Start Read Batch after Generating
Indicate whether the messages generated in a multi-company network must be
automatically processed in the receiving company. Yes
The batch for processing generated messages is automatically started in the
company for which the messages are meant.
No
The generated messages are not immediately processed in the company for which
they are meant.
7.   General Reference
References for outgoing messages can be recorded by network or as general
references. Yes
The references for outgoing messages are based on the parameters in the session
"Maintain EDI Parameters (tcedi0100m000)".
No
The references for outgoing messages are based on the parameters in the session
"Maintain Networks (tcedi0120m000)".
If you enter "No" the system will ignore the following fields in the session
"Maintain Networks (tcedi0120m000)" when determining the reference number of
outgoing EDI messages:
•   Fixed Part
•   Date Format
•   First Free Number
•   Action on First Message on New Date
8.   Fixed Part
Outgoing messages should always have a reference. The structure of the reference
number is defined in the following fields:
•   Fixed Part
•   Date Format
•   First Free Number
The following possibilities are available:
•   Fixed Part/Date/Sequence Number
•   Fixed Part/Sequence Number
•   Date/Sequence Number
Reference numbers are always fourteen positions long. This means that the
sequence number occupies the positions which are not occupied by:
•   Fixed Part and/or Date Enter the fixed part of your reference number.
9.   Date Format
The date format used as part of the reference number. When selecting the date
format, you should take into account that the reference number has a length of
14 positions.
10.   First Free Number
The first free number used as reference number in the next outgoing message.
Example:
Fixed Part   : COMPANY
Date Format   : Without Century Number
First Free Number: 5
The first free reference number will be: COMPANY9401015
The first free number is automatically incremented whenever an outgoing message
is created. You can adjust the first free number manually.
11.   Action on First Message on New Date
Start with 0
The first outgoing message on a day has sequence number 0.
Start with 1
The first outgoing message on a day has sequence number 1.
Last Number + 1
The first outgoing message has as sequence number the number of the last message
to have been sent plus 1. Select one of the three options available.

tcedi0120m000   single-occ (1) < Form 2-2
+--+
| Maintain Networks   Company: 000 |

```
|-------------------------------------------------------------------------|
|                                                                         |
|  Network              : 1_____   2_____         |
|                                                                         |
|  Record Separator     : 3.........                                      |
|  Field Type           : 4..............                                 |
|                                                                         |
|  Separator Sign       : 5          Sign Around Strings  : 7             |
|  Replacement Sign     : 6          Replacement Sign     : 8             |
|                                                                         |
|  Leading Zeroes       : 9....                                           |
|                                                                         |
|  Suppress Standard    : 10...                                           |
|  Communication                                                          |
|                                                                         |
|  Generate Outgoing    : 11...                                           |
|  Messages before                                                        |
|  Connection                                                             |
|                                                                         |
+-------------------------------------------------------------------------+
```

1.   Network
The code uniquely identifying the network.
2.   Description
The description of the network.
3.   Record Separator
Depending on the system on which your EDI conversion program is implemented,
records in ASCII files will be separated by different separator signs.
<CR><LF> Mainly applicable to Personal Computers. Lines are separated by two
signs.
<LF> Mainly applicable to UNIX-type Operating Systems. Lines are separated by
one sign. The value you enter here depends on the line separator sign required
by your EDI conversion software.
4.   Field Type
ASCII files come in two base formats. Fixed Length
Each field always occupies a fixed number of positions.
Example:
<Order Number><Sender><Item>
0000000002332JOHNSON   ARMCHAIR
0000000440001PATTERSON MISCELL
0000000065500FINCH   ARMCHAIR
Delimited
Fields are separated by field separators. This separator can be defined
separately.
Example (separator is a comma): Order Number,Sender,Item 2332,JOHNSON,ARMCHAIR
440001,PATTERSON,MISCELL 65500,FINCHI,ARMCHAIR
The field type entered here depends on the data format expected by the external
EDI conversion software.
5.   Separator Sign
The field separator used (only relevant in case of files with "delimited"
fields). Enter the field separator that is expected by the external EDI software
(if the files contain field separators). A frequently used field separator is
the comma - 'comma-delimited'.
6.   Replacement Sign
The data in outgoing messages may not include characters identical to field
separators. This field contains a substitute character.
Enter a separator sign that is not identical to the field separator (if the
files contain field separators).
Example: The field separator is a comma (,) The replacing separator is a semi-
colon (;) Data is (Dear Sir,) Data becomes (Dear Sir;)
7.   Sign Around Strings
The special signs round string fields in EDI conversion packages.
Enter the sign here.
Example: "JOHNSON","ADDITIONAL TEXT"

8.   Replacement Sign
The fields in outgoing messages may not include signs identical to the sign
enclosing strings. This field contains a substitute sign.
Enter another sign than the sign surrounding strings.
Example:
*   Sign surrounding strings (")
*   Replacing sign (')
*   Data is (Note: item number is "355444")
*   Data becomes ("Note: item number is '355444'")
9.   Leading Zeroes
Some EDI conversion packages expect numeric fields to have leading zeros, so
that they do not contain alphanumeric characters (only relevant with fields of a
fixed length). Your choice in this field depends on the EDI conversion package.
Yes
The space in front of a number is filled with zeroes.
No
The space in front of a number is filled with spaces.
10.   Suppress Communication
Indicates whether or not communication with the external EDI network should be
suppressed (see also: Communication (tcedi00060)).
No
The standard communication procedure of the external EDI communication software
is executed.
Yes
The standard communication procedure is suppressed. Please ensure that the
messages generated within this network are manually removed from the APPL_FROM
directory. The status of a generated message is not changed into "Read by
Relation" until all files associated with the message have been removed.
Incoming messages must be placed in the APPL_TO directory manually.
11.   Generate Outgoing Message before Connection
The session "EDI Interchange Controller (tcedi7210m000)" handles outgoing
messages in two different ways.
Yes
The system generates outgoing messages before initiating the communication with
the network.
No
The system merely sends messages to the network which are waiting to be sent. It
does not generate any outgoing messages.
6.2   Maintain Connect Frequencies by Network (tcedi0122m000)
SESSION OBJECTIVE
To define the connect frequencies of the networks to be used in EDI.
SEE ALSO KEYWORD(S)
*   Connect Frequencies by Network
tcedi0122m000   multi/group (3   Form 1-1
+--+
Maintain Connect Frequencies by Network   Company: 000
Network   : 1.....   2_____
Status   : 3..............
Date   from : 4........
Date   to   : 5........
Day   from : 6........
Day   to   : 7........
Time   from :   8....
Time   to   :   9....

```
|  Interval     [min]:    10..                                            |
|                                                                         |
+-------------------------------------------------------------------------+
```
1.   Network
The code uniquely identifying the network.
2.   Description
The description of the network.
3.   Status
For each connection schedule you can define two periods which may overlap.
Active
During this period communication with the network takes place.
Inactive
During this period there is no communication with the network. Inactive periods
have a higher priority than active periods. If an active and an inactive period
overlap, the overlapping part becomes inactive.
4.   Date
The start date of the period.
5.   Date
The end date of the period.
6.   Day
Apart from a range of periods, you can also specify a range of days within a
week. Possibility 1 The start ("from") day is earlier than or the same as the
end ("to") day.
Example:
•   start day is Monday
•   end day is Friday
So Mo Tu We Th Fr Sa
   |------------|
The period runs from Monday to Friday (inclusive)
Possibility 2 The start ("from") day is later than the end ("to") day.
Example:
•   Start day is Saturday
•   End day is Sunday
So Ma Tu We Th Fr Sa
-| |-
The period runs from Saturday to Sunday (inclusive).
7.   Day
Apart from a range of periods, you can also specify a range of days within a
week.
8.   Time
In addition to the period and day ranges, you can specify a time range per day.
Possibility 1 The start ("from") time is earlier than or the same as the end
("to") time.
Example:
•   start time is 6:00 hours
•   end time is 18:00 hours
0 3 6 9 12 15 18 21 24
      |-----------|
Possibility 2 The start ("from") time is later than the end ("to") time.
Example
•   start time is 18:00 hours
•   end time is 6:00 hours
0 3 6 9 12 15 18 21 24
------| |-------
9.   Time
In addition to the period and day ranges, you can specify a time range per day.
10.   Interval
For an active period you can record the interval between connections with the
network in minutes.
6.3   Maintain Connect Times by Network (tcedi0125m000)
SESSION OBJECTIVE
To define the connect times of the networks to be used in EDI.
SEE ALSO KEYWORD(S)

•   Connect Times by Network
tcedi0125m000   multi-occ (2)   Form 1-1

```
+--------------------------------------------------------------------+
| Maintain Connect Times by Network                  Company: 000   |
|--------------------------------------------------------------------|
|                                                                    |
| Network     Description                    Date        Time        |
|                                                                    |
|    1.....   2_____ 3......... 4....        |
|                                                                    |
+--------------------------------------------------------------------+
```

1.   Network
The code uniquely identifying the network.
2.   Description
The description of the network.
3.   Date
The date of connection with the network.
4.   Time
The time of connection with the network.
6.4   Generate Connect Times by Network (tcedi0225m000)
SESSION OBJECTIVE
To generate the connect times defined in the session "Maintain Connect
Frequencies by Network (tcedi0122m000)".
SEE ALSO KEYWORD(S)
•   Connect Times by Network
tcedi0225m000   single-occ (4)   Form 1-1

```
+--------------------------------------------------------------------+
| Generate Connect Times by Network                  Company: 000   |
|--------------------------------------------------------------------|
|                                                                    |
| Network      from :   1.....                                       |
|              to   :   2.....                                       |
|                                                                    |
| Date         from : 3.........                                     |
|              to   : 4........                                      |
|                                                                    |
| 5_____   6_____                                                |
+--------------------------------------------------------------------+
```

1.   Network from
2.   Network to
3.   Date from
4.   Date to
5.   Current Network
6.   Current Date
6.5   Maintain Relation Data by Network (tcedi0128m000)
SESSION OBJECTIVE
To define the network data of each relation to be used in EDI.
SEE ALSO KEYWORD(S)
•   Relations by Network
tcedi0128m000   multi/group (3   Form 1-1

```
+--------------------------------------------------------------------+
| Maintain Relation Data by Network                  Company: 000   |
|--------------------------------------------------------------------|
|                                                                    |
| Relation      : 1.....  2_____            |
|                                                                    |
| Network   Description          Network Address   New Batch Number  |
|                                                                    |
|   3.....  4_____ 5...............  6.............. |
|                                                                    |
+--------------------------------------------------------------------+
```

1.   Relation

An outgoing message for this relation is sent to the network address of the
parent relation. For both relations the field "Network Address" in the session
"Maintain Relation Data by Network (tcedi0128m000)" must be filled.

2.   Description
3.   Network
The code uniquely identifying the network. A multicompany network (the field
"Multicompany" is on "Yes") is only allowed if the conditions described at the
field "Relation" have been met.

4.   Description
The description of the network.

5.   Network Address
The network address of this relation for the network.

6.   New Batch Number
By Message
A new reference is generated for each outgoing message.

By Message Group
As many outgoing messages as possible are grouped under one reference, for
instance: all invoices for a specific relation.

By Recipient
All messages for one and the same relation are collected and referred to by one
reference.

7   Other Print Sessions
7.1   Print Networks (tcedi0420m000)

tcedi0420m000   single-occ (4)   Form 1-1
+---+
Print Networks   Company: 000
Network   From : 1.....
To   : 2.....
+---+

1.   Network From
2.   Network to

7.2   Print Connect Frequencies by Network (tcedi0422m000)
tcedi0422m000   single-occ (4)   Form 1-1
+---+
Print Connect Frequencies by Network   Company: 000
Network   from :   1.....
to   :   2.....
Date   from : 3........
to   : 4........
+---+

1.   Network from
2.   Network to
3.   Date from
4.   Date to

7.3   Print Connect Times by Network (tcedi0425m000)
tcedi0425m000   single-occ (4)   Form 1-1
+---+
Print Connect Times by Network   Company: 000
Network   from :   1.....
to   :   2.....

```
|                                                       |        |
|  Date        from : 3........                         |        |
|              to   : 4........                         |        |
|                                                       |        |
+-----------------------------------------------------------------+
1.    Network from
2.    Network to
3.    Date from
4.    Date to
7.4   Print Relation Identification by Network (tcedi0428m000)
tcedi0428m000                          single-occ (4)    Form 1-1
+-----------------------------------------------------------------+
|                                                                 |
|  Print Relation Identification by Network        Company: 000   |
|-----------------------------------------------------------------|
|                                                                 |
|  Relation            from : 1.....                              |
|                      to   : 2.....                              |
|                                                                 |
|  Network             from : 3.....                              |
|                      to   : 4.....                              |
|                                                                 |
+-----------------------------------------------------------------+
1.    Relation from
2.    Relation to
3.    Network from
4.    Network to
8     Introduction to Coding and Conversion Data
8.1   General
```

OBJECTIVE OF BUSINESS OBJECT

This b-object allows you to control codes and conversion data for incoming and outgoing messages. Such information must prevent interpretation problems from arising between senders and receivers of EDI messages.

Such codes can be defined at two levels:

- Codes having a 1:1 relation with fields and functions in BAAN IV (i.e. which can be exchanged), for instance:
- Address Types
- Discounts
- Codes which can not be used directly in BAAN IV. They can only be used by including them in text fields. For instance:
- Schedule Release Frequencies
- Packing Code IDs

TERMS AND DEFINITIONS

Code IDs are codes giving information about other codes. For instance:

- address code ID "16" indicates that a code is a ZIP code
- item code ID "CL" indicates that a code is a color code

Display the procedure and show the sessions in:

- Coding and Conversion Data Procedure

8.2   Session Overview

Seq.	Session	Description	Session Usage
1	tcedi2128m000	Maintain Terms of Delivery	Mandatory
2	tcedi3100m000	Maint Conv of Terms of Deliv Codes (in)	Mandatory
3	tcedi4130m000	Maint Conv of Terms of Deliv Codes (out	Mandatory
4	tcedi2126m000	Maintain Countries	Mandatory
5	tcedi3102m000	Maint Conversion of Country Codes (in)	Mandatory

```
|   6 | tcedi4140m000 | Maint Conversion of Country Codes (out)| Mandatory
|
|   7 | tcedi2130m000 | Maintain Units                        | Mandatory
|
|   8 | tcedi3104m000 | Maintain Conversion of Unit Codes (in) | Mandatory
|
|   9 | tcedi4142m000 | Maintain Conversion of Unit Codes (out)| Mandatory
|
|  10 | tcedi2132m000 | Maintain Item Code IDs                | Mandatory
|
|  11 | tcedi3106m000 | Maint Conv of Item Codes by Rel (in)  | Mandatory
|
|  12 | tcedi3122m000 | Maint Conv of Item Codes (General) (in)| Mandatory
|
|  13 | tcedi4144m000 | Maint Conv of Item Codes by Rel (out) | Mandatory
|
|  14 | tcedi4160m000 | Maintain Conversion of Item Codes (out)| Mandatory
|
|  15 | tcedi2140m000 | Maintain Tax Code IDs                 | Mandatory
|
|  16 | tcedi2142m000 | Maintain Tax Codes                    | Mandatory
|
|  17 | tcedi3108m000 | Maintain Conversion of Tax Codes (in) | Mandatory
|
|  18 | tcedi4146m000 | Maintain Conversion of Tax Codes (out)| Mandatory
|
|  19 | tcedi2118m000 | Maintain Address Code IDs             | Mandatory
|
|  20 | tcedi3110m000 | Maint Conv Deliv Addr Codes by Cust (in| Mandatory
|
|  21 | tcedi3112m000 | Maint Conv Postal Addr Codes by Cust  | Mandatory
|
|  22 | tcedi3113m000 | Maint Conv Postal Addr Codes by Supplie| Mandatory
|
|  23 | tcedi4148m000 | Maint Conv of Deliv Addr Codes by Cust | Mandatory
|
|  24 | tcedi4150m000 | Maint Conv of Postal Addr Codes by Cust| Mandatory
|
|  25 | tcedi4151m000 | Maint Conv of Postal Addr Codes by Supp| Mandatory
|
|  26 | tcedi2192m000 | Maintain Currencies                   | Mandatory
|
|  27 | tcedi3124m000 | Maint Conversion of Currency Codes (in)| Mandatory
|
|  28 | tcedi4138m000 | Maint Conversion of Currency Codes (out| Mandatory
|
|  29 | tcedi2194m000 | Maint Terms of Payment/Late Payment Sur| Mandatory
|
|  30 | tcedi3126m000 | Maint Conv of Terms of Payment Codes (i| Mandatory
|
|  30 | tcedi4166m000 | Maint Conv of Terms of Payment Codes (o| Mandatory
|
|  31 | tcedi3130m000 | Maint Conv of Late Payment Surcharges  | Mandatory
|
|  31 | tcedi4170m000 | Maint Conv of Late Payment Surcharges  | Mandatory
|
|  32 | tcedi2148m000 | Maintain Third Parties                | Mandatory
|
|  33 | tcedi3128m000 | Maint Conv of Third Party Codes by Re(i| Mandatory
|
|  34 | tcedi4168m000 | Maint Conv of Third Party Codes by Re(o| Mandatory
|
```

35	tcedi2100m000	Maintain Order Types	Mandatory
36	tcedi4132m000	Maintain Conv of Order Types (out)	Mandatory
37	tcedi2124m000	Maintain Address Types	Mandatory
38	tcedi4134m000	Maintain Conv of Address Types (out)	Mandatory
39	tcedi2120m000	Maintain Reference Number Types	Mandatory
40	tcedi4136m000	Maint Conv of Reference Number Types (o	Mandatory
42	tcedi4162m000	Maint Conv of Warehouse Addresses (out)	Mandatory
43	tcedi4108m000	Maintain Character Conversion Codes	Mandatory
44	tcedi4109m000	Maintain Character Conversions (out)	Mandatory
45	tcedi2145m000	Maintain Allowances and Charges	Mandatory
46	tcedi4172m000	Maint Conv of Allowances and Charges (o	Mandatory
47	tcedi2144m000	Maintain Discounts and Surcharges	Mandatory
80	tcedi3200m000	Check/Clear Conv of Item Codes by Re(in	Additional
81	tcedi4200m000	Check/Clear Conv of Item Codes by Re(ou	Additional
82	tcedi7200m000	Copy Conversion Tables	Additional
101	tcedi2428m000	Print Terms of Delivery	Print
102	tcedi3400m000	Print Conv of Terms of Deliv Codes (in)	Print
103	tcedi4430m000	Print Conv Terms of Delivery Codes (out	Print
104	tcedi2426m000	Print Countries	Print
105	tcedi3402m000	Print Conversion of Country Codes (in)	Print
106	tcedi4440m000	Print Conversion of Country Codes (out)	Print
107	tcedi2430m000	Print Units	Print
108	tcedi3404m000	Print Conversion of Unit Codes (in)	Print
109	tcedi4442m000	Print Conversion of Unit Codes (out)	Print
110	tcedi2432m000	Print Item Code IDs	Print
111	tcedi3406m000	Print Conv of Item Codes by Relation (i	Print
112	tcedi3422m000	Print Conv of Item Codes (General) (in)	Print
113	tcedi4444m000	Print Conv of Item Codes by Relation (o	Print
114	tcedi4460m000	Print Conversion of Item Codes (out)	Print
115	tcedi2440m000	Print Tax Code IDs	Print
115	tcedi3430m000	Print Conv of Late Payment Surcharges(i	Print

```
| 116 | tcedi2442m000 | Print Tax Codes                         | Print
| 117 | tcedi3408m000 | Print Conversion of Tax Codes (in)      | Print
| 118 | tcedi4446m000 | Print Conversion of Tax Codes (out)     | Print
| 119 | tcedi2418m000 | Print Address Code IDs                  | Print
| 120 | tcedi3410m000 | Print Conv of Deliv Addr Codes by Custo| Print
| 121 | tcedi3412m000 | Print Conv of Postal Addr Codes by Cust| Print
| 122 | tcedi3413m000 | Print Conv of Postal Addr Codes by Supp| Print
| 123 | tcedi4448m000 | Print Conv of Del Addr Codes by Cust (o| Print
| 124 | tcedi4450m000 | Print Conv of Postal Addr Codes by Cust| Print
| 124 | tcedi4451m000 | Print Conv of Postal Addr Codes by Supp| Print
| 125 | tcedi4462m000 | Print Conv of Warehouse Addresses (out)| Print
| 126 | tcedi2492m000 | Print Currencies                        | Print
| 127 | tcedi3424m000 | Print Conversion of Currency Codes (in)| Print
| 128 | tcedi4438m000 | Print conversion of Currency Codes (out| Print
| 129 | tcedi2494m000 | Print Terms of Payment/Late Payment Sur| Print
| 129 | tcedi4470m000 | Print Conv of Late Payment Surcharges   | Print
| 130 | tcedi3426m000 | Print Conv of Terms of Payment Codes (i| Print
| 131 | tcedi4466m000 | Print Conversion of Terms of Payment (o| Print
| 132 | tcedi2448m000 | Print Third Parties                     | Print
| 133 | tcedi3428m000 | Print Conv of Third Party Code by Rel(i| Print
| 134 | tcedi4468m000 | Print Conv of Third Party Code by Rel(o| Print
| 135 | tcedi2400m000 | Print Order Types                       | Print
| 136 | tcedi4432m000 | Print Conversion of Order Types (out)   | Print
| 136 | tcedi4436m000 | Print Conv of Reference Number Types (o| Print
| 137 | tcedi2424m000 | Print Address Types                     | Print
| 138 | tcedi4434m000 | Print Conversion of Address Types (out)| Print
| 139 | tcedi2420m000 | Print Reference Number Types            | Print
| 141 | tcedi4408m000 | Print Character Conversion Codes (out)  | Print
| 142 | tcedi4409m000 | Print Character Conversions (out)       | Print
| 201 | tcedi2500s000 | Display Order Types                     | Display
| 201 | tcedi4532s000 | Display Conversion of Order Types (out)| Display
```

| 202 | tcedi2545s000 | Display Allowances and Charges | Display
| 203 | tcedi2518s000 | Display Address Code IDs | Display
| 204 | tcedi2520s000 | Display Reference Number Types | Display
| 204 | tcedi4536s000 | Display Conv of Ref Number Types (out) | Display
| 205 | tcedi2524s000 | Display Address Types | Display
| 205 | tcedi4534s000 | Display Conversion of Address Types (ou| Display
| 206 | tcedi2526s000 | Display Countries | Display
| 206 | tcedi4540s000 | Display Conversion of Country Codes (ou| Display
| 207 | tcedi2528s000 | Display Terms of Delivery | Display
| 207 | tcedi4530s000 | Display Conv of Terms of Del Codes (out| Display
| 208 | tcedi2530s000 | Display Units | Display
| 208 | tcedi4542s000 | Display Conversion of Unit Codes (out) | Display
| 209 | tcedi2532s000 | Display Item Code IDs | Display
| 209 | tcedi4544s000 | Display Conv of Item Codes by Rel (out)| Display
| 210 | tcedi2540s000 | Display Tax Code IDs | Display
| 210 | tcedi4546s000 | Display Conversion of Tax Codes (out) | Display
| 211 | tcedi2542s000 | Display Tax Codes | Display
| 212 | tcedi2548s000 | Display Third Parties | Display
| 213 | tcedi2592s000 | Display Currencies | Display
| 213 | tcedi4538s000 | Display Conversion of Currency Codes (o| Display
| 214 | tcedi2594s000 | Display Terms of Payment/Late Pay Surch| Display
| 215 | tcedi4548s000 | Display Conv of Del Addr Codes by Rel(o| Display
| 216 | tcedi4550s000 | Display Conv of Postal Addr Code by Rel| Display
| 217 | tcedi4552s000 | Display Conv of Sales Contract Code by | Display
| 218 | tcedi4554s000 | Display Conv of Project Codes by Rel(ou| Display
| 219 | tcedi4556s000 | Display Conv of Forw Agent Code by Rel | Display
| 220 | tcedi4558s000 | Display Conv of Employee Code by Rel (o| Display
| 221 | tcedi4560s000 | Display Conversion of Item Codes (out) | Display
| 222 | tcedi4508s000 | Display Character Conversion Codes (out| Display
| 223 | tcedi4509s000 | Display Character Conversions (out) | Display

9   Mandatory Sessions
9.1   Maintain Terms of Delivery (tcedi2128m000)

SESSION OBJECTIVE
To maintain terms of delivery codes. This is necessary in order to be able to
send or receive messages containing these.
SEE ALSO KEYWORD(S)
• 	Terms of Delivery
tcedi2128m000   multi/group (3   Form 1-1
+---+
Maintain Terms of Delivery   Company: 000
Organization   : 1.. 2_____
Code in Message   Description
3.....   4...........................
+---+

1.   Organization
The code which uniquely identifies the organization.
2.   Description
3.   Code in Message
The code used in the message.
4.   Description
The description for the code in the EDI message.
9.2   Maintain Conversion of Terms of Delivery Codes (in) (tcedi3100m000)
SESSION OBJECTIVE
To maintain the conversion data for the terms of delivery in incoming messages.
SEE ALSO KEYWORD(S)
• 	Conversion of Delivery Condition Codes (in)
tcedi3100m000   multi/group (3   Form 1-1
+---+
Maintain Conversion of Terms of Delivery Codes (in)   Company: 000
Organization   : 1.. 2_____
Code in Message   Code in Application   Description
3..... 4_____   5.. 6_____
+---+
1.   Organization
The code which uniquely identifies the organization.
2.   Description
3.   Code in Message
The code used in the message.
4.   Description
The description for the code in the EDI message.
5.   Code in Application
The code used in BAAN IV.
6.   Description
9.3   Maintain Conversion of Terms of Delivery Codes (out) (tcedi4130m000)
SESSION OBJECTIVE
To maintain the conversion data for the terms of delivery codes in outgoing
messages. This will allow you to send messages for which this conversion is
necessary.
SEE ALSO KEYWORD(S)
• 	Conversion of Terms of Delivery Codes (out)
tcedi4130m000   multi/group (3   Form 1-1
+---+
Maintain Conversion of Terms of Delivery Codes (out)   Company: 000

```
|                                                                              |
|  Organization: 1..  2_____                        |
|                                                                              |
|  Code in Application                      Code in Message                    |
|                                                                              |
|  3..  4_____        5.....  6_____|
|                                                                              |
+------------------------------------------------------------------------------+
```

1.   Organization
The code which uniquely identifies the organization.
2.   Description
3.   Code in Appl.
The code used in BAAN IV.
4.   Description
5.   Code in Message
The code used in the message.
6.   Description
The description for the code in the EDI message.
9.4   Maintain Countries (tcedi2126m000)
SESSION OBJECTIVE
To maintain country codes. This is necessary in order to be able to send or
receive messages to/from different countries.
SEE ALSO KEYWORD(S)
•   Countries
tcedi2126m000   multi/group (3   Form 1-1

```
+------------------------------------------------------------------------------+
|  Maintain Countries                                        Company: 000   |
|------------------------------------------------------------------------------|
|                                                                              |
|  Organization        : 1..  2_____                |
|                                                                              |
|  Code in Message        Description                                          |
|                                                                              |
|  3.....                 4..........................                          |
|                                                                              |
+------------------------------------------------------------------------------+
```

1.   Organization
The code which uniquely identifies the organization.
2.   Description
3.   Code in Message
The code used in the message.
4.   Description
The description for the code in the EDI message.
9.5   Maintain Conversion of Country Codes (in) (tcedi3102m000)
SESSION OBJECTIVE
To maintain the conversion data for the country codes in incoming messages.
HOW TO USE THE SESSION
•   Conversion of Country Codes (in)
tcedi3102m000   multi/group (3   Form 1-1

```
+------------------------------------------------------------------------------+
|  Maintain Conversion of Country Codes (in)                 Company: 000   |
|------------------------------------------------------------------------------|
|                                                                              |
|  Organization        : 1..  2_____                |
|                                                                              |
|  Code in Message                    Code in Application   Description        |
|                                                                              |
|  3.....  4_____        5..  6_____         |
|                                                                              |
+------------------------------------------------------------------------------+
```

1.   Organization
The code which uniquely identifies the organization.
2.   Description

3.   Code in Message
The code used in the message.
4.   Description
The description for the code in the EDI message.
5.   Code in Application
The code used in BAAN IV.
6.   Description
9.6   Maintain Conversion of Country Codes (out) (tcedi4140m000)
SESSION OBJECTIVE
To maintain the conversion data for the country codes in outgoing messages.
This will allow you to send messages for which this conversion is necessary.
SEE ALSO KEYWORD(S)
•   Conversion of Country Codes (out)
tcedi4140m000   multi/group (3   Form 1-1
+---+
Maintain Conversion of Country Codes (out)   Company: 000
Organization   : 1.. 2_____
Code in Application   Code in Message
3.. 4_____   5..... 6_____
+---+
1.   Organization
The code which uniquely identifies the organization.
2.   Description
3.   Code in Application
The code used in BAAN IV.
4.   Description
5.   Code in Message
The code used in the message.
6.   Description
The description for the code in the EDI message.
9.7   Maintain Units (tcedi2130m000)
SESSION OBJECTIVE
To maintain unit codes. This is necessary in order to be able to send or receive
messages containing these.
SEE ALSO KEYWORD(S)
•   Units
tcedi2130m000   multi/group (3   Form 1-1
+---+
Maintain Units   Company: 000
Organization   : 1.. 2_____
Code in Message   Description
3.....   4...........................
+---+
1.   Organization
The code which uniquely identifies the organization.
2.   Description
3. Code in Message
The code used in the message.
4.   Description
The description for the code in the EDI message.
9.8   Maintain Conversion of Unit Codes (in) (tcedi3104m000)
SESSION OBJECTIVE
To maintain the conversion data for the unit codes in incoming messages.

SEE ALSO KEYWORD(S)
• Conversion of Unit Codes (in)

tcedi3104m000   multi/group (3   Form 1-1
+---+
Maintain Conversion of Unit Codes (in)   Company: 000
Organization   : 1.. 2_____
Code in Message   Code in Application
3..... 4_____ 5.. 6_____
+---+

1.   Organization
The code which uniquely identifies the organization.
2.   Description
3.   Code in Message
The code used in the message.
4.   Description
The description for the code in the EDI message.
5.   Code in Application
The code used in BAAN IV.
6. Description
9.9   Maintain Conversion of Unit Codes (out) (tcedi4142m000)
SESSION OBJECTIVE
To maintain the conversion data for the unit codes in outgoing messages. This
will allow you to send messages for which this conversion is necessary.
SEE ALSO KEYWORD(S)
• Conversion of Unit Codes (out)

tcedi4142m000   multi/group (3   Form 1-1
+---+
Maintain Conversion of Unit Codes (out)   Company: 000
Organization   : 1.. 2_____
Code in Application   Code in Message
3.. 4_____   5..... 6_____
+---+

1.   Organization
The code which uniquely identifies the organization.
2.   Description
3.   Code in Application
The code used in BAAN IV.
4.   Description
5.   Code in Message
The code used in the message.
6.   Description
The description for the code in the EDI message.
9.10 Maintain Item Code IDs (tcedi2132m000)
SESSION OBJECTIVE
To maintain item code IDs. This is necessary in order to be able to send or
receive messages containing these.
SEE ALSO KEYWORD(S)
• Item Code IDs

tcedi2132m000   multi/group (3   Form 1-1
+---+
Maintain Item Code IDs   Company: 000

```
| Organization        : 1..  2_____      |
|                                                                     |
| Code in Message       Description              Item Code System     |
|                                                                     |
| 3.....                4............................  5..            |
+---------------------------------------------------------------------+
```

1.   Organization
The code which uniquely identifies the organization.
2.   Description
3.   Code in Message
The code used in the message.
4.   Description
The description for the code in the EDI message.
5.   Item Code System
For further information, see keyword(s)
"Item Code Systems".

9.11 Maintain Conversion of Item Codes by Relation (in) (tcedi3106m000)
SESSION OBJECTIVE
To maintain the conversion data for the item codes in incoming messages. The
items may be standard as well as customized items.
When converting incoming messages the system first consults the conversion data
entered in this session, and only then the general conversion data for items as
recorded in the session "Maintain Conversion of Item Codes (General) (in)
(tcedi3122m000)".
SEE ALSO KEYWORD(S)
•   Conversion of Item Codes by Relation (in)

```
tcedi3106m000                         multi/group (3    Form 1-1
+---------------------------------------------------------------------+
| Maintain Conversion of Item Codes by Relation (in)   Company: 000   |
|---------------------------------------------------------------------|
|                                                                     |
| Relation           : 1.....  3_____          |
| Organization       :   4..  5_____          |
| Item Code ID       : 6.....  7_____          |
|                                                                     |
|Code in Message                    Proj.  Code in Appl.              |
|                                                                     |
|8................................. 9..... 10.............. 2_____ 11.|
|                                                                     |
+---------------------------------------------------------------------+
```

1.   Relation
An outgoing message for this relation is sent to the network address of the
parent relation. For both relations the field "Network Address" in the session
"Maintain Relation Data by Network (tcedi0128m000)" must be filled.
2.   Description
3.   Description
4.   Organization
The code which uniquely identifies the organization.
5.   Description
6.   Item Code ID
The code type of the code in the message.
7.   Description
The description for the code in the EDI message.
8.   Code of Relation
The code used in the message.
9.   Project
The project within which the item has been defined. If this field is left empty,
the item is a standard instead of a project item.
10.   Code in Application
The code used in BAAN IV.
11.   Container

A container is a particular type of package in which an item occurs. The container unit must be part of the unit set. (see also the field "Containerized" in the session "Maintain Item Data (tiitm0101m000)")
For further information, see keyword(s)
•   Units
•   Units By Unit Set
For further information, see method(s)
•   Using Containers
•   Containerized Items

9.12 Maintain Conversion of Item Codes (General) (in) (tcedi3122m000)
SESSION OBJECTIVE
To maintain the conversion data for the item codes in incoming messages. This will allow you to process received messages for which this conversion is necessary.
HOW TO USE THE SESSION
If the "Code in Message" exists in the table which you defined in the session "Maintain Conversion of Item Codes by Relation (in) (tcedi3106m000)" for the relevant relation, that conversion will be used instead of this one.
If the "Code in Message" is already used for a relation (entered in session "Maintain Conversion of Item Codes by Relation (in) (tcedi3106m000)"), the system will ask you whether the conversions recorded there may be deleted. It will do so only if you choose option "Continue [cont.process]", and the "code in BAAN IV is equal to the one defined here.
SEE ALSO KEYWORD(S)
•   Conversion of Item Codes (General) (in)

```
tcedi3122m000                                    multi/group (3     Form 1-1
+----------------------------------------------------------------------------+
|  Maintain Conversion of Item Codes (General) (in)          Company: 000  |
|--------------------------------------------------------------------------|
|                                                                          |
|  Organization         :    1..   2_____       |
|  Item Code ID         : 3.....   4_____       |
|                                                                          |
|  Code in Message                       Code in Appl.                     |
|                                                                          |
|  5...................................  6............  8_____  7.. |
|                                                                          |
+----------------------------------------------------------------------------+
```

1.   Organization
The code which uniquely identifies the organization.
2.   Description
3.   Item Code ID
The code type of the code in the message.
4.   Description
The description for the code in the EDI message.
5.   Code in Message
The code used in the message.
6.   Code in Application
The code used in BAAN IV.
7.   Container
A container is a particular type of package in which an item occurs. The container unit must be part of the unit set. (see also the field "Containerized" in the session "Maintain Item Data (tiitm0101m000)")
For further information, see keyword(s)
•   Units
•   Units By Unit Set
For further information, see method(s)
•   Using Containers
•   Containerized Items
8.   Description

9.13 Maintain Conversion of Item Codes by Relation (out) (tcedi4144m000)
SESSION OBJECTIVE

To maintain the conversion data for the item codes by relation in outgoing
messages. This will allow you to send messages for which this conversion is
necessary.
SEE ALSO KEYWORD(S)
•   Conversion of Item Codes by Relation (out)

tcedi4144m000   multi/group (3   Form 1-1
+---+
Maintain Conversion of Item Codes by Relation (out)   Company: 000
Relation   : 1.....   3_____
Organization   :   4..   5_____
Project   : 6.....   7_____
Code in Appl.   Item Code in Message
C. ID
8.............. 2_____   9.. 10.... 11........................ .
+---+

1.   Relation
An outgoing message for this relation is sent to the network address of the
parent relation. For both relations the field "Network Address" in the session
"Maintain Relation Data by Network (tcedi0128m000)" must be filled.
2.   Description
3.   Description
4.   Organization
The code which uniquely identifies the organization.
5.   Description
6.   Project
The project within which the item has been defined. If this field is left empty,
the item is a standard instead of a project item.
7.   Description
8.   Code in Application
The code used in BAAN IV.
9.   Container
A container is a particular type of package in which an item occurs. The
container unit must be part of the unit set. (see also the field "Containerized"
in the session "Maintain Item Data (tiitm0101m000)")
For further information, see keyword(s)
•   Units
•   Units By Unit Set
For further information, see method(s)
•   Using Containers
•   Containerized Items
10.   Item Code ID
The code type of the code in the message.
11.   Code in Message
The code used in the message.
9.14 Maintain Conversion of Item Codes (out) (tcedi4160m000)
SESSION OBJECTIVE
To maintain the conversion data for the item codes in outgoing messages. This
will allow you to send messages for which this conversion is necessary.
HOW TO USE THE SESSION
Upon sending messages, the "Code in BAAN IV will be converted to "Code in
message". If the "Code in BAAN IV is found in the table recorded in the session
"Maintain Conversion of Item Codes by Relation (out) (tcedi4144m000)", that
conversion will be selected instead of the other.
If the "Code in message" that you record belongs to a relation, the system will
ask you whether the conversions recorded there may be deleted. This will only
occur if you answered the question by "yes" and the "Code in Message" and "Item
Code ID" are equal to the ones defined here.
SEE ALSO KEYWORD(S)

- Conversion of Item Codes (out)

tcedi4160m000   multi/group (3   Form 1-1

```
+----------------------------------------------------------------------+
| Maintain Conversion of Item Codes (out)          Company: 000 |
|----------------------------------------------------------------------|
|                                                                      |
|  Organization        : 1..  2_____            |
|                                                                      |
| Code in Appl.                     Item    Code in Message            |
|                                   Code ID                            |
|                                                                      |
| 3.............. 5_____  4..  6..... 7........................ |
|                                                                      |
+----------------------------------------------------------------------+
```

1.   Organization
The code which uniquely identifies the organization.
2.   Description
3.   Code in Application
The code used in BAAN IV.
4.   Container
A container is a particular type of package in which an item occurs. The
container unit must be part of the unit set. (see also the field "Containerized"
in the session "Maintain Item Data (tiitm0101m000)")
For further information, see keyword(s)
- Units
- Units By Unit Set
For further information, see method(s)
- Using Containers
- Containerized Items
5. Description
6.   Item Code ID
The code type of the code in the message.
7.   Code in Message
The code used in the message.

9.15 Maintain Tax Code IDs (tcedi2140m000)
SESSION OBJECTIVE
To maintain Tax code IDs. This is necessary in order to be able to send or
receive messages containing these.
SEE ALSO KEYWORD(S)
- Tax Code IDs

tcedi2140m000   multi/group (3   Form 1-1

```
+----------------------------------------------------------------------+
| Maintain Tax Code IDs                            Company: 000 |
|----------------------------------------------------------------------|
|                                                                      |
|  Organization        : 1..  2_____            |
|                                                                      |
| Code in Message        Description                                   |
|                                                                      |
| 3.....                 4...........................                  |
|                                                                      |
+----------------------------------------------------------------------+
```

1.   Organization
The code which uniquely identifies the organization.
2.   Description
3.   Code in Message
The code used in the message.
4.   Description
The description for the code in the EDI message.

9.16 Maintain Tax Codes (tcedi2142m000)
SESSION OBJECTIVE
To maintain Tax codes. This is necessary in order to be able to send or receive
messages containing these.

SEE ALSO KEYWORD(S)
•   Tax Codes

tcedi2142m000   multi/group (3   Form 1-1

```
+------------------------------------------------------------------------+
| Maintain Tax Codes                                      Company: 000   |
|------------------------------------------------------------------------|
|                                                                        |
| Organization        : 1..  2_____             |
|                                                                        |
| Code in Message        Description                                     |
|                                                                        |
| 3.....                 4...........................                    |
|                                                                        |
+------------------------------------------------------------------------+
```

1.   Organization
The code which uniquely identifies the organization.
2.   Description
3.   Code in Message
The code used in the message.
4.   Description
The description for the code in the EDI message.
9.17 Maintain Conversion of Tax Codes (in) (tcedi3108m000)
SESSION OBJECTIVE
To maintain the conversion data for the Tax codes in incoming messages. This
will allow you to process received messages for which this conversion is
necessary.

SEE ALSO KEYWORD(S)
•   Conversion of Tax Codes (in)

tcedi3108m000   multi/group (3   Form 1-1

```
+------------------------------------------------------------------------+
| Maintain Conversion of Tax Codes (in)                   Company: 000   |
|------------------------------------------------------------------------|
|                                                                        |
| Organization        : 1..    2_____                    |
| Country             : 3..    4_____                    |
| Tax Code ID         : 5.....  6_____                   |
|                                                                        |
| Code in Message      Description      Code in Application  Description  |
|                                                                        |
| 7.....               8_____          9........ 10_____     |
|                                                                        |
+------------------------------------------------------------------------+
```

1.   Organization
The code which uniquely identifies the organization.
2.   Description
3.   Country
The country for which this Tax code is used in BAAN IV.
4.   Description
5.   Tax Code ID
The code type of the code in the message.
6.   Description
The description for the code in the EDI message.
7.   Code in Message
The code used in the message.
8.   Description
The description for the code in the EDI message.
9.   Code in Application
The code used in BAAN IV.
10.   Description
9.18 Maintain Conversion of Tax Codes (out) (tcedi4146m000)
SESSION OBJECTIVE
To maintain the conversion data for the Tax codes in outgoing messages. This
will allow you to send messages for which this conversion is necessary.

SEE ALSO KEYWORD(S)
- Conversion of Tax Codes (out)

tcedi4146m000   multi/group (3   Form 1-1
+--+
Maintain Conversion of Tax Codes (out)   Company: 000
Organization   : 1.. 2_____
Country   : 3.. 4_____
Code in Application   Tax Code ID   Code in Message
5........ 6_____ 7..... 8_____ 9..... 10_____
+--+

1.   Organization
The code which uniquely identifies the organization.
2.   Description
3.   Country
The country for which this Tax code is used in BAAN IV.
4.   Description
5.   Code in Application
The code used in BAAN IV.
6.   Description
7.   Tax Code ID
The code type of the code in the message.
8.   Description
The description for the code in the EDI message.
9.   Code in Message
The code used in the message.
10.   Description
The description for the code in the EDI message.

9.19 Maintain Address Code IDs (tcedi2118m000)
SESSION OBJECTIVE
To maintain address code IDs. This is necessary in order to be able to send or
receive messages containing these.
SEE ALSO KEYWORD(S)
- Address Code IDs

tcedi2118m000   multi/group (3   Form 1-1
+--+
Maintain Address Code IDs   Company: 000
Organization   : 1.. 2_____
Code in Message   Description
3.....   4...........................
+--+

1.   Organization
The code which uniquely identifies the organization.
2.   Description
3.   Code in Message
The code used in the message.
4.   Description
Enter a clear description here.

9.20 Maintain Conv. of Delivery Address Codes by Customer (in) (tcedi3110m000)
SESSION OBJECTIVE
To maintain the conversion data for the delivery address codes in incoming
messages. This will allow you to process received messages for which this
conversion is necessary.
SEE ALSO KEYWORD(S)

tcedi3110m000   multi/group (3   Form 1-1
+---+
Maintain Conv. of Delivery Address Codes by Customer (in)   Company: 000
Customer   : 1..... 2_____
Organization   :   3.. 4_____
Address Code ID   : 5..... 6_____
Code in Message   Code in Application
7...................   8.. 9_____
+---+

1.   Customer
The customer associated with the relation.
2.   Name
The first part of the customer's name.
3.   Organization
The code which uniquely identifies the organization.
4.   Description
5.   Address Code ID
The code type of the code in the message.
6.   Description
7.   Code in Message
The code used in the message.
8.   Code in Application
The code used in BAAN IV.
9.   Name
The first part of the customer name.

9.21 Maintain Conversion of Postal Address Codes by Customer (in)
(tcedi3112m000)
SESSION OBJECTIVE
To maintain the conversion data for the postal address codes in incoming
messages from customers. This will allow you to process received messages for
which this conversion is necessary.
SEE ALSO KEYWORD(S)
• Conversion of Postal Address Codes by Customer (in)
tcedi3112m000   multi/group (3   Form 1-1
+---+
Maintain Conversion of Postal Address Codes by Customer (in) Company: 000
Customer   : 1..... 2_____
Organization   :   3.. 4_____
Address Code ID: 5..... 6_____
Code in Message   Code in Appl.   Name
7...................   8.. 9_____
+---+

1.   Customer
The customer associated with the relation.
2.   Name
The first part of the customer's name.
3.   Organization
The code which uniquely identifies the organization.
4.   Description
5.   Address Code ID
The code type of the code in the message.
6.   Description

7.   Code in Message
The code used in the message.
8.   Code in Application
The code used in BAAN IV.
9.   Name
The first part of the customer name.

9.22 Maintain Conversion of Postal Address Codes by Supplier (in) (tcedi3113m000)

SESSION OBJECTIVE
To maintain the conversion data for the postal address codes in incoming messages from suppliers. This will allow you to process received messages for which this conversion is necessary.
SEE ALSO KEYWORD(S)
•   Conversion of Postal Address Codes by Supplier (in)

```
tcedi3113m000                              multi/group (3    Form 1-1
+------------------------------------------------------------------------+
| Maintain Conversion of Postal Address Codes by Supplier (in)  Company: 000 |
|------------------------------------------------------------------------|
|                                                                        |
| Supplier        : 1.....   2_____          |
| Organization    :   3..  4_____             |
| Address Code ID: 5.....   6_____            |
|                                                                        |
| Code in Message        Code in Appl.     Name                          |
|                                                                        |
| 7...................                8..  9_____ |
|                                                                        |
+------------------------------------------------------------------------+
```

1.   Supplier
The supplier linked to the relation.
2.   Name
The first part of the supplier's name.
3.   Organization
The code which uniquely identifies the organization.
4.   Description
5.   Address Code ID
The code type of the code in the message.
6.   Description
7.   Code in Message
The code used in the message.
8.   Code in Application
The code used in BAAN IV.
9.   Name
The first part of the supplier's name.

9.23 Maintain Conv. of Delivery Address Codes by Customer (out) (tcedi4148m000)

SESSION OBJECTIVE
To maintain the conversion data for the delivery address codes by customer in outgoing messages. This will allow you to send messages for which this conversion is necessary.
SEE ALSO KEYWORD(S)
•   Conversion of Delivery Address Codes by Customer (out)

```
tcedi4148m000                              multi/group (3    Form 1-1
+------------------------------------------------------------------------+
| Maintain Conv. of Delivery Address Codes by Customer (out)   Company: 000 |
|------------------------------------------------------------------------|
|                                                                        |
| Customer          : 1.....   2_____        |
| Organization      :   3..  4_____           |
|                                                                        |
| Code in Application              Address Code ID  Code in Message      |
|                                                                        |
| 5.. 6_____    7_____    8.....        9.................. |
|                                                                        |
```

```
+------------------------------------------------------------------------------+
```
1.   Customer
The customer associated with the relation.
2.   Name
The first part of the customer's name.
3.   Organization
The code which uniquely identifies the organization.
4.   Description
5.   Code in Application
The code used in BAAN IV.
6.   Name
The first part of the customer name.
7.   City
The city where the customer is established.
For tax provider users, the city and state or province where the customer is
established. The city and state or province should be separated by a comma ","
such as "Menlo Park, CA".
For further information, see method(s)
•   Address Verification for Tax Provider
8.   Address Code ID
The code type of the code in the message.
9.   Code in Message
The code used in the message.

9.24 Maintain Conv. of Postal Address Codes by Customer (out) (tcedi4150m000)
SESSION OBJECTIVE
To maintain the conversion data for the postal address codes by customer in
outgoing messages. This will allow you to send messages for which this
conversion is necessary.
SEE ALSO KEYWORD(S)
•   Conversion of Postal Address Codes by Customer (out)

tcedi4150m000   multi/group (3   Form 1-1
```
+------------------------------------------------------------------------------+
| Maintain Conv. of Postal Address Codes by Customer (out)    Company: 000 |
|------------------------------------------------------------------------------|
|                                                                          |
| Customer        : 1.....   2_____            |
| Organization    :    3..   4_____                |
|                                                                          |
| Code in Appl.  Name        Address Code ID  Description   Code in Message |
|                                                                          |
|        5..  6_____   7.....          8_____   9.............. |
|                                                                          |
+------------------------------------------------------------------------------+
```
1.   Customer
The customer associated with the relation.
2.   Name
The first part of the customer's name.
3.   Organization
The code which uniquely identifies the organization.
4.   Description
5.   Code in Application
The code used in BAAN IV.
6.   Name
The first part of the customer name.
7.   Address Code ID
The code type of the code in the message.
8.   Description
9.   Code in Message
The code used in the message.

9.25 Maintain Conv. of Postal Address Codes by Supplier (out) (tcedi4151m000)
SESSION OBJECTIVE

To maintain the conversion data for the postal address codes by supplier in
outgoing messages. This will allow you to send messages for which this
conversion is necessary.
SEE ALSO KEYWORD(S)
•   Conversion of Postal Address Codes by Supplier (out)

```
tcedi4151m000                           multi/group (3    Form 1-1
+--------------------------------------------------------------------------+
| Maintain Conv. of Postal Address Codes by Supplier (out)   Company: 000  |
|--------------------------------------------------------------------------|
|                                                                          |
|  Supplier       : 1.....  2_____        |
|  Organization   :   3..   4_____                  |
|                                                                          |
|  Code in Appl.  Name        Address Code ID  Description    Code in Message |
|                                                                          |
|        5..  6_____  7.....          8_____   9..............      |
|                                                                          |
+--------------------------------------------------------------------------+
```

1.   Supplier
The supplier linked to the relation.
2.   Name
The first part of the supplier's name.
3.   Organization
The code which uniquely identifies the organization.
4.   Description
5.   Code in Application
The code used in BAAN IV.
6.   Name
The first part of the supplier's name.
7.   Address Code ID
The code type of the code in the message.
8.   Description
9.   Code in Message
The code used in the message.

9.26 Maintain Currencies (tcedi2192m000)
SESSION OBJECTIVE
To maintain currency codes. This is necessary in order to be able to send or
receive messages containing these.
SEE ALSO KEYWORD(S)
•   Currencies

```
tcedi2192m000                           multi/group (3    Form 1-1
+--------------------------------------------------------------------------+
|  Maintain Currencies                                      Company: 000    |
|--------------------------------------------------------------------------|
|                                                                          |
|  Organization        : 1..  2_____                |
|                                                                          |
|  Code in Message        Description                                       |
|                                                                          |
|  3.....                 4...........................                      |
|                                                                          |
+--------------------------------------------------------------------------+
```

1.   Organization
The code which uniquely identifies the organization.
2.   Description
3.   Code in Message
The code used in the message.
4.   Description
The description for the code in the EDI message.

9.27 Maintain Conversion of Currency Codes (in) (tcedi3124m000)
SESSION OBJECTIVE

To maintain the conversion data for the currency codes in incoming messages.
This will allow you to process received messages for which this conversion is
necessary.
SEE ALSO KEYWORD(S)
- Conversion of Currency Codes (in)

tcedi3124m000   multi/group (3   Form 1-1

```
+-------------------------------------------------------------------------+
| Maintain Conversion of Currency Codes (in)            Company: 000  |
|-------------------------------------------------------------------------|
|                                                                         |
| Organization       : 1.. 2_____                 |
|                                                                         |
| Code in Message        Description    Code in Application  Description   |
|                                                                         |
| 3.....            4_____           5.. 6_____  |
|                                                                         |
+-------------------------------------------------------------------------+
```

1.   Organization
The code which uniquely identifies the organization.
2.   Description
3.   Code in Message
The code used in the message.
4.   Description
The description for the code in the EDI message.
5.   Code in Application
The code used in BAAN IV.
6.   Description

9.28 Maintain Conversion of Currency Codes (out) (tcedi4138m000)
SESSION OBJECTIVE
To maintain the conversion data for the currency codes in outgoing messages.
This will allow you to send messages for which this conversion is necessary.
SEE ALSO KEYWORD(S)
- Conversion of Currency Codes (out)

tcedi4138m000   multi/group (3   Form 1-1

```
+-------------------------------------------------------------------------+
| Maintain Conversion of Currency Codes (out)           Company: 000  |
|-------------------------------------------------------------------------|
|                                                                         |
| Organization       : 1.. 2_____                 |
|                                                                         |
| Code in Application              Code in Message                        |
|                                                                         |
| 3.. 4_____   5..... 6_____    |
|                                                                         |
+-------------------------------------------------------------------------+
```

1.   Organization
The code which uniquely identifies the organization.
2.   Description
3.   Code in Application
The code used in BAAN IV.
4.   Description
5.   Code in Message
The code used in the message.
6.   Description
The description for the code in the EDI message.

9.29 Maintain Terms of Payment / Late Payment Surcharges (tcedi2194m000)
SESSION OBJECTIVE
To maintain terms of payment. This is necessary in order to be able to send or
receive messages containing these.
SEE ALSO KEYWORD(S)
- Terms of Payment

tcedi2194m000   multi/group (3   Form 1-1

```
+-------------------------------------------------------------------------+
```

```
| Maintain Terms of Payment / Late Payment Surcharges        Company: 000 |
|------------------------------------------------------------------------|
|                                                                        |
|  Organization : 1..  2_____                     |
|                                                                        |
|  Code in Message              Description                              |
|                                                                        |
|  3.....                       4............................            |
|                                                                        |
+------------------------------------------------------------------------+
```

1.   Organization
The organization within which the code is valid.
2.   Description
3.   Code in Message
The code used in the message.
4.   Description
The description for the code in the EDI message.
9.30 Maintain Conversion of Terms of Payment Codes (in) (tcedi3126m000)
SESSION OBJECTIVE
To maintain the conversion data for the terms of payment codes in incoming
messages. This will allow you to process received messages for which this
conversion is necessary.
SEE ALSO KEYWORD(S)
•   Conversion of Terms of Payment (in)
tcedi3126m000   multi/group (3   Form 1-1

```
+-------------------------------------------------------------------------+
| Maintain Conversion of Terms of Payment Codes (in)        Company: 000  |
|-------------------------------------------------------------------------|
|                                                                         |
|  Organization : 1..  2_____                      |
|                                                                         |
|  Code in Message                     Code in Application                |
|                                                                         |
|  3.....  4_____     5..  6_____      |
|                                                                         |
+-------------------------------------------------------------------------+
```

1.   Organization
The code which uniquely identifies the organization.
2.   Description
3.   Code in Message
The code used in the message.
4.   Description
The description for the code in the EDI message.
5.   Code in Application
The code used in BAAN IV.
6.   Description
9.31 Maintain Conversion of Terms of Payment Codes (out) (tcedi4166m000)
SESSION OBJECTIVE
To maintain the conversion data for the terms of payment codes by customer in
outgoing messages. This will allow you to send messages for which this
conversion is necessary.
SEE ALSO KEYWORD(S)
•   Conversion of Terms of Payment (out)
tcedi4166m000   multi/group (3   Form 1-1

```
+-------------------------------------------------------------------------+
| Maintain Conversion of Terms of Payment Codes (out)       Company: 000  |
|-------------------------------------------------------------------------|
|                                                                         |
|  Organization : 1..  2_____                      |
|                                                                         |
|  Code in Application                  Code in Message                   |
|                                                                         |
|  3..  4_____        5.....  6_____   |
```

```
|                                                                           |
+---------------------------------------------------------------------------+
1.    Organization
The code which uniquely identifies the organization.
2.    Description
3.    Code in Application
The code used in BAAN IV.
4.    Description
5.    Code in Message
The code used in the message.
6.    Description
The description for the code in the EDI message.
9.32  Maintain Conversion of Late Payment Surcharges (in) (tcedi3130m000)
SESSION OBJECTIVE
To maintain the conversion data for the late payment surcharge codes in incoming
messages. This will allow you to process received messages for which this
conversion is necessary.
SEE ALSO KEYWORD(S)
•     Conversion of Late Payment Surcharges (in)
tcedi3130m000                                multi/group (3     Form 1-1
+---------------------------------------------------------------------------+
| Maintain Conversion of Late Payment Surcharges (in)      Company: 000  |
|---------------------------------------------------------------------------|
|                                                                           |
| Organization  : 1..   2_____                      |
|                                                                           |
| Code in Message                        Code in Application                |
|                                                                           |
| 3.....   4_____      5..  6_____ |
|                                                                           |
+---------------------------------------------------------------------------+
1.    Organization
The code which uniquely identifies the organization.
2.    Description
3.    Code in Message
The code used in the message.
4.    Description
The description for the code in the EDI message.
5.    Code in Application
The code used in BAAN IV.
6.    Description
9.33  Maintain Conversion of Late Payment Surcharges (out) (tcedi4170m000)
SESSION OBJECTIVE
To maintain the conversion data for the late payment surcharge codes in outgoing
messages. This will allow you to send messages for which this conversion is
necessary.
SEE ALSO KEYWORD(S)
•     Conversion of Late Payment Surcharges (out)
tcedi4170m000                                multi/group (3     Form 1-1
+---------------------------------------------------------------------------+
| Maintain Conversion of Late Payment Surcharges (out)     Company: 000  |
|---------------------------------------------------------------------------|
|                                                                           |
| Organization  : 1..   2_____                      |
|                                                                           |
| Code in Application                     Code in Message                   |
|                                                                           |
| 3..  4_____         5.....  6_____ |
|                                                                           |
+---------------------------------------------------------------------------+
1.    Organization
The code which uniquely identifies the organization.
2.    Description
```

3.   Code in Application
The code used in BAAN IV.
4.   Description
5.   Code in Message
The code used in the message.
6.   Description
The description for the code in the EDI message.

9.34 Maintain Third Parties (tcedi2148m000)

SESSION OBJECTIVE
To maintain relation codes. This is necessary in order to be able to send or
receive messages containing these.

SEE ALSO KEYWORD(S)
•   Third Parties

tcedi2148m000   multi/group (3   Form 1-1
+---+
Maintain Third Parties   Company: 000
Organization   : 1.. 2_____
Code in Message   Description
3.....   4...................
+---+

1. Organization
The code which uniquely identifies the organization.
2. Description
3. Code in Message
The code used in the message.
4. Description
The description for the code in the EDI message.

9.35 Maintain Conversion of Third Party Codes by Relation (in) (tcedi3128m000)

SESSION OBJECTIVE
To maintain the conversion data for the third party codes in incoming messages
from relations. This will allow you to process received messages for which this
conversion is necessary.

SEE ALSO KEYWORD(S)
•   Conversion of Third Party Codes by Relation (in)

tcedi3128m000   multi/group (3   Form 1-1
+---+
Maintain Conversion of Third Party Codes by Relation (in) Company: 000
Relation   : 1..... 2_____
Organization   :   3.. 4_____
Address Code ID : 5..... 6_____
Code in Message   Third Party Relation Description
7...................   8..... 2_____
+---+

1. Relation
An outgoing message for this relation is sent to the network address of the
parent relation. For both relations the field "Network Address" in the session
"Maintain Relation Data by Network (tcedi0128m000)" must be filled.
The relation code field may be skipped. This will indicate that the conversion
is a general one for a number of relations, e.g. in case of EAN codes.
2. Description
3. Organization
The code which uniquely identifies the organization.
4. Description

5. Address Code ID
The code type of the code in the message.
6. Description
7. Code in Message
The code used in the message.
8. Third Party Relation
The code used in BAAN IV.
9.36 Maintain Conversion of Third Party Codes by Relation (out) (tcedi4168m000)
SESSION OBJECTIVE
To maintain the conversion data for the third party codes by relation in
outgoing messages. This will allow you to send messages for which this
conversion is necessary.
SEE ALSO KEYWORD(S)
•   Conversion of Third Party Codes by Relation (out)
tcedi4168m000   multi/group (3   Form 1-1
+--+
Maintain Conversion of Third Party Codes by Relation (out)   Company: 000
Relation   : 1..... 2_____
Organization   :   3.. 4_____
Third Party Relation Description   Address Code ID Code in Message
5..... 2_____ 6.....   7...............
+--+

1. Relation
An outgoing message for this relation is sent to the network address of the
parent relation. For both relations the field "Network Address" in the session
"Maintain Relation Data by Network (tcedi0128m000)" must be filled.
The relation code field may be skipped. This will indicate that the conversion
is a general one for a number of relations, e.g. in case of EAN codes.
2. Description
3. Organization
The code which uniquely identifies the organization.
4. Description
5. Third Party Relation
The code used in BAAN IV.
6. Address Code ID
The code type of the code in the message.
7. Code in Message
The code used in the message.
9.37 Maintain Order Types (tcedi2100m000)
SESSION OBJECTIVE
To maintain the order types that will be used in EDI. This session must be
executed before you can receive and send sales orders.
SEE ALSO KEYWORD(S)
•   Order Types
tcedi2100m000   multi/group (3   Form 1-1
+--+
Maintain Order Types   Company: 000
Organization   : 1.. 2_____
EDI   Description   Code in Message   Description
Message
3..... 4_____   5.............................. 6............
+--+

1. Organization

The code which uniquely identifies the organization.
2. Description
3. EDI Message
This code uniquely identifies an EDI message. Depending on the direction, it identifies an incoming or outgoing message.
4. Description
The description associated with the message code.
5. Code
The code used in the message.
6. Description
Indicates the type of received order.
Normal Order
The order is a normal order. The associated order type may not be of the category "return order".
Return Order
The order is a return order. The associated order type must be of the category "return order".
9.38 Maintain Conversion of Order Types (out) (tcedi4132m000)
SESSION OBJECTIVE
To maintain the conversion data for the order types in outgoing messages. This will allow you to send messages for which this conversion is necessary.
SEE ALSO KEYWORD(S)
•   Conversion of Order Types (out)
tcedi4132m000   multi/group (3   Form 1-1
+--+
Maintain Conversion of Order Types (out)   Company: 000
Organization   :   1..   3_____
EDI Message   : 4.....   2_____
Code in Application   Code in Message
5..   6_____   7.....
+--+
1. Organization
The code which uniquely identifies the organization.
2. Description
The description associated with the message code.
3. Description
4. EDI Message
This code uniquely identifies an EDI message. Depending on the direction, it identifies an incoming or outgoing message.
5. Code in Appl.
The code used in BAAN IV.
6. Description
7. Code in Message
The code used in the message.
9.39 Maintain Address Types (tcedi2124m000)
SESSION OBJECTIVE
To maintain address types. This is necessary in order to be able to send or receive messages containing these.
SEE ALSO KEYWORD(S)
•   Address Types
tcedi2124m000   multi/group (3   Form 1-1
+--+
Maintain Address Types   Company: 000
Organization   : 1..   2_____
Code in Message   Description

```
|                                                                      |
|   3.....                   4...............                          |
|                                                                      |
+----------------------------------------------------------------------+
```

1. Organization
The code which uniquely identifies the organization.
2. Description
3. Code in Message
The code used in the message.
4. Description
Indicates which type of address is used:
Invoice Address
The address is an invoice address.
Delivery Address
The address is a delivery address.
Customer Address
The address is the customer's address.
Shop Address
The address is the address of the shop.

9.40 Maintain Conversion of Address Types (out) (tcedi4134m000)

SESSION OBJECTIVE
To maintain the conversion data for the address types in outgoing messages. This
will allow you to send messages for which this conversion is necessary.

SEE ALSO KEYWORD(S)
•   Conversion of Address Types (out)

tcedi4134m000   multi/group (3   Form 1-1

```
+----------------------------------------------------------------------+
|  Maintain Conversion of Address Types (out)        Company: 000  |
|----------------------------------------------------------------------|
|                                                                      |
|   Organization       : 1..  2_____          |
|                                                                      |
|   Code in Application   Code in Message                              |
|                                                                      |
|   3...................  4.....  5_____        |
|                                                                      |
+----------------------------------------------------------------------+
```

1.   Organization
The code which uniquely identifies the organization.
2.   Description
3.   Code in Application
The address types that can occur in the application.
4.   Code in Message
The code used in the message.
5.   Description

9.41 Maintain Reference Number Types (tcedi2120m000)

SESSION OBJECTIVE
To maintain reference number types. This is necessary in order to be able to
send or receive messages containing these.

SEE ALSO KEYWORD(S)
•   Reference Number Types

tcedi2120m000   multi/group (3   Form 1-1

```
+----------------------------------------------------------------------+
|  Maintain Reference Number Types                   Company: 000  |
|----------------------------------------------------------------------|
|                                                                      |
|   Organization       : 1..  2_____          |
|                                                                      |
|   Code in Message        Description                                 |
|                                                                      |
|   3.....                 4...............                            |
|                                                                      |
+----------------------------------------------------------------------+
```

1.   Organization
The code which uniquely identifies the organization.
2.   Description
3.   Code in Message
The code used in the message.
4.   Description
The description for the code in the EDI message.
9.42 Maintain Conversion of Reference Number Types (out) (tcedi4136m000)
SESSION OBJECTIVE
To maintain the conversion data for the reference number types in outgoing
messages. This will allow you to send messages for which this conversion is
necessary.
SEE ALSO KEYWORD(S)
•   Conversion of Reference Number Types (out)

tcedi4136m000   multi/group (3   Form 1-1
+---+
Maintain Conversion of Reference Number Types (out)   Company: 000
Organization   : 1..   2_____
Code in Application   Code in Message
3................   4..... 5_____
+---+

1.   Organization
The code which uniquely identifies the organization.
2.   Description
3.   Code in Application
The code used in BAAN IV.
4.   Code in Message
The code used in the message.
5.   Description
The description for the code in the EDI message.
9.43 Maintain Conversion of Warehouse Addresses (out) (tcedi4162m000)
SESSION OBJECTIVE
To maintain the conversion data for the warehouse address codes by customer in
outgoing messages. This will allow you to send messages for which this
conversion is necessary.
SEE ALSO KEYWORD(S)
•   Conversion of Warehouse Addresses (out)

tcedi4162m000   multi/group (3   Form 1-1
+---+
Maintain Conversion of Warehouse Addresses (out)   Company: 000
Relation   : 1..... 2_____
Organization   :   3.. 4_____
Code in Application   Address Code ID Code in Message
5.. 6_____ 7.....   8..................
+---+

1.   Relation
An outgoing message for this relation is sent to the network address of the
parent relation. For both relations the field "Network Address" in the session
"Maintain Relation Data by Network (tcedi0128m000)" must be filled.
If the relation code is skipped, the relation is a general one, applying to all
relations.
2.   Description
3.   Organization

The code which uniquely identifies the organization.
4.   Description
5.   Code in Application
The code used in BAAN IV.
6.   Description
7.   Address Code ID
The code type of the code in the message.
8.   Code in Message
The code used in the message.
9.44 Maintain Character Conversion Codes (tcedi4108m000)
SESSION OBJECTIVE
To maintain character conversion codes. Character conversion codes identify
different character conversions.
SEE ALSO KEYWORD(S)
•   Character Conversion Codes (out)

```
tcedi4108m000                                   multi-occ (2)    Form 1-1
+----------------------------------------------------------------------+
| Maintain Character Conversion Codes                    Company: 000  |
|----------------------------------------------------------------------|
|                                                                      |
| Char. Conv. Code    Description                                      |
|                                                                      |
|          1.....   2...........................                       |
|                                                                      |
+----------------------------------------------------------------------+
```

1.   Character Conversion
The code uniquely identifying the character conversion.
2.   Description
The description of the character conversion code.
9.45 Maintain Character Conversions (out) (tcedi4109m000)
SESSION OBJECTIVE
To maintain the conversion data for characters in outgoing messages. This will
allow you to send messages for which this conversion is necessary.
SEE ALSO KEYWORD(S)
•   Character Conversions (out)

```
tcedi4109m000                                   multi/group (3    Form 1-1
+----------------------------------------------------------------------+
| Maintain Character Conversions (out)                   Company: 000  |
|----------------------------------------------------------------------|
|                                                                      |
| Char. Conv. Code  : 1.....   2_____          |
|                                                                      |
| Code in Appl.   Code in Message                                      |
|                                                                      |
| 3               4..                                                  |
|                                                                      |
+----------------------------------------------------------------------+
```

1.   Character Conversion
The code uniquely identifying the character conversion.
2.   Description
The description of the character conversion code.
3.   Code in Appl.
The characters from BAAN IV.
4.   Code in Message
The characters to be included in the message.
9.46 Maintain Allowances and Charges (tcedi2145m000)
SESSION OBJECTIVE
To maintain allowances and charges.
SEE ALSO KEYWORD(S)
•   Allowances and Charges

```
tcedi2145m000                                   multi/group (3    Form 1-1
+----------------------------------------------------------------------+
| Maintain Allowances and Charges                        Company: 000  |
```

```
|-----------------------------------------------------------------------|
|                                                                       |
|   Organization    : 1..  2_____           |
|                                                                       |
|   Code in Message                         Description                 |
|                                                                       |
|    3................................... 4.............................  |
|                                                                       |
+-----------------------------------------------------------------------+
```

1.   Organization
The code which uniquely identifies the organization.
2.   Description
3.   Code in Message
The code used in the message.
4.   Description
The description for the code in the EDI message.
9.47 Maintain Conversion of Allowances and Charges (out) (tcedi4172m000)
SESSION OBJECTIVE
To maintain the conversion data for the allowances and charges codes in outgoing
invoices. This will allow you to send invoices for which this conversion is
necessary.
SEE ALSO KEYWORD(S)
•   Conversion of Allowances and Charges (out)
tcedi4172m000   multi/group (3   Form 1-1

```
+-----------------------------------------------------------------------+
|  Maintain Conversion of Allowances and Charges (out)   Company: 000   |
|-----------------------------------------------------------------------|
|                                                                       |
|   Organization         : 1..  2_____      |
|                                                                       |
|   Allowance / Charge Type               Code in Message               |
|                                                                       |
|    3...................... 4........    5...........................  |
|                                                                       |
+-----------------------------------------------------------------------+
```

1.   Organization
The code which uniquely identifies the organization.
2.   Description
3.   Allowance / Charge Type
The cost types which are possible as output in an EDI invoice. In the field
"Allowance / Charge" you can indicate if the entered cost type involves an
allowance (discount) or charge (surcharge).
Cost Item
Cost items which have been entered manually during order entry.
Additional Costs
Automatically added additional cost lines.
Order Discount
The order discount, without any line discounts.
Prepaid Amount
Prepaid amounts.
Invoiced Installment
Installment to be paid on this invoice.
Late Payment Surcharge
Late payment surcharge.
4.   Allowance / Charge
Indicates whether a discount or a surcharge is involved.
5.   Code in Message
The code used in the message.
9.48 Maintain Discounts and Surcharges (tcedi2144m000)
SESSION OBJECTIVE
To maintain discount and surcharge codes. This is necessary in order to be able
to send or receive messages containing these.
SEE ALSO KEYWORD(S)

```
+------------------------------------------------------------------------+
| Maintain Discounts and Surcharges                    Company: 000      |
|------------------------------------------------------------------------|
|                                                                        |
| Organization        : 1.. 2_____           |
|                                                                        |
| Code in Message        Description                                     |
|                                                                        |
| 3.....                 4.......                                        |
|                                                                        |
+------------------------------------------------------------------------+
```

1.   Organization
The code which uniquely identifies the organization.
2.   Description
3.   Code in Message
The code used in the message.
4.   Description
Indicates whether a discount or a surcharge is involved.
10   Other Maintenance Sessions
10.1 Check/Clear Conversion of Item Codes by Relation (in) (tcedi3200m000)
SESSION OBJECTIVE
To delete item code conversions by relation that also exist in the general item
conversion table.
HOW TO USE THE SESSION
If codes are identical, i.e. the same code is defined in the general tables in
BAAN IV and in the table by relation, the conversion for the relation is
deleted. If codes are not identical, this information is printed on a report.
SEE ALSO KEYWORD(S)
• Conversion of Item Codes (General) (in)
tcedi3200m000   single-occ (4)   Form 1-1

```
+------------------------------------------------------------------------+
| Check/Clear Conversion of Item Codes by Relation (in)   Company: 000   |
|------------------------------------------------------------------------|
|                                                                        |
| Organization        from : 1..                                        |
|                     to   : 2..                                         |
|                                                                        |
| Checking only            : 3....                                      |
|                                                                        |
+------------------------------------------------------------------------+
```

1.   Organization from
2.   Organization to
3.   Checking only
4.   Code of Relation
The code used in the message.
10.2 Check/Clear Conversion of Item Codes by Relation (out) (tcedi4200m000)
SESSION OBJECTIVE
Delete item code conversions by relation that also exist in the general item
conversion table.
HOW TO USE THE SESSION
If two codes are identical, i.e. the same code is defined in the general tables
in BAAN IV and in the table by relation, the conversion for the relation is
deleted. If codes are not identical, this information is printed on a report.
SEE ALSO KEYWORD(S)
• Conversion of Item Codes (out)
tcedi4200m000   single-occ (4)   Form 1-1

```
+------------------------------------------------------------------------+
| Check/Clear Conversion of Item Codes by Relation (out)   Company: 000  |
|------------------------------------------------------------------------|
|                                                                        |
| Organization             from : 1..                                   |
```

```
|                                  to    : 2..                                   |
|                                                                                |
| Checking only                   : 3....                                        |
|                                                                                |
+--------------------------------------------------------------------------------+
```

1.   Organization from
2.   Organization to
3.   Checking only
4.   Code in Application
The code used in BAAN IV.
10.3 Copy Conversion Tables (tcedi7200m000)
SESSION OBJECTIVE
To replace incoming conversion tables by outgoing ones or vice versa.
tcedi7200m000   single-occ (4)   Form 1-1

```
+--------------------------------------------------------------------------------+
|  Copy Conversion Tables                                      Company: 000  |
|------------------------------------------------------------------------------|
|                                                                              |
|  Direction                 : 1............................                   |
|                                                                              |
|  Overwrite message codes : 2....                                             |
|                                                                              |
|  Copy message type         : 3......................                         |
|                                                                              |
+--------------------------------------------------------------------------------+
```

1.   Direction
Indicate if the conversion tables are to be copied from incoming to outgoing or
vice versa.
2.   Overwrite message codes
Indicate if existing codes may be overwritten.
3.   Copy message type
Specify the conversion table to be copied.
4.   Endmark in ASCII File (DCS)
This field displays process information.
11   Other Print Sessions
11.1 Print Terms of Delivery (tcedi2428m000)
tcedi2428m000   single-occ (4)   Form 1-1

```
+--------------------------------------------------------------------------------+
|  Print Terms of Delivery                                    Company: 000  |
|------------------------------------------------------------------------------|
|                                                                              |
|  Organization          From : 1..                                            |
|                        To   : 2..                                            |
|                                                                              |
|  Code in Message       From : 3.....                                         |
|                        To   : 4.....                                         |
|                                                                              |
+--------------------------------------------------------------------------------+
```

1.   Organization from
2.   Organization to
3.   Code in Message from
4.   Code in Message to
11.2 Print Conversion of Terms of Delivery Codes (in) (tcedi3400m000)
tcedi3400m000   single-occ (4)   Form 1-1

```
+--------------------------------------------------------------------------------+
|  Print Conversion of Terms of Delivery Codes (in)           Company: 000  |
|------------------------------------------------------------------------------|
|                                                                              |
|  Organization          from : 1..                                            |
|                        to   : 2..                                            |
|                                                                              |
|  Code in Message       from : 3.....                                         |
|                        to   : 4.....                                         |
```

```
|                                                                          |
+--------------------------------------------------------------------------+
1.     Organization from
2.     Organization to
3.     Code in Message from
4.     Code in Message to
11.3  Print Conversion Terms of Delivery Codes (out) (tcedi4430m000)
tcedi4430m000                                  single-occ (4)    Form 1-1
+--------------------------------------------------------------------------+
|  Print Conversion Terms of Delivery Codes (out)        Company: 000  |
|--------------------------------------------------------------------------|
|                                                                      |
|  Organization    from : 1..                                          |
|                  to   : 2..                                          |
|                                                                      |
|  Code in Appl.   from : 3..                                          |
|                  to   : 4..                                          |
|                                                                      |
+--------------------------------------------------------------------------+
1.     Organization from
2.     Organization to
3.     Code in Appl. from
4.     Code in Appl. to
11.4  Print Countries (tcedi2426m000)
tcedi2426m000                                  single-occ (4)    Form 1-1
+--------------------------------------------------------------------------+
|  Print Countries                                       Company: 000  |
|--------------------------------------------------------------------------|
|                                                                      |
|  Organization         From : 1..                                     |
|                       To   : 2..                                     |
|                                                                      |
|  Code in Message      From : 3.....                                  |
|                       To   : 4.....                                  |
|                                                                      |
+--------------------------------------------------------------------------+
1.     Organization from
2.     Organization to
3.     Code in Message from
4.     Code in Message to
11.5  Print Conversion of Country Codes (in) (tcedi3402m000)
tcedi3402m000                                  single-occ (4)    Form 1-1
+--------------------------------------------------------------------------+
|  Print Conversion of Country Codes (in)                Company: 000  |
|--------------------------------------------------------------------------|
|                                                                      |
|  Organization         from : 1..                                     |
|                       to   : 2..                                     |
|                                                                      |
|  Code in Message      from : 3.....                                  |
|                       to   : 4.....                                  |
|                                                                      |
+--------------------------------------------------------------------------+
1.     Organization from
2.     Organization to
3.     Code in Message from
4.     Code in Message to
11.6  Print Conversion of Country Codes (out) (tcedi4440m000)
tcedi4440m000                                  single-occ (4)    Form 1-1
+--------------------------------------------------------------------------+
|  Print Conversion of Country Codes (out)               Company: 000  |
|--------------------------------------------------------------------------|
|                                                                      |
```

```
|  Organization            from : 1..                                    |
|                          to   : 2..                                    |
|                                                                        |
|  Code in Application     from : 3..                                    |
|                          to   : 4..                                    |
|                                                                        |
+------------------------------------------------------------------------+
1.    Organization from
2.    Organization to
3.    Code in Application from
4.    Code in Application to
```

11.7 Print Units (tcedi2430m000)

```
tcedi2430m000                          single-occ (4)   Form 1-1
+------------------------------------------------------------------------+
| Print Units                                          Company: 000 |
|------------------------------------------------------------------------|
|                                                                        |
|  Organization           From : 1..                                    |
|                         To   : 2..                                    |
|                                                                        |
|  Code in Message        From : 3.....                                 |
|                         To   : 4.....                                 |
|                                                                        |
+------------------------------------------------------------------------+
1.    Organization from
2.    Organization to
3.    Code in Message from
4.    Code in Message to
```

11.8 Print Conversion of Unit Codes (in) (tcedi3404m000)

```
tcedi3404m000                          single-occ (4)   Form 1-1
+------------------------------------------------------------------------+
| Print Conversion of Unit Codes (in)                  Company: 000 |
|------------------------------------------------------------------------|
|                                                                        |
|  Organization           from : 1..                                    |
|                         to   : 2..                                    |
|                                                                        |
|  Code in Message        from : 3.....                                 |
|                         to   : 4.....                                 |
|                                                                        |
+------------------------------------------------------------------------+
1.    Organization from
2.    Organization to
3.    Code in Message from
4.    Code in Message to
```

11.9 Print Conversion of Unit Codes (out) (tcedi4442m000)

```
tcedi4442m000                          single-occ (4)   Form 1-1
+------------------------------------------------------------------------+
| Print Conversion of Unit Codes (out)                 Company: 000 |
|------------------------------------------------------------------------|
|                                                                        |
|  Organization           from : 1..                                    |
|                         to   : 2..                                    |
|                                                                        |
|  Code in Application    from : 3..                                    |
|                         to   : 4..                                    |
|                                                                        |
+------------------------------------------------------------------------+
1.    Organization from
2.    Organization to
3.    Code in Application from
4.    Code in Application to
```

11.10 Print Item Code IDs (tcedi2432m000)

```
tcedi2432m000                        single-occ (4)    Form 1-1
+--------------------------------------------------------------------+
| Print Item Code IDs                                 Company: 000   |
|--------------------------------------------------------------------|
|                                                                    |
| Organization         From : 1..                                   |
|                      To   : 2..                                    |
|                                                                    |
| Code in Message      From : 3.....                                |
|                      To   : 4.....                                |
|                                                                    |
+--------------------------------------------------------------------+
1.    Organization from
2.    Organization to
3.    Code in Message from
4.    Code in Message to
11.11 Print Conversion of Item Codes by Relation (in) (tcedi3406m000)
tcedi3406m000                        single-occ (4)    Form 1-1
+--------------------------------------------------------------------+
| Print Conversion of Item Codes by Relation (in)     Company: 000   |
|--------------------------------------------------------------------|
|                                                                    |
| Relation             from : 1.....                                |
|                      to   : 2.....                                |
|                                                                    |
| Organization         from :    3..                                |
|                      to   :    4..                                 |
|                                                                    |
| Item Code ID         from : 5.....                                |
|                      to   : 6.....                                 |
|                                                                    |
| Project              from : 7.....                                |
|                      to   : 8.....                                 |
|                                                                    |
| Code in Message      from : 9...................................  |
|                      to   : 10..................................  |
|                                                                    |
+--------------------------------------------------------------------+
1.    Relation from
2.    Relation to
3.    Organization from
4.    Organization to
5.    Item Code ID from
6.    Item Code ID to
7.    Project from
8.    Project to
9.    Code in Message from
10.   Code in Message to
11.12 Print Conversion of Item Codes (General) (in) (tcedi3422m000)
tcedi3422m000                        single-occ (4)    Form 1-1
+--------------------------------------------------------------------+
| Print Conversion of Item Codes (General) (in)       Company: 000   |
|--------------------------------------------------------------------|
|                                                                    |
| Organization         from : 1..                                   |
|                      to   : 2..                                    |
|                                                                    |
| Item Code ID         from : 3.....                                |
|                      to   : 4.....                                 |
|                                                                    |
| Code in Message      from : 5...................................  |
|                      to   : 6...................................  |
|                                                                    |
```

```
+-----------------------------------------------------------------------+
1.     Organization from
2.     Organization to
3.     Item Code ID from
4.     Item Code ID to
5.     Code in Message from
6.     Code in Message to
11.13 Print Conversion of Item Codes by Relation (out) (tcedi4444m000)
tcedi4444m000                              single-occ (4)   Form 1-1
+-----------------------------------------------------------------------+
| Print Conversion of Item Codes by Relation (out)      Company: 000    |
|-----------------------------------------------------------------------|
|                                                                       |
| Relation             from : 1.....                                    |
|                      to   : 2.....                                     |
|                                                                       |
| Organization         from :    3..                                    |
|                      to   :    4..                                     |
|                                                                       |
| Project              from : 5.....                                    |
|                      to   : 6.....                                     |
|                                                                       |
| Code in Application  from : 7...............           / 8..          |
|                      to   : 9...............           / 10.          |
|                                                                       |
+-----------------------------------------------------------------------+
1.     Relation from
2.     Relation to
3.     Organization from
4.     Organization to
5.     Project from
6.     Project to
7.     Code in Application from
8.     Unit
9.     Code in Application to
10.    Unit
11.14 Print Conversion of Item Codes (out) (tcedi4460m000)
tcedi4460m000                              single-occ (4)   Form 1-1
+-----------------------------------------------------------------------+
| Print Conversion of Item Codes (out)                  Company: 000    |
|-----------------------------------------------------------------------|
|                                                                       |
| Organization         from : 1..                                       |
|                      to   : 2..                                        |
|                                                                       |
| Code in Application  from : 3...............           / 4..          |
|                      to   : 5...............           / 6..          |
|                                                                       |
+-----------------------------------------------------------------------+
1.     Organization from
2.     Organization to
3.     Code in Application from
4.     Unit
5.     Code in Application to
6.     Unit
11.15 Print Tax Code IDs (tcedi2440m000)
tcedi2440m000                              single-occ (4)   Form 1-1
+-----------------------------------------------------------------------+
| Print Tax Code IDs                                    Company: 000    |
|-----------------------------------------------------------------------|
|                                                                       |
| Organization         From : 1..                                       |
|                      To   : 2..                                        |
|                                                                       |
```

```
|                                                                          |
| Code in Message      From : 3.....                                       |
|                      To   : 4.....                                       |
|                                                                          |
+--------------------------------------------------------------------------+
1.    Organization from
2.    Organization to
3.    Code in Message from
4.    Code in Message to
```

11.16 Print Conversion of Late Payment Surcharges (in) (tcedi3430m000)

```
tcedi3430m000                              single-occ (4)   Form 1-1
+--------------------------------------------------------------------------+
| Print Conversion of Late Payment Surcharges (in)       Company: 000 |
|--------------------------------------------------------------------------|
|                                                                          |
| Organization    from : 1..                                               |
|                 to   : 2..                                               |
|                                                                          |
| Code in Message from : 3.....                                            |
|                 to   : 4.....                                            |
|                                                                          |
+--------------------------------------------------------------------------+
1.    Organization from
2.    Organization to
3.    Code in Message from
4.    Code in Message to
```

11.17 Print Tax Codes (tcedi2442m000)

```
tcedi2442m000                              single-occ (4)   Form 1-1
+--------------------------------------------------------------------------+
| Print Tax Codes                                        Company: 000 |
|--------------------------------------------------------------------------|
|                                                                          |
| Organization         From : 1..                                         |
|                      To   : 2..                                         |
|                                                                          |
| Code in Message      From : 3.....                                      |
|                      To   : 4.....                                      |
|                                                                          |
+--------------------------------------------------------------------------+
1.    Organization from
2.    Organization to
3.    Code in Message from
4.    Code in Message to
```

11.18 Print Conversion of Tax Codes (in) (tcedi3408m000)

```
tcedi3408m000                              single-occ (4)   Form 1-1
+--------------------------------------------------------------------------+
| Print Conversion of Tax Codes (in)                     Company: 000 |
|--------------------------------------------------------------------------|
|                                                                          |
| Organization         from : 1..                                         |
|                      to   : 2..                                         |
|                                                                          |
| Country              from : 3..                                         |
|                      to   : 4..                                         |
|                                                                          |
| Tax Code ID          from : 5.....                                      |
|                      to   : 6.....                                      |
|                                                                          |
| Code in Message      from : 7.....                                      |
|                      to   : 8.....                                      |
|                                                                          |
+--------------------------------------------------------------------------+
1.    Organization from
```

```
2.      Organization to
3.      Country from
4.      Country to
5.      Tax Code ID from
6.      Tax Code ID to
7.      Code in Message from
8.      Code in Message to
```

11.19 Print Conversion of Tax Codes (out) (tcedi4446m000)

```
tcedi4446m000                           single-occ (4)    Form 1-1
+---------------------------------------------------------------------+
|  Print Conversion of Tax Codes (out)               Company: 000  |
|---------------------------------------------------------------------|
|                                                                     |
|  Organization         from : 1..                                    |
|                       to   : 2..                                    |
|                                                                     |
|  Country              from : 3..                                    |
|                       to   : 4..                                    |
|                                                                     |
|  Code in Application  from : 5.......                               |
|                       to   : 6.......                               |
|                                                                     |
+---------------------------------------------------------------------+
```

```
1.      Organization from
2.      Organization to
3.      Country from
4.      Country to
5.      Code in Application from
6.      Code in Application to
```

11.20 Print Address Code IDs (tcedi2418m000)

```
tcedi2418m000                           single-occ (4)    Form 1-1
+---------------------------------------------------------------------+
|  Print Address Code IDs                            Company: 000  |
|---------------------------------------------------------------------|
|                                                                     |
|  Organization         From : 1..                                    |
|                       To   : 2..                                    |
|                                                                     |
|  Code in Message      From : 3.....                                 |
|                       To   : 4.....                                 |
|                                                                     |
+---------------------------------------------------------------------+
```

```
1.      Organization from
2.      Organization to
3.      Code in Message from
4.      Code in Message to
```

11.21 Print Conversion of Delivery Address Codes by Customer (in)
(tcedi3410m000)

```
tcedi3410m000                           single-occ (4)    Form 1-1
+---------------------------------------------------------------------+
|  Print Conversion of Delivery Address Codes by Customer (in)  Company: 000  |
|---------------------------------------------------------------------|
|                                                                     |
|  Customer            from : 1.....                                  |
|                      to   : 2.....                                  |
|                                                                     |
|  Organization        from :    3..                                 |
|                      to   :    4..                                  |
|                                                                     |
|  Address Code ID from : 5.....                                      |
|                      to   : 6.....                                  |
|                                                                     |
|  Code in Message from : 7..................                         |
```

```
|                 to   : 8...................                          |
|                                                                      |
+----------------------------------------------------------------------+
1.     Customer from
2.     Customer to
3.     Organization from
4.     Organization to
5.     Address Code ID from
6.     Address Code ID to
7.     Code in Message from
8.     Code in Message to
11.22 Print Conversion of Postal Address Codes by Customer (in) (tcedi3412m000)
tcedi3412m000                             single-occ (4)   Form 1-1
+----------------------------------------------------------------------+
| Print Conversion of Postal Address Codes by Customer (in)   Company: 000 |
|----------------------------------------------------------------------|
|                                                                      |
| Customer        from : 1.....                                        |
|                 to   : 2.....                                        |
|                                                                      |
| Organization    from :    3..                                       |
|                 to   :    4..                                        |
|                                                                      |
| Address Code ID from : 5.....                                        |
|                 to   : 6.....                                        |
|                                                                      |
| Code in Message from : 7...................                          |
|                 to   : 8...................                          |
|                                                                      |
+----------------------------------------------------------------------+
1.     Customer from
2.     Customer to
3.     Organization from
4.     Organization to
5.     Address Code ID from
6.     Address Code ID to
7.     Code in Message from
8.     Code in Message to
11.23 Print Conversion of Postal Address Codes by Supplier (in) (tcedi3413m000)
tcedi3413m000                             single-occ (4)   Form 1-1
+----------------------------------------------------------------------+
| Print Conversion of Postal Address Codes by Supplier (in)   Company: 000 |
|----------------------------------------------------------------------|
|                                                                      |
| Supplier        from : 1.....                                        |
|                 to   : 2.....                                        |
|                                                                      |
| Organization    from :    3..                                       |
|                 to   :    4..                                        |
|                                                                      |
| Address Code ID from : 5.....                                        |
|                 to   : 6.....                                        |
|                                                                      |
| Code in Message from : 7...................                          |
|                 to   : 8...................                          |
|                                                                      |
+----------------------------------------------------------------------+
1.     Supplier from
2.     Supplier to
3.     Organization from
4.     Organization to
5.     Address Code ID from
6.     Address Code ID to
```

```
7.     Code in Message from
8.     Code in Message to
11.24 Print Conversion of Delivery Address Codes by Customer (out)
(tcedi4448m000)
tcedi4448m000                               single-occ (4)    Form 1-1
+---------------------------------------------------------------------+
| Print Conversion of Delivery Address Codes by Customer (out)  Company: 000 |
|---------------------------------------------------------------------|
|                                                                     |
| Customer              from : 1.....                                 |
|                       to   : 2.....                                 |
|                                                                     |
| Organization          from :    3..                                |
|                       to   :    4..                                 |
|                                                                     |
| Code in Application from :    5..                                   |
|                       to   :    6..                                 |
|                                                                     |
+---------------------------------------------------------------------+
1.     Customer from
2.     Customer to
3.     Organization from
4.     Organization to
5.     Code in Application from
6.     Code in Application to
11.25 Print Conversion of Postal Address Codes by Customer (out) (tcedi4450m000)
tcedi4450m000                               single-occ (4)    Form 1-1
+---------------------------------------------------------------------+
| Print Conversion of Postal Address Codes by Customer (out)   Company: 000 |
|---------------------------------------------------------------------|
|                                                                     |
| Customer              from : 1.....                                 |
|                       to   : 2.....                                 |
|                                                                     |
| Organization          from :    3..                                |
|                       to   :    4..                                 |
|                                                                     |
| Code in Application from :    5..                                   |
|                       to   :    6..                                 |
|                                                                     |
+---------------------------------------------------------------------+
1.     Customer from
2.     Customer to
3.     Organization from
4.     Organization to
5.     Code in Application from
6.     Code in Application to
11.26 Print Conversion of Postal Address Codes by Supplier (out) (tcedi4451m000)
tcedi4451m000                               single-occ (4)    Form 1-1
+---------------------------------------------------------------------+
| Print Conversion of Postal Address Codes by Supplier (out)   Company: 000 |
|---------------------------------------------------------------------|
|                                                                     |
| Supplier              from : 1.....                                 |
|                       to   : 2.....                                 |
|                                                                     |
| Organization          from :    3..                                |
|                       to   :    4..                                 |
|                                                                     |
| Code in Application from :    5..                                   |
|                       to   :    6..                                 |
|                                                                     |
+---------------------------------------------------------------------+
```

```
1.    Supplier from
2.    Supplier to
3.    Organization from
4.    Organization to
5.    Code in Application from
6.    Code in Application to
```

11.27 Print Conversion of Warehouse Addresses (out) (tcedi4462m000)

```
tcedi4462m000                              single-occ (4)   Form 1-1
+------------------------------------------------------------------------+
|  Print Conversion of Warehouse Addresses (out)        Company: 000  |
|------------------------------------------------------------------------|
|                                                                        |
|  Relation            from : 1.....                                     |
|                      to   : 2.....                                     |
|                                                                        |
|  Organization        from :    3..                                     |
|                      to   :    4..                                     |
|                                                                        |
|  Code in Application from :    5..                                     |
|                      to   :    6..                                     |
|                                                                        |
+------------------------------------------------------------------------+
```

```
1.    Relation from
2.    Relation to
3.    Organization from
4.    Organization to
5.    Code in Application from
6.    Code in Application to
```

11.28 Print Currencies (tcedi2492m000)

```
tcedi2492m000                              single-occ (4)   Form 1-1
+------------------------------------------------------------------------+
|  Print Currencies                                     Company: 000  |
|------------------------------------------------------------------------|
|                                                                        |
|  Organization        From : 1..                                        |
|                      To   : 2..                                        |
|                                                                        |
|  Code in Message     From : 3.....                                     |
|                      To   : 4.....                                     |
|                                                                        |
+------------------------------------------------------------------------+
```

```
1.    Organization from
2.    Organization to
3.    Code in Message from
4.    Code in Message to
```

11.29 Print Conversion of Currency Codes (in) (tcedi3424m000)

```
tcedi3424m000                              single-occ (4)   Form 1-1
+------------------------------------------------------------------------+
|  Print Conversion of Currency Codes (in)              Company: 000  |
|------------------------------------------------------------------------|
|                                                                        |
|  Organization        from : 1..                                        |
|                      to   : 2..                                        |
|                                                                        |
|  Code in Message     from : 3.....                                     |
|                      to   : 4.....                                     |
|                                                                        |
+------------------------------------------------------------------------+
```

```
1.    Organization from
2.    Organization to
3.    Code in Message from
4.    Code in Message to
```

11.30 Print conversion of Currency Codes (out) (tcedi4438m000)

```
tcedi4438m000                          single-occ (4)    Form 1-1
+--------------------------------------------------------------------+
| Print conversion of Currency Codes (out)          Company: 000     |
|--------------------------------------------------------------------|
|                                                                    |
| Organization        from : 1..                                    |
|                     to   : 2..                                    |
|                                                                    |
| Code in Application from : 3..                                    |
|                     to   : 4..                                    |
|                                                                    |
+--------------------------------------------------------------------+
1.    Organization from
2.    Organization to
3.    Code in Application from
4.    Code in Application to
11.31 Print Terms of Payment / Late Payment Surcharges (tcedi2494m000)
tcedi2494m000                          single-occ (4)    Form 1-1
+--------------------------------------------------------------------+
| Print Terms of Payment / Late Payment Surcharges   Company: 000    |
|--------------------------------------------------------------------|
|                                                                    |
| Organization      from : 1..                                      |
|                   to   : 2..                                      |
|                                                                    |
| Code in Message from : 3.....                                     |
|                 to   : 4.....                                     |
|                                                                    |
+--------------------------------------------------------------------+
1.    Organization from
2.    Organization to
3.    Code in Message from
4.    Code in Message to
11.32 Print Conversion of Late Payment Surcharges (out) (tcedi4470m000)
tcedi4470m000                          single-occ (4)    Form 1-1
+--------------------------------------------------------------------+
| Print Conversion of Late Payment Surcharges (out)  Company: 000    |
|--------------------------------------------------------------------|
|                                                                    |
| Organization        from : 1..                                    |
|                     to   : 2..                                    |
|                                                                    |
| Code in Application from : 3..                                    |
|                     to   : 4..                                    |
|                                                                    |
+--------------------------------------------------------------------+
1.    Organization from
2.    Organization to
3.    Code in Application from
4.    Code in Application to
11.33 Print Conversion of Terms of Payment Codes (in) (tcedi3426m000)
tcedi3426m000                          single-occ (4)    Form 1-1
+--------------------------------------------------------------------+
| Print Conversion of Terms of Payment Codes (in)    Company: 000    |
|--------------------------------------------------------------------|
|                                                                    |
| Organization      from : 1..                                      |
|                   to   : 2..                                      |
|                                                                    |
| Code in Message from : 3.....                                     |
|                 to   : 4.....                                     |
|                                                                    |
+--------------------------------------------------------------------+
```

```
1.      Organization from
2.      Organization to
3.      Code in Message from
4.      Code in Message to
11.34 Print Conversion of Terms of Payment (out) (tcedi4466m000)
tcedi4466m000                               single-occ (4)   Form 1-1
+-------------------------------------------------------------------+
|  Print Conversion of Terms of Payment (out)        Company: 000   |
|-------------------------------------------------------------------|
|                                                                   |
|  Organization         from : 1..                                  |
|                       to   : 2..                                  |
|                                                                   |
|  Code in Application from : 3..                                   |
|                       to   : 4..                                  |
|                                                                   |
+-------------------------------------------------------------------+
1.      Organization from
2.      Organization to
3.      Code in Application from
4.      Code in Application to
11.35 Print Third Parties (tcedi2448m000)
tcedi2448m000                               single-occ (4)   Form 1-1
+-------------------------------------------------------------------+
|  Print Third Parties                               Company: 000   |
|-------------------------------------------------------------------|
|                                                                   |
|  Organization         From : 1..                                  |
|                       To   : 2..                                  |
|                                                                   |
|  Code in Message      From : 3.....                               |
|                       To   : 4.....                               |
|                                                                   |
+-------------------------------------------------------------------+
1.      Organization from
2.      Organization to
3.      Code in Message from
4.      Code in Message to
11.36 Print Conversion of Third Party Codes by Relation (in) (tcedi3428m000)
tcedi3428m000                               single-occ (4)   Form 1-1
+-------------------------------------------------------------------+
|  Print Conversion of Third Party Codes by Relation (in)  Company: 000 |
|-------------------------------------------------------------------|
|                                                                   |
|  Relation           from : 1.....                                 |
|                     to   : 2.....                                 |
|                                                                   |
|  Organization       from :    3..                                 |
|                     to   :    4..                                 |
|                                                                   |
|  Address Code ID from : 5.....                                    |
|                   to   : 6.....                                   |
|                                                                   |
|  Code in Message from : 7...................                      |
|                   to   : 8...................                     |
|                                                                   |
+-------------------------------------------------------------------+
1.      Relation from
2.      Relation to
3.      Organization from
4.      Organization to
5.      Address Code ID from
6.      Address Code ID to
```

7.   Code in Message from
8.   Code in Message to
11.37 Print Conversion of Third Party Codes by Relation (out) (tcedi4468m000)
tcedi4468m000   single-occ (4)   Form 1-1

```
+------------------------------------------------------------------------+
| Print Conversion of Third Party Codes by Relation (out)  Company: 000  |
|------------------------------------------------------------------------|
|                                                                        |
| Relation              from : 1.....                                    |
|                       to   : 2.....                                    |
|                                                                        |
| Organization          from :    3..                                    |
|                       to   :    4..                                    |
|                                                                        |
| Third Party Relation from : 5.....                                     |
|                       to   : 6.....                                    |
|                                                                        |
+------------------------------------------------------------------------+
```

1.   Relation from
2.   Relation to
3.   Organization from
4.   Organization to
5.   Third Party Relation from
6.   Third Party Relation to
11.38 Print Order Types (tcedi2400m000)
tcedi2400m000   single-occ (4)   Form 1-1

```
+------------------------------------------------------------------------+
| Print Order Types                                        Company: 000  |
|------------------------------------------------------------------------|
|                                                                        |
| Organization   from :    1..                                           |
|                to   :    2..                                           |
|                                                                        |
| EDI Message    from : 3.....                                           |
|                to   : 4.....                                           |
|                                                                        |
+------------------------------------------------------------------------+
```

1.   Organization from
2.   Organization to
3.   EDI Message from
4.   EDI Message to
11.39 Print Conversion of Order Types (out) (tcedi4432m000)
tcedi4432m000   single-occ (4)   Form 1-1

```
+------------------------------------------------------------------------+
| Print Conversion of Order Types (out)                    Company: 000  |
|------------------------------------------------------------------------|
|                                                                        |
| Organization   from :    1..                                           |
|                to   :    2..                                           |
|                                                                        |
| EDI Message    from : 3.....                                           |
|                to   : 4.....                                           |
|                                                                        |
| Code in Appl.  from :    5..                                           |
|                to   :    6..                                           |
|                                                                        |
+------------------------------------------------------------------------+
```

1.   Organization from
2.   Organization to
3.   EDI Message from
4.   EDI Message to
5.   Code in Appl. from
6.   Code in Appl. to

11.40 Print Conversion of Reference Number Types (out) (tcedi4436m000)

tcedi4436m000   single-occ (4)   Form 1-1

```
+--------------------------------------------------------------------------+
| Print Conversion of Reference Number Types (out)       Company: 000 |
|--------------------------------------------------------------------------|
|                                                                          |
| Organization           from : 1..                                        |
|                        to   : 2..                                        |
|                                                                          |
| Code in Application    from : 3................                          |
|                        to   : 4...............                           |
|                                                                          |
+--------------------------------------------------------------------------+
```

1.   Organization from
2.   Organization to
3.   Code in Application from
4.   Code in Application to

11.41 Print Address Types (tcedi2424m000)

tcedi2424m000   single-occ (4)   Form 1-1

```
+--------------------------------------------------------------------------+
| Print Address Types                                    Company: 000 |
|--------------------------------------------------------------------------|
|                                                                          |
| Organization           From : 1..                                        |
|                        To   : 2..                                        |
|                                                                          |
| Code in Message        From : 3.....                                     |
|                        To   : 4.....                                     |
|                                                                          |
+--------------------------------------------------------------------------+
```

1.   Organization from
2.   Organization to
3.   Code in Message from
4.   Code in Message to

11.42 Print Conversion of Address Types (out) (tcedi4434m000)

tcedi4434m000   single-occ (4)   Form 1-1

```
+--------------------------------------------------------------------------+
| Print Conversion of Address Types (out)               Company: 000 |
|--------------------------------------------------------------------------|
|                                                                          |
| Organization           from : 1..                                        |
|                        to   : 2..                                        |
|                                                                          |
| Code in Application    from : 3..................                        |
|                        to   : 4..................                        |
|                                                                          |
+--------------------------------------------------------------------------+
```

1.   Organization from
2.   Organization to
3.   Code in Application from
4.   Code in Application to

11.43 Print Reference Number Types (tcedi2420m000)

tcedi2420m000   single-occ (4)   Form 1-1

```
+--------------------------------------------------------------------------+
| Print Reference Number Types                           Company: 000 |
|--------------------------------------------------------------------------|
|                                                                          |
| Organization           From : 1..                                        |
|                        To   : 2..                                        |
|                                                                          |
| Code in Message        From : 3.....                                     |
|                        To   : 4.....                                     |
|                                                                          |
```

```
+-------------------------------------------------------------------------+
1.    Organization from
2.    Organization to
3.    Code in Message from
4.    Code in Message to
11.44 Print Character Conversion Codes (out) (tcedi4408m000)
tcedi4408m000                           single-occ (4)   Form 1-1
+-------------------------------------------------------------------------+
| Print Character Conversion Codes (out)              Company: 000  |
|-------------------------------------------------------------------------|
|                                                                         |
| Char. Conv. Code      from : 1.....                                     |
|                       to   : 2.....                                     |
|                                                                         |
+-------------------------------------------------------------------------+
1.    Character Conversion from
2.    Character Conversion to
11.45 Print Character Conversions (out) (tcedi4409m000)
tcedi4409m000                           single-occ (4)   Form 1-1
+-------------------------------------------------------------------------+
| Print Character Conversions (out)                  Company: 000  |
|-------------------------------------------------------------------------|
|                                                                         |
| Char. Conv. Code      from : 1.....                                     |
|                       to   : 2.....                                     |
|                                                                         |
+-------------------------------------------------------------------------+
1.    Character Conversion from
2.    Character Conversion to
```

12   Introduction to Additional Conversion Data

12.1 General

OBJECTIVE OF BUSINESS OBJECT

This b-object allows you to control the remaining conversion data required to prevent interpretation problems from arising between senders and receivers of EDI messages.

This b-object involves the following data sets:
• Conversion of Sales Contract Codes by Relation (in)
• Conversion of Sales Contract Codes by Relation (out)
• Conversion of Project Codes by Relation (in)
• Conversion of Project Codes by Relation (out)
• Conversion of Forwarding Agent Codes by Relation (in)
• Conversion of Forwarding Agent Codes by Relation (out)
• Conversion of Employee Codes by Relation (in)
• Conversion of Employee Codes by Relation (out)

Display the procedure and show the sessions in:
• Additional Conversion Data Procedure

12.2 Session Overview

Seq.	Session	Description	Session Usage
1	tcedi3114m000	Maint Conv of Sales Contract Code by Re	Mandatory
2	tcedi4152m000	Maint Conv of Sales Contract Code by Re	Mandatory
3	tcedi3116m000	Maint Conv of Project Codes by Relation	Mandatory
4	tcedi4154m000	Maint Conv of Project Codes by Relation	Mandatory
5	tcedi3118m000	Maint Conv of Forwarding Agent Codes by	Mandatory
6	tcedi4156m000	Maint Conv of Forw Agent Code by Rel (o	Mandatory

```
|    7 | tcedi3120m000 | Maint Conv of Employee Code by Relation| Mandatory
|
|    8 | tcedi3132m000 | Maint Conv of Discount Codes by Relatio| Mandatory
|
|    8 | tcedi4158m000 | Maint Conv of Employee Codes by Rel (ou| Mandatory
|
|    9 | tcedi4174m000 | Maint Conv of Discount Code by Rel (out| Mandatory
|
|   10 | tcedi3133m000 | Maint Conv of Discount Methods by Rel(i| Mandatory
|
|   11 | tcedi4175m000 | Maint Conv of Discount Methods by Rel(o| Mandatory
|
|   12 | tcedi3134m000 | Maint Conv of Lot Selection Code by Rel| Mandatory
|
|   13 | tcedi4176m000 | Maint Conv of Lot Selection Code by Rel| Mandatory
|
|   14 | tcedi3135m000 | Maint Conv of Lot Code ID. by Rel(in)  | Mandatory
|
|   15 | tcedi4177m000 | Maint Conv of Lot Code ID. by Rel (out)| Mandatory
|
|   20 | tcedi3115m000 | Maint Conv of Purchase Contr Codes by R| Additional
|
|   21 | tcedi3415m000 | Print Conv of Sales Contr Code by Rel(i| Print
|
|   40 | tcedi4153m000 | Maint Conv of Purchase Contr Code by Re| Additional
|
|   41 | tcedi4453m000 | Print Conv of Purchase Contr Code by Re| Print
|
|  101 | tcedi3414m000 | Print Conv of Purchase Contr Code by Re| Print
|
|  102 | tcedi4452m000 | Print Conv of Sales Contr Code by Rel(o| Print
|
|  103 | tcedi3416m000 | Print Conv of Project Code by Relation | Print
|
|  104 | tcedi4454m000 | Print Conv of Project Code by Rel (out)| Print
|
|  105 | tcedi3418m000 | Print Conv of Forw Agent Code by Rel (i| Print
|
|  106 | tcedi4456m000 | Print Conv of Forw Agent Code by Rel (o| Print
|
|  107 | tcedi3420m000 | Print Conv of Employee Code by Rel (in)| Print
|
|  108 | tcedi4458m000 | Print Conv of Employee Code by Rel (out| Print
|
```

13   Mandatory Sessions
13.1 Maintain Conversion of Sales Contract Codes by Relation (in)
(tcedi3114m000)
SESSION OBJECTIVE
To maintain the conversion data for the sales contract codes in incoming
messages from relations. This will allow you to process received messages for
which this conversion is necessary.
SEE ALSO KEYWORD(S)
•   Conversion of Sales Contract Codes by Relation (in)

```
tcedi3114m000                            multi/group (3     Form 1-1
+-------------------------------------------------------------------------+
| Maintain Conversion of Sales Contract Codes by Relation (in)  Company: 000 |
|-------------------------------------------------------------------------|
|                                                                         |
|  Relation          : 1.....  2_____            |
|                                                                         |
|  Code in Message       Code in Application   Description                |
|                                                                         |
```

```
|   3..................    4.....  5_____  |
|                                                                |
+----------------------------------------------------------------+
```

1.   Relation
An outgoing message for this relation is sent to the network address of the
parent relation. For both relations the field "Network Address" in the session
"Maintain Relation Data by Network (tcedi0128m000)" must be filled.
2.   Description
3.   Code in Message
The code used in the message.
4.   Code in Application
The code used in BAAN IV.
5.   Description
The contract description.

13.2 Maintain Conv. of Sales Contract Codes by Relation (out) (tcedi4152m000)

SESSION OBJECTIVE
To maintain the conversion data for the sales contract codes by relation in
outgoing messages. This will allow you to send messages for which this
conversion is necessary.
SEE ALSO KEYWORD(S)
•   Conversion of Sales Contract Codes by Relation (out)

```
tcedi4152m000                            multi/group (3    Form 1-1
+----------------------------------------------------------------+
| Maintain Conv. of Sales Contract Codes by Relation (out)   Company: 000 |
|----------------------------------------------------------------|
|                                                                |
| Relation            : 1.....  2_____     |
|                                                                |
| Code in Application   Description            Code in Message   |
|                                                                |
|            3.....  4_____   5.....       |
|                                                                |
+----------------------------------------------------------------+
```

1.   Relation
An outgoing message for this relation is sent to the network address of the
parent relation. For both relations the field "Network Address" in the session
"Maintain Relation Data by Network (tcedi0128m000)" must be filled.
2.   Description
3.   Code in Application
The code used in BAAN IV.
4.   Description
The contract description.
5.   Code in Message
The code used in the message.

13.3 Maintain Conversion of Project Codes by Relation (tcedi3116m000)

SESSION OBJECTIVE
To maintain the conversion data for the project codes in incoming messages from
relations. This will allow you to process received messages for which this
conversion is necessary.
SEE ALSO KEYWORD(S)
•   Conversion of Project Codes by Relation (in)

```
tcedi3116m000                            multi/group (3    Form 1-1
+----------------------------------------------------------------+
| Maintain Conversion of Project Codes by Relation        Company: 000 |
|----------------------------------------------------------------|
|                                                                |
| Relation            : 1.....  2_____     |
|                                                                |
| Code in Message        Code in Application   Description       |
|                                                                |
| 3..................          4.....  5_____ |
|                                                                |
+----------------------------------------------------------------+
```

1.   Relation
An outgoing message for this relation is sent to the network address of the
parent relation. For both relations the field "Network Address" in the session
"Maintain Relation Data by Network (tcedi0128m000)" must be filled.
2.   Description
3.   Code in Message
The code used in the message.
4.   Code in Application
The code used in BAAN IV.
5.   Description

13.4 Maintain Conversion of Project Codes by Relation (out) (tcedi4154m000)
SESSION OBJECTIVE
To maintain the conversion data for the project codes by relation in outgoing
messages. This will allow you to send messages for which this conversion is
necessary.
SEE ALSO KEYWORD(S)
•   Conversion of Project Codes by Relation (out)

tcedi4154m000   multi/group (3   Form 1-1
+--+
Maintain Conversion of Project Codes by Relation (out)   Company: 000
Relation   : 1..... 2_____
Code in Application   Description   Code in Message
3.....   4_____   5.....
+--+

1.   Relation
An outgoing message for this relation is sent to the network address of the
parent relation. For both relations the field "Network Address" in the session
"Maintain Relation Data by Network (tcedi0128m000)" must be filled.
2.   Description
3.   Code in Application
The code used in BAAN IV.
4.   Description
5.   Code in Message
The code used in the message.

13.5 Maintain Conv. of Forwarding Agent Codes by Relation (in) (tcedi3118m000)
SESSION OBJECTIVE
To maintain the conversion data for the forwarding agent codes in incoming
messages from relations. This will allow you to process received messages for
which this conversion is necessary.
SEE ALSO KEYWORD(S)
•   Conversion of Forwarding Agent Codes by Relation (in)

tcedi3118m000   multi/group (3   Form 1-1
+--+
Maintain Conv. of Forwarding Agent Codes by Relation (in)   Company: 000
Relation   : 1..... 2_____
Code in Message   Code in Application   Description
3...................   4.. 5_____
+--+

1.   Relation
An outgoing message for this relation is sent to the network address of the
parent relation. For both relations the field "Network Address" in the session
"Maintain Relation Data by Network (tcedi0128m000)" must be filled.
2.   Description

3.   Code in Message
The code used in the message.
4.   Code in Application
The code used in BAAN IV.
5.   Description

13.6 Maintain Conv. of Forwarding Agent Codes by Relation (out) (tcedi4156m000)

SESSION OBJECTIVE

To maintain the conversion data for the forwarding agent codes by relation in outgoing messages. This will allow you to send messages for which this conversion is necessary.

SEE ALSO KEYWORD(S)

•   Conversion of Forwarding Agent Codes by Relation (out)

```
tcedi4156m000                              multi/group (3    Form 1-1
+--------------------------------------------------------------------+
| Maintain Conv. of Forwarding Agent Codes by Relation (out)  Company: 000 |
|--------------------------------------------------------------------|
|                                                                    |
| Relation            : 1.....  2_____        |
|                                                                    |
| Code in Application   Description                 Code in Message   |
|                                                                    |
|              3..  4_____  5.....             |
|                                                                    |
+--------------------------------------------------------------------+
```

1.   Relation
An outgoing message for this relation is sent to the network address of the parent relation. For both relations the field "Network Address" in the session "Maintain Relation Data by Network (tcedi0128m000)" must be filled.
2.   Description
3.   Code in Application
The code used in BAAN IV.
4.   Description
5.   Code in Message
The code used in the message.

13.7 Maintain Conversion of Employee Codes by Relation (tcedi3120m000)

SESSION OBJECTIVE

To maintain the conversion data for the employee codes in incoming messages from relations. This will allow you to process received messages for which this conversion is necessary.

SEE ALSO KEYWORD(S)

•   Conversion of Employee Codes by Relation (in)

```
tcedi3120m000                              multi/group (3    Form 1-1
+--------------------------------------------------------------------+
| Maintain Conversion of Employee Codes by Relation     Company: 000 |
|--------------------------------------------------------------------|
|                                                                    |
| Relation            : 1.....  2_____        |
|                                                                    |
| Code in Message      Code in Application   Name                     |
|                                                                    |
| 3.....                          4.....  5_____   |
|                                                                    |
+--------------------------------------------------------------------+
```

1.   Relation
An outgoing message for this relation is sent to the network address of the parent relation. For both relations the field "Network Address" in the session "Maintain Relation Data by Network (tcedi0128m000)" must be filled.
2.   Description
3.   Code in Message
The code used in the message.
4.   Code in Application
The code used in BAAN IV.
5.   Name

The employee's name.

13.8 Maintain Conv. of Discount Codes by Relation (in) (tcedi3132m000)

SESSION OBJECTIVE

To maintain the conversion data for the discount codes in incoming messages received from relations. This will allow the processing of received messages requiring conversion.

SEE ALSO KEYWORD(S)

•   Conversion of Discount Codes by Relation (in)

```
tcedi3132m000                                multi/group (3    Form 1-1
+------------------------------------------------------------------------+
| Maintain Conv. of Discount Codes by Relation (in)      Company: 000  |
|------------------------------------------------------------------------|
|                                                                        |
| Relation              : 1.....  2_____         |
|                                                                        |
| Code in Message       Code in Application   Description               |
|                                                                        |
| 3..................                  4..  5_____ |
|                                                                        |
+------------------------------------------------------------------------+
```

1.   Relation
An outgoing message for this relation is sent to the network address of the parent relation. For both relations the field "Network Address" in the session "Maintain Relation Data by Network (tcedi0128m000)" must be filled.
2.   Description
3.   Code in Message
The code used in the message.
4.   Code in Application
For further information, see keyword(s)
"Discount Codes".
5.   Description

13.9 Maintain Conversion of Employee Codes by Relation (out) (tcedi4158m000)

SESSION OBJECTIVE

To maintain the conversion data for the employee codes by relation in outgoing messages. This will allow you to send messages for which this conversion is necessary.

SEE ALSO KEYWORD(S)

•   Conversion of Employee Codes by Relation (out)

```
tcedi4158m000                                multi/group (3    Form 1-1
+------------------------------------------------------------------------+
| Maintain Conversion of Employee Codes by Relation (out)   Company: 000 |
|------------------------------------------------------------------------|
|                                                                        |
| Relation              : 1.....  2_____         |
|                                                                        |
| Code in Application   Name                      Code in Message       |
|                                                                        |
|            3          4_____  5.....           |
|                                                                        |
+------------------------------------------------------------------------+
```

1.   Relation
An outgoing message for this relation is sent to the network address of the parent relation. For both relations the field "Network Address" in the session "Maintain Relation Data by Network (tcedi0128m000)" must be filled.
2.   Description
3.   Code in Application
The code used in BAAN IV.
4.   Name
The employee's name.
5.   Code in Message
The code used in the message.

13.10 Maintain Conv. of Discount Codes by Relation (out) (tcedi4174m000)

SESSION OBJECTIVE

To maintain the conversion data for the discount codes by relation in outgoing messages. This will allow you to send messages that require this conversion.
SEE ALSO KEYWORD(S)
- Conversion of Discount Codes by Relation (out)

tcedi4174m000   multi/group (3   Form 1-1

```
+-------------------------------------------------------------------------+
| Maintain Conv. of Discount Codes by Relation (out)      Company: 000 |
|-------------------------------------------------------------------------|
|                                                                         |
| Relation              : 1..... 2_____           |
|                                                                         |
| Code in Application  Description               Code in Message          |
|                                                                         |
|              3.. 4_____  5..................    |
|                                                                         |
+-------------------------------------------------------------------------+
```

1.   Relation
An outgoing message for this relation is sent to the network address of the parent relation. For both relations the field "Network Address" in the session "Maintain Relation Data by Network (tcedi0128m000)" must be filled.
2.   Description
3.   Code in Application
The code used in BAAN IV.
4.   Description
5.   Code in Message
The code used in the message.

13.11 Maintain Conv. of Discount Methods by Relation (in) (tcedi3133m000)
SESSION OBJECTIVE
To maintain the conversion data for the discount methods in incoming messages received from relations. This will allow processing of received messages that require conversion.
SEE ALSO KEYWORD(S)
- Conversion of Discount Methods by Relation (in)

tcedi3133m000   multi/group (3   Form 1-1

```
+-------------------------------------------------------------------------+
| Maintain Conv. of Discount Methods by Relation (in)     Company: 000 |
|-------------------------------------------------------------------------|
|                                                                         |
| Relation              : 1..... 2_____           |
|                                                                         |
| Code in Message       Description                                       |
|                                                                         |
| 3..................  4.......................                           |
|                                                                         |
+-------------------------------------------------------------------------+
```

1.   Relation
An outgoing message for this relation is sent to the network address of the parent relation. For both relations the field "Network Address" in the session "Maintain Relation Data by Network (tcedi0128m000)" must be filled.
2.   Description
3.   Code in Message
The code used in the message.
4.   Code in Application
The code used in BAAN IV.

13.12 Maintain Conv. of Discount Methods by Relation (out) (tcedi4175m000)
SESSION OBJECTIVE
To maintain the conversion data for the discount methods by relation in outgoing messages. This will allow you to send messages that require this conversion.
SEE ALSO KEYWORD(S)
- Conversion of Discount Methods by Relation (out)

tcedi4175m000   multi/group (3   Form 1-1

```
+-------------------------------------------------------------------------+
| Maintain Conv. of Discount Methods by Relation (out)     Company: 000 |
```

```
|-----------------------------------------------------------------------|
|                                                                       |
|  Relation              : 1.....  2_____         |
|                                                                       |
|  Description                    Code in Message                       |
|                                                                       |
|  3........................      4...................                  |
|                                                                       |
+-----------------------------------------------------------------------+
```

1.   Relation
An outgoing message for this relation is sent to the network address of the
parent relation. For both relations the field "Network Address" in the session
"Maintain Relation Data by Network (tcedi0128m000)" must be filled.
2.   Description
3.   Code in Application
The code used in BAAN IV.
4.   Code in Message
The code used in the message.

13.13 Maintain Conv. of Lot Selection Codes by Relation (in) (tcedi3134m000)
SESSION OBJECTIVE
To maintain the conversion data for the lot selection codes in incoming messages
received from relations. This will allow processing of received messages that
require conversion.
SEE ALSO KEYWORD(S)
•   Conversion of Lot Selection Methods by Relation (in)

```
tcedi3134m000                          multi/group (3    Form 1-1
+-----------------------------------------------------------------------+
|  Maintain Conv. of Lot Selection Codes by Relation (in)   Company: 000 |
|-----------------------------------------------------------------------|
|                                                                       |
|  Relation              : 1.....  2_____         |
|                                                                       |
|  Code in Message       Description                                    |
|                                                                       |
|  3...................   4...........                                  |
|                                                                       |
+-----------------------------------------------------------------------+
```

1.   Relation
An outgoing message for this relation is sent to the network address of the
parent relation. For both relations the field "Network Address" in the session
"Maintain Relation Data by Network (tcedi0128m000)" must be filled.
2.   Description
3.   Code in Message
The code used in the message.
4.   Code in Application
The code used in BAAN IV.

13.14 Maintain Conv. of Lot Selection Codes by Relation (out) (tcedi4176m000)
SESSION OBJECTIVE
To maintain the conversion data for the lot selection codes by relation in
outgoing messages. This will allow you to send messages that require this
conversion.
SEE ALSO KEYWORD(S)
•   Conversion of Lot Selection Methods by Relation (out)

```
tcedi4176m000                          multi/group (3    Form 1-1
+-----------------------------------------------------------------------+
|  Maintain Conv. of Lot Selection Codes by Relation (out)  Company: 000 |
|-----------------------------------------------------------------------|
|                                                                       |
|  Relation              : 1.....  2_____         |
|                                                                       |
|  Description                    Code in Message                       |
|                                                                       |
|  3..........            4...................                          |
```

```
|                                                                              |
+------------------------------------------------------------------------------+
```

1.   Relation
An outgoing message for this relation is sent to the network address of the
parent relation. For both relations the field "Network Address" in the session
"Maintain Relation Data by Network (tcedi0128m000)" must be filled.
2.   Description
3.   Code in Application
The code used in BAAN IV.
4.   Code in Message
The code used in the message.
13.15 Maintain Conv. of Lot Code ID. by Relation (in) (tcedi3135m000)
SESSION OBJECTIVE
To maintain the conversion data for the lot identifications in incoming messages
received from relations. This will allow processing of received messages that
require conversion.
SEE ALSO KEYWORD(S)
•   Conversion of Lot Code ID by Relation (in)
tcedi3135m000   multi/group (3   Form 1-1

```
+------------------------------------------------------------------------------+
| Maintain Conv. of Lot Code ID. by Relation (in)         Company: 000  |
|------------------------------------------------------------------------------|
|                                                                              |
| Relation                : 1.....  2_____              |
|                                                                              |
| Code in Message        Description                                           |
|                                                                              |
| 3.....                  4.................                                    |
|                                                                              |
+------------------------------------------------------------------------------+
```

1.   Relation
An outgoing message for this relation is sent to the network address of the
parent relation. For both relations the field "Network Address" in the session
"Maintain Relation Data by Network (tcedi0128m000)" must be filled.
2.   Description
3.   Code in Message
The code used in the message.
4.   Code in Application
The code used in BAAN IV.
13.16 Maintain Conv. of Lot Code ID. by Relation (out) (tcedi4177m000)
SESSION OBJECTIVE
To maintain the conversion data for the lot code identifications by relation in
outgoing messages. This will allow you to send messages that require this
conversion.
SEE ALSO KEYWORD(S)
•   Conversion of Lot Code ID by Relation (out)
tcedi4177m000   multi/group (3   Form 1-1

```
+------------------------------------------------------------------------------+
| Maintain Conv. of Lot Code ID. by Relation (out)         Company: 000  |
|------------------------------------------------------------------------------|
|                                                                              |
| Relation                : 1.....  2_____              |
|                                                                              |
| Description            Code in Message                                       |
|                                                                              |
| 3.................      4.....                                               |
|                                                                              |
+------------------------------------------------------------------------------+
```

1.   Relation
An outgoing message for this relation is sent to the network address of the
parent relation. For both relations the field "Network Address" in the session
"Maintain Relation Data by Network (tcedi0128m000)" must be filled.
2.   Description

3.   Code in Application
The code used in BAAN IV.
4.   Code in Message
The code used in the message.
14   Other Maintenance Sessions
14.1 Maintain Conversion of Purchase Contract Codes by Rel. (in)
(tcedi3115m000)
SESSION OBJECTIVE
To modify conversion data for purchase contract codes per relation on incoming
messages, allowing you to receive messages in which these codes are converted.
SEE ALSO KEYWORD(S)
•   Conversion of Purchase Contract Codes by Relation (in)
tcedi3115m000   multi/group (3   Form 1-1
+--+
Maintain Conversion of Purchase Contract Codes by Rel. (in)   Company: 000
Relation   : 1..... 2_____
Code in Message   Code in Appl. Description
3..................   4..... 5_____
+--+
1.   Relation
An outgoing message for this relation is sent to the network address of the
parent relation. For both relations the field "Network Address" in the session
"Maintain Relation Data by Network (tcedi0128m000)" must be filled.
2.   Description
3.   Code in Message
The code used in the message.
4.   Code in Application
The code used in BAAN IV.
5.   Description
The contract description is used to sort or retrieve contracts. It is often
displayed after the contract number.
14.2 Maintain Conv. of Purchase Contract Codes by Relation (out)
(tcedi4153m000)
SESSION OBJECTIVE
To modify conversion data for purchase contract codes per relation on outgoing
messages, allowing you to receive messages in which these codes are converted.
SEE ALSO KEYWORD(S)
•   Conversion of Purchase Contract Codes by Relation (out)
tcedi4153m000   multi/group (3   Form 1-1
+--+
Maintain Conv. of Purchase Contract Codes by Relation (out)   Company: 000
Relation   : 1..... 2_____
Code in Appl. Description   Code in Message
3..... 4_____   5..................
+--+
1.   Relation
An outgoing message for this relation is sent to the network address of the
parent relation. For both relations the field "Network Address" in the session
"Maintain Relation Data by Network (tcedi0128m000)" must be filled.
2.   Description
3.   Code in Application
The code used in BAAN IV.
4.   Description

The contract description is used to sort or retrieve contracts. It is often
displayed after the contract number.
5.   Code in Message
The code used in the message.
15   Other Print Sessions
15.1   Print Conversion of Sales Contract Codes by Relation (in) (tcedi3415m000)
tcedi3415m000   single-occ (4)   Form 1-1
+--+
Print Conversion of Sales Contract Codes by Relation (in)   Company: 000
Relation   from : 1.....
to   : 2.....
Code in Message from : 3...................
to   : 4...................
+--+
1.   Relation
2.   Relation
3.   Long Code in Message
4.   Long Code in Message
15.2   Print Conv. of Purchase Contract Codes by Relation (out) (tcedi4453m000)
tcedi4453m000   single-occ (4)   Form 1-1
+--+
Print Conv. of Purchase Contract Codes by Relation (out)   Company: 000
Relation   from : 1.....
to   : 2.....
Code in Application from : 3.....
to   : 4.....
+--+
1.   Relation
2.   Relation
3.   Contract Number
4.   Contract Number
15.3   Print Conversion of Purchase Contract Codes by Relation (in)
(tcedi3414m000)
tcedi3414m000   single-occ (4)   Form 1-1
+--+
Print Conversion of Purchase Contract Codes by Relation (in) Company: 000
Relation   from : 1.....
to   : 2.....
Code in Message   from : 3...................
to   : 4...................
+--+
1.   Relation from
2.   Relation to
3.   Code in Message from
4.   Code in Message to
15.4   Print Conversion of Sales Contract Codes by Relation (out) (tcedi4452m000)
tcedi4452m000   single-occ (4)   Form 1-1
+--+
Print Conversion of Sales Contract Codes by Relation (out)   Company: 000

```
|  Relation               from : 1.....                                |
|                         to   : 2.....                                |
|                                                                      |
|  Code in Application    from : 3.....                                |
|                         to   : 4.....                                |
|                                                                      |
+----------------------------------------------------------------------+
1.    Relation from
2.    Relation to
3.    Code in Application from
4.    Code in Application to
```

15.5 Print Conversion of Project Codes by Relation (in) (tcedi3416m000)

tcedi3416m000   single-occ (4)   Form 1-1

```
+----------------------------------------------------------------------+
|  Print Conversion of Project Codes by Relation (in)      Company: 000 |
|----------------------------------------------------------------------|
|                                                                      |
|  Relation               from : 1.....                                |
|                         to   : 2.....                                |
|                                                                      |
|  Code in Message        from : 3..................                   |
|                         to   : 4..................                   |
|                                                                      |
+----------------------------------------------------------------------+
1.    Relation from
2.    Relation to
3.    Code in Message from
4.    Code in Message to
```

15.6 Print Conversion of Project Codes by Relation (out) (tcedi4454m000)

tcedi4454m000   single-occ (4)   Form 1-1

```
+----------------------------------------------------------------------+
|  Print Conversion of Project Codes by Relation (out)     Company: 000 |
|----------------------------------------------------------------------|
|                                                                      |
|  Relation               from : 1.....                                |
|                         to   : 2.....                                |
|                                                                      |
|  Code in Application    from : 3.....                                |
|                         to   : 4.....                                |
|                                                                      |
+----------------------------------------------------------------------+
1.    Relation from
2.    Relation to
3.    Code in Application from
4.    Code in Application to
```

15.7 Print Conversion of Forwarding Agent Codes by Relation (in)
(tcedi3418m000)

tcedi3418m000   single-occ (4)   Form 1-1

```
+----------------------------------------------------------------------+
|  Print Conversion of Forwarding Agent Codes by Relation (in)  Company: 000 |
|----------------------------------------------------------------------|
|                                                                      |
|  Relation               from : 1.....                                |
|                         to   : 2.....                                |
|                                                                      |
|  Code in Message        from : 3..................                   |
|                         to   : 4..................                   |
|                                                                      |
+----------------------------------------------------------------------+
1.    Relation from
2.    Relation to
3.    Code in Message from
4.    Code in Message to
```

15.8 Print Conversion of Forwarding Agent Codes by Relation (out)
(tcedi4456m000)
tcedi4456m000   single-occ (4)   Form 1-1
+--+
Print Conversion of Forwarding Agent Codes by Relation (out) Company: 000
Relation   from : 1.....
to   : 2.....
Code in Application   from : 3..
to   : 4..
+--+
1.   Relation from
2.   Relation to
3.   Code in Application from
4.   Code in Application to
15.9 Print Conversion of Employee Codes by Relation (in) (tcedi3420m000)
tcedi3420m000   single-occ (4)   Form 1-1
+--+
Print Conversion of Employee Codes by Relation (in)   Company: 000
Relation   from : 1.....
to   : 2.....
Code in Message   from : 3...................
to   : 4...................
+--+
1.   Relation from
2.   Relation to
3.   Code in Message from
4.   Code in Message to
15.10 Print Conversion of Employee Codes by Relation (out) (tcedi4458m000)
tcedi4458m000   single-occ (4)   Form 1-1
+--+
Print Conversion of Employee Codes by Relation (out)   Company: 000
Relation   from : 1.....
to   : 2.....
Code in Application   from : 3.....
to   : 4.....
+--+
1.   Relation from
2.   Relation to
3.   Code in Application from
4.   Code in Application to
16   Introduction to Additional Coding Data
16.1 General
OBJECTIVE OF BUSINESS OBJECT
This b-object allows to manage the remaining codes and associated data.
This b-object involves the following data sets:
•   Schedule Release Frequencies
•   Type of Delivery Specifier
•   Schedule Status Indicators
•   Schedule Release Categories
•   Item Status Indicators
Display the procedure and show the sessions in:

Seq.	Session	Description	Session Usage
1	tcedi2102m000	Maint Schedule Release Frequencies	Mandatory
2	tcedi2104m000	Maint Type of Delivery Specifier	Mandatory
3	tcedi2106m000	Maintain Schedule Status Indicators	Mandatory
4	tcedi2108m000	Maintain Schedule Release Categories	Mandatory
5	tcedi2110m000	Maintain Item Status Indicators	Mandatory
6	tcedi2112m000	Maintain Production Schedule Types	Mandatory
7	tcedi2114m000	Maintain Packing Code IDs	Mandatory
8	tcedi2122m000	Maintain Dates/Times	Mandatory
9	tcedi2134m000	Maintain Transport Types	Mandatory
10	tcedi2136m000	Maintain Periods	Mandatory
11	tcedi2138m000	Maintain Discounts	Mandatory
12	tcedi2144m000	Maintain Discounts and Surcharges	Mandatory
13	tcedi2150m000	Maintain Message Function	Mandatory
14	tcedi2152m000	Maintain Time Zone Specifier	Mandatory
15	tcedi2154m000	Maintain Contact Function	Mandatory
16	tcedi2156m000	Maintain Communication Channel	Mandatory
17	tcedi2158m000	Maintain Terms of Delivery Function	Mandatory
18	tcedi2160m000	Maint Type of Supplementary Information	Mandatory
19	tcedi2162m000	Maint Type of Contract and Carriage Con	Mandatory
20	tcedi2164m000	Maintain Type of Monetary Amount	Mandatory
21	tcedi2166m000	Maintain Charge Category	Mandatory
22	tcedi2168m000	Maintain Dimension Qualifier	Mandatory
23	tcedi2170m000	Maintain Temperature Qualifier	Mandatory
24	tcedi2172m000	Maintain Plus/Minus Indicator	Mandatory
25	tcedi2174m000	Maintain Measurement Qualifier	Mandatory
26	tcedi2176m000	Maintain Type of Packages	Mandatory
27	tcedi2178m000	Maintain Transport Stage	Mandatory
28	tcedi2180m000	Maintain Equipment Qualifier	Mandatory

```
|   29 | tcedi2182m000 | Maint Shipper-Supplied Equipment Indica| Mandatory
|
|   30 | tcedi2184m000 | Maintain Dangerous Goods Regulations   | Mandatory
|
|   31 | tcedi2186m000 | Maint Government Involvement Indicator | Mandatory
|
|   32 | tcedi2188m000 | Maintain Government Agencies           | Mandatory
|
|   33 | tcedi2190m000 | Maintain Government Actions            | Mandatory
|
|  101 | tcedi2402m000 | Print Schedule Release Frequencies     | Print
|
|  102 | tcedi2404m000 | Print Type of Delivery Specifier       | Print
|
|  103 | tcedi2406m000 | Print Schedule Status Indicators       | Print
|
|  104 | tcedi2408m000 | Print Schedule Release Categories      | Print
|
|  105 | tcedi2410m000 | Print Item Status Indicators           | Print
|
|  106 | tcedi2412m000 | Print Production Schedule Types        | Print
|
|  107 | tcedi2414m000 | Print Packing Code IDs                 | Print
|
|  108 | tcedi2422m000 | Print Dates/Times                      | Print
|
|  109 | tcedi2434m000 | Print Transport Types                  | Print
|
|  110 | tcedi2436m000 | Print Periods                          | Print
|
|  111 | tcedi2438m000 | Print Discounts                        | Print
|
|  112 | tcedi2444m000 | Print Discounts and Surcharges         | Print
|
|  113 | tcedi2450m000 | Print Message Function                 | Print
|
|  114 | tcedi2452m000 | Print Time Zone Specifier              | Print
|
|  115 | tcedi2454m000 | Print Contact Function                 | Print
|
|  116 | tcedi2456m000 | Print Communication Channel            | Print
|
|  117 | tcedi2458m000 | Print Terms of Delivery Function       | Print
|
|  118 | tcedi2460m000 | Print Type of Supplementary Information| Print
|
|  119 | tcedi2462m000 | Print Type of Contract and Carriage Con| Print
|
|  120 | tcedi2464m000 | Print Type of Monetary Amount          | Print
|
|  121 | tcedi2466m000 | Print Charge Category                  | Print
|
|  122 | tcedi2468m000 | Print Dimension Qualifier              | Print
|
|  123 | tcedi2470m000 | Print Temperature Qualifier            | Print
|
|  124 | tcedi2472m000 | Print Plus/Minus Indicator             | Print
|
|  125 | tcedi2474m000 | Print Measurement Qualifier            | Print
|
|  126 | tcedi2476m000 | Print Type of Packages                 | Print
|
```

```
| 127 | tcedi2478m000 | Print Transport Stage                    | Print
|
| 128 | tcedi2480m000 | Print Equipment Qualifier                | Print
|
| 129 | tcedi2482m000 | Print Shipper-Supplied Equipment Indica| Print
|
| 130 | tcedi2484m000 | Print Dangerous Goods Regulations        | Print
|
| 131 | tcedi2486m000 | Print Government Involvement Indicator  | Print
|
| 132 | tcedi2488m000 | Print Government Agencies                | Print
|
| 133 | tcedi2490m000 | Print Government Actions                 | Print
|
| 201 | tcedi2502s000 | Display Schedule Release Frequencies    | Display
|
| 202 | tcedi2504s000 | Display Type of Delivery Specifier      | Display
|
| 203 | tcedi2506s000 | Display Schedule Status Indicators      | Display
|
| 204 | tcedi2508s000 | Display Schedule Release Categories     | Display
|
| 205 | tcedi2510s000 | Display Item Status Indicators          | Display
|
| 206 | tcedi2512s000 | Display Production Schedule Types       | Display
|
| 207 | tcedi2514s000 | Display Packing Code IDs                | Display
|
| 208 | tcedi2522s000 | Display Dates/Times                     | Display
|
| 209 | tcedi2534s000 | Display Transport Types                 | Display
|
| 210 | tcedi2536s000 | Display Periods                         | Display
|
| 211 | tcedi2538s000 | Display Discounts                       | Display
|
| 212 | tcedi2544s000 | Display Discounts and Surcharges        | Display
|
| 213 | tcedi2550s000 | Display Message Function                | Display
|
| 214 | tcedi2552s000 | Display Time Zone Specifier             | Display
|
| 215 | tcedi2554s000 | Display Contact Function                | Display
|
| 216 | tcedi2556s000 | Display Communication Channel           | Display
|
| 217 | tcedi2558s000 | Display Terms of Delivery Function      | Display
|
| 218 | tcedi2560s000 | Display Type of Supplementary Informati| Display
|
| 219 | tcedi2562s000 | Display Type of Contr and Carriage Cond| Display
|
| 220 | tcedi2564s000 | Display Type of Monetary Amount         | Display
|
| 221 | tcedi2566s000 | Display Charge Category                 | Display
|
| 222 | tcedi2568s000 | Display Dimension Qualifier             | Display
|
| 223 | tcedi2570s000 | Display Temperature Qualifier           | Display
|
| 224 | tcedi2572s000 | Display Plus/Minus Indicator            | Display
|
```

```
|   225 | tcedi2574s000 | Display Measurement Qualifier          | Display
|
|   226 | tcedi2576s000 | Display Type of Packages               | Display
|
|   227 | tcedi2578s000 | Display Transport Stages               | Display
|
|   228 | tcedi2580s000 | Display Equipment Qualifier            | Display
|
|   229 | tcedi2582s000 | Display Shipper-Supplied Equipment Indi| Display
|
|   230 | tcedi2584s000 | Display Dangerous Goods Regulations    | Display
|
|   231 | tcedi2586s000 | Display Government Involvement Indicato| Display
|
|   232 | tcedi2588s000 | Display Government Agencies            | Display
|
|   233 | tcedi2590s000 | Display Government Actions             | Display
|
```

---

17   Mandatory Sessions

17.1 Maintain Schedule Release Frequencies (tcedi2102m000)

SESSION OBJECTIVE

To maintain the schedule release frequencies that will be used in incoming and outgoing messages.

SEE ALSO KEYWORD(S)

•   Schedule Release Frequencies

tcedi2102m000   multi/group (3   Form 1-1

```
+--------------------------------------------------------------------------+
|  Maintain Schedule Release Frequencies              Company: 000  |
|--------------------------------------------------------------------------|
|                                                                          |
|  Organization        : 1..  2_____               |
|                                                                          |
|  Code in Message        Description                                      |
|                                                                          |
|  3.....                 4...........................                     |
|                                                                          |
+--------------------------------------------------------------------------+
```

1.   Organization
The code which uniquely identifies the organization.
2.   Description
3.   Code in Message
The code used in the message.
4.   Description
Enter a clear description here.

17.2 Maintain Type of Delivery Specifier (tcedi2104m000)

SESSION OBJECTIVE

To maintain delivery types. This is necessary in order to be able to send or receive messages containing these.

SEE ALSO KEYWORD(S)

•   Type of Delivery Specifier

tcedi2104m000   multi/group (3   Form 1-1

```
+--------------------------------------------------------------------------+
|  Maintain Type of Delivery Specifier              Company: 000  |
|--------------------------------------------------------------------------|
|                                                                          |
|  Organization        : 1..  2_____               |
|                                                                          |
|  Code in Message        Description                                      |
|                                                                          |
|  3.....                 4...........................                     |
|                                                                          |
+--------------------------------------------------------------------------+
```

1.   Organization
The code which uniquely identifies the organization.
2.   Description
3.   Code in Message
The code used in the message.
4.   Description
The description for the code in the EDI message.
17.3 Maintain Schedule Status Indicators (tcedi2106m000)
SESSION OBJECTIVE
To maintain schedule status indicators. This is necessary in order to be able to
send or receive messages containing these.
SEE ALSO KEYWORD(S)
•   Schedule Status Indicators
tcedi2106m000   multi/group (3   Form 1-1
+---+
Maintain Schedule Status Indicators   Company: 000
Organization   : 1.. 2_____
Code in Message   Description
3.....   4...........................
+---+
1.   Organization
The code which uniquely identifies the organization.
2.   Description
3.   Code in Message
The code used in the message.
4.   Description
The description for the code in the EDI message.
17.4 Maintain Schedule Release Categories (tcedi2108m000)
SESSION OBJECTIVE
To maintain schedule release categories. This is necessary in order to be able
to send or receive messages containing these.
SEE ALSO KEYWORD(S)
•   Schedule Release Categories
tcedi2108m000   multi/group (3   Form 1-1
+---+
Maintain Schedule Release Categories   Company: 000
Organization   : 1.. 2_____
Code in Message   Description
3.....   4.....................
+---+
1.   Organization
The code which uniquely identifies the organization.
2.   Description
3.   Code in Message
The code used in the message.
4.   Description
Indicates how the order line is added to the order system.
Replace All from Date
Delete all the lines of a sales contract and item from this delivery date
onwards. Next, add this line.
Replace as Specified
Delete the line of the sales contract and item with this delivery date. Next,
add this line.

17.5 Maintain Item Status Indicators (tcedi2110m000)
SESSION OBJECTIVE
To maintain item status indicators. This is necessary in order to be able to
send or receive messages containing these.
SEE ALSO KEYWORD(S)
• Item Status Indicators
tcedi2110m000   multi/group (3   Form 1-1
+--+
Maintain Item Status Indicators   Company: 000
Organization   : 1.. 2_____
Code in Message   Description
3.....   4...........................
+--+
1.   Organization
The code which uniquely identifies the organization.
2.   Description
3.   Code in Message
The code used in the message.
4.   Description
The description for the code in the EDI message.
17.6 Maintain Production Schedule Types (tcedi2112m000)
SESSION OBJECTIVE
To maintain production schedule types. This is necessary in order to be able to
send or receive messages containing these.
SEE ALSO KEYWORD(S)
• Production Schedule Types
tcedi2112m000   multi/group (3   Form 1-1
+--+
Maintain Production Schedule Types   Company: 000
Organization   : 1.. 2_____
Code in Message   Description
3.....   4...........................
+--+
1.   Organization
The code which uniquely identifies the organization.
2.   Description
3.   Code in Message
The code used in the message.
4.   Description
The description for the code in the EDI message.
17.7 Maintain Packing Code IDs (tcedi2114m000)
SESSION OBJECTIVE
To maintain packing code IDs. This is necessary in order to be able to send or
receive messages containing these.
SEE ALSO KEYWORD(S)
• Packing Code IDs
tcedi2114m000   multi/group (3   Form 1-1
+--+
Maintain Packing Code IDs   Company: 000
Organization   : 1.. 2_____

```
| Code in Message        Description                                    |
|                                                                       |
| 3.....                 4...........................                    |
|                                                                       |
+-----------------------------------------------------------------------+
```

1.   Organization
The code which uniquely identifies the organization.
2.   Description
3.   Code in Message
The code used in the message.
4.   Description
The description for the code in the EDI message.
17.8 Maintain Dates/Times (tcedi2122m000)
SESSION OBJECTIVE
To maintain dates and times. This is necessary in order to be able to send or
receive messages containing these.
SEE ALSO KEYWORD(S)
•   Dates/Times
tcedi2122m000   multi/group (3   Form 1-1

```
+-----------------------------------------------------------------------+
| Maintain Dates/Times                              Company: 000  |
|-----------------------------------------------------------------------|
|                                                                       |
| Organization        : 1..   2_____             |
|                                                                       |
| Code in Message        Description                                    |
|                                                                       |
| 3.....                 4.............                                  |
|                                                                       |
+-----------------------------------------------------------------------+
```

1.   Organization
The code which uniquely identifies the organization.
2.   Description
3.   Code in Message
The code used in the message.
4.   Description
The description for the code in the EDI message.
17.9 Maintain Transport Types (tcedi2134m000)
SESSION OBJECTIVE
To maintain transport types codes. This is necessary in order to be able to send
or receive messages containing these.
SEE ALSO KEYWORD(S)
•   Transport Types
tcedi2134m000   multi/group (3   Form 1-1

```
+-----------------------------------------------------------------------+
| Maintain Transport Types                          Company: 000  |
|-----------------------------------------------------------------------|
|                                                                       |
| Organization        : 1..   2_____             |
|                                                                       |
| Code in Message        Description                                    |
|                                                                       |
| 3.....                 4...........................                    |
|                                                                       |
+-----------------------------------------------------------------------+
```

1.   Organization
The code which uniquely identifies the organization.
2.   Description
3.   Code in Message
The code used in the message.
4.   Description
The description for the code in the EDI message.
17.10 Maintain Periods (tcedi2136m000)

SESSION OBJECTIVE
To maintain period codes. This is necessary in order to be able to send or
receive messages containing these.
SEE ALSO KEYWORD(S)
•   Periods
tcedi2136m000   multi/group (3   Form 1-1
+---+
Maintain Periods   Company: 000
Organization   : 1.. 2_____
Code in Message   Description
3.....   4........
+---+
1.   Organization
The code which uniquely identifies the organization.
2.   Description
3.   Code in Message
The code used in the message.
4.   Description
The description for the code in the EDI message.
17.11 Maintain Discounts (tcedi2138m000)
SESSION OBJECTIVE
To maintain discount codes. This is necessary in order to be able to send or
receive messages containing these.
SEE ALSO KEYWORD(S)
•   Discounts
tcedi2138m000   multi/group (3   Form 1-1
+---+
Maintain Discounts   Company: 000
Organization   : 1.. 2_____
Code in Message   Description
3.....   4...................
+---+
1.   Organization
The code which uniquely identifies the organization.
2.   Description
3.   Code in Message
The code used in the message.
4.   Description
Indicates one of the following types of discounts:
Cash Discount
Late Payment Surcharge
17.12 Maintain Discounts and Surcharges (tcedi2144m000)
SESSION OBJECTIVE
To maintain discount and surcharge codes. This is necessary in order to be able
to send or receive messages containing these.
SEE ALSO KEYWORD(S)
•   Discounts and Surcharges
tcedi2144m000   multi/group (3   Form 1-1
+---+
Maintain Discounts and Surcharges   Company: 000
Organization   : 1.. 2_____

```
|                                                                    |
| Code in Message       Description                                  |
|                                                                    |
| 3.....                4.......                                     |
|                                                                    |
+--------------------------------------------------------------------+
```

1.   Organization
The code which uniquely identifies the organization.
2.   Description
3.   Code in Message
The code used in the message.
4.   Description
Indicates whether a discount or a surcharge is involved.

17.13 Maintain Message Function (tcedi2150m000)

SESSION OBJECTIVE
To maintain message function codes. This is necessary in order to be able to
send or receive messages containing these.

SEE ALSO KEYWORD(S)
•   Message Functions

tcedi2150m000   multi/group (3   Form 1-1
```
+--------------------------------------------------------------------+
| Maintain Message Function                        Company: 000      |
|--------------------------------------------------------------------|
|                                                                    |
| Organization        : 1..   2_____         |
|                                                                    |
| Code in Message       Description                                  |
|                                                                    |
| 3.....                4..................                          |
|                                                                    |
+--------------------------------------------------------------------+
```

1.   Organization
The code which uniquely identifies the organization.
2.   Description
3.   Code in Message
The code used in the message.
4.   Description
The description for the code in the EDI message.

17.14 Maintain Time Zone Specifier (tcedi2152m000)

SESSION OBJECTIVE
To maintain time zone specifiers. This is necessary in order to be able to send
or receive messages containing these.

SEE ALSO KEYWORD(S)
•   Time Zone Specifiers

tcedi2152m000   multi/group (3   Form 1-1
```
+--------------------------------------------------------------------+
| Maintain Time Zone Specifier                     Company: 000      |
|--------------------------------------------------------------------|
|                                                                    |
| Organization        : 1..   2_____         |
|                                                                    |
| Code in Message       Description                                  |
|                                                                    |
| 3.....                4...........................                 |
|                                                                    |
+--------------------------------------------------------------------+
```

1.   Organization
The code which uniquely identifies the organization.
2.   Description
3.   Code in Message
The code used in the message.
4.   Description
The description for the code in the EDI message.

17.15 Maintain Contact Function (tcedi2154m000)
SESSION OBJECTIVE
To maintain contact functions. This is necessary in order to be able to send or
receive messages containing these.
SEE ALSO KEYWORD(S)
•   Contact Functions

```
tcedi2154m000                              multi/group (3     Form 1-1
+-----------------------------------------------------------------------+
|  Maintain Contact Function                            Company: 000  |
|-----------------------------------------------------------------------|
|                                                                       |
|  Organization        : 1..  2_____           |
|                                                                       |
|  Code in Message        Description                                   |
|                                                                       |
|  3.....                  4.......................                     |
|                                                                       |
+-----------------------------------------------------------------------+
```

1.   Organization
The code which uniquely identifies the organization.
2.   Description
3.   Code in Message
The code used in the message.
4.   Description
The description for the code in the EDI message.
17.16 Maintain Communication Channel (tcedi2156m000)
SESSION OBJECTIVE
To maintain communication channel codes. This is necessary in order to be able
to send or receive messages using these.
SEE ALSO KEYWORD(S)
•   Communication Channels

```
tcedi2156m000                              multi/group (3     Form 1-1
+-----------------------------------------------------------------------+
|  Maintain Communication Channel                       Company: 000  |
|-----------------------------------------------------------------------|
|                                                                       |
|  Organization        : 1..  2_____           |
|                                                                       |
|  Code in Message        Description                                   |
|                                                                       |
|  3.....                  4.......                                     |
|                                                                       |
+-----------------------------------------------------------------------+
```

1.   Organization
The code which uniquely identifies the organization.
2.   Description
3.   Code in Message
The code used in the message.
4.   Description
The description for the code in the EDI message.
17.17 Maintain Terms of Delivery Function (tcedi2158m000)
SESSION OBJECTIVE
To maintain terms of delivery functions. This is necessary in order to be able
to send or receive messages containing these.
SEE ALSO KEYWORD(S)
•   Terms of Delivery Functions

```
tcedi2158m000                              multi/group (3     Form 1-1
+-----------------------------------------------------------------------+
|  Maintain Terms of Delivery Function                  Company: 000  |
|-----------------------------------------------------------------------|
|                                                                       |
|  Organization        : 1..  2_____           |
|                                                                       |
```

```
| Code in Message        Description                                    |
|                                                                       |
| 3.....                 4................                              |
|                                                                       |
+-----------------------------------------------------------------------+
```
1.   Organization
The code which uniquely identifies the organization.
2.   Description
3.   Code in Message
The code used in the message.
4.   Description
The description for the code in the EDI message.
17.18 Maintain Type of Supplementary Information (tcedi2160m000)
SESSION OBJECTIVE
To maintain types of supplementary information. This is necessary in order to be
able to send or receive messages containing these.
SEE ALSO KEYWORD(S)
•   Types of Supplementary Information
tcedi2160m000   multi/group (3   Form 1-1
```
+-----------------------------------------------------------------------+
| Maintain Type of Supplementary Information            Company: 000    |
|-----------------------------------------------------------------------|
|                                                                       |
| Organization        : 1..  2_____             |
|                                                                       |
| Code in Message        Description                                    |
|                                                                       |
| 3.....                 4......................                        |
|                                                                       |
+-----------------------------------------------------------------------+
```
1.   Organization
The code which uniquely identifies the organization.
2.   Description
3.   Code in Message
The code used in the message.
4.   Description
The description for the code in the EDI message.
17.19 Maintain Type of Contract and Carriage Condition (tcedi2162m000)
SESSION OBJECTIVE
To maintain types of contract and carriage conditions. This is necessary in
order to be able to send or receive messages containing these.
SEE ALSO KEYWORD(S)
•   Types of Contract and Carriage Condition
tcedi2162m000   multi/group (3   Form 1-1
```
+-----------------------------------------------------------------------+
| Maintain Type of Contract and Carriage Condition      Company: 000    |
|-----------------------------------------------------------------------|
|                                                                       |
| Organization        : 1..  2_____             |
|                                                                       |
| Code in Message        Description                                    |
|                                                                       |
| 3.....                 4....................                          |
|                                                                       |
+-----------------------------------------------------------------------+
```
1.   Organization
The code which uniquely identifies the organization.
2.   Description
3.   Code in Message
The code used in the message.
4.   Description
The description for the code in the EDI message.
17.20 Maintain Type of Monetary Amount (tcedi2164m000)

SESSION OBJECTIVE
To maintain types of monetary amounts. This is necessary in order to be able to
send or receive messages containing these.
SEE ALSO KEYWORD(S)
•   Types of Monetary Amount

tcedi2164m000   multi/group (3   Form 1-1

```
+--------------------------------------------------------------------+
| Maintain Type of Monetary Amount                  Company: 000     |
|--------------------------------------------------------------------|
|                                                                    |
| Organization        : 1.. 2_____            |
|                                                                    |
| Code in Message        Description                                 |
|                                                                    |
| 3.....                 4.................                          |
|                                                                    |
+--------------------------------------------------------------------+
```

1.   Organization
The code which uniquely identifies the organization.
2.   Description
3.   Code in Message
The code used in the message.
4.   Description
The description for the code in the EDI message.

17.21 Maintain Charge Category (tcedi2166m000)
SESSION OBJECTIVE
To maintain charge categories. This is necessary in order to be able to send or
receive messages containing these.
SEE ALSO KEYWORD(S)
•   Charge Categories

tcedi2166m000   multi/group (3   Form 1-1

```
+--------------------------------------------------------------------+
| Maintain Charge Category                          Company: 000     |
|--------------------------------------------------------------------|
|                                                                    |
| Organization        : 1.. 2_____            |
|                                                                    |
| Code in Message        Description                                 |
|                                                                    |
| 3.....                 4.....................                      |
|                                                                    |
+--------------------------------------------------------------------+
```

1.   Organization
The code which uniquely identifies the organization.
2.   Description
3.   Code in Message
The code used in the message.
4.   Description
The description for the code in the EDI message.

17.22 Maintain Dimension Qualifier (tcedi2168m000)
SESSION OBJECTIVE
To maintain dimension qualifiers of consignments. This is necessary in order to
be able to send or receive messages containing these.
SEE ALSO KEYWORD(S)
•   Dimension Qualifiers

tcedi2168m000   multi/group (3   Form 1-1

```
+--------------------------------------------------------------------+
| Maintain Dimension Qualifier                      Company: 000     |
|--------------------------------------------------------------------|
|                                                                    |
| Organization        : 1.. 2_____            |
|                                                                    |
| Code in Message        Description                                 |
```

```
|                                                                  |
|   3.....              4...........................               |
|                                                                  |
+------------------------------------------------------------------+
1.    Organization
The code which uniquely identifies the organization.
2.    Description
3.    Code in Message
The code used in the message.
4.    Description
The description for the code in the EDI message.
17.23 Maintain Temperature Qualifier (tcedi2170m000)
SESSION OBJECTIVE
To maintain temperature qualifiers of consignments. This is necessary in order
to be able to send or receive messages containing these.
SEE ALSO KEYWORD(S)
•    Temperature Qualifiers
tcedi2170m000                              multi/group (3    Form 1-1
+------------------------------------------------------------------+
|   Maintain Temperature Qualifier                  Company: 000   |
|------------------------------------------------------------------|
|                                                                  |
|   Organization        : 1..   2_____       |
|                                                                  |
|   Code in Message       Description                              |
|                                                                  |
|   3.....              4.................                         |
|                                                                  |
+------------------------------------------------------------------+
1.    Organization
The code which uniquely identifies the organization.
2.    Description
3.    Code in Message
The code used in the message.
4.    Description
The description for the code in the EDI message.
17.24 Maintain Plus/Minus Indicator (tcedi2172m000)
SESSION OBJECTIVE
To maintain plus and minus indicators. This is necessary in order to be able to
send or receive messages containing these.
SEE ALSO KEYWORD(S)
•    Plus/Minus Indicators
tcedi2172m000                              multi/group (3    Form 1-1
+------------------------------------------------------------------+
|   Maintain Plus/Minus Indicator                   Company: 000   |
|------------------------------------------------------------------|
|                                                                  |
|   Organization        : 1..   2_____       |
|                                                                  |
|   Code in Message       Description                              |
|                                                                  |
|   3.....              4...........................               |
|                                                                  |
+------------------------------------------------------------------+
1.    Organization
The code which uniquely identifies the organization.
2.    Description
3.    Code in Message
The code used in the message.
4.    Description
The description for the code in the EDI message.
17.25 Maintain Measurement Qualifier (tcedi2174m000)
SESSION OBJECTIVE
```

To maintain measurement qualifiers of consignments. This is necessary in order
to be able to send or receive messages containing these.
SEE ALSO KEYWORD(S)
•   Measurement Qualifiers

tcedi2174m000   multi/group (3   Form 1-1

```
+-------------------------------------------------------------------+
| Maintain Measurement Qualifier               Company: 000 |
|-------------------------------------------------------------------|
|                                                                   |
| Organization      : 1..  2_____           |
|                                                                   |
| Code in Message       Description                                 |
|                                                                   |
| 3.....                4.............................              |
|                                                                   |
+-------------------------------------------------------------------+
```

1.   Organization
The code which uniquely identifies the organization.
2.   Description
3.   Code in Message
The code used in the message.
4.   Description
The description for the code in the EDI message.

17.26 Maintain Type of Packages (tcedi2176m000)
SESSION OBJECTIVE
To maintain type of package codes. This is necessary in order to be able to send
or receive messages containing these.
SEE ALSO KEYWORD(S)
•   Types of Packages

tcedi2176m000   multi/group (3   Form 1-1

```
+-------------------------------------------------------------------+
| Maintain Type of Packages                    Company: 000 |
|-------------------------------------------------------------------|
|                                                                   |
| Organization      : 1..  2_____           |
|                                                                   |
| Code in Message       Description                                 |
|                                                                   |
| 3.....                4.............................              |
|                                                                   |
+-------------------------------------------------------------------+
```

1.   Organization
The code which uniquely identifies the organization.
2.   Description
3.   Code in Message
The code used in the message.
4.   Description
The description for the code in the EDI message.

17.27 Maintain Transport Stage (tcedi2178m000)
SESSION OBJECTIVE
To maintain transport stage codes. This is necessary in order to be able to send
or receive messages containing these.
SEE ALSO KEYWORD(S)
•   Transport Stages

tcedi2178m000   multi/group (3   Form 1-1

```
+-------------------------------------------------------------------+
| Maintain Transport Stage                     Company: 000 |
|-------------------------------------------------------------------|
|                                                                   |
| Organization      : 1..  2_____           |
|                                                                   |
| Code in Message       Description                                 |
|                                                                   |
```

```
|   3.....                    4...........................                   |
|                                                                           |
+---------------------------------------------------------------------------+
```

1.   Organization
The code which uniquely identifies the organization.
2.   Description
3.   Code in Message
The code used in the message.
4.   Description
The description for the code in the EDI message.

17.28 Maintain Equipment Qualifier (tcedi2180m000)

SESSION OBJECTIVE
To maintain equipment qualifiers. This is necessary in order to be able to send
or receive messages containing these.

SEE ALSO KEYWORD(S)
•   Equipment Qualifiers

tcedi2180m000   multi/group (3   Form 1-1

```
+---------------------------------------------------------------------------+
|  Maintain Equipment Qualifier                            Company: 000  |
|---------------------------------------------------------------------------|
|                                                                           |
|  Organization        : 1..  2_____                      |
|                                                                           |
|  Code in Message       Description                                        |
|                                                                           |
|  3.....                    4...........................                   |
|                                                                           |
+---------------------------------------------------------------------------+
```

1.   Organization
The code which uniquely identifies the organization.
2.   Description
3.   Code in Message
The code used in the message.
4.   Description
The description for the code in the EDI message.

17.29 Maintain Shipper-Supplied Equipment Indicator (tcedi2182m000)

SESSION OBJECTIVE
To maintain shipper-supplied equipment indicators. This is necessary in order to
be able to send or receive messages containing these.

SEE ALSO KEYWORD(S)
•   Shipper-Supplied Equipment Indicators

tcedi2182m000   multi/group (3   Form 1-1

```
+---------------------------------------------------------------------------+
|  Maintain Shipper-Supplied Equipment Indicator           Company: 000  |
|---------------------------------------------------------------------------|
|                                                                           |
|  Organization        : 1..  2_____                      |
|                                                                           |
|  Code in Message       Description                                        |
|                                                                           |
|  3.....                    4...........................                   |
|                                                                           |
+---------------------------------------------------------------------------+
```

1.   Organization
The code which uniquely identifies the organization.
2.   Description
3.   Code in Message
The code used in the message.
4.   Description
The description for the code in the EDI message.

17.30 Maintain Dangerous Goods Regulations (tcedi2184m000)

SESSION OBJECTIVE

To maintain dangerous goods regulations. This is necessary in order to be able
to send or receive messages containing these.
SEE ALSO KEYWORD(S)
• Dangerous Goods Regulations

```
tcedi2184m000                                 multi/group (3    Form 1-1
+------------------------------------------------------------------------+
| Maintain Dangerous Goods Regulations                    Company: 000   |
|------------------------------------------------------------------------|
|                                                                        |
| Organization        : 1.. 2_____                    |
|                                                                        |
| Code in Message        Description                                     |
|                                                                        |
| 3.....                 4............................                   |
|                                                                        |
+------------------------------------------------------------------------+
```

1.   Organization
The code which uniquely identifies the organization.
2.   Description
3.   Code in Message
The code used in the message.
4.   Description
The description for the code in the EDI message.

17.31 Maintain Government Involvement Indicator (tcedi2186m000)
SESSION OBJECTIVE
To maintain government involvement indicators. This is necessary in order to be
able to send or receive messages containing these.
SEE ALSO KEYWORD(S)
• Government Involvement Indicators

```
tcedi2186m000                                 multi/group (3    Form 1-1
+------------------------------------------------------------------------+
| Maintain Government Involvement Indicator               Company: 000   |
|------------------------------------------------------------------------|
|                                                                        |
| Organization        : 1.. 2_____                    |
|                                                                        |
| Code in Message        Description                                     |
|                                                                        |
| 3.....                 4............................                   |
|                                                                        |
+------------------------------------------------------------------------+
```

1.   Organization
The code which uniquely identifies the organization.
2.   Description
3.   Code in Message
The code used in the message.
4.   Description
The description for the code in the EDI message.

17.32 Maintain Government Agencies (tcedi2188m000)
SESSION OBJECTIVE
To maintain government codes. This is necessary in order to be able to send or
receive messages containing these.
SEE ALSO KEYWORD(S)
• Government Codes

```
tcedi2188m000                                 multi/group (3    Form 1-1
+------------------------------------------------------------------------+
| Maintain Government Agencies                            Company: 000   |
|------------------------------------------------------------------------|
|                                                                        |
| Organization        : 1.. 2_____                    |
|                                                                        |
| Code in Message        Description                                     |
|                                                                        |
```

```
|   3.....                 4.........................          |
|                                                              |
+--------------------------------------------------------------+
```

1.   Organization
The code which uniquely identifies the organization.
2.   Description
3.   Code in Message
The code used in the message.
4.   Description
The description for the code in the EDI message.

17.33 Maintain Government Actions (tcedi2190m000)
SESSION OBJECTIVE
To maintain government actions. This is necessary in order to be able to send or receive messages containing these.
SEE ALSO KEYWORD(S)
•   Government Actions

tcedi2190m000   multi/group (3   Form 1-1

```
+--------------------------------------------------------------+
|  Maintain Government Actions                   Company: 000  |
|--------------------------------------------------------------|
|                                                              |
|   Organization       : 1..  2_____    |
|                                                              |
|   Code in Message       Description                          |
|                                                              |
|   3.....                 4.........................          |
|                                                              |
+--------------------------------------------------------------+
```

1.   Organization
The code which uniquely identifies the organization.
2.   Description
3.   Code in Message
The code used in the message.
4.   Description
The description for the code in the EDI message.

18   Other Print Sessions
18.1 Print Schedule Release Frequencies (tcedi2402m000)

tcedi2402m000   single-occ (4)   Form 1-1

```
+--------------------------------------------------------------+
|  Print Schedule Release Frequencies            Company: 000  |
|--------------------------------------------------------------|
|                                                              |
|   Organization        From : 1..                            |
|                       To   : 2..                            |
|                                                              |
|   Code in Message     From : 3.....                         |
|                       To   : 4.....                         |
|                                                              |
+--------------------------------------------------------------+
```

1.   Organization From
2.   Organization to
3.   Code in Message From
4.   Code in Message to

18.2 Print Type of Delivery Specifier (tcedi2404m000)

tcedi2404m000   single-occ (4)   Form 1-1

```
+--------------------------------------------------------------+
|  Print Type of Delivery Specifier              Company: 000  |
|--------------------------------------------------------------|
|                                                              |
|   Organization        From : 1..                            |
|                       To   : 2..                            |
|                                                              |
|   Code in Message     From : 3.....                         |
```

```
|                         To   : 4.....                                       |
|                                                                             |
+-----------------------------------------------------------------------------+
1.    Organization from
2.    Organization to
3.    Code in Message from
4.    Code in Message to
18.3  Print Schedule Status Indicators (tcedi2406m000)
tcedi2406m000                              single-occ (4)   Form 1-1
+-----------------------------------------------------------------------------+
|  Print Schedule Status Indicators                      Company: 000  |
|-----------------------------------------------------------------------------|
|                                                                             |
|  Organization          From : 1..                                           |
|                        To   : 2..                                           |
|                                                                             |
|  Code in Message       From : 3.....                                        |
|                        To   : 4.....                                        |
|                                                                             |
+-----------------------------------------------------------------------------+
1.    Organization from
2.    Organization to
3.    Code in Message from
4.    Code in Message to
18.4  Print Schedule Release Categories (tcedi2408m000)
tcedi2408m000                              single-occ (4)   Form 1-1
+-----------------------------------------------------------------------------+
|  Print Schedule Release Categories                     Company: 000  |
|-----------------------------------------------------------------------------|
|                                                                             |
|  Organization          From : 1..                                           |
|                        To   : 2..                                           |
|                                                                             |
|  Code in Message       From : 3.....                                        |
|                        To   : 4.....                                        |
|                                                                             |
+-----------------------------------------------------------------------------+
1.    Organization from
2.    Organization to
3.    Code in Message from
4.    Code in Message to
18.5  Print Item Status Indicators (tcedi2410m000)
tcedi2410m000                              single-occ (4)   Form 1-1
+-----------------------------------------------------------------------------+
|  Print Item Status Indicators                          Company: 000  |
|-----------------------------------------------------------------------------|
|                                                                             |
|  Organization          From : 1..                                           |
|                        To   : 2..                                           |
|                                                                             |
|  Code in Message       From : 3.....                                        |
|                        To   : 4.....                                        |
|                                                                             |
+-----------------------------------------------------------------------------+
1.    Organization from
2.    Organization to
3.    Code in Message from
4.    Code in Message to
18.6  Print Production Schedule Types (tcedi2412m000)
tcedi2412m000                              single-occ (4)   Form 1-1
+-----------------------------------------------------------------------------+
|  Print Production Schedule Types                        Company: 000  |
|-----------------------------------------------------------------------------|
```

```
|                                                                              |
| Organization         From : 1..                                             |
|                      To   : 2..                                             |
|                                                                              |
| Code in Message      From : 3.....                                          |
|                      To   : 4.....                                          |
|                                                                              |
+------------------------------------------------------------------------------+

1.    Organization from
2.    Organization to
3.    Code in Message from
4.    Code in Message to
```

18.7 Print Packing Code IDs (tcedi2414m000)

```
tcedi2414m000                           single-occ (4)   Form 1-1
+------------------------------------------------------------------------------+
| Print Packing Code IDs                                    Company: 000 |
|------------------------------------------------------------------------------|
|                                                                              |
| Organization         From : 1..                                             |
|                      To   : 2..                                             |
|                                                                              |
| Code in Message      From : 3.....                                          |
|                      To   : 4.....                                          |
|                                                                              |
+------------------------------------------------------------------------------+

1.    Organization from
2.    Organization to
3.    Code in Message from
4.    Code in Message to
```

18.8 Print Dates/Times (tcedi2422m000)

```
tcedi2422m000                           single-occ (4)   Form 1-1
+------------------------------------------------------------------------------+
| Print Dates/Times                                         Company: 000 |
|------------------------------------------------------------------------------|
|                                                                              |
| Organization         From : 1..                                             |
|                      To   : 2..                                             |
|                                                                              |
| Code in MeBaange     From : 3.....                                          |
|                      To   : 4.....                                          |
|                                                                              |
+------------------------------------------------------------------------------+

1.    Organization from
2.    Organization to
3.    Code in MeBaange from
4.    Code in MeBaange to
```

18.9 Print Transport Types (tcedi2434m000)

```
tcedi2434m000                           single-occ (4)   Form 1-1
+------------------------------------------------------------------------------+
| Print Transport Types                                     Company: 000 |
|------------------------------------------------------------------------------|
|                                                                              |
| Organization         From : 1..                                             |
|                      To   : 2..                                             |
|                                                                              |
| Code in MeBaange     From : 3.....                                          |
|                      To   : 4.....                                          |
|                                                                              |
+------------------------------------------------------------------------------+

1.    Organization from
2.    Organization to
3.    Code in MeBaange from
4.    Code in MeBaange to
```

18.10 Print Periods (tcedi2436m000)

```
tcedi2436m000                          single-occ (4)   Form 1-1
+-----------------------------------------------------------------------+
| Print Periods                                      Company: 000 |
|-----------------------------------------------------------------------|
|                                                                       |
| Organization         From : 1..                                       |
|                      To   : 2..                                        |
|                                                                       |
| Code in MeBaange     From : 3.....                                     |
|                      To   : 4.....                                     |
|                                                                       |
+-----------------------------------------------------------------------+
```

1.   Organization from
2.   Organization to
3.   Code in MeBaange from
4.   Code in MeBaange to

18.11 Print Discounts (tcedi2438m000)

```
tcedi2438m000                          single-occ (4)   Form 1-1
+-----------------------------------------------------------------------+
| Print Discounts                                    Company: 000 |
|-----------------------------------------------------------------------|
|                                                                       |
| Organization         From : 1..                                       |
|                      To   : 2..                                        |
|                                                                       |
| Code in MeBaange     From : 3.....                                     |
|                      To   : 4.....                                     |
|                                                                       |
+-----------------------------------------------------------------------+
```

1.   Organization From
2.   Organization to
3.   Code in MeBaange From
4.   Code in MeBaange to

18.12 Print Discounts and Surcharges (tcedi2444m000)

```
tcedi2444m000                          single-occ (4)   Form 1-1
+-----------------------------------------------------------------------+
| Print Discounts and Surcharges                     Company: 000 |
|-----------------------------------------------------------------------|
|                                                                       |
| Organization         From : 1..                                       |
|                      To   : 2..                                        |
|                                                                       |
| Code in MeBaange     From : 3.....                                     |
|                      To   : 4.....                                     |
|                                                                       |
+-----------------------------------------------------------------------+
```

1.   Organization from
2.   Organization to
3.   Code in MeBaange from
4.   Code in MeBaange to

18.13 Print MeBaange Function (tcedi2450m000)

```
tcedi2450m000                          single-occ (4)   Form 1-1
+-----------------------------------------------------------------------+
| Print MeBaange Function                            Company: 000 |
|-----------------------------------------------------------------------|
|                                                                       |
| Organization         From : 1..                                       |
|                      To   : 2..                                        |
|                                                                       |
| Code in MeBaange     From : 3.....                                     |
|                      To   : 4.....                                     |
|                                                                       |
```

```
+----------------------------------------------------------------------+
1.      Organization from
2.      Organization to
3.      Code in MeBaange from
4.      Code in MeBaange to
18.14 Print Time Zone Specifier (tcedi2452m000)
tcedi2452m000                            single-occ (4)    Form 1-1
+----------------------------------------------------------------------+
|  Print Time Zone Specifier                          Company: 000  |
|----------------------------------------------------------------------|
|                                                                      |
|  Organization         From : 1..                                  |
|                       To   : 2..                                  |
|                                                                      |
|  Code in MeBaange     From : 3.....                               |
|                       To   : 4.....                               |
|                                                                      |
+----------------------------------------------------------------------+
1.      Organization from
2.      Organization to
3.      Code in MeBaange from
4.      Code in MeBaange to
18.15 Print Contact Function (tcedi2454m000)
tcedi2454m000                            single-occ (4)    Form 1-1
+----------------------------------------------------------------------+
|  Print Contact Function                             Company: 000  |
|----------------------------------------------------------------------|
|                                                                      |
|  Organization         From : 1..                                  |
|                       To   : 2..                                  |
|                                                                      |
|  Code in MeBaange     From : 3.....                               |
|                       To   : 4.....                               |
|                                                                      |
+----------------------------------------------------------------------+
1.      Organization from
2.      Organization to
3.      Code in MeBaange from
4.      Code in MeBaange to
18.16 Print Communication Channel (tcedi2456m000)
tcedi2456m000                            single-occ (4)    Form 1-1
+----------------------------------------------------------------------+
|  Print Communication Channel                        Company: 000  |
|----------------------------------------------------------------------|
|                                                                      |
|  Organization         From : 1..                                  |
|                       To   : 2..                                  |
|                                                                      |
|  Code in MeBaange     From : 3.....                               |
|                       To   : 4.....                               |
|                                                                      |
+----------------------------------------------------------------------+
1.      Organization from
2.      Organization to
3.      Code in MeBaange from
4.      Code in MeBaange to
18.17 Print Terms of Delivery Function (tcedi2458m000)
tcedi2458m000                            single-occ (4)    Form 1-1
+----------------------------------------------------------------------+
|  Print Terms of Delivery Function                   Company: 000  |
|----------------------------------------------------------------------|
|                                                                      |
|  Organization         From : 1..                                  |
```

```
|                        To   : 2..                                        |
|                                                                          |
| Code in MeBaange        From : 3.....                                    |
|                        To   : 4.....                                     |
|                                                                          |
+--------------------------------------------------------------------------+
1.     Organization from
2.     Organization to
3.     Code in MeBaange from
4.     Code in MeBaange to
18.18 Print Type of Supplementary Information (tcedi2460m000)
tcedi2460m000                              single-occ (4)    Form 1-1
+--------------------------------------------------------------------------+
| Print Type of Supplementary Information              Company: 000 |
|--------------------------------------------------------------------------|
|                                                                          |
| Organization           From : 1..                                       |
|                        To   : 2..                                        |
|                                                                          |
| Code in MeBaange        From : 3.....                                    |
|                        To   : 4.....                                     |
|                                                                          |
+--------------------------------------------------------------------------+
1.     Organization from
2.     Organization to
3.     Code in MeBaange from
4.     Code in MeBaange to
18.19 Print Type of Contract and Carriage Condition (tcedi2462m000)
tcedi2462m000                              single-occ (4)    Form 1-1
+--------------------------------------------------------------------------+
| Print Type of Contract and Carriage Condition        Company: 000 |
|--------------------------------------------------------------------------|
|                                                                          |
| Organization           From : 1..                                       |
|                        To   : 2..                                        |
|                                                                          |
| Code in MeBaange        From : 3.....                                    |
|                        To   : 4.....                                     |
|                                                                          |
+--------------------------------------------------------------------------+
1.     Organization from
2.     Organization to
3.     Code in MeBaange from
4.     Code in MeBaange to
18.20 Print Type of Monetary Amount (tcedi2464m000)
tcedi2464m000                              single-occ (4)    Form 1-1
+--------------------------------------------------------------------------+
| Print Type of Monetary Amount                        Company: 000 |
|--------------------------------------------------------------------------|
|                                                                          |
| Organization           From : 1..                                       |
|                        To   : 2..                                        |
|                                                                          |
| Code in MeBaange        From : 3.....                                    |
|                        To   : 4.....                                     |
|                                                                          |
+--------------------------------------------------------------------------+
1.     Organization from
2.     Organization to
3.     Code in MeBaange from
4.     Code in MeBaange to
18.21 Print Charge Category (tcedi2466m000)
tcedi2466m000                              single-occ (4)    Form 1-1
```

```
+-----------------------------------------------------------------------+
|  Print Charge Category                               Company: 000  |
|-----------------------------------------------------------------------|
|                                                                   |
|  Organization           From : 1..                                |
|                         To   : 2..                                |
|                                                                   |
|  Code in MeBaange       From : 3.....                             |
|                         To   : 4.....                             |
|                                                                   |
+-----------------------------------------------------------------------+
1.    Organization from
2.    Organization to
3.    Code in MeBaange from
4.    Code in MeBaange to
18.22 Print Dimension Qualifier (tcedi2468m000)
tcedi2468m000                          single-occ (4)   Form 1-1
+-----------------------------------------------------------------------+
|  Print Dimension Qualifier                           Company: 000  |
|-----------------------------------------------------------------------|
|                                                                   |
|  Organization           From : 1..                                |
|                         To   : 2..                                |
|                                                                   |
|  Code in MeBaange       From : 3.....                             |
|                         To   : 4.....                             |
|                                                                   |
+-----------------------------------------------------------------------+
1.    Organization from
2.    Organization to
3.    Code in MeBaange from
4.    Code in MeBaange to
18.23 Print Temperature Qualifier (tcedi2470m000)
tcedi2470m000                          single-occ (4)   Form 1-1
+-----------------------------------------------------------------------+
|  Print Temperature Qualifier                         Company: 000  |
|-----------------------------------------------------------------------|
|                                                                   |
|  Organization           From : 1..                                |
|                         To   : 2..                                |
|                                                                   |
|  Code in MeBaange       From : 3.....                             |
|                         To   : 4.....                             |
|                                                                   |
+-----------------------------------------------------------------------+
1.    Organization from
2.    Organization to
3.    Code in MeBaange from
4.    Code in MeBaange to
18.24 Print Plus/Minus Indicator (tcedi2472m000)
tcedi2472m000                          single-occ (4)   Form 1-1
+-----------------------------------------------------------------------+
|  Print Plus/Minus Indicator                          Company: 000  |
|-----------------------------------------------------------------------|
|                                                                   |
|  Organization           From : 1..                                |
|                         To   : 2..                                |
|                                                                   |
|  Code in MeBaange       From : 3.....                             |
|                         To   : 4.....                             |
|                                                                   |
+-----------------------------------------------------------------------+
1.    Organization from
```

```
2.     Organization to
3.     Code in MeBaange from
4.     Code in MeBaange to
18.25 Print Measurement Qualifier (tcedi2474m000)
tcedi2474m000                              single-occ (4)   Form 1-1
+-------------------------------------------------------------------------+
| Print Measurement Qualifier                          Company: 000 |
|-------------------------------------------------------------------------|
|                                                                         |
| Organization            From : 1..                                      |
|                         To   : 2..                                      |
|                                                                         |
| Code in MeBaange        From : 3.....                                   |
|                         To   : 4.....                                   |
|                                                                         |
+-------------------------------------------------------------------------+
1.     Organization from
2.     Organization to
3.     Code in MeBaange from
4.     Code in MeBaange to
18.26 Print Type of Packages (tcedi2476m000)
tcedi2476m000                              single-occ (4)   Form 1-1
+-------------------------------------------------------------------------+
| Print Type of Packages                               Company: 000 |
|-------------------------------------------------------------------------|
|                                                                         |
| Organization            From : 1..                                      |
|                         To   : 2..                                      |
|                                                                         |
| Code in MeBaange        From : 3.....                                   |
|                         To   : 4.....                                   |
|                                                                         |
+-------------------------------------------------------------------------+
1.     Organization from
2.     Organization to
3.     Code in MeBaange from
4.     Code in MeBaange to
18.27 Print Transport Stage (tcedi2478m000)
tcedi2478m000                              single-occ (4)   Form 1-1
+-------------------------------------------------------------------------+
| Print Transport Stage                                Company: 000 |
|-------------------------------------------------------------------------|
|                                                                         |
| Organization            From : 1..                                      |
|                         To   : 2..                                      |
|                                                                         |
| Code in MeBaange        From : 3.....                                   |
|                         To   : 4.....                                   |
|                                                                         |
+-------------------------------------------------------------------------+
1.     Organization from
2.     Organization to
3.     Code in MeBaange from
4.     Code in MeBaange to
18.28 Print Equipment Qualifier (tcedi2480m000)
tcedi2480m000                              single-occ (4)   Form 1-1
+-------------------------------------------------------------------------+
| Print Equipment Qualifier                            Company: 000 |
|-------------------------------------------------------------------------|
|                                                                         |
| Organization            From : 1..                                      |
|                         To   : 2..                                      |
|                                                                         |
```

```
|  Code in MeBaange       From : 3.....                                 |
|                         To   : 4.....                                 |
|                                                                       |
+-----------------------------------------------------------------------+
1.     Organization from
2.     Organization to
3.     Code in MeBaange from
4.     Code in MeBaange to
18.29 Print Shipper-Supplied Equipment Indicator (tcedi2482m000)
tcedi2482m000                           single-occ (4)   Form 1-1
+-----------------------------------------------------------------------+
|  Print Shipper-Supplied Equipment Indicator          Company: 000  |
|-----------------------------------------------------------------------|
|                                                                       |
|  Organization           From : 1..                                    |
|                         To   : 2..                                    |
|                                                                       |
|  Code in MeBaange       From : 3.....                                 |
|                         To   : 4.....                                 |
|                                                                       |
+-----------------------------------------------------------------------+
1.     Organization from
2.     Organization to
3.     Code in MeBaange from
4.     Code in MeBaange to
18.30 Print Dangerous Goods Regulations (tcedi2484m000)
tcedi2484m000                           single-occ (4)   Form 1-1
+-----------------------------------------------------------------------+
|  Print Dangerous Goods Regulations                   Company: 000  |
|-----------------------------------------------------------------------|
|                                                                       |
|  Organization           From : 1..                                    |
|                         To   : 2..                                    |
|                                                                       |
|  Code in MeBaange       From : 3.....                                 |
|                         To   : 4.....                                 |
|                                                                       |
+-----------------------------------------------------------------------+
1.     Organization from
2.     Organization to
3.     Code in MeBaange from
4.     Code in MeBaange to
18.31 Print Government Involvement Indicator (tcedi2486m000)
tcedi2486m000                           single-occ (4)   Form 1-1
+-----------------------------------------------------------------------+
|  Print Government Involvement Indicator              Company: 000  |
|-----------------------------------------------------------------------|
|                                                                       |
|  Organization           From : 1..                                    |
|                         To   : 2..                                    |
|                                                                       |
|  Code in MeBaange       From : 3.....                                 |
|                         To   : 4.....                                 |
|                                                                       |
+-----------------------------------------------------------------------+
1.     Organization from
2.     Organization to
3.     Code in MeBaange from
4.     Code in MeBaange to
18.32 Print Government Agencies (tcedi2488m000)
tcedi2488m000                           single-occ (4)   Form 1-1
+-----------------------------------------------------------------------+
|  Print Government Agencies                           Company: 000  |
```

```
|------------------------------------------------------------------------------|
|                                                                              |
| Organization            From : 1..                                           |
|                         To   : 2..                                           |
|                                                                              |
| Code in MeBaange        From : 3.....                                         |
|                         To   : 4.....                                         |
|                                                                              |
+------------------------------------------------------------------------------+
```

1.   Organization from
2.   Organization to
3.   Code in MeBaange from
4.   Code in MeBaange to

18.33 Print Government Actions (tcedi2490m000)

tcedi2490m000   single-occ (4)   Form 1-1

```
+------------------------------------------------------------------------------+
| Print Government Actions                               Company: 000 |
|------------------------------------------------------------------------------|
|                                                                              |
| Organization            From : 1..                                           |
|                         To   : 2..                                           |
|                                                                              |
| Code in MeBaange        From : 3.....                                         |
|                         To   : 4.....                                         |
|                                                                              |
+------------------------------------------------------------------------------+
```

1.   Organization from
2.   Organization to
3.   Code in MeBaange from
4.   Code in MeBaange to

19   Introduction to Conversion Parameters

19.1 General

OBJECTIVE OF BUSINESS OBJECT

This b-object controls the definitions and relations of ASCII files (in-house
files). This will enable you to store the data in as flexible and compact a
manner as possible. The ASCII files constitute the link between EDI software and
the BAAN IV application. This flexibility will make it possible to give your own
interpretation to the meBaange content per meBaange and relation.

This b-object involves the following data sets:
•   Conversion Setups (Names)
•   Conversion Setups (Definitions)
•   Conversion Setups (Relationships)
•   Evaluation Expressions

A meBaange arrives as an ASCII file. A normal ASCII file is a text format
(arrangement) that cannot be read very quickly by BAAN IV. It must therefore be
converted into an "in-house" file: a file that BAAN IV is able to read. This is
done by the EDI software.

ASCII files consist of records which in turn consist of fields which contain the
actual information. Examples of fields are: "Customer Number", "Name" and
"Address".

If several files are related to each other, these are called relational. This is
the case, for instance, if several addresses have been recorded for one
customer. In this example, the customer number is the key. In the address file
you can search for the addresses using the customer number. A key may consist of
more than one field. If, for instance, more than one telephone number is
recorded for one address, the key is the customer number together with the
address.

Display the procedure and show the sessions in:
•   Conversion Parameter Procedure

More than one conversion setup can be defined by organization and meBaange type.
The only restriction is that the format of the ASCII files must be identical for
each organization and meBaange type. This means that relationships are defined

for a combination of organization and meBaange type in session "Maintain Conversion Setups (Relationships) (tcedi5112m000)".
The general meBaange data are also recorded once for each organization and meBaange type. This 'overhead' applies to all conversion setups for the organization and meBaange type concerned.
A conversion setup consists of a name, a definition, and a relationship table. When the module is installed, the basic data is loaded, allowing you to start working immediately.
First choose a similar conversion setup which can then be copied. Failing this, you can create a new setup. When you zoom to the definition, an empty definition is generated. In the definition you can only modify fields with the destination 'Header' and 'Line'.

19.2 Session Overview

Seq.	Session	Description	Session Usage
1	tcedi5110m000	Maintain Conversion Setups	Optional
1	tcedi5111s000	Maint Definitions of Conversion Setups	Optional
2	tcedi5112m000	Maint Conversion Setups (Relationships)	Optional
2	tcedi5115s000	Maint Definitions of Conversion Setups	Mandatory
3	tcedi5105m000	Maintain Evaluation Expressions	Mandatory
101	tcedi5410m000	Print Conversion Setups	Print
102	tcedi5405m000	Print Evaluation Expressions	Print
103	tcedi5415m000	Print Mapping Information	Print
201	tcedi5510s000	Display Conversion Setups (Names)	Display
202	tcedi5512s000	Display Conv Setups (Relationships)	Display
203	tcedi5505s000	Display Evaluation Expressions List	Display
204	tcedi5506s000	Display Evaluation Expressions	Display

20   Mandatory Sessions
20.1 Maintain Definitions of Conversion Setups (tcedi5115s000)
SESSION OBJECTIVE
To record the fields, the sequence of working, and options for the conversion of meBaanges on receipt.
HOW TO USE THE SESSION
The session is protected, so that it cannot be run simultaneously with sessions with interfere with it or with which it may interfere.
If fields are separated, the optimum processing rate is achieved by converting by level whenever possible, in the sequence in which the data is contained in the files (i.e. from left to right). If "qualifiers" are used, they are read before the file itself is read.
At least two fields of iterative levels must be read. You cannot set the fields "Sequence when Iterative Level" and "Sequence when Key does not Match" to "Yes" for one line. Choosing option "Change Order [change.order]" enables you to choose whether the fields should be displayed in the sequence of field name or processing sequence. Before you can add lines, choose option "Start Group [start.set]" to choose the right destination.
SEE ALSO KEYWORD(S)
•   Conversion Setups (Definitions)

tcedi5115s000   multi/group (3   Form 1-4 >

```
+--Maintain Definitions of Conversion Setups------------------------------------
----+
|
|
| Organization          :   1.. 2_____        Direction           :
3....
| EDI MeBaange          : 4..... 5_____        Field Type          :
6....
| Destination           : 7...... Conversion Setup   : 8.....
9_____
|
|
| Field  Seq Lev Start Index Length Next Sequence Write Mult Conv  Action when
Eva
| No.  Pos.  Rec. Iter Key  Record  Fact Table         not found
Expression
|
| 10 11  12      13    14    15   16  17 18  19    20.. 21 22... 23.. 24. 25_____
26____
|
+-------------------------------------------------------------------------------
----+
```
1.   Organization
The code which uniquely identifies the organization.
2.   Description
3.   Direction
The meBaange can be incoming or outgoing.
4.   EDI MeBaange
This code uniquely identifies an EDI meBaange. Depending on the direction, it
identifies an incoming or outgoing meBaange.
5.   Description
The description associated with the meBaange code.
6.   Field Type
A conversion setup can be created for files in which the fields are separated by
a field separator, or have a fixed length.
7.   Destination
The destination of the field in case of receiving information or the source of
the field in case of sending information, as defined in the session "Maintain
Conversion Setups (Relationships) (tcedi5112m000)".
MeBaange Overhead
General data relevant to the processing of EDI meBaanges, including for example
sequence numbers and EDI references.
Header (Order) header data.
Line (Order) line data.
Footer
Data relating to the meBaange as a whole, but only known as soon as the
meBaanges is completed, e.g. totals.
8.   Conversion Setup
The code identifying the conversion setup.
9.   Description
The description of the conversion setup.
10.   Field
The name of the field, e.g. "tdsls040.cuno". For outgoing conversion setups,
constants may be used. These should start with double quotes ("). All text
following the double quotes and preceding a closing quotation mark (if present)
is placed in the meBaange. If you wish to use double quotes within the text
string itself, you have to type in double quotes twice ("").
11.   Sequence No.
The sequence number of the field, which means that the same fields may be
included more than once. However, this only applies to outgoing conversion
setups.
12.   Processing Sequence
In this field you indicate the sequence in which the fields are to be processed.

13.   Level
A reference to the level, as defined in the session "Maintain Conversion Setups (Relationships) (tcedi5112m000)".
14.   Start Position
The position of the field in the line. The meaning depends on the field type set in the session "Maintain Networks (tcedi0120m000)".
Fixed Length
You must enter the physical starting position of the field.
Delimited
You must enter the field number. The first field has number 1.
15.   Element
In the case of an index field, the index element can be entered here. Example:
Field   tdsls041.dper   (standard depth = 3 levels)
Level 1   10
      2   15
      3   8
The value 0 outputs the entire field: "010015008", this option will only be used for internal communication. The values 1 and 3 output the following elements only: "010","008". This means the field can also be used for external communication.
In the case of a string variable, the start position within the string can be specified here; this field - in combination with the field "Length" - allows you to specify a substring, e.g. string "ABCDEFGHIJKLMNOP" the value 3 with a length of 5 produces the following output: "CDEFG".
These options are valid for both outgoing and incoming meBaanges.
16.   Length
The physical length of the field.
17.   Read Next Record
Indicates whether a new record should be read for processing the contents of the field. Based on this, it can be determined when a new line is to be read from the same file.
Yes
Incoming meBaanges: A new record will be read for this level.
Outgoing meBaanges: A new record of the table, belonging to the field, will be read.
No
New records will not be read, but the current records remain active.
18.   Sequence when Iterative Level
Indicate the sequence number to which the cursor is to go after processing the field. It is only used if it is the last field of an iterative level or the last field of the conversion setup.
Example: You want to enter a text field containing data from an ASCII file in an order header, which is done iteratively. Once the last text field has been filled, the cursor is returned to the field with sequence number 3 using the above field. The key and 3 text fields are included in each line of level 2.

Field	Level	Sequence Number	Back Iterative
Order No.	1	1	
Reference	1	2	
Text Field	2	3	
Text Field	2	4	
Text Field	2	5	3

19.   Sequence when Key does not Match
If, after reading a new record, the key is not valid, this field indicates the sequence number to which the cursor is returned. This field only needs to be filled if "New record" is on "yes".
Example 1.   Iterative processing After all text fields have been processed, the customer number is read. Level 2 is iterative.

Field	Level Iter.	Key	Sequence in record	Back	Back	New
Order No.	1		1			
Reference	1		2			
Text Field	2		3		6	yes
Text Field	2		4			

| Text Field | 2 | 5 | | | 3 |
| Customer | 1 | 6 | | | |

Example 2. Sequential processing When all order lines have been filled (level 2) a new order can be present (level 1).

Field	Level	Sequence in	Back Iter.	Back Key	New record
Order No.	1	1			yes
Reference	1	2			
Customer	1	3			
Item	2	4		1	yes
Quantity	2	5			
Delivery Date	2	6	2		

20.   Write Record

Incoming meBaanges: This field indicates whether a record must be added to the relevant table after processing a field. The destination of the field (overhead, header or line) determines in which table meBaanges will be saved.

Example:

Field	Destination	Write record
Order No.	header	
Reference	header	
Customer	header	yes
Item	line	
Quantity	line	
Delivery Date	line	yes

Fields processed after a write action for the same destination are not added to the relevant table. You cannot start several write actions for the same record (e.g. order line).

Due to the hierarchy of destinations, it is checked whether all "higher" destinations have been written. If not, the relevant destinations are written before the specified destination is written. The hierarchy is:

• Overhead
• Header
• Line

Example:

Field	Destination	Write record
Order No.	header	
Reference	header	
Customer	header	
Item	line	
Quantity	line	
Delivery Date	line	yes

Because no header has been written yet, the header is written first, followed by the line. If there is no overhead, it is written before the header.

Outgoing meBaanges: A record is written for the specified level, depending on the result of the output expression.

21.   Multiplication Factor

The multiplication factor for a numeric field. Herewith you can make percentages or amounts negative, etc.

22.   Conversion Table

The conversion table used to convert the field. You define outgoing conversion tables for outgoing meBaanges and incoming conversion tables for incoming meBaanges.

23.   Action in Conv. Table

This field enables you to indicate what should be done if the conversion cannot be carried out, i.e. the field is not found in the conversion table.

Discard MeBaange
The generation of the meBaange is aborted.

Original Value
The value searched for is included in the meBaange, i.e. there will be no conversion.

Empty the Field
The field is cleared.

Default Value
This is similar to "Original Value".
24.   Evaluation Expression
The expression you can enter here determines whether or not the field is
included in the meBaange. It is a logical expression: it results in a "true" or
"false". The default value of this field is 1, i.e. "true". The system executes
the expression before placing the field in the meBaange. This means that the
associated reading and writing actions are always executed.
In fact, the expression is an equation. For the field "Street" in an address,
the expression might for instance be: strip(tdsls040.cdel)="". This is true if
the address is not filled.
In an expression, the following operators may be used:
Arithmetical:
()   brackets (priority)
-                 reverses sign (requires an argument), e.g. a=-b
*   multiplication, e.g. 3*5=15
/   division, e.g. 6/2=3
\   remainder after division, e.g. 8\3=2
&   linking up strings, e.g. "A"&"B"="AB"
+   addition, e.g. 2+3=5
-                 subtraction, e.g. 3-2=1

Relational (comparing):
= or EQ   is equal to, e.g. 3=5 is false
<> or NE   is unequal to, e.g. 3<>5 is true
> or GT   is greater than, e.g. 3>5 is false
< or LT   is less than, e.g. 3<5 is true
>= or GE   is greater than or equal to, e.g. 3>=5 is false
<= or LE   is less than or equal to, e.g. 3<=5 is true

Logical:
AND   and (both are true), e.g. a=b AND b=c
OR   or (one of the two is true), e.g. a=b OR a=c
NOT   not (is not true), e.g. NOT (a=b AND b=c)

Others:
condition?true:false
                  if <condition> is true, <true> is executed, otherwise
                  <false> (always place brackets around <condition>, as
                  this has the lowest priority)

The priority is as follows:
()
-        (reverse sign)
* / \
&
+ -   (subtract)
= > < <> <= >=

NOT
AND
OR
?:

An expression may contain the following constants:

PI   3.1415926535..
TRUE   Always true.
FALSE   Always false.

An expression may contain the following functions:

abs(N)   Produces the absolute value of N

acos(N)	Produces the angle (in radials) of which N is the cosine.
asc(S)	Produces the total of the ASCII values of the characters in S, e.g. asc("ABC")=65+66+67=198
asin(N)	Produces the angle (in radials) of which N is the sine.
atan(N)	Produces the angle (in radials) of which N is the tangent.
chr(N)	Produces the character of which N is the ASCII value, e.g. chr(65)="A"
cos(N)	Produces the cosine for angle N (in radials).
cosh(N)	Produces the hyperbolic cosine for angle N (in radials)
date()	Produces the current day number.
date(J,M,D)	Produces the day number in the date represented by D, M and J.
exp(N)	Produces 2.718128.. to the power of N.
int(N)	Produces the integer of N (rounded down).
len(S)	Produces the number of characters in S, e.g. len("ABC")=3.
log(N)	Produces the natural logarithm of N.
log10(N)	Produces the 10-logarithm of N.
max(N,M)	Produces the greater value of N or M.
min(N,M)	Produces the lesser value of N or M.
pos(S,T)	Produces the first position where T occurs in S, e.g. pos("ABCDEFEF","EF")=5.
pow(N,M)	Produces N to the power of M.
round(N,D,M)	Produces the value of N rounded to D decimals. If M=0, N is rounded down, e.g. round(1.99,2,0)=1.00. If M=1, N is rounded off normally, e.g. round(1.49,2,1)=1.00 and round(1.50,2,1)=2.00. If M=2, N is rounded up, e.g. round(1.01,2,2)=2.00.
rpos(S,T)	Produces the last position where T occurs in S, e.g. rpos("ABCDEFEF,"EF")=7.
sin(N)	Produces the sine of angle N (in radials).
sinh(N)	Produces the hyperbolic sine of angle N (in radials).
sqrt(N)	Produces the non-negative square root of N.
str(N)	Creates a string of N, e.g. str(1.04)="1.04"
strip(S)	Returns S without the spaces following it.
tan(N)	Produces the tangent of angle N (in radials).
tanh(N)	Produces the hyperbolic tangent of angle N (in radials).
time()	Produces the current time in UUMM format.
val(S)	Produces the numerical value of S, e.g. val("1.04")=1.04.

Numerical ranges can also be used:

a IN [10,20] is equal to.a>=20 AND a<=30
a IN [10,20][30,40][50,60] is equal to a>=10 AND a<=20 OR a>=30
AND a<=40 OR a>=50 AND a<=60

25.   Description
The description of the evaluation expression.
26.   Field Description
The field description, which is modified if you switch lines.
tcedi5115s000   multi/group (3 < Form 2-4 >
+--Maintain Definitions of Conversion Setups-----------------------------------
----+
|
|
| Organization   :   1.. 2_____ Direction   :
3....
| EDI MeBaange   : 4..... 5_____ Field Type   :
6....
| Destination   : 7............... Conversion Setup   : 8.....
9_____
|
|
| Field   Qualifier 1
Qualifier 2 |
| Pos Length Default Conv. Table NF Pos Length Default Conv. Table   NF
|
| 10_____ 11_____ 12   13   14   15............ 16............
|
+--
----+
1.   Organization
The code which uniquely identifies the organization.
2.   Description
3.   Direction
The meBaange can be incoming or outgoing.
4.   EDI MeBaange
This code uniquely identifies an EDI meBaange. Depending on the direction, it
identifies an incoming or outgoing meBaange.
5.   Description
The description associated with the meBaange code.
6.   Field Type
A conversion setup can be created for files in which the fields are separated by
a field separator, or have a fixed length.
7.   Destination
The destination of the field in case of receiving information or the source of
the field in case of sending information, as defined in the session "Maintain
Conversion Setups (Relationships) (tcedi5112m000)".
MeBaange Overhead
General data relevant to the processing of EDI meBaanges, including for example
sequence numbers and EDI references.
Header (Order) header data.
Line (Order) line data.
Footer
Data relating to the meBaange as a whole, but only known as soon as the
meBaanges is completed, e.g. totals.
8.   Conversion Setup
The code identifying the conversion setup.
9.   Description
The description of the conversion setup.
10.   Field
The name of the field, e.g. "tdsls040.cuno". For outgoing conversion setups,
constants may be used. These should start with double quotes ("). All text
following the double quotes and preceding a closing quotation mark (if present)
is placed in the meBaange. If you wish to use double quotes within the text
string itself, you have to type in double quotes twice ("").
11.   Field Description
The field description, which is modified if you switch lines.
12.   Start Pos. Qualifier

The position of a qualifier. The meaning depends on the field type set in the session "Maintain Networks (tcedi0120m000)".
Fixed Length
You must enter the physical starting position of the key.
Delimited
You must enter the field number. The first field has number 1.
13.   Qualifier Length
The physical length of the qualifier. This length can only be entered if the field type as recorded in the session "Maintain EDI Parameters (tcedi0100m000)" is "Fixed Length".
14.   Default Qualifier
Incoming meBaanges: This value is used if no qualifier has been received.
Outgoing meBaanges: If table "Item Codes by Item Code System" is chosen for outgoing item conversion, the value for the field "Item Code System" can be entered here; the value of this qualifier can be converted via the table "Item Code IDs" to the value that will be used in the meBaange. The value entered here, can be overruled by filling in the field "Item Code System".
15.   Qualifier Conv. Table
The conversion table used to convert the qualifier. You should define outgoing conversion tables for outgoing meBaanges and incoming conversion tables for incoming meBaanges.
16.   Action in Conv. Table
This field enables you to indicate what should be done if the conversion cannot be carried out, i.e. the qualifier is not found in the conversion table.
Discard MeBaange
The generation of the meBaange is aborted.
Original Value
The value searched for is included in the meBaange, i.e. there will be no conversion.
Empty the Field
The field is cleared.
Default Value
The default value which you have defined is adopted.

```
tcedi5115s000                               multi/group (3  < Form 3-4 >
+--Maintain Definitions of Conversion Setups-------------------------------
----+
                                   |
| Organization      :   1.. 2_____      Direction      :
3....
| EDI MeBaange      : 4..... 5_____      Field Type     :
6....
| Destination       : 7...... Conversion Setup   : 8.....
9_____
|
|
| Field   Max. Number of  Maximum Number of Text Segments   Textfields per
Segment
|
| 10_____ 11_____              12                     13.
|
+--------------------------------------------------------------------------
----+
```

1.   Organization
The code which uniquely identifies the organization.
2.   Description
3.   Direction
The meBaange can be incoming or outgoing.
4.   EDI MeBaange
This code uniquely identifies an EDI meBaange. Depending on the direction, it identifies an incoming or outgoing meBaange.
5.   Description
The description associated with the meBaange code.
6.   Field Type

A conversion setup can be created for files in which the fields are separated by a field separator, or have a fixed length.

7.   Destination
The destination of the field in case of receiving information or the source of the field in case of sending information, as defined in the session "Maintain Conversion Setups (Relationships) (tcedi5112m000)".

MeBaange Overhead
General data relevant to the processing of EDI meBaanges, including for example sequence numbers and EDI references.
Header (Order) header data.
Line (Order) line data.
Footer
Data relating to the meBaange as a whole, but only known as soon as the meBaanges is completed, e.g. totals.

8.   Conversion Setup
The code identifying the conversion setup.

9.   Description
The description of the conversion setup.

10.   Field
The name of the field, e.g. "tdsls040.cuno". For outgoing conversion setups, constants may be used. These should start with double quotes ("). All text following the double quotes and preceding a closing quotation mark (if present) is placed in the meBaange. If you wish to use double quotes within the text string itself, you have to type in double quotes twice ("").

11.   Field Description
The field description, which is modified if you switch lines.

12.   Maximum Number of Text Segments
Texts in a meBaange have a special structure, so that they must be processed separately. The reason is that each text consists of a number of segments, each made up of a number of fields. In this field you enter the maximum number segments in a text.

13.   Maximum Number of Text Fields per Text Segment
Texts in a meBaange have a special structure, so that they must be processed separately. The reason is that each text consists of a number of segments each made up of a number of fields. In this
field you enter the maximum number of fields in a segment.

```
tcedi5115s000                                   multi/group (3  < Form 4-4
+--Maintain Definitions of Conversion Setups------------------------------
----+
|
|
| Organization          :    1.. 2_____      Direction        :
3....
| EDI MeBaange          : 4..... 5_____      Field Type       :
9....
| Destination           : 8..... Conversion Setup   : 6.....
7_____
|
|
| Field  Field Mapping Info   Mapping Information         Mapping
Information                           |
| Qualifier 1                  Qualifier 2
|
|
| 10_____   11_____   12.............  13.............
14.......
|
+-------------------------------------------------------------------------
----+
```

1.   Organization
The code which uniquely identifies the organization.
2.   Description
3.   Direction

The meBaange can be incoming or outgoing.
4.   EDI MeBaange
This code uniquely identifies an EDI meBaange. Depending on the direction, it
identifies an incoming or outgoing meBaange.
5.   Description
The description associated with the meBaange code.
6.   Conversion Setup
The code identifying the conversion setup.
7.   Description
The description of the conversion setup.
8.   Destination
The destination of the field in case of receiving information or the source of
the field in case of sending information, as defined in the session "Maintain
Conversion Setups (Relationships) (tcedi5112m000)".
MeBaange Overhead
General data relevant to the processing of EDI meBaanges, including for example
sequence numbers and EDI references.
Header (Order) header data.
Line (Order) line data.
Footer
Data relating to the meBaange as a whole, but only known as soon as the
meBaanges is completed, e.g. totals.
9.   Field Type
A conversion setup can be created for files in which the fields are separated by
a field separator, or have a fixed length.
10.   Field
The name of the field, e.g. "tdsls040.cuno". For outgoing conversion setups,
constants may be used. These should start with double quotes ("). All text
following the double quotes and preceding a closing quotation mark (if present)
is placed in the meBaange. If you wish to use double quotes within the text
string itself, you have to type in double quotes twice ("").
11.   Field Description
The field description, which is modified if you switch lines.
12.   Field Mapping Information
Mapping information for this field and the corresponding data element in the EDI
meBaange.
13.   Qualifier 1 Mapping Information
Mapping information for the first qualifier and the corresponding data element
in the EDI meBaange.
14.   Qualifier 2 Mapping Information
Mapping information for the second qualifier and the corresponding data element
in the EDI meBaange.
20.2 Maintain Evaluation Expressions (tcedi5105m000)
SESSION OBJECTIVE
To maintain evaluation expressions.
SEE ALSO KEYWORD(S)
•   Evaluation Expressions
tcedi5105m000   single-occ (1)   Form 1-1
+---+
Maintain Evaluation Expressions   Company: 000
Evaluation Expression   : 1..
Description   : 3............................
Evaluation Text   : 4____
2_____
2_____
2_____
2_____
2_____
2_____

```
|   2_____|
|   2_____|
|   2_____|
|   2_____|
|                                                                          |
+--------------------------------------------------------------------------+
```

1.   Evaluation Expression
The unique code of the evaluation expression.
2.   Evaluation Text
3.   Description
The description of the evaluation expression.
4.   txta.yn
21 . Optional Sessions
21.1 Maintain Conversion Setups (tcedi5110m000)
SESSION OBJECTIVE
To maintain conversion setups. For each organization and meBaange type, you can
link a code, direction and description to a conversion setup code.
SEE ALSO KEYWORD(S)
•   Conversion Setups (Names)

```
tcedi5110m000                           multi/group (3    Form 1-1
+--------------------------------------------------------------------------+
| Maintain Conversion Setups                              Company: 000 |
|--------------------------------------------------------------------------|
|                                                                          |
|  Organization     :   1..  2_____                 |
|  EDI MeBaange     : 3.....  4_____                 |
|  Direction        : 5....  6_____                  |
|  Field Type       : 7.......................                             |
|                                                                          |
|   Code    Description                       Group MeBaanges Setup Text   |
|                                                                          |
|    8..... 9............................  10...          11___            |
|                                                                          |
+--------------------------------------------------------------------------+
```

1.   Organization
The code which uniquely identifies the organization.
2.   Description
3.   EDI MeBaange
This code uniquely identifies an EDI meBaange. Depending on the direction, it
identifies an incoming or outgoing meBaange.
4.   Description
The description associated with the meBaange code.
5.   Direction
The meBaange can be incoming or outgoing.
6.   Description
The description of the meBaange.
7.   Field Type
A conversion setup can be created for files in which the fields are separated by
a field separator, or have a fixed length.
8.   Conversion Setup
The code identifying the conversion setup.
For each combination of:
•   Organization
•   EDI MeBaange
•   Direction
•   Field Type
an "overhead" setup (GLOBAL OVERHEAD) is defined, in which the header data of
the meBaange is placed. The field "Conversion Setup" ("Code") remains empty.
In addition, you can create various ways of reading or generating ASCII files,
which can then be linked to a relation and meBaange. The field "Conversion
Setup" must be filled with a code.
9.   Description
The description of the conversion setup.

10.   Group the MeBaanges
Yes
This conversion setup can be used to group outgoing meBaanges under one
"overhead".
No
This conversion setup can only be used to generate one meBaange by "overhead".
11.   Setup Text

21.2 Maintain Definitions of Conversion Setups (tcedi5111s000)

SESSION OBJECTIVE
To record the fields, the sequence of working, and options for the conversion of
meBaanges on receipt.

HOW TO USE THE SESSION
The session is protected, so that it cannot be run simultaneously with sessions
with interfere with it or with which it may interfere.
If fields are separated, the optimum processing rate is achieved by converting
by level whenever possible, in the sequence in which the data is contained in
the files (i.e. from left to right). If "qualifiers" are used, they are read
before the file itself is read.
At least two fields of iterative levels must be read. You cannot set the fields
"Sequence when Iterative Level" and "Sequence when Key does not Match" to "Yes"
for one line. Choosing option "Change Order [change.order]" enables you to
choose whether the fields should be displayed in the sequence of field name or
processing sequence. Before you can add lines, choose option "Start Group
[start.set]" to choose the right destination.

SEE ALSO KEYWORD(S)
•   Conversion Setups (Definitions)

```
tcedi5111s000                                    multi/group (3    Form 1-3 >
+--Maintain Definitions of Conversion Setups-------------------------------------
----+
|
|
| Organization         :    1.. 2_____    Direction         :
3....
| EDI MeBaange         : 4..... 5_____    Field Type        :
6....
| Destination          : 7..... Conversion Setup   : 8..... 9_____
|
|
| Field  Seq Seq. Lev Start Index Length  Next  Seq  Write Conv Field Action on
CT
| No.        Pos.            Rec.  Iter Key Record       Action      Conv
err                          |
|
|
| 10.. 11  12  13   14   15   16  17... 18  19 20.. 21... 22... 23... 24...
25____
|
+--------------------------------------------------------------------------
----+
```

1.   Organization
The code which uniquely identifies the organization.
2.   Description
3.   Direction
The meBaange can be incoming or outgoing.
4.   EDI MeBaange
This code uniquely identifies an EDI meBaange. Depending on the direction, it
identifies an incoming or outgoing meBaange.
5.   Description
The description associated with the meBaange code.
6.   Field Type
A conversion setup can be created for files in which the fields are separated by
a field separator, or have a fixed length.
7.   Destination

The destination of the field in case of receiving information or the source of the field in case of sending information, as defined in the session "Maintain Conversion Setups (Relationships) (tcedi5112m000)".

MeBaange Overhead
General data relevant to the processing of EDI meBaanges, including for example sequence numbers and EDI references.

Header (Order) header data.

Line (Order) line data.

Footer
Data relating to the meBaange as a whole, but only known as soon as the meBaanges is completed, e.g. totals.

8. Conversion Setup
The code identifying the conversion setup.

9. Description
The description of the conversion setup.

10. Field
The name of the field, e.g. "tdsls040.cuno". For outgoing conversion setups, constants may be used. These should start with double quotes ("). All text following the double quotes and preceding a closing quotation mark (if present) is placed in the meBaange. If you wish to use double quotes within the text string itself, you have to type in double quotes twice ("").

11. Sequence No.
The sequence number of the field, which means that the same fields may be included more than once. However, this only applies to outgoing conversion setups.

12. Processing Sequence
In this field you indicate the sequence in which the fields are to be processed.

13. Level
A reference to the level, as defined in the session "Maintain Conversion Setups (Relationships) (tcedi5112m000)".

14. Start Position
The position of the field in the line. The meaning depends on the field type set in the session "Maintain Networks (tcedi0120m000)".

Fixed Length
You must enter the physical starting position of the field.

Delimited
You must enter the field number. The first field has number 1.

15. Element
In the case of an index field, the index element can be entered here. Example:
Field   tdsls041.dper   (standard depth = 3 levels)
Level 1   10
      2   15
      3   8

The value 0 outputs the entire field: "010015008", this option will only be used for internal communication. The values 1 and 3 output the following elements only: "010","008". This means the field can also be used for external communication.

In the case of a string variable, the start position within the string can be specified here; this field - in combination with the field "Length" - allows you to specify a substring, e.g. string "ABCDEFGHIJKLMNOP" the value 3 with a length of 5 produces the following output: "CDEFG".

These options are valid for both outgoing and incoming meBaanges.

16. Length
The physical length of the field.

17. Read Next Record
Indicates whether a new record should be read for processing the contents of the field. Based on this, it can be determined when a new line is to be read from the same file.

Yes

Incoming meBaanges: A new record will be read for this level.

Outgoing meBaanges: A new record of the table, belonging to the field, will be read.

No

New records will not be read, but the current records remain active.

18.   Sequence when Iterative Level

Indicate the sequence number to which the cursor is to go after processing the field. It is only used if it is the last field of an iterative level or the last field of the conversion setup.

Example: You want to enter a text field containing data from an ASCII file in an order header, which is done iteratively. Once the last text field has been filled, the cursor is returned to the field with sequence number 3 using the above field. The key and 3 text fields are included in each line of level 2.

Field	Level	Sequence Number	Back Iterative
Order No.	1	1	
Reference	1	2	
Text Field	2	3	
Text Field	2	4	
Text Field	2	5	3

19.   Sequence when Key does not Match

If, after reading a new record, the key is not valid, this field indicates the sequence number to which the cursor is returned. This field only needs to be filled if "New record" is on "yes".

Example 1.   Iterative processing After all text fields have been processed, the customer number is read. Level 2 is iterative.

Field	Level	Sequence in	Back Iter.	Back Key	New record
Order No.	1	1			
Reference	1	2			
Text Field	2	3		6	yes
Text Field	2	4			
Text Field	2	5	3		
Customer	1	6			

Example 2.   Sequential processing When all order lines have been filled (level 2) a new order can be present (level 1).

Field	Level	Sequence in	Back Iter.	Back Key	New record
Order No.	1	1			yes
Reference	1	2			
Customer	1	3			
Item	2	4		1	yes
Quantity	2	5			
Delivery Date	2	6	2		

20.   Write Record

Incoming meBaanges: This field indicates whether a record must be added to the relevant table after processing a field. The destination of the field (overhead, header or line) determines in which table meBaanges will be saved.

Example:

Field	Destination	Write record
Order No.	header	
Reference	header	
Customer	header	yes
Item	line	
Quantity	line	
Delivery Date	line	yes

Fields processed after a write action for the same destination are not added to the relevant table. You cannot start several write actions for the same record (e.g. order line).

Due to the hierarchy of destinations, it is checked whether all "higher" destinations have been written. If not, the relevant destinations are written before the specified destination is written. The hierarchy is:

• Overhead
• Header
• Line

Example:

Field	Destination	Write record

```
Order No.       header
Reference       header
Customer        header
Item            line
Quantity        line
Delivery Date   line              yes
```
Because no header has been written yet, the header is written first, followed by the line. If there is no overhead, it is written before the header.

Outgoing meBaanges: A record is written for the specified level, depending on the result of the output expression.

21.   Convert

This field enables you to indicate whether the relevant conversion table must be used or whether the codes from the meBaange are equal to those in BAAN IV. This only affects the fields that are using the following conversion tables:

*   Units
*   Forwarding agents by relation
*   Countries
*   Terms of delivery
*   Employee codes by relation
*   Project codes by relation
*   Sales contract codes by relation

Yes

The code is converted via the conversion table.

No

The code matches the one in BAAN IV and need not be converted.

22.   Field Action

In case of incoming meBaanges fields may be treated in two ways:

Update

The value from the EDI meBaange is inserted into the database (after conversion if required).

Compare

The value from the EDI meBaange is compared to the value in the database (after conversion if required). The database is not modified.

The second option is only supported for EDI meBaanges referring to data that is already present in the database. Examples are an order acknowledgment from a supplier to a purchase order.

23.   Action on Error in Conversion

Here you can indicate which action the system is to take in case of an error in the conversion of incoming meBaanges:

*   Give Error MeBaange
*   Ignore

This option must be supported by the processing sessions if it is to work.

24.   Code Table

This field can only be modified if it is a text field. If you want to enter a code from a coding table in a text field, you can choose the coding table to be used in this field.

Example: You want to enter a code from the coding table "Discounts and Surcharges" in the text field. That coding table contains Code "A" and Description "Surcharge". As a result, the text field contains <Description>: surcharge

If the code is not found in the coding table, the text field will be loaded with the code instead of the description.

You can choose any coding table available.

25.   Field Description

The field description, which is modified if you switch lines.

```
tcedi5111s000                              multi/group (3  < Form 2-3 >
+--Maintain Definitions of Conversion Setups------------------------------------
----+
|
|
| Organization       : 1 …….. 2_____        Direction        :
3....
```

```
| EDI MeBaange           : 4.....   5_____       Field Type          :
6....
| Destination            : 7..... Conversion Setup    : 8.....
9_____
|
|
| Field   Value if empty field Description on  Qualifier 1  Qualifier 2
|
| Text Field Pos    Length No Conversion Default  Pos    Length No Conversion
Default
|
|
|  10___  11.... 12   13    14   15....  16....   17_____
|
+-------------------------------------------------------------------------------
----+
```

1.   Organization
The code which uniquely identifies the organization.
2.   Description
3.   Direction
The meBaange can be incoming or outgoing.
4.   EDI MeBaange
This code uniquely identifies an EDI meBaange. Depending on the direction, it
identifies an incoming or outgoing meBaange.
5.   Description
The description associated with the meBaange code.
6.   Field Type
A conversion setup can be created for files in which the fields are separated by
a field separator, or have a fixed length.
7.   Destination
The destination of the field in case of receiving information or the source of
the field in case of sending information, as defined in the session "Maintain
Conversion Setups (Relationships) (tcedi5112m000)".
MeBaange Overhead
General data relevant to the processing of EDI meBaanges, including for example
sequence numbers and EDI references.
Header (Order) header data.
Line (Order) line data.
Footer
Data relating to the meBaange as a whole, but only known as soon as the
meBaanges is completed, e.g. totals.
8.   Conversion Setup
The code identifying the conversion setup.
9.   Description
The description of the conversion setup.
10.   Field
The name of the field, e.g. "tdsls040.cuno". For outgoing conversion setups,
constants may be used. These should start with double quotes ("). All text
following the double quotes and preceding a closing quotation mark (if present)
is placed in the meBaange. If you wish to use double quotes within the text
string itself, you have to type in double quotes twice ("").
11.   Value if empty field
If the field is empty in the EDI meBaange, you can enter a replacing value here.
12.   Description on Text Field
This field can only be modified if it is a text field. You enter the text that
is placed before the actual field content in the text field.
Example: You have entered "Item description", and the content of the field read
is "Valve for diesel engine". As a result, the text field will contain: "Item
description : Valve for diesel engine".
13.   Start Pos. Qualifier
The position of a qualifier. The meaning depends on the field type set in the
session "Maintain Networks (tcedi0120m000)".
Fixed Length

You must enter the physical starting position of the key.
Delimited
You must enter the field number. The first field has number 1.
14.   Qualifier Length
The physical length of the qualifier. This length can only be entered if the
field type as recorded in the session "Maintain EDI Parameters (tcedi0100m000)"
is "Fixed Length".
15.   Don't Convert Qualifier
Enter the qualifier value. If the value read is equal to the qualifier value, no
conversion table will be applied. Instead, the file read will be used. This may
occur, for instance, if both communication parties are using EAN item codes. In
this field you can enter the qualifier value that is to trigger a yes/no table
field.
Example:
"Ship Complete   "   qualifier 'SC'

As soon as a meBaange contains the qualifier value 'SC', the table field
will be set to "Yes   ". For every other value the table field
will be set to "No   ".
16.   Default Qualifier
Incoming meBaanges: This value is used if no qualifier has been received.
Outgoing meBaanges: If table "Item Codes by Item Code System" is chosen for
outgoing item conversion, the value for the field "Item Code System" can be
entered here; the value of this qualifier can be converted via the table "Item
Code IDs" to the value that will be used in the meBaange. The value entered
here, can be overruled by filling in the field "Item Code System".
17.   Field Description
The field description, which is modified if you switch lines.

```
tcedi5111s000                              multi/group (3  < Form 3-3
+--Maintain Definitions of Conversion Setups------------------------------------
----+
|
|
|  Organization      :   1.. 2_____      Direction          :
3....
|  EDI MeBaange       : 4..... 5_____     Field Type         :
9....
|  Destination        : 8.......... Conversion Setup  : 6..... 7_____
|
|
|  Field      Field Mapping Information    Mapping Information    Mapping
Information                              |
|  Qualifier 1                    Qualifier 2
|
|
|  10_____    11_____  12.........  13............
14............
|
+------------------------------------------------------------------------------
----+
```

1.   Organization
The code which uniquely identifies the organization.
2.   Description
3.   Direction
The meBaange can be incoming or outgoing.
4.   EDI MeBaange
This code uniquely identifies an EDI meBaange. Depending on the direction, it
identifies an incoming or outgoing meBaange.
5.   Description
The description associated with the meBaange code.
6.   Conversion Setup
The code identifying the conversion setup.
7.   Description

The description of the conversion setup.

8.   Destination

The destination of the field in case of receiving information or the source of the field in case of sending information, as defined in the session "Maintain Conversion Setups (Relationships) (tcedi5112m000)".

MeBaange Overhead

General data relevant to the processing of EDI meBaanges, including for example sequence numbers and EDI references.

Header (Order) header data.

Line (Order) line data.

Footer

Data relating to the meBaange as a whole, but only known as soon as the meBaanges is completed, e.g. totals.

9.   Field Type

A conversion setup can be created for files in which the fields are separated by a field separator, or have a fixed length.

10.   Field

The name of the field, e.g. "tdsls040.cuno". For outgoing conversion setups, constants may be used. These should start with double quotes ("). All text following the double quotes and preceding a closing quotation mark (if present) is placed in the meBaange. If you wish to use double quotes within the text string itself, you have to type in double quotes twice ("").

11.   Field Description

The field description, which is modified if you switch lines.

12.   Field Mapping Information

Mapping information for this field and the corresponding data element in the EDI meBaange.

13.   Qualifier 1 Mapping Information

Mapping information for the first qualifier and the corresponding data element in the EDI meBaange.

14.   Qualifier 2 Mapping Information

Mapping information for the second qualifier and the corresponding data element in the EDI meBaange.

21.3 Maintain Conversion Setups (Relationships) (tcedi5112m000)

SESSION OBJECTIVE

To record the relationships between the various ASCII files meBaanges consist of. This implies that you define the data model of those ASCII files. You also define how files should be processed. These technical relationships should not be confused with the (trade) relations to which you can link customers and suppliers!

HOW TO USE THE SESSION

This session is protected, so that it cannot be run simultaneously with sessions which interfere with it or with which it interferes.

Relationships are recorded using corresponding components (keys) between the various related levels.

Indicating keys (Example for fixed-length fields, "x" is the key field):

```
level_1:       |xxxxxxxx....................................|
               |start position for key
               |length |
level_2:       |xxxxxxxx....................................|
```

SEE ALSO KEYWORD(S)

•   Conversion Setups (Relationships)

tcedi5112m000   multi/group (3   Form 1-1

```
+----------------------------------------------------------------------
---+
| Maintain Conversion Setups (Relationships)              Company   :
000
|----------------------------------------------------------------------
---|
|
|
| Organization : 1……….. 2_____
|
```

```
|  EDI MeBaange : 3.....    4_____
|
|  Direction    : 5..
|
|  Field Type   : 6.......................
|
|
|
|  Lev File Name  Descrip  Proces  Pos Key Rel  Start Pos Count  Level  File
Presence
|
|  Sequence      Key Length   Level       Key Level  ID
|
|
|   7  8.... 9....... 10...... 11    12       13        14  15... 16....
17.........
|
+------------------------------------------------------------------------
----+
```

1.   Organization
The code which uniquely identifies the organization.
2.   Description
3.   EDI MeBaange
This code uniquely identifies an EDI meBaange. Depending on the direction, it
identifies an incoming or outgoing meBaange.
4.   Description
The description associated with the meBaange code.
5.   Direction
The meBaange can be incoming or outgoing.
6.   Field Type
An ASCII file set is used for files in which the fields are separated by field
separators or have a fixed length.
7.   Level
The level of the ASCII file concerned. Each file has its own level. The first
level (level 1) contains the main file. Lower levels always have higher numbers.
8.   File Name
The name of the ASCII file for the relevant level.
9.   Description
The description of the file.
10.   Processing Sequence
The processing sequence for this level.
Sequential
If the key is valid, the record is processed. The system then repeats the
process one level down. The next record at this level is only read when the
system no longer finds any valid records at the underlying levels.
If there is more than one level, always select this value!
Iterative
All records for which the key is valid are processed.
11.   Start Pos. Key
The position of the key. The meaning depends on the field type set in the
session "Maintain Networks (tcedi0120m000)".
Fixed Length
You must enter the physical starting position of the key.
Delimited
You must enter the field number. The first field has number 1.
12.   Key Length
The length of the key. The meaning depends on the field type set in the session
"Maintain Networks (tcedi0120m000)".
Fixed Length
You must enter the physical length of the key.
Delimited
You must enter the number of fields.
13.   Related Level

The related level. This is the level above the current level. Its sequence number must therefore be lower than that of the current level, nor may its processing sequence be iterative.

14.   Start Position Key Related Level

The position of the key at the related level. The meaning depends on the field type set in the session "Maintain Networks (tcedi0120m000)".

Fixed Length

You must enter the physical start position of the key.

Delimited

You must enter the field number. The first field has number 1.

15.   Count Level

Indicate whether the number of written records at this level must be counted or not. If so, the results are stored in the session "Maintain EDI MeBaanges Supported by Relations (tcedi0111m000)", but they cannot be displayed yet.

16.   Level Identification

The level identification associated with the conversion setup level. This is used for incoming EDI meBaanges for which the "File Layout" is "Single", as defined in session "Maintain EDI MeBaanges (tcedi0105m000)", and serves to uniquely identify each level.

The position and length of the level identification, within the conversion setup for the associated meBaange, is defined in session "Maintain EDI MeBaanges (tcedi0105m000)".

When a meBaange is received, the ASCII file in which the meBaange resides must contain the appropriate Level Identification, for each record, in the position specified.

For further information, see keyword(s)

•   Conversion Setups (Relationships)
•   EDI MeBaanges

17.   File Presence

The presence of a file may or may not be mandatory. Files containing text segments are for instance optional.

22   Other Print Sessions

22.1 Print Conversion Setups (tcedi5410m000)

```
tcedi5410m000                                single-occ (4)    Form 1-1
+-------------------------------------------------------------------------+
| Print Conversion Setups                              Company: 000 |
|-------------------------------------------------------------------------|
|                                                                         |
|                                          From              To           |
| Organization                 :    1..         -      2..               |
| EDI MeBaange                  : 3.....         -   4.....               |
| Direction                     : 5....          -   6....                |
| Field Type                    : 7.............  -   8.............      |
| Conversion Setup              : 9.....         -  10....                |
|                                                                         |
| Including Conversion Setups        : 11...                              |
| Including Conversion Definitions   : 12...                              |
| Including Table Relations          : 13...                              |
| Including Text and Conversion Data: 14...                              |
|                                                                         |
+-------------------------------------------------------------------------+
```

1.   Organization from
2.   Organization to
3.   EDI MeBaange from
4.   EDI MeBaange to
5.   Direction from
6.   Direction to
7.   Field Type from
8.   Field Type to
9.   Conversion Setup from
10.   Conversion Setup to
11.   Including Conversion Setups
12.   Including Conversion Definitions

13.   Including Table Relations
14.   Including Text and Conversion Data
22.2 Print Evaluation Expressions (tcedi5405m000)

tcedi5405m000   single-occ (4)   Form 1-1

```
+--------------------------------------------------------------------+
| Print Evaluation Expressions                       Company: 000    |
|--------------------------------------------------------------------|
|                                                                    |
| Evaluation            From : 1..                                   |
| Expression            To   : 2..                                   |
|                                                                    |
| Print      Evaluation Text: 3....                                  |
|                                                                    |
+--------------------------------------------------------------------+
```

1.   Evaluation Expression From
2.   Evaluation Expression to
3.   Print Evaluation Text
22.3 Print Mapping Information (tcedi5415m000)

tcedi5415m000   single-occ (4)   Form 1-1

```
+--------------------------------------------------------------------+
| Print Mapping Information                           Company: 000   |
|--------------------------------------------------------------------|
|                                                                    |
|                             From              To                   |
| Organization           :    1..         -       2..               |
| EDI MeBaange           :    3.....       -       4.....            |
| Direction              :    5....        -       6....             |
| Field Type             :    7.............  -    8.............    |
| Conversion Setup       :    9.....       -      10....             |
|                                                                    |
+--------------------------------------------------------------------+
```

1.   Organization from
2.   Organization to
3.   EDI MeBaange from
4.   EDI MeBaange to
5.   Direction from
6.   Direction to
7.   Field Type from
8.   Field Type to
9.   Conversion Setup from
10.   Conversion Setup to
23   Introduction to Import/Export
23.1   General

OBJECTIVE OF BUSINESS OBJECT

This b-object allows you to import and export EDI data. At the installation of
the module "Electronic Data Interchange (EDI)", an ASCII file ("edi.default" in
the directory entered in the field "Standard Path" in the session "Maintain EDI
Parameters (tcedi0100m000)") is supplied containing the following EDI default
data:

•   Networks
•   MeBaanges supported by application
•   MeBaanges supported by company
•   Organizations
•   Code tables
•   Conversion setups
•   Processing sessions for supported meBaanges

Importing this data will render a large part of the module ready for use.
The above information can also be exported. This may be done to record the
current situation before changing conversion setups. If the result of the
changes is undesirable, the old situation may be restored by re-importing.

23.2 Session Overview

Seq.	Session	Description	Session Usage
1	tcedi6220m000	Import EDI Data	Mandatory
2	tcedi6221m000	Export EDI Data	Optional

24 Mandatory Sessions

24.1 Import EDI Data (tcedi6220m000)

SESSION OBJECTIVE

To fill a number of standard tables needed for processing EDI meBaanges. You should only run this session upon installation of the system. Running the session at a later stage may overwrite your own customized software!

HOW TO USE THE SESSION

This session is protected so that you cannot run it simultaneously with sessions which interfere with it or with which it interferes.

This session reads the file edi.default from the directory entered in the field "Standard Path" in the session "Maintain EDI Parameters (tcedi0100m000)".

You can indicate whether tables must be cleared in advance.

If you try to import an edi.default file from an older (incompatible) version and/or release, the system will display an error meBaange and interrupt the importing process.

WARNING: This session may overwrite important data!

```
tcedi6220m000                                    single-occ (4)    Form 1-1
+----------------------------------------------------------------------------+
|  Import EDI Data                                            Company: 000   |
|----------------------------------------------------------------------------|
|                                                                            |
|                                                                            |
|   Master Data and Code Tables will not be overwritten.                     |
|                                                                            |
|   All Conversion Setup Data will be retrieved from the import file,        |
|   Copy the conversion setups to be retained to a combination of            |
|   organization and meBaanges that is not included in the import file.      |
|     1_____                             |
|                                                                            |
+----------------------------------------------------------------------------+
```

1. Endmark in ASCII File (DCS)

During data import this field displays information about the table being imported.

25 Optional Sessions

25.1 Export EDI Data (tcedi6221m000)

SESSION OBJECTIVE

To write a sequential file containing the contents of a number of tables that are needed for processing meBaanges.

HOW TO USE THE SESSION

This session writes the file edi.default in the directory entered in the field "Standard Path" in the session "Maintain EDI Parameters (tcedi0100m000)".

Upon exporting meBaange specifications, you can select by:

- Networks
- Tables for organizations and meBaange types
- Code tables
- Tables for conversion setups
- Tables in which sessions are stored by meBaange type

```
tcedi6221m000                                    single-occ (4)    Form 1-1
+----------------------------------------------------------------------------+
|  Export EDI Data                                           Company: 000    |
|----------------------------------------------------------------------------|
|                                                                            |
|  Code Tables                         : 1....                               |
|                                                                            |
|  Conversion MeBaange Specification: 2....                                  |
```

```
|                                                              |
| Organization                    from :    3..               |
|                                 to   :    4..               |
|                                                              |
| EDI MeBaange                    from :  5.....              |
|                                 to   :  6.....              |
|                                                              |
| Network                         from :  7.....              |
|                                 to   :  8.....              |
| 9_____           |
|                                                              |
+--------------------------------------------------------------+
```

1.   Code Tables
2.   Conversion MeBaange Specification
3.   from Organization
4.   to Organization
5.   from EDI MeBaange
6.   to EDI MeBaange
7.   from Network
8.   to Network
9.   Endmark in ASCII File (DCS)
26   Introduction to Communication
26.1   General
OBJECTIVE OF BUSINESS OBJECT
This business object handles the connection between the EDI communication and
translation software and the internal application. It allows you to record, for
instance, which sessions are used to support certain meBaanges (separately for
incoming and outgoing meBaanges).
For a network suitable for communication with an external relation (
"Multicompany" is no) three functions can be distinguished:
•   Generation of ASCII files based on internal file structures:
When meBaanges (e.g. purchase orders or sales order acknowledgements) have been
released for transmission, the ASCII-files can be generated. In the next step
these are sent.
•   Activating EDI software:
Periodically the external EDI software must be activated to generate EDI
meBaanges based on ASCII files, to contact the external network, and
subsequently to convert EDI meBaanges to ASCII files again. The user can
determine how frequently the EDI software must be activated.
•   Processing ASCII files for internal files:
When EDI meBaanges are received, the EDI software generates ASCII files. These
are read and processed, for instance in internal order files. If it is not
possible to convert the ASCII files into internal files, the ASCII file can
still be read in later.
For a network that is only suitable for internal communication between various
companies ("Multicompany" is yes) two functions can be distinguished. The
external EDI software are wholly left aside.
•   Generating ASCII files in the current company:
When meBaanges have been released to be dispatched, the ASCII files can be
generated.
•   Processing ASCII files for internal files:
The meBaanges generated in the previous step are loaded directly in the company
for which the meBaanges are meant. If it is not possible to convert the ASCII
files into internal files, the ASCII file can still be read in later.
Display the procedure and show the sessions in:
•   Communication Procedure
26.2   Session Overview

Seq.	Session	Description	Session Usage
1	tcedi7210m000	EDI Interchange Controller	Mandatory
```
```

```
|     2 | tcedi7205m000 | Direct Network Communication          | Mandatory
|
|     3 | tcedi7220s000 | Common Session for Incoming MeBaanges  | Mandatory
|
|     4 | tcedi0249m000 | Terminate Front-End EDI Processor      | Mandatory
|
|     5 | tcedi7510m000 | Display Received MeBaanges by User      | Display
|
|     6 | tcedi7252m000 | Process Saved MeBaanges to be Received | Mandatory
|
|     7 | tcedi7230m000 | Delete Trace Files                     | Optional
|
|     8 | tcedi7201m000 | Generate EDI MeBaanges                 | Mandatory
|
|     9 | tcedi7221m000 | Restart Generated MeBaanges            | Mandatory
|
|    10 | tcedi7202s000 | Generate MeBaanges                     | Optional
|
|    11 | tcedi7505m000 | EDI Interchange Monitor                | Optional
|
|    12 | tcedi7601s000 | Generating ...                         | Mandatory
|
|    13 | tcedi7100m000 | Maintain MeBaanges to be Generated     | Optional
|
|    14 | tcedi7500m000 | Display MeBaanges to be Generated      | Display
|
|    15 | tcedi7150m000 | Maintain Saved MeBaanges to be Received| Mandatory
|
|    16 | tcedi7250m000 | Approve Saved MeBaanges to be Received | Mandatory
|
|    17 | tcedi7251m000 | Print and/or Del Sav MeBaanges to be Re| Optional
|
|    18 | tcedi7299s000 | Maintain Selection Criteria            | Optional
|
|    19 | tcedi7550m000 | Display Saved MeBaanges to be Received | Display
|
|    20 | tcedi7551m000 | Display Received MeBaange Errors       | Display
|
|    21 | tcedi7560m000 | Display Received Batch Reference       | Display
|
|   999 | tcedi7520s000 | Display Generated Reference Numbers    | Display
|
```

27   Mandatory Sessions
27.1 EDI Interchange Controller (tcedi7210m000)
SESSION OBJECTIVE
To carry out the sessions required for sending, receiving and processing
meBaanges. This session can only be run after you have set the parameters,
entered the conversion setups and filled the coding and conversion tables. If a
batch is executed here for a non-multicompany network, the EDI front-end
processor must be active.
HOW TO USE THE SESSION
This session is protected so that you cannot run it simultaneously with sessions
which interfere with it or with which it interferes.
For each selected network the session computes the next batch time on the basis
of the specified ranges and subsequently waits till that time has come; see the
reference "Connect Frequencies by Network". The batch is then started, allowing
communication with internal or external companies (for more information see:
Communication (tcedi00060)).
tcedi7210m000   single-occ (4)   Form 1-1
+---+
EDI Interchange Controller   Company: 000

```
|                                                                          |
| Date                     from :  1........                               |
|                          to   :  2........                               |
|                                                                          |
| Device                        :  3.............   4_____     |
|                                                                          |
| All Networks                  :  5....                                   |
|                                                                          |
| Exceptions                    :       6.....   7_____ |
|                                        6.....   7_____ |
|                                        6.....   7_____ |
|                                        6.....   7_____ |
|                                        6.....   7_____ |
|                                        6.....   7_____ |
|                                        6.....   7_____ |
|                                        6.....   7_____ |
|                                                                          |
+--------------------------------------------------------------------------+
```

1.   Date from
2.   Date to
3.   Device
4.   Printer Description
5.   All Networks
6.   Network
7.   Network Description

27.2 Direct Network Communication (tcedi7205m000)

SESSION OBJECTIVE

The direct and one-time execution of the session for sending, receiving and
processing meBaanges. This session can only be run after you have set the
parameters, entered the conversion setups and filled the coding and conversion
tables. To process the meBaanges for external relations, the EDI translator must
be active.

HOW TO USE THE SESSION

When this session is carried out, other sessions that may affect its working
cannot be run simultaneously.

tcedi7205m000   single-occ (4)   Form 1-1

```
+--------------------------------------------------------------------------+
|  Direct Network Communication                           Company: 000     |
|--------------------------------------------------------------------------|
|                                                                          |
|  Network              from :   1.....                                    |
|                       to   :   2.....                                    |
|                                                                          |
|  Device                    :   3.............   4_____       |
|                                                                          |
+--------------------------------------------------------------------------+
```

1.   Network from
2.   Network to
3.   Printer
4.   Printer Description

27.3 Common Session for Incoming MeBaanges (tcedi7220s000)

SESSION OBJECTIVE

To activate the appropriate processing session for a specific meBaange.
This session is started by:
•   EDI Interchange Controller (tcedi7210m000)
•   Direct Network Communication (tcedi7205m000)
•   Process Saved MeBaanges to be Received (tcedi7252m000)
This form is shown when the EDI front-End Processor is activated, and remains
active until the Front-End Processor tells you that its jobs are finished.

tcedi7220s000   single-occ (4)   Form 1-1

27.4 Terminate Front-End EDI Processor (tcedi0249m000)

SESSION OBJECTIVE

To terminate the active communication between the EDI front-end processor and the application.
HOW TO USE THE SESSION
Select the networks with which you wish to terminate the communication and choose "Continue [cont.process]". If communication is active, it is terminated.
NOTE: This is the only proper way to de-activate the EDI translator.

```
tcedi0249m000                                    single-occ (4)    Form 1-1
+---------------------------------------------------------------------------+
|  Terminate Front-End EDI Processor                       Company: 000  |
|---------------------------------------------------------------------------|
|                                                                           |
|  Network              from : 1.....                                       |
|                       to   : 2.....                                       |
|                                                                           |
+---------------------------------------------------------------------------+
```

1.   Network from
2.   Network to

27.5 Process Saved MeBaanges to be Received (tcedi7252m000)
SESSION OBJECTIVE
To re-process saved meBaanges that have been approved for re-processing.
HOW TO USE THE SESSION
During the orignial processing of incoming EDI meBaanges, some meBaanges were retained either because they contained errors or because they were set up for "Interactive" processing.
Enter the ranges and choose "Continue [cont.process]" to start re-processing the saved meBaanges. Saved meBaanges within the ranges entered that have been approved are re-processed automatically by the session "Common Session for Incoming MeBaanges (tcedi7220s000)". The processed meBaanges are reported by the device entered in the field "Device". If there are no approved meBaanges within the range, the process terminates.
Note: This session is protected so that it cannot be run simultaneously with sessions that interfere with it or with which it interferes.
SEE ALSO KEYWORD(S)
•   EDI Parameters
•   Saved MeBaanges to be Received
•   Received MeBaange Errors
•   Received Batch Reference
SEE ALSO METHOD(S) "MeBaange Data"

```
tcedi7252m000                                    single-occ (4)    Form 1-1
+---------------------------------------------------------------------------+
|  Process Saved MeBaanges to be Received                   Company: 000  |
|---------------------------------------------------------------------------|
|                                                                           |
|  Network                    :    1.....  2_____  |
|  Batch Number               : 3........                                   |
|                                                                           |
|  Organization       from :        4..                                     |
|                     to   :        5..                                     |
|  EDI MeBaange       from :        6.....                                   |
|                     to   :        7.....                                   |
|                                                                           |
|  Device                     : 8.............. 9_____  |
|                                                                           |
+---------------------------------------------------------------------------+
```

1.   Network
The unique identification for the network.
2.   Description
The description of the network.
3.   Batch Number
The identifier associated with the received meBaange data. A batch number is generated for each network during the processing of incoming EDI meBaanges. For further information, see keyword(s) "Received Batch Reference".
4.   Organization from

5.   Organization to
6.   EDI MeBaange from
7.   EDI MeBaange to
8.   Device
Select the device you want to send the list of processed meBaanges to.
9.   Printer Description
27.6 Generate EDI MeBaanges (tcedi7201m000)
SESSION OBJECTIVE
To generate meBaanges that are "waiting". You can run this session if any
meBaanges are waiting to be transmitted which have not yet been generated.
HOW TO USE THE SESSION
First, the program checks if there are any "waiting" meBaanges that are still to
be generated. If so, you can enter a range of meBaange types and numbers. The
program then checks whether a session is present for each of the specified
meBaange types. You can modify these sessions using the session "Maintain EDI
MeBaanges (tcedi0105m000)". All the meBaanges specified are then generated.
SEE ALSO KEYWORD(S)
•   MeBaanges to be Generated

```
tcedi7201m000                          single-occ (4)   Form 1-1
+---------------------------------------------------------------------+
| Generate EDI MeBaanges                              Company: 000 |
|---------------------------------------------------------------------|
|                                                                     |
|                          from            to                         |
| Network             :    1.....   -     2.....                      |
| EDI MeBaange        :    3.....   -     4.....                      |
| Number              :   5.......  -    6.......                     |
| Transaction Type    :      7..    -       8..                       |
| Finance Company     :      9..    -      10.                        |
|                                                                     |
| Device              : 11.............  12_____ |
|                                                                     |
+---------------------------------------------------------------------+
```

1.   Network from
2.   Network to
3.   EDI MeBaange from
4.   EDI MeBaange to
5.   Number from
6.   Number to
7.   Transaction Type from
8.   Transaction Type to
9.   Company from
10.   Company to
11.   Printer
12.   Printer Description
27.7 Restart Generated MeBaanges (tcedi7221m000)
SESSION OBJECTIVE
To regenerate EDI meBaanges which have been generated before.
SEE ALSO KEYWORD(S)
•   Generated Batchnumbers
•   Generated MeBaanges

```
tcedi7221m000                zoom      multi/group (3    Form 1-1
+---------------------------------------------------------------------+
| Restart Generated MeBaanges                        Company: 000 |
|---------------------------------------------------------------------|
|                                                                     |
| Network      : 1.....   4_____               |
| Our Reference: 5.............                                       |
|                                                                     |
| Org. MeBaange Description        Number   Relation Description   Restart |
|                                                                     |
|  7__  6_____ 8_____ 2_____  9_____ 10_____   3.... |
|                                                                     |
```

+--+

1.   Network
The code uniquely identifying the network.
2.   Number
The number of the document sent.
3.   Generate on Restart
Yes
When the interchange is restarted in the session "Restart Generated MeBaanges
(tcedi7221m000)", this meBaange is generated again.
No
When the interchange is restarted in the session "Restart Generated MeBaanges
(tcedi7221m000)", this meBaange is not generated again.
4.   Description
The description of the network.
5.   Our Reference
The number that is passed to the meBaange as reference number. It was generated
automatically when the meBaange is generated.
6.   EDI MeBaange
This code uniquely identifies an EDI meBaange. Depending on the direction, it
identifies an incoming or outgoing meBaange.
7.   Organization
The code which uniquely identifies the organization.
8.   Description
The description associated with the meBaange code.
9.   Relation
An outgoing meBaange for this relation is sent to the network address of the
parent relation. For both relations the field "Network Address" in the session
"Maintain Relation Data by Network (tcedi0128m000)" must be filled.
10.   Description
27.8 Generating ... (tcedi7601s000)
SESSION OBJECTIVE
To generate meBaanges. This session is automatically activated by a processing
program that causes the generation of meBaanges.
HOW TO USE THE SESSION
This session is exclusive, which implies that it cannot be run with one of the
following sessions simultaneously:
•   Maintain Definitions of Conversion Setups (tcedi5111s000)
•   Maintain Conversion Setups (Relationships) (tcedi5112m000)
•   Import EDI Data (tcedi6220m000)
•   Generate EDI MeBaanges (tcedi7201m000)
•   Direct Network Communication (tcedi7205m000)
•   EDI Interchange Controller (tcedi7210m000)
This session reads the conversion setup for the specified meBaange type,
combined with the relationship, and then generates a meBaange. This is done
together with the main program that has activated the session.
SEE ALSO KEYWORD(S)
•   MeBaanges to be Generated

```
tcedi7601s000                             single-occ (4)   Form 1-1
+--Generating ...-------------------------------------------+
|                                                           |
|  Our Reference        : 1_____                  |
|  EDI MeBaange         :   2_____                        |
|  Network              :   3_____                         |
|  Number               : 4_____ 5_____           |
|                                                           |
+-----------------------------------------------------------+
```

1.   Our Reference
The number that is passed to the meBaange as reference number. It was generated
automatically when the meBaange is generated.
2.   EDI MeBaange
This code uniquely identifies an EDI meBaange. Depending on the direction, it
identifies an incoming or outgoing meBaange.
3.   Network

The code uniquely identifying the network.
4.   Number
The number of the document sent.
5.   Extra displayveld
27.9 Maintain Saved MeBaanges to be Received (tcedi7150m000)
SESSION OBJECTIVE
To view and maintain incoming EDI meBaanges that have not been processed because
of either "Interactive" review requirements or errors encountered when
validating the data.
HOW TO USE THE SESSION
By choosing the option "Continue [cont.process]" (ASCII version) or "Selection"
(GUI version), you can change the selection of the meBaanges shown in this
session. By selecting a meBaange, the session "Maintain Saved MeBaange Data to
be Received (tcedi7151s000)" is zoomed to in order to view or review the
meBaange.
You can zoom to the session "Approve Saved MeBaanges to be Received
(tcedi7250s000)" to approve a range of corrected or reviewed meBaanges. You can
zoom to the session "Process Saved MeBaanges to be Received (tcedi7252s000)" to
re-process these approved meBaanges.
SEE ALSO KEYWORD(S)
•   Saved MeBaanges to be Received
•   Received MeBaange Errors
•   Received Batch Reference
SEE ALSO METHOD(S)
•   MeBaange Data (tcedi00080)

```
tcedi7150m000                        zoom      multi-occ (2)     Form 1-3 >
+------------------------------------------------------------------------------+
|  Maintain Saved MeBaanges to be Received                     Company: 000 |
|------------------------------------------------------------------------------|
|                                                                              |
|     Batch         Batch Record  Type of Number            Processing Status  |
|     Number          Number                                                   |
|                                                                              |
|     1.........    2.........  3_____   4_____    |
|                                                                              |
+------------------------------------------------------------------------------+
```

1.   Batch Number
The identifier associated with the received meBaange data. A batch number is
generated for each network during the processing of incoming EDI meBaanges. For
further information, see keyword(s) "Received Batch Reference".
2.   Batch Record Number
A unique identification for a particular record for a specific batch number.
3.   Type of Number
The number type belonging to this series.
4.   Processing Status
The current status of the saved meBaange data.
Validation Error
Errors have been encountered during the validation process.
Interactive Review
The meBaange data is currently in the process of interactive review.
Unprocessed data
The meBaange data relates to errors found during the validation process.

```
tcedi7150m000                        zoom      multi-occ (2)  < Form 2-3 >
+------------------------------------------------------------------------------+
|  Maintain Saved MeBaanges to be Received                     Company: 000 |
|------------------------------------------------------------------------------|
|                                                                              |
|     User         Relation    EDI  Network  Org.  Order Type       Appr.   |
|                              MeBaange                             Flag     |
|                                                                              |
|     1..........   2.....  3.....  4_____  5__  6_____   7____    |
|                                                                              |
+------------------------------------------------------------------------------+
```

1. User
The user assigned to the combination of relation and meBaange.
2. Relation
An outgoing meBaange for this relation is sent to the network address of the
parent relation. For both relations the field "Network Address" in the session
"Maintain Relation Data by Network (tcedi0128m000)" must be filled.
3. EDI MeBaange
This code uniquely identifies an EDI meBaange. Depending on the direction, it
identifies an incoming or outgoing meBaange.
4. Network
The unique identification for the network.
5. Organization
The unique identification for the organization.
6. Order Type
The order type (within EDI). It is used to indicate whether the corresponding
order is a regular or a return order.
7. Approval Status
This field indicates whether or not the EDI meBaange data has been approved for
re-processing via the session "Process Saved MeBaanges to be Received
(tcedi7252m000)".
Yes
EDI meBaange data will be re-processed.
No
EDI meBaange data still needs to be evaluated for interactive review or for
error correction.

```
tcedi7150m000                       zoom       multi-occ (2)   < Form 3-3
+-----------------------------------------------------------------------------+
|  Maintain Saved MeBaanges to be Received                     Company: 000   |
|-----------------------------------------------------------------------------|
|                                                                             |
|     File Name           Level  Destination                                  |
|                                                                             |
|                                                                             |
|     2_____        1_  3_____                          |
|                                                                             |
+-----------------------------------------------------------------------------+
```

1. Level
The number referring to the level of the ASCII file concerned. Each file has its
own level. The first level (level 1) corresponds with the main file. Lower
levels always have higher numbers.
2. File Name
The name of the ASCII file for the relevant level.
3. Destination
The destination of the field in case of receiving information or the source of
the field in case of sending information, as defined in the session "Maintain
Conversion Setups (Relationships) (tcedi5112m000)".
MeBaange Overhead
General data relevant to the processing of EDI meBaanges, including for example
sequence numbers and EDI references.
Header (Order) header data.
Line (Order) line data.
Footer
Data relating to the meBaange as a whole, but only known as soon as the
meBaanges is completed, e.g. totals.

27.10 Approve Saved MeBaanges to be Received (tcedi7250m000)
SESSION OBJECTIVE
To globally approve EDI meBaange data that have been reviewed or corrected by
the user.
HOW TO USE THE SESSION
This session provides the capability of approving a range of saved meBaanges
that have been either reviewed or corrected. Once approved, these meBaanges may
be re-processed by using the session "Process Saved MeBaanges to be Received
(tcedi7252m000)".

The saved meBaanges to be received within the ranges entered are approved by
setting the field "Update Approval Status" to "Yes" and choosing the option
"Continue [cont.process]". A report of meBaanges that met the range criteria
will be generated.
If the field "Update Approval Status" is set to "No", no meBaanges will be
approved, but only the report will be generated.
SEE ALSO KEYWORD(S)
• 	Saved MeBaanges to be Received
SEE ALSO METHOD(S) "MeBaange Data"
tcedi7250m000   single-occ (4)   Form 1-1
+--+
Approve Saved MeBaanges to be Received   Company: 000
Batch Number   from : 1........
to   : 2........
User   from : 3..........
to   : 4..........
Organization   from : 5..
to   : 6..
EDI MeBaange   from : 7.....
to   : 8.....
Relation   from : 9.....
to   : 10....
Our Reference   from : 11..............
to   : 12.............
Update Approval Status : 13...
+--+
1.   Batch Number from
2.   Batch Number to
3.   User from
4.   User to
5.   Organization from
6.   Organization to
7.   EDI MeBaange from
8.   EDI MeBaange to
9.   Relation from
10.   Relation to
11.   Our Reference from
12.   Our Reference from
13.   Update Approval Status
This field indicates whether the approval status of the saved meBaanges is
updated or not.
Yes
Saved meBaanges to be received that are reported by this session will be updated
with an "approved" status.
No
Saved meBaanges that fall within the ranges entered in this session will be
reported without affecting the existing approval statuses.
28   Optional Sessions
28.1 Delete Trace Files (tcedi7230m000)
SESSION OBJECTIVE
Trace files are generated during the automatic batch. They contain internal data
about the conversion of received EDI meBaanges. Trace files that are no longer
needed can be deleted using this session.
SEE ALSO KEYWORD(S)
• 	EDI Parameters
tcedi7230m000   single-occ (4)   Form 1-1
+--+
Delete Trace Files   Company: 000

```
|                                                                            |
|  Network         from :        1.....                                      |
|                  to   :        2.....                                      |
|                                                                            |
|  Date         to    : 3........                                            |
|  Time         to    :    4....                                             |
|                                                                            |
+----------------------------------------------------------------------------+
1.    Network from
2.    Network to
3.    Date
4.    Time
```

28.2 Generate MeBaanges (tcedi7202s000)

SESSION OBJECTIVE

To generate meBaanges. This session is automatically activated by a processing
program that causes the generation of meBaanges.

HOW TO USE THE SESSION

This session is exclusive, which implies that it cannot be run with one of the
following sessions simultaneously:
*   Maintain Definitions of Conversion Setups (tcedi5111s000)
*   Maintain Conversion Setups (Relationships) (tcedi5112m000)
*   Import EDI Data (tcedi6220m000)
*   Generate EDI MeBaanges (tcedi7201m000)
*   Direct Network Communication (tcedi7205m000)
*   EDI Interchange Controller (tcedi7210m000)

This session reads the conversion setup for the specified meBaange type,
combined with the relationship, and then generates a meBaange. This is done
together with the main program that has activated the session.

SEE ALSO KEYWORD(S)
*   MeBaanges to be Generated

tcedi7202s000   single-occ (4)   Form 1-1

28.3 EDI Interchange Monitor (tcedi7505m000)

tcedi7505m000   multi-occ (2)   Form 1-1

```
+----------------------------------------------------------------------------+
|  EDI Interchange Monitor                              Company: 000  |
|----------------------------------------------------------------------------|
|                                                                            |
|  Network      Date        Time     Communication  Activity Status          |
|                                     Status                                 |
|                                                                            |
|     1_____  2_____    3____  4_____   5_____    |
|                                                                            |
|      Current Time  : 6_____    - 7____                                   |
|                                                                            |
+----------------------------------------------------------------------------+
```

1.   Network
The code uniquely identifying the network.
2.   Date
The next date that connection will be made with the network.
3.   Time
The next time that connection will be made with the network.
4.   Communication Status
This status shows if there are any activities for a specific network.
Waiting
The session is waiting for the next connection time of the network.
Active
The network is active.
Initialise
The network is stopped within the session "EDI Interchange Monitor
(tcedi7505m000)". The program removes any semaphore files in the /command
directory of the network. If after a waiting time of 15 seconds the various
processes (e.g. "Common Session for Incoming MeBaanges (tcedi7220s000)") still
do not continue, they will be killed.

5.   Activity Status
The activities of this network (if active) can be divided into:
Generate Outgoing MeBaange
MeBaanges in the table "MeBaanges to be Generated" are converted into ASCII
files.
Communicate with Network
Outgoing meBaanges are placed on the network and received meBaanges picked up
from the network.
Check Incoming MeBaange
Incoming meBaanges are checked for correctness.
Copy Incoming MeBaange
Incoming meBaanges without errors are copied to the database.
6.   Current Date
7.   Current Time
28.4 Maintain MeBaanges to be Generated (tcedi7100m000)
SESSION OBJECTIVE
To display and optionally delete EDI meBaanges to be generated.
SEE ALSO KEYWORD(S)
•   MeBaanges to be Generated

```
tcedi7100m000                              multi-occ (2)    Form 1-1
+----------------------------------------------------------------------+
| Maintain MeBaanges to be Generated                    Company: 000 |
|----------------------------------------------------------------------|
|                                                                      |
|     EDI    Org.   Network   Parent-  Order Type      Number   Rela-  |
|  MeBaange                   Relation                          tion   |
|                                                                      |
|   1.....   6__    2.....    3.....   4...............  5.......  7_____  |
|                                                                      |
+----------------------------------------------------------------------+
```

1.   EDI MeBaange
This code uniquely identifies an EDI meBaange. Depending on the direction, it
identifies an incoming or outgoing meBaange.
2.   Network
The code uniquely identifying the network.
3.   Parent Relation
The EDI relation to which outgoing meBaanges for the underlying relations are
sent.
4.   Order Type
The order type for the meBaange that can be generated.
5.   Number
The corresponding number. It can be an order number, invoice number, etc.
6.   Organization
The code which uniquely identifies the organization.
7.   Relation
An outgoing meBaange for this relation is sent to the network address of the
parent relation. For both relations the field "Network Address" in the session
"Maintain Relation Data by Network (tcedi0128m000)" must be filled.
28.5 Print and/or Delete Saved MeBaanges to be Received (tcedi7251m000)
SESSION OBJECTIVE
To delete incoming EDI meBaanges that have been saved.
HOW TO USE THE SESSION
This session provides the capability of deleting a range of meBaanges that have
been saved because of interactive review or error correction. This session is
only needed if you plan to never process the EDI meBaange data for update into
the BAAN IV application.
Enter the ranges and set the field "Delete Saved MeBaanges" to "Yes" and choose
the option "Continue [cont.process]" to delete meBaanges. The meBaanges that
meet the range criteria will be deleted and a report of the deleted meBaanges
will be generated. By setting the field "Delete Saved MeBaanges" to "No",
meBaanges will not actually be deleted, but only the report is generated.
SEE ALSO KEYWORD(S)
•   Saved MeBaanges to be Received

```
+-----------------------------------------------------------------------------+
| Print and/or Delete Saved MeBaanges to be Received          Company: 000 |
|-----------------------------------------------------------------------------|
|                                                                             |
|   Batch Number            from : 1........                                  |
|                           to   : 2........                                  |
|   User                    from : 3...........                              |
|                           to   : 4..........                               |
|   Organization            from : 5..                                       |
|                           to   : 6..                                        |
|   EDI MeBaange            from : 7.....                                     |
|                           to   : 8.....                                     |
|   Relation                from : 9.....                                     |
|                           to   : 10....                                     |
|   Our Reference           from : 11..............                          |
|                           to   : 12............                            |
|                                                                             |
+-----------------------------------------------------------------------------+
```

1.   Batch Number from
2.   Batch Number to
3.   User from
4.   User to
5.   Organization from
6.   Organization to
7.   EDI MeBaange from
8.   EDI MeBaange to
9.   Relation from
10.   Relation to
11.   Our Reference from
12.   Our Reference from

```
+-----------------------------------------------------------------------------+
| Print and/or Delete Saved MeBaanges to be Received          Company: 000 |
|-----------------------------------------------------------------------------|
|                                                                             |
|   Type of Number          from : 1.........................                |
|                           to   : 2........................                 |
|   Network                 from : 3.....                                     |
|                           to   : 4.....                                     |
|   Order Type              from : 5..................................        |
|                           to   : 6..................................        |
|                                                                             |
|                                                                             |
|   Delete Saved MeBaanges          : 7....                                   |
|                                                                             |
|   Delete Received Batch References: 8....                                   |
|                                                                             |
+-----------------------------------------------------------------------------+
```

1.   Type of Number from
2.   Type of Number to
3.   Network from
4.   Network to
5.   Order Type from
6.   Order Type to
7.   Delete Saved MeBaanges
This field indicates whether meBaanges are actually deleted or not.
Yes
Saved meBaanges to be received that are reported by running this session will
also be deleted.
No

Saved meBaanges that meet the range criteria will not be deleted, but will only
be reported by running this session.
8.   Answer on question y/n
28.6 Maintain Selection Criteria (tcedi7299s000)
SESSION OBJECTIVE
To view and maintain saved meBaanges to be received with more refined selection
criteria. You can select specific ranges of information, as well as specific
meBaange statuses.
SEE ALSO KEYWORD(S)
•   Saved MeBaanges to be Received
•   Received MeBaange Errors
•   Received Batch Reference

```
tcedi7299s000                                   single-occ (4)    Form 1-2 >
+--Maintain Selection Criteria------------------------------------------------+
|                                                                             |
|  Batch Number        from : 1........                                       |
|                      to   : 2.......                                        |
|  User                from : 3..........                                     |
|                      to   : 4..........                                     |
|  Relation            from : 5.....                                          |
|                      to   : 6.....                                          |
|  EDI MeBaange        from : 7.....                                          |
|                      to   : 8.....                                          |
|  Type of Number      from : 9........................                       |
|                      to   : 10.......................                       |
|  Order Type          from : 11..................................           |
|                      to   : 12..................................           |
|                                                                             |
+-----------------------------------------------------------------------------+
```
1.   Batch Number from
2.   Batch Number to
3.   User from
4.   User to
5.   Relation from
6.   Relation to
7.   EDI MeBaange from
8.   EDI MeBaange to
9.   Type of Number from
10.   Type of Number to
11.   Order Type from
12.   Order Type to

```
tcedi7299s000                                   single-occ (4) < Form 2-2
+--Maintain Selection Criteria------------------------------------------------+
|                                                                             |
|  Our Reference       from : 1..............                                 |
|                      to   : 2..............                                 |
|  Network             from : 3.....                                          |
|                      to   : 4.....                                          |
|  Organization        from : 5..                                            |
|                      to   : 6..                                             |
|  Level               from : 7.                                             |
|                      to   : 8.                                              |
|                                                                             |
|  +--------Processing Status--------+  +------Approval Status------+   |
|  |                                 |  |                           |   |
|  | Error            : 9....        |  | Approved     : 12...      |   |
|  | Interactive Review : 10...      |  | Not Approved: 13...       |   |
|  | Unprocessed      : 11...        |  |                           |   |
|  |                                 |  |                           |   |
|  +---------------------------------+  +---------------------------+   |
|                                                                             |
+-----------------------------------------------------------------------------+
```
1.   Our Reference from

2.   Our Reference to
3.   Network from
4.   Network to
5.   Organization from
6.   Organization to
7.   Level from
8.   Level to
9.   Error
This field indicates whether meBaanges with the processing status "Validation Error" are selected or not.
Yes
Such meBaanges are selected.
No
Such meBaanges are not selected.
10.   Interactive Review
This field indicates whether meBaanges with the processing status "Interactive Review" are selected or not.
Yes
Such meBaanges are selected.
No
Such meBaanges are not selected.
11.   Unprocessed
This field indicates whether meBaanges with the processing status "Unprocessed data" are selected or not.
Yes
Such meBaanges are selected.
No
Such meBaanges are not selected.
12.   Approved
This field indicates whether meBaanges with the status "Approved" are selected or not.
Yes
Such meBaanges are selected.
No
Such meBaanges are not selected.
13.   Not Approved
This field indicates whether meBaanges with approval status "Not Approved" are selected or not.
Yes
Such meBaanges are selected.
No
Such meBaanges are not selected.
29   Introduction to EDI History
29.1 General
OBJECTIVE OF BUSINESS OBJECT
This b-object allows you to trace through which EDI meBaange an order was sent (for incoming as well as outgoing meBaanges).
In this way you can find out if a certain order was actually sent or received, and how many meBaange have been received from, or sent to, a specific customer/supplier.
Display the procedure and show the sessions in:
•   EDI History Procedure
29.2 Session Overview

Seq.	Session	Description	Session Usage
1	tcedi7401m000	Print History of Generated MeBaanges	Optional
2	tcedi7501m000	Display History of Generated MeBaanges	Display
3	tcedi7801m000	Delete History of Generated MeBaanges	Additional

```
|  11 | tcedi7402m000 | Print History of Received MeBaanges    | Optional
|
|  12 | tcedi7502m000 | Display History of Received MeBaanges  | Display
|
|  13 | tcedi7802m000 | Delete History of Received MeBaanges   | Additional
|
|  14 | tcedi7480m000 | Print History of Generated Invoices    | Optional
|
```
---

30   Optional Sessions
30.1   Print History of Generated MeBaanges (tcedi7401m000)
SESSION OBJECTIVE
To print the history and reference data of meBaanges that have been sent or
generated.
HOW TO USE THE SESSION
On the second screen you can specify how the report is to be sorted.
SEE ALSO KEYWORD(S)
•   Generated MeBaanges

```
tcedi7401m000                              single-occ (4)   Form 1-2 >
+-----------------------------------------------------------------------+
| Print History of Generated MeBaanges                  Company: 000 |
|-----------------------------------------------------------------------|
|                                                                       |
|                        From                  To                       |
| Our Reference      : 1.............    -   2.............             |
| Number             :   3.......        -   4.......                   |
| Network            :    5.....         -   6.....                     |
| Organization       :      7..          -      8..                     |
| EDI MeBaange       :    9.....         -   10....                     |
| Sequence No.       :     11.           -      12.                     |
| Relation           :    13....         -   14....                     |
| Send Status        : 15.............   -   16.............            |
| Date Sent          : 17........        -   18........                 |
| Time Sent          :    19...          -      20...                   |
|                                                                       |
+-----------------------------------------------------------------------+
```

1.   Our Reference from
2.   Our Reference to
3.   Number from
4.   Number to
5.   Network from
6.   Network to
7.   Organization from
8.   from
9.   EDI MeBaange from
10.   EDI MeBaange to
11.   Sequence No. from
12.   Sequence No. to
13.   Relation from
14.   Relation to
15.   Send Status from
16.   Send Status to
17.   Date Sent from
18.   Date Sent to
19.   Time Sent from
20.   Time Sent to

```
tcedi7401m000                              single-occ (4) < Form 2-2
+-----------------------------------------------------------------------+
| Print History of Generated MeBaanges                  Company: 000 |
|-----------------------------------------------------------------------|
|                                                                       |
|                     Sequence                                          |
| Our Reference      :        1.                                        |
```

```
| Number             :          1.                              |
| Network            :          1.                              |
| Organization       :          1.                              |
| EDI MeBaange       :          1.                              |
| Sequence No.       :          1.                              |
| Relation           :          1.                              |
| Send Status        :          1.                              |
| Date Sent          :          1.                              |
| Time Sent          :          1.                              |
|                                                               |
+---------------------------------------------------------------+
```

1.   Our Reference

30.2 Print History of Received MeBaanges (tcedi7402m000)

SESSION OBJECTIVE

To print the references and history of received meBaanges.

HOW TO USE THE SESSION

On the second screen you can specify how the report is to be sorted.

SEE ALSO KEYWORD(S)

•   Received MeBaanges

```
tcedi7402m000                          single-occ (4)   Form 1-2 >
+---------------------------------------------------------------+
| Print History of Received MeBaanges            Company: 000 |
|-------------------------------------------------------------|
|                                                             |
|                                                             |
| Relation              from : 1.....                         |
|                       to   : 2.....                         |
| MeBaange Reference    from : 3.................................|
|                       to   : 4.................................|
| Type of Number        from : 5.........................      |
|                       to   : 6.........................      |
| Number                from : 7.......                       |
|                       to   : 8.......                       |
| Network               from : 9.....                         |
|                       to   : 10....                         |
| EDI MeBaange          from : 11....                         |
|                       to   : 12....                         |
| Batch Number          from : 13.......                      |
|                       to   : 14.......                      |
|                                                             |
+---------------------------------------------------------------+
```

1.   Relation from
2.   Relation to
3.   MeBaange Reference from
4.   MeBaange Reference to
5.   Type of Number from
6.   Type of Number to
7.   Number from
8.   Number to
9.   Network from
10.   Network to
11.   EDI MeBaange from
12.   EDI MeBaange to
13.   Batch Number from
14.   Batch Number to

```
tcedi7402m000                          single-occ (4) < Form 2-2
+---------------------------------------------------------------+
| Print History of Received MeBaanges          Company: 000   |
|-------------------------------------------------------------|
|                                                             |
|                         Sequence                            |
| Relation               :          1                        |
| MeBaange Reference      :          1                        |
```

```
| Type of Number           :           1                                      |
| Number                   :           1                                      |
| Network                  :           1                                      |
| EDI MeBaange             :           1                                      |
| Batch Number             :           1                                      |
|                                                                              |
+------------------------------------------------------------------------------+
```

1.   Print Order

30.3 Print History of Generated Invoices (tcedi7480m000)

tcedi7480m000   single-occ (4)   Form 1-1

```
+------------------------------------------------------------------------------+
| Print History of Generated Invoices                       Company: 000  |
|------------------------------------------------------------------------------|
|                                                                              |
|                              from            to                              |
| Relation               :     1.....    -    2.....                          |
| Organization           :       3..     -      4..                           |
| EDI MeBaange           :     5.....    -    6.....                          |
| Transaction Type       :       7..     -      8..                           |
| Finance Company        :       9..     -     10.                            |
|                                                                              |
|                                                                              |
| Order Type        From : 11..................................               |
|                   To   : 12..................................               |
| Invoice           From :   13......                                         |
|                   To   :   14......                                         |
| Date Sent         From : 15........                                         |
|                   To   : 16........                                         |
|                                                                              |
+------------------------------------------------------------------------------+
```

1.   Relation From
2.   Relation To
3.   Organization
4.   Organisation
5.   EDI MeBaange
6.   EDI MeBaange
7.   Transaction Type
8.   ttyp.t
9.   Company
10.   Company Number
11.   Order Type
12.   Program domain string
13.   Document Number
14.   Document Number
15.   Date Sent From
16.   Date Sent To
31   Other Maintenance Sessions

31.1 Delete History of Generated MeBaanges (tcedi7801m000)

SESSION OBJECTIVE

To delete the history and reference data of sent or generated meBaanges.

SEE ALSO KEYWORD(S)

•   Generated MeBaanges

tcedi7801m000   single-occ (4)   Form 1-1

```
+------------------------------------------------------------------------------+
| Delete History of Generated MeBaanges                     Company: 000  |
|------------------------------------------------------------------------------|
|                                                                              |
| Date Sent          to  : 1........                                          |
| Time Sent          to  :   2....                                            |
|                                                                              |
|   +------------------------+                                                 |
|   | EDI MeBaange :   3_____ |                                                |
|   | Number       : 4_____ |                                               |
```

```
|   +----------------------+                                                    |
|                                                                               |
+-------------------------------------------------------------------------------+
```
1.   Date Sent
2.   Time Sent
3.   EDI MeBaange
This code uniquely identifies an EDI meBaange. Depending on the direction, it
identifies an incoming or outgoing meBaange.
4.   Number
The number of the document sent.
31.2 Delete History of Received MeBaanges (tcedi7802m000)
SESSION OBJECTIVE
To delete the history and reference data of received meBaanges.
SEE ALSO KEYWORD(S)
•   Received MeBaanges

tcedi7802m000   single-occ (4)   Form 1-1
```
+-------------------------------------------------------------------------------+
| Delete History of Received MeBaanges                          Company: 000 |
|-------------------------------------------------------------------------------|
|                                                                               |
|  Batch Number              from : 1........                                   |
|                            to   : 2.......                                    |
|                                                                               |
|  Organization              from :        3..                                  |
|                            to   :        4..                                  |
|                                                                               |
|  EDI MeBaange              from :     5.....                                  |
|                            to   :     6.....                                  |
|                                                                               |
|  Delete Received Batch References: 7....                                      |
|                                                                               |
|  +-------------------------+                                                   |
|  | EDI MeBaange :      8_____|                                                 |
|  | Number       : 9_____ |                                                |
|  +-------------------------+                                                   |
|                                                                               |
+-------------------------------------------------------------------------------+
```
1.   Batch Number from
2.   Batch Number to
3.   Organization from
4.   Organization to
5.   EDI MeBaange from
6.   EDI MeBaange to
7.   Answer on question y/n
8.   EDI MeBaange
This code uniquely identifies an EDI meBaange. Depending on the direction, it
identifies an incoming or outgoing meBaange.
9.   Number
The internal number (generated within BAAN IV). It may for instance be an order
number.
32   Introduction to MeBaange Data
32.1 General
OBJECTIVE OF BUSINESS OBJECT
This business object allows you to manage EDI meBaanges that have not yet been
successfully processed.
For outgoing EDI meBaanges, this includes "MeBaanges to be Generated", which
represent the meBaange data that has been collected, but for which the outgoing
ASCII file has not yet been generated. For these outgoing EDI meBaanges, you may
display and remove any meBaanges to be generated.
For incoming EDI meBaanges, this includes the "Saved MeBaanges to be Received",
which represent the incoming EDI meBaanges (ASCII files) that were not
successfully processed and updated into the BAAN IV application for which they
were destined. These EDI meBaanges are unsuccessfully processed and updated
either because they had erred data, or because they were set up for interactive

processing for the relation from whom it was received and they were thus stored as "Saved MeBaanges to be Received" without validation.

For these incoming EDI meBaanges, you may display, report, maintain and approve these "Saved MeBaanges to be Received", as well as view any associated errors and warnings ("Received MeBaange Errors"). These EDI meBaanges may not be reprocessed until approved. If it is desired to never reprocess these meBaanges, this business object allows you to delete "saved meBaanges to be received" as well.

Display the procedure and show the sessions in:
- Incoming MeBaange Data
- Outgoing MeBaange Data

32.2 Session Overview

Seq.	Session	Description	Session Usage
1	tcedi7150m000	Maint Saved MeBaanges to be Received	Mandatory
2	tcedi7550m000	Display Saved MeBaanges to be Received	Display
3	tcedi7551m000	Display Received MeBaange Errors	Display
4	tcedi7560m000	Display Received Batch Reference	Display
5	tcedi7450m000	Print Saved MeBaanges to be Received	Print
6	tcedi7451m000	Print Received MeBaange Errors	Print
7	tcedi7250m000	Approve Saved MeBaanges to be Received	Mandatory
8	tcedi7251m000	Print and/or Del Sav MeBaanges to be Re	Optional
9	tcedi7100m000	Maintain MeBaanges to be Generated	Optional
10	tcedi7500m000	Display MeBaanges to be Generated	Display
11	tcedi7552s000	Display Saved MeBaange Data to be Recei	Optional
12	tcedi7299s000	Maintain Selection Criteria	Optional

33 Mandatory Sessions

33.1 Maintain Saved MeBaanges to be Received (tcedi7150m000)

SESSION OBJECTIVE

To view and maintain incoming EDI meBaanges that have not been processed because of either "Interactive" review requirements or errors encountered when validating the data.

HOW TO USE THE SESSION

By choosing the option "Continue [cont.process]" (ASCII version) or "Selection" (GUI version), you can change the selection of the meBaanges shown in this session. By selecting a meBaange, the session "Maintain Saved MeBaange Data to be Received (tcedi7151s000)" is zoomed to in order to view or review the meBaange.

You can zoom to the session "Approve Saved MeBaanges to be Received (tcedi7250s000)" to approve a range of corrected or reviewed meBaanges. You can zoom to the session "Process Saved MeBaanges to be Received (tcedi7252s000)" to re-process these approved meBaanges.

SEE ALSO KEYWORD(S)
- Saved MeBaanges to be Received
- Received MeBaange Errors
- Received Batch Reference

SEE ALSO METHOD(S)
- MeBaange Data (tcedi00080)

```
+------------------------------------------------------------------------+
|  Maintain Saved MeBaanges to be Received                 Company: 000  |
|------------------------------------------------------------------------|
|                                                                        |
|      Batch        Batch Record   Type of Number        Processing Status |
|      Number          Number                                            |
|                                                                        |
|     1........     2.........   3_____  4_____  |
|                                                                        |
+------------------------------------------------------------------------+
```

1.   Batch Number
The identifier associated with the received meBaange data. A batch number is
generated for each network during the processing of incoming EDI meBaanges. For
further information, see keyword(s) "Received Batch Reference".
2.   Batch Record Number
A unique identification for a particular record for a specific batch number.
3.   Type of Number
The number type belonging to this series.
4.   Processing Status
The current status of the saved meBaange data.
Validation Error
Errors have been encountered during the validation process.
Interactive Review
The meBaange data is currently in the process of interactive review.
Unprocessed data
The meBaange data relates to errors found during the validation process.

```
+------------------------------------------------------------------------+
|  Maintain Saved MeBaanges to be Received                 Company: 000  |
|------------------------------------------------------------------------|
|                                                                        |
|     User          Relation      EDI  Network  Org.  Order Type    Appr.  |
|                              MeBaange                              Flag  |
|                                                                        |
|    1..........   2.....  3.....  4_____  5__  6_____   7____  |
|                                                                        |
+------------------------------------------------------------------------+
```

1.   User
The user assigned to the combination of relation and meBaange.
2.   Relation
An outgoing meBaange for this relation is sent to the network address of the
parent relation. For both relations the field "Network Address" in the session
"Maintain Relation Data by Network (tcedi0128m000)" must be filled.
3.   EDI MeBaange
This code uniquely identifies an EDI meBaange. Depending on the direction, it
identifies an incoming or outgoing meBaange.
4.   Network
The unique identification for the network.
5.   Organization
The unique identification for the organization.
6.   Order Type
The order type (within EDI). It is used to indicate whether the corresponding
order is a regular or a return order.
7.   Approval Status
This field indicates whether or not the EDI meBaange data has been approved for
re-processing via the session "Process Saved MeBaanges to be Received
(tcedi7252m000)".
Yes
EDI meBaange data will be re-processed.
No
EDI meBaange data still needs to be evaluated for interactive review or for
error correction.

```
+----------------------------------------------------------------------+
|  Maintain Saved MeBaanges to be Received                Company: 000 |
|----------------------------------------------------------------------|
|                                                                      |
|      File Name        Level  Destination                            |
|                                                                      |
|                                                                      |
|      2_____     1_   3_____                    |
|                                                                      |
+----------------------------------------------------------------------+
```

1.   Level
The number referring to the level of the ASCII file concerned. Each file has its
own level. The first level (level 1) corresponds with the main file. Lower
levels always have higher numbers.
2.   File Name
The name of the ASCII file for the relevant level.
3.   Destination
The destination of the field in case of receiving information or the source of
the field in case of sending information, as defined in the session "Maintain
Conversion Setups (Relationships) (tcedi5112m000)".
MeBaange Overhead
General data relevant to the processing of EDI meBaanges, including for example
sequence numbers and EDI references.
Header (Order) header data.
Line (Order) line data.
Footer
Data relating to the meBaange as a whole, but only known as soon as the
meBaanges is completed, e.g. totals.
33.2 Approve Saved MeBaanges to be Received (tcedi7250m000)
SESSION OBJECTIVE
To globally approve EDI meBaange data that have been reviewed or corrected by
the user.
HOW TO USE THE SESSION
This session provides the capability of approving a range of saved meBaanges
that have been either reviewed or corrected. Once approved, these meBaanges may
be re-processed by using the session "Process Saved MeBaanges to be Received
(tcedi7252m000)".
The saved meBaanges to be received within the ranges entered are approved by
setting the field "Update Approval Status" to "Yes" and choosing the option
"Continue [cont.process]". A report of meBaanges that met the range criteria
will be generated.
If the field "Update Approval Status" is set to "No", no meBaanges will be
approved, but only the report will be generated.
SEE ALSO KEYWORD(S)
•   Saved MeBaanges to be Received
SEE ALSO METHOD(S) "MeBaange Data"

tcedi7250m000   single-occ (4)   Form 1-1

```
+----------------------------------------------------------------------+
|  Approve Saved MeBaanges to be Received                 Company: 000 |
|----------------------------------------------------------------------|
|                                                                      |
|    Batch Number      from : 1........                                |
|                      to   : 2.......                                 |
|    User              from : 3...........                             |
|                      to   : 4..........                              |
|    Organization      from : 5..                                      |
|                      to   : 6..                                      |
|    EDI MeBaange      from : 7.....                                   |
|                      to   : 8.....                                   |
|    Relation          from : 9.....                                   |
|                      to   : 10....                                   |
|    Our Reference     from : 11.............                          |
```

```
|                          to    : 12..............                       |
|                                                                         |
|  Update Approval Status  : 13...                                        |
|                                                                         |
+-------------------------------------------------------------------------+
1.     Batch Number from
2.     Batch Number to
3.     User from
4.     User to
5.     Organization from
6.     Organization to
7.     EDI MeBaange from
8.     EDI MeBaange to
9.     Relation from
10.    Relation to
11.    Our Reference from
12.    Our Reference from
13.    Update Approval Status
```

This field indicates whether the approval status of the saved meBaanges is
updated or not.

Yes

Saved meBaanges to be received that are reported by this session will be updated
with an "approved" status.

No

Saved meBaanges that fall within the ranges entered in this session will be
reported without affecting the existing approval statuses.

34   Optional Sessions

34.1 Print and/or Delete Saved MeBaanges to be Received (tcedi7251m000)

SESSION OBJECTIVE

To delete incoming EDI meBaanges that have been saved.

HOW TO USE THE SESSION

This session provides the capability of deleting a range of meBaanges that have
been saved because of interactive review or error correction. This session is
only needed if you plan to never process the EDI meBaange data for update into
the BAAN IV application.

Enter the ranges and set the field "Delete Saved MeBaanges" to "Yes" and choose
the option "Continue [cont.process]" to delete meBaanges. The meBaanges that
meet the range criteria will be deleted and a report of the deleted meBaanges
will be generated. By setting the field "Delete Saved MeBaanges" to "No",
meBaanges will not actually be deleted, but only the report is generated.

SEE ALSO KEYWORD(S)

•   Saved MeBaanges to be Received

SEE ALSO METHOD(S) "MeBaange Data"

```
tcedi7251m000                              single-occ (4)    Form 1-2 >
+-------------------------------------------------------------------------+
|  Print and/or Delete Saved MeBaanges to be Received    Company: 000 |
|-------------------------------------------------------------------------|
|                                                                         |
|  Batch Number          from : 1........                                 |
|                        to   : 2........                                 |
|  User                  from : 3...........                              |
|                        to   : 4..........                               |
|  Organization          from : 5..                                       |
|                        to   : 6..                                       |
|  EDI MeBaange          from : 7.....                                    |
|                        to   : 8.....                                    |
|  Relation              from : 9.....                                    |
|                        to   : 10....                                    |
|  Our Reference         from : 11..............                          |
|                        to   : 12..............                          |
|                                                                         |
+-------------------------------------------------------------------------+
1.     Batch Number from
```

```
2.    Batch Number to
3.    User from
4.    User to
5.    Organization from
6.    Organization to
7.    EDI MeBaange from
8.    EDI MeBaange to
9.    Relation from
10.   Relation to
11.   Our Reference from
12.   Our Reference from
```

```
+-----------------------------------------------------------------------+
| Print and/or Delete Saved MeBaanges to be Received     Company: 000 |
|-----------------------------------------------------------------------|
|                                                                       |
| Type of Number            from : 1........................           |
|                           to   : 2........................           |
| Network                   from : 3.....                              |
|                           to   : 4.....                              |
| Order Type                from : 5...............................    |
|                           to   : 6...............................    |
|                                                                       |
|                                                                       |
| Delete Saved MeBaanges         : 7....                               |
|                                                                       |
| Delete Received Batch References: 8....                              |
|                                                                       |
+-----------------------------------------------------------------------+
```

```
1.    Type of Number from
2.    Type of Number to
3.    Network from
4.    Network to
5.    Order Type from
6.    Order Type to
7.    Delete Saved MeBaanges
```
This field indicates whether meBaanges are actually deleted or not.
Yes
Saved meBaanges to be received that are reported by running this session will
also be deleted.
No
Saved meBaanges that meet the range criteria will not be deleted, but will only
be reported by running this session.
```
8.    Answer on question y/n
```
34.2 Maintain MeBaanges to be Generated (tcedi7100m000)
SESSION OBJECTIVE
To display and optionally delete EDI meBaanges to be generated.
SEE ALSO KEYWORD(S)
•   MeBaanges to be Generated

```
+-----------------------------------------------------------------------+
| Maintain MeBaanges to be Generated                     Company: 000 |
|-----------------------------------------------------------------------|
|                                                                       |
|    EDI    Org.   Network  Parent-  Order Type         Number   Rela- |
| MeBaange                  Relation                             tion  |
|                                                                       |
|   1.....   6__   2.....   3.....  4................   5.......  7_____ |
|                                                                       |
+-----------------------------------------------------------------------+
```

```
1.    EDI MeBaange
```
This code uniquely identifies an EDI meBaange. Depending on the direction, it
identifies an incoming or outgoing meBaange.

2.   Network
The code uniquely identifying the network.
3.   Parent Relation
The EDI relation to which outgoing meBaanges for the underlying relations are
sent.
4.   Order Type
The order type for the meBaange that can be generated.
5.   Number
The corresponding number. It can be an order number, invoice number, etc.
6.   Organization
The code which uniquely identifies the organization.
7.   Relation
An outgoing meBaange for this relation is sent to the network address of the
parent relation. For both relations the field "Network Address" in the session
"Maintain Relation Data by Network (tcedi0128m000)" must be filled.

34.3 Display Saved MeBaange Data to be Received (tcedi7552s000)

```
tcedi7552s000                        zoom        single-occ (4)   Form 1-5 >
+-Display Saved MeBaange Data to be Received--------------------------------+
|                                                                          |
| Batch Number : 1_____                                               |
|                                                                          |
| 2_____  : 3...................................... 4_____ |
| 2_____  : 3...................................... 4_____ |
| 2_____  : 3...................................... 4_____ |
| 2_____  : 3...................................... 4_____ |
| 2_____  : 3...................................... 4_____ |
| 2_____  : 3...................................... 4_____ |
| 2_____  : 3...................................... 4_____ |
| 2_____  : 3...................................... 4_____ |
| 2_____  : 3...................................... 4_____ |
| 2_____  : 3...................................... 4_____ |
|                                                                          |
| Error/Warning: 5_____ |
|               6_____  |
|                                                                          |
| More MeBaanges: 7_____                                                    |
|                                                                          |
+--------------------------------------------------------------------------+
```

1.   Batch Number
The identifier associated with the received meBaange data. A batch number is
generated for each network during the processing of incoming EDI meBaanges. For
further information, see keyword(s) "Received Batch Reference".
2.   Program domain string
3.   Program domain string
4.   Program domain string
5.   Description 1
The first line of the error/warning meBaange associated with the incoming EDI
data.
6.   Description 2
The second line of the error/warning meBaange associated to the incoming EDI
data.
7.   More Error/Warning

```
tcedi7552s000                        zoom        single-occ (4) < Form 2-5 >
+-Display Saved MeBaange Data to be Received--------------------------------+
|                                                                          |
| Batch Number : 1_____                                               |
|                                                                          |
| 2_____  : 3...................................... 4_____ |
| 2_____  : 3...................................... 4_____ |
| 2_____  : 3...................................... 4_____ |
| 2_____  : 3...................................... 4_____ |
| 2_____  : 3...................................... 4_____ |
| 2_____  : 3...................................... 4_____ |
```

```
| 2_____ : 3...................................... 4_____ |
| 2_____ : 3...................................... 4_____ |
| 2_____ : 3...................................... 4_____ |
| 2_____ : 3...................................... 4_____ |
|                                                                           |
| Error/Warning: 5_____    |
|                6_____    |
|                                                                           |
| More MeBaanges: 7_____                                                     |
|                                                                           |
+---------------------------------------------------------------------------+
```

1.   Batch Number
The identifier associated with the received meBaange data. A batch number is
generated for each network during the processing of incoming EDI meBaanges. For
further information, see keyword(s) "Received Batch Reference".
2.   Program domain string
3.   Program domain string
4.   Program domain string
5.   Description 1
The first line of the error/warning meBaange associated with the incoming EDI
data.
6.   Description 2
The second line of the error/warning meBaange associated to the incoming EDI
data.
7.   More Error/Warning

```
tcedi7552s000                    zoom       single-occ (4) < Form 3-5 >
+-Display Saved MeBaange Data to be Received--------------------------------+
|                                                                           |
| Batch Number : 1_____                                                |
|                                                                           |
| 2_____ : 3...................................... 4_____ |
| 2_____ : 3...................................... 4_____ |
| 2_____ : 3...................................... 4_____ |
| 2_____ : 3...................................... 4_____ |
| 2_____ : 3...................................... 4_____ |
| 2_____ : 3...................................... 4_____ |
| 2_____ : 3...................................... 4_____ |
| 2_____ : 3...................................... 4_____ |
| 2_____ : 3...................................... 4_____ |
| 2_____ : 3...................................... 4_____ |
|                                                                           |
| Error/Warning: 5_____    |
|                6_____    |
|                                                                           |
| More MeBaanges: 7_____                                                     |
|                                                                           |
+---------------------------------------------------------------------------+
```

1.   Batch Number
The identifier associated with the received meBaange data. A batch number is
generated for each network during the processing of incoming EDI meBaanges. For
further information, see keyword(s) "Received Batch Reference".
2.   Program domain string
3.   Program domain string
4.   Program domain string
5.   Description 1
The first line of the error/warning meBaange associated with the incoming EDI
data.
6.   Description 2
The second line of the error/warning meBaange associated to the incoming EDI
data.
7.   More Error/Warning

```
tcedi7552s000                    zoom       single-occ (4) < Form 4-5 >
+-Display Saved MeBaange Data to be Received--------------------------------+
```

```
|                                                                             |
| Batch Number : 1_____                                                  |
|                                                                             |
| 2_____ : 3........................................ 4_____ |
| 2_____ : 3........................................ 4_____ |
| 2_____ : 3........................................ 4_____ |
| 2_____ : 3........................................ 4_____ |
| 2_____ : 3........................................ 4_____ |
| 2_____ : 3........................................ 4_____ |
| 2_____ : 3........................................ 4_____ |
| 2_____ : 3........................................ 4_____ |
| 2_____ : 3........................................ 4_____ |
| 2_____ : 3........................................ 4_____ |
|                                                                             |
| Error/Warning: 5_____ |
|                6_____ |
|                                                                             |
| More MeBaanges: 7_____                                                      |
|                                                                             |
+-----------------------------------------------------------------------------+
```

1.   Batch Number
The identifier associated with the received meBaange data. A batch number is
generated for each network during the processing of incoming EDI meBaanges. For
further information, see keyword(s) "Received Batch Reference".
2.   Program domain string
3.   Program domain string
4.   Program domain string
5.   Description 1
The first line of the error/warning meBaange associated with the incoming EDI
data.
6.   Description 2
The second line of the error/warning meBaange associated to the incoming EDI
data.
7.   More Error/Warning

```
tcedi7552s000                      zoom        single-occ (4) < Form 5-5
+-Display Saved MeBaange Data to be Received------------------------------+
|                                                                          |
| Batch Number : 1_____                                               |
|                                                                          |
| 2_____ : 3..................................... 4_____     |
| 2_____ : 3..................................... 4_____     |
| 2_____ : 3..................................... 4_____     |
| 2_____ : 3..................................... 4_____     |
| 2_____ : 3..................................... 4_____     |
| 2_____ : 3..................................... 4_____     |
| 2_____ : 3..................................... 4_____     |
| 2_____ : 3..................................... 4_____     |
| 2_____ : 3..................................... 4_____     |
| 2_____ : 3..................................... 4_____     |
|                                                                          |
| Error/Warning: 5_____  |
|                6_____  |
|                                                                          |
| More MeBaanges: 7_____                                                   |
|                                                                          |
+--------------------------------------------------------------------------+
```

1.   Batch Number
The identifier associated with the received meBaange data. A batch number is
generated for each network during the processing of incoming EDI meBaanges. For
further information, see keyword(s) "Received Batch Reference".
2.   Program domain string
3.   Program domain string
4.   Program domain string

5.   Description 1
The first line of the error/warning meBaange associated with the incoming EDI
data.
6.   Description 2
The second line of the error/warning meBaange associated to the incoming EDI
data.
7.   More Error/Warning
34.4 Maintain Selection Criteria (tcedi7299s000)
SESSION OBJECTIVE
To view and maintain saved meBaanges to be received with more refined selection
criteria. You can select specific ranges of information, as well as specific
meBaange statuses.
SEE ALSO KEYWORD(S)
•   Saved MeBaanges to be Received
•   Received MeBaange Errors
•   Received Batch Reference

```
tcedi7299s000                                single-occ (4)   Form 1-2 >
+--Maintain Selection Criteria-------------------------------------------+
|                                                                        |
|  Batch Number          from : 1........                                |
|                        to   : 2.......                                 |
|  User                  from : 3..........                              |
|                        to   : 4..........                             |
|  Relation              from : 5.....                                  |
|                        to   : 6.....                                   |
|  EDI MeBaange          from : 7.....                                   |
|                        to   : 8.....                                   |
|  Type of Number        from : 9........................               |
|                        to   : 10.......................                |
|  Order Type            from : 11..................................     |
|                        to   : 12..................................     |
|                                                                        |
+------------------------------------------------------------------------+
```
1.   Batch Number from
2.   Batch Number to
3.   User from
4.   User to
5.   Relation from
6.   Relation to
7.   EDI MeBaange from
8.   EDI MeBaange to
9.   Type of Number from
10.   Type of Number to
11.   Order Type from
12.   Order Type to
```
tcedi7299s000                                single-occ (4) < Form 2-2
+--Maintain Selection Criteria-------------------------------------------+
|                                                                        |
|  Our Reference         from : 1..............                          |
|                        to   : 2..............                          |
|  Network               from : 3.....                                   |
|                        to   : 4.....                                   |
|  Organization          from : 5..                                      |
|                        to   : 6..                                      |
|  Level                 from : 7.                                       |
|                        to   : 8.                                       |
|                                                                        |
|  +--------Processing Status-------+  +------Approval Status------+     |
|  |                                |  |                           |  |  |
|  |  Error             : 9....     |  |  Approved    : 12...       |  |  |
|  |  Interactive Review : 10...    |  |  Not Approved: 13...       |  |  |
|  |  Unprocessed       : 11...     |  |                           |  |  |
|  |                                |  |                           |  |  |
```

```
|   +-----------------------------+  +------------------------+   |
|                                                                 |
+-----------------------------------------------------------------+
1.    Our Reference from
2.    Our Reference to
3.    Network from
4.    Network to
5.    Organization from
6.    Organization to
7.    Level from
8.    Level to
9.    Error
```
This field indicates whether meBaanges with the processing status "Validation
Error" are selected or not.
Yes
Such meBaanges are selected.
No
Such meBaanges are not selected.
10.   Interactive Review
This field indicates whether meBaanges with the processing status "Interactive
Review" are selected or not.
Yes
Such meBaanges are selected.
No
Such meBaanges are not selected.
11.   Unprocessed
This field indicates whether meBaanges with the processing status "Unprocessed
data" are selected or not.
Yes
Such meBaanges are selected.
No
Such meBaanges are not selected.
12.   Approved
This field indicates whether meBaanges with the status "Approved" are selected
or not.
Yes
Such meBaanges are selected.
No
Such meBaanges are not selected.
13.   Not Approved
This field indicates whether meBaanges with approval status "Not Approved" are
selected or not.
Yes
Such meBaanges are selected.
No
Such meBaanges are not selected.
35   Other Print Sessions
35.1 Print Saved MeBaanges to be Received (tcedi7450m000)
SESSION OBJECTIVE
To print ranges of meBaanges to be received.
HOW TO USE THE SESSION
You can print a list of meBaanges depending on approval status and you can
choose to include error/warning meBaanges.
SEE ALSO KEYWORD(S)
•   Saved MeBaanges to be Received

```
tcedi7450m000                          single-occ (4)   Form 1-2 >
+----------------------------------------------------------------------+
| Print Saved MeBaanges to be Received              Company: 000 |
|----------------------------------------------------------------------|
|                                                                      |
| Batch Number         from : 1........                                |
|                      to   : 2........                                |
| User                 from : 3..........                             |
```

```
|                          to    : 4...........                           |
|  Relation              from  : 5.....                                    |
|                          to    : 6.....                                  |
|  EDI MeBaange          from  : 7.....                                     |
|                          to    : 8.....                                   |
|  Type of Number        from  : 9........................                 |
|                          to    : 10......................                |
|                                                                          |
+--------------------------------------------------------------------------+
1.    Batch Number from
2.    Batch Number to
3.    User from
4.    User to
5.    Relation from
6.    Relation to
7.    EDI MeBaange from
8.    EDI MeBaange to
9.    Type of Number from
10.   Type of Number to
```

tcedi7450m000   single-occ (4) < Form 2-2

```
+--------------------------------------------------------------------------+
|  Print Saved MeBaanges to be Received                   Company: 000  |
|--------------------------------------------------------------------------|
|                                                                          |
|  Network               from  : 1.....                                    |
|                          to    : 2.....                                   |
|  Organization          from  : 3..                                       |
|                          to    : 4..                                      |
|  Order Type            from  : 5................................         |
|                          to    : 6................................        |
|  Our Reference         from  : 7..............                           |
|                          to    : 8..............                          |
|  Processing Status     from  : 9................                         |
|                          to    : 10...............                       |
|                                                                          |
|  Approval Status               : 11........                              |
|  Print MeBaange Errors         : 12...                                   |
|                                                                          |
+--------------------------------------------------------------------------+
1.    Network from
2.    Network to
3.    Organization from
4.    Organization to
5.    Order Type from
6.    Order Type to
7.    Our Reference from
8.    Our Reference to
9.    Processing Status from
10.   Processing Status to
11.   Approval Status
```
This field indicates whether EDI meBaanges that are approved, unapproved or
meBaanges with either status are printed.
Approved
Only approved EDI meBaange data will be reported.
Not Approved
Only unapproved EDI meBaange data will be reported.
ALL
All EDI meBaange data will be reported, regardless of approval status.
12.   Print MeBaange Errors
This field indicates whether error/warning meBaanges associated with the saved
meBaange to be received are included in the report or not.
Yes

Error/warning meBaanges associated to the incoming EDI meBaange data will be included in the report.
No
Error/warning meBaanges will not be included in the report.
35.2 Print Received MeBaange Errors (tcedi7451m000)
SESSION OBJECTIVE
To print errors that have been encountered while validating the incoming EDI meBaanges.
HOW TO USE THE SESSION
The validation errors or warnings associated with the meBaanges within the entered ranges are printed. Choose "Continue [cont.process]" to print the receive meBaange errors either by batch number or by user, relation and meBaange.
SEE ALSO KEYWORD(S)
•   Received MeBaange Errors

```
tcedi7451m000                              single-occ (4)    Form 1-1
+--------------------------------------------------------------------+
| Print Received MeBaange Errors                    Company: 000 |
|--------------------------------------------------------------------|
|                                                                    |
| Batch Number         from : 1........                              |
|                      to   : 2.......                               |
| Batch Record Number from : 3.......                               |
|                      to   : 4.......                               |
| User                 from : 5..........                            |
|                      to   : 6..........                            |
| Relation             from : 7.....                                 |
|                      to   : 8.....                                 |
| EDI MeBaange         from : 9.....                                 |
|                      to   : 10....                                 |
|                                                                    |
+--------------------------------------------------------------------+
```

1.   Batch Number from
2.   Batch Number to
3.   Batch Record Number from
4.   Batch Record Number to
5.   User from
6.   User to
7.   Relation from
8.   Relation to
9.   EDI MeBaange from
10.   EDI MeBaange to
GLO - Global Localization

1   Introduction to Global Localisation
1.1   Session Overview

Seq.	Session	Description	Session Usage
10	tcmcsl140m000	Maintain Tax Authority Group Codes	Optional
11	tcmcsl137m000	Maintain Tax Authority Codes	Optional
12	tcmcsl136m000	Maintain Tax Codes by Postal Code	Mandatory
13	tcmcsl138m000	Maintain Exceptions for Taxes - Sales	Optional
14	tcmcsl139m000	Maintain Exceptions by Tax Location	Optional
15	tcmcsl199m000	Test Tax Structure	Additional

16	tcmcs1141m000	Maintain Reasons for Tax Exemptions	Optional
17	tcmcs1142m000	Maint Tax Exemp for Cust by Tax Authori	Optional
18	tcmcs1143m000	Maintain States	Mandatory
18	tcmcs1201m000	Globally Change Tax Rates by Tax Author	Optional
19	tcmcs1543m000	Display States	Display
20	tcmcs1443m000	Print States	Print
100	tcmcs1436m000	Print Tax Codes by Postal Code	Print
101	tcmcs1437m000	Print Tax Authority Codes	Print
102	tcmcs1438m000	Print Exceptions for Taxes - Sales	Print
103	tcmcs1439m000	Print Exceptions by Tax Location	Print
104	tcmcs1440m000	Print Tax Authority Group Codes	Print
105	tcmcs1536m000	Display Tax Codes by Postal Code	Display
106	tcmcs1536s000	Display Tax Codes by Postal Code	Display
107	tcmcs1537m000	Display Tax Authority Codes	Display
108	tcmcs1537s000	Display Tax Authority Codes	Display
109	tcmcs1538m000	Display Exceptions for Taxes - Sales	Display
110	tcmcs1538s000	Display Exceptions for Taxes - Sales	Display
111	tcmcs1539m000	Display Exceptions by Tax Location	Display
112	tcmcs1539s000	Display Exceptions by Tax Location	Display
113	tcmcs1540m000	Display Tax Authority Groups	Display
114	tcmcs1540s000	Display Tax Authority Groups	Display
115	tcmcs1541m000	Display Reasons for Tax Exemptions	Optional
116	tcmcs1541s000	Display Reasons for Tax Exemptions	Optional
117	tcmcs1542m000	Display Tax Exemp for Cust by Tax Autho	Optional
118	tcmcs1441m000	Print Reasons for Tax Exemptions	Print
119	tcmcs1442m000	Print Tax Exemp for Cust by Tax Authori	Print
201	tccom1136m000	Maintain Supplier's 1099 Details	Mandatory
202	tccom1436m000	Print Supplier's 1099 Details	Print
203	tccom1536m000	Display Supplier's 1099 Details	Display
204	tccom1536s000	Display Supplier's 1099 Details	Display
205	tccom1137m000	Maintain Payer's 1099 Details	Mandatory

| 206 | tccoml537m000 | Display Payer's 1099 Details | Display |
| 207 | tccoml437m000 | Print Payer's 1099 Details | Print |

2   Mandatory Sessions
2.1   Maintain Tax Codes by Postal Code (tcmcsl136m000)

SESSION OBJECTIVE

To define the default Tax Code related to a destination Postal Code. These
defaults are used when maintaining orders or invoices within BAAN IV.
The mapping of Postal Codes to Tax Codes is done by range. Specific or partial
codes may be used to define the range. Only the 'from' Postal Code is entered.
Any destination Postal Code which is equal to or greater than the 'from code'
entered on a line and less than the 'from code' entered on the following line
will default to the tax code assigned to that line.

SEE ALSO METHOD(S)
•   Tables for Destination Sales Tax

SEE ALSO KEYWORD(S)
•   Tax Codes by Postal Code

HOW TO USE THE SESSION

This session can be executed if the parameter "Destination Taxes Applicable"
(dstx) is set to 'Yes' in the Maintain COM Parameters (tccom0000m000) session.
Tax Codes are assigned to Postal Codes per country. The country codes and the
Tax Codes must be defined before this session can be executed.

```
tcmcsl136m000                                    multi/group (3    Form 1-1
+----------------------------------------------------------------------+
| Maintain Tax Codes by Postal Code                     Company: 000  |
|----------------------------------------------------------------------|
|                                                                      |
|  Country: 1..   2_____                       |
|                                                                      |
|  From Postal Code   Tax Code   Description                           |
|                                                                      |
|  3........          4.......  5_____         |
|                                                                      |
+----------------------------------------------------------------------+
```

1.   Country
The code of the Country for which Tax Codes are to be defined by Postal Code.
The data to be entered must be defined in the session "Maintain Countries
(tcmcs0110m000)"

2.   Description

3.   Postal Code
The Postal Codes which are to be mapped to the appropriate Tax Codes. This is a
'From' value which is used to define a range, so partial Postal Codes are
accepted.
Example:
The following Postal Codes and Tax Codes are entered

From Postal Code	Tax Code
	400
94	200
94880	500
95050	100
9999999999	300

Any Postal Code which is less than 94 will default to a Tax Code of 400, any
Postal Code which is greater than or equal to 94 but less than 94880 will
default to a Tax Code of 200, and so on.

4.   Tax Code
This is the Tax Code to be linked the range of Postal Codes between the 'from
code' defined on this line and the 'from code' defined on the following line.
The Tax Code should have already been defined in the Maintain Tax Codes
(tcmcs0137m000) session.

5.   Description

2.2 Maintain States (tcmcsl143m000)

SESSION OBJECTIVE

To maintain state codes for a country. State codes are used in electronic filing of 1099-MISC Income. They are assigned to both the payer (company) and payee (supplier) in the Maintain Payer's 1099 Details (tccoml137m000) and Maintain Supplier's 1099 Details (tccoml136m000) sessions.

SEE ALSO KEYWORD(S)

• States

HOW TO USE THE SESSION

Select the "Insert Record(s) [add.set]" option to insert a new state code.

```
tcmcsl143m000                                   multi/group (3   Form 1-1
+----------------------------------------------------------------------+
| Maintain States                                        Company: 000  |
|----------------------------------------------------------------------|
|                                                                      |
| Country: 1.. 2_____                                |
|                                                                      |
| State   Description                                                  |
|                                                                      |
|    3.  4............................                                 |
|                                                                      |
+----------------------------------------------------------------------+
```

1. Country

The code by which the country is recognized in BAAN IV.

2. Description

3. State

The code by which the state is recognized for the corresponding country.

4. Description

The description of the state belonging to the country code.

2.3 Maintain Supplier's 1099 Details (tccoml136m000)

SESSION OBJECTIVE

To identify a particular supplier as one who receives 1099-MISC Income payments. Any payments to this supplier which reference a payment reason code that is associated to a 1099-MISC Income box number will be included in 1099-MISC Income reporting for the year.

SEE ALSO KEYWORD(S)

• Supplier's 1099 Details

SEE ALSO METHOD(S)

• IRS 1099-MISC Reporting

HOW TO USE THE SESSION

Choose option "Insert Record(s) [add.set]" to enter 1099 details for a supplier. The supplier must have already been created with the Maintain Suppliers (tccom2101m000) session. tccoml136m000   single-occ (1)   Form 1-1

```
+----------------------------------------------------------------------+
| Maintain Supplier's 1099 Details                       Company: 000  |
|----------------------------------------------------------------------|
|                                                                      |
| Supplier Number                : 1.....  2_____      |
|                                                                      |
| 1099 Name                      : 3.................................  |
| Payee Name Control             : 4...                                |
| Country                        :    5__  6_____     |
| City                           : 7...............................    |
| State                          :    8.  9_____      |
| ZIP Code                       : 10........                          |
| Foreign (non-U.S.) Entity      : 11...                               |
| Direct Sales Indicator         : 12...                               |
| Type of Tax ID                 : 13.                                 |
| Income Tax Reporting Site      : 14.................                 |
| Income Tax Type                : 15.................                 |
| Account Number 1099            : 16..........................        |
| 2nd TIN                        : 17...                               |
```

```
|   State/Payer's State Number Box 12: 18.................                    |
|                                                                             |
+-----------------------------------------------------------------------------+
```
1.   Supplier Number
2.   Name
The first part of the supplier's name.
3.   1099 Name
The 1099 Name is used to override the first line of the supplier's name from the
Maintain Suppliers (tccom2101m000) session when reporting 1099-MISC Income.
This field should be used in cases where an individual is doing business under a
fictitious business name. For example, John Smith does business as JS
Consulting. Payments are created in the name of JS Consulting, but 1099-MISC
forms must show his actual name of John Smith.
If this field is left empty, the name from the supplier master will be used for
1099-MISC Income reporting.
4.   Payee Name Control
The payee name control defaults to the first four characters of the payee's 1099
name. If the payee's 1099 name is null, then the payee name control defaults to
the first four characters of the supplier's name.
5.   Country
The country where the supplier is established. The country code is:
•   printed on documents;
•   used in combination with the Tax code of the item in order to retrieve the
correct Tax percentage;
•   used as sorting criterion for the purchase statistics.
6.   Description
7.   City
The payee's 1099 city. This defaults to the city from the supplier table.
Note: State should not be included in this field
8.   State
The state code of the country to which the payee (supplier) belongs.
9.   Description
The description of the state belonging to the country code.
10.   ZIP Code
The payee's 1099 ZIP code. This defaults to the postal code from the supplier
table.
11.   Foreign (non-U.S.) Entity
The foreign country indicator is required for electronic filing of 1099
information.
Yes
This indicates that the payee is in a foreign country.
No
This indicates that the payee is not in a foreign country.
12.   Direct Sales Indicator
Indicates sales of $5,000 or more for consumer products to a person on a
buy/sell, deposit/commission, or other commission basis for resale anywhere
other than in a permanent retail establishment.
Yes
An "X" will be printed on box 9 of the 1099 paper form and the appropriate
position will be flagged in 1099 electronic filing.
No
No direct sales indicator will be in included on paper or electonic filing of
1099 informaton.
13.   Type of Tax ID
Enter the type of tax ID. The type of tax ID is required for electronic filing
of 1099-MISC Income information.
SSN The supplier is an individual and the tax ID number is a Social Security
Number
EIN The supplier is a partnership or corporation and the tax ID number is an
Employer Identification Number.
N/A The type of tax ID number is not known
14.   Income Tax Reporting Site

This field is used to record the place where 1099-MISC Income is to be reported. This is for information purposes only, it has no impact on the 1099-MISC Income forms or electronic filing.

15.   Income Tax Type

This field is used to record the tax type of the supplier. For example, individual, partnership, or corporation. This is for information purposes and has no impact on 1099-MISC Income forms or electronic filing.

16.   Account Number 1099

The 1099-MISC Income account number is an optional field. It can be used as a way of identifying the supplier to you when looking at the printed 1099-MISC forms. It will appear in the lower left corner of the 1099-MISC Income form.

17.   2nd TIN

The 2nd TIN Number field is used to indicate that 2 notices have already been received from the IRS for an incorrect taxpayer identification number given by the supplier.

Yes

An "X" will be printed in the 2nd TIN number box on the bottom of the 1099 MISC Income form for the supplier to indicate to the IRS that no more notices should be sent to you.No

An "X" will not be printed in the 2nd TIN number box of the 1099-MISC Income form to indicate to the IRS that you should be notified if the supplier's TIN number is incorrect.

18.   State/Payer's State Number Box 12

The State Payer's State Number is used to record your state taxpayer's identification number for the state where this supplier is located. It will be printed in box 12 of the
1099-MISC Income form.

The State Payer's number will not be included if filing electronically.

2.4   Maintain Payer's 1099 Details (tccoml137m000)

SESSION OBJECTIVE

To maintain payer's 1099 details

SEE ALSO KEYWORD(S)

•   Payer's 1099 Details

SEE ALSO METHOD(S)

•   IRS 1099-MISC Reporting

HOW TO USE THE SESSION

Choose option "Insert Record(s) [add.set]" to add 1099 details for a company

```
tccoml137m000                                    single-occ (1)    Form 1-1
+-----------------------------------------------------------------------------+
| Maintain Payer's 1099 Details                            Company: 000  |
|-----------------------------------------------------------------------------|
|                                                                             |
| Company                       : 1..  2_____    |
|                                                                             |
| Country                       : 3__  4_____      |
| City                          : 5...........................              |
| State                         :  6.  7_____      |
| ZIP Code                      : 8.........                                |
| Foreign (non-U.S.) Entity: 9....                                          |
| Payer Name Control            : 10..                                      |
| Transmitter Control Code : 11...                                          |
|                                                                             |
+-----------------------------------------------------------------------------+
```

1.   Company

2.   Company Name

The company's name.

3.   Country

The country code of the country where the company is established.

4.   Description

5.   City

The payer's 1099 city. This defaults to the city from the company table.

Note: The state should not be included in this field

6.   State

The state code of the country to which the payer (company) belongs.
7.   Description
The description of the state belonging to the country code.
8.   ZIP Code
The payer's 1099 ZIP code. This defaults to the postal code from the company table.
9.   Foreign (non-U.S.) Entity
The foreign country indicator is required for electronic filing of 1099 information
Yes
This indicates the payer (company) is in a foreign country.
No
This indicates the payer (company) is not in a foreign country.
10.   Payer Name Control
The payer name control defaults to the first four characters of the payer's (company's) name.
11.   Transmitter Control Code
Enter the five character transmitter control code assigned by the IRS.
3   Optional Sessions
3.1   Maintain Tax Authority Group Codes (tcmcsl140m000)
SESSION OBJECTIVE
To maintain tax Authority Group Codes for the purpose of categorizing tax authority codes.
Tax Authorities are assigned to Tax Authority Groups in the Maintain Tax Authority Codes (tcmcsl137m000) session. Tax Authorities can be grouped geographically, by type of jurisdiction, or by any other means that will be meaningful when selecting or sorting tax information for reporting purposes.
SEE ALSO KEYWORD(S)
•   Tax Authority Groups
•   Tax Authority Codes
SEE ALSO METHOD(S)
•   Tables for Destination Sales Tax
HOW TO USE THE SESSION
Select the "Insert Record(s) [add.set]" option to insert a new Tax Authority Group code.

```
tcmcsl140m000                                  multi-occ (2)    Form 1-1
+--------------------------------------------------------------------------+
| Maintain Tax Authority Group Codes                        Company: 000   |
|--------------------------------------------------------------------------|
|                                                                          |
| Auth.        Description                                                 |
| Group                                                                    |
|                                                                          |
|         1..  2.............................                              |
|                                                                          |
+--------------------------------------------------------------------------+
```

1.   Code Tax Authority Group
This is the code which identifies a Tax Authority Group. Tax Authority Groups are used to group similar tax authorities for reporting purposes. For example, Tax Authorities associated to the same type of jurisdiction, such as States, Cities, Counties, or Provinces might be grouped together. Another common way to group Tax Authorities is by geographic area, such as all Cities and Counties within a State.
2.   Description
Description for the Tax Authority Group.
3.2   Maintain Tax Authority Codes (tcmcsl137m000)
SESSION OBJECTIVE
To maintain codes for the tax authorities to which sales taxes must be paid.
Tax Authorities are assigned to Tax Codes by tax line (either single or multiple level). Tax authorities are defined for single level Tax codes in the session Maintain Tax Codes by Country (tcmcs0136m000). For multiple level Tax Codes, they are defined inthe session Maintain Tax Rates by Tax Code (tcmcs0135s000)

Before maintaining Tax Authority Codes, the Tax Authority Groups must be
maintained in the Maintain Tax Authority Group Codes (tcmcsl140m000) session.
Tax reports can be sorted on the tax authority codes entered here with the Print
Tax Summary by Tax Authorities (tfgld1436m000) and the Print Tax Analysis
(tfgld1420m000) sessions.

HOW TO USE THE SESSION

Insert new tax authority codes by using option "Insert Record(s) [add.set]".

```
tcmcsl137m000                                     multi-occ (2)   Form 1-1
+--------------------------------------------------------------------------+
| Maintain Tax Authority Codes                             Company: 000    |
|--------------------------------------------------------------------------|
|                                                                          |
|                                                                          |
| Tax Auth.  Description                   Auth. Description               |
| Code                                     Group                           |
|                                                                          |
| 1........ 2...........................   3.. 4_____    |
|                                                                          |
+--------------------------------------------------------------------------+
```

1.   Tax Authority Code

A Tax Authority is a Government Body with jurisdiction over the sales taxes in a
specific area. The state of California, the province of Ontario, the county of
Dade, and the city of Atlanta are all examples of Tax Authorities. Tax Authority
Codes are maintained here.

2.   Description

Description of the Tax Authority Code is maintained here.

3.   Code Tax Authority Group

This is the code which identifies a Tax Authority Group. Tax Authority Groups
are used to group similar tax authorities for reporting purposes. For example,
Tax Authorities associated to the same type of jurisdiction, such as States,
Cities, Counties, or Provinces might be grouped together. Another common way to
group Tax Authorities is by geographic area, such as all Cities and Counties
within a State.

Tax Authority Group Codes should have already been defined in the Maintain Tax
Authority Group Codes (tcmcsl140m000) session.

4.   Description

Description for the Tax Authority Group.

3.3   Maintain Exceptions for Taxes - Sales (tcmcsl138m000)

SESSION OBJECTIVE

This session is used to maintain exceptions to the default Tax Codes defined in
the Maintain Tax Codes by Postal Code (tcmcsl136m000) and Maintain Exceptions by
Tax Location (tcmcsl139m000) sessions and has a higher priority than both of
these.

The exceptions are defined for 'Sales' transactions and are considered in the
following modules:

Sales
Sales Quotations
Service and Maintenance
Product Configuration
Transport Order Control   (BAAN Transportation)
Warehousing Order Control (BAAN Transportation)

SEE ALSO KEYWORD(S)

•   Exceptions for Taxes - Sales

SEE ALSO METHOD(S)

•   Procedure for Deriving Default Tax Code

HOW TO USE THE SESSION

Exceptions can be defined for a country, customer, item group, project item or
budget item, item, postal code, or any combination of these.

All fields except country code can be left empty. The priority for seeking the
defined combination is as follows:

Country	Customer	Project	Budget	Item	Item-Grp	Postal-code
x	x	x		x	x	x
x	x		x	x	x	x

X	X			X	X	X
X	X	X		X		X
X	X		X	X		X
X	X			X		X
X	X	X		X	X	
X	X		X	X	X	
X	X			X	X	
X	X	X		X		
X	X		X	X		
X	X			X		
X	X				X	X
X	X				X	
X	X					X
X	X					
X		X		X	X	X
X			X	X	X	X
X				X	X	X
X		X		X	X	
X			X	X	X	
X				X	X	
X		X		X	X	
X			X	X	X	
X				X	X	
X		X		X		
X			X	X		
X				X		
X					X	X
X					X	
X						X
X						

Before exceptions can be maintained, the Country Code, Customer, Item Group, Project, Budget, Postal Code, and Tax Code must be maintained.
Blanks will indicate that all customers meeting the rest of the selection criteria should be included
If entered then this customer should have already been defined in the Maintain Customers (tccom1101m000) session. tcmcsl138m000
multi/group (3   Form 1-1

```
+------------------------------------------------------------------------+
| Maintain Exceptions for Taxes - Sales                    Company: 000  |
|------------------------------------------------------------------------|
|                                                                        |
| Country          :           1..  2_____   |
| Customer         :           3..... 4_____  |
| Item Group       :           5..... 6_____   |
| Project          :           7..... 8_____   |
| Budget           :           9..... 10_____   |
| Item             : 11.............  12_____   |
|                                                                        |
| Postal Code  Tax Code   Description                                    |
|                                                                        |
| 13........   14.......   15_____                  |
|                                                                        |
+------------------------------------------------------------------------+
```

1.   Country
This is the Country for which tax code exceptions are to be defined.
The data to be entered must be defined in the session Maintain Countries (tcmcs0110m000).
2.   Description
3.   Customer
This is the Customer Code for which tax code exceptions are to be defined.
Blanks will indicate that all customers meeting the rest of the selection criteria should be included

If entered, the customer should have already defined in the Maintain Customers (tccom1101m000) session.

4.   Name
The first part of the customer's name.

5.   Item Group
This is the Item Group Code for which tax code exceptions are to be defined.

6.   Description

7.   Project
This is the Project Code for which tax code exceptions are to be defined.

8.   Description

9.   Budget
This is the Budget Code for which tax code exceptions are to be defined.

10.   Description
The first line for the description of the budget.

11.   Item
This is the Item Code for which tax code exceptions are to be defined.

12.   Description

13.   Postal Code
This is the Postal Code for which tax code Exceptions are to be defined.

14.   Tax Code
This is the exception Tax Code to be used as a default when the combination of Country, Customer, Item Group, Project, Budget, and Item defined above occurs on an order or invoice.

15.   Description

3.4   Maintain Exceptions by Tax Location (tcmcsl139m000)

SESSION OBJECTIVE
This session is used for maintaining exceptions to the tax codes assigned by postal code in the Maintain Tax Codes by Postal Code (tcmcsl136m000) session. This is neceBaanry when the tax liability for a particular destination is dependent on where the shipment of the goods originated.
Exceptions are only used for determining the tax codes related to Sales, they do not apply to tax on Purchases.

SEE ALSO KEYWORD(S)
•   Exceptions by Tax Location

SEE ALSO METHOD(S)
•   Tables for Destination Sales Tax
•   Procedure for Deriving Default Tax Code

HOW TO USE THE SESSION
Select the "Start Group [start.set]" option to add tax codes for a new country and destination postal code combination.
Select the "OPadd.set" option to add tax codes for an existing country and destination postal code combination

```
tcmcsl139m000                              multi/group (3    Form 1-1
+--------------------------------------------------------------------+
| Maintain Exceptions by Tax Location           Company: 000         |
|--------------------------------------------------------------------|
|                                                                    |
| Country                    : 1.. 2_____         |
| Postal Code Destination    : 3........                             |
|                                                                    |
|     Postal Code For                                                |
| Origin        Postal Add.     Tax Code   Description               |
|                                                                    |
| 4........     5........        6........  7_____ |
|                                                                    |
+--------------------------------------------------------------------+
```

1.   Country
This is the Country code for which "Tax Exceptions by Locations" are to be entered. The data to be entered must be defined in the session Maintain Countries (tcmcs0110m000)

2.   Description

3.   Postal Code Destination

This the Postal Code of the destination location for which "Exceptions by Tax Location" must be entered. In the case of Sales, the Customer's delivery address Postal Code is the Destination Postal Code.

4.   Postal Code Origin

This Origin Postal Code is the Postal Code from where goods are delivered. In the case of Sales, the origin Postal Code is the Postal Code on the address of the warehouse the goods are shipped from.

5.   Postal Code Order Acceptance

This is the Postal Code on the Postal Address of the customer. This field is used if the tax code is dependent on order origin in addition to the shipment origin for a particular destination.

6.   Tax Code

7.   Description

3.5   Maintain Reasons for Tax Exemptions (tcmcsl141m000)

SESSION OBJECTIVE

To define reason codes for Tax Exemptions. Tax exemptions are defined and reason codes are assigned to them in the Maintain Tax Exemptions for Customer by Tax Authority (tcmcsl142m000) session. Tax will not be charged on sales activity which is before the expiration date for a particular customer and tax authority which have been defined as exempt.

Tax exempt sales can be reported in the Print Tax Exemption Analysis (tfgldl410m000) session.

SEE ALSO KEYWORD(S)

•   Reasons for Tax Exemptions
•   Tax Exemptions for Customer by Tax Authority

SEE ALSO METHOD(S)

•   Tax Calculations

HOW TO USE THE SESSION

Select the "Insert Record(s) [add.set]" option to insert a new tax exemption reason code.

```
tcmcsl141m000                              multi-occ (2)    Form 1-1
+-------------------------------------------------------------------------+
|  Maintain Reasons for Tax Exemptions                    Company: 000  |
|-------------------------------------------------------------------------|
|                                                                         |
|  Reason Code  Description                                               |
|                                                                         |
|         1..  2.................................................         |
|                                                                         |
+-------------------------------------------------------------------------+
```

1.   Reason Code

This is a description for the tax exemption reason code specified.

2.   Description

This code specifies the reason why a customer is exempted from sales tax for a particular tax authority. For example, the goods they purchase may be for resale only and thus not subject to tax.

3.6   Maintain Tax Exemptions for Customer by Tax Authority (tcmcsl142m000)

SESSION OBJECTIVE

To define when a customer is exempt from sales tax for a particular tax authority. Any sales activity occuring prior to the expiration date defined for a particular customer and tax authority will not be subject to sales tax. Exempted sales activity can be printed in the Print Tax Exemption Analysis (tfgldl410m000) session.

SEE ALSO KEYWORD(S)

•   Reasons for Tax Exemptions
•   Tax Exemptions for Customer by Tax Authority

SEE ALSO METHOD(S)

•   Tax Calculations

HOW TO USE THE SESSION

Select the "Start Group [start.set]" option to add exemption information for a new customer.

Select the "Insert Record(s) [add.set]" option to add additional exemption information for a particular tax authority and an existing customer.

Note: Tax exemption functionality is only available when the parameters for the tax provider interface are set to no in the Maintain API Parameters (tcapil136m000) and Maintain Tax Provider Parameters (tccoml150m000) sessions.

tcmcsl142m000   multi/group (3   Form 1-1

```
+--------------------------------------------------------------------------+
| Maintain Tax Exemptions for Customer by Tax Authority     Company: 000   |
|--------------------------------------------------------------------------|
|                                                                          |
| Customer: 1.....   2_____                        |
|                                                                          |
| Tax Authority              Expiry Dt.  Exemption Number     Reason       |
|                                                                          |
| 3........  4_____      5........  6...................  7..  8_____ |
|                                                                          |
+--------------------------------------------------------------------------+
```

1.   Customer
This is the customer for which tax exemption information is to be entered.
2.   Name
The first part of the customer's name.
3.   Tax Authority Code
This is the tax authority code for which a particular customer tax exemption is to be entered. Tax authority codes are tied to tax codes in the Maintain Tax Codes by Country (tcmcs0136m000) and Maintain Tax Rates by Tax Code (tcmcs0135s000) sessions for single and multiple level tax codes.
4.   Description
Description of the Tax Authority Code is maintained here.
5.   Expiry Date
This is the date after which the customer's tax exemption will expire for this tax authority. Activity taking place after this date will be subject to sales tax.
6.   Exemption Number
This is the exemption number which has been assigned to the customer by this tax authority. The exemption number can be printed on orders and invoices if the print flag is set to yes for the country of the customer in the Maintain Countries (tcmcs0110m000) session.
7.   Reason Code
This is the reason code for the exemption of tax for this customer and tax authority. Reason codes are defined in the Maintain Reasons for Tax Exemptions (tcmcsl141m000) session.
8.   Description
This code specifies the reason why a customer is exempted from sales tax for a particular tax authority. For example, the goods they purchase may be for resale only and thus not subject to tax.

3.7   Globally Change Tax Rates by Tax Authority (tcmcsl201m000)
SESSION OBJECTIVE
To change the Tax Rates for a Tax Authority Code.
HOW TO USE THE SESSION
Select a Tax Authority Code for which the rate is to be changed. The Tax Authority Code must have been maintained in the Maintain Tax Authority Codes (tcmcsl137m000) session. The new tax rates will be added in the Maintain Single Tax Rates (tcmcs0132s000) and/or Maintain Multiple Tax Rates (tcmcs0133s000) sessions, depending on whether a single or multiple level tax code is involved, wherever the Tax Authority Code is used. If a record already exists for this effective date, it will be replaced by the new values. tcmcsl201m000

zoom   single-occ (4)   Form 1-1

```
+--------------------------------------------------------------------------+
| Globally Change Tax Rates by Tax Authority              Company: 000     |
|--------------------------------------------------------------------------|
|                                                                          |
| Tax Authority Code  : 1........   2_____         |
|                                                                          |
| Tax Authority Group :           3__  4_____      |
|                                                                          |
```

```
| Effective Date        : 5........                                            |
|                                                                              |
| New Rate              :        6..                                           |
| Maximum Tax Amount    : 7.............                                       |
| Tax Base Amount       : 8.............                                       |
| Rate for Excess       :        9..                                          |
|                                                                              |
+------------------------------------------------------------------------------+
```

1.   Tax Authority Code
The Tax Authority Code for which the Tax Rate is to be changed. The Tax rates
will be replaced with the new rate in all the places where this Tax Authority
Code is used.
2.   Description
Description of the Tax Authority Code is maintained here.
3.   Code Tax Authority Group
This is the code which identifies a Tax Authority Group. Tax Authority Groups
are used to group similar tax authorities for reporting purposes. For example,
Tax Authorities associated to the same type of jurisdiction, such as States,
Cities, Counties, or Provinces might be grouped together. Another common way to
group Tax Authorities is by geographic area, such as all Cities and Counties
within a State.
4.   Description
Description for the Tax Authority Group.
5.   Effective Date
The effective date for the new Tax rate. If a rate already exists as of this
date, it will be replaced by the new rate.
6.   New Rate
The new tax rate for the tax authority code.
7.   Maximum Tax Amount
SEE ALSO METHOD(S)
•   Currency Formats
The new maximum tax amount. For further information see "Maximum Tax Amount"
8.   Tax Base Amount
SEE ALSO METHOD(S)
•   Currency Formats
The new maximum tax amount. For further information see "Tax Base Amount"
9.   Rate for Excess Amount
The new maximum tax amount. For further information see "Rate for Excess Amount"
3.8   Display Reasons for Tax Exemptions (tcmcsl541m000)
This session is used to display the reason codes which have been created with
the Maintain Reasons for Tax Exemptions (tcmcsl141m000) session. Reason codes
are associated to a customer and tax authority in the Maintain Tax Exemptions
for Customer by Tax Authority (tcmcsl142m000) session.

```
tcmcsl541m000                                 multi-occ (2)    Form 1-1
+------------------------------------------------------------------------------+
| Display Reasons for Tax Exemptions                        Company: 000  |
|------------------------------------------------------------------------------|
|                                                                              |
| Reason Code  Description                                                     |
|                                                                              |
|      1..  2_____                  |
|                                                                              |
+------------------------------------------------------------------------------+
```

1.   Reason Code
This is a description for the tax exemption reason code specified.
This is a description for the tax exemption reason code specified.
2.   Description
This code specifies the reason why a customer is exempted from sales tax for a
particular tax authority. For example, the goods they purchase may be for
resale only and thus not subject to tax. This code specifies the reason why a
customer is exempted from sales tax for a particular tax authority. For
example, the goods they purchase may be for resale only and thus not subject to
tax.

3.9   Display Reasons for Tax Exemptions (tcmcsl541s000)
This session is used to display the reason codes which have been created with
the Maintain Reasons for Tax Exemptions (tcmcsl141m000) session. Reason codes
are associated to a customer and tax authority in the Maintain Tax Exemptions
for Customer by Tax Authority (tcmcsl142m000) session.

```
tcmcsl541s000                                    multi-occ (2)     Form 1-1
+--Display Reasons for Tax Exemptions------------------------------+
|                                                                  |
|   Reason Code   Description                                      |
|                                                                  |
|        1..    2_____         |
|                                                                  |
+------------------------------------------------------------------+
```

1.   Reason Code
This is a description for the tax exemption reason code specified.
This is a description for the tax exemption reason code specified.
2.   Description
This code specifies the reason why a customer is exempted from sales tax for a
particular tax authority. For example, the goods they purchase may be for
resale only and thus not subject to tax. This code specifies the reason why a
customer is exempted from sales tax for a particular tax authority. For
example, the goods they purchase may be for resale only and thus not subject to
tax.
3.10 Display Tax Exemptions for Customer by Tax Authority (tcmcsl542m000)

```
tcmcsl542m000                                    multi/group (3     Form 1-1
+---------------------------------------------------------------------------+
| Display Tax Exemptions for Customer by Tax Authority      Company: 000    |
|---------------------------------------------------------------------------|
|                                                                           |
|  Customer: 1.....    2_____                    |
|                                                                           |
|  Tax Authority          Expiry Dt.  Exemption Number      Reason          |
|                                                                           |
|  3........  4_____   5........  6_____   7__  8_____   |
|                                                                           |
+---------------------------------------------------------------------------+
```

1.   Customer
This is the customer for which tax exemption information is to be entered.
2.   Name
The first part of the customer's name.
3.   Tax Authority Code
This is the tax authority code for which a particular customer tax exemption is
to be entered. Tax authority codes are tied to tax codes in the Maintain Tax
Codes by Country (tcmcs0136m000) and Maintain Tax Rates by Tax Code
(tcmcs0135s000) sessions for single and multiple level tax codes.
4.   Description
Description of the Tax Authority Code is maintained here.
5.   Expiry Date
This is the date after which the customer's tax exemption will expire for this
tax authority. Activity taking place after this date will be subject to sales
tax.
6.   Exemption Number
This is the exemption number which has been assigned to the customer by this tax
authority. The exemption number can be printed on orders and invoices if the
print flag is set to yes for the country of the customer in the Maintain
Countries (tcmcs0110m000) session.
7.   Reason Code
This is the reason code for the exemption of tax for this customer and tax
authority. Reason codes are defined in the Maintain Reasons for Tax Exemptions
(tcmcsl141m000) session.
8.   Description

This code specifies the reason why a customer is exempted from sales tax for a particular tax authority. For example, the goods they purchase may be for resale only and thus not subject to tax.

4   Other Maintenance Sessions

4.1   Test Tax Structure (tcmcsl199m000)

SESSION OBJECTIVE

To test the tax structure defined with the Maintain Tax Codes by Postal Code (tcmcsl136m000), Maintain Exceptions for Taxes - Sales (tcmcsl138m000), Maintain Exceptions for Taxes - Purchase (tcmcsl146m000), and Maintain Exceptions by Tax Location (tcmcsl139m000) sessions.

The default tax codes which will be used in the following modules can be tested with this session:

1 Sales Control (SLS)
2 Service & Maintenance (SMA)
3 Product Configuration (PCF)
4 Transport Order Control (TOC)
5 Warehouse Order Control (WOC)
6 Purchase Control (PUR)
7 Transport Fuel Control (TFC)

Modules 1 through 5 have the characteristics of Sales. That is, the exceptions defined in the Maintain Exceptions for Taxes - Sales (tcmcsl138m000) session are taken into consideration. In addition to these modules, the Sales Quotation (SLQ) submodule may also be tested.

Modules 6 and 7 have the characteristics of Purchases. The exceptions defined in the Maintain Exceptions for Taxes - Purchase (tcmcsl146m000) session are taken into consideration.

HOW TO USE THE SESSION

The default tax code is derived from the origin, destination and postal address postal codes.

For sales, the origin postal code is the postal code of the warehouse (maintained in the Maintain Warehouses (tcmcs0103m000) session) or in its absence, the postal code of the company (maintained in the Maintain Company Data (tccom0100m000) session). The destination postal code for sales is either the postal code from the specific delivery address, delivery address or customer address, in that order.

For purchases, the origin postal code is that of the supplier address (maintained in the Maintain Suppliers (tccom2101m000) session) and the destination postal code is that of specific delivery, warehouse or company, in that order.

The search path or priority for selecting the default tax code is as follows:

1.   Maintain Exceptions for Taxes - Sales (tcmcsl138m000) for sales or Maintain Exceptions for Taxes - Purchase (tcmcsl146m000) for purchases
2.   Maintain Exceptions by Tax Location (tcmcsl139m000)
3.   Maintain Tax Codes by Postal Code (tcmcsl136m000)

```
tcmcsl199m000                          zoom        single-occ (4)    Form 1-1
+------------------------------------------------------------------------------+
| Test Tax Structure                                          Company: 000  |
|------------------------------------------------------------------------------|
|                                                                              |
|  Module                       :              1..                             |
|  Country                      :              2..                             |
|  Customer/Supplier            :            3.....                            |
|  Item                         : 4...............                            |
|  Postal Code                                                                 |
|  Warehouse                    : 5.........                                  |
|  Specific Delivery/Delivery   : 6.........                                  |
|  Postal Address               : 7.........                                  |
|  Customer/Supplier            : 8.........                                  |
|                                                                              |
|  Project/Budget               :            9.....                           |
|                                                                              |
|  Tax Code                     :       10_____                            |
|                                                                              |
```

```
+--------------------------------------------------------------------------+
1.      Module
2.      Country
3.      Customer
4.      Item Code
5.      Postcode
6.      Postcode
7.      Postcode
8.      Postcode
9.      Project
10.     VAT Code
5       Other Print Sessions
5.1     Print States (tcmcsl443m000)
SESSION OBJECTIVE
To print state codes for a country
SEE ALSO KEYWORD(S)
•       States
tcmcsl443m000                           single-occ (4)    Form 1-1
-----------------------------------------------------------------------------+
| Print States                                          Company: 000  |
|----------------------------------------------------------------------------|
|                                                                    |
| Country   From: 1..                                                |
|           To: 2..                                                  |
|                                                                    |
| State     From:  3.                                                |
|           To:  4.                                                  |
|                                                                    |
+----------------------------------------------------------------------------+
1.      Country
2.      Country
3.      State
4.      State
5.2     Print Tax Codes by Postal Code (tcmcsl436m000)
SESSION AIM To print the details of table "Tax Codes by Postal Code".
tcmcsl436m000                           single-occ (4)    Form 1-1
+----------------------------------------------------------------------------+
| Print Tax Codes by Postal Code                        Company: 000  |
|----------------------------------------------------------------------------|
|                                                                    |
| Country                    From: 1..                               |
|                            To: 2..                                 |
|                                                                    |
| Postal Code                From: 3........                         |
|                            To: 4........                           |
|                                                                    |
+----------------------------------------------------------------------------+
```

1.   Country
Enter the first of the range of Countries for which you want to print the data.
2.   Country
Enter the last of the range of the Countries for which you want to print the data.
3.   Postcode
Enter the first of the range of Postal Codes for which you want to print the data.
4.   Postcode
Enter the last of the range of the Postal Codes for which you want to print the data.
5.3   Print Tax Authority Codes (tcmcsl437m000)
SESSION AIM To print the details of table "Tax Authority Codes". tcmcsl437m000
single-occ (4)   Form 1-1

```
+----------------------------------------------------------------------------+
| Print Tax Authority Codes                             Company: 000  |
```

```
|---------------------------------------------------------------------------|
|                                                                           |
|  Tax Authority Code            From: 1........                            |
|                                  To: 2........                            |
|                                                                           |
+---------------------------------------------------------------------------+
```

1.   Tax Authority Code
Enter the first of the range of the Tax Authority Codes for which you want to
print the data.
2.   Tax Authority Code
Enter the last of the range of the Tax Authority codes for which you want to
print the data.
5.4   Print Exceptions for Taxes - Sales (tcmcsl438m000)
SESSION AIM To print the details of table "Exceptions for Taxes". tcmcsl438m000
single-occ (4)   Form 1-1

```
+---------------------------------------------------------------------------+
|  Print Exceptions for Taxes - Sales                      Company: 000     |
|---------------------------------------------------------------------------|
|                                                                           |
|  Country                From: 1..                                         |
|                           To: 2..                                         |
|                                                                           |
|  Customer               From: 3.....                                      |
|                           To: 4.....                                      |
|                                                                           |
|  Item Group             From: 5..                                         |
|                           To: 6..                                         |
|                                                                           |
|  Item                   From: 7..............                             |
|                           To: 8..............                             |
|                                                                           |
|  Postal Code            From: 9........                                    |
|                           To: 10.......                                   |
|                                                                           |
+---------------------------------------------------------------------------+
```

1.   Country
Enter the first of the range of Countries for which you want to print the data.
2.   Country
Enter the last of the range of the Countries for which you want to print the
data.
3.   Customer
Enter the first of the range of Customers for which you want to print the data.
4.   Customer
Enter the last of the range of Customers for which you want to print the data.
5.   Item Group
Enter the first of the range of Item Group Codes for which you want to print the
data.
6.   Item Group
Enter the last of the range of Item Group Codes for which you want to print the
data.
7.   Item Code
Enter the first of the range of Item Codes for which you want to print the data.
8.   Item Code
Enter the last of the range of Item Codes for which you want to print the data.
9.   Postcode
Enter the first of the range of Postal Codes for which you want to print the
data.
10.   Postcode
Enter the last of the range of Postal Codes for which you want to print the
data.
5.5   Print Exceptions by Tax Location (tcmcsl439m000)
SESSION AIM For printing Exceptions by Tax Locations.
tcmcsl439m000   single-occ (4)   Form 1-1

```
+-----------------------------------------------------------------------+
|  Print Exceptions by Tax Location                      Company: 000   |
|-----------------------------------------------------------------------|
|                                                                       |
|   Country                      From: 1..                              |
|                                  To: 2..                              |
|                                                                       |
|   Postal Code Destination    From: 3.........                         |
|                                To: 4.........                         |
|                                                                       |
|   Postal Code Origin         From: 5.........                         |
|                                To: 6.........                         |
|                                                                       |
|   Postal Add.                From: 7.........                         |
|                                To: 8.........                         |
|                                                                       |
+-----------------------------------------------------------------------+
```

1.   Country
Enter first of the range of Countries for which you want to print the data.
2.   Country
Enter last of the range of Countries for which you want to print the data.
3.   Postcode
Enter first of the range of Postal Codes (Destination) for which you want to
print the data.
4.   Postcode
Enter last of the range of Postal Codes (Destination) for which you want to
print the data.
5.   Postcode
Enter first of the range of Postal Codes (Origin) for which you want to print
the data.
6.   Postcode
Enter last of the range of Postal Codes (Origin) for which you want to print the
data.
7.   Postcode
Enter first of the range of Postal Codes (Postal Address) for which you want to
print the data.
8.   Postcode
Enter last of the range of Postal Codes (Postal Address) for which you want to
print the data.
5.6   Print Tax Authority Group Codes (tcmcsl440m000)
SESSION AIM Print details of Tax Authority Groups. tcmcsl440m000
single-occ (4)   Form 1-1

```
+-----------------------------------------------------------------------+
|  Print Tax Authority Group Codes                       Company: 000   |
|-----------------------------------------------------------------------|
|                                                                       |
|   Code Tax Authority Group     From: 1..                              |
|                                  To: 2..                              |
|                                                                       |
+-----------------------------------------------------------------------+
```

1.   Code Tax Authority Group from
Enter the first of the range of Tax Authority Group Codes for which you want to
print the data.
2.   Code Tax Authority Group to
Enter the last of the range of Tax Authority Group Codes for which you want to
print the data.
5.7   Print Reasons for Tax Exemptions (tcmcsl441m000)
tcmcsl441m000   single-occ (4)   Form 1-1

```
+-----------------------------------------------------------------------+
|  Print Reasons for Tax Exemptions                      Company: 000   |
|-----------------------------------------------------------------------|
|                                                                       |
|   Reason Code  From: 1..                                              |
```

```
|                    To: 2..                                              |
|                                                                         |
+-------------------------------------------------------------------------+
1.      Reason for Tax Exemption
2.      Reason for Tax Exemption
5.8    Print Tax Exemptions for Customer by Tax Authority (tcmcsl442m000)
tcmcsl442m000                              single-occ (4)    Form 1-1
+-------------------------------------------------------------------------+
| Print Tax Exemptions for Customer by Tax Authority      Company: 000 |
|-------------------------------------------------------------------------|
|                                                                         |
| Customer              From:    1.....                                   |
|                         To:    2.....                                   |
|                                                                         |
| Tax Authority Code    From: 3........                                   |
|                         To: 4........                                   |
|                                                                         |
| Expiry Date           From: 5........                                   |
|                         To: 6........                                   |
|                                                                         |
+-------------------------------------------------------------------------+
1.      Customer
2.      Customer
3.      Tax Authority Code
4.      Tax Authority Code
5.      Date
6.      Date
5.9    Print Supplier's 1099 Details (tccoml436m000)
tccoml436m000                              single-occ (4)    Form 1-1
+-------------------------------------------------------------------------+
| Print Supplier's 1099 Details                          Company: 000 |
|-------------------------------------------------------------------------|
|                                                                         |
| Supplier Number          from : 1.....                                 |
|                          to   : 2.....                                 |
|                                                                         |
+-------------------------------------------------------------------------+
1.      Supplier Number
2.      Supplier Number
5.10   Print Payer's 1099 Details (tccoml437m000)
SESSION OBJECTIVE
To print payer's 1099 details
SEE ALSO KEYWORD(S)
•      Payer's 1099 Details
tccoml437m000                              single-occ (4)    Form 1-1
+-------------------------------------------------------------------------+
| Print Payer's 1099 Details                             Company: 000 |
|-------------------------------------------------------------------------|
|                                                                         |
| Company  From: 1..                                                      |
|           To: 2..                                                       |
|                                                                         |
+-------------------------------------------------------------------------+
1.      Company Number
2.      Company Number
6      Introduction to Global Localisation (Tax Provider)
6.1   General
OBJECTIVE OF BUSINESS OBJECT
```

This i-function allows you to interface between BAAN IV and third-party tax providers such as TAXWARE's Master Tax System or Vertex's Quantum for Sales and Use Tax for United States (U.S.) and Canadian taxes. The tax provider interface is optional and if used, the tax provider will perform tax computations and provide tax registers for auditing and tax reporting purposes.

Currently, the interface is not integrated with BAAN Project (tptp-20010) or BAAN Transportation (trtr-20010). Additionally, the ability to update the tax provider tax register is not provided within BAAN Finance (tftf-20010).

SEE ALSO METHOD(S)
- Parameters for Tax Provider
- Tables for Tax Provider
- Address Verification for Tax Provider
- Tax Calculations for Tax Provider
- Tax Impact on Sales Installments for Tax Provider
- Conversion Considerations for Tax Provider
- Technical Implementation Considerations

Some terms require further explanation:
- Tax Provider
- GEO Codes

A tax provider is a third-party software product that facilitates the computation of tax for U.S. and Canadian taxes. To facilitate the calculation of tax within the U.S. and Canada an interface to TAXWARE's Master Tax System and Vertex's Quantum for Sales and Use Tax is provided.

A GEO code is a code used together or in lieu of address information such as the city, state/province, and ZIP/postal code to uniquely identify a taxing jurisdiction. The tax provider determines the GEO code based upon the address information entered and the county and city limits selected.

The format of the GEO code varies by tax provider. TAXWARE uses a two-digit GEO code; the GEO code together with the city, state, and ZIP code, identifies a taxing jurisdiction. Quantum uses a nine-digit GEO code comprised of a two-digit state code, three-digit county code, and a four-digit city code. A tenth digit is used to identify if the jurisdiction is inside or outside of the city limits.

6.2 Session Overview

Seq.	Session	Description	Session Usage
10	tcapil136m000	Maintain API Parameters	Mandatory
11	tccoml140m000	Maintain Country Tax Provider Register	Mandatory
12	tccoml910m000	Address Jurisdic Verification Utility	Additional
13	tccoml911m000	Address Format Conversion Utility	Additional
14	tccoml150m000	Maintain Tax Provider Parameters	Mandatory
15	tccoml151s000	Tax Provider Initialization Process	Mandatory
16	tccoml138m000	Maintain Product Categories	Optional
17	tccoml538m000	Display Product Categories	Display
18	tccoml538s000	Display Product Categories	Display
19	tccoml438m000	Print Product Categories	Optional
20	tccoml139m000	Maintain Product Category Tax Matrix	Optional
21	tccoml539m000	Display Product Category Tax Matrix	Display
22	tccoml539s000	Display Product Category Tax Matrix	Display
23	tccoml439m000	Print Product Category Tax Matrix	Print
24	tccoml912m000	Tax Provider Calculation Utility	Optional

7   Mandatory Sessions
7.1   Maintain API Parameters (tcapil136m000)

tcapil136m000   single-occ (1)   Form 1-1
+--+
Maintain API Parameters   Company: 000
API type   : 1..................
Interface Provider   : 2.............................
Interface Used   : 3....
+--+

1.   API type
The types of external applications that interface with BAAN IV's API.
Tax Provider
BAAN IV interface to an external tax provider.
2.   Interface Provider
The available interface providers for the specified API type.
TAXWARE's Master Tax System
BAAN IV will interface to TAXWARE's Master Tax System.
Quantum for Sales/Use Tax
BAAN IV will interface to Quantum for Sales/Use Tax.
None
No external tax provider interface will be used.
3.   Interface Used
Indicate whether or not the specified API interface is being used by BAAN IV.
Yes
BAAN IV will interface with the selected provider for the specified API type.
No
No interface for the specified API type is active.
7.2   Maintain Country Tax Provider Register (tccoml140m000)
SESSION OBJECTIVE
To register countries for the tax provider interface.
SEE ALSO KEYWORD(S)
•   Country Tax Provider Register
See also help about Global Localisation (Tax Provider).

tccoml140m000   multi-occ (2)   Form 1-1
+--+
Maintain Country Tax Provider Register   Company: 000
Country Description   Address Type
1.. 2_____   3..................
+--+

1.   Country Code
The code by which the country is recognized in BAAN IV.
2.   Description
3.   Address Type
The type of address that is associated with the registered country.
United States
The address is in the United States format.
Canada
The address is in the Canadian format.
7.3   Maintain Tax Provider Parameters (tccoml150m000)

tccoml150m000   single-occ (1)   Form 1-1
+--+
Maintain Tax Provider Parameters   Company: 000

```
|                                                                        |
|  Using Tax Provider                          : 1....                   |
|                                                                        |
|  Point of Title PaBaange                     : 2..................     |
|                                                                        |
|  Warn if Tax on ACR Invoices                 : 3....                   |
|                                                                        |
+------------------------------------------------------------------------+
```

1.   Tax Provider
2.   Point of Title PaBaange
3.   Warn if Tax on ACP invoices

7.4   Tax Provider Initialization Process (tccoml151s000)

SESSION OBJECTIVE

To recalculate tax on all invoiced sales installations based on call-outs to the
external tax provider. Additionally, all tax codes will be defined as singular
within Tax Codes by Country (tcmcs036).

```
tccoml151s000                                single-occ (4)   Form 1-1
+--Tax Provider Initialization Process--------------------------+
|                                                               |
|   1_____         |
|   +---------------------------------+                         |
|   | 2_____  3_____       |                        |
|   | 4_____  5_____       |                        |
|   | 6_____  7_____       |                        |
|   +---------------------------------+                         |
|                                                               |
+---------------------------------------------------------------+
```

1.   Program domain string
2.   Program domain string
3.   Program domain string
4.   Program domain string
5.   Program domain string
6.   Program domain string
7.   Program domain string
8   Optional Sessions
8.1 Maintain Product Categories (tccoml138m000)

SESSION OBJECTIVE

To define different product categories to be used by an exteranl tax provider
for tax computations. Product categories need to be further detailed in the
session "Maintain Product Category Tax Matrix (tccoml139m000)".

SEE ALSO KEYWORD(S)
•   Product Category
See also help about Global Localisation (Tax Provider).

```
tccoml138m000                                multi-occ (2)    Form 1-1
+------------------------------------------------------------------------+
|  Maintain Product Categories                        Company: 000       |
|------------------------------------------------------------------------|
|                                                                        |
|  Product Category                Description                           |
|                                                                        |
|  1.................................. 2............................     |
|                                                                        |
+------------------------------------------------------------------------+
```

1.   Product Category
The code used to identify a specific product category which will be used to
classify different types of products bought or sold.
For further information, see keyword(s)
Product Category (tccom938)
2.   Description
The description of the product category.
8.2 Print Product Categories (tccoml438m000)

```
tccoml438m000                                single-occ (4)   Form 1-1
+------------------------------------------------------------------------+
```

```
| Print Product Categories                                    Company: 000  |
|---------------------------------------------------------------------------|
|                                                                           |
| Product Category from : 1.................................                 |
|               to    : 2...............................                     |
|                                                                           |
+---------------------------------------------------------------------------+
1.     Product Category from
2.     Product Category to
```

8.3 Maintain Product Category Tax Matrix (tccoml139m000)

SESSION OBJECTIVE

To define product category tax matrices which associate product categories with
selected ranges of information such as items, item groups, etc. Effectivity and
expiration dates can also be associated to the product category tax matrices.

SEE ALSO KEYWORD(S)
•   Product Category Tax Matrix
See also help about Global Localisation (Tax Provider).

tccoml139m000   single-occ (1)   Form 1-1

```
+---------------------------------------------------------------------------+
| Maintain Product Category Tax Matrix                        Company: 000  |
|---------------------------------------------------------------------------|
|                                                                           |
|   Product Category    : 1...............................                   |
|   Product Relation    : 2..............                                    |
|                                                                           |
|   Item Group From     : 3..                                               |
|   Item Group To       : 4..                                               |
|   Item From           : 5..............                                    |
|   Item To             : 6..............                                    |
|   Contract Type From : 7..                                                |
|   Contract Type To    : 8..                                               |
|   Account Number From: 9...........                                        |
|   Account Number To   : 10..........                                       |
|                                                                           |
|   Effectivity Date    : 11........                                         |
|   Expiration Date     : 12.......                                          |
|                                                                           |
+---------------------------------------------------------------------------+
```

1.   Product Category
The code used to identify a specific product category which will be used to
classify different types of products bought or sold.
For further information, see keyword(s)
Product Category (tccom938)
2.   Product Relation
The relation type that is associated with the product category. Product
categories can be associated to item codes, item groups, contract types, and GL
account number. An item, item group or contract type can be associated with
only one product category for a given date.
Item
Associate a range of items to the product category.
Item Group
Associate a range of item groups to the product category.
Contract Type
Associate a range of contract types to the product category.
Account Number
Associate a range of account numbers to the product category.
3.   Item Group From
The beginning of the range of item groups that is associated to the product
category/product relation combination.
4.   Item Group To
The end of the range of item groups that is associated to the product
category/product relation combination.
5.   Item From

The beginning of the range of item codes that is associated to the product category/product relation combination.

6.   Item To
The end of the range of item codes that is associated to the product category/product relation combination.

7.   Contract Type From
The beginning of the range of contract types that is associated to the product category/product relation combination.

8.   Contract Type To
The end of the range of contract types that is associated to the product category/product relation combination.

9.   Account Number From
The beginning of the range of GL account numbers that is associated to the product category/product relation combination.

10.   Account Number To
The end of the range of GL account numbers that is associated to the product category/product relation combination.

11.   Effectivity Date
The date that the product category tax matrix become effective.

12.   Expiration Date
The date that the product category tax matrix becomes inactive.

8.4   Tax Provider Calculation Utility (tccoml912m000)

SESSION OBJECTIVE
To provide data input for the visibility and maintenance of information provided by the tax provider interface.

HOW TO USE THE SESSION
The parameter Tax Provider must be set to Yes in order to run this session. You can define this parameter in the session Maintain Tax Provider Parameters (tccoml150m000).

The utility has two main features:
•   Display Tax Provider Amounts/Rates (tccoml913s000)
•   Process Tax Provider Adjustments (tccoml914s000)

See also help about Global Localisation (Tax Provider).

tccoml912m000   single-occ (4)   Form 1-1
+---+
Tax Provider Calculation Utility   Company: 000
Order Type   : 1.......
2_____ : 3.....   4_____
Service Location   : 5........
6_____ : 7..
Country   : 8..   9_____
10_____ : 11............................
12_____ : 13............................
14_____15 16_____
17_____18 19...
Product Category   : 20..............................
Description   : 21_____
Order Quantity   : 22.....
Gross Amount   : 23.............
Transaction Date   : 24.......
+---+

1.   Service/Rental Use Indicators
2.   Program domain string
3.   Customer
4.   Name V
5.   serv.loc
6.   Program domain string
7.   Delivery Address

8. Country
9. Description
10. Program domain string
11. Name V
12. Program domain string
13. Name V
14. Program domain string
15. Program domain of string length 1
16. GEO Code
17. Program domain string
18. Program domain of string length 1
19. Answer on question y/n
20. Product Category
21. Description
22. Order Quantity
23. Gross Amount
SEE ALSO METHOD(S)
• Currency Formats
24. Date
9 Other Maintenance Sessions
9.1 Address Jurisdiction Verification Utility (tccoml910m000)

SESSION OBJECTIVE

To verify that address information stored within BAAN IV is properly associated with the correct tax jurisdiction (GEO code) required by external tax providers.

HOW TO USE THE SESSION

This utility can be used as a periodic verification tool, or as a mechanism to initially associate tax jurisdictions with existing address information. The parameter '%FFtccoml150m0001txpr' must be set to Yes in order to run this session. You can define this parameter in the session Maintain Tax Provider Parameters (tccoml150m000).

GEO Code Verification For each table containing address information within the selected range, the utility will procedurally execute the following:

• Processing criteria: GEO code jurisdiction will only be associated to address data correlating to countries registered in the table Country Tax Provider Register. Countries can be registered in the session Maintain Country Tax Provider Register (tccoml140m000).

• Format Verification: Address information should be in the proper format in order to parse the address information for input into the tax provider. Run the session Address Format Conversion Utility (tccoml911m000) in order to verify the existing address data formats. In addition to format structure, verification of valid state codes such as CA (California) or province codes such as QB (Quebec) is also done by the utility.

For Canadian addresses, there is an additional verification for valid province/postal code association (The first 2 characters of the postal code uniquely correspond to a specific province).

Based on the address information, the tax provider will attempt to validate the existing tax jurisdiction association.

One of the following cases will occur:

1) No jurisdiction - Address information does not correspond to a valid jurisdiction in the tax provider. (error meBaange reported by utility).

2) Unique jurisdiction - GEO code returned will be compared to the existing jurisdiction that is associated to the address information. Utility will change the jurisdiction association only if it is different.

3) Multiple jurisdictions - More than one jurisdiction can be valid for a specific address. If multiple GEO codes are valid, the utility will change the jurisdiction to the first GEO code passed back from the tax provider only if the existing association is not valid.

If using the tax provider Vertex, all modified jurisdictions will be defaulted to be "inside city limits".

The utility can be run for a specific range of addresses that exist within BAAN IV. You also have the option to run the utility without actually updating the existing data. Reports will be generated to show modified GEO code associations and address data that was not processed due to errors.

```
+----------------------------------------------------------------------+
| Address Jurisdiction Verification Utility           Company: 000     |
|----------------------------------------------------------------------|
|                                                                      |
| Table                 from : 1........................               |
|                       to   : 2.......................                |
|                                                                      |
| Update GEO Code Jurisdiction: 3....                                  |
|                                                                      |
| +----------------------------------------+                           |
| | Table: 4_____                        |                           |
| | Index: 5_____ |                          |
| +----------------------------------------+                           |
|                                                                      |
+----------------------------------------------------------------------+
```

1.   Tax Address Tables
2.   Tax Address Tables
3.   Update GEO Code Jurisdiction
Utility option which allows users to update the database.
Yes
Valid jurisdiction changes that are reported by the utility will be updated
within the database.
No
Utility will run in "report only" mode without affecting the existing
jurisdiction associations that are stored within the database.
4.   Tax Address Tables
5.   Program domain of string length 30
9.2   Address Format Conversion Utility (tccoml911m000)
SESSION OBJECTIVE
To allow the user to convert address information stored within BAAN IV into a
pre-defined address format required by external tax providers.
HOW TO USE THE SESSION
The utility assumes that existing address data has been input into BAAN IV in
one of 3 format types. Only these formats will be recognized by the utility for
conversion.
The 3 formats that will be converted are:

Line 1 of Address   Line 2 of Address

Type 1	AAA, BBB CCC	
Type 2	AAA	BBB CCC
Type 3	AAA, BBB	CCC

Legend:
AAA - City
BBB - State (for US address) or Province (for Canadian address)
CCC - Zip Code (for US address) or Postal Code (for Canadian address)
These formats will be converted to:

Line 1: AAA, BBB
Line 2: CCC

The utility can be run for a specific range of addresses that exist within BAAN
IV. You also have the option to run the utility without actually updating the
existing data. Reports will be generated to show the converted address data and
address data that was not converted due to errors.
See also help about Global Localisation (Tax Provider)

```
+----------------------------------------------------------------------+
| Address Format Conversion Utility                   Company: 000     |
```

```
|----------------------------------------------------------------------|
|                                                                      |
|   Table              from : 1......................                  |
|                      to   : 2......................                  |
|                                                                      |
|   Convert Address Format: 3....                                      |
|                                                                      |
|   +---------------------------------------+                          |
|   | Table: 4_____                       |                          |
|   | Index: 5_____|                          |
|   +---------------------------------------+                          |
|                                                                      |
+----------------------------------------------------------------------+
```

1.   Tax Address Tables
2.   Tax Address Tables
3.   Convert Address Format
Utility option which allows users to update the database.
Yes
Valid address information that is reported by the utility will be converted to
the new format within the database.
No
Utility will run in "report only" mode without affecting the existing address
information stored within the database.
4.   Tax Address Tables
5.   Program domain of string length 30
10   Other Print Sessions
10.1 Print Product Category Tax Matrix (tccoml439m000)

tccoml439m000   single-occ (4)   Form 1-2 >
```
+----------------------------------------------------------------------+
|  Print Product Category Tax Matrix                      Company: 000  |
|----------------------------------------------------------------------|
|                                                                      |
|   Product Category     from: 1...............................        |
|                        to  : 2...............................        |
|                                                                      |
|   Product Relation     from: 3..............                         |
|                        to  : 4..............                         |
|                                                                      |
|   Check Validity Date       : 5....                                  |
|   Check Date                : 6........                              |
|                                                                      |
+----------------------------------------------------------------------+
```

1.   Product Category
2.   Product Category
3.   Product Relation
4.   Product Relation
5.   Check Validity Date
Use this parameter for selective reporting of product category tax matrices.
Yes
Only product category tax matrices within the product category/product relation
ranges that are effective on the entered check date will be reported.
No
All product category tax matrices within the product category/product relation
ranges will be reported.
6.   Check Date

tccoml439m000   single-occ (4) < Form 2-2
```
+----------------------------------------------------------------------+
|  Print Product Category Tax Matrix                      Company: 000  |
|----------------------------------------------------------------------|
|                                                                      |
|                             From              To                     |
|                                                                      |
|   Item Group From    :            1.. -               2..            |
```

```
|  Item Group To        :              3.. -              4..          |
|                                                                      |
|  Item From            : 5............... - 6...............          |
|  Item To              : 7............... - 8...............          |
|                                                                      |
|  Contract Type From :              9.. -              10.            |
|  Contract Type To   :              11. -              12.            |
|                                                                      |
|  Account Number From: 13..........    - 14..........                 |
|  Account Number To  : 15..........    - 16..........                 |
|                                                                      |
+----------------------------------------------------------------------+
```

1.   Item Group From
2.   Item Group From
3.   Item Group To
4.   Item Group To
5.   Item From
6.   Item From
7.   Item To
8.   Item To
9.   Contract Type From
10.   Contract Type From
11.   Contract Type To
12.   Contract Type To
13.   Account Number From
14.   Account Number From
15.   Account Number To
16.   Account Number To

****

QMS - Quality Management System

1   Quality Management System (QMS)
1.1   General
OBJECTIVE OF THIS MODULE
The Quality Management System (QMS) supports both quality management throughout
the entire company as well as quality control of intermediate and end products.
QMS governs the activities required to control the flow of products selected for
inspection.
QMS is linked to other BAAN IV modules and packages at various points in the
production process so as to provide extensive quality checks.
The following points in the production process are examples of points at which
these quality checks may take place:
•   after purchase receipt;
•   before sales deliveries;
•   before raw material issue;
•   after the production process (final inspection);
•   during production process operations;
•   in storage.
The following list displays the links of Quality Management System (QMS) with
other BAAN IV modules/packages or major areas of packages:
•   BAAN Distribution
•   Sales Control (SLS)
•   Purchase Control (PUR)
•   Inventory Control (INV)
•   Location Control (ILC)
•   BAAN Manufacturing
•   Shop Floor Control (SFC)
•   Routing (ROU)
•   BOM Control (BOM)
•   Repetitive Manufacturing (RPT)
•   BAAN Process

- Routing (ROU)
- Formula Management (FRM)
- Batch Control
2   Introduction to Master Data
2.1   General
OBJECTIVE OF BUSINESS OBJECT
In QMS Master Data, the following data can be specified:
- Characteristics
- Aspects and Characteristics by Aspects (tcqms003)
- Options and Option Sets (tcqms013)
- Tests and Tests by Characteristic (tcqms005)
- Instruments
- Test Areas
- Quality Groups and Items by Quality Group (tcqms020)
Display the procedure and show the sessions in:
- Master Data Procedure
2.2   Session Overview

Seq.	Session	Description	Session Usage
10	tcqms0101m000	Maintain Characteristics	Mandatory
11	tcqms0102m000	Maintain Aspects	Mandatory
12	tcqms0103m000	Maintain Characteristics by Aspect	Mandatory
13	tcqms0106m000	Maintain Tests	Mandatory
14	tcqms0107m000	Maintain Test Areas	Mandatory
15	tcqms0108m000	Maintain Test Instruments	Mandatory
16	tcqms0105m000	Maintain Tests by Characteristic	Mandatory
30	tcqms0114m000	Maintain Options	Mandatory
31	tcqms0113m000	Maintain Option Sets	Mandatory
101	tcqms0401m000	Print Characteristics	Print
102	tcqms0402m000	Print Aspects	Print
103	tcqms0405m000	Print Tests by Characteristic	Print
104	tcqms0406m000	Print Tests	Print
105	tcqms0407m000	Print Test Areas	Print
106	tcqms0408m000	Print Test Instruments	Print
107	tcqms0413m000	Print Option Sets	Print
108	tcqms0414m000	Print Options	Print
109	tcqms0420m000	Print Items by Quality Group	Print
110	tcqms0437m000	Print Characteristics by Test Group	Print
111	tcqms0403m000	Print Characteristics by Aspect	Print
201	tcqms0501m000	Display Characteristics	Display

```
| 202 | tcqms0502m000 | Display Aspects                          | Display
|
| 203 | tcqms0503m000 | Display Characteristics by Aspect        | Display
|
| 204 | tcqms0505m000 | Display Tests by Characteristic          | Display
|
| 205 | tcqms0506m000 | Display Tests                            | Display
|
| 206 | tcqms0507m000 | Display Test Areas                       | Display
|
| 207 | tcqms0508m000 | Display Test Instruments                 | Display
|
| 208 | tcqms0513m000 | Display Option Sets                      | Display
|
| 209 | tcqms0514m000 | Display Options                          | Display
|
| 211 | tcqms0537m000 | Display Characteristics by Test Group    | Display
|
| 212 | tcqms0501s000 | Display Characteristics                  | Display
|
| 214 | tcqms0502s000 | Display Aspects                          | Display
|
| 215 | tcqms0503s000 | Display Characteristics by Aspect        | Display
|
| 216 | tcqms0505s000 | Display Tests by Characteristic          | Display
|
| 217 | tcqms0507s000 | Display Test Areas                       | Display
|
| 218 | tcqms0508s000 | Display Test Instruments                 | Display
|
| 220 | tcqms0513s000 | Display Option Sets                      | Display
|
| 221 | tcqms0514s000 | Display Options                          | Display
|
| 223 | tcqms0537s000 | Display Characteristics by Test Group    | Display
|
| 224 | tcqms0506s000 | Display Tests                            | Display
|
| 225 | tcqms0520m000 | Display Items by Quality Group           | Display
|
| 226 | tcqms0524s000 | Display Characteristic Data              | Display
|
```

3 Mandatory Sessions
3.1 Maintain Characteristics (tcqms0101m000)

SESSION OBJECTIVE

To maintain quality characteristics.

SEE ALSO KEYWORD(S)

• Characteristics

```
tcqms0101m000                    zoom      single-occ (1)   Form 1-1
+-------------------------------------------------------------------------+
| Maintain Characteristics                                Company: 000    |
|-------------------------------------------------------------------------|
|                                                                         |
| Characteristic              : 1.......  2...........................    |
|                                                                         |
| Search Key                  : 3..............                          |
| Characteristic Type         : 4..............                          |
| Method                      : 5..............                          |
| Characteristic Unit         : 6..  7_____           |
| Characteristic Standard     : 8.......                                 |
| Default Test                : 9......  10_____  |
| Algorithm                   : 11....  12_____    |
```

```
| Fixed Characteristic Value    : 13......                              |
| Skill                         : 14..  15_____|
| Test Area                     : 16.  17_____ |
| Employee                      : 18....  19_____|
| Instrument                    : 20....  21_____|
| Text                          : 22___                                 |
|                                                                       |
+-----------------------------------------------------------------------+
```

1.   Characteristic
For further information, see keyword(s)
•   Characteristics
2.   Description
3.   Search Key
A search key is an optional field which is used to search on specific keywords.
There are no specific rules for the definition of search keys.
Example:
Search Key
If sort order "Search Key" is chosen and a search is initiated for 'Test', the
system will list the first record with that search key.
4.   Characteristic Type
The type of characteristic is the type of value which may be measured by means
of an instrument. Fraction
A ratio of two expressions or numbers other than zero representing part of an
integer (written with a decimal point followed by one or more numbers).
Integer
An exact whole number as opposed to a number with decimals.
Option
For this type of characteristic, various options may be defined. For further
information, see keyword(s)
•   Option Sets
•   Options

Characteristic Type	Example
Fraction	3.145
Integer	123
Option	Blue

5.   Method
The type of characteristic value or the way in which the characteristic value is
calculated. Fixed
The characteristic value is determined once and can be entered in field "Fixed
Characteristic Value". It is used to compare results or in algorithms. The
results are entered in session "Enter Test Data (tcqms1115m000)".
Variable
Characteristic values are measured immediately by means of an instrument. The
results are entered in session "Enter Test Data (tcqms1115m000)".
Algorithm
The characteristic is calculated by means of an algorithm, using the inspection
results of variable or fixed characteristics.
For further information, see keyword(s)
•   Algorithms
See also field "Algorithm".

Method	Characteristic	Example
Fixed	Pi	3.14..
Variable	Length	4 meters
```
```

```
|                          |                |             |          |
|Algorithm                 | Voltage        | I * R       |          |
|                          |                |             |          |
+-------------------------------------------------------------------+
```
6.   Characteristic Unit
The unit in which a characteristic value, e.g. the norm, is specified.

Characteristic Type	Mandatory
Fraction	Yes
Integer	Yes
Option	N/A

For further information, see keyword(s)
•   Units
For further information, see method(s)
•   Units and Quantities in QMS
7.   Description
8.   Characteristic Standard
The standard normally used for characteristics. This is an informative field.
Example:
A DIN standard.
9.   Default Test
For further information, see keyword(s)
•   Tests
10.   Description
11.   Algorithm
For further information, see keyword(s)
•   Algorithms
This default only applies to method "Algorithm". Enter the algorithm by means of
which the characteristic is calculated.
12.   Description
13.   Fixed Characteristic Value
The value of a constant (i.e. a fixed characteristic) which is used in
algorithms.
Example:
Characteristic [TF@tcqms001.chGravity
Fixed Characteristic Value
Only applies to method "Fixed".
If the characteristic is of type "Integer", the value of the characteristic is
rounded up to the nearest integer.
Example:

User Entry	Rounded Value
10.5	11
10.4	10
10.6	11

14.   Skill
For further information, see keyword(s)
"Skills".
Enter the default skill required for the person who executes the test.
15.   Description
16.   Test Area
For further information, see keyword(s)
•   Test Areas
Enter the default test area in which the characteristic is tested.
17.   Description
18.   Employee
The default employee to execute the test for this characteristic.
For further information, see keyword(s)
•   Employees
Enter the default employee to execute the test for this characteristic.
19.   Name
The employee's name.
20.   Instrument
For further information, see keyword(s)
•   Instruments

Enter the default instrument to measure the characteristic.
21.   Description
22.   Answer on question y/n
3.2   Maintain Aspects (tcqms0102m000)
SESSION OBJECTIVE
To maintain aspects by means of which the same characteristic can be used more
than once for the same item.
SEE ALSO KEYWORD(S)
•   Aspects

tcqms0102m000   multi-occ (2)   Form 1-1
```
+-----------------------------------------------------------------------------+
| Maintain Aspects                                           Company: 000 |
|-----------------------------------------------------------------------------|
|                                                                             |
| Aspect     Description                           Text                       |
|                                                                             |
| 1.......   2.............................  3____                            |
|                                                                             |
+-----------------------------------------------------------------------------+
```
1.   Aspect
For further information, see keyword(s)
•   Aspects
2.   Description
3.   Text
3.3   Maintain Characteristics by Aspect (tcqms0103m000)
SESSION OBJECTIVE
To customize and group characteristics by aspect. Different parts of an item
(which may or may not have common characteristics) may have to be tested. IN
QMS, these parts are referred to as aspects.
SEE ALSO KEYWORD(S)
•   Characteristics by Aspects

tcqms0103m000   zoom   multi/group (3   Form 1-1
```
+-----------------------------------------------------------------------------+
| Maintain Characteristics by Aspect                         Company: 000 |
|-----------------------------------------------------------------------------|
|                                                                             |
| Aspect          : 1.......  2_____                       |
|                                                                             |
| Characteristic  Description       Default   Description          Text       |
|                                   Test                                      |
|                                                                             |
|     3.......  4_____     5.......  6_____     7____ |
|                                                                             |
+-----------------------------------------------------------------------------+
```
1.   Aspect
For further information, see keyword(s)
•   Aspects
2.   Description
3.   Characteristic
For further information, see keyword(s)
•   Characteristics
4.   Description
5.   Default Test
For further information, see keyword(s)
•   Tests
6.   Description
7.   Answer on question y/n
3.4   Maintain Tests (tcqms0106m000)
SESSION OBJECTIVE
To maintain the tests which are used to inspect characteristics.
SEE ALSO KEYWORD(S)
•   Tests

tcqms0106m000   multi-occ (2)   Form 1-1

```
+------------------------------------------------------------------------+
| Maintain Tests                                         Company: 000   |
|------------------------------------------------------------------------|
|                                                                        |
|  Test      Description                                                 |
|                                                                        |
|  1.......  2...........................                                |
|                                                                        |
+------------------------------------------------------------------------+
```
1.   Test
For further information, see keyword(s)
•   Tests
2.   Description
3.5   Maintain Test Areas (tcqms0107m000)
SESSION OBJECTIVE
To maintain the areas where tests take place.
SEE ALSO KEYWORD(S)
•   Test Areas
Test areas can be part of:
•   a work center;
•   a warehouse;
•   inventory locations within a warehouse.
tcqms0107m000   single-occ (1)   Form 1-1
```
+------------------------------------------------------------------------+
|  Maintain Test Areas                                    Company: 000  |
|------------------------------------------------------------------------|
|                                                                        |
|  Test Area                 : 1.. 2...........................         |
|                                                                        |
|  Work Center               : 3.. 4_____       |
|  Warehouse                 : 5.. 6_____       |
|  Inventory Locations       : 7.......                                 |
|                                                                        |
+------------------------------------------------------------------------+
```
1.   Test Area
For further information, see keyword(s)
•   Test Areas
2.   Description
3.   Work Center
For further information, see keyword(s)
"Work Centers".
4.   Description
The description of the work center.
5.   Warehouse
For further information, see keyword(s)
"Warehouses".
6.   Description
7.   Inventory Locations
The location where the lot is stored.
For further information, see keyword(s)
•   Locations
Only applies if module "Location Control (ILC)" is implemented.
3.6   Maintain Test Instruments (tcqms0108m000)
SESSION OBJECTIVE
To maintain instruments which will be used to test items for specific
characteristic.
SEE ALSO KEYWORD(S)
•   Instruments
tcqms0108m000   single-occ (1)   Form 1-1
```
+------------------------------------------------------------------------+
|  Maintain Test Instruments                              Company: 000  |
|------------------------------------------------------------------------|
|                                                                        |
```

```
| Instrument                      :   1.....  2..............................  |
| Test Area                       :   3..   4_____  |
| Skill                           :   5...  6_____  |
| Least Measurable Quantity [7.. ]:   8.                                       |
|                                                                              |
|   +-Calibration Data------------------------------------------+             |
|   | Interval Type                  :  9...................  |             |
|   | Interval [Days/Times Used]     : 10......              |             |
|   | Last Calibration Date          : 11_____            |             |
|   | Next Calibration Date          : 12_____            |             |
|   | Next Calibration [Times Used]  : 13_____              |             |
|   | Blocked for Calibration        : 14...                  |             |
|   | Actual Times Used              : 15_____            |             |
|   | Instrument Text                : 16___                  |             |
|   | Calibration Text               : 17___                  |             |
|   +------------------------------------------------------+             |
|                                                                              |
+------------------------------------------------------------------------------+
```

1.   Instrument
For further information, see keyword(s)
•   Instruments
2.   Description
3.   Test Area
For further information, see keyword(s)
•   Test Areas
This is the default test location for this instrument.
4.   Description
5.   Skill
For further information, see keyword(s)
"Skills".
Enter the default skill required for the person who executes the test.
6.   Description
7.   Least Measurable Unit
This field is used to enter the unit in which the least measurable value is
expressed.
The physical unit of the least measurable value must be equal to the
characteristic unit of the characteristic value that is measured by the
instrument.
For further information, see keyword(s)
•   Units
For further information, see method(s)
•   Units and Quantities in QMS
Example:
A micrometer screw gage.

A micrometer screw gage can measure, for example, a minumum of 10 micrometers.
As a result, micrometer can be entered as the "Least Measurable Unit" and 10 as
the "Least Measurable Quantity".
8.   Least Measurable Quantity
The minimum value which can be measured by an instrument.
Example:
A micrometer screw gage.

A micrometer screw gage can measure, for example, a minumum of 10 micrometers.
As a result, micrometer can be entered as the "Least Measurable Unit" and 10 as
the "Least Measurable Quantity".
9.   Calibration Interval Type
The frequency of calibration depends on Time or the Number of Times Used. It is
also possible that it is not neceBaanry to calibrate the instrument. Not
Applicable
The instrument does not need calibration. No data is entered in the fields
related to calibration.
Time

The instrument is calibrated after a specific time interval. It is selected for calibration on or after the next calibration date.

Number of Times Used

The instrument is calibrated after 'n' times used. That is to say, the instrument is selected for calibration when it has been used 'n' or more times. See also session "Select Instruments for Calibration (tcqms3201m000)".

10.   Calibration Interval [Days/Times Used]

Indication when calibration is to take place:
• 	after n days;
• 	after n times used.
Where 'n' is the value of this field.

11.   Last Calibration Date

The last time the instrument was calibrated.

12.   Next Calibration Date

The date on which the next calibration of the instrument is to take place. The date on which the next calibration of the instrument is to take place.

13.   Next Calibration [Times Used]

Indication of the number of times used after which the next calibration of the instrument is to take place. Indication of the number of times used after which the next calibration of the instrument is to take place.

14.   Blocked for Calibration

Indication that an instrument is being calibrated and is blocked for use. A blocked instrument can be used for inspections, but a calibration warning is giffen. Yes

An instrument is automatically blocked when it is selected for calibration in session "Select Instruments for Calibration (tcqms3201m000)". No calibration-related data can be maintained when an instrument is blocked.

No

An instrument can be unblocked by means of session "Enter Calibration Dates (tcqms3202m000)"

Indication that an instrument is being calibrated and is blocked for use. A blocked instrument can be used for inspections, but a calibration warning is giffen.

15.   Actual Times Used

The number of times or the number of days the instrument is used for testing since the last calibration. The number of times or the number of days the instrument is used for testing since the last calibration.

16.   Text

17.   Calibration Text

3.7   Maintain Tests by Characteristic (tcqms0105m000)

SESSION OBJECTIVE

To maintain the tests which are used to inspect characteristics.

HOW TO USE THE SESSION

The characteristic data is default for many fields.

SEE ALSO KEYWORD(S)

• 	Tests by Characteristic

```
tcqms0105m000                              multi/group (3     Form 1-1
+-----------------------------------------------------------------------+
| Maintain Tests by Characteristic                        Company: 000  |
|-----------------------------------------------------------------------|
|                                                                       |
| Aspect        : 1.......  2_____  Char. Type : 5_____ |
| Characteristic : 3.......  4_____  Char. Unit : 6__      |
|                                                                       |
| Test     Description           Test  Destructive  Result Type   Text  |
|                                Unit                                   |
|                                                                       |
| 7.......  8_____  9..  10...       11............ 12___ |
|                                                                       |
|-----------------------------------------------------------------------|
| Test Std. : 13......            Employee  : 18.... 19_____   |
| Skill     : 14.. 15_____  Instrument: 20.... 21_____  |
| Test Area : 16.  17_____                                    |
```

| | | |
+--+
1.   Aspect
For further information, see keyword(s)
•   Aspects
Skip this field to define a general test for a characteristic.
2.   Description
3.   Characteristic
For further information, see keyword(s)
•   Characteristics
Enter a characteristic.
For further information, see keyword(s)
•   Characteristics by Aspects
4.   Description
5.   Characteristic Type
The type of characteristic is the type of value which may be measured by means
of an instrument.
6.   Characteristic Unit
The unit in which a characteristic value, e.g. the norm, is specified.

Characteristic Type	Mandatory
Fraction	Yes
Integer	Yes
Option	N/A

For further information, see keyword(s)
•   Units
For further information, see method(s)
•   Units and Quantities in QMS
7.   Test
For further information, see keyword(s)
•   Tests
8.   Description
9.   Test Unit
The unit in which the test results are defined or calculated.
For further information, see keyword(s)
•   "Units"
For further information, see method(s)
•   •   "Units and Quantities in QMS" This field does not apply to
characteristics of type "Option".
The characteristic unit is the default value. The test unit and the
characteristic unit must have the same physical quantity.
10.   Destructive
Indication that the test is destructive and that the item cannot be used after
testing.
For further information, see method(s)
•   Using Destructive Tests
11.   Result Type
The type of result which is reported to the user. Quantitative
A quantitative value is reported after testing, e.g. "40 cm".
Qualitative
A qualitative value is reported after testing, e.g. "Acceptable" or "Not
Acceptable".
12.   Text
13.   Test Standard
The standard normally used for the test.
Example:
A DIN standard.
14.   Skill
For further information, see keyword(s)
"Skills".
Enter the default skill required for the person who executes the test.
15.   Description
16.   Test Area
For further information, see keyword(s)

• Test Areas
Enter the default test area in which the characteristic is tested.
17.   Description
18.   Employee
The default employee to execute the test for this characteristic.
For further information, see keyword(s)
•   Employees
The value entered for characteristic data is a default value. This field is used
to indicate the default value while tests are being defined by quality ID.
19.   Name
The employee's name.
20.   Instrument
For further information, see keyword(s)
•   Instruments
Enter the default instrument to measure the characteristic.
21.   Description
3.8   Maintain Options (tcqms0114m000)
SESSION OBJECTIVE
To create options for an option set and characteristic.
SEE ALSO KEYWORD(S)
•   Options
tcqms0114m000   multi/group (3   Form 1-1
+--+
Maintain Options   Company: 000
Characteristic : 1....... 2_____
Option Set   : 3..... 4_____
Option   Description   Option Type
5....... 6.........................   7..............
+--+
1.   Characteristic
For further information, see keyword(s)
•   Characteristics
The characteristic must be of type "Option".
2.   Description
3.   Option Set
For further information, see keyword(s)
•   Option Sets
4.   Description
5.   Option
For further information, see keyword(s)
•   Options
6.   Description
7.   Option Type
Indication whether the option (= result of the test) is acceptable or not. If
the result is acceptable, the item passes the test for this characteristic.
3.9   Maintain Option Sets (tcqms0113m000)
SESSION OBJECTIVE
To create option sets for a quality characteristic of type "Option".
SEE ALSO KEYWORD(S)
•   Option Sets
tcqms0113m000   zoom   multi/group (3   Form 1-1
+--+
Maintain Option Sets   Company: 000
Characteristic: 1....... 2_____
Option Set   Description

```
|                                                                          |
|          3.....   4...........................                          |
|                                                                          |
+--------------------------------------------------------------------------+
1.     Characteristic
For further information, see keyword(s)
•      Characteristics
The characteristic must be of type "Option".
2.     Description
3.     Option Set
For further information, see keyword(s)
•      Option Sets
4.     Description
4      Other Print Sessions
4.1    Print Characteristics (tcqms0401m000)
tcqms0401m000                                single-occ (4)    Form 1-1
+--------------------------------------------------------------------------+
|  Print Characteristics                              Company: 000  |
|--------------------------------------------------------------------------|
|                                                                          |
|  Characteristic            from : 1.......                              |
|                            to   : 2.......                              |
|                                                                          |
|  Print Characteristic Text      : 3....                                 |
|                                                                          |
+--------------------------------------------------------------------------+
1.     Characteristic from
2.     Characteristic to
3.     Print Text
4.2    Print Aspects (tcqms0402m000)
tcqms0402m000                                single-occ (4)    Form 1-1
+--------------------------------------------------------------------------+
|  Print Aspects                                      Company: 000  |
|--------------------------------------------------------------------------|
|                                                                          |
|  Aspect                    from : 1.......                              |
|                            to   : 2.......                              |
|                                                                          |
|  Print Aspect Text              : 3....                                 |
|                                                                          |
+--------------------------------------------------------------------------+
1.     Aspect from
2.     Aspect to
3.     Print Text
4.3    Print Tests by Characteristic (tcqms0405m000)
tcqms0405m000                                single-occ (4)    Form 1-1
+--------------------------------------------------------------------------+
|  Print Tests by Characteristic                      Company: 000  |
|--------------------------------------------------------------------------|
|                                                                          |
|  Aspect                    from : 1.......                              |
|                            to   : 2.......                              |
|                                                                          |
|  Characteristic            from : 3......                               |
|                            to   : 4......                               |
|                                                                          |
|  Test                      from : 5.......                              |
|                            to   : 6.......                              |
|                                                                          |
|  Print Aspect Text              : 7....                                 |
|                                                                          |
|  Print Characteristic Text      : 8....                                 |
|                                                                          |
```

```
|  Print Test Text                      : 9....                                |
|                                                                              |
+------------------------------------------------------------------------------+
1.      Aspect from
2.      Aspect to
3.      Characteristic from
4.      Characteristic to
5.      Test from
6.      Test to
7.      Print Aspect Text
8.      Print Characteristic Text
9.      Print Test Text
4.4     Print Tests (tcqms0406m000)
tcqms0406m000                                  single-occ (4)   Form 1-1
+------------------------------------------------------------------------------+
|  Print Tests                                            Company: 000  |
|------------------------------------------------------------------------------|
|                                                                              |
|  Test         from : 1.......                                         |
|               to   : 2.......                                         |
|                                                                              |
+------------------------------------------------------------------------------+
1.      from
2.      to
4.5     Print Test Areas (tcqms0407m000)
tcqms0407m000                                  single-occ (4)   Form 1-1
+------------------------------------------------------------------------------+
|  Print Test Areas                                       Company: 000  |
|------------------------------------------------------------------------------|
|                                                                              |
|  Test Area              from : 1..                                    |
|                         to   : 2..                                    |
|                                                                              |
+------------------------------------------------------------------------------+
1.      From
2.      To
4.6     Print Test Instruments (tcqms0408m000)
tcqms0408m000                                  single-occ (4)   Form 1-1
+------------------------------------------------------------------------------+
|  Print Test Instruments                                 Company: 000  |
|------------------------------------------------------------------------------|
|                                                                              |
|  Instrument                    from : 1.....                          |
|                                to   : 2.....                          |
|                                                                              |
|  Print Instruments                  : 3..............                 |
|                                                                              |
|  Print Instrument Text              : 4....                           |
|                                                                              |
|  Print Calibration Text             : 5....                           |
|                                                                              |
+------------------------------------------------------------------------------+
1.      Instrument from
2.      Instrument to
3.      Print Instruments
The following print options are available:
Not Blocked
Only the instruments which are not blocked and not due for calibration.
Blocked
Only the instruments which are blocked for calibration.
All
All instruments.
4.      Print Text
```

5.   Print Calibration Text
4.7   Print Option Sets (tcqms0413m000)

tcqms0413m000   single-occ (4)   Form 1-1
+---+
Print Option Sets   Company: 000
Characteristic   from : 1.......
to   : 2.......
Option Set   from : 3.....
to   : 4.....
+---+

1.   from
2.   to
3.   from
4.   to

4.8   Print Options (tcqms0414m000)

tcqms0414m000   single-occ (4)   Form 1-1
+---+
Print Options   Company: 000
Characteristic   from : 1.......
to   : 2.......
Option Set   from : 3.....
to   : 4.....
Option   from : 5.......
to   : 6.......
+---+

1.   Characteristic From
2.   Characteristic To
3.   Option Set from
4.   Option Set to
5.   Option from
6.   Option to

4.9   Print Items by Quality Group (tcqms0420m000)

tcqms0420m000   single-occ (4)   Form 1-1
+---+
Print Items by Quality Group   Company: 000
Quality Group   from : 1.....
to   : 2.....
Project   from : 3.....
to   : 4.....
Item   from : 5..............
to   : 6..............
+---+

1.   Quality Group from
2.   Quality Group to
3.   Project from
4.   Project to
5.   Item from
6.   Item to

4.10   Print Characteristics by Test Group (tcqms0437m000)

```
+-----------------------------------------------------------------------+
|  Print Characteristics by Test Group                   Company: 000   |
|-----------------------------------------------------------------------|
|                                                                       |
|   Quality ID                from : 1.........                         |
|                             to   : 2.........                         |
|                                                                       |
|   Test Group                from : 3..                                |
|                             to   : 4..                                |
|                                                                       |
|   Aspect                    from : 5......                            |
|                             to   : 6......                            |
|                                                                       |
|   Characteristic            from : 7......                            |
|                             to   : 8......                            |
|                                                                       |
+-----------------------------------------------------------------------+
```

1.   Quality ID from
2.   Quality ID to
3.   Test Group from
4.   Test Group to
5.   Aspect from
6.   Aspect to
7.   Characteristic from
8.   Characteristic to

4.11 Print Characteristics by Aspect (tcqms0403m000)

```
+-----------------------------------------------------------------------+
|  Print Characteristics by Aspect                       Company: 000   |
|-----------------------------------------------------------------------|
|                                                                       |
|   Aspect                    from : 1......                            |
|                             to   : 2......                            |
|                                                                       |
|   Characteristic            from : 3......                            |
|                             to   : 4......                            |
|                                                                       |
|   Print Characteristic Text     : 5....                               |
|                                                                       |
+-----------------------------------------------------------------------+
```

1.   Aspect from
2.   Aspect to
3.   Characteristic from
4.   Characteristic to
5.   Print Characteristic Text

5   Introduction to Algorithms

5.1   General

OBJECTIVE OF BUSINESS OBJECT

Lab recording is not simply a matter of taking measurements. Based on measurements, complex calculations can be performed which may or may not include product specifications as part of the calculation. For this purpose, algorithms are created and used.

Example: By measuring the amount of sugar in wine, it is possible to determine the amount of alcohol it is going to contain.

First, it is neceBaanry to define the variables needed to define algorithms. Standard mathematical expressions (logarithms, sine, cosine, etc.) can also be used within algorithms.

Based on the defined algorithm, variables can be assinged to characteristics and/or combinations of aspects and characteristics. The used characteristics and combinations of aspects and characteristics must be of characteristic type "Fraction" or "Integer". Consequently, a numeric value is to be entered instead of an option.

The result of calculating an algorithm is entered in session "Enter Test Data (tcqms1115m000)".
Display the procedure and show the sessions in:
•   Algorithm Procedure

5.2   Session Overview

Seq.	Session	Description	Session Usage
10	tcqms0123m000	Maintain Algorithm Variables	Mandatory
20	tcqms0121m000	Maintain Algorithms	Mandatory
30	tcqms0122m000	Maintain Variables by Algorithm	Mandatory
101	tcqms0421m000	Print Algorithms	Print
201	tcqms0522s000	Display Variables by Algorithm	Display
202	tcqms0521m000	Display Algorithms	Display
203	tcqms0521s000	Display Algorithms	Display

6   Mandatory Sessions
6.1   Maintain Algorithm Variables (tcqms0123m000)

SESSION OBJECTIVE

To maintain the variable codes for algorithms. A maximum of 99 variable codes can be maintained. In this session, only the code of the variable can be defined. For each algorithm, the variable which is used is defined as well as the characteristic which must be assigned to it. See also session "Maintain Variables by Algorithm (tcqms0122s000)".

HOW TO USE THE SESSION

If the variable is used by an algorithm, it cannot be changed. If a variable is removed, the system deletes the space in front of each variable so that there is no space in between the variables.

SEE ALSO KEYWORD(S)
•   Algorithm Variables
•   Variables by Algorithm

tcqms0123m000   single-occ (1)   Form 1-1

```
+-----------------------------------------------------------------------+
| Maintain Algorithm Variables                          Company: 000  |
|-----------------------------------------------------------------------|
|                                                                       |
|  +Algorithm Variables--------------------------------------------+    |
|                                                                       |
|  1.     1.     1.     1.     1.     1.     1.     1.     1.     1.   |
|  1.     1.     1.     1.     1.     1.     1.     1.     1.     1.   |
|  1.     1.     1.     1.     1.     1.     1.     1.     1.     1.   |
|  1.     1.     1.     1.     1.     1.     1.     1.     1.     1.   |
|  1.     1.     1.     1.     1.     1.     1.     1.     1.     1.   |
|  1.     1.     1.     1.     1.     1.     1.     1.     1.     1.   |
|  1.     1.     1.     1.     1.     1.     1.     1.     1.     1.   |
|  1.     1.     1.     1.     1.     1.     1.     1.     1.     1.   |
|  1.     1.     1.     1.     1.     1.     1.     1.     1.          |
|  1.     1.     1.     1.     1.     1.     1.     1.     1.          |
|                                                                       |
+-----------------------------------------------------------------------+
```

1.   Variables
A short code for a variable which is used in an algorithm.
For further information, see keyword(s)
•   Algorithm Variables

6.2   Maintain Algorithms (tcqms0121m000)

SESSION OBJECTIVE
To maintain algorithms.
HOW TO USE THE SESSION
A maximum of 99 variable codes can be used to formulate the expression of an
algorithm (see session "Maintain Algorithm Variables (tcqms0123m000)"). Any
desired variable can be defined and assigned to a variable code by means of
subsession "Maintain Variables by Algorithm (tcqms0122s000)".
Note:
If the expression for an algorithm is not valid, the algorithm cannot be used in
sessions "Maintain Inspection Order Lines (tcqms1101s000)" and "Maintain Order-
Specific Inspection Data (Lines) (tcqms0151s000)".
If an algorithm is inserted, the general data must be entered and saved first by
means of option "Save Record(s) [update.db]". After this, it is possible to
enter an expression.
SEE ALSO KEYWORD(S)
•   Algorithms
SEE ALSO METHOD(S)
•   Using Algorithms

```
tcqms0121m000                        zoom      single-occ (1)    Form 1-1
+---------------------------------------------------------------------------+
|  Maintain Algorithms                                       Company: 000   |
|---------------------------------------------------------------------------|
|                                                                           |
|   Algorithm                    : 1.....                                   |
|                                                                           |
|   Description                  : 2...........................             |
|   Search Key                   : 3..............                          |
|   Expression                   : 4.....................................   |
|   Algorithm Unit               : 5..  6_____    |
|                                                                           |
|   Text                         : 7____                                    |
|                                                                           |
+---------------------------------------------------------------------------+
```

1.   Algorithm
For further information, see keyword(s)
•   Algorithms
2.   Description
3.   Search Key
A search key is an optional field which is used to search on specific keywords.
There are no specific rules for the definition of search keys.
Example:
Search Key
If sort order "Search Key" is chosen and a search is initiated for 'Test', the
system will list the first record with that search key.
4.   Expression
The expression indicates the way in which the algorithm value is calculated. For
further information, see method(s)
•   Syntax for Expressions
If an expression is entered, the system will check the validity of the
expression. Errors will be reported in the form of bshell meBaanges.
5.   Algorithm Unit
The unit in which the result of the algorithm calculation is expressed.
For further information, see method(s)
•   Using Algorithms
•   Units and Quantities in QMS
6.   Description
7.   Answer on question y/n
6.3   Maintain Variables by Algorithm (tcqms0122m000)
SESSION OBJECTIVE
To assign variables to characteristics so that these variables can be used in
algorithms.
HOW TO USE THE SESSION

A characteristic can be assigned to a specific variable code. All variable codes which are defined in session "Maintain Algorithm Variables (tcqms0123m000)" can be used.
Example:
Algorithmlecteristic X1   V   Value X134 X2
V   Value X256
SEE ALSO KEYWORD(S)
•   Variables by Algorithm
tcqms0122m000   multi/group (3   Form 1-1
+--+
Maintain Variables by Algorithm   Company: 000
Algorithm   : 1..... 2_____
Variable   Aspect   Description   Characteristic Description
3.   4...... 5_____   6...... 7_____
+--+
1.   Algorithm
For further information, see keyword(s)
•   Algorithms
2.   Description
3.   Variable
For further information, see keyword(s)
•   Algorithm Variables
•   Variables by Algorithm
4.   Aspect
For further information, see keyword(s)
•   Aspects
5.   Description
6.   Characteristic
For further information, see keyword(s)
•   Characteristics
7.   Description
7   Other Print Sessions
7.1   Print Algorithms (tcqms0421m000)
tcqms0421m000   single-occ (4)   Form 1-1
+--+
Print Algorithms   Company: 000
Algorithm   from : 1.....
to   : 2.....
Print Algorithm Text   : 3....
+--+
1.   Algorithm
2.   Algorithm
3.   Print Text
8   Introduction to Quality IDs
8.1   General
OBJECTIVE OF BUSINESS OBJECT
Quality IDs are used for groups of items with the same quality standards and tests. This is done to reduce the time spent defining quality standards and tests for each item separately in specific situations. Consequently, different characteristics and quality groups can be linked to a quality ID.
All kinds of data which is linked to quality IDs can be defined:
•   Characteristics by Quality ID
•   Tests by Quality ID
•   Test Groups by Quality ID

Characteristics can be assigned to each quality ID. The characteristic data is
default and can be changed.
Quality combinations are used to link a quality ID to an origin. The origin
indicates which other modules are used or are influenced by the use of an
inspection order. The origins are the same as the module names in BAAN IV. These
quality combinations are the primary input for the creation of inspection
orders.
For further information, see keyword(s)
• "Quality Combinations".
Display the procedure and show the sessions in:
• Quality Control Procedure

8.2   Session Overview

Seq.	Session	Description	Session Usage
10	tcqms0110m000	Maintain Quality IDs	Mandatory
11	tcqms0136m000	Maintain Test Groups by Quality ID	Mandatory
12	tcqms0137m000	Maintain Characteristics by Test Group	Mandatory
13	tcqms0115m000	Maintain Characteristics by Quality ID	Mandatory
14	tcqms0117m000	Maintain Tests by Quality ID	Mandatory
15	tcmcs0129m000	Maintain Quality Groups	Mandatory
16	tcqms0120m000	Maintain Items by Quality Group	Mandatory
17	tcqms0111m000	Maintain Quality Combinations	Mandatory
19	tcqms0220m000	Copy Item Range to Quality Group	Additional
20	tcqms0221m000	Delete Item Range from Quality Group	Additional
101	tcqms0410m000	Print Quality IDs	Print
102	tcqms0415m000	Print Characteristics by Quality ID	Print
103	tcqms0417m000	Print Tests by Quality ID	Print
104	tcqms0436m000	Print Test Groups by Quality ID	Print
105	tcqms0411m000	Print Quality Combinations	Print
106	tcmcs0429m000	Print Quality Groups	Print
201	tcqms0510m000	Display Quality IDs	Display
202	tcqms0512m000	Display Where-Used Quality IDs	Display
203	tcqms0515m000	Display Characteristics by Quality ID	Display
204	tcqms0517m000	Display Tests by Quality ID	Display
205	tcqms0536m000	Display Test Groups by Quality ID	Display
206	tcqms0510s000	Display Quality IDs	Display
207	tcqms0512s000	Display Where-Used Quality IDs	Display

```
| 208 | tcqms0515s000 | Display Characteristics by Quality ID | Display |
| 209 | tcqms0517s000 | Display Tests by Quality ID           | Display |
| 210 | tcqms0536s000 | Display Test Groups by Quality ID     | Display |
| 211 | tcqms0511m000 | Display Quality Combinations          | Display |
| 212 | tcmcs0529m000 | Display Quality Groups                | Display |
```

9 Mandatory Sessions

9.1 Maintain Quality IDs (tcqms0110m000)

SESSION OBJECTIVE
To maintain quality IDs which group all quality data.
SEE ALSO KEYWORD(S)
• Quality IDs

```
tcqms0110m000                          multi-occ (2)    Form 1-1
+---------------------------------------------------------------------+
| Maintain Quality IDs                              Company: 000 |
|---------------------------------------------------------------------|
|                                                                     |
| Quality ID       Description                                        |
|                                                                     |
|     1.........   2...........................                       |
|                                                                     |
+---------------------------------------------------------------------+
```

1.   Quality ID
All quality data is linked to one or more items by means of a quality ID.
For further information, see keyword(s)
• Quality IDs
2.   Description

9.2 Maintain Test Groups by Quality ID (tcqms0136m000)

SESSION OBJECTIVE
To maintain test groups by quality ID. Data defined by test group applies to all
the characteristics defined for that test group. See also session "Maintain
Characteristics by Test Group (tcqms0137m000)".
SEE ALSO KEYWORD(S)
• Test Groups by Quality ID
SEE ALSO METHOD(S)
• Using Destructive Tests
• Example Test Types
• Units and Quantities in QMS

```
tcqms0136m000              zoom        multi/group (3    Form 1-1
+---------------------------------------------------------------------+
| Maintain Test Groups by Quality ID                 Company: 000 |
|---------------------------------------------------------------------|
|                                                                     |
| Quality ID    : 1.........  2_____          |
|                                                                     |
|   Test Description  Test Type     Sample Size---------------+ Quality|
|   Group                           %     Unit Total Quantity  Level  |
|                                                                %    |
|     3.. 4.........  5................ 8..  9.. 10............. 11.  |
|                                                                     |
|---------------------------------------------------------------------|
| Frequency Unit : 6..                         Text    : 12___        |
| Frequency      : 7.............                                     |
|                                                                     |
+---------------------------------------------------------------------+
```

1.   Quality ID
All quality data is linked to one or more items by means of a quality ID.
For further information, see keyword(s)

- Quality IDs
2. Description
3. Test Group
For further information, see keyword(s)
- Test Groups by Quality ID
For every test group, one or more samples are drawn from the lot to test the quality. The total quantity of all samples per test group is referred to as the sample size. See also session "Maintain Samples (tcqms1110m000)".
SEE ALSO METHOD(S)
- Units and Quantities in QMS
- Using Destructive Tests
4. Description
5. Test Type
The test type specifies the way in which the samples are drawn from the order quantity. 100 %
All items are inspected. The "Sample Size" and the order quantity have the same value.
Single Sampling
One sample out of the entire order quantity is inspected.
Continuous Sampling
This type of sampling only takes place in case of mass production and is used to control processing. After a particular interval, a sample is drawn as large as the sample size. A decision is taken as to whether to continue the production or to stop and take corrective action. For this test type, data must be entered in the following fields:
- Frequency Unit
- Frequency
For further information, see method(s)
- Example Test Types
- Using Destructive Tests
- Units and Quantities in QMS
6. Frequency Unit
The frequency unit specifies the unit in which the sample size is expressed. The frequency unit and the unit of the order quantity do not have to be identical, in which case, however, a correct conversion factor is essential.
For further information, see keyword(s)
- Units
For further information, see method(s)
- Units and Quantities in QMS

Test Type	Unit
100 % [ENtcqms.tsty.hundred.perc]	Order Unit
Single Sampling	- Sample Size [%] = Order Unit
	- Sample Size = Sample Unit
Continuous Sampling	- Sample Unit = Frequency Unit

7. Frequency
The frequency of continuous inspection expressed in the frequency unit.
Example:
Sample Size [TF@tcqms0310spieces
Frequency [TF@tcqms036100epieces

A new sample of 10 pieces is drawn for every 100 pieces.
For further information, see method(s)

•   Example Test Types
8.   Percentage
The sample size is the total quantity that is to be tested. In this field, it is expressed as a percentage of either the order quantity or the frequency (in case of "Continuous Sampling").
Example:

Test Type	Single Sampling		
Order Quantity	10000	20000	pieces
Percentage	1%	1%	
Sample Size	100*	200*	pieces

* The sample size is automatically updated when the order quantity is changed.
For further information, see method(s)
•   Example Test Types
•   Units and Quantities in QMS

Test Type	Sample Size
100 % [ENtcqms.tsty.hundred.perc]	Order Quantity
Single Sampling	n % of order quantity or n units
Continuous Sampling	n % of frequency or n units

9.   Sample Unit
The sample unit specifies the unit in which the sample size is expressed. If the sample size is expressed as a percentage, the system will use the unit of the order quantity.
The sample unit and the unit of the order quantity do not have to be identical, in which case, however, a correct conversion factor is essential.
For further information, see keyword(s)
•   Units
For further information, see method(s)
•   Units and Quantities in QMS

Test Type	Unit
100 % [ENtcqms.tsty.hundred.perc]	Order Unit
Single Sampling	- Sample Size [%] = Order Unit - Sample Size = Sample Unit
Continuous Sampling	- Sample Unit = Frequency Unit

10.   Sample Size
The sample size is the total quantity of all samples which are to be tested out of the order quantity, expressed in the unit of the sample size. In this field, it is expressed as a fixed quantity.
Example:

Order Quantity	10000	20000	pieces
Percentage	0%	0%	
Sample Size	50	50	pieces

For further information, see method(s)
- Example Test Types
- Units and Quantities in QMS

+--+
| Test Type | Sample Size |
| | |
|-------------------------------+------------------------------------|
100 %	Order Quantity
[ENtcqms.tsty.hundred.p	
erc]	
-------------------------------+------------------------------------
Single Sampling	n % of order quantity or n units
-------------------------------+------------------------------------
Continuous Sampling	n % of frequency or n units
+--+

11.   Acceptable Quality Level
The acceptable quality level is the percentage of all test quantities of all
samples of an inspection order which must pass the test successfully to accept:
- the entire order quantity (Single Sampling)
- the entire frequency quantity (Continuous Sampling)
The percentage can be determined by experience or statistics.
For further information, see method(s)
- Example Test Types
Examples

Single Sampling
Acceptable Quality Level
Sample Size   30 pieces

Sample	le	Result
1	5 pieces	Good
2	10 pieces	Bad
3	15 pieces	Good

Actual Quality Level = [(5 + 15) / (5 + 10 + 15)] x 100 % = 66,67 %
The actual quality is higher than the acceptable quality level.
Consequently, the order quantity is accepted.

Continuous Sampling
Acceptable Quality Level
Order Quantity [TF@tcqms120.oqua300 pieces
Frequency   100 pieces
Sample Size   10 pieces

Sample	le [TF@tcqms110.sActual Quality Level
1	10 pieces	70 % good
2	10 pieces	50 % good
3	10 pieces	80 % good

        Compare the results to the "Acceptable Quality Level
".

Sample	Quality Level		Quantity	
	Actual	Acceptable	Accepted	Rejected
1	70 %	60 %	100	0
2	50 %	60 %	0	100
3	80 %	60 %	100	0
			----	----
		Total	200	100

This field does not apply to tests of type 100 %.
12.   Answer on question y/n

9.3   Maintain Characteristics by Test Group (tcqms0137m000)
SESSION OBJECTIVE
To maintain groups of characteristics which are inspected in the same sample for a specific quality ID.
When inspection orders are generated, the system will also generate:
- an inspection order for each test group;
- an inspection order line for each characteristic.
All characteristics by test group are tested on the same sample.
HOW TO USE THE SESSION
Before groups of characteristics can be maintained for a test group, specific sample data must be defined in session "Maintain Test Groups by Quality ID (tcqms0136m000)".
SPECIAL OPTIONS
- Copy Characteristics [tcqms0137m0001.user.0]
Only those aspects/characteristics are copied which are not used by any test group for the quality ID defined in session "Maintain Characteristics by Quality ID (tcqms0115m000)". Validity dates are not checked during copying.
SEE ALSO KEYWORD(S)
- Characteristics by Test Group

```
tcqms0137m000                              multi/group (3     Form 1-1
+-------------------------------------------------------------------------+
|  Maintain Characteristics by Test Group              Company: 000  |
|-------------------------------------------------------------------------|
|                                                                         |
|  Quality ID    : 1.........   2_____   |
|  Test Group    : 3..  4_____               |
|                                                                         |
|  Aspect    Description        Characteristic Description     Test Seq. |
|                                                                         |
|  5....... 6_____       7....... 8_____     9.. |
|                                                                         |
+-------------------------------------------------------------------------+
```

1.   Quality ID
All quality data is linked to one or more items by means of a quality ID.
For further information, see keyword(s)
- Quality IDs
2.   Description
3.   Test Group
For further information, see keyword(s)
- Test Groups by Quality ID
4.   Description
5.   Aspect
For further information, see keyword(s)
- Aspects
6.   Description
7.   Characteristic
For further information, see keyword(s)
- Characteristics
8.   Description
9.   Test Sequence
The test sequence specifies the sequence in which the characteristics in a test group are tested. Zero test sequence indicates that the sequence of this aspect/characteristic is not important for testing. An aspect or a characteristic with zero test sequence will be tested after all other tests have taken place.
Example:

	Destructive	Sequence
Test 1	No	1
Test 2	Yes	2

Explanation:
The destructive test will take place last.

The sequence number can be the same for more than one characteristic. In this case, the tests will be sorted by aspect/characteristic, unless the test sequence number is zero.

9.4   Maintain Characteristics by Quality ID (tcqms0115m000)

SESSION OBJECTIVE

To define the quality requirements for characteristics. The characteristics defined for a quality ID apply to all the quality combinations to which the quality ID is assigned.

HOW TO USE THE SESSION

The default data of characteristics can be changed.

SEE ALSO KEYWORD(S)
•   Characteristics by Quality ID

SEE ALSO METHOD(S)
•   Using Destructive Tests

```
tcqms0115m000                         multi/group (3    Form 1-2 >
+-------------------------------------------------------------------+
| Maintain Characteristics by Quality ID          Company: 000 |
|-------------------------------------------------------------------|
| Quality ID     : 1.........  2_____  |
| Aspect         : 3.......  4_____  |
|                                                                   |
| Characteristic For   Character. Method   Test      Type of   Char Text |
|             Algo. Type                              Limit     Unit      |
| 5...... 6 7.. 8.... 9......... 10....... 11...... 12....... 13.   32___  |
|                                                                   |
|-------------------------------------------------------------------|
| Effective Date   : 14........    Norm            [22_]: 23........... |
| Expiry Date      : 15........    Upper Limit     [24_]: 25........... |
| Fixed Char. Value: 16............  Lower Limit   [26_]: 27........... |
| Algorithm        : 17.... 18_____  Upper Tolerance [ 28]: 29.    |
| Option Set       : 19.... 20_____  Lower Tolerance [ 30]: 31.    |
| 21_____                                   |
+-------------------------------------------------------------------+
```

1.   Quality ID
All quality data is linked to one or more items by means of a quality ID.
For further information, see keyword(s)
•   Quality IDs
2.   Description
3.   Aspect
For further information, see keyword(s)
•   Aspects
4.   Description
5.   Characteristic
For further information, see keyword(s)
•   Characteristics
6.   Slash Character
7.   Sequence
If a sequence is specified, it is possible to define, for example, the same characteristic twice but with different expiry dates.
8.   For Algorithm
Indication that this characteristic can be used as a variable or constant in the algorithm of another characteristic.
For further information, see keyword(s)
•   Algorithms
•   Variables by Algorithm
9.   Characteristic Type
The type of characteristic is the type of value which may be measured by means of an instrument. Fraction
A ratio of two expressions or numbers other than zero representing part of an integer (written with a decimal point followed by one or more numbers).
Integer
An exact whole number as opposed to a number with decimals.
Option

For this type of characteristic, various options may be defined. For further information, see keyword(s)

- Option Sets
- Options

Characteristic Type	Example
Fraction	3.145
Integer	123
Option	Blue

10. Method

The type of characteristic value or the way in which the characteristic value is calculated. Fixed

The characteristic value is determined once and can be entered in field "Fixed Characteristic Value". It is used to compare results or in algorithms. The results are entered in session "Enter Test Data (tcqms1115m000)".

Variable

Characteristic values are measured immediately by means of an instrument. The results are entered in session "Enter Test Data (tcqms1115m000)".

Algorithm

The characteristic is calculated by means of an algorithm, using the inspection results of variable or fixed characteristics.

For further information, see keyword(s)

- Algorithms

See also field "Algorithm".

Method	Characteristic	Example
Fixed	Pi	3.14..
Variable	Length	4 meters
Algorithm	Voltage	I * R

11. Test

For further information, see keyword(s)

- Tests

12. Type of Limit

The type of limit indicates the way in which the upper and lower limits are entered, namely as a value or tolerance. Value

The limits are entered as values on the following fields:

- Upper Limit
- Lower Limit

Tolerance

The limits are entered as relative values (percentages of the norm) on the following fields:

- Upper Tolerance
- Lower Tolerance

This field only applies to variable characteristics of type "Fraction" or "Integer".

13. Characteristic Unit

The unit in which a characteristic value, e.g. the norm, is specified.

Characteristic Type	Mandatory
Fraction	Yes
Integer	Yes
Option	N/A

For further information, see keyword(s)

- Units

For further information, see method(s)
- Units and Quantities in QMS

14. Effective Date

The date as of which a test can be used to inspect items.

15. Expiry Date

The date as of which a test can no longer be used to inspect the characteristic for this quality ID. The default date is zero (i.e. no expiry date).

16. Fixed Characteristic Value

The value of a constant (i.e. a fixed characteristic) which is used in algorithms.

Example:

Characteristic [TF@tcqms001.chGravity

Fixed Characteristic Value

Only applies to method "Fixed".

If the characteristic is of type "Integer", the value of the characteristic is rounded up to the nearest integer.

Example:

User Entry	Rounded Value
10.5	11
10.4	10
10.6	11

17. Algorithm

For further information, see keyword(s)
- Algorithms

Enter an algorithm if the characteristic is measured by means of method "Algorithm".

For more information see
- Method

18. Description

19. Option Set

For further information, see keyword(s)
- Option Sets

Enter an option set if the characteristic is of type "Option". See also "Characteristic Type" in session "Maintain Characteristics (tcqms0101m000)".

20. Description

21. Description

22. Unit

23. Norm

The norm is the desired quality for this characteristic, expressed in the characteristic unit. Does not apply if the method is "Fixed" or if the type is "Option".

24. Unit

25. Upper Limit

The highest characteristic value for which quality is acceptable, expressed in the characteristic unit. The "Upper Limit" must be greater than or equal to the "Norm".

26. Unit

27. Lower Limit

The lowest characteristic value for which quality is acceptable, expressed in the characteristic unit. The "Lower Limit" must be smaller than or equal to the "Norm".

28. Upper Tolerance Percentage

29. Upper Tolerance

The upper limit, expressed as a relative value (a percentage of the norm). The system will automatically calculate the value of the upper limit.

30. Lower Tolerance Percentage

31. Lower Tolerance

The lower limit, expressed as a relative value (a percentage of the norm). The system will automatically calculate the value of the lower limit.

32. Text

```
| Maintain Characteristics by Quality ID                    Company: 000  |
|-------------------------------------------------------------------------|
| Quality ID      : 1.........  2_____           |
| Aspect          : 3.......  4_____              |
|                                                                         |
| Characteristic Description                 Char. Standard               |
|                                                                         |
| 5...... 6 7.. 8_____        9.......                 |
|                                                                         |
|-------------------------------------------------------------------------|
| Effective Date   : 10_____      Norm            [17_]: 18_____ |
| Expiry Date      : 11_____      Upper Limit     [19_]: 20_____  |
| Fixed Char. Value: 12_____        Lower Limit     [21_]: 22_____  |
| Algorithm        : 13____ 14_____   Upper Tolerance [ 23]:    24_     |
| Option Set       : 15____ 16_____   Lower Tolerance [ 25]:    26_     |
|                                                                         |
+-------------------------------------------------------------------------+
```

1.   Quality ID
All quality data is linked to one or more items by means of a quality ID.
For further information, see keyword(s)
•   Quality IDs
2.   Description
3.   Aspect
For further information, see keyword(s)
•   Aspects
4.   Description
5.   Characteristic
For further information, see keyword(s)
•   Characteristics
6.   Slash Character
7.   Sequence
If a sequence is specified, it is possible to define, for example, the same
characteristic twice but with different expiry dates.
8.   Description
9.   Characteristic Standard
The standard normally used for characteristics. This is an informative field.
Example:
A DIN standard.
10.   Effective Date
The date as of which a test can be used to inspect items.
11.   Expiry Date
The date as of which a test can no longer be used to inspect the characteristic
for this quality ID. The default date is zero (i.e. no expiry date).
12.   Fixed Characteristic Value
The value of a constant (i.e. a fixed characteristic) which is used in
algorithms.
Example:
Characteristic [TF@tcqms001.chGravity
Fixed Characteristic Value
13.   Algorithm
For further information, see keyword(s)
•   Algorithms
14.   Description
15.   Option Set
For further information, see keyword(s)
•   Option Sets
16.   Description
17.   Unit
The unit in which a characteristic value, e.g. the norm, is specified.

Characteristic Type	Mandatory
Fraction	Yes
Integer	Yes
Option	N/A

For further information, see keyword(s)
- Units

For further information, see method(s)
- Units and Quantities in QMS

18.   Norm

The norm is the desired quality for this characteristic, expressed in the characteristic unit.

19.   Unit

The unit in which a characteristic value, e.g. the norm, is specified.

Characteristic Type	Mandatory
Fraction	Yes
Integer	Yes
Option	N/A

For further information, see keyword(s)
- Units

For further information, see method(s)
- Units and Quantities in QMS

20.   Upper Limit

The highest characteristic value for which quality is acceptable, expressed in the characteristic unit.

21.   Unit

The unit in which a characteristic value, e.g. the norm, is specified.

Characteristic Type	Mandatory
Fraction	Yes
Integer	Yes
Option	N/A

For further information, see keyword(s)
- Units

For further information, see method(s)
- Units and Quantities in QMS

22.   Lower Limit

The lowest characteristic value for which quality is acceptable, expressed in the characteristic unit.

23.   Upper Tolerance Percentage
24.   Upper Tolerance

The upper limit, expressed as a relative value (a percentage of the norm). The system will automatically calculate the value of the upper limit.

25.   Lower Tolerance Percentage
26.   Lower Tolerance

The lower limit, expressed as a relative value (a percentage of the norm). The system will automatically calculate the value of the lower limit.

9.5   Maintain Tests by Quality ID (tcqms0117m000)

SESSION OBJECTIVE

To define the alternative tests for a specific quality ID and a characteristic. The default data of tests by characteristic can be used and customized for this specific quality ID. A single test may be used for several quality IDs and a single quality ID may have several tests.

SEE ALSO KEYWORD(S)
- Tests by Quality ID

SEE ALSO METHOD(S)
- Using Destructive Tests
- Quality Control Procedure

SPECIAL OPTIONS

Copy Default Data [tcqms0117m0001.user.0]

The default data defined in session "Maintain Tests by Characteristic (tcqms0105m000)" can be copied. Tests by quality ID which were previously defined in this session can be overwritten with the defaults.

```
tcqms0117m000                                  multi/group (3     Form 1-1
+------------------------------------------------------------------------------+
| Maintain Tests by Quality ID                               Company: 000  |
|------------------------------------------------------------------------------|
|                                                                          |
| Quality ID    : 1........  2_____                          |
```

```
| Aspect         : 3.......  4_____    Char. Type : 7_____ |
| Characteristic: 5.......  6_____    Char. Unit : 8__           |
|                                                                                |
|    Test        Description        Unit  Destructive  Result Type      Text     |
|                                                                                |
|    9.......  10_____    11.  12...        13.............  14___     |
|                                                                                |
|--------------------------------------------------------------------------------|
| Test Std.  : 15......              Employee  : 20.... 21_____         |
| Skill      : 16..  17_____ Instrument: 22.... 23_____         |
| Test Area  : 18.  19_____                                              |
|                                                                                |
+--------------------------------------------------------------------------------+
```

1.   Quality ID
All quality data is linked to one or more items by means of a quality ID.
For further information, see keyword(s)
•   Quality IDs
The system uses quality IDs when quality combinations, characteristics by
quality ID, and characteristic tests by quality ID are defined.
2.   Description
3.   Aspect
For further information, see keyword(s)
•   Aspects
4.   Description
5.   Characteristic
For further information, see keyword(s)
•   Characteristics
Enter a characteristic.
For further information, see keyword(s)
•   Characteristics by Aspects
6.   Description
7.   Characteristic Type
The type of characteristic is the type of value which may be measured by means
of an instrument.
8.   Characteristic Unit
The unit in which a characteristic value, e.g. the norm, is specified.

Characteristic Type	Mandatory
Fraction	Yes
Integer	Yes
Option	N/A

For further information, see keyword(s)
•   Units
For further information, see method(s)
•   Units and Quantities in QMS
9.   Test
For further information, see keyword(s)
•   Tests
All the tests required to test the quality of this combination of an aspect and
a characteristic.
10.   Description
11.   Test Unit
The unit in which the test results are defined or calculated.
For further information, see keyword(s)
•   "Units"
For further information, see method(s)
•   •   "Units and Quantities in QMS" Does not apply to characteristics of
type "Option".
12.   Destructive
Indication that the test is destructive and that the item cannot be used after
testing.
For further information, see method(s)
•   Using Destructive Tests
13.   Result Type

The type of result which is reported to the user. Quantitative
A quantitative value is reported after testing, e.g. "40 cm".
Qualitative
A qualitative value is reported after testing, e.g. "Acceptable" or "Not
Acceptable".
14.   Text
15.   Test Standard
The standard normally used for the test.
Example:
A DIN standard.
16.   Skill
For further information, see keyword(s)
"Skills".
17.   Description
18.   Test Area
For further information, see keyword(s)
•   Test Areas
19.   Description
20.   Employee
The default employee to execute the test for this characteristic.
For further information, see keyword(s)
•   Employees
21.   Name
The employee's name.
22.   Instrument
For further information, see keyword(s)
•   Instruments
23.   Description
9.6   Maintain Quality Groups (tcmcs0129m000)
SESSION OBJECTIVE
To maintain quality groups.
SEE ALSO KEYWORD(S)
•   Quality Groups

```
tcmcs0129m000                       zoom      multi-occ (2)    Form 1-1
+----------------------------------------------------------------------+
| Maintain Quality Groups                            Company: 000  |
|----------------------------------------------------------------------|
|                                                                      |
| Quality Group  Description                                           |
|                                                                      |
|      1.....  2...........................                            |
|                                                                      |
+----------------------------------------------------------------------+
```

1.   Quality Group
For further information, see keyword(s)
"Quality Groups".
2.   Description
Enter a clear description here.
9.7   Maintain Items by Quality Group (tcqms0120m000)
SESSION OBJECTIVE
To group items with similar quality standards. An item can be grouped in one
group only.
HOW TO USE THE SESSION
The quality data defined for a quality group will apply to all the items of that
group unless quality data was defined for specific items within that group.
The containers of a containerized item are included with that item.
SEE ALSO KEYWORD(S)
•   Items by Quality Group

```
tcqms0120m000                             multi/group (3    Form 1-1
+----------------------------------------------------------------------+
| Maintain Items by Quality Group                    Company: 000  |
|----------------------------------------------------------------------|
|                                                                      |
```

```
| Quality Group: 1..... 2_____            |
|                                                                 |
| Project  Description    Item                                    |
|                                                                 |
|  3..... 4_____   5.............. 6_____   |
|                                                                 |
+-----------------------------------------------------------------+
```

1.   Quality Group
For further information, see keyword(s)
"Quality Groups".
Standard and customized items with the same quality are grouped by quality
group.
2.   Description
3.   Project
The project which applies to the customized item for which a certain quality
inspection is desired. A value must also be entered in field "Item".
For further information, see keyword(s)
•   Projects
Enter a project code for customized items. Skip this field for standard items.
4.   Description
5.   Item
For further information, see keyword(s)
•   Items
Only applies to items of type:
•   Manufactured
•   Purchased
•   Subcontracting
6.   Description
9.8   Maintain Quality Combinations (tcqms0111m000)
SESSION OBJECTIVE
To define quality combinations which, generally speaking, consist of three
parts:
•   the module from which the inspection originates;
•   the item(s) that apply to the combination;
•   the quality ID that applies to the combination.
Defining the desired quality for an item can be done at several levels.
A single quality ID can be used for more than one quality combination.
HOW TO USE THE SESSION
Within this module, this is an important session. For more information on how to
enter these quality combinations, see •   "Defining Quality Combinations".
SEE ALSO KEYWORD(S)
•   Quality Combinations
SPECIAL OPTIONS
•   Validate Quality ID [tcqms0111m0001.user.0]
This option can be used to validate a quality ID. A quality ID is valid when
inspection data can be generated. This means that:
•   The quality ID has at least one test group (Maintain Test Groups by
Quality ID (tcqms0136m000));
•   At least one test group has a combination of an aspect and characteristic
(Maintain Characteristics by Test Group (tcqms0137m000)); NOTE: A characteristic
of method Algorithm is valid when all combinations of an aspect and
characteristic needed by the algorithm are present and valid.
•   The current date falls between the effective date and the expiry date of
the combination of an aspect and characteristic of the quality ID (Maintain
Characteristics by Quality ID (tcqms0115m000));
•   Only one test type can have destructive tests (Maintain Tests by Quality
ID (tcqms0117m000)). NOTE: The total sample percentage of the test groups with
destructive tests can be max. 100%. For more information on destructive tests,
see • "Using Destructive Tests".

```
tcqms0111m000                      zoom      single-occ (1)   Form 1-1
+-----------------------------------------------------------------------+
| Maintain Quality Combinations                       Company: 000  |
|-----------------------------------------------------------------------|
```

```
| Origin                : 1....................                                    |
| Quality Group         : 2.....   3_____                        |
| Project               : 4.....   5_____                        |
| Item                  : 6..............   7_____         |
| Container             : 8..  9_____                      |
| Customer              : 10....  11_____                       |
| Supplier              : 12....  13_____                       |
| Position              : 14.                                                      |
| Standard/Customized   : 15....................                                   |
| Sub-Item              : 16.............   17_____              |
| Container             : 18.  9_____                      |
| Routing               : 19....  20_____                       |
| Operation             : 21.                                                      |
| Task                  : 22..  23_____                          |
| Only Recommended      : 24...                                                    |
| Blocking Method       : 25......................                                 |
| Quality ID            : 26.......  27_____                     |
| Text                  : 28___                                                    |
+----------------------------------------------------------------------------------+
```

1.   Origin
Quality inspections are executed within a module or package. This field is used
to select one of the implemented modules or packages of BAAN IV.
See also session "Maintain QMS Parameters (tcqms0100m000)" for the implemented
modules and packages. For further information, see method(s)
•   Defining Quality Combinations
2.   Quality Group
The quality group, and all the items in it, for which a certain quality
inspection is desired.
For further information, see keyword(s)
•   Quality Groups
•   Items by Quality Group
For further information, see method(s)
•   Defining Quality Combinations
3.   Description
4.   Project
The project which applies to the customized item for which a certain quality
inspection is desired. A value must also be entered in field "Item".
For further information, see keyword(s)
•   Projects
For further information, see method(s)
•   Defining Quality Combinations
5.   Description
6.   Item
The item for which a certain quality inspection is desired. The quality
combination of the item overrules the quality combination of the quality group
to which the item belongs.
For further information, see keyword(s)
•   Items
For further information, see method(s)
•   Defining Quality Combinations
7.   Description
8.   Container
The container in which the item is packaged and for which a certain quality
inspection is desired. See also field "Containerized" in session "Maintain Item
Data (tiitm0101m000)".
For further information, see keyword(s)
•   Units
•   Units By Unit Set
For further information, see method(s)
•   Containerized Items
For further information, see method(s)
•   Defining Quality Combinations
9.   Description

10. Customer

The customer for whom a certain quality inspection is desired.
For further information, see keyword(s)
• Customers
For further information, see method(s)
• Defining Quality Combinations

11. Name

The first part of the customer's name.

12. Supplier

The supplier for whom a certain quality inspection is desired.
For further information, see keyword(s)
• Suppliers
For further information, see method(s)
• Defining Quality Combinations

13. Name

The first part of the supplier's name.

14. Position

The position in the bill of material or formula at which point a certain quality
inspection is to take place. For further information, see method(s)
• Defining Quality Combinations

15. Standard/Custom ized

Indication whether the item is a Standard Item or a Customized Item. For further
information, see method(s)
• Defining Quality Combinations

16. Sub-Item

The sub-item for which a certain quality inspection is desired.
A sub-item may be:
1. a component item used in the bill of material;
2. a material used in the formula.
Field "Position" refers to the line in the BOM or formula.
For further information, see method(s)
• Defining Quality Combinations

17. Description

18. Container

The container in which the sub-item is packaged. See also field "Containerized"
in session "Maintain Item Data (tiitm0101m000)".
For further information, see keyword(s)
• Units
• Units By Unit Set
For further information, see method(s)
• Containerized Items
For further information, see method(s)
• Defining Quality Combinations

19. Routing

The routing that is used in combination with an operation. During or after this
operation a certain quality inspection is to take place.
This field applies to a standard routing if field "Item" is skipped.
For further information, see keyword(s)
• Routing Codes by Item (BAAN Manufacturing)
• Routing Codes by Formula (BAAN Process)
For further information, see method(s)
• Defining Quality Combinations

20. Routing

21. Operation

The operation of the routing. During or after this operation, a certain quality
inspection must take place.
For further information, see keyword(s)
• Routing (BAAN Manufacturing)
• Routing Operations (BAAN Process) For further information, see method(s)
• Defining Quality Combinations

22. Task

The task which is executed during the operation. If there is only one task for
this operation, a value cannot be entered in this field.

For further information, see keyword(s)
- Tasks

For further information, see method(s)
- Defining Quality Combinations

23. Description
The description of the task.

24. Only Recommended
Indication that the use of QMS results is mandatory or recommended.
If the use of QMS results is mandatory, it is not possible to use destructive tests.
This field makes it possible to overrule the value of the (general) parameter "QMS recommendation for ...". See also session "Maintain QMS Parameters (tcqms0100m000)".
A value can only be entered in this field if a quality combination is added.

For further information, see keyword(s)
- Defining Quality Combinations

25. Blocking Method for Inspections
The blocking method refers to the way in which production, purchase, or sales is blocked and is based on the point in the logistical process at which time the inspection takes place. Block
It is not possible to continue production before the inspection results are known.
Continue
It is possible to continue production before the results of previous inspections are known. If the previous field "Only Recommended" is set to "No", this option cannot be used.
Block before Posting
Production is blocked before posting to stock.
Block after Posting
Production is blocked after posting to stock. If the previous field "Only Recommended" is set to "No", this option cannot be used.
Block on Operation
Production is blocked during the operation.
Block on Compl. Operation
Production is blocked upon completion of the operation. If the previous field "Only Recommended" is set to "No", this option cannot be used.

26. Quality ID
All quality data is linked to one or more items by means of a quality ID.

For further information, see keyword(s)
- Quality IDs

For further information, see method(s)
- Defining Quality Combinations

27. Description
28. Text

10   Other Maintenance Sessions
10.1 Copy Item Range to Quality Group (tcqms0220m000)
SESSION OBJECTIVE
To copy a range of standard or customized items to a quality group.
HOW TO USE THE SESSION
The quality group is the target quality group to which the item range will be copied. It is also possible to move items which were already assigned to the selected quality group by means of field "Overwrite Group".
SEE ALSO KEYWORD(S)
- Quality Groups

tcqms0220m000   single-occ (4)   Form 1-1
+---+
Copy Item Range to Quality Group   Company: 000
Quality Group   : 1.....   2_____
Item Group   from : 3.....
to : 4.....

```
|                                                               |
| Project                      from : 5.....                   |
|                              to   : 6.....                   |
|                                                               |
| Item                         from : 7...............         |
|                              to   : 8..............          |
|                                                               |
| Overwrite Group                  : 9....                     |
| Print Report                     : 10...                     |
|                                                               |
| +-Item----------------------------+                          |
| | 11_____                |                         |
| +----------------------------------+                          |
+---------------------------------------------------------------+
```

1.   Quality Group
The selected item range will be copied to this quality group.
2.   Description
3.   Item Group from
4.   Item Group to
5.   Project from
6.   Project to
7.   Item from
8.   Item to
9.   Overwrite Group
If this option is used, the items which are selected are assigned to the
selected quality group. If the items were previously assigned to another group,
they are moved to the selected group.
10.   Print Report
It is possible to print a list of the items which were assigned to the quality
group.
11.   Item
For further information, see keyword(s)
•   Items
10.2 Delete Item Range from Quality Group (tcqms0221m000)
SESSION OBJECTIVE
To delete an item range from a quality group.
HOW TO USE THE SESSION
It is possible to delete a range of customized items from a quality group by
entering the project range.

```
tcqms0221m000                              single-occ (4)    Form 1-1
+---------------------------------------------------------------+
| Delete Item Range from Quality Group          Company: 000    |
|---------------------------------------------------------------|
|                                                               |
| Quality Group                from : 1.....                   |
|                              to   : 2.....                   |
|                                                               |
| Item Group                   from : 3.....                   |
|                              to   : 4.....                   |
|                                                               |
| Project                      from : 5.....                   |
|                              to   : 6.....                   |
|                                                               |
| Item                         from : 7...............         |
|                              to   : 8.............           |
|                                                               |
| Print Report                     : 9....                     |
|                                                               |
| +-Item----------------------------+                          |
| | 10_____                |                         |
| +----------------------------------+                          |
+---------------------------------------------------------------+
```

1.   Quality Group from

2.   Quality Group to
3.   Item Group from
4.   Item Group to
5.   Project from
6.   Project to
7.   Item from
8.   Item to
9.   Print Report
It is possible to print a list of the items which were deleted from particular
quality groups.
10.   Item
For further information, see keyword(s)
•   Items
11   Other Print Sessions
11.1 Print Quality IDs (tcqms0410m000)

tcqms0410m000   single-occ (4)   Form 1-1
+--+
Print Quality IDs   Company: 000
Quality ID   from : 1.........
to   : 2.........
+--+

1.   Quality ID from
2.   Quality ID to
11.2 Print Characteristics by Quality ID (tcqms0415m000)

tcqms0415m000   single-occ (4)   Form 1-1
+--+
Print Characteristics by Quality ID   Company: 000
Quality ID   from : 1.........
to   : 2.........
Aspect   from : 3.......
to   : 4.......
Characteristic   from : 5......
to   : 6......
Sequence   from : 7..
to   : 8..
Print Characteristic Text   : 9....
+--+

1.   Quality ID from
2.   Quality ID to
3.   Aspect from
4.   Aspect to
5.   Characteristic from
6.   Characteristic to
7.   Sequence from
8.   Sequence to
9.   Print Characteristic Text
11.3 Print Tests by Quality ID (tcqms0417m000)

tcqms0417m000   single-occ (4)   Form 1-1
+--+
Print Tests by Quality ID   Company: 000
Quality ID   from : 1.........

```
|                              to    : 2.........                              |
|                                                                              |
| Aspect                       from  : 3.......                                |
|                              to    : 4.......                                |
|                                                                              |
| Characteristic              from   : 5.......                                |
|                              to    : 6.......                                |
|                                                                              |
| Test                        from   : 7.......                                |
|                              to    : 8.......                                |
|                                                                              |
| Print Test Text                    : 9....                                   |
|                                                                              |
+------------------------------------------------------------------------------+
1.   Quality ID from
2.   Quality ID to
3.   Aspect from
4.   Aspect to
5.   Characteristic from
6.   Characteristic to
7.   Test from
8.   Test to
9.   Print Test Text
```

11.4 Print Test Groups by Quality ID (tcqms0436m000)

tcqms0436m000   single-occ (4)   Form 1-1

```
+------------------------------------------------------------------------------+
| Print Test Groups by Quality ID                        Company: 000 |
|------------------------------------------------------------------------------|
|                                                                              |
| Quality ID                  from  : 1.........                              |
|                              to    : 2........                               |
|                                                                              |
| Test Group                  from  : 3..                                     |
|                              to    : 4..                                     |
|                                                                              |
| Print Test Group Text              : 5....                                   |
|                                                                              |
+------------------------------------------------------------------------------+
1.   Quality ID from
2.   Quality ID to
3.   Test Group from
4.   Test Group to
5.   Print Test Group Text
```

11.5 Print Quality Combinations (tcqms0411m000)

tcqms0411m000   single-occ (4)   Form 1-2 >

```
+------------------------------------------------------------------------------+
| Print Quality Combinations                             Company: 000 |
|------------------------------------------------------------------------------|
|                                                                              |
|                      From                      To                            |
|                                                                              |
| Origin             : 1....................   - 2....................         |
| Quality Group      : 3.....                  - 4.....                        |
| Project            : 5.....                  - 6.....                        |
|                                                                              |
| Item        from   : 7..............                                         |
|             to      : 8..............                                        |
|                                                                              |
| Container          : 9..                     - 10.                           |
| Customer           : 11....                  - 12....                        |
| Supplier           : 13....                  - 14....                        |
| Position           : 15.                     - 16.                           |
|                                                                              |
```

```
+-------------------------------------------------------------------------+
  1.      Origin of Inspection
  2.      Origin of Inspection
  3.      Quality Group
  4.      Quality Group
  5.      Project
  6.      Project
  7.      From Item
  8.      To Item
  9.      Unit
  10.     Unit
  11.     Customer
  12.     Customer
  13.     Supplier Number
  14.     Supplier Number
  15.     Position
  16.     Position
  tcqms0411m000                              single-occ (4) < Form 2-2
+-------------------------------------------------------------------------+
| Print Quality Combinations                         Company: 000 |
|-------------------------------------------------------------------------|
|                                                                         |
|                         From                    To                      |
|                                                                         |
| Item Type            : 1....................  - 2.................... |
|                                                                         |
| Sub-Item       from : 3...............                                  |
|                to   : 4...............                                  |
|                                                                         |
| Container            : 5..                    - 6..                     |
| Routing              : 7.....                  - 8.....                 |
| Operation            : 9..                    - 10.                     |
| Task                 : 11..                   - 12..                    |
| Quality ID           : 13.......              - 14.......               |
|                                                                         |
| Print Text           : 15...                                           |
|                                                                         |
+-------------------------------------------------------------------------+
  1.      Item Type
  2.      Item Type
  3.      Item Code
  4.      Item Code
  5.      Unit
  6.      Unit
  7.      opro.f
  8.      opro.t
  9.      Operation Number
  10.     Operation Number
  11.     Task Number
  12.     Task Number
  13.     Quality ID From
  14.     Quality ID To
  15.     Print Text
  11.6  Print Quality Groups (tcmcs0429m000)
  tcmcs0429m000                              single-occ (4)   Form 1-1
+-------------------------------------------------------------------------+
| Print Quality Groups                               Company: 000 |
|-------------------------------------------------------------------------|
|                                                                         |
| Quality Group          from : 1.....                                   |
|                        to   : 2.....                                   |
|                                                                         |
+-------------------------------------------------------------------------+
```

1.   Quality Group
2.   Quality Group
12   Introduction to Calibrations
12.1 General
OBJECTIVE OF BUSINESS OBJECT
Based on the instrument data (specified in business object "Master Data"), the instruments which need to be calibrated can be selected. These selected instruments receive status "Blocked for calibration".
After the instruments are calibrated, the calibration date can be entered. The instruments for which a calibration date was entered are unblocked.
For each instrument, a history of calibration dates is kept by the system based on the instrument and/or the date. This calibration history can be deleted based on instruments and dates.
Although instruments were selected for calibration, they can still be assigned to inspection orders. This is useful for planning purposes. When a blocked instrument is selected for calibration, the system will generate a signal so as to inform the user that the instrument is blocked.
Display the procedure and show the sessions in:
•   Calibration Procedure
12.2 Session Overview

Seq.	Session	Description	Session Usage
0	tcqms3201m000	Select Instruments for Calibration	Mandatory
1	tcqms3202m000	Enter Calibration Dates	Mandatory
2	tcqms3500m000	Display Calibration History	Display
3	tcqms3400m000	Print Calibration History	Print
4	tcqms3200m000	Delete Calibration History	Optional

13   Mandatory Sessions
13.1 Select Instruments for Calibration (tcqms3201m000)
SESSION OBJECTIVE
To select instruments which must be calibrated.
Instruments are due for calibration when the defined interval has elapsed This interval is defined in session "Maintain Test Instruments (tcqms0108m000)". See also the following fields:
•   Calibration Interval Type
•   Calibration Interval   [Days/Times Used]
•   Next Calibration [Times Used]
•   Next Calibration Date
All the instruments selected for calibration are blocked for use.
SEE ALSO KEYWORD(S)
•   Instruments

tcqms3201m000   single-occ (4)   Form 1-1
+--+
Select Instruments for Calibration   Company: 000
Instrument   from: 1.....
to : 2.....
Also Select Instruments in Use   : 3....
Print Report   : 4....
+--+

1.   from Instrument

2.   to
3.   Also Select Instruments in Use
Instruments can still be in use when the moment has come that they are to be
calibrated based on the time or the number of times they have been used. This
option can be used to select
these instruments for calibration.
4.   Print Report
It is possible to print a report of all selected instruments.
13.2 Enter Calibration Dates (tcqms3202m000)
SESSION OBJECTIVE
To enter the calibration dates of instruments which have been calibrated and to
unblock calibrated instruments so that they can be used for inspection again.
All instruments shown in this session are blocked for calibration.
HOW TO USE THE SESSION
•   Unblock one instrument by marking a record and select the unblock option.
•   Unblock all instruments by selecting the unblock option without marking
any record.
SEE ALSO KEYWORD(S)
•   Instruments

```
tcqms3202m000                              multi-occ (2)   Form 1-1
+----------------------------------------------------------------------+
|  Enter Calibration Dates                              Company: 000  |
|--------------------------------------------------------------------|
|                                                                    |
|  Instrument  Description                    Calibration  Calibration |
|                                                 Date       Text     |
|                                                                    |
|     1.....  2_____    3.........  4____     |
|                                                                    |
+----------------------------------------------------------------------+
```

1.   Instrument
For further information, see keyword(s)
•   Instruments
2.   Description
3.   Calibration Date
The date on which the instrument is (to be) calibrated.
4.   Text Company
14   Optional Sessions
14.1 Delete Calibration History (tcqms3200m000)
SESSION OBJECTIVE
To delete the calibration history of instruments.
SEE ALSO KEYWORD(S)
•   Calibration History

```
tcqms3200m000                              single-occ (4)   Form 1-1
+----------------------------------------------------------------------+
|  Delete Calibration History                           Company: 000  |
|--------------------------------------------------------------------|
|                                                                    |
|  Instrument            from : 1.....                               |
|                        to   : 2.....                               |
|                                                                    |
|  Calibration Date      from : 3.........                           |
|                        to   : 4.........                           |
|                                                                    |
|  Print Report               : 5....                               |
|                                                                    |
|  Print Text                 : 6....                               |
|                                                                    |
|                                                                    |
|  +-Instrument--------------------------+                           |
|  | 7_____  8_____ |                        |
|  +--------------------------------------+                          |
|                                                                    |
```

```
+----------------------------------------------------------------------------+
```
1.   Instrument from
2.   Instrument to
3.   Date from
4.   Date to
5.   Print
It is possible to print a report of all deleted calibration history data.
6.   Print Text
7.   Instrument
For further information, see keyword(s)
•   Instruments
8.   Description
15   Other Print Sessions
15.1   Print Calibration History (tcqms3400m000)
tcqms3400m000   single-occ (4)   Form 1-1
```
+----------------------------------------------------------------------------+
|  Print Calibration History                               Company: 000  |
|----------------------------------------------------------------------------|
|                                                                            |
|  Instrument            from : 1.....                                       |
|                        to   : 2.....                                       |
|                                                                            |
|  Calibration Date      from : 3........                                    |
|                        to   : 4........                                    |
|                                                                            |
|  Print Text                 : 5....                                        |
|                                                                            |
+----------------------------------------------------------------------------+
```
1.   Instrument
2.   Instrument
3.   from
4.   to
5.   Print Text
16   Introduction to Standard Inspections
16.1   General
OBJECTIVE OF BUSINESS OBJECT
Inspection orders can be created automatically by means of predefined quality
combinations. It is possible to maintain, add, or delete inspection orders based
on the origin of the order.
All inspection orders are linked to sales, purchase, or production
orders/batches through the origin.
For each inspection order, different samples with different sample sizes and
different dates and times can be created. The system always checks if the total
of all samples matches the sample size.
It is possible to enter the test data for each item of a sample after the
inspection on each sample item. This test data can be entered either by unit or
by characteristic. When the test data is entered, the system will generate the
answers, if defined for that specific characteristic.
If an algorithm was defined for a characteristic, this algorithm can be
calculated during inspection. Each algorithm is only calculated when the
variables (characteristics) needed for that algorithm are entered. This applies
only to each sample of an inspection order.
The results for all characteristics and aspects in the inspection order are
recorded for each piece in a sample.
Inspection orders can be completed collectively by order, origin, or storage
inspection. If an inspection order is completed, the system checks if all test
data is entered. If not, the inspection order cannot be completed.
Inspection orders can be processed by inspection order, by origin, and by
storage inspection to let the system determine the "good" and the "bad" pieces
in the sample size. Based on this the system calculates the actual accepted and
rejected quantities. These accepted and rejected quantities are compared with
the acceptable quality level (AQL). If the percentage of accepted quantity is
less than the AQL, the entire order or lot is rejected.

For each item, the inspection order sequence, the quantity ordered, the recommended and actual quantities accepted, and the recommended and actual quantities rejected, and the status of the order can be shown.
While the order quantities are updated, the system checks if the "destructive" field is set to "yes". If so, the system subtracts the sample quantity from the order quantity.
All test data and inspection orders can be deleted collectively by inspection order, by origin, and by storage inspection order.
Display the procedure and show the sessions in:
• Inspection Procedure

16.2 Session Overview

Seq.	Session	Description	Session Usage
10	tcqms1120m000	Maintain Standard Inspections by Origin	Mandatory
11	tcqms1100s000	Maintain Inspection Orders	Mandatory
12	tcqms1101s000	Maintain Inspection Order Lines	Additional
13	tcqms1110m000	Maintain Samples	Mandatory
14	tcqms1115m000	Enter Test Data	Mandatory
15	tcqms1202m000	Complete Inspection Orders Collectively	Additional
16	tcqms1203m000	Delete Inspection Orders Collectively	Additional
17	tcqms1204m000	Process Inspection Orders	Additional
18	tcqms1205m000	Check and Close Standard Inspections	Optional
19	tcqms1215m000	Delete Test Data Collectively	Optional
101	tcqms1400m000	Print Inspection Orders	Print
102	tcqms1410m000	Print Samples	Print
103	tcqms1415m000	Print Test Data	Print
201	tcqms1500s000	Display Inspection Orders	Display
202	tcqms1510m000	Display Samples	Display
203	tcqms1515m000	Display Test Data by Characteristic	Display
204	tcqms1520m000	Display Standard Inspections	Display
206	tcqms1501s000	Display Inspection Order Lines	Display
207	tcqms1502s000	Maintain Inspection Orders	Display
208	tcqms1510s000	Display Samples	Display
209	tcqms1504s000	Display Inspec Orders (Standard Inspect	Display
210	tcqms1505s000	Display Inspection Order Lines	Display
211	tcqms1516m000	Display Test Data by Unit	Display

17.1 Maintain Standard Inspections by Origin (tcqms1120m000)

SESSION OBJECTIVE

To maintain inspections by origin. In this session, the order numbers of the orders in other BAAN IV modules for which an inspection order exists are shown. It is also possible to manually enter new inspection orders.

HOW TO USE THE SESSION

Options "Select Record [mark.occur]" and "Zoom [zoom]" are used to maintain the inspection order(s) for a specific order.

Only inspections with status "Free" can be deleted.

SEE ALSO KEYWORD(S)

• Inspection Orders

SEE ALSO METHOD(S)

• Inspection Order and Order Line Status

• Integrations

```
tcqms1120m000                    zoom    multi/group (3    Form 1-3 >
+-----------------------------------------------------------------------+
| Maintain Standard Inspections by Origin              Company: 000 |
|-----------------------------------------------------------------------|
|                                                                       |
| Origin                  : 1...................                        |
|                                                                       |
|    Origin Pos. Opr. Receipt/  Inbound/ Seq. Only   Blocking Method Insp.|
|    Order          Delivery  Outbound      Recom.                 Status |
|                                                                       |
|    2..... 3... 4..        5. 6......  7. 8.... 9.............. 10_____||
|                                                                       |
+-----------------------------------------------------------------------+
```

1. Origin

The origin of the inspection is an integrated package or module.

See also session "Maintain QMS Parameters (tcqms0100m000)" for the implemented modules and packages.

2. Origin Order

The order number of the origin of the inspection:

+--+
| Origin | Origin Order |
|---------------------------------+--------------------------------------|
Sales (SLS)	Sales Orders
Purchase (PUR)	Purchase Orders
Production (SFC)	Production Orders
Material (BOM)	Production Orders
Routing (TI)	Production Orders
Production (PMG)	Production Batches
Material (FRM)	Production Batches
Routing (PS)	Production Batches
+--+

3. Position

The position number on the order to which the inspection order applies, namely:

• the position of the sales order;
• the position of the purchase order;
• the position of the estimated materials;
• the position of the estimated co- by-products;
• the position of the estimated end items.

4. Operation

The operation of the routing. During or after this operation, a certain quality inspection must take place.

For further information, see keyword(s)

- Routing (BAAN Manufacturing)
- Routing Operations (BAAN Process)

5.   Receipt/Delivery

A sequence number representing the number of:
- the receipt line (Purchase (PUR));
- the delivery line (Sales (SLS)).

6.   Inbound/Outbound

The sequence number of a partial delivery or receipt when multiple inbound or outbound lines are used in module "Location Control (ILC)".
For lot items, the number may be the number of:
- the inbound line for the same partial delivery (Purchase (PUR));
- the outbound line for the same partial delivery (Purchase (PUR), Material (BOM), Material (FRM)).

7.   Sequence Number

The sequence number of the inspection order on the basis of which characteristics are tested on different samples. Does not apply to the following origins:
- Sales (SLS)
- Purchase (PUR)

8.   Only Recommended

Indication that the use of QMS results is mandatory or recommended.
If the use of QMS results is mandatory, it is not possible to use destructive tests.
This field makes it possible to overrule the value of the (general) parameter "QMS recommendation for ...". See also session "Maintain QMS Parameters (tcqms0100m000)".

9.   Blocking Method for Inspections

The blocking method refers to the way in which production, purchase, or sales is blocked and is based on the point in the logistical process at which time the inspection takes place. Block
It is not possible to continue production before the inspection results are known.
Continue
It is possible to continue production before the results of previous inspections are known. If the previous field "Only Recommended" is set to "No", this option cannot be used.
Block before Posting
Production is blocked before posting to stock.
Block after Posting
Production is blocked after posting to stock. If the previous field "Only Recommended" is set to "No", this option cannot be used.
Block on Operation
Production is blocked during the operation.
Block on Compl. Operation
Production is blocked upon completion of the operation. If the previous field "Only Recommended" is set to "No", this option cannot be used.

10.   Inspection Status

The inspection status indicates the current status of the inspection order. The status is changed during several sessions:

Session	Inspection Status
Maintain Inspection Orders (tcqms1100s000)	Free
Maintain Storage Inspections (tcqms2120m000)	Free
Enter Test Data (tcqms1115m000)	Active
Complete Inspection Orders Collectively	Completed

```
| (tcqms1202m000)                              |                          |
|----------------------------------------------+--------------------------|
| Process Inspection Orders (tcqms1204m000)    | Processed                |
|                                              |                          |
|----------------------------------------------+--------------------------|
| Check and Close Standard Inspections         | Closed                   |
| (tcqms1205m000)                              |                          |
+----------------------------------------------------------------------------+
```

For further information, see method(s)
•   Inspection Order and Order Line Status
tcqms1120m000   zoom   single/grp (3) < Form 2-3 >

```
+-------------------------------------------------------------------------------+
|  Maintain Standard Inspections by Origin                     Company: 000  |
|-------------------------------------------------------------------------------|
|                                                                               |
|  Origin                  : 1...................                               |
|                                                                               |
|  Origin Order            : 2.....          Insp. Status  : 17_____      |
|  Position                : 3...            Order Quantity: 18_____      |
|  Operation               : 4..             Order Unit    : 19_                |
|  Receipt/Delivery        : 5.                                                 |
|  Inbound/Outbound        : 6.......        Warehouse     : 20_                |
|  Sequence Number         : 7.              Description   : 21_____     |
|  Only Recommended        : 8....           Location      : 22_____           |
|  Blocking Method         : 9................ Lot          : 23_____     |
|  Reason for Rejection: 10.                 Date          : 24_____         |
|  Description             : 11_____ Storage Unit  : 25_                |
|                                                                               |
|  Project                 : 12____  13_____          |
|  Item                    : 14_____                                     |
|  Description             : 15_____                        |
|  Container               : 16_                                                |
+-------------------------------------------------------------------------------+
```

1.   Origin
The origin of the inspection is an integrated package or module.
See also session "Maintain QMS Parameters (tcqms0100m000)" for the implemented modules and packages.
2.   Origin Order
The order number of the origin of the inspection:

Origin	Origin Order
Sales (SLS)	Sales Orders
Purchase (PUR)	Purchase Orders
Production (SFC)	Production Orders
Material (BOM)	Production Orders
Routing (TI)	Production Orders
Production (PMG)	Production Batches
Material (FRM)	Production Batches
Routing (PS)	Production Batches

3.   Position
The position number on the order to which the inspection order applies, namely:
•   the position of the sales order;
•   the position of the purchase order;
•   the position of the estimated materials;

- the position of the estimated co- by-products;
- the position of the estimated end items.

4.   Operation

The operation of the routing. During or after this operation, a certain quality inspection must take place.

For further information, see keyword(s)

- Routing (BAAN Manufacturing)
- Routing Operations (BAAN Process)

5.   Receipt/Delivery

A sequence number representing the number of:

- the receipt line (Purchase (PUR));
- the delivery line (Sales (SLS)).

6.   Inbound/Outbound

The sequence number of a partial delivery or receipt when multiple inbound or outbound lines are used in module "Location Control (ILC)".

For lot items, the number may be the number of:

- the inbound line for the same partial delivery (Purchase (PUR));
- the outbound line for the same partial delivery (Purchase (PUR), Material (BOM), Material (FRM)).

7.   Sequence Number

The sequence number of the inspection order on the basis of which characteristics are tested on different samples. Does not apply to the following origins:

- Sales (SLS)
- Purchase (PUR)

8.   Only Recommended

Indication that the use of QMS results is mandatory or recommended.

If the use of QMS results is mandatory, it is not possible to use destructive tests.

This field makes it possible to overrule the value of the (general) parameter "QMS recommendation for ...". See also session "Maintain QMS Parameters (tcqms0100m000)".

9.   Blocking Method for Inspections

The blocking method refers to the way in which production, purchase, or sales is blocked and is based on the point in the logistical process at which time the inspection takes place. Block

It is not possible to continue production before the inspection results are known.

Continue

It is possible to continue production before the results of previous inspections are known. If the previous field "Only Recommended" is set to "No", this option cannot be used.

Block before Posting

Production is blocked before posting to stock.

Block after Posting

Production is blocked after posting to stock. If the previous field "Only Recommended" is set to "No", this option cannot be used.

Block on Operation

Production is blocked during the operation.

Block on Compl. Operation

Production is blocked upon completion of the operation. If the previous field "Only Recommended" is set to "No", this option cannot be used.

10.   Reason for Rejection

For further information, see keyword(s)

"Reasons for Rejection".

11.   Description

12.   Project

The project code which applies to the customized item.

For further information, see keyword(s)

- Projects

13.   Project Description

14.   Item

The item which is to be inspected.

For further information, see keyword(s)
- Items

15. Description
16. Container
The container in which the item is packaged.
For further information, see keyword(s)
- Units
- Units By Unit Set

17. Inspection Status
The inspection status indicates the current status of the inspection order. The status is changed during several sessions:

Session	Inspection Status
Maintain Inspection Orders (tcqms1100s000)	Free
Maintain Storage Inspections (tcqms2120m000)	Free
Enter Test Data (tcqms1115m000)	Active
Complete Inspection Orders Collectively (tcqms1202m000)	Completed
Process Inspection Orders (tcqms1204m000)	Processed
Check and Close Standard Inspections (tcqms1205m000)	Closed

For further information, see method(s)
- Inspection Order and Order Line Status

18. Order Quantity
The order quantity is the inspected quantity which may originate from several modules. It is expressed in the unit related to the module from which it originates:

Origin	Order Quantity	Unit
Sales (SLS)	Delivered Quantity	Purchase Unit
Purchase (PUR)	Received Quantity	Sales Unit
Production (SFC)	Order Quantity	Inventory Unit
Material (BOM)	Order Quantity	Inventory Unit
Routing (TI)	Order Quantity	Inventory Unit
Production (PMG)	Batch Quantity	Inventory Unit
Material (FRM)	Batch Quantity	Inventory Unit
Routing (PS)	Batch Quantity	Inventory Unit

Note:
In case of project items, the unit is the "Inventory Unit" as defined for the customized item.

19.   Order Unit
The order quantity is the inspected quantity which may originate from several
modules. It is expressed in the unit related to the module from which it
originates:

+--+
| Origin | Order Quantity | Unit |
| | | |
|-----------------------------+---------------------+----------------|
Sales (SLS)	Delivered Quantity	Purchase Unit
Purchase (PUR)	Received Quantity	Sales Unit
Production (SFC)	Order Quantity	Inventory Unit
Material (BOM)	Order Quantity	Inventory Unit
Routing (TI)	Order Quantity	Inventory Unit
Production (PMG)	Batch Quantity	Inventory Unit
Material (FRM)	Batch Quantity	Inventory Unit
Routing (PS)	Batch Quantity	Inventory Unit
+--+

Note:
In case of project items, the unit is the "Inventory Unit" as defined for the
customized item.
20.   Warehouse
For further information, see keyword(s)
"Warehouses".
21.   Description
22.   Location
The location where the lot is stored.
For further information, see keyword(s)
•   Locations
23.   Lot
For further information, see keyword(s)
•   Lots
24.   Date
The date assigned to the item/lot at the time it is stored. For more
information, see also field "Date" in "Location Control (ILC)".
25.   Storage Unit
The storage unit is the unit in which items are stored. The storage unit is used
in module "Location Control (ILC)".
For further information, see method(s)
•   Units and Quantities in QMS
The result of the inspection in the form of accepted and rejected quantities.
Example:

```
+Quantities-----------------------------------Order Unit---------+
|Recommended Quantity Accepted                            kg      |
|Recommended Quantity Rejected                            kg      |
|Actual Quantity Accepted [TFtcqms1202050,0000            kg      |
|Actual Quantity Rejected [TFtcqms120.400,0000            kg      |
|Rec. Quantity Destroyed [TFtcqms120.rd50,0000            kg      |
+----------------------------------------------------------------+
```

SEE ALSO METHOD(S)
•   Units and Quantities in QMS

```
tcqms1120m000                      zoom      single/grp (3) < Form 3-3
+----------------------------------------------------------------------+
|  Maintain Standard Inspections by Origin               Company: 000  |
|----------------------------------------------------------------------|
|                                                                      |
```

```
| Origin                    : 1...................                               |
|                                                                                |
| Origin Order              : 2.....        Insp. Status  : 3_____|
| Position                  : 4...          Order Quantity : 5_____|
| Operation                 : 6..           Order Unit    : 7__                  |
| Receipt/Delivery          : 8.                                                 |
| Inbound/Outbound          : 9.......                                           |
| Sequence Number           : 10                                                 |
|                                                                                |
|+-Quantities-----------------------------+                                      |
|| Recommended Accepted: 11_____7__ |                                    |
|| Recommended Rejected: 12_____7__ |                                    |
|| Actual Accepted     : 13_____7__ |                                    |
|| Actual Rejected     : 14_____7__ |                                    |
|| Destroyed           : 15_____7__ |                                    |
|+-----------------------------------------+                                     |
|                                                                                |
+--------------------------------------------------------------------------------+
```

1.   Origin

The origin of the inspection is an integrated package or module.
See also session "Maintain QMS Parameters (tcqms0100m000)" for the implemented
modules and packages.

2.   Origin Order

The order number of the origin of the inspection:

Origin	Origin Order
Sales (SLS)	Sales Orders
Purchase (PUR)	Purchase Orders
Production (SFC)	Production Orders
Material (BOM)	Production Orders
Routing (TI)	Production Orders
Production (PMG)	Production Batches
Material (FRM)	Production Batches
Routing (PS)	Production Batches

3.   Inspection Status

The inspection status indicates the current status of the inspection order. The
status is changed during several sessions:

Session	Inspection Status
Maintain Inspection Orders (tcqms1100s000)	Free
Maintain Storage Inspections (tcqms2120m000)	Free
Enter Test Data (tcqms1115m000)	Active
Complete Inspection Orders Collectively (tcqms1202m000)	Completed
Process Inspection Orders (tcqms1204m000)	Processed

```
|                                               |                       |
|-----------------------------------------------+-----------------------|
| Check and Close Standard Inspections          | Closed                |
| (tcqms1205m000)                               |                       |
+-------------------------------------------------------------------------+
```

For further information, see method(s)
•   Inspection Order and Order Line Status
4.   Position
The position number on the order to which the inspection order applies, namely:
•   the position of the sales order;
•   the position of the purchase order;
•   the position of the estimated materials;
•   the position of the estimated co- by-products;
•   the position of the estimated end items.
5.   Order Quantity
The order quantity is the inspected quantity which may originate from several modules. It is expressed in the unit related to the module from which it originates:

Origin	Order Quantity	Unit
Sales (SLS)	Delivered Quantity	Purchase Unit
Purchase (PUR)	Received Quantity	Sales Unit
Production (SFC)	Order Quantity	Inventory Unit
Material (BOM)	Order Quantity	Inventory Unit
Routing (TI)	Order Quantity	Inventory Unit
Production (PMG)	Batch Quantity	Inventory Unit
Material (FRM)	Batch Quantity	Inventory Unit
Routing (PS)	Batch Quantity	Inventory Unit

Note:
In case of project items, the unit is the "Inventory Unit" as defined for the customized item.
6.   Operation
The operation of the routing. During or after this operation, a certain quality inspection must take place.
For further information, see keyword(s)
•   Routing (BAAN Manufacturing)
•   Routing Operations (BAAN Process)
7.   Order Unit
The order quantity is the inspected quantity which may originate from several modules. It is expressed in the unit related to the module from which it originates:

Origin	Order Quantity	Unit
Sales (SLS)	Delivered Quantity	Purchase Unit
Purchase (PUR)	Received Quantity	Sales Unit
Production (SFC)	Order Quantity	Inventory Unit
Material (BOM)	Order Quantity	Inventory Unit

Routing (TI)	Order Quantity	Inventory Unit	
Production (PMG)	Batch Quantity	Inventory Unit	
Material (FRM)	Batch Quantity	Inventory Unit	
Routing (PS)	Batch Quantity	Inventory Unit	

Note:
In case of project items, the unit is the "Inventory Unit" as defined for the customized item.

8.   Receipt/Delivery
A sequence number representing the number of:
*   the receipt line (Purchase (PUR));
*   the delivery line (Sales (SLS)).

9.   Inbound/Outbound
The sequence number of a partial delivery or receipt when multiple inbound or outbound lines are used in module "Location Control (ILC)".
For lot items, the number may be the number of:
*   the inbound line for the same partial delivery (Purchase (PUR));
*   the outbound line for the same partial delivery (Purchase (PUR), Material (BOM), Material (FRM)).

10.   Sequence Number
The sequence number of the inspection order on the basis of which characteristics are tested on different samples. Does not apply to the following origins:
*   Sales (SLS)
*   Purchase (PUR)

11.   Recommended Quantity Accepted
The quantity to be accepted, as recommended by QMS, expressed in the order unit (or inventory unit for "Storage Inspection"). The total of all sample quantities which passed the tests successfully.
This quantity is updated by means of session "Process Inspection Orders (tcqms1204m000)".

12.   Recommended Quantity Rejected
The quantity to be rejected, as recommended by QMS, expressed in the order unit (or inventory unit for "Storage Inspection"). The total of all sample quantities which do not have the required quality level.
This quantity is updated by means of session "Process Inspection Orders (tcqms1204m000)".

13.   Actual Quantity Accepted
The actual quantity that is accepted, expressed in the order unit (or the inventory unit for "Storage Inspection"). The actual quantity can be adjusted until the inspection order is closed.
Only Recommended
If parameter field "Only Recommended" is set to "No", the results are mandatory. Consequently, this field is the same as field "Recommended Quantity Accepted". However, storage inspections are always only recommended. All inventory of the storage inspection order will be unblocked.

14.   Actual Quantity Rejected
The actual quantity which is rejected, expressed in the order unit (or the inventory unit for "Storage Inspection"). The actual quantity can be adjusted until the inspection order is closed.
Only Recommended
If field "Only Recommended" is set to "No", the results are mandatory. Consequently, the value of this field is the same as the value of field "Recommended Quantity Rejected". However, storage inspections are always "Only Recommended". All inventory of the storage inspection order will be unblocked.

15.   Rec. Quantity Destroyed

The total quantity which is destroyed during a destructive test, expressed in
the order unit. This quantity is equal to the sample size of the inspection
orders which are tested by means of destructive tests.
The destroyed quantity does not have any impact on the accepted or rejected
quantities. The system only calculates which quantity is destroyed according to
the test.
This quantity is automatically updated in session "Process Inspection Orders
(tcqms1204m000)".

17.2 Maintain Inspection Orders (tcqms1100s000)

SESSION OBJECTIVE
To maintain the inspection orders which were generated by default or to manually
add new inspection orders.

HOW TO USE THE SESSION
Inspection order headers can only be modified if the "Inspection Status" is
either "Free" or "Active" and if no order lines have an "Order Line Status"
greater than "Active".

SEE ALSO KEYWORD(S)
•   Inspection Orders

SEE ALSO METHOD(S)
•   Generating Standard Inspections
•   Inspection Order and Order Line Status
•   Using Destructive Tests
•   Inspection Procedure

```
tcqms1100s000                          zoom         single/grp (3)   Form 1-2 >
+-----------------------------------------7_____8-9_____-+
| Origin          : 1_____       Receipt/Delivery:      4_  |
| Origin Order    :              2_____     Inbound/Outbound: 6_____   |
| 3_____ :              5___       Order Qty. [10_]: 11_____  |
|                                                                     |
| Inspection Order : 12 13...... 14_____  +-Sample Data----------------+ |
| Quality ID       : 15........ 16_____   | Percentage : 22          | |
| Test Group       : 17. 18_____    | Unit       : 23.         | |
| Test Type        : 19....................    | Size       : 24...........| |
| Frequency  [20. ]: 21.............           +---------------------------+ |
|                                                                     |
+---------------------------------------------------------------------+
```

1.   Origin
The origin of the inspection is an integrated package or module.
See also session "Maintain QMS Parameters (tcqms0100m000)" for the implemented
modules and packages.
2.   Origin Order
The order number of the origin of the inspection:

+---+
Origin	Origin Order
Sales (SLS)	Sales Orders
Purchase (PUR)	Purchase Orders
Production (SFC)	Production Orders
Material (BOM)	Production Orders
Routing (TI)	Production Orders
Production (PMG)	Production Batches
Material (FRM)	Production Batches
Routing (PS)	Production Batches
+---+

3.   Origin Order Origin
4.   Receipt/Delivery

A sequence number representing the number of:
- the receipt line (Purchase (PUR));
- the delivery line (Sales (SLS)).

5.   Position/Operation

For more information, see the help information on:
- Position
- Operation

6.   Inbound/Outbound

The sequence number of a partial delivery or receipt when multiple inbound or outbound lines are used in module "Location Control (ILC)".

For lot items, the number may be the number of:
- the inbound line for the same partial delivery (Purchase (PUR));
- the outbound line for the same partial delivery (Purchase (PUR), Material (BOM), Material (FRM)).

7.   Description
8.   Program domain of string length 1
9.   Status

The inspection status indicates the current status of the inspection order. The status is changed during several sessions:

Session	Inspection Status
Maintain Inspection Orders (tcqms1100s000)	Free
Maintain Storage Inspections (tcqms2120m000)	Free
Enter Test Data (tcqms1115m000)	Active
Complete Inspection Orders Collectively (tcqms1202m000)	Completed
Process Inspection Orders (tcqms1204m000)	Processed
Check and Close Standard Inspections (tcqms1205m000)	Closed

For further information, see method(s)
- Inspection Order and Order Line Status

10.   Unit

The order quantity is the inspected quantity which may originate from several modules. It is expressed in the unit related to the module from which it originates:

Origin	Order Quantity	Unit
Sales (SLS)	Delivered Quantity	Purchase Unit
Purchase (PUR)	Received Quantity	Sales Unit
Production (SFC)	Order Quantity	Inventory Unit
Material (BOM)	Order Quantity	Inventory Unit
Routing (TI)	Order Quantity	Inventory Unit
Production (PMG)	Batch Quantity	Inventory Unit

Material (FRM)	Batch Quantity	Inventory Unit
Routing (PS)	Batch Quantity	Inventory Unit

Note:
In case of project items, the unit is the "Inventory Unit" as defined for the customized item.

11.   Order Quantity
The order quantity is the inspected quantity which may originate from several modules. It is expressed in the unit related to the module from which it originates:

| Origin | Order Quantity | Unit |
Sales (SLS)	Delivered Quantity	Purchase Unit
Purchase (PUR)	Received Quantity	Sales Unit
Production (SFC)	Order Quantity	Inventory Unit
Material (BOM)	Order Quantity	Inventory Unit
Routing (TI)	Order Quantity	Inventory Unit
Production (PMG)	Batch Quantity	Inventory Unit
Material (FRM)	Batch Quantity	Inventory Unit
Routing (PS)	Batch Quantity	Inventory Unit

Note:
In case of project items, the unit is the "Inventory Unit" as defined for the customized item.

12.   Inspection Order
13.   Inspection Order
The number of the inspection order.
For further information, see keyword(s)
•   Inspection Orders
14.   Description
15.   Quality ID
All quality data is linked to one or more items by means of a quality ID.
For further information, see keyword(s)
•   Quality IDs
16.   Description
17.   Test Group
For further information, see keyword(s)
•   Test Groups by Quality ID
18.   Description
19.   Test Type
The test type specifies the way in which the samples are drawn from the order quantity. 100 %
All items are inspected. The "Sample Size" and the order quantity have the same value.
Single Sampling
One sample out of the entire order quantity is inspected.
Continuous Sampling
This type of sampling only takes place in case of mass production and is used to control processing. After a particular interval, a sample is drawn as large as the sample size. A decision is taken as to whether to continue the production or

to stop and take corrective action. For this test type, data must be entered in the following fields:
- Frequency Unit
- Frequency

For further information, see method(s)
- Example Test Types
- Using Destructive Tests
- Units and Quantities in QMS

20.   Frequency Unit

The frequency unit specifies the unit in which the sample size is expressed. The frequency unit and the unit of the order quantity do not have to be identical, in which case, however, a correct conversion factor is essential.
For further information, see keyword(s)
- Units

For further information, see method(s)
- Units and Quantities in QMS

+--+
| Test Type | Unit |
| | |
|----------------------------+---|
100 %	Order Unit
[ENtcqms.tsty.hundred.p	
erc]	
----------------------------+---
Single Sampling	- Sample Size [%] = Order Unit
	- Sample Size = Sample Unit
----------------------------+---
Continuous Sampling	- Sample Unit = Frequency Unit
+--+

21.   Frequency

The frequency of continuous inspection expressed in the frequency unit.
Example:
Sample Size [TF@tcqms0310spieces
Frequency [TF@tcqms036100epieces

A new sample of 10 pieces is drawn for every 100 pieces.
For further information, see method(s)
- Example Test Types

22.   Percentage

The sample size is the total quantity that is to be tested. In this field, it is expressed as a percentage of either the order quantity or the frequency (in case of "Continuous Sampling").
Example:

Test Type	Single Sampling		
Order Quantity	10000	20000	pieces
Percentage	1%	1%	
Sample Size	100*	200*	pieces

* The sample size is automatically updated when the order quantity is changed.
For further information, see method(s)
- Example Test Types
- Units and Quantities in QMS

+--+
| Test Type | Sample Size |
| | |
|----------------------------+---|
100 %	Order Quantity
[ENtcqms.tsty.hundred.p	
erc]	
----------------------------+---

Single Sampling	n % of order quantity or n units
Continuous Sampling	n % of frequency or n units

23. Sample Unit

The sample unit specifies the unit in which the sample size is expressed. If the sample size is expressed as a percentage, the system will use the unit of the order quantity.
The sample unit and the unit of the order quantity do not have to be identical, in which case, however, a correct conversion factor is essential.
For further information, see keyword(s)
• Units
For further information, see method(s)
• Units and Quantities in QMS

Test Type	Unit

100 %
    [ENtcqms.tsty.hundred.p
    erc]
	Order Unit

Single Sampling	- Sample Size [%] = Order Unit - Sample Size = Sample Unit
Continuous Sampling	- Sample Unit = Frequency Unit

24. Sample Size

The sample size is the total quantity of all samples which are to be tested out of the order quantity, expressed in the unit of the sample size. In this field, it is expressed as a fixed quantity.
Example:

Order Quantity	10000	20000	pieces
Percentage	0%	0%	
Sample Size	50	50	pieces

For further information, see method(s)
• Example Test Types
• Units and Quantities in QMS

Test Type	Sample Size

100 %
    [ENtcqms.tsty.hundred.p
    erc]
	Order Quantity

Single Sampling	n % of order quantity or n units
Continuous Sampling	n % of frequency or n units

```
tcqms1100s000                      zoom        single/grp (3) < Form 2-2
+---------------------------------------------3_____4-5_____-+
|  Origin           : 1_____  | Container   : 11_      |
|  Origin Order     :              2_____   | Order Qty. [6__]: 7_____ |
|  Project/Item     : 8_____/9_____  10_____  |
|                                                                          |
```

```
| Inspection Order : 12......        Text              : 16___     |
| Order Date       : 13........      Acc. Quality Level : 17.   %   |
| Effective Date   : 14........                                     |
| Completion Date  : 15_____                                     |
|                                                                   |
+-------------------------------------------------------------------+
```

1.   Origin
The origin of the inspection is an integrated package or module.
See also session "Maintain QMS Parameters (tcqms0100m000)" for the implemented
modules and packages.
2.   Origin Order
The order number of the origin of the inspection:

```
+------------------------------------------------------------------+
| Origin                         | Origin Order                    |
|--------------------------------+---------------------------------|
| Sales (SLS)                    | Sales Orders                    |
| Purchase (PUR)                 | Purchase Orders                 |
|                                |                                 |
| Production (SFC)               | Production Orders               |
|                                |                                 |
| Material (BOM)                 | Production Orders               |
|                                |                                 |
| Routing (TI)                   | Production Orders               |
|                                |                                 |
| Production (PMG)               | Production Batches              |
|                                |                                 |
| Material (FRM)                 | Production Batches              |
|                                |                                 |
| Routing (PS)                   | Production Batches              |
|                                |                                 |
+------------------------------------------------------------------+
```

3.   Description
4.   Program domain of string length 1
5.   Status
The inspection status indicates the current status of the inspection order. The
status is changed during several sessions:

```
+------------------------------------------------------------------+
| Session                             | Inspection Status          |
|                                     |                            |
|-------------------------------------+----------------------------|
| Maintain Inspection Orders (tcqms1100s000) | Free                |
|                                     |                            |
|-------------------------------------+----------------------------|
| Maintain Storage Inspections        | Free                       |
| (tcqms2120m000)                     |                            |
|-------------------------------------+----------------------------|
| Enter Test Data (tcqms1115m000)     | Active                     |
|                                     |                            |
|-------------------------------------+----------------------------|
| Complete Inspection Orders Collectively | Completed              |
| (tcqms1202m000)                     |                            |
|-------------------------------------+----------------------------|
| Process Inspection Orders (tcqms1204m000) | Processed            |
|                                     |                            |
|-------------------------------------+----------------------------|
| Check and Close Standard Inspections | Closed                    |
| (tcqms1205m000)                     |                            |
+------------------------------------------------------------------+
```

For further information, see method(s)
•   Inspection Order and Order Line Status
6.   Unit

The order quantity is the inspected quantity which may originate from several modules. It is expressed in the unit related to the module from which it originates:

Origin	Order Quantity	Unit
Sales (SLS)	Delivered Quantity	Purchase Unit
Purchase (PUR)	Received Quantity	Sales Unit
Production (SFC)	Order Quantity	Inventory Unit
Material (BOM)	Order Quantity	Inventory Unit
Routing (TI)	Order Quantity	Inventory Unit
Production (PMG)	Batch Quantity	Inventory Unit
Material (FRM)	Batch Quantity	Inventory Unit
Routing (PS)	Batch Quantity	Inventory Unit

Note:
In case of project items, the unit is the "Inventory Unit" as defined for the customized item.

7.   Order Quantity

The order quantity is the inspected quantity which may originate from several modules. It is expressed in the unit related to the module from which it originates:

Origin	Order Quantity	Unit
Sales (SLS)	Delivered Quantity	Purchase Unit
Purchase (PUR)	Received Quantity	Sales Unit
Production (SFC)	Order Quantity	Inventory Unit
Material (BOM)	Order Quantity	Inventory Unit
Routing (TI)	Order Quantity	Inventory Unit
Production (PMG)	Batch Quantity	Inventory Unit
Material (FRM)	Batch Quantity	Inventory Unit
Routing (PS)	Batch Quantity	Inventory Unit

Note:
In case of project items, the unit is the "Inventory Unit" as defined for the customized item.

8.   Project

The project which applies to the customized item for which a certain quality inspection is desired. A value must also be entered in field "Item".
For further information, see keyword(s)

•   Projects

9.   Item

The item which is to be inspected.
For further information, see keyword(s)

- Items
10. Description
11. Container
The container in which the item is packaged and for which a certain quality inspection is desired. See also field "Containerized" in session "Maintain Item Data (tiitm0101m000)".
For further information, see keyword(s)
- Units
- Units By Unit Set
For further information, see method(s)
- Containerized Items
12. Inspection Order
The number of the inspection order.
For further information, see keyword(s)
- Inspection Orders
13. Order Date
The date on which the inspection order is/was created.
14. Effective Date
The date as of which a test can be used to inspect items.
15. Completion Date
The completion date is the date on which all inspection order lines are completed. This date is updated automatically in session "Complete Inspection Orders Collectively (tcqms1202m000)" and cannot be entered manually.
16. Text
17. Acceptable Quality Level
The acceptable quality level is the percentage of all test quantities of all samples of an inspection order which must pass the test successfully to accept:
- the entire order quantity (Single Sampling)
- the entire frequency quantity (Continuous Sampling)
The percentage can be determined by experience or statistics.
For further information, see method(s)
- Example Test Types
Examples

Single Sampling
Acceptable Quality Level
Sample Size   30 pieces

Sample	le	Result
1	5 pieces	Good
2	10 pieces	Bad
3	15 pieces	Good

Actual Quality Level = [(5 + 15) / (5 + 10 + 15)] x 100 % = 66,67 %
The actual quality is higher than the acceptable quality level. Consequently, the order quantity is accepted.

Continuous Sampling
Acceptable Quality Level
Order Quantity [TF@tcqms120.oqua300 pieces
Frequency   100 pieces
Sample Size   10 pieces

Sample	le [TF@tcqms110.sActual Quality Level	
1	10 pieces	70 % good
2	10 pieces	50 % good
3	10 pieces	80 % good

Compare the results to the "Acceptable Quality Level ".

Sample	Quality Level		Quantity	
	Actual	Acceptable	Accepted	Rejected

```
1      70 %        60 %           100            0
2      50 %        60 %             0          100
3      80 %        60 %           100            0
                                  ----         ----
                    Total         200          100
```
This field does not apply to tests of type 100 %.

17.3 Maintain Samples (tcqms1110m000)

SESSION OBJECTIVE

To maintain samples, based on the sample size of the inspection order. The total of all sample quantities cannot exceed the "Maximum Size".

HOW TO USE THE SESSION

Inspections should be maintained in session "Maintain Inspection Orders (tcqms1100s000)" before the samples can be maintained. It is not possible to modify those samples for which the test data has already been entered.

SEE ALSO KEYWORD(S)

*   Samples

SEE ALSO METHOD(S)

*   Generating Standard Inspections
*   Inspection Order and Order Line Status
*   Inspection Procedure

```
tcqms1110m000                      zoom      multi/group (3    Form 1-1
+----------------------------------------------------------------------+
|  Maintain Samples                                      Company: 000   |
|----------------------------------------------------------------------|
|                                                                      |
|   Inspection Order: 1.......       Origin            : 2_____  |
|   Insp. Status    : 3_____  Origin Order       : 4_____        |
|   Project         : 5_____         Operation/Position No: 6___        |
|   Item/Container  : 7_____        8 9__                         |
|   Maximum Size    : 10_____11_                                  |
|                                                                      |
|   Sample    Test Quantity  Sample Quantity  Date      Time    Test Data |
|                                                                      |
|   12......  13...........   14..........15....... 16......   17___    |
|                                                                      |
|                     +-------------+                                  |
|   Total Quantity    : 18_____11_                               |
+----------------------------------------------------------------------+
```

1.   Inspection Order

The number of the inspection order.

For further information, see keyword(s)

*   Inspection Orders

2.   Origin

The origin of the inspection is an integrated package or module.

See also session "Maintain QMS Parameters (tcqms0100m000)" for the implemented modules and packages.

3.   Result Status

The inspection status indicates the current status of the inspection order. The status is changed during several sessions:

Session	Inspection Status
Maintain Inspection Orders (tcqms1100s000)	Free
Maintain Storage Inspections (tcqms2120m000)	Free
Enter Test Data (tcqms1115m000)	Active
Complete Inspection Orders Collectively	Completed

```
| (tcqms1202m000)                        |                          |
|----------------------------------------+--------------------------|
| Process Inspection Orders (tcqms1204m000) | Processed             |
|                                        |                          |
|----------------------------------------+--------------------------|
| Check and Close Standard Inspections   | Closed                   |
| (tcqms1205m000)                        |                          |
+-----------------------------------------------------------------+
```

For further information, see method(s)
- Inspection Order and Order Line Status

4. Origin Order
The order number of the origin of the inspection:

```
+-----------------------------------------------------------------+
| Origin                          | Origin Order                  |
|---------------------------------+-------------------------------|
| Sales (SLS)                     | Sales Orders                  |
| Purchase (PUR)                  | Purchase Orders               |
|                                 |                               |
| Production (SFC)                | Production Orders             |
|                                 |                               |
| Material (BOM)                  | Production Orders             |
|                                 |                               |
| Routing (TI)                    | Production Orders             |
|                                 |                               |
| Production (PMG)                | Production Batches            |
|                                 |                               |
| Material (FRM)                  | Production Batches            |
|                                 |                               |
| Routing (PS)                    | Production Batches            |
|                                 |                               |
+-----------------------------------------------------------------+
```

5. Project
The project which applies to the customized item for which a certain quality
inspection is desired. A value must also be entered in field "Item".
For further information, see keyword(s)
- Projects

6. Position Number
The position number on the order to which the inspection order applies, namely:
- the position of the sales order;
- the position of the purchase order;
- the position of the estimated materials;
- the position of the estimated co- by-products;
- the position of the estimated end items.

7. Item
The item which is to be inspected.
For further information, see keyword(s)
- Items

8. Program domain of string length 1

9. Container
The container in which the item is packaged and for which a certain quality
inspection is desired. See also field "Containerized" in session "Maintain Item
Data (tiitm0101m000)".
For further information, see keyword(s)
- Units
- Units By Unit Set
For further information, see method(s)
- Containerized Items

10. Maximum Size
The maximum size of the sample quantity depends on the test type:
- 100 % or Single Sampling
 Maximum Size
 = "Sample Size
"

- Continuous Sampling

Maximum Size =

$$\frac{\text{Order Quantity}}{\text{Frequency}} \quad e$$

The sample of continuous sampling is equal to the sample size.

11. Sample Unit

The sample unit specifies the unit in which the sample size is expressed. If the sample size is expressed as a percentage, the system will use the unit of the order quantity.

The sample unit and the unit of the order quantity do not have to be identical, in which case, however, a correct conversion factor is essential.

For further information, see keyword(s)
- Units

For further information, see method(s)
- Units and Quantities in QMS

12. Sample

For further information, see keyword(s)
- Samples

The default sample number which is generated by the system can be modified.

13. Test Quantity

The test quantity is a part, an exact factor of the sample size, that is tested each time and is expressed in the same unit as the sample size. For each test quantity, the result of the test can be entered in session "Enter Test Data (tcqms1115m000)".

Example:

Sample Size	5 kilogram
Test Quantity	kilogram

Explanation:

A 5 kg sample will be tested by testing 1 kg at a time.

For further information, see method(s)
- Example Test Types
- Units and Quantities in QMS

14. Sample Quantity

The actual quantity that is drawn from the total quantity.

Example:

Sample Size   : 200 pieces

Sample	Sample Quantity
1	50
2	40
3	50
4	60

The total of all sample quantities must be less than or equal to the sample size.

For continuous sampling, the sample quantity is always equal to the sample size.

For further information, see method(s)
- Units and Quantities in QMS

15. Sample Date

The date on which the samples are taken.

16. Time [hh:mm:ss]

The time at which the samples are taken.

17. Test Data Present

Indication whether test data already exists in session "Enter Test Data (tcqms1115m000)". The value of this field is set to "Yes", even if the all test data lines are empty (zero result).

18. Total Quantity

The total quantity of all samples. This quantity must be less than or equal to the sample size.

17.4 Enter Test Data (tcqms1115m000)

SESSION OBJECTIVE

To enter the actual test data after each sample item has been inspected. The test data can be entered for valid inspection order lines only.
SEE ALSO KEYWORD(S)
• Inspection Data
SEE ALSO METHOD(S)
• Inspection Order and Order Line Status
• Storage Inspection Procedure
Evaluate Algorithm [tcqms1115m0001.user.1]
Evaluate the value of the algoritm characteristic based on the data of other characteristics. It is not possible to modify the calculated results.
This option applies to orders with status "Active".
The line for an algorithm is influenced by the variables used in the algoritm expression:

+---+
| Variable | Option Result |
|---------------+---|
Modified	Algorithm value will change
Inserted	A new line of the algorithm will be inserted
Deleted	The line of the algorithm will be deleted
+---+

Toggle Status Active/Complete [tcqms1115m0001.user.2]
Switch between line status "Active" and line status "Completed".
If this option is used for an algorithm characteristic, the status of the lines of the variables (characteristics) will also change to "Completed".
Conditions:
• The total quantity of samples is equal to the sample size;
• The inspection data is entered for all samples defined for this order line;
• The status of an inspection order line can only change back to "Active" if the inspection status is not yet "Completed".
Create Test Data Lines [tcqms1115m0001.user.3]
Either generate the test data lines which must be entered based on the test quantity;
Example: Sample Quantity Test Quantity [TF@tcqms120.pieces
Explanation: 100 divided by 20 makes 5. Consequently, 5 lines will be generated.
Or generate a test data line for each position of the inspection order.
Example: If an inspection order has 4 positions with a characteristic, 4 lines will be generated;
Depending on the chosen order.
No lines are created for algorithm characteristics. Use option "Evaluate Algorithm [tcqms1115m0001.user.1]" to accomplish this.
Display Drawings [tcqms1115m0001.user.4]
This option is used to display a drawing of how an item is to be tested for a specific characteristic.
OTHER FEATURES
Reset Inspection Line Status
Inspection order line: "Active"
If all inspection order lines are deleted or all test data, the status of the order line will change to "Free".
The Number of Times an Instrument is Used
Incremented If all test data is entered for a sample and the test results are available, the number of times used is incremented by 1.
Changed It is possible to change the instrument. The system will correct the number of times used for both instruments.

tcqms1115m000   multi/group (3   Form 1-2 >
+---+
Enter Test Data   Company: 000
Inspection Order   : 1.......   Line Status   : 4_____
Sample   : 2.......   Aspect   : 5_____ 6_____
Position   : 3..   Characteristic : 7_____ 8_____
Serial   Test Date Test Time Measurement Unit Option   Option   Result

```
| Number                         Value        Set                  |
|                                                                  |
| 9...... 10.......    11...... 12......... 13_   14____ 15...... 16.........|
|                                                                  |
|------------------------------------------------------------------|
| Test Area   : 17.  18_____  Char. Type    : 23_____    |
| Employee    : 19.... 20_____  Overall Result : 24_____       |
| Instrument  : 21.... 22_____                             |
+------------------------------------------------------------------+
```

1.   Inspection Order
The number of the inspection order.
For further information, see keyword(s)
•   Inspection Orders
2.   Sample
For further information, see keyword(s)
•   Samples
3.   Position
The position number of the sample identifies the line in which the test data can
be found. A line is inserted for each test quantity.
For further information, see method(s)
•   Units and Quantities in QMS
The inspection order line number which is maintained in session "Maintain
Inspection Orders (tcqms1100s000)".
4.   Order Line Status
The order line status indicates the current status of the inspection line. The
status is changed in several sessions:

+---+
| Session | Order Line Status |
| | |
|--+--------------------------|
| Maintain Inspection Order Lines | Free |
| (tcqms1101s000) | |
|--+--------------------------|
| Print Inspection Orders (tcqms1400m000)| Printed |
| | |
|--+--------------------------|
| Enter Test Data (tcqms1115m000) | Active |
| | |
|--+--------------------------|
| Complete Inspection Orders Collectively| Completed |
| (tcqms1202m000) | |
+---+

For further information, see method(s)
•   Inspection Order and Order Line Status
5.   Aspect
For further information, see keyword(s)
•   Aspects
6.   Description
7.   Characteristic
For further information, see keyword(s)
•   Characteristics
8.   Description
9.   Serial Number
Default serial numbers can be generated by the system by means of option "Toggle
Status Active/Complete [tcqms1115m0001.user.2]". The total of the serial numbers
cannot exceed the value of the sample quantity divided by the test quantity.
10.   Test Date
The date on which the test takes place. The default date is the current date.
11.   Time [hhmmss]
12.   Measurement Value
A numeric value is entered if the result type for the inspection order line is
"Quantitative" and the characteristic type is not "Option". If the algorithm is

specified for the inspection order line, the numeric value is calculated based on the algorithm. It is not possible to modify the result.

13.   Test Unit

The unit in which the test results are defined or calculated.
For further information, see keyword(s)
•   "Units"
For further information, see method(s)
•   •   "Units and Quantities in QMS"

14.   Option Set

For further information, see keyword(s)
•   Option Sets

15.   Option

This option (i.e. the test result) was found during the test for the option set which applies to this test. Depending on the result type ("Option Type") the result is either good or bad.

16.   Result

The result of the inspection is "Good" or "Bad". This value of this field is automatically generated by the system.

+--+
| Characteristic Type | Good | Bad |
| | | |
|----------------------+----------------------+---------------------|
| Integer/Fraction | Between Limits | Outside Limits |
| Option | Acceptable | Not Acceptable |
+--+

These quality limits can be defined in the following sessions:
•   Maintain Characteristics by Quality ID (tcqms0115m000) (to define the limits);
•   Maintain Options (tcqms0114m000) (to define the acceptability).

17.   Test Area

For further information, see keyword(s)
•   Test Areas

18.   Description

19.   Employee

The default employee to execute the test for this characteristic.
For further information, see keyword(s)
•   Employees

20.   Name

The employee's name.

21.   Instrument

For further information, see keyword(s)
•   Instruments

22.   Description

23.   Characteristic Type

The type of characteristic is the type of value which may be measured by means of an instrument.

24.   Result

The overall result for a test quantity which is tested for various characteristics.
Good
All characteristics are good.
Bad
One or more characteristics are bad as a result of which the entire test quantity is bad.
Empty One or more characteristics are not yet tested while the characteristics which were tested are good.
Example:
Item 'A' is tested for the characteristics 'Weight' and 'Length':

Characteristic	ult
Weight	Bad
Length	Good

The overall result is "Bad   ".
tcqms1115m000   multi/group (3 < Form 2-2
+---+
Enter Test Data   Company: 000
Inspection Order   : 1.......
Sample   : 2.......
Serial Number   : 3.......   Overall Result : 4_____
Pos. Test Date Test Time Measurement Unit Option   Option Result Line
Value   Set   Status
5.. 6.........   7....... 8.......... 9__   10____ 11...... 12...... 13____
Test Area : 14. 15_____   Aspect : 20_____ 21_____
Employee   : 16.... 17_____ Charact.: 22_____ 23_____
Instrument : 18.... 19_____ Ch. Type: 24_____
+---+
1.   Inspection Order
The number of the inspection order.
For further information, see keyword(s)
•   Inspection Orders
2.   Sample
For further information, see keyword(s)
•   Samples
3.   Serial Number
Default serial numbers can be generated by the system by means of option "Toggle
Status Active/Complete [tcqms1115m0001.user.2]". The total of the serial numbers
cannot exceed the value of the sample quantity divided by the test quantity.
4.   Result
The overall result for a test quantity which is tested for various
characteristics.
Good
All characteristics are good.
Bad
One or more characteristics are bad as a result of which the entire test
quantity is bad.
Empty One or more characteristics are not yet tested while the characteristics
which were tested are good.
Example:
Item 'A' is tested for the characteristics 'Weight' and 'Length':

Characteristic   ult
Weight   Bad
Length   Good

The overall result is "Bad".
5.   Position
The position number of the sample identifies the line in which the test data can
be found. A line is inserted for each test quantity.
For further information, see method(s)
•   Units and Quantities in QMS
The inspection order line number which is maintained in session "Maintain
Inspection Orders (tcqms1100s000)".
6.   Test Date
The date on which the test takes place. The default date is the current date.
7.   Time [hhmmss]
8.   Measurement Value
A numeric value is entered if the result type for the inspection order line is
"Quantitative" and the characteristic type is not "Option". If the algorithm is
specified for the inspection order line, the numeric value is calculated based
on the algorithm. It is not possible to modify the result.

9.   Test Unit
The unit in which the test results are defined or calculated.
For further information, see keyword(s)
•   "Units"
For further information, see method(s)
•   •   "Units and Quantities in QMS"
10.   Option Set
For further information, see keyword(s)
•   Option Sets
11.   Option
This option (i.e. the test result) was found during the test for the option set which applies to this test. Depending on the result type ("Option Type") the result is either good or bad.
12.   Result
The result of the inspection is "Good" or "Bad". This value of this field is automatically generated by the system.

+---+
| Characteristic Type | Good | Bad |
| | | |
|----------------------+------------------+--------------------|
| Integer/Fraction | Between Limits | Outside Limits |
| Option | Acceptable | Not Acceptable |
+---+

These quality limits can be defined in the following sessions:
•   Maintain Characteristics by Quality ID (tcqms0115m000) (to define the limits);
•   Maintain Options (tcqms0114m000) (to define the acceptability).
13.   Order Line Status
The order line status indicates the current status of the inspection line. The status is changed in several sessions:

+---+
| Session | Order Line Status |
| | |
|--+----------------------|
| Maintain Inspection Order Lines | Free |
| (tcqms1101s000) | |
|--+----------------------|
| Print Inspection Orders (tcqms1400m000) | Printed |
| | |
|--+----------------------|
| Enter Test Data (tcqms1115m000) | Active |
| | |
|--+----------------------|
| Complete Inspection Orders Collectively | Completed |
| (tcqms1202m000) | |
+---+

For further information, see method(s)
•   Inspection Order and Order Line Status
14.   Test Area
For further information, see keyword(s)
•   Test Areas
15.   Description
16.   Employee
The default employee to execute the test for this characteristic.
For further information, see keyword(s)
•   Employees
17.   Name
The employee's name.
18.   Instrument
For further information, see keyword(s)
•   Instruments
19.   Description
20.   Aspect

21.   Description
22.   Characteristic
23.   Description
24.   Characteristic Type
The type of characteristic is the type of value which may be measured by means
of an instrument.
18   Optional Sessions
18.1 Check and Close Standard Inspections (tcqms1205m000)
SESSION OBJECTIVE
To check the results of inspection orders and/or to close inspection orders.
HOW TO USE THE SESSION
When you start processing, the system will report the recommended and actual
quantities completed (accepted) and rejected of the selected inspection orders.
Whether the selected inspection orders will be closed depends on the setting of
field "Close Inspection Orders" and the status of the inspection order and the
production order/batch.
SEE ALSO METHOD(S)
•   Using QMS for Manufacturing Operations
•   Using QMS in Production (SFC)
•   Using QMS for Process Operations
•   Using QMS in Production (PMG)
SEE ALSO KEYWORD(S)
•   Inspection Orders
•   Inspections by Origin

tcqms1205m000   single-occ (4) < Form 1-1 >
+--+
Check and Close Standard Inspections   Company: 000
From   To
Origin   : 1.................   - 2.................
Origin Order   : 3.....   - 4.....
Position   : 5...   - 6...
Operation   : 7..   - 8..
Receipt/Delivery   : 9.   - 10
Inbound/Outbound   : 11......   - 12......
Close Inspection Orders : 13...
+--+
1.   Origin of Inspection
2.   Origin of Inspection
3.   Origin Order
4.   Origin Order
5.   Position
6.   Position
7.   Operation
8.   Operation
9.   Receipt/Delivery
10.   Receipt/Delivery
11.   Inbound/Outbound
12.   Inbound/Outbound
13.   Close Inspection Orders
Indicates whether the system will close the selected inspection orders.
The system only closes an inspection order if the following conditions are met:
•   field "Inspection Status" in session "Maintain Standard Inspections by
Origin (tcqms1120m000)" is set to "Processed";
•   field "Blocking Method for Inspections" in session "Maintain Standard
Inspections by Origin (tcqms1120m000)" is set to "Continue" or "Block after
Posting";
•   the status of the production order/batch is set to "Completed".

18.2 Delete Test Data Collectively (tcqms1215m000)
SESSION OBJECTIVE
To collectively delete ranges of test data.
HOW TO USE THE SESSION
Specify Range After the field "Processing By" and other optional fields, specify
the range by means of option "Continue [cont.process]".
Delete Data For processing types "Origin" and "Storage Inspection", only
inspection data with a status prior to status "Processed" can be deleted. All
data related to an inspection order will be deleted. See also field "Delete
Samples".
SEE ALSO METHOD(S)
•   Inspection Order and Order Line Status
SEE ALSO KEYWORD(S)
•   Inspection Data
tcqms1215m000   single-occ (4)   Form 1-4 >
+---+
Delete Test Data Collectively   Company: 000
Process by   : 1.....................
Delete Samples   : 2....
Print Report   : 3   1 - No Report
2 - By Characteristic
3 - By Serial Number
+---+
1.   Processing By
The range of inspection orders may be entered by:
•   Origin;
•   Storage Inspection;
•   Inspection Order.
2.   Delete Samples
All related samples can be deleted.
3.   Print Report
It is possible to print a report with the deleted test data, by serial number or
by characteristic.
tcqms1215m000   single-occ (4) < Form 2-4 >
+---+
Delete Test Data Collectively   Company: 000
Delete by Origin
From   To
Origin   : 1..................... - 2.....................
Origin Order   : 3..... - 4.....
Position   : 5... - 6...
Operation   : 7.. - 8..
Receipt/Delivery : 9. - 10
Inbound/Outbound : 11...... - 12......
+---+
1.   Origin from
2.   Origin to
3.   Origin Order from
4.   Origin Order to
5.   Position from
6.   Position to
7.   Operation from
8.   Operation to

9.   Receipt/Delivery from
10.   Receipt/Delivery to
11.   Inbound/Outbound from
12.   Inbound/Outbound to
tcqms1215m000   single-occ (4) < Form 3-4 >

```
+----------------------------------------------------------------------+
| Delete Test Data Collectively                       Company: 000 |
|----------------------------------------------------------------------|
|                                                                      |
| Delete by Storage Inspection                                         |
|                                                                      |
| Project                      from : 1.....                           |
|                              to   : 2.....                           |
|                                                                      |
| Item                         from : 3..............                  |
|                              to   : 4..............                  |
|                                                                      |
| Container                    from : 5..                              |
|                              to   : 6..                              |
|                                                                      |
| Sequence                     from : 7..                              |
|                              to   : 8..                              |
|                                                                      |
+----------------------------------------------------------------------+
```

1.   Project from
2.   Project to
3.   Item from
4.   Item to
5.   Container from
6.   Container to
7.   Storage Inspection Sequence from
8.   Storage Inspection Sequence to
tcqms1215m000   single-occ (4) < Form 4-4

```
+----------------------------------------------------------------------+
| Delete Test Data Collectively                       Company: 000 |
|----------------------------------------------------------------------|
|                                                                      |
| Delete by Inspection Order                                           |
|                              From            To                      |
|                                                                      |
| Inspection Order            : 1.......   - 2.......                  |
|                                                                      |
| Position                    : 3..        - 4..                       |
|                                                                      |
| Sample                      : 5.......   - 6.......                  |
|                                                                      |
| Test Date                   : 7........  - 8.........               |
|                                                                      |
| Test Time                   : 9.......   - 10......                  |
|                                                                      |
+----------------------------------------------------------------------+
```

1.   Inspection Order from
2.   Inspection Order to
3.   Position from
4.   Position to
5.   Sample from
6.   Sample to
7.   Test Date from
8.   Test Date to
9.   Test Time from
10.   Test Time to
19   Other Maintenance Sessions
19.1 Maintain Inspection Order Lines (tcqms1101s000)

SESSION OBJECTIVE
To maintain inspection order lines. For each combination of an aspect and a
characteristic, an inspection line is available. The data related to the
characteristic can be changed for this specific inspection order.
SEE ALSO KEYWORD(S)
•   Inspection Orders
SEE ALSO METHOD(S)
•   Generating Standard Inspections
•   Inspection Order and Order Line Status
•   Using Destructive Tests
•   Inspection Procedure

```
+------------------------------------------------------------------------+
| Insp. Order    : 1_____                                             |
| Position       : 2..          Order Line Status    : 16_____|
| Aspect         : 3....... 4_____  Fixed Char. Value   : 17........ |
| Characteristic : 5....... 6_____  Char. Standard      : 18...... |
| Char. Type     : 7.............   Norm         [19_ ]: 20........ |
| Char. Unit     : 8.. 9_____  Upper Limit  [21_ ]: 22........ |
| For Algorithm  : 10...         Lower Limit  [23_ ]: 24........ |
| Option Set     : 11.... 12_____  Actual Start Date   : 25_____ |
| Method         : 13.............  Actual Compl. Date  : 26_____ |
| Algorithm      : 14.... 15_____                                 |
|                                                                        |
+------------------------------------------------------------------------+
```

1.   Inspection Order
The number of the inspection order.
For further information, see keyword(s)
•   Inspection Orders
2.   Position
The line number which identifies the inspection order line.
3.   Aspect
For further information, see keyword(s)
•   Aspects
The combination of an aspect and a characteristic must be valid for the current
date as defined in session "Maintain Characteristics by Quality ID
(tcqms0115m000)". The characteristic lines related to the quality ID which is
defined in the inspection order are default.
4.   Description
5.   Characteristic
For further information, see keyword(s)
•   Characteristics
6.   Description
7.   Characteristic Type
The type of characteristic is the type of value which may be measured by means
of an instrument. Fraction
A ratio of two expressions or numbers other than zero representing part of an
integer (written with a decimal point followed by one or more numbers).
Integer
An exact whole number as opposed to a number with decimals.
Option
For this type of characteristic, various options may be defined. For further
information, see keyword(s)
•   Option Sets
•   Options

Characteristic Type	Example
Fraction	3.145
Integer	123

```
|Option                        | Blue             |
|                              |                  |
+------------------------------------------------+
```
8.   Characteristic Unit
The unit in which a characteristic value, e.g. the norm, is specified.

Characteristic Type   Mandatory
Fraction   Yes
Integer   Yes
Option   N/A

For further information, see keyword(s)
•   Units
For further information, see method(s)
•   Units and Quantities in QMS
9.   Description
10.   For Algorithm
Indication that this characteristic can be used as a variable or constant in the algorithm of another characteristic.
For further information, see keyword(s)
•   Algorithms
•   Variables by Algorithm
11.   Option Set
For further information, see keyword(s)
•   Option Sets
12.   Description
13.   Method
The type of characteristic value or the way in which the characteristic value is calculated. Fixed
The characteristic value is determined once and can be entered in field "Fixed Characteristic Value". It is used to compare results or in algorithms. The results are entered in session "Enter Test Data (tcqms1115m000)".
Variable
Characteristic values are measured immediately by means of an instrument. The results are entered in session "Enter Test Data (tcqms1115m000)".
Algorithm
The characteristic is calculated by means of an algorithm, using the inspection results of variable or fixed characteristics.
For further information, see keyword(s)
•   Algorithms
See also field "Algorithm".

```
+------------------------------------------------------------+
|Method                 | Characteristic   | Example        |
|                       |                  |                |
|-----------------------+------------------+----------------|
|Fixed                  | Pi               | 3.14..         |
|Variable               | Length           | 4 meters       |
|                       |                  |                |
|Algorithm              | Voltage          | I * R          |
|                       |                  |                |
+------------------------------------------------------------+
```
14.   Algorithm
For further information, see keyword(s)
•   Algorithms
Enter an algorithm if the characteristic is measured by means of method "Algorithm".
For more information see
•   Method
15.   Description
16.   Order Line Status
The order line status indicates the current status of the inspection line. The status is changed in several sessions:

```
+-------------------------------------------------------------------+
| Session                              | Order Line Status          |
|                                      |                            |
```

Maintain Inspection Order Lines (tcqms1101s000)	Free
Print Inspection Orders (tcqms1400m000)	Printed
Enter Test Data (tcqms1115m000)	Active
Complete Inspection Orders Collectively (tcqms1202m000)	Completed

For further information, see method(s)
• Inspection Order and Order Line Status
17. Fixed Characteristic Value
The value of a constant (i.e. a fixed characteristic) which is used in algorithms.
Example:
Characteristic [TF@tcqms001.chGravity
Fixed Characteristic Value
Only applies to method "Fixed".
If the characteristic is of type "Integer", the value of the characteristic is rounded up to the nearest integer.
Example:

User Entry	Rounded Value
10.5	11
10.4	10
10.6	11

18. Characteristic Standard
The standard normally used for characteristics. This is an informative field.
Example:
A DIN standard.
19. Norm Unit
20. Norm
The norm is the desired quality for this characteristic, expressed in the characteristic unit. Does not apply if the method is "Fixed" or if the type is "Option".
21. Limit Unit
22. Upper Limit
The highest characteristic value for which quality is acceptable, expressed in the characteristic unit. The "Upper Limit" must be greater than or equal to the "Norm".
23. Limit Unit
24. Lower Limit
The lowest characteristic value for which quality is acceptable, expressed in the characteristic unit. The "Lower Limit" must be smaller than or equal to the "Norm".
25. Actual Start Date
The date on which the first data is entered for the inspection order line. This date is updated in session "Enter Test Data (tcqms1115m000)" and cannot be modified.
26. Actual Completion Date
The date on which the inspection is reported completed. This date is updated in session "Complete Inspection Orders Collectively (tcqms1202m000)" and cannot be changed.

tcqms1101s000   single/grp (3) < Form 2-2

```
+------------------------------------------------------------------+
| Insp. Order   : 1_____                                         |
| Position      : 2..              Line Status   : 13_____  |
| Test          : 3....... 4_____  Char.Drawing : 14............... |
| Test Area     : 5..      6_____  Test Drawing : 15............... |
| Destructive   : 7....             Skill        : 16..  17_____ |
```

```
| Result Type    : 8.............     Employee    : 18.... 19_____ |
| Test Unit      : 9..      10_____  Instrument  : 20.... 21_____ |
| Test Sequence  : 11.                 Text        : 22___              |
| Test Standard  : 12......                                            |
|                                                                      |
+----------------------------------------------------------------------+
```

1.   Inspection Order
The number of the inspection order.
For further information, see keyword(s)
•   Inspection Orders
2.   Position
The line number which identifies the inspection order line.
3.   Test
For further information, see keyword(s)
•   Tests
4.   Description
5.   Test Area
For further information, see keyword(s)
•   Test Areas
6.   Description
7.   Destructive
Indication that the test is destructive and that the item cannot be used after testing.
For further information, see method(s)
•   Using Destructive Tests
8.   Result Type
The type of result which is reported to the user. Quantitative
A quantitative value is reported after testing, e.g. "40 cm".
Qualitative
A qualitative value is reported after testing, e.g. "Acceptable" or "Not Acceptable".
9.   Test Unit
The unit in which the test results are defined or calculated.
For further information, see keyword(s)
•   "Units"
For further information, see method(s)
•   •   "Units and Quantities in QMS" Does not apply to characteristics of type "Option".
10.   Description
11.   Test Sequence
The sequence in which the tests should take place. This is not a mandatory field. If there are more than one inspection order lines with the same sequence, these tests can be carried out simultaneously. If the test sequence is not specified, the sequence is not important.
12.   Test Standard
The standard normally used for the test.
Example:
A DIN standard.
13.   Order Line Status
The order line status indicates the current status of the inspection line. The status is changed in several sessions:

Session	Order Line Status
Maintain Inspection Order Lines (tcqms1101s000)	Free
Print Inspection Orders (tcqms1400m000)	Printed
Enter Test Data (tcqms1115m000)	Active

```
|-----------------------------------------------+---------------------------|
| Complete Inspection Orders Collectively        | Completed                 |
| (tcqms1202m000)                                |                           |
+-----------------------------------------------------------------------------+
```

For further information, see method(s)
•   Inspection Order and Order Line Status
14.   Characteristic Drawing
The file name of the drawing located in the directory specified in session
"Maintain QMS Parameters (tcqms0100m000)" on field "Directory Name for Drawing".
15.   Test Drawing
The file name of the drawing located in the directory specified in session
"Maintain QMS Parameters (tcqms0100m000)" on field "Directory Name for Drawing".
16.   Skill
For further information, see keyword(s)
"Skills".
17.   Description
18.   Employee
The default employee to execute the test for this characteristic.
For further information, see keyword(s)
•   Employees
19.   Name
The employee's name.
20.   Instrument
For further information, see keyword(s)
•   Instruments
21.   Description
22.   Text
19.2   Complete Inspection Orders Collectively (tcqms1202m000)
SESSION OBJECTIVE
To complete a range of inspection orders and inspection order lines
collectively.
HOW TO USE THE SESSION
Specify Range After entering data in field "Processing By" and the other
optional fields, specify the range by means of option "Continue [cont.process]".
Complete Order Lines Depending on the origin, a check is made to verify if there
are any inspections lines with status "Active".
Inspection Status
While the inspection orders by origin and by storage inspection are being
completed, all the positions of the inspection orders lines for that origin or
storage inspection must have order line status "Completed" so that the
inspection status will change to "Completed".
SEE ALSO METHOD(S)
•   Inspection Order and Order Line Status
SEE ALSO KEYWORD(S)
•   Inspection Orders
tcqms1202m000   single-occ (4)   Form 1-4 >
```
+-----------------------------------------------------------------------------+
|  Complete Inspection Orders Collectively                   Company: 000     |
|-----------------------------------------------------------------------------|
|                                                                             |
|   Process by                    : 1....................                     |
|                                                                             |
|   Print Report                  : 2    1 - Completion                       |
|                                        2 - Error                            |
|                                        3 - Both                             |
|                                                                             |
|                                                                             |
|   Evaluate Algorithm before                                                 |
|   Completion                    : 3....                                     |
|                                                                             |
+-----------------------------------------------------------------------------+
```
1.   Processing By
The range of inspection orders may be entered by:

- Origin;
- Storage Inspection;
- Inspection Order.

2. Print Report

A report can be printed of all completed inspection orders, all inspection orders with errors, or all selected inspection orders.

3. Evaluate Algorithm before Completion

This option is used to calculate the test data of all inspection order lines with characteristics of type "Algorithm".

Note:

After the algorithm has been evaluated, it is still possible that the inspection order line cannot be completed, because of incomplete test data.

tcqms1202m000   single-occ (4) < Form 2-4 >

```
+------------------------------------------------------------------------+
| Complete Inspection Orders Collectively              Company: 000      |
|------------------------------------------------------------------------|
|                                                                        |
| Complete by Origin                                                     |
|                            From                      To                |
|                                                                        |
| Origin            : 1....................   - 2....................|
| Origin Order      : 3.....                  - 4.....                   |
| Position          : 5...                    - 6...                     |
|                                                                        |
| Operation         : 7..                     - 8..                      |
| Receipt/Delivery  : 9.                      - 10                       |
| Inbound/Outbound  : 11......                - 12......                 |
|                                                                        |
+------------------------------------------------------------------------+
```

1. Origin from
2. Origin to
3. Origin Order from
4. Origin Order to
5. Position from
6. Position to
7. Operation from
8. Operation to
9. Receipt/Delivery from
10. Receipt/Delivery to
11. Inbound/Outbound from
12. Inbound/Outbound to

tcqms1202m000   single-occ (4) < Form 3-4 >

```
+------------------------------------------------------------------------+
| Complete Inspection Orders Collectively              Company: 000      |
|------------------------------------------------------------------------|
|                                                                        |
| Complete by Storage Inspection                                         |
|                                                                        |
| Project                    from : 1.....                               |
|                            to   : 2.....                               |
|                                                                        |
| Item                       from : 3..............                      |
|                            to   : 4..............                      |
|                                                                        |
| Container                  from : 5..                                  |
|                            to   : 6..                                  |
|                                                                        |
| Sequence                   from : 7..                                  |
|                            to   : 8..                                  |
|                                                                        |
+------------------------------------------------------------------------+
```

1. Project from
2. Project to

```
3.      Item from
4.      Item to
5.      Container from
6.      Container to
7.      Sequence from
8.      Sequence to
```

```
+------------------------------------------------------------------------+
|  Complete Inspection Orders Collectively              Company: 000  |
|------------------------------------------------------------------------|
|                                                                        |
|   Complete by Inspection Order                                         |
|                                                                        |
|   Inspection Order                      from : 1.......               |
|                                         to   : 2......                 |
|                                                                        |
|   Position                              from : 3..                     |
|                                         to   : 4..                     |
|                                                                        |
+------------------------------------------------------------------------+
```

```
1.      Inspection Order from
2.      Inspection Order to
3.      Position from
4.      Position to
```

19.3 Delete Inspection Orders Collectively (tcqms1203m000)

SESSION OBJECTIVE

To delete a range of inspection orders

HOW TO USE THE SESSION

Specify Range After entering data in field "Processing By" and using the print option, specify the range by means of option "Continue [cont.process]".

Delete Data The following data will be deleted:

- Inspection Orders
- Inspection Order Lines
- Samples
- Inspection Orders

Inspection orders with status "Processed" or "Closed" cannot be deleted.

Algorithms (tcqms021)

If an order line has method "Algorithm" the field "For Algorithm" is set to "No". That will be done for all order lines used by the algorithm. Order lines which are used in other algorithms are skipped.

Inspection, Header, Lines If all the inspection order lines of an inspection order are deleted, the inspection order header is also deleted. If all the inspection order headers of a particular origin are deleted, the inspection by origin or storage inspection is also deleted.

SEE ALSO METHOD(S)

- Inspection Order and Order Line Status

SEE ALSO KEYWORD(S)

- Inspection Orders

```
+------------------------------------------------------------------------+
|  Delete Inspection Orders Collectively                Company: 000  |
|------------------------------------------------------------------------|
|                                                                        |
|   Process by                            : 1...................         |
|                                                                        |
|   Print Report                          : 2....                        |
|                                                                        |
+------------------------------------------------------------------------+
```

```
1.      Processing By
```

The range of inspection orders may be entered by:

- Origin;
- Storage Inspection;
- Inspection Order.

2. Print Report
A report can be printed of all deleted inspection orders.

```
+------------------------------------------------------------------------+
| Delete Inspection Orders Collectively              Company: 000 |
|------------------------------------------------------------------------|
|                                                                        |
| Delete by Origin                                                       |
|                           From                       To                |
|                                                                        |
| Origin               : 1....................  - 2....................|
| Origin Order         : 3.....                 - 4.....                 |
| Position             : 5...                   - 6...                   |
|                                                                        |
| Operation            : 7..                    - 8..                    |
| Receipt/Delivery     : 9.                     - 10                     |
| Inbound/Outbound     : 11......               - 12......               |
|                                                                        |
+------------------------------------------------------------------------+
```

1.   Origin from
2.   Origin to
3.   Origin Order from
4.   Origin Order to
5.   Position from
6.   Position to
7.   Operation from
8.   Operation to
9.   Receipt/Delivery from
10. Receipt/Delivery to
11. Inbound/Outbound from
12. Inbound/Outbound to

```
+------------------------------------------------------------------------+
| Delete Inspection Orders Collectively              Company: 000 |
|------------------------------------------------------------------------|
|                                                                        |
| Delete by Storage Inspection                                           |
|                                                                        |
| Project                    from : 1.....                               |
|                            to   : 2.....                               |
|                                                                        |
| Item                       from : 3..............                      |
|                            to   : 4..............                      |
|                                                                        |
| Container                  from : 5..                                  |
|                            to   : 6..                                  |
|                                                                        |
| Sequence                   from : 7..                                  |
|                            to   : 8..                                  |
|                                                                        |
+------------------------------------------------------------------------+
```

1.   Project from
2.   Project to
3.   Item from
4.   Item to
5.   Container from
6.   Container to
7.   Sequence from
8.   Sequence to

```
+------------------------------------------------------------------------+
| Delete Inspection Orders Collectively              Company: 000 |
|------------------------------------------------------------------------|
```

```
|                                                                    |
|  Delete by Inspection Order                                        |
|                                                                    |
|  Inspection Order              from : 1......                      |
|                                to   : 2......                      |
|                                                                    |
|  Position                      from : 3..                          |
|                                to   : 4..                          |
|                                                                    |
+--------------------------------------------------------------------+
```

1.   Inspection Order from
2.   Inspection Order to
3.   Position from
4.   Position to

19.4 Process Inspection Orders (tcqms1204m000)

SESSION OBJECTIVE

To process inspection orders with status "Completed".

HOW TO USE THE SESSION

After entering data in field "Processing By", specify the range by means of option "Continue [cont.process]".

Processing involves the following steps:

- the system selects all the inspection orders for each origin with status "Completed".
- the system selects inspections by "Test Type":

1)   Single Sampling
2)   100 % or Continuous Sampling.

- for each inspection order, the samples are also selected.
- for each sample selected, the system determines the number of:
- "Good" pieces
- "Bad" pieces.

The system consolidates the inspection results for all the samples.

- the system calculates the actual acceptance percentage and compares the result with AQL. If the "Acceptable Quality Level" is reached, the order quantity is accepted.

The next step depends on the origin of the order:

Origin	Session
Sales (SLS)	Maintain Deliveries (tdsls4120m000)
Purchase (PUR)	Maintain Approvals (tdpur4121m000)
Production (SFC) [ENtcqms.orgn.production] Material (BOM) Routing (TI) Production (PMG) Material (FRM) Routing (PS)	Check and Close Standard Inspections (tcqms1205m000)

SEE ALSO METHOD(S)

- Inspection Order and Order Line Status
- Inspection Procedure

SEE ALSO KEYWORD(S)

```
+-----------------------------------------------------------------------+
|  Process Inspection Orders                           Company: 000  |
|-----------------------------------------------------------------------|
|                                                                   |
|  Process by                    : 1....................            |
|                                                                   |
+-----------------------------------------------------------------------+
```

1.   Processing By
The range of inspection orders may be entered by:
•   Origin;
•   Storage Inspection;
•   Inspection Order.

```
+-----------------------------------------------------------------------+
|  Process Inspection Orders                           Company: 000  |
|-----------------------------------------------------------------------|
|                                                                   |
|  Process by Origin                                                |
|                          From                     To              |
|                                                                   |
|  Origin            : 1....................  - 2....................|
|  Origin Order      : 3.....                 - 4.....              |
|  Position          : 5...                   - 6...                |
|                                                                   |
|  Operation         : 7..                    - 8..                 |
|  Receipt/Delivery  : 9.                      - 10                 |
|  Inbound/Outbound  : 11......               - 12......            |
|                                                                   |
|   +-Inspection Order----+                                         |
|   | 13_____            |                                         |
|   +---------------------+                                         |
|                                                                   |
+-----------------------------------------------------------------------+
```

1.   Origin from
2.   Origin to
3.   Origin Order from
4.   Origin Order to
5.   Position from
6.   Position to
7.   Operation from
8.   Operation to
9.   Receipt/Delivery from
10.   Receipt/Delivery to
11.   Inbound/Outbound from
12.   Inbound/Outbound to
13.   Inspection Order
The number of the inspection order.
For further information, see keyword(s)
•   Inspection Orders

```
+-----------------------------------------------------------------------+
|  Process Inspection Orders                           Company: 000  |
|-----------------------------------------------------------------------|
|                                                                   |
|  Process by Storage Inspection                                    |
|                                                                   |
|  Project                       from : 1.....                      |
|                                to  : 2.....                       |
|                                                                   |
|  Item                          from : 3..............             |
|                                to  : 4..............              |
```

```
|                                                                    |
|  Container                        from : 5..                       |
|                                   to   : 6..                       |
|                                                                    |
|  Sequence                         from : 7..                       |
|                                   to   : 8..                       |
|                                                                    |
+--------------------------------------------------------------------+
```

1.   Project from
2.   Project to
3.   Item from
4.   Item to
5.   Container from
6.   Container to
7.   Sequence from
8.   Sequence to
20   Other Print Sessions
20.1 Print Inspection Orders (tcqms1400m000)

SESSION OBJECTIVE

To print inspection orders and the related inspection order lines. This session may be optional or mandatory depending on parameter "Mandatory Printing of Inspection Order Documents" in session "Maintain QMS Parameters (tcqms0100m000)".

```
tcqms1400m000                              single-occ (4)   Form 1-4 >
+--------------------------------------------------------------------+
|  Print Inspection Orders                        Company: 000       |
|--------------------------------------------------------------------|
|                                                                    |
|  Processing by                       : 1.....................      |
|                                                                    |
|  Print Already Printed Order Lines   : 2....                       |
|                                                                    |
|  Print Text                          : 3....                       |
|                                                                    |
+--------------------------------------------------------------------+
```

1.   Processing By
2.   Answer on question y/n
3.   Answer on question y/n

```
tcqms1400m000                              single-occ (4) < Form 2-4 >
+--------------------------------------------------------------------+
|  Print Inspection Orders                        Company: 000       |
|--------------------------------------------------------------------|
|                                                                    |
|  Print by Origin                                                   |
|                             From                   To              |
|                                                                    |
|  Origin           : 1...................  - 2.................     |
|  Origin Order     : 3.....                - 4.....                 |
|  Position         : 5...                  - 6...                   |
|                                                                    |
|  Operation        : 7..                   - 8..                    |
|  Receipt/Delivery : 9.                    - 10                     |
|  Inbound/Outbound : 11......              - 12......               |
|  Inspection Status: 13............        - 14............         |
|                                                                    |
+--------------------------------------------------------------------+
```

1.   Origin
2.   Origin
3.   Origin Order
4.   Origin Order
5.   Position
6.   Position
7.   Operation

```
8.     Operation
9.     Receipt/Delivery
10.    Receipt/Delivery
11.    Inbound/Outbound
12.    Inbound/Outbound
13.    Inspection Status
14.    Inspection Status
tcqms1400m000                      single-occ (4) < Form 3-4 >
+----------------------------------------------------------------------+
| Print Inspection Orders                           Company: 000 |
|----------------------------------------------------------------------|
|                                                                      |
| Print by Storage Inspection                                          |
|                                                                      |
| Project                    from : 1.....                             |
|                            to   : 2.....                             |
|                                                                      |
| Item                       from : 3..............                    |
|                            to   : 4..............                    |
|                                                                      |
| Container                  from : 5..                                |
|                            to   : 6..                                |
|                                                                      |
| Sequence                   from : 7..                                |
|                            to   : 8..                                |
|                                                                      |
| Inspection Status          from : 9.............                     |
|                            to   : 10............                     |
|                                                                      |
+----------------------------------------------------------------------+
1.     Project
2.     Project
3.     Item Code
4.     Item Code
5.     Container
6.     Unit
7.     Storage Inspection Sequence
8.     Sequence
9.     Inspection Status
10.    Inspection Status
tcqms1400m000                      single-occ (4) < Form 4-4
+----------------------------------------------------------------------+
| Print Inspection Orders                           Company: 000 |
|----------------------------------------------------------------------|
|                                                                      |
| Print by Inspection Order                                            |
|                                                                      |
| Inspection Order           from : 1.......                           |
|                            to   : 2.......                           |
|                                                                      |
| Position                   from : 3..                                |
|                            to   : 4..                                |
|                                                                      |
| Inspection Status          from : 5.............                     |
|                            to   : 6.............                     |
|                                                                      |
+----------------------------------------------------------------------+
1.     Position
2.     Inspection Order
3.     Position
4.     Position
5.     Inspection Status
6.     Inspection Status
```

20.2 Print Samples (tcqms1410m000)

```
+----------------------------------------------------------------------+
| Print Samples                                       Company: 000  |
|----------------------------------------------------------------------|
|                                                                      |
| Processing by               : 1....................                  |
|                                                                      |
+----------------------------------------------------------------------+
```

1.   Processing By

```
+----------------------------------------------------------------------+
| Print Samples                                       Company: 000  |
|----------------------------------------------------------------------|
|                                                                      |
| Print by Origin                                                      |
|                          From                    To                  |
|                                                                      |
| Origin            : 1....................  - 2....................|
| Origin Order      : 3.....                 - 4.....                  |
| Position          : 5...                   - 6...                    |
|                                                                      |
| Operation         : 7..                    - 8..                     |
| Receipt/Delivery  : 9.                      - 10                     |
| Inbound/Outbound  : 11......                - 12......               |
|                                                                      |
+----------------------------------------------------------------------+
```

1.   From Origin
2.   To Origin
3.   From Origin Order
4.   To Origin Order
5.   From Position
6.   To Position
7.   From Operation
8.   To Operation
9.   From Receipt/Delivery
10.   To Receipt/Delivery
11.   From Inbound/Outbound
12.   To Inbound/Outbound

```
+----------------------------------------------------------------------+
| Print Samples                                       Company: 000  |
|----------------------------------------------------------------------|
|                                                                      |
| Print by Storage Inspection                                          |
|                                                                      |
| Project               from : 1.....                                  |
|                       to   : 2.....                                  |
|                                                                      |
| Item                  from : 3..............                         |
|                       to   : 4..............                         |
|                                                                      |
| Container             from : 5..                                     |
|                       to   : 6..                                     |
|                                                                      |
| Sequence              from : 7..                                     |
|                       to   : 8..                                     |
|                                                                      |
+----------------------------------------------------------------------+
```

1.   From Project
2.   To Project
3.   From Item
4.   To Item

```
5.     From Container
6.     To Container
7.     From Sequence
8.     To Sequence
tcqms1410m000                          single-occ (4) < Form 4-4
+----------------------------------------------------------------------+
|  Print Samples                                      Company: 000  |
|----------------------------------------------------------------------|
|                                                                      |
|  Print by Inspection Order                                           |
|                                                                      |
|  Inspection Order                from : 1.......                     |
|                                  to   : 2......                      |
|                                                                      |
+----------------------------------------------------------------------+
1.     From Inspection Order
2.     To Inspection Order
20.3  Print Test Data (tcqms1415m000)
tcqms1415m000                          single-occ (4)   Form 1-4 >
+----------------------------------------------------------------------+
|  Print Test Data                                    Company: 000  |
|----------------------------------------------------------------------|
|                                                                      |
|  Process by                  : 1....................                 |
|                                                                      |
|  Print Report                : 2         1 - By Characteristic       |
|                                          2 - By Serial Number        |
|                                                                      |
+----------------------------------------------------------------------+
1.     Processing By
2.     Print Report
tcqms1415m000                          single-occ (4) < Form 2-4 >
+----------------------------------------------------------------------+
|  Print Test Data                                    Company: 000  |
|----------------------------------------------------------------------|
|                                                                      |
|  Print by Origin                                                     |
|                         From                     To                  |
|                                                                      |
|  Origin             : 1....................  - 2....................  |
|  Origin Order       : 3.....                 - 4.....                |
|  Position           : 5...                   - 6...                  |
|                                                                      |
|  Operation          : 7..                    - 8..                   |
|  Receipt/Delivery   : 9.                     - 10                    |
|  Inbound/Outbound   : 11......               - 12......              |
|                                                                      |
+----------------------------------------------------------------------+
1.     From Origin
2.     To Origin
3.     From Origin Order
4.     To Origin Order
5.     From Position
6.     To Position
7.     From Operation
8.     To Operation
9.     From Receipt/Delivery
10.    To Receipt/Delivery
11.    From Inbound/Outbound
12.    To Inbound/Outbound
tcqms1415m000                          single-occ (4) < Form 3-4 >
+----------------------------------------------------------------------+
|  Print Test Data                                    Company: 000  |
```

```
|-------------------------------------------------------------------------------|
|                                                                               |
|  Print by Storage Inspection                                                  |
|                                                                               |
|  Project                          from : 1.....                               |
|                                   to   : 2.....                               |
|                                                                               |
|  Item                             from : 3...............                     |
|                                   to   : 4...............                     |
|                                                                               |
|  Container                        from : 5..                                  |
|                                   to   : 6..                                  |
|                                                                               |
|  Sequence                         from : 7..                                  |
|                                   to   : 8..                                  |
|                                                                               |
+-------------------------------------------------------------------------------+
```

1.   From Project
2.   To Project
3.   From Item
4.   To Item
5.   From Container
6.   To Container
7.   From Sequence
8.   To Sequence

tcqms1415m000   single-occ (4) < Form 4-4

```
+-------------------------------------------------------------------------------+
|  Print Test Data                                        Company: 000          |
|-------------------------------------------------------------------------------|
|                                                                               |
|  Print by Inspection Order                                                    |
|                                                                               |
|  Inspection Order                 from :  1.......                            |
|                                   to   :  2.......                            |
|                                                                               |
|  Sample                           from :  3.......                            |
|                                   to   :  4.......                            |
|                                                                               |
|  Position                         from :  5..                                 |
|                                   to   :  6..                                 |
|                                                                               |
|  Serial Number                    from :  7.......                            |
|                                   to   :  8.......                            |
|                                                                               |
+-------------------------------------------------------------------------------+
```

1.   Position
2.   Inspection Order
3.   Sample
4.   Sample
5.   Position
6.   Position
7.   Serial Number
8.   Serial Number

21   Introduction to Storage Inspections
21.1 General
OBJECTIVE OF BUSINESS OBJECT
It is possible to generate storage inspection orders based on item, warehouse,
location, lot, date, or inventory unit. While the storage inspection order is
generated, the system uses the quality combination and quality ID for the
default inspection data.
The generated storage inspection orders can be adjusted or new storage
inspection orders can be created.

When an item is selected for storage inspection, it is possible to make
different groups. For each group of lots, warehouses, locations, dates, or
inventory units, a separate storage inspection order can be created. This makes
it possible to inspect, for example, one group more extensively than another
group because of different data.
The main part of the storage inspection is identical to 'standard' inspection.
See also the procedure of this business object.
All inventory selected for inspection will be blocked. While the storage
inspection is closed, the system checks for all processed storage inspections
and unblocks all inventory. The rejected quantities can be subtracted from
inventory by using an inventory transfer.
Display the procedure and show the sessions in:
•   Storage Inspection Procedure
21.2 Session Overview

Seq.	Session	Description	Session Usage
10	tcqms2110m000	Maintain Samples (Storage Inspections)	Mandatory
11	tcqms2120m000	Maintain Storage Inspections	Mandatory
12	tcqms2120s000	Maintain Storage Inspection Inventory	Additional
13	tcqms2220m000	Generate Storage Inspections	Additional
14	tcqms2221m000	Print and Close Storage Inspections	Mandatory
15	tcqms1102s000	Maintain Inspection Orders	Mandatory
201	tcqms2510m000	Display Samples (Storage Inspections)	Display
202	tcqms2520m000	Display Storage Inspections	Display
203	tcqms2510s000	Display Samples (Storage Inspections)	Display
204	tcqms2520s000	Display Storage Inspection Inventory	Display
205	tcqms1506s000	Display Inspection Orders	Display
206	tcqms2521s000	Display Storage Inspections	Display
207	tcqms1509s000	Display Inspec Orders (Storage Inspecti	Display

22   Mandatory Sessions
22.1 Maintain Samples (Storage Inspections) (tcqms2110m000)
SESSION OBJECTIVE
To maintain samples for storage inspections.
HOW TO USE THE SESSION
Before maintaining samples for a storage inspection order, inventory should be
maintained in session "Maintain Storage Inspection Inventory (tcqms2120s000)".
SEE ALSO KEYWORD(S)
•   Samples
SEE ALSO METHOD(S)
•   Storage Inspections
•   Storage Inspection Procedure
tcqms2110m000   zoom   single/grp (3)   Form 1-1
+--+
Maintain Samples (Storage Inspections)   Company: 000
Inspection Order : 1......   Maximum Size : 2_____3__

```
|                                  Total Quantity : 4_____5__  |
|  Project            : 6..... 7_____          |
|  Item               : 8............. 9_____   |
|  Container          : 10. 11_____           |
|                                                                         |
|  Sample             : 12......    Test Data Present   : 13___            |
|  Warehouse          : 14. 15_____            |
|  Location           : 16......                                          |
|  Lot                : 17..............                                  |
|  Date               : 18........                                        |
|  Storage Unit       : 19. 20_____           |
|  Test Quantity      : 21............. 22_                               |
|  Sample Quantity    : 23............. 24_                               |
|  Sample Date        : 25........                                        |
|  Sample Time        : 26......                                          |
|                                                                         |
+-------------------------------------------------------------------------+
```

1.   Inspection Order
The number of the inspection order.
For further information, see keyword(s)
•   Inspection Orders
2.   Maximum Size
The maximum size of the sample quantity depends on the test type:
•   100 % or Single Sampling
Maximum Size = "Sample Size"
•   Continuous Sampling
Maximum Size = Order Quantity e

      Frequency
The sample of continuous sampling is equal to the sample size.
3.   Sample Unit
The sample unit specifies the unit in which the sample size is expressed. If the sample size is expressed as a percentage, the system will use the unit of the order quantity.
The sample unit and the unit of the order quantity do not have to be identical, in which case, however, a correct conversion factor is essential.
For further information, see keyword(s)
•   Units
For further information, see method(s)
•   Units and Quantities in QMS
4.   Total Quantity
The total quantity of all samples. This quantity must be less than or equal to the sample size.
5.   Sample Unit
The sample unit specifies the unit in which the sample size is expressed. If the sample size is expressed as a percentage, the system will use the unit of the order quantity.
The sample unit and the unit of the order quantity do not have to be identical, in which case, however, a correct conversion factor is essential.
For further information, see keyword(s)
•   Units
For further information, see method(s)
•   Units and Quantities in QMS
6.   Project
The project code which applies to the customized item.
For further information, see keyword(s)
•   Projects
7.   Description
8.   Item
The item which is to be inspected.
For further information, see keyword(s)
•   Items
9.   Item

10. Container
The container in which the item is packaged.
For further information, see keyword(s)
•   Units
•   Units By Unit Set
11. Description
12. Sample
For further information, see keyword(s)
•   Samples
The default sample number which is generated by the system can be modified.
13. Test Data Present
Indication whether test data already exists in session "Enter Test Data
(tcqms1115m000)". The value of this field is set to "Yes", even if the all test
data lines are empty (zero result).
14. Warehouse
For further information, see keyword(s)
"Warehouses".
15. Description
16. Location
The location where the lot is stored.
For further information, see keyword(s)
•   Locations
17. Lot
For further information, see keyword(s)
•   Lots
18. Inventory Date
The date assigned to the item/lot at the time it is stored. For more
information, see also field "Date" in "Location Control (ILC)".
19. Storage Unit
The storage unit is the unit in which items are stored. The storage unit is used
in module "Location Control (ILC)".
For further information, see method(s)
•   Units and Quantities in QMS
20. Description
21. Test Quantity
The test quantity is a part, an exact factor of the sample size, that is tested
each time and is expressed in the same unit as the sample size. For each test
quantity, the result of the test can be entered in session "Enter Test Data
(tcqms1115m000)".
Example:
Sample Size   5 kilogram
Test Quantity   kilogram

Explanation:
A 5 kg sample will be tested by testing 1 kg at a time.
For further information, see method(s)
•   Example Test Types
•   Units and Quantities in QMS
22. Sample Unit
The sample unit specifies the unit in which the sample size is expressed. If the
sample size is expressed as a percentage, the system will use the unit of the
order quantity.
The sample unit and the unit of the order quantity do not have to be identical,
in which case, however, a correct conversion factor is essential.
For further information, see keyword(s)
•   Units
For further information, see method(s)
•   Units and Quantities in QMS
23. Sample Quantity
The actual quantity that is drawn from the total quantity.
Example:
Sample Size   : 200 pieces

```
Sample                          Sample Quantity
1                               50
2                               40
3                               50
4                               60
```
The total of all sample quantities must be less than or equal to the sample
size.
For continuous sampling, the sample quantity is always equal to the sample size.
For further information, see method(s)
•   Units and Quantities in QMS
24.   Sample Unit
The sample unit specifies the unit in which the sample size is expressed. If the
sample size is expressed as a percentage, the system will use the unit of the
order quantity.
The sample unit and the unit of the order quantity do not have to be identical,
in which case, however, a correct conversion factor is essential.
For further information, see keyword(s)
•   Units
For further information, see method(s)
•   Units and Quantities in QMS
25.   Sample Date
The date on which the samples are taken.
26.   Time [hh:mm:ss]
22.2 Maintain Storage Inspections (tcqms2120m000)
SESSION OBJECTIVE
To maintain storage inspections.
HOW TO USE THE SESSION
Storage inspections can be generated as well as adjusted by means of session
"Generate Storage Inspections (tcqms2220m000)".
From this session, inventory can be grouped to link to an inspection order. Use
options "Select Record [mark.occur]" and "Zoom [zoom]" to maintain the
inspection order for the inventory selected.
Deleting storage inspections Only inspections with status "Free" can be deleted.
If a storage inspection is deleted, all inventory records for that inspection
are automatically updated.
SEE ALSO KEYWORD(S)
•   Inspections by Origin
SEE ALSO METHOD(S)
•   Inspection Order and Order Line Status
```
tcqms2120m000                       zoom      multi/group (3     Form 1-3 >
+-----------------------------------------------------------------------------+
|  Maintain Storage Inspections                          Company: 000 |
|-----------------------------------------------------------------------------|
|                                                                     |
|   Project      : 1.....  2_____             |
|   Item         : 3.............. 4_____         |
|   Container    : 5..  6_____            Quantity Unit: 7__ |
|                                                                     |
|   Sequence    Quantity       Accepted Quantities----------+  Status |
|               Ordered        Recommended     Actual                 |
|                                                                     |
|       8..  9_____  10_____  11_____  12_____ |
|                                                                     |
+-----------------------------------------------------------------------------+
```
1.   Project
The project code which applies to the customized item.
For further information, see keyword(s)
•   Projects
2.   Description
3.   Item
The item which is to be inspected.
For further information, see keyword(s)
•   Items

4.   Description
5.   Container
The container in which the item is packaged.
For further information, see keyword(s)
•   Units
•   Units By Unit Set
6.   Description
7.   Unit
The inventory unit of the item.
8.   Sequence
The sequence number identifies the storage inspections for a particular item. A
common inspection is done for different parts of inventory. The inventory to be
inspected can be assigned to the sequence in session "Maintain Storage
Inspection Inventory (tcqms2120s000)".
The default number is the highest number incremented by 1.
9.   Quantity Ordered
The quantity which is to be inspected. Quantities which are blocked for other
reasons and storage inspections are not taken for inspection.
Maintain Storage Inspection Inventory (tcqms2120s000) The on-hand inventory is
default.
Maintain Storage Inspections (tcqms2120m000)
The quantity ordered is the total of all the order quantities which are taken
for storage inspection.
10.   Recommended Quantity Accepted
The quantity to be accepted, as recommended by QMS, expressed in the order unit
(or inventory unit for "Storage Inspection"). The total of all sample quantities
which passed the tests successfully.
This quantity is updated by means of session "Process Inspection Orders
(tcqms1204m000)".
11.   Actual Quantity Accepted
The actual quantity that is accepted, expressed in the order unit (or the
inventory unit for "Storage Inspection"). The actual quantity can be adjusted
until the inspection order is closed.
Only Recommended
If parameter field "Only Recommended" is set to "No", the results are mandatory.
Consequently, this field is the same as field "Recommended Quantity Accepted".
However, storage inspections are always only recommended. All inventory of the
storage inspection order will be unblocked.
12.   Result Status
The inspection status indicates the current status of the inspection order. The
status is changed during several sessions:

+---+---------------------------------+
| Session | Inspection Status |
Maintain Inspection Orders (tcqms1100s000)	Free
Maintain Storage Inspections	Free
(tcqms2120m000)	
Enter Test Data (tcqms1115m000)	Active
Complete Inspection Orders Collectively	Completed
(tcqms1202m000)	
Process Inspection Orders (tcqms1204m000)	Processed
Check and Close Standard Inspections	Closed
(tcqms1205m000)	
+---+---------------------------------+

For further information, see method(s)
- Inspection Order and Order Line Status

```
+----------------------------------------------------------------------+
| Maintain Storage Inspections                        Company: 000     |
|----------------------------------------------------------------------|
|                                                                      |
|   Project       : 1.....   2_____         |
|   Item          : 3.............. 4_____          |
|   Container     : 5.. 6_____          Quantity Unit: 7__          |
|                                                                      |
|   Sequence    Quantity       Rejected Quantities----------+  Status   |
|               Ordered        Recommended    Actual                    |
|                                                                      |
|        8..  9_____   10_____  11_____  12_____ |
|                                                                      |
+----------------------------------------------------------------------+
```

1.   Project
The project code which applies to the customized item.
For further information, see keyword(s)
- Projects
2.   Description
3.   Item
The item which is to be inspected.
For further information, see keyword(s)
- Items
4.   Description
5.   Container
The container in which the item is packaged.
For further information, see keyword(s)
- Units
- Units By Unit Set
6.   Description
7.   Unit
The inventory unit of the item.
8.   Sequence
The sequence number identifies the storage inspections for a particular item. A
common inspection is done for different parts of inventory. The inventory to be
inspected can be assigned to the sequence in session "Maintain Storage
Inspection Inventory (tcqms2120s000)".
9.   Quantity Ordered
The quantity which is to be inspected. Quantities which are blocked for other
reasons and storage inspections are not taken for inspection.
Maintain Storage Inspection Inventory (tcqms2120s000) The on-hand inventory is
default.
Maintain Storage Inspections (tcqms2120m000)
The quantity ordered is the total of all the order quantities which are taken
for storage inspection.
10.   Recommended Quantity Rejected
The quantity to be rejected, as recommended by QMS, expressed in the order unit
(or inventory unit for "Storage Inspection"). The total of all sample quantities
which do not have the required quality level.
This quantity is updated by means of session "Process Inspection Orders
(tcqms1204m000)".
11.   Actual Quantity Rejected
The actual quantity which is rejected, expressed in the order unit (or the
inventory unit for "Storage Inspection"). The actual quantity can be adjusted
until the inspection order is closed.
Only Recommended
If field "Only Recommended" is set to "No", the results are mandatory.
Consequently, the value of this field is the same as the value of field
"Recommended Quantity Rejected". However, storage inspections are always "Only
Recommended". All inventory of the storage inspection order will be unblocked.

12.   Inspection Status
The inspection status indicates the current status of the inspection order. The status is changed during several sessions:

Session	Inspection Status
Maintain Inspection Orders (tcqms1100s000)	Free
Maintain Storage Inspections (tcqms2120m000)	Free
Enter Test Data (tcqms1115m000)	Active
Complete Inspection Orders Collectively (tcqms1202m000)	Completed
Process Inspection Orders (tcqms1204m000)	Processed
Check and Close Standard Inspections (tcqms1205m000)	Closed

For further information, see method(s)
•   Inspection Order and Order Line Status

```
tcqms2120m000                         zoom      multi/group (3  < Form 3-3
+-----------------------------------------------------------------------+
|  Maintain Storage Inspections                         Company: 000  |
|---------------------------------------------------------------------|
|                                                                     |
|   Project      : 1..... 3_____               |
|   Item         : 4.............. 5_____    |
|   Container    : 6.. 7_____              Quantity Unit: 8__  |
|                                                                     |
|   Sequence      Quantity        Reason for     Description          |
|                 Destroyed       Rejection                           |
|                                                                     |
|      9..    2_____              10.   11_____ |
|                                                                     |
+-----------------------------------------------------------------------+
```

1.   Project
The project code which applies to the customized item.
For further information, see keyword(s)
•   Projects
2.   Rec. Quantity Destroyed
The total quantity which is destroyed during a destructive test, expressed in the order unit. This quantity is equal to the sample size of the inspection orders which are tested by means of destructive tests.
The destroyed quantity does not have any impact on the accepted or rejected quantities. The system only calculates which quantity is destroyed according to the test.
This quantity is automatically updated in session "Process Inspection Orders (tcqms1204m000)".
3.   Description
4.   Item
The item which is to be inspected.
For further information, see keyword(s)
•   Items
5.   Description
6.   Container
The container in which the item is packaged.

For further information, see keyword(s)
* Units
* Units By Unit Set
7.   Description
8.   Unit
9.   Sequence
The sequence number identifies the storage inspections for a particular item. A
common inspection is done for different parts of inventory. The inventory to be
inspected can be assigned to the sequence in session "Maintain Storage
Inspection Inventory (tcqms2120s000)".
10.   Reason for Rejection
The reason why the order is rejected.
For further information, see keyword(s)
* Reasons for Rejection
11.   Description

22.3 Print and Close Storage Inspections (tcqms2221m000)

SESSION OBJECTIVE
To print and close storage inspections. The inventory quantity will be unblocked
if option "Print Processed Inspections" is used. Storage inspections can only be
closed if status is "Processed".

```
tcqms2221m000                              single-occ (4)   Form 1-1
+---------------------------------------------------------------------------+
|  Print and Close Storage Inspections                     Company: 000  |
|---------------------------------------------------------------------------|
|                                                                         |
|   Project                  from : 1.....                               |
|                            to   : 2.....                               |
|   Item                     from : 3..............                      |
|                            to   : 4..............                      |
|   Container                from : 5..                                  |
|                            to   : 6..                                  |
|   Sequence                 from : 7..                                  |
|                            to   : 8..                                  |
|                                                                         |
|   Close Inspections             : 9....                                |
|                                                                         |
|   Print Processed Inspections   : 10...                                |
|                                                                         |
|   Print Closed Inspections      : 11...                                |
|                                                                         |
+---------------------------------------------------------------------------+
```

1.   from
2.   to
3.   from Item
4.   to
5.   from Container
6.   to
7.   from Sequence
8.   to
9.   Print Processed Inspections
This option is used to close storage inspections.
10.   Close Inspections
This option is used to print all processed storage inspections.
11.   Print Closed Inspections
This option is used to print the results of closed storage inspections.

22.4 Maintain Inspection Orders (tcqms1102s000)

SESSION OBJECTIVE
To maintain the inspection orders which were generated by default or to manually
add new inspection orders.
HOW TO USE THE SESSION
Inspection order headers can only be modified if the "Inspection Status" is
either "Free" or "Active" and if no order lines have an "Order Line Status"
greater than "Active".

SEE ALSO KEYWORD(S)
- Inspection Orders

SEE ALSO METHOD(S)
- Generating Standard Inspections
- Inspection Order and Order Line Status
- Using Destructive Tests
- Inspection Procedure

```
tcqms1102s000                      zoom        single/grp (3)   Form 1-2 >
+------------------------------------7_____8-9_____ ----------+
| Project          : 1_____                                                 |
| Item/Container   : 2_____  3_____ 4 5__    |
| Sequence         : 6__               Order Quantity  [10_]: 11_____  |
|                                                                           |
| Inspection Order : 12 13...... 14_____  +-Sample Data--------------+ |
| Quality ID       : 15........ 16_____   | Percentage : 22          | |
| Test Group       : 17.        18_____   | Unit       : 23.         | |
| Test Type        : 19...................     | Size       : 24..........| |
| Frequency [20. ]: 21.............            +--------------------------+ |
|                                                                           |
+---------------------------------------------------------------------------+
```

1.   Project
The project which applies to the customized item for which a certain quality
inspection is desired. A value must also be entered in field "Item".
For further information, see keyword(s)
- Projects

2.   Item
The item which is to be inspected.
For further information, see keyword(s)
- Items

3.   Description
4.   Program domain of string length 1
5.   Container
The container in which the item is packaged and for which a certain quality
inspection is desired. See also field "Containerized" in session "Maintain Item
Data (tiitm0101m000)".
For further information, see keyword(s)
- Units
- Units By Unit Set
For further information, see method(s)
- Containerized Items

6.   Storage Inspection Sequence
The sequence number identifies the storage inspections for a particular item. A
common inspection is done for different parts of inventory. The inventory to be
inspected can be assigned to
the sequence in session "Maintain Storage Inspection Inventory (tcqms2120s000)".

7.   Description
8.   Program domain of string length 1
9.   Status
The inspection status indicates the current status of the inspection order. The
status is changed during several sessions:

Session	Inspection Status
Maintain Inspection Orders (tcqms1100s000)	Free
Maintain Storage Inspections (tcqms2120m000)	Free
Enter Test Data (tcqms1115m000)	Active

Complete Inspection Orders Collectively (tcqms1202m000)	Completed
Process Inspection Orders (tcqms1204m000)	Processed
Check and Close Standard Inspections (tcqms1205m000)	Closed

For further information, see method(s)
•   Inspection Order and Order Line Status
10.   Unit
The inventory unit of the item.
11.   Order Quantity
The quantity which is to be inspected. Quantities which are blocked for other reasons and storage inspections are not taken for inspection.
Maintain Storage Inspection Inventory (tcqms2120s000) The on-hand inventory is default.
Maintain Storage Inspections (tcqms2120m000)
The quantity ordered is the total of all the order quantities which are taken for storage inspection.
12.   Inspection Order
13.   Inspection Order
The number of the inspection order.
For further information, see keyword(s)
•   Inspection Orders
14.   Description
15.   Quality ID
All quality data is linked to one or more items by means of a quality ID.
For further information, see keyword(s)
•   Quality IDs
16.   Description
17.   Test Group
For further information, see keyword(s)
•   Test Groups by Quality ID
18.   Description
19.   Test Type
The test type specifies the way in which the samples are drawn from the order quantity. 100 %
All items are inspected. The "Sample Size" and the order quantity have the same value.
Single Sampling
One sample out of the entire order quantity is inspected.
Continuous Sampling
This type of sampling only takes place in case of mass production and is used to control processing. After a particular interval, a sample is drawn as large as the sample size. A decision is taken as to whether to continue the production or to stop and take corrective action. For this test type, data must be entered in the following fields:
•   Frequency Unit
•   Frequency
For further information, see method(s)
•   Example Test Types
•   Using Destructive Tests
•   Units and Quantities in QMS
20.   Frequency Unit
The frequency unit specifies the unit in which the sample size is expressed. The frequency unit and the unit of the order quantity do not have to be identical, in which case, however, a correct conversion factor is essential.
For further information, see keyword(s)
•   Units
For further information, see method(s)
•   Units and Quantities in QMS

+--+
| Test Type | Unit |
100 %	Order Unit
[ENtcqms.tsty.hundred.p|	
erc]	
Single Sampling	- Sample Size [%] = Order Unit
	- Sample Size = Sample Unit
Continuous Sampling	- Sample Unit = Frequency Unit
+--+

21.   Frequency
The frequency of continuous inspection expressed in the frequency unit.
Example:
Sample Size [TF@tcqms0310spieces
Frequency [TF@tcqms036100epieces

A new sample of 10 pieces is drawn for every 100 pieces.
For further information, see method(s)
•   Example Test Types
22.   Percentage
The sample size is the total quantity that is to be tested. In this field, it is
expressed as a percentage of either the order quantity or the frequency (in case
of "Continuous Sampling").
                 Example:
Example:
Test Type   Single Sampling
Order Quantity   10000   20000   pieces
Percentage   1%   1%
Sample Size   100*   200*   pieces

* The sample size is automatically updated when the order quantity is changed.
For further information, see method(s)
•   Example Test Types
•   Units and Quantities in QMS

+--+
| Test Type | Sample Size |
100 %	Order Quantity
[ENtcqms.tsty.hundred.p|	
erc]	
Single Sampling	n % of order quantity or n units
Continuous Sampling	n % of frequency or n units
+--+

23.   Sample Unit
The sample unit specifies the unit in which the sample size is expressed. If the
sample size is expressed as a percentage, the system will use the unit of the
order quantity.
The sample unit and the unit of the order quantity do not have to be identical,
in which case, however, a correct conversion factor is essential.
For further information, see keyword(s)
•   Units
For further information, see method(s)

- Units and Quantities in QMS

+--+
| Test Type | Unit |
100 %	Order Unit
[ENtcqms.tsty.hundred.p	
erc]	
Single Sampling	- Sample Size [%] = Order Unit
	- Sample Size = Sample Unit
Continuous Sampling	- Sample Unit = Frequency Unit
+--+

24.   Sample Size
The sample size is the total quantity of all samples which are to be tested out
of the order quantity, expressed in the unit of the sample size. In this field,
it is expressed as a fixed quantity.
Example:

Order Quantity   10000   20000   pieces
Percentage   0%   0%
Sample Size   50   50   pieces

For further information, see method(s)
- Example Test Types
- Units and Quantities in QMS

+--+
| Test Type | Sample Size |
100 %	Order Quantity
[ENtcqms.tsty.hundred.p	
erc]	
Single Sampling	n % of order quantity or n units
Continuous Sampling	n % of frequency or n units
+--+

tcqms1102s000   zoom   single/grp (3) < Form 2-2
+--7_____8-9_____-----------+
| Project   : 1_____ |
| Item/Container : 2_____ 3_____ 4 5__ |
| Sequence   : 6__   Order Quantity [10_]: 11_____ |
| |
| Inspection Order : 12......   Text   : 16___ |
| Order Date   : 13........   Acc. Quality Level : 17.   % |
| Effective Date   : 14........ |
| Completion Date : 15_____ |
| |
+--+

1.   Project
The project which applies to the customized item for which a certain quality
inspection is desired. A value must also be entered in field "Item".
For further information, see keyword(s)
- Projects
2.   Item
The item which is to be inspected.
For further information, see keyword(s)
- Items

3.   Description
4.   Program domain of string length 1
5.   Container
The container in which the item is packaged and for which a certain quality
inspection is desired. See also field "Containerized" in session "Maintain Item
Data (tiitm0101m000)".
For further information, see keyword(s)
•   Units
•   Units By Unit Set
For further information, see method(s)
•   Containerized Items
6.   Storage Inspection Sequence
The sequence number identifies the storage inspections for a particular item. A
common inspection is done for different parts of inventory. The inventory to be
inspected can be assigned to
the sequence in session "Maintain Storage Inspection Inventory (tcqms2120s000)".
7.   Description
8.   Program domain of string length 1
9.   Status
The inspection status indicates the current status of the inspection order. The
status is changed during several sessions:

Session	Inspection Status
Maintain Inspection Orders (tcqms1100s000)	Free
[SEtcqms1100s000]	
Maintain Storage Inspections	Free
(tcqms2120m000)	
Enter Test Data (tcqms1115m000)	Active
[SEtcqms1115m000]	
Complete Inspection Orders Collectively	Completed
(tcqms1202m000)	
Process Inspection Orders (tcqms1204m000)	Processed
[SEtcqms1204m000]	
Check and Close Standard Inspections	Closed
(tcqms1205m000)	

For further information, see method(s)
•   Inspection Order and Order Line Status
10.   Unit
The inventory unit of the item.
11.   Order Quantity
The quantity which is to be inspected. Quantities which are blocked for other
reasons and storage inspections are not taken for inspection.
Maintain Storage Inspection Inventory (tcqms2120s000) The on-hand inventory is
default.
Maintain Storage Inspections (tcqms2120m000)
The quantity ordered is the total of all the order quantities which are taken
for storage inspection.
12.   Inspection Order
The number of the inspection order.
For further information, see keyword(s)
•   Inspection Orders
13.   Order Date
The date on which the inspection order is/was created.
14.   Effective Date
The date as of which a test can be used to inspect items.

15.   Completion Date
The completion date is the date on which all inspection order lines are completed. This date is updated automatically in session "Complete Inspection Orders Collectively (tcqms1202m000)" and cannot be entered manually.
16.   Text
17.   Acceptable Quality Level
The acceptable quality level is the percentage of all test quantities of all samples of an inspection order which must pass the test successfully to accept:
*   the entire order quantity (Single Sampling)
*   the entire frequency quantity (Continuous Sampling)
The percentage can be determined by experience or statistics.
For further information, see method(s)
*   Example Test Types
Examples

Single Sampling
Acceptable Quality Level
Sample Size   30 pieces

Sample	le	Result
1	5 pieces	Good
2	10 pieces	Bad
3	15 pieces	Good

Actual Quality Level = [(5 + 15) / (5 + 10 + 15)] x 100 % = 66,67 %
The actual quality is higher than the acceptable quality level.
Consequently, the order quantity is accepted.

Continuous Sampling
Acceptable Quality Level
Order Quantity [TF@tcqms120.oqua300 pieces
Frequency   100 pieces
Sample Size   10 pieces

Sample	le [TF@tcqms110.s	Actual Quality Level
1	10 pieces	70 % good
2	10 pieces	50 % good
3	10 pieces	80 % good

          Compare the results to the "Acceptable Quality Level
".

Sample	Quality Level		Quantity	
	Actual	Acceptable	Accepted	Rejected
1	70 %	60 %	100	0
2	50 %	60 %	0	100
3	80 %	60 %	100	0
			----	----
		Total	200	100

This field does not apply to tests of type 100 %.
23   Other Maintenance Sessions
23.1 Maintain Storage Inspection Inventory (tcqms2120s000)
SESSION OBJECTIVE
To assign inventory which is taken for storage inspection.
HOW TO USE THE SESSION
This session can be activated in session "Maintain Storage Inspections (tcqms2120m000)". The inventory under a particular sequence number is inspected together with a set of inspection orders. Only inventory of the same project / item / container can be inspected together.
The inventory lines cannot be deleted or added if:
*   the storage inspection status is not "Free", or
*   the storage inspection status is "Active" and one of the inspection order lines has status "Completed".

The inventory lines can be deleted or added if:
• the storage inspection status is "Free", or
• the storage inspection status is "Active" and none of the inspection order lines has status "Completed".
"Quantity Ordered" can be modified if:
• the storage inspection status is "Free", or
• the storage inspection status is "Active" and none of the inspection orders line has status "Completed".
• If new inventory lines are added or the "Quantity Ordered" is increased, the sample sizes will be updated for all the inspection orders of this inspection due to the new order quantity.
• The existing inventory lines can be deleted or the "Quantity Ordered" can be decreased, provided that the new sample sizes that are required (because of the new order quantity after the deleting/changing) are not smaller than the total sample quantity already drawn for any inspection order of this inspection by session "Maintain Samples (tcqms1110m000)".
Inventory cannot be taken for storage inspection if:
• it is blocked for any reason,
• it is already under cycle counting,
• it is already taken for storage inspection.
The "Quantity Ordered" seen in session "Maintain Storage Inspections (tcqms2120m000)" for that inspection is also updated by the system.
The quantity fields "Actual Quantity Accepted" and "Actual Quantity Rejected" can be modified only if the inspection status is "Processed".
If the "Actual Quantity Accepted" is modified, the "Actual Quantity Rejected" is automatically adjusted by the system so that the total of two quantities is equal to the "Quantity Ordered". The reverse is also true.
SEE ALSO KEYWORD(S)
• Inspection Results by Origin (Storage Inspection)

```
tcqms2120s000                          multi/group (3    Form 1-2 >
+--Maintain Storage Inspection Inventory--------------------------------------+
|                                                                             |
|  Project      : 1.....  2_____                       |
|  Item         : 3.............. 4_____               |
|  Container    : 5..  6_____           Insp. Status : 7_____         |
|  Sequence     : 8..                       Quantity Unit: 9__                 |
|                                                                             |
|  Warehouse  Location  Lot              Date        Storage    Order Quantity |
|                                                    Unit                      |
|                                                                             |
|  11    12.  13......  14..............  15.......     16.  17.............|
|                                                                             |
|  Total Order Quantity: 10_____  9__                                   |
+-----------------------------------------------------------------------------+
```

1.   Project
The project code which applies to the customized item.
For further information, see keyword(s)
•   Projects
2.   Description
3.   Item
The item which is to be inspected.
For further information, see keyword(s)
•   Items
4.   Description
5.   Container
The container in which the item is packaged.
For further information, see keyword(s)
•   Units
•   Units By Unit Set
6.   Description
7.   Result Status
The inspection status indicates the current status of the inspection order. The status is changed during several sessions:

Session	Inspection Status
Maintain Inspection Orders (tcqms1100s000)	Free
Maintain Storage Inspections (tcqms2120m000)	Free
Enter Test Data (tcqms1115m000)	Active
Complete Inspection Orders Collectively (tcqms1202m000)	Completed
Process Inspection Orders (tcqms1204m000)	Processed
Check and Close Standard Inspections (tcqms1205m000)	Closed

For further information, see method(s)
• Inspection Order and Order Line Status
8. Sequence
The sequence number identifies the storage inspections for a particular item. A common inspection is done for different parts of inventory. The inventory to be inspected can be assigned to the sequence in session "Maintain Storage Inspection Inventory (tcqms2120s000)".
9. Unit
The inventory unit of the item.
10. Total Order Quantity
The total of all the order quantities taken for storage inspection.
11. Serial Number
12. Warehouse
For further information, see keyword(s)
"Warehouses".
If ILC is not implemented, the default warehouse for customized items is generated by the system. This default warehouse is the same warehouse as the warehouse maintained in the customized item data.
13. Location
The location where the lot is stored.
For further information, see keyword(s)
• Locations
14. Lot
For further information, see keyword(s)
• Lots
15. Date
The date assigned to the item/lot at the time it is stored. For more information, see also field "Date" in "Location Control (ILC)".
Can only be entered if "Lot Control (LTC)" is implemented.
16. Storage Unit
The storage unit is the unit in which items are stored. The storage unit is used in module "Location Control (ILC)".
For further information, see method(s)
• Units and Quantities in QMS
17. Quantity Ordered
The quantity which is to be inspected. Quantities which are blocked for other reasons and storage inspections are not taken for inspection.
Maintain Storage Inspection Inventory (tcqms2120s000) The on-hand inventory is default.
Maintain Storage Inspections (tcqms2120m000)

The quantity ordered is the total of all the order quantities which are taken
for storage inspection.

```
tcqms2120s000                              multi/group (3  < Form 2-2
+--Maintain Storage Inspection Inventory-----------------------------------+
|                                                                          |
|   Project        : 1.....   3_____             |
|   Item           : 4............... 5_____             |
|   Container      : 6..   7_____          Insp. Status : 8_____   |
|   Sequence       : 9..                       Quantity Unit: 10_           |
|                                                                          |
|   Accepted Quantities---------+ Rejected Quantities---------+  Quantity   |
|   Recommended      Actual        Recommended      Actual      Destroyed   |
|                                                                          |
|11 12_____13............14_____15............2_____|
|                                                                          |
| Total Order Quantity: 16_____ 10_                                |
+--------------------------------------------------------------------------+
```

1.   Project
The project code which applies to the customized item.
For further information, see keyword(s)
•   Projects
2.   Rec. Quantity Destroyed
The total quantity which is destroyed during a destructive test, expressed in
the order unit. This quantity is equal to the sample size of the inspection
orders which are tested by means of destructive tests.
The destroyed quantity does not have any impact on the accepted or rejected
quantities. The system only calculates which quantity is destroyed according to
the test.
This quantity is automatically updated in session "Process Inspection Orders
(tcqms1204m000)".
3.   Description
4.   Item
The item which is to be inspected.
For further information, see keyword(s)
•   Items
5.   Description
6.   Container
The container in which the item is packaged.
For further information, see keyword(s)
•   Units
•   Units By Unit Set
7.   Description
8.   Result Status
The inspection status indicates the current status of the inspection order. The
status is changed during several sessions:

Session	Inspection Status
Maintain Inspection Orders (tcqms1100s000)	Free
Maintain Storage Inspections (tcqms2120m000)	Free
Enter Test Data (tcqms1115m000)	Active
Complete Inspection Orders Collectively (tcqms1202m000)	Completed
Process Inspection Orders (tcqms1204m000)	Processed

Check and Close Standard Inspections	Closed
(tcqms1205m000)	

For further information, see method(s)
•   Inspection Order and Order Line Status
9.   Sequence
The sequence number identifies the storage inspections for a particular item. A common inspection is done for different parts of inventory. The inventory to be inspected can be assigned to the sequence in session "Maintain Storage Inspection Inventory (tcqms2120s000)".
10.   Unit
The inventory unit of the item.
11.   Serial Number
12.   Recommended Quantity Accepted
The quantity to be accepted, as recommended by QMS, expressed in the order unit (or inventory unit for "Storage Inspection"). The total of all sample quantities which passed the tests successfully.
This quantity is updated by means of session "Process Inspection Orders (tcqms1204m000)".
13.   Actual Quantity Accepted
The actual quantity that is accepted, expressed in the order unit (or the inventory unit for "Storage Inspection"). The actual quantity can be adjusted until the inspection order is closed.
Only Recommended
If parameter field "Only Recommended" is set to "No", the results are mandatory. Consequently, this field is the same as field "Recommended Quantity Accepted". However, storage inspections are always only recommended. All inventory of the storage inspection order will be unblocked. If the inspection status is "Processed", the quantity can be changed. If the quantity is changed, the system automatically updates the value of the "Actual Quantity Rejected" so that the sum of these fields is equal to the value of the "Quantity Ordered".
14.   Recommended Quantity Rejected
The quantity to be rejected, as recommended by QMS, expressed in the order unit (or inventory unit for "Storage Inspection"). The total of all sample quantities which do not have the required quality level.
This quantity is updated by means of session "Process Inspection Orders (tcqms1204m000)".
15.   Actual Quantity Rejected
The actual quantity which is rejected, expressed in the order unit (or the inventory unit for "Storage Inspection"). The actual quantity can be adjusted until the inspection order is closed.
Only Recommended
If field "Only Recommended" is set to "No", the results are mandatory. Consequently, the value of this field is the same as the value of field "Recommended Quantity Rejected". However, storage inspections are always "Only Recommended". All inventory of the storage inspection order will be unblocked.
16.   Total Order Quantity
The total of all the order quantities taken for storage inspection.
23.2 Generate Storage Inspections (tcqms2220m000)
SESSION OBJECTIVE
To generate storage inspection orders if parameter "QMS Implemented for Storage Inspection" is set to 'Yes'.
HOW TO USE THE SESSION
Storage inspection orders can be generated for a specified range of projects, items, containers, etc. The generated orders can be maintained in session "Maintain Storage Inspections (tcqms2120m000)".
Inventory cannot be taken for storage inspection if:
1.   It is blocked for any reason;
2.   It is already under cycle counting;
3.   It is already taken for storage inspection.
To generate inspection orders, the system first searches for the quality ID. If no quality ID is found, the inspection orders are not generated.

The system uses the information in the following sessions to generate storage
inspection orders:
1.   Maintain Test Groups by Quality ID (tcqms0136m000)
2.   Maintain Characteristics by Test Group (tcqms0137m000)
3.   Maintain Characteristics by Quality ID (tcqms0115m000)
If BAAN Process is not implemented, there are no containerized items and the
"Container" field will remain blank.
If "Location Control (ILC)" is not implemented, warehouse, location, inventory
date, and storage unit fields will not be used for selection.
Note:
Field "Frequency for Storage Inspection (In Days)" in session "Maintain Item
Data (tiitm0101m000)" must be specified to be able to generate storage
inspections.

```
tcqms2220m000                            single-occ (4)   Form 1-1
+---------------------------------------------------------------------------+
| Generate Storage Inspections                            Company: 000  |
|---------------------------------------------------------------------------|
|                                                                           |
| Generation Method         : 1..................                          |
|                                                                           |
|                                 From                    To               |
| Project                   : 2.....        -    3.....                    |
| Item            from   : 4..............                                  |
|                 to     : 5..............                                  |
| Container                 : 6..           -    7..                       |
| Warehouse                 : 8..           -    9..                        |
| Location                  : 10......      -    11......                   |
| Lot                       : 12............. -   13.............           |
| Inventory Date            : 14........     -    15........                |
| Storage Unit              : 16.           -    17.                        |
|                                                                           |
|+-------------------------------------------------------+                  |
|| Project        :                        18____      |                  |
|| Item/Container : 19_____              /20_|                  |
|+-------------------------------------------------------+                  |
+---------------------------------------------------------------------------+
```

1.   Generation Method for Storage Inspection Order
Indication of the method used to combine the various inspections of item
inventory into one inspection.
Example:
An item is stored in one warehouse in four different locations (e.g. LOC1, LOC2,
LOC3, LOC4) and the user wishes to do a general inspection for all or some of
the inventory stored in these locations. In this case, the user can use
generation method "Item" or "Warehouse".
Item
All inventory of each item is combined for inspection.
Warehouse
All inventory of each item/warehouse is combined for inspection.
Location
All inventory of each item/warehouse/warehouse location is combined for
inspection.
Lot
All inventory of each item/warehouse/warehouse location/lot is combined for
inspection.
Date
All inventory of each item/warehouse/warehouse location/lot/inventory date is
combined for inspection.
Storage Unit
All inventory of each item/warehouse/warehouse location/lot/inventory
date/storage unit is combined for inspection.
Select a method to generate storage inspections.
Based on the generation method for the following location and lot data, this
session is used to group the inspection orders as shown below.

Example:
```
Project Item   Container Warehouse Location  Lot   Inv.Date  St.Unit
1 -     ITEM1  -         VAR01     LOCA1     LOT1  10/02/94  kg
2 -     ITEM1  -         VAR01     LOCA1     LOT1  10/02/94  gm
3 -     ITEM1  -         VAR01     LOCA1     LOT2  11/03/94  gm
4 -     ITEM1  -         VAR01     LOCA1     LOT2  12/04/94  kg
5 -     ITEM1  -         VAR01     LOCA2     LOT3  20/04/95  kg
6 -     ITEM1  -         VAR02     LOCA1     LOT1  25/04/95  gm
7 -     ITEM2  -         VAR01     LOCA1     LOT1  10/02/94  kg
```

Generation Method	Standard inspection for the following lots
Item	1, 2, 3, 4, 5, 6/ 7
Warehouse	1, 2, 3, 4, 5/ 6/ 7
Location	1, 2, 3, 4/ 5/ 6/ 7
Lot	1, 2/ 3, 4/ 5/ 6/ 7
Date	1, 2/ 3/ 4/ 5/ 6/ 7
Storage Unit	1/ 2/ 3/ 4/ 5/ 6/ 7

2.   Project
3.   Project
4.   Item Code
5.   Item Code
6.   Unit
7.   Unit
8.   Warehouse
9.   Warehouse
10. loca.f
11. loca.t
12. clot.f
13. clot.t
14. Date
15. Date
16. Unit
17. Unit
18. Project
19. Item
20. Container
24   Introduction to Order-Specific Inspections
24.1 General
OBJECTIVE OF BUSINESS OBJECT
In some situations, order-specific inspections are required. Based on sales, purchase, and production orders or batches specific inspection data can be entered.
When sales, purchase, or production orders or batches are created, it is possible to create an inspection order linked to that sales, purchase, or production order or batch. While an inspection order is created, BAAN IV searches for the quality combination and the predefined inspection data linked to that combination. The default inspection data can then be modified and changed into order-specific inspection data. This order-specific inspection data only applies to that specific order in that specific situation.
Display the procedure and show the sessions in:
•   Order-Specific Inspection Procedure
24.2 Session Overview

Seq.	Session	Description	Session Usage
10	tcqms0149m000	Maintain Order-Specific Inspections	Additional
11	tcqms0150s000	Maint Order-Specific Inspec Data (Heade	Additional
12	tcqms0151s000	Maint Order-Specific Inspec Data (Lines	Additional

| 13 | tcqms0250m000 | Global Update of Order-Spec Inspec Data| Additional
|
| 101 | tcqms0450m000 | Print Order-Specific Inspection Data | Print
|
| 190 | tcqms0549m000 | Display Order-Specific Inspections | Display
|
| 201 | tcqms0550s000 | Display Order-Specific Inspec Data (Hea| Display
|
| 202 | tcqms0551s000 | Display Order-Specific Inspec Data (Lin| Display
|
| 203 | tcqms0552s000 | Maintain Order-Specific Inspection Data| Display
|
| 204 | tcqms0553s000 | Maint Order-Specific Inspec Data (Lines| Display
|
| 205 | tcqms0554s000 | Display Order-Specific Inspec Data (Lin| Display
|

---

25 Other Maintenance Sessions

25.1 Maintain Order-Specific Inspections (tcqms0149m000)

SESSION OBJECTIVE

To maintain order-specific inspections. In this session, the order number of
orders in other BAAN IV modules for which order-specific inspection data exists
is shown. It is also possible to enter new order-specific data manually.

HOW TO USE THE SESSION

The origins for which order-specific inspection data exists depend on the
parameter settings. See also fields "...Order-Specific Inspection Data" in
session "Maintain QMS Parameters (tcqms0100m000)", for example "Sales (SLS)
Order-Specific Inspection Data".

SEE ALSO KEYWORD(S)
• Order-Specific Inspections

```
tcqms0149m000                        zoom     multi/group (3    Form 1-1
+------------------------------------------------------------------------+
| Maintain Order-Specific Inspections                      Company: 000  |
|------------------------------------------------------------------------|
|                                                                        |
| Origin                  : 1...................                         |
|                                                                        |
|     Origin Position Operation  Only Recommended  Blocking Method       |
|     Order                                                              |
|                                                                        |
|     2.....     3...     4..          5....  6.......................   |
|                                                                        |
+------------------------------------------------------------------------+
```

1. Origin
The origin of the inspection is an integrated package or module.
See also session "Maintain QMS Parameters (tcqms0100m000)" for the implemented
modules and packages.

2. Order
The order number of the origin of the inspection:

+--+
| Origin | Origin Order |
|---------------------------------+------------------------------------|
Sales (SLS)	Sales Orders
Purchase (PUR)	Purchase Orders
Production (SFC)	Production Orders
Material (BOM)	Production Orders
Routing (TI)	Production Orders
Production (PMG)	Production Batches

```
| Material (FRM)                    | Production Batches                    |
|                                   |                                       |
| Routing (PS)                      | Production Batches                    |
|                                   |                                       |
+----------------------------------------------------------------------------+
```

3.   Position

The position number on the order to which the inspection order applies, namely:
*   the position of the sales order;
*   the position of the purchase order;
*   the position of the estimated materials;
*   the position of the estimated co- by-products;
*   the position of the estimated end items.

4.   Operation

The operation of the routing. During or after this operation, a certain quality inspection must take place.

For further information, see keyword(s)
*   Routing (BAAN Manufacturing)
*   Routing Operations (BAAN Process)

5.   Only Recommended

Indication that the use of QMS results is mandatory or recommended.

If the use of QMS results is mandatory, it is not possible to use destructive tests.

This field makes it possible to overrule the value of the (general) parameter "QMS recommendation for ...". See also session "Maintain QMS Parameters (tcqms0100m000)".

6.   Blocking Method for Inspections

The blocking method refers to the way in which production, purchase, or sales is blocked and is based on the point in the logistical process at which time the inspection takes place. Block

It is not possible to continue production before the inspection results are known.

Continue

It is possible to continue production before the results of previous inspections are known. If the previous field "Only Recommended" is set to "No", this option cannot be used.

Block before Posting

Production is blocked before posting to stock.

Block after Posting

Production is blocked after posting to stock. If the previous field "Only Recommended" is set to "No", this option cannot be used.

Block on Operation

Production is blocked during the operation.

Block on Compl. Operation

Production is blocked upon completion of the operation. If the previous field "Only Recommended" is set to "No", this option cannot be used.

25.2 Maintain Order-Specific Inspection Data (Header) (tcqms0150s000)

SESSION OBJECTIVE

To maintain the test and sample data of order-specific inspections. The copied standard data can be modified.

SEE ALSO METHOD(S)
*   Order-Specific Inspection Procedure
*   Using Destructive Tests

SEE ALSO KEYWORD(S)
*   Order-Specific Inspections

tcqms0150s000   single/grp (3)   Form 1-1

```
+----------------------------------------------------------------------------+
| Origin      : 1_____     Order        : 2_____ |
| Project     : 5_____                   Position     : 3___    |
| Item        : 6_____         Operation    : 4__     |
| Container   : 7__                        Inventory Unit :  8__  |
|                                                                |
| Sequence            : 9..               +-Sample Data-------------------+|
| Quality ID          : 10....... 11_____ | Percentage  : 18.          ||
```

```
| Test Group      : 12. 13_____  | Unit         : 19.           ||
| Test Type       : 14.................   | Size         : 20............||
| Frequency  [15. ]: 16.............      +-------------------------------+|
| Effective Date  : 17........            Acc. Quality Level: 21.    %    |
| Text            : 22___                                                 |
+------------------------------------------------------------------------+
```

1.   Origin
The origin of the inspection is an integrated package or module.
See also session "Maintain QMS Parameters (tcqms0100m000)" for the implemented
modules and packages.
2.   Order
The order number of the origin of the inspection:

```
+------------------------------------------------------------------------+
| Origin                          | Origin Order                         |
|---------------------------------+--------------------------------------|
| Sales (SLS)                     | Sales Orders                         |
| Purchase (PUR)                  | Purchase Orders                      |
|                                 |                                      |
| Production (SFC)                | Production Orders                    |
|                                 |                                      |
| Material (BOM)                  | Production Orders                    |
|                                 |                                      |
| Routing (TI)                    | Production Orders                    |
|                                 |                                      |
| Production (PMG)                | Production Batches                   |
|                                 |                                      |
| Material (FRM)                  | Production Batches                   |
|                                 |                                      |
| Routing (PS)                    | Production Batches                   |
|                                 |                                      |
+------------------------------------------------------------------------+
```

3.   Position
The position number on the order to which the inspection order applies, namely:
•   the position of the sales order;
•   the position of the purchase order;
•   the position of the estimated materials;
•   the position of the estimated co- by-products;
•   the position of the estimated end items.
4.   Operation
The operation of the routing. During or after this operation, a certain quality
inspection must take place.
For further information, see keyword(s)
•   Routing (BAAN Manufacturing)
•   Routing Operations (BAAN Process)
5.   Project
The project code which applies to the customized item.
For further information, see keyword(s)
•   Projects
6.   Item
The item which is to be inspected.
For further information, see keyword(s)
•   Items
7.   Container
The container in which the item is packaged. See also field "Containerized" in
session "Maintain Item Data (tiitm0101m000)".
For further information, see keyword(s)
•   Units
•   Units By Unit Set
For further information, see method(s)
•   Containerized Items
8.   Inventory unit
The inventory unit of the item.
9.   Sequence

The sequence number of the order. For each sequence, one or more samples are drawn to test the characteristics.
For further information, see method(s)
- Using Destructive Tests
10. Quality ID
All quality data is linked to one or more items by means of a quality ID.
For further information, see keyword(s)
- Quality IDs
Enter a quality ID. All data related to this quality ID, e.g. test groups, characteristics, and tests, is used as the default. Once this order-specific inspection data has been saved, any changes in the master data will not influence the inspection data.
The selection of another quality ID will overwrite all existing data with the current master data.
11. Description
12. Test Group
For further information, see keyword(s)
- Test Groups by Quality ID
13. Description
14. Test Type
The test type specifies the way in which the samples are drawn from the order quantity. 100 %
All items are inspected. The "Sample Size" and the order quantity have the same value.
Single Sampling
One sample out of the entire order quantity is inspected.
Continuous Sampling
This type of sampling only takes place in case of mass production and is used to control processing. After a particular interval, a sample is drawn as large as the sample size. A decision is taken as to whether to continue the production or to stop and take corrective action. For this test type, data must be entered in the following fields:
- Frequency Unit
- Frequency
For further information, see method(s)
- Example Test Types
- Using Destructive Tests
- Units and Quantities in QMS
15. Frequency Unit
The frequency unit specifies the unit in which the sample size is expressed.
The frequency unit and the unit of the order quantity do not have to be identical, in which case, however, a correct conversion factor is essential.
For further information, see keyword(s)
- Units
For further information, see method(s)
- Units and Quantities in QMS
16. Frequency
The frequency of continuous inspection expressed in the frequency unit.
Example:
Sample Size [TF@tcqms0310spieces
Frequency [TF@tcqms036100epieces

A new sample of 10 pieces is drawn for every 100 pieces.
For further information, see method(s)
- Example Test Types
17. Effective Date
The date as of which a test can be used to inspect items.
18. Percentage
The sample size is the total quantity that is to be tested. In this field, it is expressed as a percentage of either the order quantity or the frequency (in case of "Continuous Sampling").
                    Example:
Example:

```
Test Type                      Single Sampling
Order Quantity                 10000      20000    pieces
Percentage                     1%         1%
Sample Size                    100*       200*     pieces
```

* The sample size is automatically updated when the order quantity is changed.
For further information, see method(s)
- Example Test Types
- Units and Quantities in QMS

Test Type	Sample Size
100 % [ENtcqms.tsty.hundred.perc]	Order Quantity
Single Sampling	n % of order quantity or n units
Continuous Sampling	n % of frequency or n units

19.   Sample Unit

The sample unit specifies the unit in which the sample size is expressed. If the sample size is expressed as a percentage, the system will use the unit of the inventory of the item.
The sample unit and the inventory unit of the item do not have to be identical, in which case, however a correct conversion factor is essential.
For further information, see keyword(s)
- Units

Test Type	Unit
100 % [ENtcqms.tsty.hundred.perc]	Order Unit
Single Sampling	- Sample Size [%] = Order Unit - Sample Size = Sample Unit
Continuous Sampling	- Sample Unit = Frequency Unit

20.   Sample Size

The sample size is the total quantity of all samples which are to be tested out of the order quantity, expressed in the unit of the sample size. In this field, it is expressed as a fixed quantity.
Example:
```
Order Quantity                 10000      20000    pieces
Percentage                     0%         0%
Sample Size                    50         50       pieces
```
For further information, see method(s)
- Example Test Types
- Units and Quantities in QMS

Test Type	Sample Size
100 %	Order Quantity

```
|    [ENtcqms.tsty.hundred.p|                                           |
|    erc]                   |                                           |
|---------------------------+-------------------------------------------|
| Single Sampling           | n % of order quantity or n units          |
|                           |                                           |
|---------------------------+-------------------------------------------|
| Continuous Sampling       | n % of frequency or n units               |
|                           |                                           |
+---------------------------------------------------------------------+
```

21.   Acceptable Quality Level
The acceptable quality level is the percentage of all test quantities of all
samples of an inspection order which must pass the test successfully to accept:
•   the entire order quantity (Single Sampling)
•   the entire frequency quantity (Continuous Sampling)
The percentage can be determined by experience or statistics.
For further information, see method(s)
•   Example Test Types
Examples

Single Sampling
Acceptable Quality Level
Sample Size   30 pieces

Sample	le	Result
1	5 pieces	Good
2	10 pieces	Bad
3	15 pieces	Good

Actual Quality Level = [(5 + 15) / (5 + 10 + 15)] x 100 % = 66,67 %
The actual quality is higher than the acceptable quality level.
Consequently, the order quantity is accepted.

Continuous Sampling
Acceptable Quality Level
Order Quantity [TF@tcqms120.oqua300 pieces
Frequency   100 pieces
Sample Size   10 pieces

Sample	le [TF@tcqms110.s	Actual Quality Level
1	10 pieces	70 % good
2	10 pieces	50 % good
3	10 pieces	80 % good

            Compare the results to the "Acceptable Quality Level
".

Sample	Quality Level		Quantity	
	Actual	Acceptable	Accepted	Rejected
1	70 %	60 %	100	0
2	50 %	60 %	0	100
3	80 %	60 %	100	0
			----	----
		Total	200	100

This field does not apply to tests of type 100 %.
22.   Text
25.3 Maintain Order-Specific Inspection Data (Lines) (tcqms0151s000)
SESSION OBJECTIVE
To maintain order-specific inspection data lines. For each combination of an
aspect and a characteristic, an inspection line is available. The data related
to this characteristic can be changed for this specific order.
SEE ALSO METHOD(S)
•   Using Destructive Tests
SEE ALSO KEYWORD(S)

```
+----------------------------------------------------------------------+
| Sequence       : 1__                                                 |
| Line Number    : 2..                                                 |
|                                                                      |
| Aspect         : 3....... 4_____  Algorithm        : 14.... 15_____|
| Characteristic : 5....... 6_____  Fixed Char. Value: 16......       |
| Char. Type     : 7..............            Char. Standard  : 17......        |
| Char. Unit     : 8.. 9_____       Norm      [18_ ]: 19......        |
| For Algorithm  : 10...                      Upper Limit[20_ ]: 21......       |
| Option Set     : 11.... 12_____   Lower Limit[22_ ]: 23......       |
| Method         : 13..........                                        |
|                                                                      |
+----------------------------------------------------------------------+
```

1.   Sequence
The sequence number of the order. For each sequence, one or more samples are
drawn to test the characteristics.
For further information, see method(s)
•   Using Destructive Tests
2.   Line Number
The line number which identifies the inspection order line.
3.   Aspect
For further information, see keyword(s)
•   Aspects
4.   Description
5.   Characteristic
For further information, see keyword(s)
•   Characteristics
6.   Description
7.   Characteristic Type
The type of characteristic is the type of value which may be measured by means
of an instrument. Fraction
A ratio of two expressions or numbers other than zero representing part of an
integer (written with a decimal point followed by one or more numbers).
Integer
An exact whole number as opposed to a number with decimals.
Option
For this type of characteristic, various options may be defined. For further
information, see keyword(s)
•   Option Sets
•   Options

Characteristic Type	Example
Fraction	3.145
Integer	123
Option	Blue

8.   Unit
The unit in which a characteristic value, e.g. the norm, is specified.

Characteristic Type	Mandatory
Fraction	Yes
Integer	Yes
Option	N/A

For further information, see keyword(s)
•   Units
For further information, see method(s)
•   Units and Quantities in QMS

9.   Description
10.   For Algorithm
Indication that this characteristic can be used as a variable or constant in the
algorithm of another characteristic.
For further information, see keyword(s)
•   Algorithms
•   Variables by Algorithm
11.   Option Set
For further information, see keyword(s)
•   Option Sets
12.   Description
13.   Method
The type of characteristic value or the way in which the characteristic value is
calculated. Fixed
The characteristic value is determined once and can be entered in field "Fixed
Characteristic Value". It is used to compare results or in algorithms. The
results are entered in session "Enter Test Data (tcqms1115m000)".
Variable
Characteristic values are measured immediately by means of an instrument. The
results are entered in session "Enter Test Data (tcqms1115m000)".
Algorithm
The characteristic is calculated by means of an algorithm, using the inspection
results of variable or fixed characteristics.
For further information, see keyword(s)
•   Algorithms
See also field "Algorithm".

```
+-------------------------------------------------------------+
|Method                    | Characteristic  | Example        |
|                          |                 |                |
|--------------------------+-----------------+----------------|
|Fixed                     | Pi              | 3.14..         |
|Variable                  | Length          | 4 meters       |
|                          |                 |                |
|Algorithm                 | Voltage         | I * R          |
|                          |                 |                |
+-------------------------------------------------------------+
```

14.   Algorithm
For further information, see keyword(s)
•   Algorithms
Enter an algorithm if the characteristic is measured by means of method
"Algorithm".
For more information see
•   Method
15.   Description
16.   Fixed Characteristic Value
The value of a constant (i.e. a fixed characteristic) which is used in
algorithms.
Example:
Characteristic [TF@tcqms001.chGravity
Fixed Characteristic Value
Only applies to method "Fixed".
If the characteristic is of type "Integer", the value of the characteristic is
rounded up to the nearest integer.
Example:
User Entry   Rounded Value
   10.5   11
   10.4   10
   10.6   11
17.   Characteristic Standard
The standard normally used for characteristics. This is an informative field.
Example:
A DIN standard.
18.   Norm Unit

19.   Norm
The norm is the desired quality for this characteristic, expressed in the
characteristic unit. Does not apply if the method is "Fixed" or if the type is
"Option".
20.   Upper limit Unit
21.   Upper Limit
The highest characteristic value for which quality is acceptable, expressed in
the characteristic unit. The "Upper Limit" must be greater than or equal to the
"Norm".
22.   Lower Limit Unit
23.   Lower Limit
The lowest characteristic value for which quality is acceptable, expressed in
the characteristic unit. The "Lower Limit" must be smaller than or equal to the
"Norm".

tcqms0151s000   single/grp (3) < Form 2-2

```
+------------------------------------------------------------------------+
|  Sequence      : 1__                                                    |
|  Line Number   : 2..                                                    |
|                                                                         |
|  Test          : 3....... 4_____  Char. Drawing : 13............. |
|  Test Area     : 5.. 6_____   Test Drawing  : 14............. |
|  Destructive   : 7....                   Skill         : 15.. 16_____ |
|  Result Type   : 8.............          Employee      : 17.... 18_____ |
|  Test Unit     : 9.. 10_____  Instrument    : 19.... 20_____ |
|  Test Sequence : 11.                     Text          : 21___          |
|  Test Standard : 12......                                               |
|                                                                         |
+------------------------------------------------------------------------+
```

1.   Sequence
The sequence number of the order. For each sequence, one or more samples are
drawn to test the characteristics.
For further information, see method(s)
•   Using Destructive Tests
2.   Line Number
The line number which identifies the inspection order line.
3.   Test
For further information, see keyword(s)
•   Tests
4.   Description
5.   Test Area
For further information, see keyword(s)
•   Test Areas
6.   Description
7.   Destructive
Indication that the test is destructive and that the item cannot be used after
testing.
For further information, see method(s)
•   Using Destructive Tests
8.   Result Type
The type of result which is reported to the user. Quantitative
A quantitative value is reported after testing, e.g. "40 cm".
Qualitative
A qualitative value is reported after testing, e.g. "Acceptable" or "Not
Acceptable".
9.   Test Unit
The unit in which the test results are defined or calculated.
For further information, see keyword(s)
•   "Units"
For further information, see method(s)
•   •   "Units and Quantities in QMS" Does not apply to characteristics of
type "Option".
10.   Description
11.   Test Sequence

The test sequence specifies the sequence in which the characteristics in a test group are tested. Zero test sequence indicates that the sequence of this aspect/characteristic is not important for testing. An aspect or a characteristic with zero test sequence will be tested after all other tests have taken place.
Example:

	Destructive	Sequence
Test 1	No	1
Test 2	Yes	2

Explanation:
The destructive test will take place last.
The sequence number can be the same for more than one characteristic. In this case, the tests will be sorted by aspect/characteristic, unless the test sequence number is zero.
12.   Test Standard
The standard normally used for the test.
Example:
A DIN standard.
13.   Characteristic Drawing
The file name of the drawing located in the directory specified in session "Maintain QMS Parameters (tcqms0100m000)" on field "Directory Name for Drawing".
14.   Test Drawing
The file name of the drawing located in the directory specified in session "Maintain QMS Parameters (tcqms0100m000)" on field "Directory Name for Drawing".
15.   Skill
For further information, see keyword(s)
"Skills".
16.   Description
17.   Employee
The default employee to execute the test for this characteristic.
For further information, see keyword(s)
•   Employees
18.   Name
The employee's name.
19.   Instrument
For further information, see keyword(s)
•   Instruments
20.   Description
21.   Text
25.4 Global Update of Order-Specific Inspection Data (tcqms0250m000)
SESSION OBJECTIVE
To update order-specific inspection data collectively.
SEE ALSO KEYWORD(S)
•   Order-Specific Inspections
•   Order-Specific Inspection Data (Header)
SEE ALSO METHOD(S)
•   Storage Inspection Procedure

```
tcqms0250m000                              single-occ (4)    Form 1-1
+----------------------------------------------------------------------+
| Global Update of Order-Specific Inspection Data       Company: 000   |
|----------------------------------------------------------------------|
|                                                                      |
| Update Mode          : 1.........                                    |
| Select Multiple Origins : 2....                                      |
|                                                                      |
|+-Origin-------------------------------------------------------------+ |
|| 1. 3...............    4. 3...............    7. 3...............  | |
|| 2. 3...............    5. 3...............    8. 3...............  | |
|| 3. 3...............    6. 3...............    9. 3...............  | |
|+-------------------------------------------------------------------+ |
|                           From                   To                  |
| Origin                  : 4................... - 5...................|
```

```
| Origin Order              : 6.....           - 7.....                    |
| Position                  : 8...            - 9...                       |
| Operation                 : 10.             - 11.                        |
|+----------------------------------------------+                          |
|| Origin          : 12_____     |                          |
|| Origin Order    : 13____                     |                          |
|+----------------------------------------------+                          |
+-------------------------------------------------------------------------+
```

1.   Update Mode
Add
To generate new order-specific inspection data.
Update
To update order-specific inspection data. The update procedure will first delete
the existing inspection data and then generate new inspection data from the
master data.
Delete
To delete order-specific inspection data.
2.   Select Multiple Origins
Various origins for inspection orders can be selected.
3.   Origin
4.   Origin
5.   Origin
6.   Origin Order
7.   Origin Order
8.   Position
9.   Position
10.   Operation
11.   Operation
12.   Origin
13.   Origin Order
26   Other Print Sessions
26.1 Print Order-Specific Inspection Data (tcqms0450m000)
tcqms0450m000   single-occ (4)   Form 1-1

```
+-------------------------------------------------------------------------+
| Print Order-Specific Inspection Data                  Company: 000      |
|-------------------------------------------------------------------------|
|                                                                         |
|                    From                      To                         |
|                                                                         |
| Origin          : 1....................   - 2................           |
| Origin Order    : 3.....                  - 4.....                      |
| Position        : 5...                    - 6...                        |
| Operation       : 7..                     - 8..                         |
| Sequence        : 9..                     - 10.                         |
| Line Number     : 11.                     - 12.                         |
|                                                                         |
| Print Text      : 13...                                                 |
|                                                                         |
+-------------------------------------------------------------------------+
```

1.   Origin
2.   Origin
3.   Origin Order
4.   Origin Order
5.   Position
6.   Position
7.   Operation
8.   Operation
9.   Storage Inspection Sequence
10.   Storage Inspection Sequence
11.   Line Number
12.   Line Number
13.   Print Text
27   Introduction to Inspection History

27.1 General
OBJECTIVE OF BUSINESS OBJECT
The history of QMS can be updated regularly with inspection results. All this data can be displayed.
27.2 Session Overview

Seq.	Session	Description	Session Usage
10	tcqms3205m000	Update Inspection History	Mandatory
20	tcqms3210m000	Delete Inspection History	Optional
101	tcqms3401m000	Print Inspection History	Print
102	tcqms3410m000	Print Sample History	Print
103	tcqms3415m000	Print Test Data History	Print
201	tcqms3501m000	Display Standard Inspection History	Display
202	tcqms3502m000	Display Storage Inspection History	Display
204	tcqms3510m000	Display Sample History	Display
205	tcqms4510m000	Display Sample History (Storage Inspec)	Display
206	tcqms3515m000	Display Test Data History by Characteri	Display
207	tcqms3509s000	Display Inspection Order History	Display
208	tcqms3516s000	Display Inspec Order His (Standard Insp	Display
209	tcqms3517s000	Display Inspection Order Line History	Display
210	tcqms3520m000	Display Test Data History by Unit	Display
211	tcqms3518s000	Display Inspec Order His (Storage Inspe	Display
212	tcqms3505s000	Display Standard Inspection Order Histo	Display
213	tcqms3506s000	Display Inspection Order Line History	Display
214	tcqms3507s000	Display Inspection Order History	Display
215	tcqms3508s000	Display Inspection Order Line History	Display

28   Mandatory Sessions
28.1 Update Inspection History (tcqms3205m000)
SESSION OBJECTIVE
To update the history by copying an inspection range to history.
HOW TO USE THE SESSION:
Only inspections with inspection status "Closed" are copied to history. The following data is copied to history:
*   Inspections by Origin
*   Inspection Orders
*   Inspection Order Lines
*   Samples
*   Inspection Data
The above data is deleted after having been posted to history.
SEE ALSO KEYWORD(S):
*   Inspection History

- Storage Inspection History
- Samples History
- Test Data History

```
+-----------------------------------------------------------------------+
| Update Inspection History                             Company: 000    |
|-----------------------------------------------------------------------|
|                                                                       |
| Processing by                    : 1.....................             |
|                                                                       |
+-----------------------------------------------------------------------+
```

1.   Processing By
A range can be entered by Origin or by Storage Inspection.

```
+-----------------------------------------------------------------------+
| Update Inspection History                             Company: 000    |
|-----------------------------------------------------------------------|
|                                                                       |
| Update History by Origin                                              |
|                                                                       |
|                           From                    To                  |
|                                                                       |
| Origin                  : 1....................  - 2................   |
| Origin Order            : 3.....                 - 4.....             |
| Position                : 5...                    - 6...               |
|                                                                       |
| Operation               : 7..                    - 8..                |
| Receipt/Delivery        : 9.                      - 10                 |
| Inbound/Outbound        : 11......                - 12......           |
|                                                                       |
+-----------------------------------------------------------------------+
```

1.   From Origin
2.   To Origin
3.   From Origin Order
4.   To Origin Order
5.   From Position
6.   To Position
7.   From Operation
8.   To Operation
9.   From Receipt/Delivery
10.   To Receipt/Delivery
11.   From Inbound/Outbound
12.   To Inbound/Outbound

```
+-----------------------------------------------------------------------+
| Update Inspection History                             Company: 000    |
|-----------------------------------------------------------------------|
|                                                                       |
| Update History by Storage Inspection                                  |
|                                                                       |
| Project                      from : 1.....                            |
|                              to   : 2.....                            |
|                                                                       |
| Item                         from : 3..............                   |
|                              to   : 4..............                   |
|                                                                       |
| Container                    from : 5..                               |
|                              to   : 6..                               |
|                                                                       |
| Sequence                     from : 7..                               |
|                              to   : 8..                               |
|                                                                       |
+-----------------------------------------------------------------------+
```

1.   From Project
2.   To Project
3.   From Item
4.   To Item
5.   From Container
6.   To Container
7.   From Sequence
8.   To Sequence
29   Optional Sessions
29.1 Delete Inspection History (tcqms3210m000)
SESSION OBJECTIVE
To delete the inspection history.
HOW TO USE THE SESSION
Select a processing method by means of which a range of data can be entered
which must be deleted for several origins or a storage inspection.
The following procedure applies:
•   Based on the specified ranges, inspections are selected from the
"Inspection History".
•   For each inspection, all orders are taken from the "Inspection Order
Header History".
•   For each order, all order lines are selected from the "Inspection Order
Lines History".
•   For each order, all samples are selected from the "Samples History".
•   For each order line, all test data is selected from the "Test Data
History".

tcqms3210m000   single-occ (4)   Form 1-3 >
+--+
Delete Inspection History   Company: 000
Processing by   : 1....................
+--+
1.   Processing By
A range can be entered by Origin or by Storage Inspection.

tcqms3210m000   single-occ (4) < Form 2-3 >
+--+
Delete Inspection History   Company: 000
Delete by Origin
From   To
Origin   : 1....................   - 2................
Origin Order   : 3.....   - 4.....
Position   : 5...   - 6...
Operation   : 7..   - 8..
Receipt/Delivery   : 9.   - 10
Inbound/Outbound   : 11......   - 12......
+--+
1.   From Origin
2.   To Origin
3.   From Origin Order
4.   To Origin Order
5.   From Position
6.   To Position
7.   From Operation
8.   To Operation
9.   From Receipt/Delivery
10.   To Receipt/Delivery
11.   From Inbound/Outbound

```
12.    To Inbound/Outbound
tcqms3210m000                               single-occ (4) < Form 3-3
+----------------------------------------------------------------------+
| Delete Inspection History                        Company: 000 |
|----------------------------------------------------------------------|
|                                                                      |
| Delete by Storage Inspection                                         |
|                                                                      |
| Project                       from : 1.....                          |
|                               to   : 2.....                          |
|                                                                      |
| Item                          from : 3..............                 |
|                               to   : 4..............                 |
|                                                                      |
| Container                     from : 5..                            |
|                               to   : 6..                            |
|                                                                      |
| Sequence                      from : 7..                            |
|                               to   : 8..                            |
|                                                                      |
+----------------------------------------------------------------------+
1.     From Project
2.     To Project
3.     From Item
4.     To Item
5.     From Container
6.     To Container
7.     From Sequence
8.     To Sequence
30     Other Print Sessions
30.1   Print Inspection History (tcqms3401m000)
tcqms3401m000                               single-occ (4)   Form 1-3 >
+----------------------------------------------------------------------+
| Print Inspection History                         Company: 000 |
|----------------------------------------------------------------------|
|                                                                      |
| Processing by                 : 1....................                |
|                                                                      |
| Print Text                    : 2....                                |
|                                                                      |
+----------------------------------------------------------------------+
1.     Processing By
A range can be entered by Origin or by Storage Inspection.
2.     Print Text
The available text can be printed.
tcqms3401m000                               single-occ (4) < Form 2-3 >
+----------------------------------------------------------------------+
| Print Inspection History                         Company: 000 |
|----------------------------------------------------------------------|
|                                                                      |
| Print by Origin                                                      |
|                          From                    To                  |
|                                                                      |
| Origin              : 1....................  - 2....................|
| Origin Order        : 3.....                 - 4.....                |
| Position            : 5...                   - 6...                  |
|                                                                      |
| Operation           : 7..                    - 8..                  |
| Receipt/Delivery    : 9.                      - 10                   |
| Inbound/Outbound    : 11......                - 12......             |
|                                                                      |
+----------------------------------------------------------------------+
1.     From Origin
```

```
2.      To Origin
3.      From Origin Order
4.      To Origin Order
5.      From Position
6.      To Position
7.      From Operation
8.      To Operation
9.      From Receipt/Delivery
10.     To Receipt/Delivery
11.     From Inbound/Outbound
12.     To Inbound/Outbound
```

```
tcqms3401m000                                   single-occ (4) < Form 3-3
+-----------------------------------------------------------------------+
|  Print Inspection History                            Company: 000  |
|-----------------------------------------------------------------------|
|                                                                       |
|  Print by Storage Inspection                                          |
|                                                                       |
|  Project                           from : 1.....                     |
|                                    to   : 2.....                     |
|                                                                       |
|  Item                              from : 3..............            |
|                                    to   : 4..............            |
|                                                                       |
|  Container                         from : 5..                        |
|                                    to   : 6..                        |
|                                                                       |
|  Sequence                          from : 7..                        |
|                                    to   : 8..                        |
|                                                                       |
+-----------------------------------------------------------------------+
```

```
1.      From Project
2.      To Project
3.      From Item
4.      To Item
5.      From Container
6.      To Container
7.      From Sequence
8.      To Sequence
```

30.2 Print Sample History (tcqms3410m000)

```
tcqms3410m000                                   single-occ (4)   Form 1-4 >
+-----------------------------------------------------------------------+
|  Print Sample History                                Company: 000  |
|-----------------------------------------------------------------------|
|                                                                       |
|  Processing by               : 1....................                 |
|                                                                       |
+-----------------------------------------------------------------------+
```

```
1.      Processing By
```

```
tcqms3410m000                                   single-occ (4) < Form 2-4 >
+-----------------------------------------------------------------------+
|  Print Sample History                                Company: 000  |
|-----------------------------------------------------------------------|
|                                                                       |
|  Print by Origin                                                      |
|                           From                      To                |
|                                                                       |
|  Origin             : 1....................    - 2....................|
|  Origin Order       : 3.....                   - 4.....               |
|  Position           : 5...                     - 6...                 |
|                                                                       |
|  Operation          : 7..                      - 8..                  |
|  Receipt/Delivery   : 9.                       - 10                   |
```

```
|   Inbound/Outbound        : 11......             - 12......          |
|                                                                       |
+-----------------------------------------------------------------------+
1.     From Origin
2.     To Origin
3.     From Origin Order
4.     To Origin Order
5.     From Position
6.     To Position
7.     From Operation
8.     To Operation
9.     From Receipt/Delivery
10.    To Receipt/Delivery
11.    From Inbound/Outbound
12.    To Inbound/Outbound
tcqms3410m000                        single-occ (4) < Form 3-4 >
+-----------------------------------------------------------------------+
|  Print Sample History                           Company: 000  |
|-----------------------------------------------------------------------|
|                                                                       |
|  Print by Storage Inspection                                          |
|                                                                       |
|  Project                       from : 1.....                          |
|                                to   : 2.....                          |
|                                                                       |
|  Item                          from : 3..............                 |
|                                to   : 4..............                 |
|                                                                       |
|  Container                     from : 5..                             |
|                                to   : 6..                             |
|                                                                       |
|  Sequence                      from : 7..                             |
|                                to   : 8..                             |
+-----------------------------------------------------------------------+
1.     From Project
2.     To Project
3.     From Item
4.     To Item
5.     From Container
6.     To Container
7.     From Sequence
8.     To Sequence
tcqms3410m000                        single-occ (4) < Form 4-4
+-----------------------------------------------------------------------+
|  Print Sample History                           Company: 000  |
|-----------------------------------------------------------------------|
|                                                                       |
|  Print by Inspection Order                                            |
|                                                                       |
|  Inspection Order              from : 1.......                        |
|                                to   : 2.......                        |
|                                                                       |
+-----------------------------------------------------------------------+
1.     From Inspection Order
2.     To Inspection Order
```

30.3 Print Test Data History (tcqms3415m000)

```
tcqms3415m000                        single-occ (4)   Form 1-4 >
+-----------------------------------------------------------------------+
|  Print Test Data History                        Company: 000  |
|-----------------------------------------------------------------------|
|                                                                       |
|  Process by                    : 1...................                 |
|                                                                       |
```

```
| Print Report                    : 2           1 - By Characteristic      |
|                                                2 - By Serial Number       |
|                                                                           |
+---------------------------------------------------------------------------+
1.      Processing By
2.      Print Report
tcqms3415m000                                   single-occ (4) < Form 2-4 >
+---------------------------------------------------------------------------+
| Print Test Data History                                   Company: 000   |
|---------------------------------------------------------------------------|
|                                                                           |
| Print by Origin                                                           |
|                             From                    To                    |
|                                                                           |
| Origin             : 1....................    - 2....................|
| Origin Order       : 3.....                   - 4.....                    |
| Position           : 5...                     - 6...                      |
|                                                                           |
| Operation          : 7..                      - 8..                       |
| Receipt/Delivery   : 9.                       - 10                        |
| Inbound/Outbound   : 11......                 - 12......                   |
|                                                                           |
+---------------------------------------------------------------------------+
1.      From Origin
2.      To Origin
3.      From Origin Order
4.      To Origin Order
5.      From Position
6.      To Position
7.      From Operation
8.      To Operation
9.      From Receipt/Delivery
10.     To Receipt/Delivery
11.     From Inbound/Outbound
12.     To Inbound/Outbound
tcqms3415m000                                   single-occ (4) < Form 3-4 >
+---------------------------------------------------------------------------+
| Print Test Data History                                   Company: 000   |
|---------------------------------------------------------------------------|
|                                                                           |
| Print by Storage Inspection                                               |
|                                                                           |
| Project                      from : 1.....                                |
|                              to   : 2.....                                |
|                                                                           |
| Item                         from : 3..............                       |
|                              to   : 4..............                       |
|                                                                           |
| Container                    from : 5..                                   |
|                              to   : 6..                                    |
|                                                                           |
| Sequence                     from : 7..                                   |
|                              to   : 8..                                    |
|                                                                           |
+---------------------------------------------------------------------------+
1.      From Project
2.      To Project
3.      From Item
4.      To Item
5.      From Container
6.      To Container
7.      From Sequence
8.      To Sequence
```

```
+---------------------------------------------------------------+
| Print Test Data History                      Company: 000     |
|---------------------------------------------------------------|
|                                                               |
| Print by Inspection Order                                     |
|                                                               |
| Inspection Order           from : 1.......                    |
|                            to   : 2......                      |
|                                                               |
| Sample                     from : 3.......                    |
|                            to   : 4......                      |
|                                                               |
| Position                   from : 5..                         |
|                            to   : 6..                         |
|                                                               |
| Serial Number              from : 7.......                    |
|                            to   : 8......                      |
|                                                               |
+---------------------------------------------------------------+
```

1.   Position
2.   Inspection Order
3.   Sample
4.   Sample
5.   Position
6.   Position
7.   Serial Number
8.   Serial Number
31   Introduction to Integrations
31.1 General
OBJECTIVE OF BUSINESS OBJECT
The BAAN IV configuration is initialized by your software vendor. This involves
setting a number of parameters in order to tailor the system to your company's
specific requirements.
Please, note that some parameters cannot be changed without MAJOR CONSEQUENCES
for data storage and data processing as soon as the system is operational!

```
+----------------------------------------------------+
| Therefore: contact your software vendor prior to   |
| changing the parameter setup.                      |
+----------------------------------------------------+
```

•   QMS Implemented for ... For example: "QMS Implemented for Sales (SLS)"
•   ... Order-Specific Inspection Data For example: "Sales (SLS) Order-
Specific Inspection Data"
•   QMS Recommendation for ... For example: "QMS Recommendation for Sales
(SLS)"
31.2 Session Overview

Seq.	Session	Description	Session Usage
1	tcqms0100m000	Maintain QMS Parameters	Mandatory

32   Mandatory Sessions
32.1 Maintain QMS Parameters (tcqms0100m000)
SESSION OBJECTIVE
To maintain the parameters of module "Quality Management System (QMS)". These
parameters make it possible to base inspections on parts of BAAN IV.
SEE ALSO KEYWORD(S)
•   QMS Parameters
SEE ALSO METHOD(S)
•   Integrations

```
+------------------------------------------------------------------------+
| Maintain QMS Parameters                               Company: 000     |
|------------------------------------------------------------------------|
|                                                                        |
|                         QMS          Order-Specific    QMS Only        |
|                         Implemented  Inspection Data   Recommends      |
|                                                                        |
| 26_____ :  1....       2....           3....        |
| 27_____ :  4....       5....           6....        |
| 28_____ :  7....       8....           9....        |
| 29_____ : 10...       11...           12...         |
| 30_____ : 13...       14...           15...         |
| 31_____ : 16...       17...           18...         |
| 32_____ : 19...       20...           21...         |
| 33_____ : 22...       23...           24...         |
| 34_____ : 25...                                     |
|                                                                        |
+------------------------------------------------------------------------+
```

1.   QMS Implemented for Sales (SLS)
Indication that module "Quality Management System (QMS)" can be used within this
package or module as a basis for inspections.
2.   Sales (SLS) Order-Specific Inspection Data
This option makes it possible to use order-specific inspection data instead of
standard inspection data. Even if changes have occurred in the master data and
order-specific inspection data does exist, the inspection orders of a specific
order will remain the same.
Example:
This option may be useful in the case of purchase orders with several receipts
over a certain period of time.
3.   QMS Recommendation for Sales (SLS)
This field is used to indicate what is to be done with the inspection results:
•   the inspection results are a recommendation for the user; the
user may overwrite these results.
•   the inspection results are mandatory; the user cannot overwrite these
results.
See also field "Only Recommended" in session "Maintain Quality Combinations
(tcqms0111m000)".
4.   QMS Implemented for Purchase (PUR)
Indication that module "Quality Management System (QMS)" can be used within this
package or module as a basis for inspections.
5.   Purchase (PUR) Order-Specific Inspection Data
This option makes it possible to use order-specific inspection data instead of
standard inspection data. Even if changes have occurred in the master data and
order-specific inspection data does exist, the inspection orders of a specific
order will remain the same.
Example:
This option may be useful in the case of purchase orders with several receipts
over a certain period of time.
6.   QMS Recommendation for Purchase (PUR)
This field is used to indicate what is to be done with the inspection results:
•   the inspection results are a recommendation for the user; the user may
overwrite these results.
•   the inspection results are mandatory; the user cannot overwrite these
results.
See also field "Only Recommended" in session "Maintain Quality Combinations
(tcqms0111m000)".
7.   QMS Implemented for Production (SFC)
Indication that module "Quality Management System (QMS)" can be used within this
package or module as a basis for inspections.
8.   Production (SFC) Order-Specific Inspection Data
This option makes it possible to use order-specific inspection data instead of
standard inspection data. Even if changes have occurred in the master data and

order-specific inspection data does exist, the inspection orders of a specific order will remain the same.
Example:
This option may be useful in the case of purchase orders with several receipts over a certain period of time.
9.   QMS Recommendation for Production
This field is used to indicate what is to be done with the inspection results:
•   the inspection results are a recommendation for the user; the   (SFC) user may overwrite these results.
•   the inspection results are mandatory; the user cannot overwrite these results.
See also field "Only Recommended" in session "Maintain Quality Combinations (tcqms0111m000)".
10.   QMS Implemented for Material (BOM)
Indication that module "Quality Management System (QMS)" can be used within this package or module as a basis for inspections.
11.   Material (BOM) Order-Specific Inspection Data
This option makes it possible to use order-specific inspection data instead of standard inspection data. Even if changes have occurred in the master data and order-specific inspection data does exist, the inspection orders of a specific order will remain the same.
Example:
This option may be useful in the case of purchase orders with several receipts over a certain period of time.
12.   QMS Recommendation for Material
This field is used to indicate what is to be done with the inspection results:
•   the inspection results are a recommendation for the user; the   (BOM) user may overwrite these results.
•   the inspection results are mandatory; the user cannot overwrite these results.
See also field "Only Recommended" in session "Maintain Quality Combinations (tcqms0111m000)".
13.   QMS Implemented for Routing (TI)
Indication that module "Quality Management System (QMS)" can be used within this package or module as a basis for inspections.
14.   Routing (TI) Order-Specific Inspection Data
This option makes it possible to use order-specific inspection data instead of standard inspection data. Even if changes have occurred in the master data and order-specific inspection data does exist, the inspection orders of a specific order will remain the same.
Example:
This option may be useful in the case of purchase orders with several receipts over a certain period of time.
15.   QMS Recommendation for Routing (TI)
This field is used to indicate what is to be done with the inspection results:
•   the inspection results are a recommendation for the user; the user may overwrite these results.
•   the inspection results are mandatory; the user cannot overwrite these results.
See also field "Only Recommended" in session "Maintain Quality Combinations (tcqms0111m000)".
16.   QMS Implemented for Production (PMG)
Indication that module "Quality Management System (QMS)" can be used within this package or module as a basis for inspections.
17.   Production (PMG) Order-Specific Inspection Data
This option makes it possible to use order-specific inspection data instead of standard inspection data. Even if changes have occurred in the master data and order-specific inspection data does exist, the inspection orders of a specific order will remain the same.
Example:
This option may be useful in the case of purchase orders with several receipts over a certain period of time.
18.   QMS Recommendation for Production (PMG)

This field is used to indicate what is to be done with the inspection results:
• the inspection results are a recommendation for the user; the user may overwrite these results.
• the inspection results are mandatory; the user cannot overwrite these results.
See also field "Only Recommended" in session "Maintain Quality Combinations (tcqms0111m000)".
19.   QMS Implemented for Material (FRM)
Indication that module "Quality Management System (QMS)" can be used within this package or module as a basis for inspections.
20.   Material (FRM) Order-Specific Inspection Data
This option makes it possible to use order-specific inspection data instead of standard inspection data. Even if changes have occurred in the master data and order-specific inspection data does exist, the inspection orders of a specific order will remain the same.
Example:
This option may be useful in the case of purchase orders with several receipts over a certain period of time.
21.   QMS Recommendation for Material (FRM)
This field is used to indicate what is to be done with the inspection results:
• the inspection results are a recommendation for the user; the user may overwrite these results.
• the inspection results are mandatory; the user cannot overwrite these results.
See also field "Only Recommended" in session "Maintain Quality Combinations (tcqms0111m000)".
22.   QMS Implemented for Routing (PS)
Indication that module "Quality Management System (QMS)" can be used within this package or module as a basis for inspections.
23.   Routing (PS) Order-Specific Inspection Data
This option makes it possible to use order-specific inspection data instead of standard inspection data. Even if changes have occurred in the master data and order-specific inspection data does exist, the inspection orders of a specific order will remain the same.
Example:
This option may be useful in the case of purchase orders with several receipts over a certain period of time.
24.   QMS Recommendation for Routing (PS)
This field is used to indicate what is to be done with the inspection results:
• the inspection results are a recommendation for the user; the user may overwrite these results.
• the inspection results are mandatory; the user cannot overwrite these results.
See also field "Only Recommended" in session "Maintain Quality Combinations (tcqms0111m000)".
25.   QMS Implemented for Storage Inspection
Indication that module "Quality Management System (QMS)" can be used for the following inventory modules:
• Inventory Control (INV)
• Location Control (ILC)
26.   Description
27.   Description
28.   Description
29.   Description
30.   Description
31.   Description
32.   Description
33.   Description
34.   Description
tcqms0100m000   single-occ (1) < Form 2-3 >
+--+
Maintain QMS Parameters   Company: 000

```
|                                                                        |
|                                                                        |
|  Series in Inspection Order Numbering            : 1........           |
|                                                                        |
|  Series for Sales (SLS) Inspection Orders        : 2..                 |
|  Series for Purchase (PUR) Inspection Orders     : 3..                 |
|  Series for Production (SFC) Inspection Orders   : 4..                 |
|  Series for Material (BOM) Inspection Orders     : 5..                 |
|  Series for Routing (TI) Inspection Orders       : 6..                 |
|  Series for Production (PMG) Inspection Orders    : 7..                 |
|  Series for Material (FRM) Inspection Orders     : 8..                 |
|  Series for Routing (PS) Inspection Orders       : 9..                 |
|  Series for Storage Inspection Orders            : 10.                 |
|                                                                        |
|  Mandatory Printing of Inspection Order Documents : 11...              |
|                                                                        |
|  Step Size for Inspection Order Lines            : 12                  |
|                                                                        |
+------------------------------------------------------------------------+
```

1.   Series in Inspection Order Numbering
This parameter makes it possible to use series for inspection order numbering.
For each origin, a different serie can be defined. See also the "Series for ..."
fields in this session
(for example: "Series for Sales (SLS) Inspection Orders").
The following options are available:
•   One Digit
A maximum of 9 series is available.
•   Two Digits
A maximum of 99 series is available.
•   No Series
No series have been defined.
For further information, see keyword(s)
•   First Free Numbers
2.   Series for Sales (SLS) Inspection Orders
The initial digit(s) for inspection orders that are generated from within this
package or module. They are used to distinguish between various types of orders.
For example, the difference
between sales inspection orders and purchase inspection orders.
3.   Series for Purchase (PUR) Inspection Orders
The initial digit(s) for inspection orders that are generated from within this
package or module. They are used to distinguish between various types of orders.
For example, the difference between sales inspection orders and purchase
inspection orders.
4.   Series for Production (SFC) Inspection Orders
The initial digit(s) for inspection orders that are generated from within this
package or module. They are used to distinguish between various types of orders.
For example, the difference between sales inspection orders and purchase
inspection orders.
5.   Series for Material (BOM) Inspection Orders
The initial digit(s) for inspection orders that are generated from within this
package or module. They are used to distinguish between various types of orders.
For example, the difference between sales inspection orders and purchase
inspection orders.
6.   Series for Routing (TI) Inspection Orders
The initial digit(s) for inspection orders that are generated from within this
package or module. They are used to distinguish between various types of orders.
For example, the difference between sales inspection orders and purchase
inspection orders.
7.   Series for Production (PMG) Inspection Orders
The initial digit(s) for inspection orders that are generated from within this
package or module. They are used to distinguish between various types of orders.
For example, the difference between sales inspection orders and purchase
inspection orders.

8.   Series for Material (FRM) Inspection Orders
The initial digit(s) for inspection orders that are generated from within this
package or module. They are used to distinguish between various types of orders.
For example, the difference between sales inspection orders and purchase
inspection orders.
9.   Series for Routing (PS) Inspection Orders
The initial digit(s) for inspection orders that are generated from within this
package or module. They are used to distinguish between various types of orders.
For example, the difference between sales inspection orders and purchase
inspection orders.
10.   Series for Storage Inspection Orders
The initial digit(s) for inspection orders that are generated from within this
package or module. They are used to distinguish between various types of orders.
For example, the difference between sales inspection orders and purchase
inspection orders.
11.   Mandatory Printing of Inspection Order Documents
This parameter determines if session "Print Inspection Orders (tcqms1400m000)"
is mandatory in the procedure. If the session is mandatory , the inspection
order is blocked until the documents are printed. If the session is not
mandatory, printing is optional.
12.   Step Size for Inspection Order Lines
The step size makes it possible to automatically increase the number of
positions available for inspection orders when:
•   inspection orders are generated;
•   inspection order lines are added manually.

tcqms0100m000   single-occ (1) < Form 3-3

```
+-----------------------------------------------------------------------------+
|  Maintain QMS Parameters                                    Company: 000  |
|-----------------------------------------------------------------------------|
|                                                                             |
|                                                                             |
|  Enter Test Data by              : 1...............                         |
|                                                                             |
|  Directory Name for Drawing      : 2......................................  |
|  Display Drawing                 : 3......................................  |
|                                                                             |
+-----------------------------------------------------------------------------+
```

1.   Enter Test Data by
This parameter is used to determine how the test data is to be entered: either
by "Characteristic" or by "Unit" in session "Enter Test Data (tcqms1115m000)".
This session is used to switch from the default method to the other method.
The method is chosen on the basis of what is easiest to test:
•   Characteristic, the same aspect or characteristic for different items;
•   Unit, all aspects or characteristics for one item.
2.   Directory Name for Drawing
The directory in which the drawing files are stored.
Example:
/test/drawings
3.   Display Drawing
A shell command which will show the drawing within a window. If a UNIX system is
used, the shell command is a UNIX command.
Example:
view [parameters]

Where view is the program which will display the drawings on the system and
[parameters] the parameters required by that program to be able to load a
drawing.
Keywords

1.1   API Parameters (tcapi936)
DEFINITION

API parameters are used to configure API interface usage. Based on the API types available, the user will be able to select an interface provider to be used by BAAN IV.

APPLICATION OF DATA

The above data is relevant for the following packages/modules:

BAAN Common
- Common Data (COM)
- Tables (MCS)

BAAN Distribution
- Location Control (ILC)
- Purchase Control (PUR)
- Sales Control (SLS)

BAAN Finance
- Accounts Payable (ACP)
- Accounts Receivable (ACR)
- Cash Management (CMG)
- General Ledger (GLD)

BAAN Manufacturing
- Product Configuration (PCF)
- Project Control (PCS)

BAAN Service
- BAAN Service Master Data (tssma10010)
- Service Contract Control (tssma10030)

1.2 Acknowledgment Codes (tcmcs038)

DEFINITION

Acknowledgment Codes are used to indicate the status of an order or order change (sales order or purchase order). These codes may be assigned to the order header or order line.

For EDI sales orders, acknowledgment codes assigned to the sales order may be referenced on the outgoing acknowledgment to indicate to the receipient of the acknowledgment (the customer) the status of the received order or order change. For purchase order acknowledgments received through EDI, this code may be received in the meBaange to indicate to you the status of, or response to, your order or order change by your relation.

SOURCE OF DATA

BAAN Common (tctc-20010): Maintain Acknowledgment Codes (tcmcs0138m000)

APPLICATION OF DATA

BAAN Distribution (tdtd-20010): Maintain Sales Order Acknowledgments Codes (tdsls7103s000) Maintain Sales Acknowledgment Code Assignments (tdsls7101m000) Maintain Purchase Order Acknowledgment Codes (tdpur7104s000)

BAAN Common (tctc-20010):
Maintain Conversion of Acknowledgment Codes (out) (tcedi4128m000)
Maintain Conversion of Acknowledgment Codes (in) (tcedi3141m000)

1.3 Additional Cost Sets (tcmcs043)

DEFINITION

Additional cost sets are used to charge general extra costs to purchase and/or sales orders.

SEE ALSO METHOD(S)
- "Adding Additional Costs".

SOURCE OF DATA

BAAN Common (tctc-20010):
Maintain Costs Sets (tcmcs0143m000)

APPLICATION OF DATA

BAAN Distribution (tdtd-20010):
Maintain Costs Set by Purchase Price List by Supplier (tdpur4127m 000)
Maintain Items by Cost Set (tdpur4128m000)
Print Cost Sets by Purchase Price List and Supplier (tdpur4427m000)
Maintain Costs Set by Sales Price List and Customer (tdsls4127m000)
Maintain Items by Cost Set (tdsls4128m000)

BAAN Transportation (trtr-20010):
Maintain Cost Sets by Customer (trtco0110m000)
Maintain Cost Sets by Price Group (trtco0120m000)
Maintain Cost Sets by Price List (trtco0130m000)

Maintain Cost Codes by Cost Set (trtco0150m000)
Split Order Lines (trtoc1103s000)
Standard Session for Transport Order Lines (All Data) (trtoc1180m 000)
Maintain Transport Order Lines (trtoc1181m000)
Maintain Transport Order Lines (trtoc1182m000)
Maintain Transport Order Lines (trtoc1183m000)
Maintain Transport Order Lines (trtoc1184m000)
Maintain Transport Order Lines (trtoc1185m000)
Maintain Transport Order Lines (trtoc1186m000)
Maintain Transport Order Lines (trtoc1187m000)
Maintain Transport Order Lines (trtoc1188m000)
Maintain Document Lines (trtoc1189s000)
Maintain Transport Order Lines (trtoc1190m000)
Maintain Transport Order Lines (trtoc1191m000)
Maintain Standard Order Lines (trtoc3101m000)

1.4 Additional Statistical Information Sets (tccom705)

DEFINITION

Additional statistical information sets are sets of data which is not available as standard information within the BAAN IV applications but is required by some of the EU member states. The extra data is used in addition to the import/export data and can be linked to order types.

SOURCE OF DATA

BAAN Common (tctc-20010):
Maintain Additional Statistical Information Sets (tccom7105m000)

APPLICATION OF DATA

BAAN Common (tctc-20010):
Maintain Import/Export Statistics (tccom7171m000)
Maintain Order Types (tcmcs0142m000)
BAAN Distribution (tdtd-20010):
Maintain Replenishment Order Types (tdrpl0104m000)
BAAN Project (tptp-20010):
Maintain PRC Parameters (tpprc0100m000)
BAAN Service (tsts-20010):
Maintain Order Types (tssma3103m000)

1.5 Address Code IDs (tcedi218)

DEFINITION

An address code ID gives information about the coding system that has produced the address code. In EDIFACT, for instance:
- "SA" denotes a code determined by the supplier
- "ZZ" denotes a code determined in mutual consultation
- "EN" denotes coding according to EANCOM

SOURCE OF DATA

The data result from input or import in the session "Import EDI Data (tcedi6220m000)".

APPLICATION OF DATA

Address code types are used in:
- defining conversion data in the b-object "Coding and Conversion Data".

1.6 Address Types (tcedi224)

DEFINITION

Address types are, for instance, collect or delivery addresses.

SOURCE OF DATA

The data result from input or import in the session "Import EDI Data (tcedi6220m000)".

APPLICATION OF DATA

Address types are used in:
- defining conversion data in the b-object "Coding and Conversion Data".

1.7 Algorithm Variables (tcqms023)

DEFINITION

Variables are characteristics, either fixed or variable, which are used in algorithms to calculate the value of other characteristics.

Example:

Code   Variables by Algorithm

```
I            Current
R            Resistance
```

SOURCE OF DATA
•   Maintain Algorithm Variables (tcqms0123m000)

APPLICATION OF DATA

Variables are used in the definition of algorithms in session Maintain
Algorithms (tcqms0121m000) on field "Expression".
Before variables can be entered in an expression, they should be assigned to
characteristics in session Maintain Variables by Algorithm (tcqms0122s000).
A maximum of 99 variables can be maintained. Each of these variables can be used
for a specific algorithm.

1.8   Algorithms (tcqms021)

DEFINITION

Algorithms are expressions which are used to compute a characteristic by means
of other variable or fixed characteristics. Obviously, characteristics of type
"Option" cannot be used for calculations.

```
  Example:
  Algorithm     : VOLTAGE
  Description   : Voltage
  Expression    : I * R
```

Where I and R are the variables defined in session "Maintain
Variables by Algorithm (tcqms0122s000)   ",
representing the characteristics Current and Resistance.

SOURCE OF DATA
•   Maintain Algorithms (tcqms0121m000)

APPLICATION OF DATA
•   Maintain Characteristics (tcqms0101m000)
•   Maintain Characteristics by Quality ID (tcqms0115m000)
•   Maintain Variables by Algorithm (tcqms0122s000)
•   Maintain Order-Specific Inspection Data (Lines) (tcqms0151s000)
•   Maintain Inspection Order Lines (tcqms1101s000)

1.9   Allowances and Charges (tcedi245)

DEFINITION

Allowances and Charges record the codes and associated descriptions of
allowances (discounts) and charges (surcharges) in outgoing invoices.

SOURCE OF DATA

The data result from input or import in the session "Import EDI Data
(tcedi6220m000)".

APPLICATION OF DATA

Allowances and charges are used in:
•   processing received meBaanges in the b-object "Communication".

1.10   Areas (tcmcs045)

DEFINITION

Areas are geographical areas; they can be used to group customers, suppliers and
employees on a geographical basis.

SOURCE OF DATA

BAAN Common (tctc-20010): Maintain Areas (tcmcs0145m000)

APPLICATION OF DATA

BAAN Common (tctc-20010): Maintain Customers (tccom1101m000) Maintain Prospects
(tccom1110m000) Maintain Suppliers (tccom2101m000) Maintain Import/Export
Statistics (tccom7171m000)
BAAN Distribution (tdtd-20010): Maintain Inquiries (tdpur1101m000) Maintain
Expiry Date for Returned Inquiry (tdpur1800s000) Enter Specific Inquiry Numbers
(tdpur1820s000) Maintain Purchase Orders (tdpur4101m000) Enter Specific Purchase
Order Numbers (tdpur4820s000) Print Purchase Order Header History
(tdpur5403m000) Maintain Quotations (tdsls1101m000) Delete Sales Quotation
(tdsls1803s000) Maintain Delivery Date in Order Lines (tdsls1809s000) Enter
Specific Quotation Numbers (tdsls1820s000) Maintain Sales Orders (tdsls4101m000)
Delete Sales Order (tdsls4803s000) Copy Bill of Material to Order

(tdsls4812s000) Enter Specific Sales Order Numbers (tdsls4820s000) Maintain
Areas by SMI Employee (tdsmi0192m000)
BAAN Project (tptp-20010): Maintain Lay-Off Forecasts by Area (tppdm1120m000)
Maintain Estimate Data (tppdm4100m000) Maintain Archived Estimates
(tppdm5190m000) Maintain Projects (tppdm6100m000) Maintain Project Status
(tppdm6107m000) Maintain Archived Projects (tppdm7190m000) Maintain Extensions
(tpptc0110m000)
BAAN Transportation (trtr-20010): Maintain Defaults by ZIP Code (tracs0130m000)
Maintain Addresses (tracs1100m000) Maintain Addresses (Fast Input)
(tracs1101s000)
Maintain Areas by Standard Route (trtop2120m000)
BAAN Service (tsts-20010): Maintain Locations (tssma1110m000)

1.11 Aspects (tcqms002)

DEFINITION
For its different parts, an item can have the same characteristic more than
once. These parts can be defined as aspects. Different characteristics can be
grouped under a particular aspect.

    Example:
    Item   : Bolt
    Aspect   : Head   Tail
    Characteristic: Diameter   Diameter
                    Thickness Length

SOURCE OF DATA
•   Maintain Aspects (tcqms0102m000)
APPLICATION OF DATA
•   Maintain Characteristics by Aspect (tcqms0103m000)
•   Maintain Tests by Characteristic (tcqms0105m000)
•   Maintain Characteristics by Quality ID (tcqms0115m000)
•   Maintain Tests by Quality ID (tcqms0117m000)
•   Maintain Variables by Algorithm (tcqms0122s000)
•   Maintain Characteristics by Test Group (tcqms0137m000)
•   Maintain Order-Specific Inspection Data (Lines) (tcqms0151s000)
•   Maintain Inspection Order Lines (tcqms1101s000)

1.12 Bank Addresses (tcmcs020)

DEFINITION
Bank addresses are the address data of banks through which your/your trade
relations' payments are effected.
SOURCE OF DATA
BAAN Common (tctc-20010): Maintain Bank Addresses (tcmcs0120m000)
APPLICATION OF DATA
BAAN Common (tctc-20010): Maintain Banks by Customer (tccom1105m000) Maintain
Banks by Supplier (tccom2105m000) Maintain Banks by Factoring Company
(tcmcs0126m000)
BAAN Finance (tftf-20010): Maintain One-Time Supplier Addresses (tfacp1102m000)
Maintain One-Time Customer Addresses (tfacr1102s000) Maintain Bank Relations
(tfcmg0110m000) Maintain One-Time Supplier Addresses (tfcmg1101m000)

1.13 Banks by Customer (tccom015)

DEFINITION
Bank addresses are the address data of banks through which your/your trade
relations' payments are effected.
SOURCE OF DATA
BAAN Common (tctc-20010): Maintain Bank Addresses (tcmcs0120m000)
APPLICATION OF DATA
BAAN Common (tctc-20010): Maintain Banks by Customer (tccom1105m000) Maintain
Banks by Supplier (tccom2105m000) Maintain Banks by Factoring Company
(tcmcs0126m000)
BAAN Finance (tftf-20010): Maintain One-Time Supplier Addresses (tfacp1102m000)
Maintain One-Time Customer Addresses (tfacr1102s000) Maintain Bank Relations
(tfcmg0110m000) Maintain One-Time Supplier Addresses (tfcmg1101m000)

1.14 Banks by Supplier (tccom025)

DEFINITION

Bank addresses are the address data of banks through which your/your trade relations' payments are effected.
SOURCE OF DATA
BAAN Common (tctc-20010): Maintain Bank Addresses (tcmcs0120m000)
APPLICATION OF DATA
BAAN Common (tctc-20010): Maintain Banks by Customer (tccom1105m000) Maintain Banks by Supplier (tccom2105m000) Maintain Banks by Factoring Company (tcmcs0126m000)
BAAN Finance (tftf-20010): Maintain One-Time Supplier Addresses (tfacp1102m000) Maintain One-Time Customer Addresses (tfacr1102s000) Maintain Bank Relations (tfcmg0110m000) Maintain One-Time Supplier Addresses (tfcmg1101m000)
1.15 Banks per Factoring Company (tcmcs026)
DEFINITION
Banks by factoring company are the bank relations of factoring companies.
SOURCE OF DATA
BAAN Common (tctc-20010): Maintain Banks by Factoring Company (tcmcs0126m000)
APPLICATION OF DATA
BAAN Common (tctc-20010): Maintain Factoring Companies (tcmcs0125m000)
1.16 COM Parameters (tccom999)
DEFINITION
Parameters are variables to which a constant value is assigned. Changing parameter values will change the way in which the module operates, allowing you to adapt the module to the specific requirements of your company.
SOURCE OF DATA
First, running the session "Initialize Parameters (tcmcs0295m000)" will assign default values to the parameters, which can subsequently be modified in the parameter sessions.
1.17 Calibration History (tcqms300)
DEFINITION
The history of all the dates on which instruments were calibrated.
SOURCE OF DATA
•   Enter Calibration Dates (tcqms3202m000)
APPLICATION OF DATA
The history provides information on the dates on which instruments were actually used, the dates on which instruments were actually calibrated, and the amount of time in between calibrations.
1.18 Change Reason Codes (tcmcs017)
DEFINITION
Change Reason Codes are used to indicate the reason a change made to an order (a sales order or purchase order).
For manually maintained orders, these codes may be assigned to the order header or line each time the order is changed, in order to log the reason for making a change, if you are set up to log order history.
For sales order changes received through EDI, these codes may optionally be passed in on the incoming change order meBaange, to indicate the reason the trading partner is making a change, and is logged in the order history, if you are set up to log sales order history. Because the
SOURCE OF DATA
BAAN Common (tctc-20010): Maintain Change Reason Codes (tcmcs0117m000)
APPLICATION OF DATA
BAAN Distribution (tdtd-20010): Maintain Sales Order Change Codes (tdsls5106s000) Maintain Sales Order Acknowledgments Codes (tdsls7103s000) '%SE@tdpur7103s000'
BAAN Common (tctc-20010): Maintain Conversion of Change Reason Codes (in) (tcedi3142m000) '%SE@tcqms4191m000'
1.19 Change Type Codes (tcedi298)
DEFINITION
Change Type Codes are used to indicate the type of change made to the order, and are specified on the order change meBaange, and may be referenced on the order change acknowledgment.
These codes may be used to correspond to EDI standard codes, such as the ANSI X12 "Change or Response Type Code", or the UN/EDIFACT "MeBaange Function Code" for header changes and "Action Request Code" for line changes.

SOURCE OF DATA

The data result from input or import in the session "Import EDI Data (tcedi6220m000)".

APPLICATION OF DATA

Countries are used in:
- defining conversion data in the b-object "Coding and Conversion Data".

1.20 Change Type Codes (tcmcs057)

DEFINITION

Change Type Codes are used to indicate the type of change made to an order (a sales order or purchase order). Each code is assigned a "Change Type", indicating the type of change made to the order (header or line).

For manually maintained orders, these codes may be assigned to the order header or line each time the order is changed, in order to log the type of change made to the order, if you are set up to log order history.

For sales order changes received through EDI, these codes are passed in on the incoming change order meBaange, and indicate the type of change the trading partner is requesting. The code is used to drive the processing of the EDI inbound order change, and is logged in the sales order history, if you are set up to log sales order history. Because the change type code received in the incoming EDI order change meBaange is ultimately validated against the codes defined in session "Maintain Change Type Codes (tcmcs0157m000)", this session provides the mechanism to govern which type of sales order changes are allowed through EDI.

SOURCE OF DATA

BAAN Common (tctc-20010): Maintain Change Type Codes (tcmcs0157m000)

APPLICATION OF DATA

BAAN Distribution (tdtd-20010): Maintain Sales Order Change Codes (tdsls5106s000) Maintain Sales Order Acknowledgments Codes (tdsls7103s000) Maintain Purchase Order Change Codes (tdpur5106s000)

BAAN Common (tctc-20010): Print Conversion of Change Type Codes (in) (tcedi3440m000) Maintain Conversion of Change Type Codes (out) (tcedi4190m000)

1.21 Character Conversion Codes (out) (tcedi408)

DEFINITION

Character conversion codes identify the characters conversions required during the generation of outgoing meBaanges.

SOURCE OF DATA

The data result from input or import in the session "Import EDI Data (tcedi6220m000)".

APPLICATION OF DATA

Conversion data for outgoing meBaanges are used in:
- processing data in the b-object "Communication"

1.22 Character Conversions (out) (tcedi409)

DEFINITION

Character conversions are rules that state how characters from the application are to be translated before they are placed in an EDI meBaange.

SOURCE OF DATA

The data result from input or import in the session "Import EDI Data (tcedi6220m000)".

APPLICATION OF DATA

A character conversion is only required if a character is to be converted to another character.

Example:

- A -> A need not be entered, contrary to:

- a -> A
  b -> B

1.23 Characteristics (tcqms001)

DEFINITION

A characteristic refers to a particular quality or distinctive mark of an item or an item part/component.

Example:

Length

```
Width
Weight
etc.
```

SOURCE OF DATA
- Maintain Characteristics (tcqms0101m000)

APPLICATION OF DATA
- Maintain Characteristics by Aspect (tcqms0103m000)
- Maintain Tests by Characteristic (tcqms0105m000)
- Maintain Test Instruments (tcqms0108m000)
- Enter Calibration Dates (tcqms3202m000)
- Maintain Option Sets (tcqms0113m000)
- Maintain Options (tcqms0114m000)
- Maintain Characteristics by Quality ID (tcqms0115m000)
- Maintain Tests by Quality ID (tcqms0117m000)
- Maintain Variables by Algorithm (tcqms0122s000)
- Maintain Characteristics by Test Group (tcqms0137m000)
- Maintain Order-Specific Inspection Data (Lines) (tcqms0151s000)
- Maintain Inspection Order Lines (tcqms1101s000)
- Enter Test Data (tcqms1115m000)

1.24 Characteristics by Aspects (tcqms003)

DEFINITION

For its different parts, an item can have the same characteristic more than once. These parts can be defined as aspects.
Several aspects can have the same characteristic and one aspect can have several characteristics.

```
  Example:
  Item           : Chair
  Aspect         : Leg           Armrest
  Characteristic: Length         Length
```

SOURCE OF DATA
- Maintain Characteristics by Aspect (tcqms0103m000)

APPLICATION OF DATA
- Maintain Tests by Characteristic (tcqms0105m000)
- Maintain Characteristics by Quality ID (tcqms0115m000)
- Maintain Tests by Quality ID (tcqms0117m000) (from Session Help)

1.25 Characteristics by Quality ID (tcqms015)

DEFINITION

Characteristics by quality ID are characteristics which are grouped by means of a quality ID and are to be inspected on the same item.

SOURCE OF DATA
- Maintain Characteristics by Quality ID (tcqms0115m000)

APPLICATION OF DATA

All quality data is linked to item(s) by means of quality combinations.

1.26 Characteristics by Test Group (tcqms037)

DEFINITION

Test groups are groups of characteristics which are tested in the same way and in the same sample.

```
  Example:
  Test Group              A1
  Sample Size             2 pieces

  Characteristic [TF@tcqms001.chSample 1      Sample 2
  Weight                  5.3 kg              5.1 kg
  Length                  3.1 m               3.5 m
  Volume                  7.1 l               6.9 l
```

All the characteristics in the example are tested in the same sample.

SOURCE OF DATA
- Maintain Characteristics by Test Group (tcqms0137m000)

APPLICATION OF DATA

When inspection orders are generated, an order is generated for every test group.

1.27 Charge Categories (tcedi266)

DEFINITION

Charge categories indicate the type of costs:
- total costs incurred
- cash on delivery charges
- transport costs
- transport costs up to a specified point/location

SOURCE OF DATA

The data result from input or import in the session "Import EDI Data (tcedi6220m000)".

APPLICATION OF DATA

Charge category codes are used in:
- processing received meBaanges in the b-object "Communication".

1.28 Commodity Codes (tcmcs028)

DEFINITION

Commodity codes serve to identify groups of items. These codes are used to collect statistical data on the export/import of goods within the EU.

SOURCE OF DATA

BAAN Common (tctc-20010): Maintain Commodity Codes (tcmcs0128m000)

APPLICATION OF DATA

BAAN Common (tctc-20010): Maintain Import/Export Statistics (tccom7171m000)
BAAN Distribution (tdtd-20010): Copy BOM Components to Quotation (tdsls1812s000)
BAAN Manufacturing (titi-20010): Maintain Item Data (GRT) (tigrt1180s000)
Maintain Customized Item Data (GRT) (tigrt2180s000) Maintain Item Data
(tiitm0101m000) Maintain Item Data (in BOM) (tiitm0108s000) Maintain Item
Default Data (tiitm0110m000) Maintain Customized Item Data (tipcs2121m000)
BAAN Project (tptp-20010): Maintain Item Default Data (tppdm0109m000) Maintain
Standard Items (tppdm0110m000) Maintain Project Items (tppdm6110m000)

1.29 Communication Channels (tcedi256)

DEFINITION

The communication channels to which a number in a meBaange may refer: telephone, fax or telex.

SOURCE OF DATA

The data result from input or import in the session "Import EDI Data (tcedi6220m000)".

APPLICATION OF DATA

Communication channel codes are used in:
- processing received meBaanges in the b-object "Communication".

1.30 Companies (tccom000)

DEFINITION

In BAAN IV a company number identifies a data set. In this way a company using BAAN IV may work with different sets of records, for its constituent legal entities, plants or for different projects.

SOURCE OF DATA

BAAN Common (tctc-20010): Maintain Company Data (tccom0100m000)

APPLICATION OF DATA

BAAN Common (tctc-20010): Maintain Customers (tccom1101m000) Maintain Prospects
(tccom1110m000) Maintain Suppliers (tccom2101m000) Maintain Sales Listing
(tccom7170m000) Maintain MeBaanges to be Generated (tcedi7100m000) Restart
Generated MeBaanges (tcedi7221m000) Delete History of Generated MeBaanges
(tcedi7801m000) Maintain Warehouses (tcmcs0103m000) Maintain First Free Numbers
(tcmcs0147m000)
BAAN Distribution (tdtd-20010): Enter Inventory Transactions (tdilc1120m000)
Enter Receipts of Serial Number Items (Collect.) (tdilc4813s000) Maintain Bill
of Enterprise (tdinv0116m000) Enter Inventory Transactions by Item
(tdinv1101m000) Maintain Planned INV Purchase Orders (tdinv3120m000) Maintain
Lots (tdltc0101m000) Copy Ranges of Lots (tdltc0103s000) Maintain Blockings by
Lot and Transaction (tdltc0120m000) Convert Non-Lot Item to Lot Item
(tdltc0130m000) Convert Lot Item to Non-Lot Item (tdltc0131m000) Maintain PST
Parameters (tdpst0100m000) Maintain Inquiries (tdpur1101m000) Maintain Expiry
Date for Returned Inquiry (tdpur1800s000) Enter Specific Inquiry Numbers

(tdpur1820s000) Maintain Purchase Orders (tdpur4101m000) Maintain Defaults by
User (Purchase) (tdpur4123m000) Enter Specific Purchase Order Numbers
(tdpur4820s000) Maintain Margin Control Parameters (tdsls0120m000) Maintain
Quotations (tdsls1101m000) Delete Sales Quotation (tdsls1803s000) Maintain
Delivery Date in Order Lines (tdsls1809s000) [SE@tdsls18
09s000] Enter Specific Quotation Numbers (tdsls1820s000) Maintain Sales Orders
(tdsls4101m000) Maintain Defaults by User (Sales) (tdsls4123m000) Delete Sales
Order (tdsls4803s000) Copy Bill of Material to Order (tdsls4812s000) Enter
Specific Sales Order Numbers (tdsls4820s000) Maintain SST Parameters
(tdsst0100m000)

BAAN Finance (tftf-20010): Maintain Matched Purchase Invoice Transactions
(tfacp1133s000) Maintain Payment Advice (tfcmg1120m000) Maintain Direct Debit
Advice (tfcmg4120m000) Maintain Ratio Variables (tffst6101m000) Maintain Group
Company Parameters (tfgld0101m000) Maintain Company Parameters (tfgld0103m000)
Maintain Chart of Accounts (tfgld0108m000)

BAAN Manufacturing (titi-20010): Maintain Plan Sites (timps1120m000) Maintain
Interplant Supplying Sites (timps2150m000) Maintain Interplant Supplying
Priorities (timps2160m000) Maintain Planned Interplant Receipts (timps3120s000)
Maintain Planned MPS Interplant Orders (timps5110m000) Maintain Planned MPS
Purchase Orders (timps5130m000) Maintain Planned MRP Purchase Orders
(timrp1121m000) Maintain Budgets (tipcs0101m000) Maintain Projects
(tipcs2101m000) Maintain Project Status (tipcs2102m000) Maintain Work Centers
(tirou0101m000) Maintain Production Orders (tisfc0101m000)

BAAN Project (tptp-20010): Maintain Invoices by Equipment Conversion Order
(tpism0113s000) Maintain Invoices by Investment (tpism1132s000)
Maintain Third Party Services Trans. by Job Order (tpism3124s000)
Maintain Standard Surcharges by Cost Type and in General (tppdm11 70m000)
Maintain Standard Surcharges by Cost Component (tppdm1171m000) Maintain Standard
Surcharges by Material (tppdm1172m000) Maintain Standard Surcharges by Labor
(tppdm1173m000) Maintain Standard Surcharges by Equipment (tppdm1174m000)
Maintain Standard Surcharges by Subcontracting (tppdm1175m000) Maintain Standard
Surcharges by Sundry Cost (tppdm1176m000) Maintain Standard Surcharges by
Revenue (tppdm1177m000) Display Standard Surcharges by Cost Type and in General
(tppdm157 0m000) Display Standard Surcharges by Cost Component (tppdm1571m000)
Display Standard Surcharges by Material (tppdm1572m000) Display Standard
Surcharges by Labor (tppdm1573m000) Display Standard Surcharges by Equipment
(tppdm1574m000) Display Standard Surcharges by Subcontracting (tppdm1575m000)
Display Standard Surcharges by Sundry Cost (tppdm1576m000) Display Standard
Surcharges by Revenue (tppdm1577m000)
Maintain Archived Estimates (tppdm5190m000) Maintain Projects (tppdm6100m000)
Maintain Project Status (tppdm6107m000) Maintain Archived Projects
(tppdm7190m000) Maintain Departments (tppdm8102m000) Maintain Material
Transactions to be Invoiced (tppin4157m000) Maintain Labor Transactions to be
Invoiced (tppin4158m000) Maintain Equipment Transactions to be Invoiced
(tppin4159m000) Maintain Subcontracting Transactions to be Invoiced
(tppin4160m00 0) Maintain Sundry Cost Transactions to be Invoiced
(tppin4161m000) Maintain Material Costs (tpppc2111m000) Maintain Labor Costs
(tpppc2131m000) Maintain Equipment Cost (tpppc2151m000) Maintain Cost Surcharges
by Material (tpppc2161m000) Maintain Cost Surcharges by Labor (tpppc2162m000)
Maintain Cost Surcharges by Equipment (tpppc2163m000) Maintain Cost Surcharges
by Subcontracting (tpppc2164m000) Maintain Cost Surcharges by Sundry Cost
(tpppc2165m000) Maintain Revenue Surcharges by Revenue Code (tpppc2166m000)
Maintain Subcontracting Costs (tpppc2171m000) Maintain Cost Surcharges by
Project (tpppc2180m000) [SE@tpppc2180
m000] Maintain Cost Surcharges by Cost Type (tpppc2181m000) Maintain Cost
Surcharges by Component (tpppc2182m000) Maintain Revenue Surcharges by Project
(tpppc2185m000) Maintain Revenue Surcharges by Cost Component (tpppc2186m000)
Maintain Sundry Costs (tpppc2191m000) Maintain Revenues (tpppc3101m000) Confirm
Material Cost Transactions (tpppc4101m000) Confirm Labor Cost Transactions
(tpppc4102m000)
Confirm Equipment Cost Transactions (tpppc4105m000) Confirm Subcontracting Cost
Transactions (tpppc4107m000) Confirm Sundry Cost Transactions (tpppc4109m000)
Confirm Revenues (tpppc4110m000) Maintain Cost and Commitment Accounts

(Material) (tpprc2110m000) Maintain Cost and Commitment Accounts (Labor) (tpprc2111m000) Maintain Cost and Commitment Accounts (Equipment) (tpprc2112m000)
Maintain Cost and Commitment Accounts (Subcontracting) (tpprc2113 m000) Maintain Cost and Commitment Accounts (Sundry Cost) (tpprc2114m00 0) Maintain Cost and Commitment Accounts by Cost Type (tpprc2122m000) Maintain Cost and Commitment Accounts by Cost Component (tpprc212 4m000) Maintain Revenue Accounts by Contract Type/Category (tpprc2131m00 0) Maintain Revenue Accounts by Category (tpprc2132m000) Maintain Revenue Accounts by Contract Type/Agreement Type (tpprc2 133m000) Maintain Revenue Accounts by Agreement Type (tpprc2134m000) Maintain Revenue Accounts by Cost Component (tpprc2135m000)
BAAN Transportation (trtr-20010): Maintain Bank Account by Company (trhec0140m000) Maintain Employee Data (HEC) (trhec1170m000) Maintain Time for Time Balance by Employee (trhec1175m000) Maintain Invoice Lines (trics1100m000) Maintain Transaction Types by Financial Company (trtcd0110m000) Maintain Costs (trtco1100m000) Maintain Fuel Intake (trtfc2100m000) Maintain Fuel Intake from FINANCE (trtfc2102s000) Check Fuel Intake Bills (trtfc2110m000) Maintain Means of Transport (trtfm1110m000) Maintain Finished Activities (trtfm4100m000) Maintain Finished Activities (from FINANCE) (trtfm4102s000) Maintain Order Procedures (trtoc0130m000) Maintain Transport Orders (trtoc1100m000) Maintain Transport Orders (trtoc1102s000) Split Order Lines (trtoc1103s000) Standard Session for Transport Order Lines (All Data) (trtoc1180m 000) Maintain Transport Order Lines (trtoc1181m000) Maintain Transport Order Lines (trtoc1182m000) Maintain Transport Order Lines (trtoc1183m000) Maintain Transport Order Lines (trtoc1184m000) Maintain Transport Order Lines (trtoc1185m000) Maintain Transport Order Lines (trtoc1186m000) Maintain Transport Order Lines (trtoc1187m000) Maintain Transport Order Lines (trtoc1188m000)
Maintain Document Lines (trtoc1189s000) Maintain Transport Order Lines (trtoc1190m000) Maintain Transport Order Lines (trtoc1191m000) Maintain Standard Orders (trtoc3100m000) Maintain Standard Order Lines (trtoc3101m000) Maintain Storage Orders (trwoc1100m000) Maintain Storage Orders (Invoicing Data) (trwoc1106m000) Maintain Storage Orders (General Data) (trwoc1107m000) Maintain Inbound Orders (trwoc2100m000) Maintain Inbound Orders (trwoc2105s000) Maintain Outbound Orders (trwoc3100m000) Maintain Outbound Orders (trwoc3105s000) Maintain Transhipment Orders (trwoc4100m000) Maintain Transhipment Orders (trwoc4105s000) Maintain Assembly Orders (trwoc5100m000) Maintain Assembly Orders (Invoicing Data) (trwoc5106m000) Maintain Assembly Orders (General Data) (trwoc5107m000)
BAAN Service (tsts-20010): Maintain Contracts (tssma2120m000) Maintain Contract Installments (tssma2121m000) Confirm Contract Installments (tssma2172m000) Maintain Service Orders (tssma3101m000) Maintain Actual Service Order Costs and Revenues (tssma3110m000) Maintain Service Orders (Telephone Screen) (tssma3140m000) Maintain Service Orders (Planning) (tssma3141m000) Report Service Orders Completed (tssma3142m000)
Close Service Orders (tssma3144m000) Maintain Service Order Cost Estimate (tssma3170m000) Display Service Orders (tssma3502s000) Enter Specific Service Order Numbers (tssma3820s000)

1.31 Concern Structure (tccom030)

DEFINITION

Concern structures describe the relationships between "Parent" and "Child" companies of your suppliers/customers.

You can use concern structures to support the sales and acquisition process. As a result, a marketing or sales department can perform effective marketing actions.

SOURCE OF DATA

BAAN Common (tctc-20010): Maintain Concern Structure of Trade Relations (tccom3101m000)

1.32 Connect Frequencies by Network (tcedi022)

DEFINITION

The connect frequency determines when and with what intervals the connection with a specific network should be established.

SOURCE OF DATA

The data result from input or import in the session "Import EDI Data (tcedi6220m000)".
APPLICATION OF DATA
Connect frequencies are used in:
•   generating connect times in the b-object "Networks".
1.33   Connect Times by Network (tcedi025)
DEFINITION
Connect times are the times when the connection with a specific network is established.
APPLICATION OF DATA
Connect times are used in:
•   making contact with the right network at the right moments in the b-object "Communication".
1.34   Contact Functions (tcedi254)
DEFINITION
Contact functions specify the function of a contact, e.g.:
•   dangerous goods contact
•   notification contact (person or department to be notified if goods will arrive)
•   information contact
•   principal placing order or contract
SOURCE OF DATA
The data result from input or import in the session "Import EDI Data (tcedi6220m000)".
APPLICATION OF DATA
Contact function codes are used in:
•   processing received meBaanges in the b-object "Communication".
1.35   Conversion Setups (Definitions) (tcedi501)
DEFINITION
Conversion setups (definitions) indicate how EDI meBaanges are to be translated.
SOURCE OF DATA
The data result from input or import in the session "Import EDI Data (tcedi6220m000)".
APPLICATION OF DATA
Conversion setup definitions are used in:
•   correctly generating ASCII files in the session "Generate EDI MeBaanges (tcedi7201m000)"
•   correctly reading ASCII files in the session "Common Session for Incoming MeBaanges (tcedi7220s000)"
1.36   Conversion Setups (Names) (tcedi500)
DEFINITION
Conversion setups (names) comprise, for each organization, meBaange, direction (and field type), a code for the basic translation of the meBaange header (global overhead) and one or more codes for the way(s) in which meBaanges can be translated.
The conversion setup code that is not filled should always contain the header data. The other conversion setup codes indicate the various ways of processing EDI meBaanges.
SOURCE OF DATA
The data result from input or import in the session "Import EDI Data (tcedi6220m000)".
APPLICATION OF DATA
Conversion setup codes are used in:
•   linking conversion setups to a combination of (business) relation and meBaange in session "Maintain EDI MeBaanges Supported by Relations (tcedi0111m000)"
•   printing mapping information in the b-object "Conversion Parameters"
1.37   Conversion Setups (Relationships) (tcedi502)
DEFINITION
Conversion setups (relation) specify the relationships between the levels that represent the different sections of the EDI meBaange (overhead, header, line, footer).

If the corresponding meBaange has a "multiple" file layout, indicating that the data in the meBaange is split across multiple ASCII files, each level corresponds to a unique ASCII file. If the corresponding meBaange has a "single" file layout, indicating that the data in the meBaange is received within a single ASCII file, each level corresponds to a unique level identification. For incoming meBaanges, this level identification is specified in the session "Maintain Conversion Setups (Relationships) (tcedi5112s000)"; for outgoing meBaanges, this may be defined within the conversion setups themselves.

SOURCE OF DATA
The data result from input or import in the session "Import EDI Data (tcedi6220m000)".

APPLICATION OF DATA
Relationship sets are required for the system to:
• select and read in the right file(s) in the session "EDI Interchange Controller (tcedi7210m000)" (incoming meBaanges)
• generate the right ASCII files in the session "Generate EDI MeBaanges (tcedi7201m000)" (outgoing meBaanges)

Relationships are defined by specifying the common parts (keys) of two levels. The related level must be specified for each separate level.

Levels which are related to other levels are always sequential. Levels without relationships with other files are always iterative.

Example:

In case of a "multiple" file layout, there are 5 ASCII files:

```
Level File
-1    orders1
-2    orders2
-3    orders3
-4    orders4
-5    orders5
```

In case of a "single" file layout, there is 1 file with 5 levels, and a unique level identifier per level:

```
Level File    Level Identifier
-1    orders  ENV
-2    orders  MISC
-3    orders  HEADER
-4    orders  ADDRES
-5    orders  LINE
```

```
                    +----------------+
                    | 1 (sequential) |
                    +----------------+
                            |
        +---------------------------------------------+
        |                                             |
+----------------+                          +----------------+
| 2 (iterative)  |                          | 3 (sequential) |
+----------------+                          +----------------+
                                                    |
                                 +--------------------+
                        +--------------+   +--------------+
                        | 4 (iterative)|   | 5 (iterative)|
                        +--------------+   +--------------+
```

You cannot refer to a level file with a higher level number than that of the current level.

1.38   Conversion of Acknowledgment Codes (In) (tcedi341)
1.39   Conversion of Acknowledgment Codes (Out) (tcedi428)

DEFINITION
Conversion data for outgoing meBaanges are neceBaanry to translate codes from the application into the codes as used in the meBaange.

APPLICATION OF DATA

Conversion data for outgoing meBaanges are used in:

• processing data in the b-object "Communication".

1.40 Conversion of Address Types (out) (tcedi434)

DEFINITION

Conversion data for outgoing meBaanges are neceBaanry to translate codes from the application into the codes as used in the meBaange.

APPLICATION OF DATA

Conversion data for outgoing meBaanges are used in:

• processing data in the b-object "Communication".

1.41 Conversion of Allowances and Charges (out) (tcedi472)

DEFINITION

Conversion data for outgoing meBaanges are neceBaanry to translate codes from the application into the codes as used in the meBaange.

APPLICATION OF DATA

Conversion data for outgoing meBaanges are used in:

• processing data in the b-object "Communication".

1.42 Conversion of Change Reason Codes (In) (tcedi342)

DEFINITION

Conversion data for incoming meBaanges are neceBaanry to translate the codes used in meBaanges to codes that are used by the application.

APPLICATION OF DATA

Conversion data for incoming meBaanges are used in:

• processing data from the b-object "Communication"

1.43 Conversion of Change Reason Codes (Out) (tcedi491)

1.44 Conversion of Change Type Codes (In) (tcedi340)

DEFINITION

Conversion data for incoming meBaanges are neceBaanry to translate the codes used in meBaanges to codes that are used by the application.

APPLICATION OF DATA

Conversion data for incoming meBaanges are used in:

• processing data from the b-object "Communication"

1.45 Conversion of Change Type Codes (out) (tcedi490)

DEFINITION

Conversion data for outgoing meBaanges are neceBaanry to translate codes from the application into the codes as used in the meBaange.

APPLICATION OF DATA

Conversion data for outgoing meBaanges are used in:

• processing data in the b-object "Communication".

1.46 Conversion of Country Codes (in) (tcedi302)

DEFINITION

Conversion data for incoming meBaanges are neceBaanry to translate the codes used in meBaanges to codes that are used by the application.

APPLICATION OF DATA

Conversion data for incoming meBaanges are used in:

• processing data from the b-object "Communication"

1.47 Conversion of Country Codes (out) (tcedi440)

DEFINITION

Conversion data for outgoing meBaanges are neceBaanry to translate codes from the application into the codes as used in the meBaange.

APPLICATION OF DATA

Conversion data for outgoing meBaanges are used in:

• processing data in the b-object "Communication".

1.48 Conversion of Currency Codes (in) (tcedi324)

DEFINITION

Conversion data for incoming meBaanges are neceBaanry to translate the codes used in meBaanges to codes that are used by the application.

APPLICATION OF DATA

Conversion data for incoming meBaanges are used in:

• processing data from the b-object "Communication"

1.49 Conversion of Currency Codes (out) (tcedi438)

DEFINITION

Conversion data for outgoing meBaanges are neceBaanry to translate codes from the application into the codes as used in the meBaange.

APPLICATION OF DATA

Conversion data for outgoing meBaanges are used in:

• processing data in the b-object "Communication".

1.50 Conversion of Delivery Address Codes by Customer (in) (tcedi310)

DEFINITION

Conversion data for incoming meBaanges are neceBaanry to translate the codes used in meBaanges to codes that are used by the application.
APPLICATION OF DATA
Conversion data for incoming meBaanges are used in:
* processing data from the b-object "Communication"
1.51   Conversion of Delivery Address Codes by Customer (out) (tcedi448)
DEFINITION
Conversion data for outgoing meBaanges are neceBaanry to translate codes from the application into the codes as used in the meBaange.
APPLICATION OF DATA
Conversion data for outgoing meBaanges are used in:
* processing data in the b-object "Communication".
1.52   Conversion of Delivery Condition Codes (in) (tcedi300)
DEFINITION
Conversion data for incoming meBaanges are neceBaanry to translate the codes used in meBaanges to codes that are used by the application.
APPLICATION OF DATA
Conversion data for incoming meBaanges are used in:
* processing data from the b-object "Communication"
1.53   Conversion of Discount Codes by Relation (in) (tcedi332)
DEFINITION
Conversion data for incoming meBaanges are neceBaanry to translate the codes used in meBaanges to codes that are used by the application.
APPLICATION OF DATA
Conversion data for incoming meBaanges are used in:
* processing data from the b-object "Communication"
1.54   Conversion of Discount Codes by Relation (out) (tcedi474)
DEFINITION
Conversion data for outgoing meBaanges are neceBaanry to translate codes from the application into the codes as used in the meBaange.
APPLICATION OF DATA
Conversion data for outgoing meBaanges are used in:
* processing data in the b-object "Communication".
1.55   Conversion of Discount Methods by Relation (in) (tcedi333)
DEFINITION
Conversion data for incoming meBaanges are neceBaanry to translate the codes used in meBaanges to codes that are used by the application.
APPLICATION OF DATA
Conversion data for incoming meBaanges are used in:
* processing data from the b-object "Communication"
1.56   Conversion of Discount Methods by Relation (out) (tcedi475)
DEFINITION
Conversion data for outgoing meBaanges are neceBaanry to translate codes from the application into the codes as used in the meBaange.
APPLICATION OF DATA
Conversion data for outgoing meBaanges are used in:
* processing data in the b-object "Communication".
1.57   Conversion of Employee Codes by Relation (in) (tcedi320)
DEFINITION
Conversion data for incoming meBaanges are neceBaanry to translate the codes used in meBaanges to codes that are used by the application.
APPLICATION OF DATA
Conversion data for incoming meBaanges are used in:
* processing data from the b-object "Communication"
1.58   Conversion of Employee Codes by Relation (out) (tcedi458)
DEFINITION
Conversion data for outgoing meBaanges are neceBaanry to translate codes from the application into the codes as used in the meBaange.
APPLICATION OF DATA
Conversion data for outgoing meBaanges are used in:
* processing data in the b-object "Communication".
1.59   Conversion of Forwarding Agent Codes by Relation (in) (tcedi318)
DEFINITION
Conversion data for incoming meBaanges are neceBaanry to translate the codes used in meBaanges to codes that are used by the application.
APPLICATION OF DATA
Conversion data for incoming meBaanges are used in:
* processing data from the b-object "Communication"
1.60   Conversion of Forwarding Agent Codes by Relation (out) (tcedi456)
DEFINITION

Conversion data for outgoing meBaanges are neceBaanry to translate codes from the application into the codes as used in the meBaange.
APPLICATION OF DATA
Conversion data for outgoing meBaanges are used in:
• processing data in the b-object "Communication".
1.61   Conversion of Item Codes (General) (in) (tcedi322)
DEFINITION
Conversion data for incoming meBaanges are neceBaanry to translate the codes used in meBaanges to codes that are used by the application.
APPLICATION OF DATA
Conversion data for incoming meBaanges are used in:
• processing data from the b-object "Communication"
1.62   Conversion of Item Codes (out) (tcedi460)
DEFINITION
Conversion data for outgoing meBaanges are neceBaanry to translate codes from the application into the codes as used in the meBaange.
APPLICATION OF DATA
Conversion data for outgoing meBaanges are used in:
• processing data in the b-object "Communication".
1.63   Conversion of Item Codes by Relation (in) (tcedi306)
DEFINITION
Conversion data for incoming meBaanges are neceBaanry to translate the codes used in meBaanges to codes that are used by the application.
APPLICATION OF DATA
Conversion data for incoming meBaanges are used in:
• processing data from the b-object "Communication"
1.64   Conversion of Item Codes by Relation (out) (tcedi444)
DEFINITION
Conversion data for outgoing meBaanges are neceBaanry to translate codes from the application into the codes as used in the meBaange.
APPLICATION OF DATA
Conversion data for outgoing meBaanges are used in:
• processing data in the b-object "Communication".
1.65   Conversion of Late Payment Surcharges (in) (tcedi330)
DEFINITION
Conversion data for incoming meBaanges are neceBaanry to translate the codes used in meBaanges to codes that are used by the application.
APPLICATION OF DATA
Conversion data for incoming meBaanges are used in:
• processing data from the b-object "Communication"
1.66   Conversion of Late Payment Surcharges (out) (tcedi470)
DEFINITION
Conversion data for outgoing meBaanges are neceBaanry to translate codes from the application into the codes as used in the meBaange.
APPLICATION OF DATA
Conversion data for outgoing meBaanges are used in:
• processing data in the b-object "Communication".
1.67   Conversion of Lot Code ID by Relation (in) (tcedi335)
DEFINITION
Conversion data for incoming meBaanges are neceBaanry to translate the codes used in meBaanges to codes that are used by the application.
APPLICATION OF DATA
Conversion data for incoming meBaanges are used in:
• processing data from the b-object "Communication"
1.68   Conversion of Lot Code ID by Relation (out) (tcedi477)
DEFINITION
Conversion data for outgoing meBaanges are neceBaanry to translate codes from the application into the codes as used in the meBaange.
APPLICATION OF DATA
Conversion data for outgoing meBaanges are used in:
• processing data in the b-object "Communication".
1.69   Conversion of Lot Selection Methods by Relation (in) (tcedi334)
DEFINITION
Conversion data for incoming meBaanges are neceBaanry to translate the codes used in meBaanges to codes that are used by the application.
APPLICATION OF DATA
Conversion data for incoming meBaanges are used in:
• processing data from the b-object "Communication"
1.70   Conversion of Lot Selection Methods by Relation (out) (tcedi476)
DEFINITION

Conversion data for outgoing meBaanges are neceBaanry to translate codes from the application into the codes as used in the meBaange.
APPLICATION OF DATA
Conversion data for outgoing meBaanges are used in:
• processing data in the b-object "Communication".
1.71 Conversion of Order Types (out) (tcedi432)
DEFINITION
Conversion data for outgoing meBaanges are neceBaanry to translate codes from the application into the codes as used in the meBaange.
APPLICATION OF DATA
Conversion data for outgoing meBaanges are used in:
• processing data in the b-object "Communication".
1.72 Conversion of Postal Address Codes by Customer (in) (tcedi312)
DEFINITION
Conversion data for incoming meBaanges are neceBaanry to translate the codes used in meBaanges to codes that are used by the application.
APPLICATION OF DATA
Conversion data for incoming meBaanges are used in:
• processing data from the b-object "Communication"
1.73 Conversion of Postal Address Codes by Customer (out) (tcedi450)
DEFINITION
Conversion data for outgoing meBaanges are neceBaanry to translate codes from the application into the codes as used in the meBaange.
APPLICATION OF DATA
Conversion data for outgoing meBaanges are used in:
• processing data in the b-object "Communication".
1.74 Conversion of Postal Address Codes by Supplier (in) (tcedi313)
DEFINITION
Conversion data for incoming meBaanges are neceBaanry to translate the codes used in meBaanges to codes that are used by the application.
APPLICATION OF DATA
Conversion data for incoming meBaanges are used in:
• processing data from the b-object "Communication"
1.75 Conversion of Postal Address Codes by Supplier (out) (tcedi451)
DEFINITION
Conversion data for outgoing meBaanges are neceBaanry to translate codes from the application into the codes as used in the meBaange.
APPLICATION OF DATA
Conversion data for outgoing meBaanges are used in:
• processing data in the b-object "Communication".
1.76 Conversion of Project Codes by Relation (in) (tcedi316)
DEFINITION
Conversion data for incoming meBaanges are neceBaanry to translate the codes used in meBaanges to codes that are used by the application.
APPLICATION OF DATA
Conversion data for incoming meBaanges are used in:
• processing data from the b-object "Communication"
1.77 Conversion of Project Codes by Relation (out) (tcedi454)
DEFINITION
Conversion data for outgoing meBaanges are neceBaanry to translate codes from the application into the codes as used in the meBaange.
APPLICATION OF DATA
Conversion data for outgoing meBaanges are used in:
• processing data in the b-object "Communication".
1.78 Conversion of Purchase Contract Codes by Relation (in) (tcedi315)
DEFINITION
Conversion data for incoming meBaanges are neceBaanry to translate the codes used in meBaanges to codes that are used by the application.
APPLICATION OF DATA
Conversion data for incoming meBaanges are used in:
• processing data from the b-object "Communication"
1.79 Conversion of Purchase Contract Codes by Relation (out) (tcedi453)
DEFINITION
Conversion data for outgoing meBaanges are neceBaanry to translate codes from the application into the codes as used in the meBaange.
APPLICATION OF DATA
Conversion data for outgoing meBaanges are used in:
• processing data in the b-object "Communication".
1.80 Conversion of Reference Number Types (out) (tcedi436)
DEFINITION

Conversion data for outgoing meBaanges are neceBaanry to translate codes from the application into the codes as used in the meBaange.
APPLICATION OF DATA
Conversion data for outgoing meBaanges are used in:
• processing data in the b-object "Communication".
1.81   Conversion of Sales Contract Codes by Relation (in) (tcedi314)
DEFINITION
Conversion data for incoming meBaanges are neceBaanry to translate the codes used in meBaanges to codes that are used by the application.
APPLICATION OF DATA
Conversion data for incoming meBaanges are used in:
• processing data from the b-object "Communication"
1.82   Conversion of Sales Contract Codes by Relation (out) (tcedi452)
DEFINITION
Conversion data for outgoing meBaanges are neceBaanry to translate codes from the application into the codes as used in the meBaange.
APPLICATION OF DATA
Conversion data for outgoing meBaanges are used in:
• processing data in the b-object "Communication".
1.83   Conversion of Tax Codes (in) (tcedi308)
DEFINITION
Conversion data for incoming meBaanges are neceBaanry to translate the codes used in meBaanges to codes that are used by the application.
APPLICATION OF DATA
Conversion data for incoming meBaanges are used in:
• processing data from the b-object "Communication"
1.84   Conversion of Tax Codes (out) (tcedi446)
DEFINITION
Conversion data for outgoing meBaanges are neceBaanry to translate codes from the application into the codes as used in the meBaange.
APPLICATION OF DATA
Conversion data for outgoing meBaanges are used in:
• processing data in the b-object "Communication".
1.85   Conversion of Terms of Delivery Codes (out) (tcedi430)
DEFINITION
Conversion data for outgoing meBaanges are neceBaanry to translate codes from the application into the codes as used in the meBaange.
APPLICATION OF DATA
Conversion data for outgoing meBaanges are used in:
• processing data in the b-object "Communication".
1.86   Conversion of Terms of Payment (in) (tcedi326)
DEFINITION
Conversion data for incoming meBaanges are neceBaanry to translate the codes used in meBaanges to codes that are used by the application.
APPLICATION OF DATA
Conversion data for incoming meBaanges are used in:
• processing data from the b-object "Communication"
1.87   Conversion of Terms of Payment (out) (tcedi466)
DEFINITION
Conversion data for outgoing meBaanges are neceBaanry to translate codes from the application into the codes as used in the meBaange.
APPLICATION OF DATA
Conversion data for outgoing meBaanges are used in:
• processing data in the b-object "Communication".
1.88   Conversion of Third Party Codes by Relation (in) (tcedi328)
DEFINITION
Conversion data for incoming meBaanges are neceBaanry to translate the codes used in meBaanges to codes that are used by the application.
APPLICATION OF DATA
Conversion data for incoming meBaanges are used in:
• processing data from the b-object "Communication"
1.89   Conversion of Third Party Codes by Relation (out) (tcedi468)
DEFINITION
Conversion data for outgoing meBaanges are neceBaanry to translate codes from the application into the codes as used in the meBaange.
APPLICATION OF DATA
Conversion data for outgoing meBaanges are used in:
• processing data in the b-object "Communication".
1.90   Conversion of Unit Codes (in) (tcedi304)
DEFINITION

Conversion data for incoming meBaanges are neceBaanry to translate the codes used in
meBaanges to codes that are used by the application.
APPLICATION OF DATA
Conversion data for incoming meBaanges are used in:
•   processing data from the b-object "Communication"
1.91   Conversion of Unit Codes (out) (tcedi442)
DEFINITION
Conversion data for outgoing meBaanges are neceBaanry to translate codes from the
application into the codes as used in the meBaange.
APPLICATION OF DATA
Conversion data for outgoing meBaanges are used in:
•   processing data in the b-object "Communication".
1.92   Conversion of Warehouse Addresses (out) (tcedi462)
DEFINITION
Conversion data for outgoing meBaanges are neceBaanry to translate codes from the
application into the codes as used in the meBaange.
APPLICATION OF DATA
Conversion data for outgoing meBaanges are used in:
•   processing data in the b-object "Communication".
1.93   Countries (tcedi226)
DEFINITION
Countries are geographical regions by which you can classify suppliers and customers.
SOURCE OF DATA
The data result from input or import in the session "Import EDI Data (tcedi6220m000)".
APPLICATION OF DATA
Countries are used in:
•   defining conversion data in the b-object "Coding and Conversion Data".
1.94   Countries (tcmcs010)
DEFINITION
Countries are the national states where your suppliers and customers are based. For each
country, such data is available as the international dialing, telex and fax codes.
Countries are used to compile statistical turnover surveys and in financial data
reporting.
SOURCE OF DATA
BAAN Common (tctc-20010): Maintain Countries (tcmcs0110m000)
APPLICATION OF DATA
BAAN Common (tctc-20010): Maintain Company Data (tccom0100m000) Maintain Customers
(tccom1101m000) Maintain Delivery Addresses (tccom1102m000) Maintain Customer Postal
Addresses (tccom1103m000) Maintain Prospects (tccom1110m000) Maintain Suppliers
(tccom2101m000) Maintain Supplier Postal Addresses (tccom2103m000) Maintain Import/Export
Statistics (tccom7171m000) Maintain Conversion of Country Codes (in) (tcedi3102m000)
Maintain Conversion of Tax Codes (in) (tcedi3108m000) Maintain Conversion of Country
Codes (out) (tcedi4140m000) Maintain Conversion of Tax Codes (out) (tcedi4146m000)
Maintain Warehouses (tcmcs0103m000) Maintain Credit Insurance Companies (tcmcs0109m000)
Maintain Bank Addresses (tcmcs0120m000) Maintain Factoring Companies (tcmcs0125m000)
Maintain Single Tax Rates (tcmcs0132s000) Maintain Multiple Tax Rates (tcmcs0133s000)
Maintain Tax Rates by Tax Code (tcmcs0135s000) Maintain Tax Codes by Country
(tcmcs0136m000)
BAAN Distribution (tdtd-20010): Maintain Inquiries (tdpur1101m000) Maintain Inquiry Lines
(tdpur1102s000) Enter Inquiry Results (tdpur1103m000) Copy Quoted Inquiry Lines to
Purchase Order (tdpur1303s000) Process Quoted Inquiry Lines (tdpur1304s000) Maintain
Expiry Date for Returned Inquiry (tdpur1800s000) Enter Specific Inquiry Numbers
(tdpur1820s000) Maintain Purchase Contracts (tdpur3101m000) Maintain Purchase Contract
Lines (tdpur3102s000) Maintain Specific Delivery Address (Purchase Contract) (tdpur3103
s000) Maintain Specific Postal Address (Purchase Contract) (tdpur3104s0 00) Maintain
Purchase Contract Status (tdpur3110m000) Copy Purchase Contracts (tdpur3801m000) Enter
Specific Purchase Contract Numbers (tdpur3820s000) Maintain Purchase Orders
(tdpur4101m000) Maintain Purchase Orders (Direct Delivery) (tdpur4102m000) Maintain
Specific Delivery Address (Purchase Order) (tdpur4103s00 0) Maintain Specific Postal
Address (Purchase Order) (tdpur4104s000)
Maintain Purchase Order (Direct Line Entry) (tdpur4105m000) Maintain Purchase Order Lines
(Fast Input) (tdpur4107m000) Maintain Back Orders (tdpur4130m000) Calculate Additional
Costs (tdpur4260s000) Calculate Purchase Order Line Discounts (tdpur4802s000) Delete
Purchase Order (tdpur4803s000) Recalculate Purchase Price and Discount (tdpur4810s000)
Enter Specific Purchase Order Numbers (tdpur4820s000) Print Purchase Order Header History
(tdpur5403m000) Maintain Quotations (tdsls1101m000) Maintain Quotation Lines
(tdsls1102s000) Maintain Specific Delivery Address (Quotations) (tdsls1103s000) Maintain
Specific Postal Address (Quotations) (tdsls1104s000) Maintain Quotation Lines (Wholesale)
(tdsls1107s000) Delete Sales Quotation (tdsls1803s000) Display Gross Profit of Quotation

Line (tdsls1808s000) Maintain Delivery Date in Order Lines (tdsls1809s000) Copy BOM
Components to Quotation (tdsls1812s000) Enter Specific Quotation Numbers (tdsls1820s000)
Maintain Sales Contracts (tdsls3101m000) Maintain Sales Contract Lines (tdsls3102s000)
Maintain Specific Delivery Address (Sales Contract) (tdsls3103s00 0) Maintain Specific
Postal Address (Sales Contract) (tdsls3104s000)
Maintain Sales Contract Status (tdsls3110m000) Copy Sales Contracts (tdsls3801m000) Enter
Specific Sales Contract Numbers (tdsls3820s000) Maintain Sales Orders (tdsls4101m000)
Maintain Specific Delivery Address (Sales Order) (tdsls4103s000) Maintain Specific Postal
Address (Sales Order) (tdsls4104s000) Maintain Installment Data (tdsls4106s000) Delete
Sales Order (tdsls4803s000) Copy Bill of Material to Order (tdsls4812s000) Enter Specific
Sales Order Numbers (tdsls4820s000) Maintain Invoice Analysis Accounts (tdsls6101m000)
Maintain Invoice Analysis Accounts by Tax Code (tdsls6103m000)
BAAN Finance (tftf-20010): Maintain One-Time Supplier Addresses (tfacp1102m000) Maintain
Purchase Invoices (tfacp1110s000) Maintain Terms of Payment (tfacp1111s000) Maintain Tax
Transactions (tfacp1112s000) Maintain Purchase Invoice Transactions (tfacp1120s000)
Match/Approve Purchase Invoices with Orders (tfacp1130m000) Approve Purchase Invoices
(tfacp1140s000) Approve Price Differences (tfacp1142m000) Maintain Purchase Invoice
Details (tfacp2100m000) Maintain Purchase Invoice Corrections (tfacp2110s000) Assign
Credit Notes to Invoices (tfacp2120s000)
Assign Invoices to Credit Notes (tfacp2121s000)
Maintain One-Time Customer Addresses (tfacr1102s000) Maintain Sales Invoices
(tfacr1110s000) Maintain Sales Invoice Transactions (tfacr1111s000) Maintain Terms of
Payment (tfacr1112s000) Maintain Sales Invoice Details (tfacr2100m000) Maintain Sales
Invoice Corrections (tfacr2110s000) Assign Credit Notes to Invoices (tfacr2120s000)
Assign Credit Notes to Invoices (tfacr2121s000)
Maintain Doubtful Sales Invoices (tfacr2140s000) Maintain Reminder Diary (tfacr3130m000)
Maintain Sales Invoice Header (tfacr4100m000) Maintain Sales Invoice Lines
(tfacr4101s000) Maintain Posting Data by Tax Code (tfcmg0150m000) Maintain One-Time
Supplier Addresses (tfcmg1101m000) Maintain Standing Orders (tfcmg1110m000) Maintain
Posting Data of Standing Orders/Stand Alone Paym. (tfcmg 1113m000) Maintain Bank
Transactions (tfcmg2100s000) Assign Unallocated/Advance Receipts to Invoices
(tfcmg2105s000) Assign Unallocated/Advance Payments to Invoices (tfcmg2106s000) Maintain
Anticipated Payments (Details) (tfcmg2116s000) Maintain Anticipated Receipts (Details)
(tfcmg2117s000) Maintain Cash Management Transactions (tfcmg2120s000) Maintain Customer
Invoice Cash Date (tfcmg3110m000) Maintain Supplier Invoice Cash Date (tfcmg3111m000)
Maintain Posting Data of Electronic Bank Statements (tfcmg5106s00 0) Maintain Relations
by Tax Position (tfgld0121m000) Assign Protocol Numbers to Documents (tfgld0235m000)
[SE@tfgld023
5m000] Maintain Journal Vouchers (tfgld1103s000) Change Document Details (tfgld1104s000)
Maintain Opening Balances (tfgld1105s000) Maintain Journal Vouchers (Summarized)
(tfgld1114s000) Maintain Journal Vouchers (Multiple Lines) (tfgld1115s000)
BAAN Manufacturing (titi-20010): Maintain Item Data (GRT) (tigrt1180s000) Maintain
Customized Item Data (GRT) (tigrt2180s000) Maintain Item Data (tiitm0101m000) Maintain
Item Data (in BOM) (tiitm0108s000) Maintain Item Default Data (tiitm0110m000) Maintain
Customized Item Data (tipcs2121m000)
BAAN Project (tptp-20010): Maintain Item Default Data (tppdm0109m000) Maintain Standard
Items (tppdm0110m000) Maintain Third Parties (tppdm0132m000) Maintain Estimate Data
(tppdm4100m000) Maintain Archived Estimates (tppdm5190m000) Maintain Projects
(tppdm6100m000) Maintain Customers by Project (tppdm6101s000) Maintain Project Status
(tppdm6107m000) Maintain Project Items (tppdm6110m000) Maintain Archived Projects
(tppdm7190m000) Maintain Pro Forma Invoice (tppin4165m000) Maintain Specific Invoice
Addresses (tppin4166m000)
BAAN Transportation (trtr-20010): Maintain Sequence of Printing Address Data
(tracs0110m000) Maintain Number of ZIP Code Characters by Country (tracs0120m000)
Maintain Defaults by ZIP Code (tracs0130m000) Maintain Addresses (tracs1100m000) Maintain
Addresses (Fast Input) (tracs1101s000)
Maintain Distance Table by ZIP Code (tracs4110m000) Maintain Fuel Refills (trcde1120s000)
Maintain Expenses (trcde1140s000) Maintain Employee Data (trecs1100m000) Maintain Daily
Reports (Expenses) (trhec3120s000) Maintain Financial Parameters (Invoice Analysis)
(trics0110m000) Maintain Countries of Establishment (trtcd0102m000) Maintain Fuel Intake
(trtfc2100m000) Maintain Fuel Intake from FINANCE (trtfc2102s000) Check Fuel Intake Bills
(trtfc2110m000) Maintain Finished Activities (trtfm4100m000) Maintain Finished Activities
(from FINANCE) (trtfm4102s000) Split Order Lines (trtoc1103s000) Standard Session for
Transport Order Lines (All Data) (trtoc1180m 000) Maintain Transport Order Lines
(trtoc1181m000) Maintain Transport Order Lines (trtoc1182m000) Maintain Transport Order
Lines (trtoc1183m000) Maintain Transport Order Lines (trtoc1184m000) Maintain Transport
Order Lines (trtoc1185m000) Maintain Transport Order Lines (trtoc1186m000) Maintain
Transport Order Lines (trtoc1187m000) Maintain Transport Order Lines (trtoc1188m000)
Maintain Document Lines (trtoc1189s000) Maintain Transport Order Lines (trtoc1190m000)
Maintain Transport Order Lines (trtoc1191m000)

Maintain Standard Order Lines (trtoc3101m000) Maintain ZIP Codes by Standard Route (trtop2110m000) Maintain Storage Orders (trwoc1100m000) Maintain Storage Orders (Invoicing Data) (trwoc1106m000) Maintain Storage Orders (General Data) (trwoc1107m000) Maintain Assembly Orders (trwoc5100m000) Maintain Assembly Orders (Invoicing Data) (trwoc5106m000) Maintain Assembly Orders (General Data) (trwoc5107m000)

BAAN Service (tsts-20010): Maintain Service Orders (tssma3101m000) Maintain Specific Postal Address (Service) (tssma3102s100) Maintain Actual Service Order Costs and Revenues (tssma3110m000) Maintain Service Orders (Telephone Screen) (tssma3140m000) Maintain Service Orders (Planning) (tssma3141m000) Report Service Orders Completed (tssma3142m000) Close Service Orders (tssma3144m000) Maintain Service Order Cost Estimate (tssma3170m000) Display Service Orders (tssma3502s000) Enter Specific Service Order Numbers (tssma3820s000) Maintain Accounts for Invoice Analyses (tssma6106m000)

1.95 Country Tax Provider Register (tccom940)

DEFINITION

Countries must be registered for the tax provider interface. Registering a country for the tax provider interface indicates the type of address validation to be performed and the labels which appear when maintaining address information. United States addresses prompt for City, State, and Zip Code. Canadian addresses prompt for City, Province, and Postal Code.

APPLICATION OF DATA

The above data is relevant for the following packages/modules:

BAAN Common
* Common Data (COM)
* Tables (MCS)

BAAN Distribution
* Location Control (ILC)
* Purchase Control (PUR)
* Sales Control (SLS)

BAAN Finance
* Accounts Payable (ACP)
* Accounts Receivable (ACR)
* Cash Management (CMG)
* General Ledger (GLD)

BAAN Manufacturing
* Product Configuration (PCF)
* Project Control (PCS)

BAAN Service
* BAAN Service Master Data (tssma10010)
* Service Contract Control (tssma10030)

1.96 Credit Insurance Companies (tcmcs009)

DEFINITION

Credit insurance companies are companies insuring the credit granted to customers.

SOURCE OF DATA

BAAN Common (tctc-20010): Maintain Credit Insurance Companies (tcmcs0109m000)

APPLICATION OF DATA

BAAN Common (tctc-20010): Maintain Customers (tccom1101m000) Maintain Prospects (tccom1110m000)

1.97 Currencies (tcedi292)

DEFINITION

The currency is the legal tender (generally used monetary unit) of a country.

SOURCE OF DATA

The data result from input or import in the session "Import EDI Data (tcedi6220m000)".

APPLICATION OF DATA

Currency codes are used in:
* defining conversion data in the b-object "Coding and Conversion Data"

1.98 Currencies (tcmcs002)

DEFINITION

Defining currencies allows you to use within BAAN IV whatever currency is used in a specific country.

SOURCE OF DATA

BAAN Common (tctc-20010): Maintain Currencies (tcmcs0102m000)

APPLICATION OF DATA

BAAN Common (tctc-20010): Maintain Company Data (tccom0100m000) Maintain Customers (tccom1101m000) Maintain Prospects (tccom1110m000) Maintain Suppliers (tccom2101m000) Maintain Sales Listing (tccom7170m000) Maintain Import/Export Statistics (tccom7171m000) Maintain Conversion of Currency Codes (in) (tcedi3124m000) Maintain Conversion of Currency Codes (out) (tcedi4138m000) Maintain Currency Rates (tcmcs0108m000) Maintain Price Lists (tcmcs0134m000)

BAAN Distribution (tdtd-20010): Maintain Inquiries (tdpur1101m000) Maintain Expiry Date for Returned Inquiry (tdpur1800s000) Enter Specific Inquiry Numbers (tdpur1820s000)

Maintain Purchase Contracts (tdpur3101m000) Maintain Purchase Contract Status (tdpur3110m000) Copy Purchase Contracts (tdpur3801m000) Enter Specific Purchase Contract Numbers (tdpur3820s000) Maintain Purchase Orders (tdpur4101m000) Enter Specific Purchase Order Numbers (tdpur4820s000) Print Purchase Order Header History (tdpur5403m000) Maintain Quotations (tdsls1101m000) Delete Sales Quotation (tdsls1803s000) Maintain Delivery Date in Order Lines (tdsls1809s000) Copy BOM Components to Quotation (tdsls1812s000) Enter Specific Quotation Numbers (tdsls1820s000) Maintain Sales Contracts (tdsls3101m000) Maintain Sales Contract Status (tdsls3110m000) Copy Sales Contracts (tdsls3801m000) Enter Specific Sales Contract Numbers (tdsls3820s000) Maintain Sales Orders (tdsls4101m000) Delete Sales Order (tdsls4803s000) Copy Bill of Material to Order (tdsls4812s000)

Enter Specific Sales Order Numbers (tdsls4820s000)

BAAN Finance (tftf-20010): Maintain Received Purchase Invoices (tfacp1100m000) Maintain Purchase Invoices (tfacp1110s000) Maintain Terms of Payment (tfacp1111s000) Maintain Tax Transactions (tfacp1112s000) Maintain Purchase Invoice Transactions (tfacp1120s000) Match/Approve Purchase Invoices with Orders (tfacp1130m000) Maintain Matched Receipts (tfacp1132s000) Maintain Matched Purchase Invoice Transactions (tfacp1133s000) Approve Purchase Invoices (tfacp1140s000) Approve Price Differences (tfacp1142m000) Maintain Purchase Invoice Details (tfacp2100m000) Maintain Purchase Invoice Corrections (tfacp2110s000) Assign Credit Notes to Invoices (tfacp2120s000)

Assign Invoices to Credit Notes (tfacp2121s000)

Maintain Sales Invoices (tfacr1110s000) Maintain Sales Invoice Transactions (tfacr1111s000) Maintain Terms of Payment (tfacr1112s000) Maintain Sales Invoice Details (tfacr2100m000) Maintain Sales Invoice Corrections (tfacr2110s000) Assign Credit Notes to Invoices (tfacr2120s000)

Assign Credit Notes to Invoices (tfacr2121s000)

Maintain Doubtful Sales Invoices (tfacr2140s000) Maintain Reminder Costs (tfacr3102s000) Maintain Reminder Advice (tfacr3110m000) Maintain Reminder Diary (tfacr3130m000) Maintain Sales Invoice Header (tfacr4100m000) Maintain Interest Invoice Advice (tfacr5110m000) Maintain Bank Relations (tfcmg0110m000) Maintain Standing Orders (tfcmg1110m000) Maintain Payment Advice (tfcmg1120m000) Maintain Bank Transactions (tfcmg2100s000) Reconciliation of Anticipated Payments/Receipts (tfcmg2102s000) Reconciliation of Receipts/Payments (tfcmg2103s000) Assign Unallocated/Advance Receipts to Invoices (tfcmg2105s000) Assign Unallocated/Advance Payments to Invoices (tfcmg2106s000) Maintain Anticipated Payments (tfcmg2110s000) Maintain Anticipated Receipts (tfcmg2111s000) Maintain Anticipated Payment Status (tfcmg2112s000) Maintain Anticipated Receipt Status (tfcmg2113s000) Maintain Check Master (tfcmg2115m000) Maintain Cash Management Transactions (tfcmg2120s000) Select for Automatic Customer Reconciliation (tfcmg2121s000) Select for Automatic Supplier Reconciliation (tfcmg2122s000) [SE@ tfcmg2122s000] Selection for Automatic Reconciliation (tfcmg2123s000) Maintain Customer Invoice Cash Date (tfcmg3110m000) Maintain Supplier Invoice Cash Date (tfcmg3111m000) Maintain Direct Debit Advice (tfcmg4120m000) Send Trade Notes/Checks to Bank (tfcmg4130m000)

Maintain Remittance Advice MeBaanges (Receipts) (tfcmg5101m000) Maintain Converted Electronic Bank Statements (tfcmg5102m000) Maintain Electronic Bank Statements (tfcmg5103m000) Maintain Posting Data of Electronic Bank Statements (tfcmg5106s00 0) Maintain Budget Master Data (tffbs0103m000) Maintain Transaction Types (tfgld0111m000) Maintain Transaction Schedules (tfgld0112m000) Maintain Currency Difference Ledger Accounts by Currency (tfgld01 19m000) Assign Protocol Numbers to Documents (tfgld0235m000) Maintain Journal Vouchers (tfgld1103s000) Change Document Details (tfgld1104s000) Maintain Opening Balances (tfgld1105s000) Maintain Journal Vouchers (Summarized) (tfgld1114s000) Maintain Journal Vouchers (Multiple Lines) (tfgld1115s000)

BAAN Manufacturing (titi-20010): Maintain Subcontracting Rates (ticpr1160m000) Maintain Simulated Purchase Prices (ticpr1170m000) Maintain Item Data (GRT) (tigrt1180s000) Maintain Customized Item Data (GRT) (tigrt2180s000) Maintain Item Data (tiitm0101m000) Maintain Item Data (in BOM) (tiitm0108s000) Maintain Item Default Data (tiitm0110m000) Maintain Generic Price Lists (tipcf4101m000) Maintain Price List Matrix Codes (tipcf4110m000) Maintain Product Variants (tipcf5101m000) Maintain Calculation Parts (tipcs0110m000) Maintain Subcontracting Rates by Budget (tipcs1131m000) Maintain Customized Item Data (tipcs2121m000) Maintain Subcontracting Rates by Project (tipcs3110m000) Maintain Planned PRP Purchase Orders (tipcs5120m000)

BAAN Project (tptp-20010): Maintain HRS Parameters (tphrs0100m000) Maintain Item Default Data (tppdm0109m000) Maintain Standard Items (tppdm0110m000) Maintain Standard Equipment (tppdm0112m000) Maintain Standard Subcontracting (tppdm0113m000) Maintain Customers by Project (tppdm6101s000) Maintain Project Items (tppdm6110m000) Maintain Project Equipment (tppdm6112m000) Maintain Project Subcontracting (tppdm6113m000)

Maintain Pro Forma Invoice (tppin4165m000) Maintain Material Recommendations (tppss6110m000) Maintain Equipment Recommendations (tppss6111m000) Maintain Subcontracting Recommendations (tppss6112m000) Maintain Purchase Budget Detail Lines (tpptc4120m000)

BAAN Transportation (trtr-20010): Maintain Fuel Refills (trcde1120s000) Maintain Expenses (trcde1140s000) Maintain Deviating Currency Rates (trhec0110m000) Maintain Expense Codes (trhec1101m000) Maintain Prepayments (trhec2100m000) Maintain Daily Reports (Expenses) (trhec3120s000) Maintain Costs (trtco1100m000) Maintain Cost Lines (trtco1101s000) Maintain Costs (Subcontracting) (trtco1105s000)

Maintain Service Stations (trtfc1100m000) Maintain Fuel Intake (trtfc2100m000) Maintain Fuel Intake from FINANCE (trtfc2102s000) Check Fuel Intake Bills (trtfc2110m000) Maintain Finished Activities (trtfm4100m000) Maintain Finished Activities (from FINANCE) (trtfm4102s000) Split Order Lines (trtoc1103s000) Maintain Subcontracting Data by Order Line (trtoc1105m000) Standard Session for Transport Order Lines (All Data) (trtoc1180m000) Maintain Transport Order Lines (trtoc1181m000) Maintain Transport Order Lines (trtoc1182m000) Maintain Transport Order Lines (trtoc1183m000) Maintain Transport Order Lines (trtoc1184m000) Maintain Transport Order Lines (trtoc1185m000) Maintain Transport Order Lines (trtoc1186m000) Maintain Transport Order Lines (trtoc1187m000) Maintain Transport Order Lines (trtoc1188m000) Maintain Document Lines (trtoc1189s000) Maintain Transport Order Lines (trtoc1190m000) Maintain Transport Order Lines (trtoc1191m000) Maintain Standard Order Lines (trtoc3101m000) Maintain Subcontracting Data by Standard Order Line (trtoc3105s00 0) Maintain Subcontracting Data by Trip (trtop4105m000) Maintain Third-Party Items (trtpi1100m000) Maintain Blocking of Third-Party Items (trtpi1101m000) Maintain Transport Rate Codes (trtrc1100m000) Maintain Storage Orders (trwoc1100m000) Maintain Storage Orders (Invoicing Data) (trwoc1106m000) Maintain Storage Orders (General Data) (trwoc1107m000) Maintain Inbound Order Lines (trwoc2101m000) Maintain Inbound Order Lines (Invoicing Data) (trwoc2106m000) Maintain Inbound Order Lines (General Data) (trwoc2107m000) Maintain Outbound Order Lines (trwoc3101m000) Maintain Outbound Order Lines (Invoicing Data) (trwoc3106m000) Maintain Outbound Order Lines (General Data) (trwoc3107m000) Maintain Transhipment Order Lines (trwoc4101m000) Maintain Transhipment Order Lines (Invoicing Data) (trwoc4106m000) Maintain Transhipment Order Lines (General Data) (trwoc4107m000) Maintain Assembly Orders (trwoc5100m000) Maintain Assembly Orders (Invoicing Data) (trwoc5106m000) Maintain Assembly Orders (General Data) (trwoc5107m000) Maintain Warehousing Rate Codes (trwrc1100m000)
Maintain Warehousing Rate Codes by Order Type (trwrc1102s000)
BAAN Service (tsts-20010): Maintain Contracts (tssma2120m000) Maintain Service Orders (tssma3101m000) Maintain Service Orders (Telephone Screen) (tssma3140m000) Maintain Service Orders (Planning) (tssma3141m000) Report Service Orders Completed (tssma3142m000) Close Service Orders (tssma3144m000) Display Service Orders (tssma3502s000) Enter Specific Service Order Numbers (tssma3820s000)

1.99   Currency Rates (tcmcs008)
DEFINITION
Currency rates are the exchange rates against which currencies can be bought or sold. They are required to convert amounts correctly.
SOURCE OF DATA
BAAN Common (tctc-20010): Maintain Currency Rates (tcmcs0108m000)

1.100   Customer Balances by Company (tccom011)
1.101   Customer Postal Addresses (tccom012)
DEFINITION
Postal addresses are the addresses that are used to send correspondence to.
SOURCE OF DATA
BAAN Common (tctc-20010): Maintain Customer Postal Addresses (tccom1103m000)
BAAN Common (tctc-20010): Maintain Customer Postal Addresses (tccom1103s000)
APPLICATION OF DATA
BAAN Common (tctc-20010): Maintain Customers (tccom1101m000) Maintain Prospects (tccom1110m000) Maintain Conversion of Postal Address Codes by Customer (in) (tcedi3112m000) Maintain Conv. of Postal Address Codes by Customer (out) (tcedi41 50m000)
BAAN Distribution (tdtd-20010): Maintain Quotations (tdsls1101m000) Delete Sales Quotation (tdsls1803s000) Maintain Delivery Date in Order Lines (tdsls1809s000) Enter Specific Quotation Numbers (tdsls1820s000) Maintain Sales Contracts (tdsls3101m000) Maintain Sales Contract Status (tdsls3110m000) Copy Sales Contracts (tdsls3801m000) Enter Specific Sales Contract Numbers (tdsls3820s000) Maintain Sales Orders (tdsls4101m000) Delete Sales Order (tdsls4803s000) Copy Bill of Material to Order (tdsls4812s000) Enter Specific Sales Order Numbers (tdsls4820s000) Maintain Marketing Projects by Relation (tdsmi1103m000) Maintain Contacts by Relation (tdsmi1105m000)
BAAN Finance (tftf-20010): Maintain Sales Invoices (tfacr1110s000) Maintain Terms of Payment (tfacr1112s000) Maintain Sales Invoice Details (tfacr2100m000) Maintain Sales Invoice Corrections (tfacr2110s000) Assign Credit Notes to Invoices (tfacr2120s000) Assign Credit Notes to Invoices (tfacr2121s000)
Maintain Doubtful Sales Invoices (tfacr2140s000) Maintain Reminder Diary (tfacr3130m000) Maintain Sales Invoice Header (tfacr4100m000) Assign Unallocated/Advance Receipts to Invoices (tfcmg2105s000) Maintain Customer Invoice Cash Date (tfcmg3110m000)
BAAN Service (tsts-20010): Maintain Locations (tssma1110m000) Maintain Contracts (tssma2120m000) Maintain Service Orders (tssma3101m000) Maintain Service Orders

(Telephone Screen) (tssma3140m000) Maintain Service Orders (Planning) (tssma3141m000)
Report Service Orders Completed (tssma3142m000)
Close Service Orders (tssma3144m000) Display Service Orders (tssma3502s000) Enter
Specific Service Order Numbers (tssma3820s000)
1.102 Customers (tccom010)
DEFINITION
Customers are the clients (persons or companies) your company supplies goods to or
provides services for.
SOURCE OF DATA
BAAN Common (tctc-20010): Maintain Customers (tccom1101m000) Maintain Prospects
(tccom1110m000)
APPLICATION OF DATA
BAAN Common (tctc-20010): Maintain Customers (tccom1101m000) Maintain Delivery Addresses
(tccom1102m000) Maintain Customer Postal Addresses (tccom1103m000) Maintain Banks by
Customer (tccom1105m000) Maintain Prospects (tccom1110m000) Maintain Suppliers
(tccom2101m000) Maintain Concern Structure of Trade Relations (tccom3101m000) Maintain
Sales Listing (tccom7170m000) Maintain Relations (tcedi0110m000) Maintain Conv. of
Delivery Address Codes by Customer (in) (tcedi3 110m000) Maintain Conversion of Postal
Address Codes by Customer (in) (tce di3112m000) Maintain Conv. of Delivery Address Codes
by Customer (out) (tcedi 4148m000) Maintain Conv. of Postal Address Codes by Customer
(out) (tcedi41 50m000)
BAAN Distribution (tdtd-20010): Maintain Prices by Customer and Item (tdsls0101m000)
Maintain Discounts by Customer and Price Group (tdsls0102m000) Maintain Discounts by
Customer (tdsls0103m000) Maintain Discount Parameters by Customer and Price Group
(tdsls01 07s000) Maintain Price Parameters by Customer and Item (tdsls0109s000) Maintain
Discount Parameters by Customer (tdsls0110s000) Maintain Quotations (tdsls1101m000)
Maintain Quotation Lines (tdsls1102s000) Maintain Quotation Lines (Wholesale)
(tdsls1107s000) Delete Sales Quotation (tdsls1803s000) Display Gross Profit of Quotation
Line (tdsls1808s000) Maintain Delivery Date in Order Lines (tdsls1809s000) Enter Specific
Quotation Numbers (tdsls1820s000) Maintain Sales Contracts (tdsls3101m000) Maintain Sales
Contract Lines (tdsls3102s000) Maintain Sales Contract Status (tdsls3110m000) Copy Sales
Contracts (tdsls3801m000) Enter Specific Sales Contract Numbers (tdsls3820s000) Maintain
Sales Orders (tdsls4101m000) Maintain Sales Orders (Wholesale) (tdsls4102m000)
Maintain Sales Orders (Wholesale) (tdsls4105m000) Maintain Item Descriptions by Customer
(tdsls4107m000) Maintain Deliveries (tdsls4120m000) Change Prices and Discounts after
`Maintain Deliveries' (tdsls412 2m000) Maintain and Confirm Back Orders (tdsls4125m000)
Maintain Costs Set by Sales Price List and Customer (tdsls4127m00 0) Link Delivery Lines
(tdsls4144s000) Signal Inventory Shortages (tdsls4801s000) Calculate Sales Order Line
Discounts (tdsls4802s000) Delete Sales Order (tdsls4803s000) Display Gross Profit of
Sales Order Line (tdsls4808s000) Update Delivery Date in Sales Order Lines
(tdsls4809s000) Recalculate Sales Price and Discount (tdsls4810s000) Copy Bill of
Material to Order (tdsls4812s000) Enter Specific Sales Order Numbers (tdsls4820s000)
Maintain SMI Parameters (tdsmi0100m000) Maintain Features by Trade Relation
(tdsmi1102s000) Maintain Marketing Projects by Relation (tdsmi1103m000) Maintain Features
by Marketing Project (tdsmi1104s000)
Maintain Contacts by Relation (tdsmi1105m000) Maintain Features by Contact
(tdsmi1106s000) Maintain Contacts by Marketing Project (tdsmi1107m000) Maintain
Activities (tdsmi2101m000) Maintain Features by Activity (tdsmi2102s000) Maintain
Appointments by Sales Rep (tdsmi2110m000) Maintain Appointments by SMI Employee
(tdsmi2116s000)
BAAN Finance (tftf-20010): Maintain Sales Invoices (tfacr1110s000) Maintain Terms of
Payment (tfacr1112s000) Maintain Sales Invoice Details (tfacr2100m000) Maintain Sales
Invoice Corrections (tfacr2110s000) Assign Credit Notes to Invoices (tfacr2120s000)
Assign Credit Notes to Invoices (tfacr2121s000)
Maintain Doubtful Sales Invoices (tfacr2140s000) Maintain Reminder Advice (tfacr3110m000)
Maintain Reminder Diary (tfacr3130m000) Maintain Action Dates (tfacr3131s000) Maintain
Sales Invoice Header (tfacr4100m000) Maintain Interest Invoice Advice (tfacr5110m000)
Reconciliation of Anticipated Payments/Receipts (tfcmg2102s000) Reconciliation of
Receipts/Payments (tfcmg2103s000) Reconciliation of Receipts/Payments (tfcmg2104s000)
Assign Unallocated/Advance Receipts to Invoices (tfcmg2105s000) Maintain Anticipated
Payments (tfcmg2110s000) Maintain Anticipated Receipts (tfcmg2111s000) Maintain
Anticipated Payment Status (tfcmg2112s000) Maintain Anticipated Receipt Status
(tfcmg2113s000) Maintain Anticipated Payments (Details) (tfcmg2116s000) Maintain
Anticipated Receipts (Details) (tfcmg2117s000) Select for Automatic Customer
Reconciliation (tfcmg2121s000) Select for Automatic Supplier Reconciliation
(tfcmg2122s000) Selection for Automatic Reconciliation (tfcmg2123s000)
Maintain Customer Invoice Cash Date (tfcmg3110m000) Maintain Direct Debit Advice
(tfcmg4120m000) Send Trade Notes/Checks to Bank (tfcmg4130m000)
Maintain Remittance Advice MeBaanges (Receipts) (tfcmg5101m000) Maintain Converted
Electronic Bank Statements (tfcmg5102m000) Maintain Electronic Bank Statements

(tfcmg5103m000) Maintain Disposals (tffas1102s000) Maintain Fixed Asset Disposals (Simulation) (tffas4118m000)

BAAN Manufacturing (titi-20010): Maintain Product Variants (tipcf5101m000) Maintain Budgets (tipcs0101m000) Maintain Projects (tipcs2101m000) Maintain Project Status (tipcs2102m000) Maintain Norm Group (tpbop4100m000) Maintain Estimate Data (tppdm4100m000) Maintain Archived Estimates (tppdm5190m000) Maintain Customers by Project (tppdm6101s000) Maintain Archived Projects (tppdm7190m000) Maintain Progress Invoice Specifications (tppin1110m000) Maintain Project Advances (tppin4150m000) Maintain Installments by Project (tppin4151m000) Maintain Advances to be Invoiced (tppin4155m000) Maintain Installments to be Invoiced (tppin4156m000) Maintain Pro Forma Invoice (tppin4165m000) Maintain Advance Invoice Lines (tppin4167s000) Maintain Installment Invoice Lines (tppin4168s000) Maintain Material Invoice Lines (tppin4169s000) Maintain Invoice Lines (Cost Plus Labor) (tppin4170s000) Maintain Invoice Lines (Cost Plus Equipment) (tppin4171s000) Maintain Invoice Lines (Cost Plus Subcontracting) (tppin4172s000)

Maintain Invoice Lines (Cost Plus Sundry Cost) (tppin4173s000) Maintain Unit Rate Invoice Lines (tppin4174s000) Maintain Revenues (tpppc3101m000) Confirm Revenues (tpppc4110m000) Maintain Extensions (tpptc0110m000)

BAAN Transportation (trtr-20010): Maintain Entry Lines (trcde1101s000) Maintain Packing Transactions (trcde1160s000) Maintain Invoice Lines (trics1100m000) Maintain Rate Codes by Customer/Transaction Code/Item (trpac0140m 000) Maintain Packing Items (trpac1100m000) Maintain Owners and Numbers by Packing Item (trpac1110m000) Maintain Packing Items by Item (trpac1140m000) Maintain Packing Transactions (trpac2100m000) Maintain Addresses by Customer (trpac2130m000) Maintain Defaults by Customer (trtcd2120m000) Maintain Cost Sets by Customer (trtco0110m000) Maintain Means of Transport (trtfm1110m000) Maintain TOC Parameters (trtoc0100m000) Maintain Transport Orders (trtoc1100m000) Maintain Transport Orders (trtoc1102s000) Split Order Lines (trtoc1103s000) Maintain Bills of Material for Logistical Units (trtoc1120s000) Collect Logistic Units (trtoc1121m000) Maintain Bills of Material for Logistical Units (trtoc1122s000) Collect Logistic Units (TDPUR Order Step) (trtoc1123m000) Standard Session for Transport Order Lines (All Data) (trtoc1180m 000) Maintain Transport Order Lines (trtoc1181m000) Maintain Transport Order Lines (trtoc1182m000) Maintain Transport Order Lines (trtoc1183m000) Maintain Transport Order Lines (trtoc1184m000)

Maintain Transport Order Lines (trtoc1185m000) Maintain Transport Order Lines (trtoc1186m000) Maintain Transport Order Lines (trtoc1187m000) Maintain Transport Order Lines (trtoc1188m000) Maintain Document Lines (trtoc1189s000) Maintain Transport Order Lines (trtoc1190m000) Maintain Transport Order Lines (trtoc1191m000) Maintain Standard Orders (trtoc3100m000) Maintain Standard Order Lines (trtoc3101m000) Maintain Contracts (trtoc4100m000) Maintain Third-Party Items (trtpi1100m000) Maintain Blocking of Third-Party Items (trtpi1101m000) Maintain Alternative Units by Third-Party Item (trtpi1110m000) Maintain Storage Conditions by Third-Party Item (trtpi1120m000) Maintain Third-Party Items by Storage Condition (trtpi1121m000) Maintain Transport Rate Codes by Customer (trtrc1140m000) Enter Item Inventory Adjustments (trwic2100m000) Maintain Blocking Statuses of Item Inventories (trwic2101m000) Maintain Inventory Remarks (trwic2105s000) Maintain Minimum Inventory of Items (trwic4100m000) Maintain Minimum Inventory of Items by Location (trwic4101m000) Maintain Storage Orders (trwoc1100m000) Maintain Storage Orders (Invoicing Data) (trwoc1106m000) [SE@trwo c1106m000] Maintain Storage Orders (General Data) (trwoc1107m000) Maintain Inbound Orders (trwoc2100m000) Maintain Inbound Order Lines (trwoc2101m000) Maintain Inbound Orders (trwoc2105s000) Maintain Inbound Order Lines (Invoicing Data) (trwoc2106m000) Maintain Inbound Order Lines (General Data) (trwoc2107m000) Maintain Outbound Orders (trwoc3100m000) Maintain Outbound Order Lines (trwoc3101m000) Maintain Outbound Orders (trwoc3105s000) Maintain Outbound Order Lines (Invoicing Data) (trwoc3106m000) Maintain Outbound Order Lines (General Data) (trwoc3107m000) Maintain Transhipment Orders (trwoc4100m000) Maintain Transhipment Order Lines (trwoc4101m000) Maintain Transhipment Orders (trwoc4105s000) Maintain Transhipment Order Lines (Invoicing Data) (trwoc4106m000) Maintain Transhipment Order Lines (General Data) (trwoc4107m000) Maintain Assembly Orders (trwoc5100m000) Maintain Assembly Order Lines (trwoc5101m000) Maintain Assembly Orders (Invoicing Data) (trwoc5106m000) Maintain Assembly Orders (General Data) (trwoc5107m000) Maintain Warehousing Rate Codes by Customer (trwrc1140m000) [SE@t rwrc1140m000] Maintain Warehousing Rate Codes by Item (trwrc1150m000)

BAAN Service (tsts-20010): Maintain Installations (tssma1102m000) Maintain Installations (tssma1103s000) Maintain Locations (tssma1110m000) Maintain Contracts (tssma2120m000) Maintain Installations by Contract (tssma2182m000) Maintain Service Orders (tssma3101m000) Maintain Hourly Rates by Customer (tssma3121m000) Maintain Service Orders (Telephone Screen) (tssma3140m000) Maintain Service Orders (Planning) (tssma3141m000) Report Service Orders Completed (tssma3142m000)

Close Service Orders (tssma3144m000) Display Service Orders (tssma3502s000) Enter Specific Service Order Numbers (tssma3820s000)

1.103 Dangerous Goods Regulations (tcedi284)

DEFINITION

Regulations concerning the transport of dangerous goods, such as:
• European Agreement concerning the International Carriage of Dangerous Goods by Road (ADR)
• International Agreement concerning the Transport of Dangerous Goods by Air (IATA)
• International Regulations concerning the Transport of Dangerous Goods by Rail (RID)

SOURCE OF DATA

The data result from input or import in the session "Import EDI Data (tcedi6220m000)".

APPLICATION OF DATA

Dangerous goods regulation codes are used in:
• processing received meBaanges in the b-object "Communication".

1.104 Dates/Times (tcedi222)

DEFINITION

Dates/times record the codes for shipping/collect dates/times (by organization).

SOURCE OF DATA

The data result from input or import in the session "Import EDI Data (tcedi6220m000)".

APPLICATION OF DATA

Dates/times are used in:
• processing received meBaanges in the b-object "Communication".

1.105 Default Charts per User per Session (tccom501)

DEFINITION

Default charts by user and session.

SOURCE OF DATA

BAAN Common (tctc-20010): Maintain Default Charts by User and Session (tccom5110m000)

1.106 Delivery Addresses (tccom013)

DEFINITION

Delivery addresses are addresses where the goods ordered are delivered.

SOURCE OF DATA

BAAN Common (tctc-20010): Maintain Delivery Addresses (tccom1102m000)

APPLICATION OF DATA

BAAN Common (tctc-20010): Maintain Customers (tccom1101m000) Maintain Prospects (tccom1110m000) Maintain Conv. of Delivery Address Codes by Customer (in) (tcedi3 110m000) Maintain Conv. of Delivery Address Codes by Customer (out) (tcedi 4148m000)
BAAN Distribution (tdtd-20010): Maintain Quotations (tdsls1101m000) Delete Sales Quotation (tdsls1803s000) Maintain Delivery Date in Order Lines (tdsls1809s000) Enter Specific Quotation Numbers (tdsls1820s000) Maintain Sales Contracts (tdsls3101m000) Maintain Sales Contract Status (tdsls3110m000) Copy Sales Contracts (tdsls3801m000) Enter Specific Sales Contract Numbers (tdsls3820s000) Maintain Sales Orders (tdsls4101m000) Delete Sales Order (tdsls4803s000) Copy Bill of Material to Order (tdsls4812s000) Enter Specific Sales Order Numbers (tdsls4820s000)
BAAN Service (tsts-20010): Maintain Locations (tssma1110m000) Maintain Service Orders (tssma3101m000) Maintain Service Orders (Telephone Screen) (tssma3140m000) Maintain Service Orders (Planning) (tssma3141m000) Report Service Orders Completed (tssma3142m000) Close Service Orders (tssma3144m000) Display Service Orders (tssma3502s000) Enter Specific Service Order Numbers (tssma3820s000)

1.107 Dimension Qualifiers (tcedi268)

DEFINITION

The dimension qualifiers of consignments specify the dimensions or size of the units, e.g.:
• gross dimensions (including packing)
• load meters (length required for goods in vehicle over its entire width and height)

SOURCE OF DATA

The data result from input or import in the session "Import EDI Data (tcedi6220m000)".

APPLICATION OF DATA

Dimension qualifiers are used in:
• processing received meBaanges in the b-object "Communication".

1.108 Dimension Types (tccon150)

1.109 Discount Codes (tcmcs021)

DEFINITION

Discount codes are linked to surcharges and discount which help to determine the payable amount and thereby, the turnover from purchase and sales orders. Surcharges and discounts may be the result from:
• standard discounts or surcharges
• payable commissions
• payable rebates

SOURCE OF DATA

BAAN Common (tctc-20010): Maintain Discount Codes (tcmcs0121m000)

APPLICATION OF DATA

BAAN Distribution (tdtd-20010): Maintain Commission Agreement Parameters (tdcms0135s000) Maintain Commissions Calculated by Order (tdcms0150m000) Maintain Rebate Agreement

Parameters (tdcms1135s000) Maintain Commissions Calculated by Relation (tdcms1150m000) Close Commissions Reserved for Employees (tdcms2102m000) Maintain Rebates Calculated by Order (tdcms2150m000) Maintain Rebates Calculated by Relation (tdcms3150m000) Maintain Prices by Supplier and Item (tdpur0101m000) Maintain Prices by Supplier and Item (tdpur0101s000) Maintain Discounts by Supplier and Price Group (tdpur0102m000) Maintain Discounts by Supplier and Price Group (tdpur0102s000) Maintain Discounts by Supplier (tdpur0103m000) Maintain Discounts by Supplier (tdpur0103s000) Maintain Prices by Price List and Item (tdpur0104m000) Maintain Prices by Price List and Item (tdpur0104s000) Maintain Discounts by Price List and Price Group (tdpur0105m000) Maintain Discounts by Price List and Price Group (tdpur0105s000) Maintain Discounts by Price List (tdpur0106m000) Maintain Discounts by Price List (tdpur0106s000) Maintain Prices by Item (tdpur0113m000) Maintain Prices by Item (tdpur0113s000) Maintain Purchase Contract Prices (tdpur3106s000) Maintain Purchase Contract Discounts (tdpur3107s000) Maintain Prices by Customer and Item (tdsls0101m000) Maintain Prices by Customer and Item (tdsls0101s000) Maintain Discounts by Customer and Price Group (tdsls0102m000) Maintain Discounts by Customer and Price Group (tdsls0102s000) Maintain Discounts by Customer (tdsls0103m000) Maintain Discounts by Customer (tdsls0103s000) Maintain Prices by Price List and Item (tdsls0104m000) Maintain Prices by Price List and Item (tdsls0104s000) Maintain Discounts by Price List and Price Group (tdsls0105m000) Maintain Discounts by Price List and Price Group (tdsls0105s000) Maintain Discounts by Price List (tdsls0106m000) Maintain Discounts by Price List (tdsls0106s000) [SE@tdsls0106s00
0] Maintain Prices by Item (tdsls0113m000) Maintain Prices by Item (tdsls0113s000) Maintain Sales Contract Prices (tdsls3106s000) Maintain Sales Contract Discounts (tdsls3107s000)
1.110 Discounts (tcedi238)
DEFINITION
Discounts record the codes and associated descriptions of late payment surcharge and cash discount.
SOURCE OF DATA
The data result from input or import in the session "Import EDI Data (tcedi6220m000)".
APPLICATION OF DATA
Discounts are used in:
•   processing received meBaanges in the b-object "Communication".
1.111 Discounts and Surcharges (tcedi244)
DEFINITION
Discounts and surcharges are codes and descriptions relating to discounts and surcharges by organization.
SOURCE OF DATA
The data result from input or import in the session "Import EDI Data (tcedi6220m000)".
APPLICATION OF DATA
Discounts and surcharges are used in:
•   processing received meBaanges in the b-object "Communication".
1.112 Document Name (tcedi246)
DEFINITION
Schedule release frequencies are schedules indicating the frequency with which the goods will be delivered. During conversion, these schedules can be recorded in text fields.
SOURCE OF DATA
The data result from input or import in the session "Import EDI Data (tcedi6220m000)".
APPLICATION OF DATA
Schedule release frequency codes are used in:
•   processing received meBaanges in the b-object "Communication".
1.113 EDI Interchange Controller (tcedi710)
DEFINITION
The system uses this table for logging network data when you run the session "EDI Interchange Controller (tcedi7210m000)".
APPLICATION OF DATA
The data from this table is shown automatically in the display session "EDI Interchange Monitor (tcedi7505m000)".
1.114 EDI MeBaanges (tcedi005)
DEFINITION
A meBaange is an electronic document (for instance, an electronic order acknowledgement) consisting of an organization and a meBaange. MeBaanges are processed as incoming and/or outgoing meBaanges in specific sessions (for instance in the modules "Sales Control (SLS)", "Purchase Control (PUR)", "Transport Order Control (TOC)" and "Accounts Payable (ACP)").
For informational purposes, you may identify the meBaange type (EDIFACT, or NON-EDIACT). EDIFACT (Electronic Data Interchange for Administration, Commerce and Transport) is a worldwide organization developing standards for electronic data interchange. There are various organizations (eg. Odette), each using its own subset of standard EDIFACT meBaanges. ANSI (American National Standards Intitute's) X12 is another standards

organization, used throughout North America and elsewhere, which has its own set of standards. There are also various organizations (eg. AIAG) which use a subset of these standards. When defining meBaanges, you may use the naming convention that coincides with the standards' naming conventions to which you are accustomed.

For incoming meBaanges, the File Layout indicates whether the data for the incoming meBaange will reside in a single file or within multiple files. If a single file, the Level Identification Position specifies the position of the Level Identifier, as defined within the conversion setup, which identifies the record in the ASCII file (eg. header, header text, line, etc).

SOURCE OF DATA

The data result from input or import in the session "Import EDI Data (tcedi6220m000)".

APPLICATION OF DATA

MeBaanges are used in:
- maintaining and printing meBaanges supported by your own application or a relation in the b-object "EDI Master Data";
- maintaining outgoing meBaanges by session in the b-object "EDI Master Data";
- maintaining and printing code and conversion tables in the b-object "Coding and Conversion Data";
- maintaining and printing conversion setups and printing mapping information in the b-object "Coding and Conversion Data";
- processing saved files in the b-object "Communication".

1.115 EDI MeBaanges Supported by Relations (tcedi011)

DEFINITION

Supported meBaanges by relation are meBaanges that are used by specific (business) relations. To a combination of relation and meBaange you can link a network and a user. Only when relation and specific meBaange (incoming and/or outgoing) have been linked can the relation communicate with your application using that particular meBaange.

The session "Display Received MeBaanges by User (tcedi7510m000)" shows the received meBaanges by person responsible within your organization.

APPLICATION OF DATA

Supported meBaanges by relation are used in:
- generating EDI meBaanges in the b-object "Communication".

1.116 EDI Parameters (tcedi000)

DEFINITION

Parameters are variables to which a constant value is assigned. Changing parameter values will change the way in which the module operates, allowing you to adapt the module to the specific requirements of your company.

SOURCE OF DATA

First, running session "Initialize Parameters (tcmcs0295m000)" will assign default values to the parameters, which can subsequently be modified in the parameter sessions.

1.117 Employees (tccom001)

DEFINITION

Employees are all people working within your company.

SOURCE OF DATA

BAAN Common (tctc-20010): Maintain Employees (tccom0101m000)
BAAN Project (tptp-20010): Maintain Employees (tppdm8101m000)

APPLICATION OF DATA

BAAN Common (tctc-20010): Maintain Customers (tccom1101m000) Maintain Prospects (tccom1110m000) Maintain Suppliers (tccom2101m000) Maintain Concern Structure of Trade Relations (tccom3101m000) Maintain Conversion of Employee Codes by Relation (tcedi3120m000)
Maintain Conversion of Employee Codes by Relation (out) (tcedi415 8m000)
BAAN Distribution (tdtd-20010): Maintain Inquiries (tdpur1101m000) Maintain Expiry Date for Returned Inquiry (tdpur1800s000) Enter Specific Inquiry Numbers (tdpur1820s000) Maintain Purchase Contracts (tdpur3101m000) Maintain Purchase Contract Status (tdpur3110m000) Copy Purchase Contracts (tdpur3801m000) Enter Specific Purchase Contract Numbers (tdpur3820s000) Maintain Purchase Orders (tdpur4101m000) Enter Specific Purchase Order Numbers (tdpur4820s000) Print Purchase Order Header History (tdpur5403m000) Maintain Quotations (tdsls1101m000) Delete Sales Quotation (tdsls1803s000) Maintain Delivery Date in Order Lines (tdsls1809s000) Copy BOM Components to Quotation (tdsls1812s000) Enter Specific Quotation Numbers (tdsls1820s000) Maintain Sales Contracts (tdsls3101m000) Maintain Sales Contract Status (tdsls3110m000) Copy Sales Contracts (tdsls3801m000) Enter Specific Sales Contract Numbers (tdsls3820s000) Maintain Sales Orders (tdsls4101m000) Delete Sales Order (tdsls4803s000) Copy Bill of Material to Order (tdsls4812s000)
Enter Specific Sales Order Numbers (tdsls4820s000) Maintain SMI Employees (tdsmi0190m000) Maintain Marketing Projects by Relation (tdsmi1103m000) Maintain Activities (tdsmi2101m000) Maintain Appointments by Sales Rep (tdsmi2110m000) Maintain Appointments by SMI Employee (tdsmi2116s000)

BAAN Finance (tftf-20010): Maintain Sales Invoices (tfacr1110s000) Maintain Terms of
Payment (tfacr1112s000) Maintain Sales Invoice Details (tfacr2100m000) Maintain Sales
Invoice Corrections (tfacr2110s000) Assign Credit Notes to Invoices (tfacr2120s000)
Assign Credit Notes to Invoices (tfacr2121s000)
Maintain Doubtful Sales Invoices (tfacr2140s000) Maintain Reminder Diary (tfacr3130m000)
Assign Unallocated/Advance Receipts to Invoices (tfcmg2105s000) Maintain Customer Invoice
Cash Date (tfcmg3110m000) Maintain Fixed Asset Master Data (tffas0106m000) Maintain Fixed
Asset Master Data (Simulation) (tffas4106m000) Maintain Dimensions (tfgld0110m000)
BAAN Enterprise Modeler (tgtg-20010): Maintain Performance Indicators (tgeis0111m000)
Maintain PI Data by Period (tgeis0112m000)
BAAN Manufacturing (titi-20010): Maintain Engineering Items (tiedm0110m000) Maintain
Engineering Item Revisions (tiedm1101m000) Maintain ECOs (tiedm3110m000) Maintain Item
Data (GRT) (tigrt1180s000) Maintain Customized Item Data (GRT) (tigrt2180s000) Enter
Hours Accounting (tihra1101m000) Maintain Budget by Employee (tihra3120m000) Maintain
Item Data (tiitm0101m000) Maintain Item Data (in BOM) (tiitm0108s000) Maintain Item
Default Data (tiitm0110m000) Maintain Plan Items (timps2101m000) Maintain Budgets
(tipcs0101m000) Maintain Calculation Parts (tipcs0110m000) Maintain Projects
(tipcs2101m000) Maintain Project Status (tipcs2102m000) Maintain Customized Item Data
(tipcs2121m000) Maintain Activities (tipcs4101m000) Maintain Activities Using Planning
Board (tipcs4105m000) Maintain Work Centers (tirou0101m000) Maintain Hours Accounting
Transactions (tphrs1100m000) Maintain Hours by Manned Equipment (tpism0176m000) Maintain
Service Hours Transactions (tpism3122m000) Maintain Item Default Data (tppdm0109m000)
Maintain Standard Items (tppdm0110m000) Maintain Employees by Responsibility
(tppdm0134m000) [SE@tppdm013
4m000] Maintain Team Resources (tppdm0145m000) Maintain Employees Responsible by Estimate
(tppdm4131m000) Maintain Appointments by Estimate (tppdm4132m000) Maintain Employees
Responsible by Project (tppdm6131m000) Maintain Appointments by Project (tppdm6132m000)
Maintain Departments (tppdm8102m000) Maintain Labor Transactions to be Invoiced
(tppin4158m000) Maintain Labor Costs (tpppc2131m000) Confirm Labor Cost Transactions
(tpppc4102m000)
Maintain Plans (tppss0110m000) Maintain Employee Calendar (tppss0133m000) Maintain Labor
Actions (tppss4111m000) Maintain Extensions (tpptc0110m000) Maintain Activity Budget
(Labor Lines) (tpptc2111m000)
BAAN Service (tsts-20010): Maintain Locations (tssma1110m000) Maintain Technicians by
Service Area (tssma1113m000) Maintain Service Orders (tssma3101m000) Maintain
Technicians' Daily Planning (tssma3105m000) Maintain Service Cars (tssma3106m000)
Maintain Blank Service Job Sheets (tssma3107m000) Maintain Actual Service Order Costs and
Revenues (tssma3110m000) Maintain Service Orders (Telephone Screen) (tssma3140m000)
Maintain Service Orders (Planning) (tssma3141m000) Report Service Orders Completed
(tssma3142m000)
Close Service Orders (tssma3144m000) Plan Service Orders (tssma3158m000) Maintain
Technicians' Daily Planning (tssma3159s000) Maintain Service Order Cost Estimate
(tssma3170m000) Display Service Orders (tssma3502s000) Enter Specific Service Order
Numbers (tssma3820s000) Maintain Skills by Technician (tssma4104m000) Maintain Working
Time Tables by Technician (tssma4110m000) Maintain Technicians' Daily Planning
(tssma4116s000)

1.118 Equipment Qualifiers (tcedi280)

DEFINITION
Equipment qualifiers indicate the type of equipment that is used, e.g. container,
pallets, trailer, etc.
SOURCE OF DATA
The data result from input or import in the session "Import EDI Data (tcedi6220m000)".
APPLICATION OF DATA
Equipment qualifiers are used in:
•   processing received meBaanges in the b-object "Communication".

1.119 Evaluation Expressions (tcedi505)

DEFINITION
Evaluation expressions determine which lines of a conversion setup definition are
executed and which are not, i.e. which fields in the ASCII file are filled and which are
not.

   Example:
   The conversion setup definitions include two types of delivery
   addresses: the regular one and a specific address. For both address
   types an evaluation expression must be created. When you send a
   purchase order, the evaluation expression sees to it that the right
   delivery address is placed in the ASCII file.

SOURCE OF DATA
The data result from input or import in the session "Import EDI Data (tcedi6220m000)".
APPLICATION OF DATA

Evaluation expressions are used in:
- selecting lines in the session "Maintain Definitions of Conversion Setups (tcedi5115s000)"

1.120 Exceptions by Tax Location (tcmcs939)

DEFINITION

Exceptions by tax location are used in cases where the origin of a shipment has an impact on the sales tax charged or remitted. Exceptions recorded here will override the general tax codes assigned by destination in the Tax Codes by Postal Code (tcmcs936) table

1.121 Exceptions for Taxes - Purchase (tcmcs946)

DEFINITION

Exceptions for Taxes are maintained in the case where a particular supplier, item group, project, budget, or item has special tax consideration within a certain country and postal code. Exceptions entered here will override the tax codes assigned in the Tax Codes by Postal Code (tcmcs936) and Exceptions by Tax Location (tcmcs939) tables

1.122 Exceptions for Taxes - Sales (tcmcs938)

DEFINITION

Exceptions for Taxes are maintained in the case where a particular customer, item group, project, budget, or item has special tax considerations within a certain country and postal code. Exceptions entered here will override the tax codes assigned in the Tax Codes by Postal Code (tcmcs936) and Exceptions by Tax Location (tcmcs939) tables

1.123 External Acknowledgment Codes (tcedi299)

DEFINITION

Acknowledgment Codes are used to indicate the status of, or response to, an order request or order change request, and may be referenced on the order acknowledgment.

These codes may be used to correspond to EDI standard codes, such as the ANSI X12 "Line Item Status Code", or the UN/EDIFACT "MeBaange Function Code" for the header and "Action Request Code" for the line.

SOURCE OF DATA

The data result from input or import in the session "Import EDI Data (tcedi6220m000)".

APPLICATION OF DATA

Countries are used in:
- defining conversion data in the b-object "Coding and Conversion Data".

1.124 External Change Reason Codes (tcedi297)

DEFINITION

Change Reason Codes are used to indicate the reason for making a change to the order, and are specified on the order change meBaange, and may be referenced on the order change acknowledgment.

These codes may be used to correspond to EDI standard codes, such as the ANSI X12 "Change Reason Code", or the UN/EDIFACT "Adjustment Reason, Coded".

SOURCE OF DATA

The data result from input or import in the session "Import EDI Data (tcedi6220m000)".

APPLICATION OF DATA

Countries are used in:
- defining conversion data in the b-object "Coding and Conversion Data".

1.125 Factoring Companies (tcmcs025)

DEFINITION

Factoring companies are external bureaus managing the trade debts for other companies.

Example:
If an invoice is to be paid to a supplier who is associated with a factoring company, the amount due will be paid to the factor instead of the supplier.

SOURCE OF DATA

BAAN Common (tctc-20010): Maintain Factoring Companies (tcmcs0125m000)

APPLICATION OF DATA

BAAN Common (tctc-20010): Maintain Suppliers (tccom2101m000) Maintain Banks by Factoring Company (tcmcs0126m000)

1.126 First Free Numbers (tcmcs047)

DEFINITION

The first free number is the first available number within a series. It is offered as default when you create orders, etc. Series enable you to group orders of the same type by assigning them order numbers starting with the same figures.

SOURCE OF DATA

BAAN Common (tctc-20010): Maintain First Free Numbers (tcmcs0147m000)

APPLICATION OF DATA

BAAN Common (tctc-20010): Maintain EDI MeBaanges Supported by Relations (tcedi0111m000)

1.127 Forwarding Agents (tcmcs080)

DEFINITION

Forwarding agents are companies who take care of the transportation of goods.

SOURCE OF DATA

BAAN Common (tctc-20010): Maintain Forwarding Agents (tcmcs0180m000)
APPLICATION OF DATA
BAAN Common (tctc-20010): Maintain Customers (tccom1101m000) Maintain Prospects
(tccom1110m000) Maintain Import/Export Statistics (tccom7171m000) Maintain Conv. of
Forwarding Agent Codes by Relation (in) (tcedi3 118m000) Maintain Conv. of Forwarding
Agent Codes by Relation (out) (tcedi 4156m000)
BAAN Distribution (tdtd-20010): Maintain Inquiries (tdpur1101m000) Maintain Expiry Date
for Returned Inquiry (tdpur1800s000) Enter Specific Inquiry Numbers (tdpur1820s000)
Maintain Purchase Contracts (tdpur3101m000) Maintain Purchase Contract Status
(tdpur3110m000) Copy Purchase Contracts (tdpur3801m000) Enter Specific Purchase Contract
Numbers (tdpur3820s000) Maintain Purchase Orders (tdpur4101m000) Enter Specific Purchase
Order Numbers (tdpur4820s000) Print Purchase Order Header History (tdpur5403m000)
Maintain Quotations (tdsls1101m000) Delete Sales Quotation (tdsls1803s000) Maintain
Delivery Date in Order Lines (tdsls1809s000) Enter Specific Quotation Numbers
(tdsls1820s000) Maintain Sales Contracts (tdsls3101m000) Maintain Sales Contract Status
(tdsls3110m000) Copy Sales Contracts (tdsls3801m000) Enter Specific Sales Contract
Numbers (tdsls3820s000) Maintain Sales Orders (tdsls4101m000) Delete Sales Order
(tdsls4803s000) Copy Bill of Material to Order (tdsls4812s000) Enter Specific Sales Order
Numbers (tdsls4820s000)
1.128 Generated Batchnumbers (tcedi720)
DEFINITION
The unique references generated when outgoing meBaanges are created.
1.129 Generated MeBaanges (tcedi701)
DEFINITION
"Generated MeBaanges" are all outgoing meBaanges of which the ASCII files are present.
APPLICATION OF DATA
"Generated MeBaanges" may be used to:
•   place EDI meBaanges in ASCII files in the b-object "Communication".
1.130 Government Actions (tcedi290)
DEFINITION
Government actions are activities carried out by government agencies with respect to
transactions or transportation.
SOURCE OF DATA
The data result from input or import in the session "Import EDI Data (tcedi6220m000)".
APPLICATION OF DATA
Government action codes are used in:
•   processing received meBaanges in the b-object "Communication".
1.131 Government Codes (tcedi288)
DEFINITION
Government codes represent government agencies involved in transactions or
transportation, e.g. the customs.
SOURCE OF DATA
The data result from input or import in the session "Import EDI Data (tcedi6220m000)".
APPLICATION OF DATA
Government codes are used in:
•   processing received meBaanges in the b-object "Communication".
1.132 Government Involvement Indicators (tcedi286)
DEFINITION
Code indicating whether an activity is required or completed on behalf of the government.
SOURCE OF DATA
The data result from input or import in the session "Import EDI Data (tcedi6220m000)".
APPLICATION OF DATA
Government involvement indicators are used in:
•   processing received meBaanges in the b-object "Communication".
1.133 Import/Export Statistics (tccom710)
DEFINITION
Import and export statistics provide information about the nature, origin and extent of
the flow of goods between EU member states.
SOURCE OF DATA
BAAN Common (tctc-20010): Maintain Import/Export Statistics (tccom7171m000)
1.134 Inspection Data (tcqms115)
DEFINITION
The inspection test data consists of the measured values of the characteristics.
SOURCE OF DATA
Test data must be entered in session Enter Test Data (tcqms1115m000).
The value of algorithms can be calculated in the same session by means of option
"Evaluate Algorithm [tcqms1115m0001.user.1]".
APPLICATION OF DATA
The test data can be used to accept or reject a lot based on the sampling results. Each
sample which is tested is classified as either Good or Bad.

1.135 Inspection History (tcqms301)
DEFINITION
Contains the data of all the inspections which are posted to history.
SOURCE OF DATA
The inspection data.
APPLICATION OF DATA
•   Display Sample History (tcqms3510m000)
1.136 Inspection Order Header History (tcqms305)
1.137 Inspection Order Lines (tcqms101)
DEFINITION
Inspections consist of the combined data needed to test an item for a certain quality.
Inspections may be generated based on the master data or order-specific data.
 The structure of standard inspections is as follows:

  - Inspection by Origin 1
    General Data of Order Origin
        - Order 1
          Sample data
          (Test Groups by Quality ID   Data)
              - Line 1
Characteristic 1 (Characteristics by Quality ID (tcqms015) Data)
              - Line 2
Characteristic 2
        - Order 2
          Sample Data
              - Line 1
Characteristic 1
              - Line 2
Characteristic 2
  - Inspection by Origin 2
    ...
      etc.

Orders The order data of inspections consists of the sample data. For an inspection with
different origins, more than one set of sample data may exist.
Lines The line of an inspection order is a combination of an aspect and a characteristic
which will be tested on each sample.
SOURCE OF DATA
Inspection orders may be automatically generated in the following modules:
•   Sales (SLS)
•   Purchase (PUR)
•   Production (SFC)
•   Material (BOM)
•   Routing (TI)
•   Production (PMG)
•   Material (FRM)
•   Routing (PS)
•   Storage Inspection
New inspection orders can also be entered manually in session "Maintain Inspection Orders
(tcqms1100s000)".
APPLICATION OF DATA
Inspection orders are used in "Quality Management System (QMS)" to test items for
characteristics.
1.138 Inspection Order Lines History (tcqms306)
1.139 Inspection Orders (tcqms100)
DEFINITION
Inspections consist of the combined data needed to test an item for a certain quality.
Inspections may be generated based on the master data or order-specific data.
 The structure of standard inspections is as follows:

  - Inspection by Origin 1
    General Data of Order Origin
        - Order 1
          Sample data
          (Test Groups by Quality ID   Data)
              - Line 1
Characteristic 1 (Characteristics by Quality ID (tcqms015) Data)
              - Line 2
Characteristic 2
        - Order 2

```
            Sample Data
                - Line 1
Characteristic 1
                - Line 2
Characteristic 2
 - Inspection by Origin 2
    ...
      etc.
```

Orders The order data of inspections consists of the sample data. For an inspection with different origins, more than one set of sample data may exist.
Lines The line of an inspection order is a combination of an aspect and a characteristic which will be tested on each sample.
SOURCE OF DATA
Inspection orders may be automatically generated in the following modules:
- Sales (SLS)
- Purchase (PUR)
- Production (SFC)
- Material (BOM)
- Routing (TI)
- Production (PMG)
- Material (FRM)
- Routing (PS)
- Storage Inspection

New inspection orders can also be entered manually in session "Maintain Inspection Orders (tcqms1100s000)".
APPLICATION OF DATA
Inspection orders are used in "Quality Management System (QMS)" to test items for characteristics.

1.140 Inspection Results by Origin (Storage Inspection) (tcqms220)
DEFINITION
The inspection results of storage inspections.
SOURCE OF DATA
- Maintain Storage Inspections (tcqms2120m000)
APPLICATION OF DATA
Contains details of accepted and rejected inventory, both recommended by qms as well as the actual. Provides the inspection status per inspection order.

1.141 Inspections by Origin (tcqms120)
DEFINITION
Inspections consist of the combined data needed to test an item for a certain quality. Inspections may be generated based on the master data or order-specific data.
 The structure of standard inspections is as follows:

```
 - Inspection by Origin 1
   General Data of Order Origin
       - Order 1
         Sample data
         (Test Groups by Quality ID          Data)
             - Line 1
Characteristic 1 (Characteristics by Quality ID (tcqms015) Data)
             - Line 2
Characteristic 2
       - Order 2
         Sample Data
             - Line 1
Characteristic 1
             - Line 2
Characteristic 2
 - Inspection by Origin 2
    ...
      etc.
```

Orders The order data of inspections consists of the sample data. For an inspection with different origins, more than one set of sample data may exist.
Lines The line of an inspection order is a combination of an aspect and a characteristic which will be tested on each sample.
SOURCE OF DATA
Inspection orders may be automatically generated in the following modules:
- Sales (SLS)
- Purchase (PUR)

- Production (SFC)
- Material (BOM)
- Routing (TI)
- Production (PMG)
- Material (FRM)
- Routing (PS)
- Storage Inspection

New inspection orders can also be entered manually in session "Maintain Inspection Orders (tcqms1100s000)".

APPLICATION OF DATA
Inspection orders are used in "Quality Management System (QMS)" to test items for characteristics.

1.142 Instruments (tcqms008)

DEFINITION
Instruments are tools which are used during tests to measure particular characteristics of items.

Example:

Instrument	Acidimeter
Characteristic	value

SOURCE OF DATA
- Maintain Test Instruments (tcqms0108m000)
- Enter Calibration Dates (tcqms3202m000)

APPLICATION OF DATA
- Maintain Characteristics (tcqms0101m000)
- Maintain Tests by Characteristic (tcqms0105m000)
- Maintain Tests by Quality ID (tcqms0117m000)
- Maintain Order-Specific Inspection Data (Lines) (tcqms0151s000)
- Maintain Inspection Order Lines (tcqms1101s000)
- Enter Test Data (tcqms1115m000)

1.143 Invoicing Methods (tcmcs055)

DEFINITION
Invoicing methods are defined to meet specific invoicing requirements your customers may make. Invoices may be created for each individual delivery or for all deliveries combined on one collective invoice.

SOURCE OF DATA
BAAN Common (tctc-20010): Maintain Invoicing Methods (tcmcs0155m000)
BAAN Project (tptp-20010): Maintain Invoicing Methods (tppdm8155m000)

APPLICATION OF DATA
BAAN Common (tctc-20010): Maintain Customers (tccom1101m000) Maintain Prospects (tccom1110m000)
BAAN Project (tptp-20010): Maintain Customers by Project (tppdm6101s000) Maintain Pro Forma Invoice (tppin4165m000)

1.144 Item Code IDs (tcedi232)

DEFINITION
An item code ID gives information about the coding system that has produced the item code. In EDIFACT, for instance:
- "SA" denotes a code determined by the supplier
- "ZZ" denotes a code determined in mutual consultation
- "EN" denotes coding according to EANCOM

SOURCE OF DATA
The data result from input or import in the session "Import EDI Data (tcedi6220m000)".

APPLICATION OF DATA
Item code IDs are used in:
- defining conversion data in the b-object "Coding and Conversion Data".

1.145 Item Code Systems (tcmcs027)

DEFINITION
Item code systems are external, alternative ways of coding items. They may be general standard systems (e.g. EAN) or specific customer or supplier dependent systems.

SOURCE OF DATA
BAAN Common (tctc-20010): Maintain Item Code Systems (tcmcs0127m000)

APPLICATION OF DATA
BAAN Common (tctc-20010): Maintain EDI MeBaanges Supported by Relations (tcedi0111m000) Maintain Item Code IDs (tcedi2132m000)
BAAN Distribution (tdtd-20010): Maintain Inquiry Parameters (tdpur1100m000) Maintain Inquiry Lines (tdpur1102s000) Enter Inquiry Results (tdpur1103m000) Copy Quoted Inquiry Lines to Purchase Order (tdpur1303s000) Process Quoted Inquiry Lines (tdpur1304s000) Maintain Purchase Contract Parameters (tdpur3100m000) Maintain Purchase Contract Lines (tdpur3102s000) Maintain Purchase Order Parameters (tdpur4100m000) Maintain Purchase Orders (Direct Delivery) (tdpur4102m000) Maintain Purchase Order Lines (tdpur4102s000)

Maintain Purchase Order (Direct Line Entry) (tdpur4105m000) Maintain Purchase Order Lines
(Wholesale) (tdpur4105s000) Maintain Purchase Order Lines (Fast Input) (tdpur4107m000)
Maintain Purchase Order Lines (Project) (tdpur4107s000) Maintain Back Orders
(tdpur4130m000) Calculate Additional Costs (tdpur4260s000) Calculate Purchase Order Line
Discounts (tdpur4802s000) Delete Purchase Order (tdpur4803s000) Recalculate Purchase
Price and Discount (tdpur4810s000) Maintain Purchase Order History Parameters
(tdpur5100m000) [SE@td
pur5100m000] Maintain Financial Integration Parameters (tdpur6100m000) Maintain Quotation
Parameters (tdsls1100m000) Maintain Quotation Lines (tdsls1102s000) Maintain Quotation
Lines (Wholesale) (tdsls1107s000) Enter Quotation Results (tdsls1108m000) Display Gross
Profit of Quotation Line (tdsls1808s000) Maintain Sales Contract Parameters
(tdsls3100m000) Maintain Sales Contract Lines (tdsls3102s000) Maintain Sales Order
Parameters (tdsls4100m000)
Maintain Sales Orders (Wholesale) (tdsls4102m000) Maintain Sales Order Lines
(tdsls4102s000) Maintain Sales Orders (Wholesale) (tdsls4105m000) Maintain Sales Order
Lines (Wholesale) (tdsls4105s000) Signal Inventory Shortages (tdsls4801s000) Calculate
Sales Order Line Discounts (tdsls4802s000) Display Gross Profit of Sales Order Line
(tdsls4808s000) Update Delivery Date in Sales Order Lines (tdsls4809s000) Recalculate
Sales Price and Discount (tdsls4810s000) Maintain Sales Order History Parameters
(tdsls5100m000) Maintain Financial Integration Parameters (tdsls6100m000)
BAAN Manufacturing (titi-20010): Maintain Item Codes by Item Code System (tiitm0112m000)
1.146 Item Groups (tcmcs023)
DEFINITION
Item groups are groups of items with common characteristics. They can be used in
combination with item types for storing various types of data. When you record items
belonging to a particular item type and group, the default values stored under the item
type/group will appear on the screen.
SOURCE OF DATA
BAAN Common (tctc-20010): Maintain Item Groups (tcmcs0123m000)
BAAN Manufacturing (titi-20010): Maintain Production Data by Item Group (tisfc1100m000)
APPLICATION OF DATA
BAAN Distribution (tdtd-20010): Maintain Storage Conditions by Item Group (tdilc0156m000)
Maintain Item Groups by Storage Condition (tdilc0157m000) Maintain Inventory and WIP
Transaction Accounts (tdinv8150m000) Maintain Purchase Orders (Direct Delivery)
(tdpur4102m000) Maintain Purchase Order (Direct Line Entry) (tdpur4105m000) Maintain
Purchase Order Lines (Fast Input) (tdpur4107m000) Maintain Back Orders (tdpur4130m000)
Calculate Additional Costs (tdpur4260s000) Calculate Purchase Order Line Discounts
(tdpur4802s000) Delete Purchase Order (tdpur4803s000) Recalculate Purchase Price and
Discount (tdpur4810s000) Copy BOM Components to Quotation (tdsls1812s000) Maintain Sales
Orders (Wholesale) (tdsls4102m000) Maintain Sales Orders (Wholesale) (tdsls4105m000)
Signal Inventory Shortages (tdsls4801s000) Calculate Sales Order Line Discounts
(tdsls4802s000) Display Gross Profit of Sales Order Line (tdsls4808s000) Update Delivery
Date in Sales Order Lines (tdsls4809s000) [SE@tds
ls4809s000] Recalculate Sales Price and Discount (tdsls4810s000) Maintain Invoice Details
Accounts (tdsls6102m000)
BAAN Finance (tftf-20010): Maintain ACP Parameters (tfacp0100m000) Maintain
Subcontracting Parameters (tfacp3100m000) Maintain Cost Objects (tfcal0104m000) Maintain
Imported Quantities (tfcal1105m000)
BAAN Manufacturing (titi-20010): Maintain Surcharges by Item Group (ticpr1110m000)
Maintain Surcharge Bases by Item Group (ticpr1120s000) Maintain Engineering Items
(tiedm0110m000) Maintain Item Data (GRT) (tigrt1180s000) Maintain Customized Item Data
(GRT) (tigrt2180s000) Maintain Item Data (tiitm0101m000) Maintain Item Data (in BOM)
(tiitm0108s000) Maintain Item Default Data (tiitm0110m000) Maintain Calculation Parts
(tipcs0110m000) Maintain Customized Item Data (tipcs2121m000)
BAAN Project (tptp-20010): Maintain Item Default Data (tppdm0109m000) Maintain Standard
Items (tppdm0110m000) Maintain Standard Equipment (tppdm0112m000) Maintain Standard
Subcontracting (tppdm0113m000) Maintain Project Items (tppdm6110m000) Maintain Project
Equipment (tppdm6112m000) Maintain Project Subcontracting (tppdm6113m000)
Maintain Supplier's Item Codes (tppdm7150m000)
BAAN Transportation (trtr-20010): Maintain Bill of Distribution (trdrp0110m000)
1.147 Item Status Indicators (tcedi210)
DEFINITION
The item status informs the supplier about the status of the item:
- new item
- obsolete item
- current item - production
- product design adjusted since previous delivery
- current item - spare parts
- etc.
SOURCE OF DATA

The data result from input or import in the session "Import EDI Data (tcedi6220m000)".
APPLICATION OF DATA
Item status indicators are used in:
• 	processing received meBaanges in the b-object "Communication".
1.148	Items by Quality Group (tcqms020)
DEFINITION
Quality groups are groups of items which have the same quality requirements. An item can belong to one quality group only.
SOURCE OF DATA
• 	Maintain Items by Quality Group (tcqms0120m000)
• 	Copy Item Range to Quality Group (tcqms0220s000)
APPLICATION OF DATA
Quality groups are used to link more than one item to a quality ID. These links are made by means of quality combinations.
• 	Maintain Quality Combinations (tcqms0111m000)
1.149	Languages (tcmcs046)
DEFINITION
Defining languages is neceBaanry in order to print (external) documents in the customer's, supplier's or employee's system language.
SOURCE OF DATA
BAAN Common (tctc-20010): Maintain Languages (tcmcs0146m000)
APPLICATION OF DATA
BAAN Common (tctc-20010): Maintain Company Data (tccom0100m000) Maintain Employees (tccom0101m000) Maintain Customers (tccom1101m000) Maintain Prospects (tccom1110m000) Maintain Suppliers (tccom2101m000) Maintain Units by Language (tcmcs0107m000)
BAAN Distribution (tdtd-20010): Maintain Inquiries (tdpur1101m000) Maintain Expiry Date for Returned Inquiry (tdpur1800s000) Enter Specific Inquiry Numbers (tdpur1820s000) Maintain Purchase Contracts (tdpur3101m000) Maintain Purchase Contract Status (tdpur3110m000) Copy Purchase Contracts (tdpur3801m000) Enter Specific Purchase Contract Numbers (tdpur3820s000) Maintain Purchase Orders (tdpur4101m000) Enter Specific Purchase Order Numbers (tdpur4820s000) Print Purchase Order Header History (tdpur5403m000) Maintain Quotations (tdsls1101m000) Delete Sales Quotation (tdsls1803s000) Maintain Delivery Date in Order Lines (tdsls1809s000) Enter Specific Quotation Numbers (tdsls1820s000) Maintain Sales Contracts (tdsls3101m000) Maintain Sales Contract Status (tdsls3110m000) Copy Sales Contracts (tdsls3801m000) Enter Specific Sales Contract Numbers (tdsls3820s000) Maintain Sales Orders (tdsls4101m000) Delete Sales Order (tdsls4803s000) Copy Bill of Material to Order (tdsls4812s000) Enter Specific Sales Order Numbers (tdsls4820s000)
Maintain Contacts by Relation (tdsmi1105m000)
BAAN Finance (tftf-20010): Maintain Reminder Data (tfacr3100m000) Maintain Reminder Line Layout (tfacr3101s000) Maintain Statement of Account Letters (tfacr3113m000) Maintain Statement of Account Variables (tfacr3114s000) Maintain Statement of Account Text (tfacr3115s000) Maintain Sales Invoice Header (tfacr4100m000) Maintain Interest Invoice Header Text (tfacr5103m000)
BAAN Manufacturing (titi-20010): Maintain Product Feature Descriptions (tipcf0151s000) Maintain Option Descriptions (tipcf0161s000) Maintain Product Feature Descriptions (tipcf1102s000) Maintain Option Descriptions (tipcf1111s000) Maintain Generic Price List Descriptions (tipcf4102s000)
BAAN Project (tptp-20010): Maintain HRS Parameters (tphrs0100m000) Maintain Customers by Project (tppdm6101s000) Maintain Employees (tppdm8101m000) Maintain Pro Forma Invoice (tppin4165m000)
BAAN Transportation (trtr-20010): Maintain Standard Descriptions (trtcd3100m000) Maintain Standard Descriptions (trtcd3101s000)
BAAN Service (tsts-20010): Maintain Contracts (tssma2120m000) Maintain Service Orders (tssma3101m000) Maintain Service Orders (Telephone Screen) (tssma3140m000) Maintain Service Orders (Planning) (tssma3141m000) Report Service Orders Completed (tssma3142m000) Close Service Orders (tssma3144m000) Display Service Orders (tssma3502s000) Enter Specific Service Order Numbers (tssma3820s000)
1.150	Late Payment Surcharges (tcmcs011)
DEFINITION
Late payment surcharges are used to encourage customers to pay timely. A late payment surcharge is a surcharge over the goods amount that must be paid by the recipient of the invoice if he fails to pay within the period specified. If he does pay in time, the surcharge may be subtracted from the invoice amount.
SOURCE OF DATA
BAAN Common (tctc-20010): Maintain Late Payment Surcharges (tcmcs0111m000)
APPLICATION OF DATA
BAAN Common (tctc-20010): Maintain Customers (tccom1101m000) Maintain Prospects (tccom1110m000) Maintain Suppliers (tccom2101m000) Maintain Conversion of Late Payment

Surcharges (in) (tcedi3130m00 0) Maintain Conversion of Late Payment Surcharges (out) (tcedi4170m0 00)

BAAN Distribution (tdtd-20010): Maintain Inquiries (tdpur1101m000) Maintain Expiry Date for Returned Inquiry (tdpur1800s000) Enter Specific Inquiry Numbers (tdpur1820s000) Maintain Purchase Contracts (tdpur3101m000) Maintain Purchase Contract Status (tdpur3110m000) Copy Purchase Contracts (tdpur3801m000) Enter Specific Purchase Contract Numbers (tdpur3820s000) Maintain Purchase Orders (tdpur4101m000) Enter Specific Purchase Order Numbers (tdpur4820s000) Print Purchase Order Header History (tdpur5403m000) Maintain Quotations (tdsls1101m000) Delete Sales Quotation (tdsls1803s000) Maintain Delivery Date in Order Lines (tdsls1809s000) Enter Specific Quotation Numbers (tdsls1820s000) Maintain Sales Contracts (tdsls3101m000) Maintain Sales Contract Status (tdsls3110m000) Copy Sales Contracts (tdsls3801m000) Enter Specific Sales Contract Numbers (tdsls3820s000) Maintain Sales Orders (tdsls4101m000) Delete Sales Order (tdsls4803s000) Copy Bill of Material to Order (tdsls4812s000) Enter Specific Sales Order Numbers (tdsls4820s000)

BAAN Finance (tftf-20010): Maintain Received Purchase Invoices (tfacp1100m000) Maintain Purchase Invoices (tfacp1110s000) Maintain Terms of Payment (tfacp1111s000) Match/Approve Purchase Invoices with Orders (tfacp1130m000) Approve Purchase Invoices (tfacp1140s000) Approve Price Differences (tfacp1142m000) Maintain Purchase Invoice Details (tfacp2100m000) Maintain Purchase Invoice Corrections (tfacp2110s000) Assign Credit Notes to Invoices (tfacp2120s000)

Assign Invoices to Credit Notes (tfacp2121s000)

Maintain Sales Invoices (tfacr1110s000) Maintain Terms of Payment (tfacr1112s000) Maintain Sales Invoice Details (tfacr2100m000) Maintain Sales Invoice Corrections (tfacr2110s000) Assign Credit Notes to Invoices (tfacr2120s000)

Assign Credit Notes to Invoices (tfacr2121s000)

Maintain Doubtful Sales Invoices (tfacr2140s000) Maintain Reminder Diary (tfacr3130m000) Maintain Sales Invoice Header (tfacr4100m000) Assign Unallocated/Advance Receipts to Invoices (tfcmg2105s000) Assign Unallocated/Advance Payments to Invoices (tfcmg2106s000) Maintain Customer Invoice Cash Date (tfcmg3110m000) Maintain Supplier Invoice Cash Date (tfcmg3111m000)

BAAN Project (tptp-20010): Maintain Customers by Project (tppdm6101s000) Maintain Pro Forma Invoice (tppin4165m000)

BAAN Transportation (trtr-20010): Maintain Transport Orders (trtoc1100m000) Maintain Transport Orders (trtoc1102s000) Maintain Standard Orders (trtoc3100m000) Maintain Storage Orders (trwoc1100m000) Maintain Storage Orders (Invoicing Data) (trwoc1106m000) Maintain Storage Orders (General Data) (trwoc1107m000) Maintain Inbound Orders (trwoc2100m000) Maintain Inbound Orders (trwoc2105s000) Maintain Outbound Orders (trwoc3100m000) Maintain Outbound Orders (trwoc3105s000) Maintain Transhipment Orders (trwoc4100m000) Maintain Transhipment Orders (trwoc4105s000) Maintain Assembly Orders (trwoc5100m000) Maintain Assembly Orders (Invoicing Data) (trwoc5106m000) Maintain Assembly Orders (General Data) (trwoc5107m000)

BAAN Service (tsts-20010): Maintain Contracts (tssma2120m000) Maintain Service Orders (tssma3101m000) Maintain Service Orders (Telephone Screen) (tssma3140m000) Maintain Service Orders (Planning) (tssma3141m000) Report Service Orders Completed (tssma3142m000) Close Service Orders (tssma3144m000) Display Service Orders (tssma3502s000) Enter Specific Service Order Numbers (tssma3820s000)

1.151 Lines of Business (tcmcs031)

DEFINITION

Lines of business are groups of customers and/or suppliers working in the same business sector. You can use lines of business as selection criteria when generating reports/inquiries of statistical or historical data.

SOURCE OF DATA

BAAN Common (tctc-20010): Maintain Lines of Business (tcmcs0131m000)

APPLICATION OF DATA

BAAN Common (tctc-20010): Maintain Customers (tccom1101m000) Maintain Prospects (tccom1110m000) Maintain Suppliers (tccom2101m000)

BAAN Distribution (tdtd-20010): Maintain Inquiries (tdpur1101m000) Maintain Expiry Date for Returned Inquiry (tdpur1800s000) Enter Specific Inquiry Numbers (tdpur1820s000) Maintain Purchase Orders (tdpur4101m000) Enter Specific Purchase Order Numbers (tdpur4820s000) Print Purchase Order Header History (tdpur5403m000) Maintain Quotations (tdsls1101m000) Delete Sales Quotation (tdsls1803s000) Maintain Delivery Date in Order Lines (tdsls1809s000) Enter Specific Quotation Numbers (tdsls1820s000) Maintain Sales Orders (tdsls4101m000) Delete Sales Order (tdsls4803s000) Copy Bill of Material to Order (tdsls4812s000) Enter Specific Sales Order Numbers (tdsls4820s000) Maintain Lines of Business by SMI Employee (tdsmi0193m000)

1.152 Link (BOM/Material, Routing/Operations) (tcqms012)

1.153 Log file conversion 3.x -> BAAN IV (tccon100)

1.154 MCS Parameters (tcmcs000)

DEFINITION

Parameters are variables to which a constant value is assigned. Changing parameter values will change the way in which the module operates, allowing you to adapt the module to the specific requirements of your company.

SOURCE OF DATA

First, running the session "Initialize Parameters (tcmcs0295m000)" will assign default values to the parameters, which can subsequently be modified in the parameter sessions.

1.155 Measurement Qualifiers (tcedi274)

DEFINITION

Measurement qualifiers specify the type of measurement a specific value refers to: gross size, gross weight, net weight.

SOURCE OF DATA

The data result from input or import in the session "Import EDI Data (tcedi6220m000)".

APPLICATION OF DATA

Measurement qualifiers are used in:
*   processing received meBaanges in the b-object "Communication".

1.156 MeBaange Functions (tcedi250)

DEFINITION

MeBaange functions are the various aims of meBaanges (by organization) - e.g.: acknowledgement, modification, addition, reminder, etc. The codes determine the meaning of a field in a received EDI meBaange.

SOURCE OF DATA

The data result from input or import in the session "Import EDI Data (tcedi6220m000)".

APPLICATION OF DATA

MeBaange function codes are used in:
*   processing received meBaanges in the b-object "Communication".

1.157 MeBaanges to be Generated (tcedi700)

DEFINITION

"MeBaanges to be Generated" are EDI meBaanges which are marked out for generating, but have not yet been included in ASCII files.

APPLICATION OF DATA

The file of "MeBaanges to be Generated" contains all documents that must be sent as EDI meBaange.

1.158 Miscellaneous descriptions (tccon167)

1.159 Multi-Company Batches to be Activated (tcedi711)

DEFINITION

The multicompany batches to be activated contain all company numbers for which meBaanges have been generated in a multicompany network.

SOURCE OF DATA

These company numbers are recorded in the case of a multicompany network (the field "Multicompany" is on "Yes"), and the field "Start Read Batch after Generating" is on "Yes".

APPLICATION OF DATA

The recorded company numbers are used to automatically process the meBaanges generated for a certain company in that company. For this purpose, the session "Common Session for Incoming MeBaanges (tcedi7220s000)" is started in the company in question.

1.160 Multiple Tax Rates (tcmcs033)

DEFINITION

The tax rate consists of multiple percentages.

SOURCE OF DATA

BAAN Common (tctc-20010): Maintain Multiple Tax Rates (tcmcs0133s000)

1.161 Networks (tcedi020)

DEFINITION

Networks manage the various data flows, for instance, communication through a Value Added Network (VAN) via an EDI-converter, or directly, without translation, to a sister company using the same software.

SOURCE OF DATA

The data result from input or import in the session "Import EDI Data (tcedi6220m000)".

APPLICATION OF DATA

Networks are used in:
*   creating combinations of meBaanges and relations in the b-object "EDI Master Data";
*   defining connection schedules in the b-object "Networks";
*   recording relation identifications by network in the b-object "Networks";
*   recording the networks with which your company will communicate (in the session "EDI Interchange Controller (tcedi7210m000)" and in the b-object Communication").

1.162 Option Sets (tcqms013)

DEFINITION

Options sets are groups of options. Several option sets can be used for one characteristic.

  Example:
  Characteristic

```
  Option Set                      ption
  COLOR                   Characteristic Color
  WIDTH                   Characteristic Width
```

SOURCE OF DATA
•   Maintain Option Sets (tcqms0113m000)
APPLICATION OF DATA
•   Maintain Options (tcqms0114m000)
•   Maintain Characteristics by Quality ID (tcqms0115m000)
•   Maintain Order-Specific Inspection Data (Lines) (tcqms0151s000)
•   Maintain Inspection Order Lines (tcqms1101s000)
1.163 Options (tcqms014)
DEFINITION
Options represent the possible values of a characteristic and are grouped in option sets.
For each option, it is possible to indicate whether it is acceptable or not.
  Example:
```
  Characteristic                 Value
  Test                     Litmus Test

  Options:      Blue            Acceptable
Red             Not Acceptable
```
SOURCE OF DATA
•   Maintain Options (tcqms0114m000)
APPLICATION OF DATA
•   Enter Test Data (tcqms1115m000)
1.164 Order Steps (tcmcs039)
DEFINITION
Order steps are sessions which may be included in specific order procedures, with some
additional features. By defining a session as an order step you mark it as a possible
step in a procedure. These steps can be arranged in a certain sequence; you can also
indicate when each step may be executed.
The order steps can be used for various order types, using the session:
•   Maintain Order Types (tcmcs0142m000)
The following order steps have been pre-defined in BAAN IV:
```
 Step  |Purchase Control (PUR)
 No.   |
 ------+-------------------------------------------------------------
 1     |Print Purchase Orders (tdpur4401m000)
 2     |Print Goods Received Notes (tdpur4410m000)
 3     |Maintain Receipts (tdpur4120m000)
 4     |Print Claims (tdpur4420m000)
 5     |Maintain Approvals (tdpur4121m000)
 6     |Print Storage Lists (tdpur4421m000)
 7     |Print Return Notes (tdpur4411m000)
 8     |Print Purchase Invoices (tdpur4404m000)
 9     |Process Delivered Purchase Orders (tdpur4223m000)


 Step  |Sales Control (SLS)
 No.   |
 ------+-------------------------------------------------------------
 1     |Print Order Acknowledgements (tdsls4401m000)
 2     |Print Picking Lists (tdsls4402m000)
 3     |Maintain Deliveries (tdsls4120m000)
 4     |Print Packing Slips (tdsls4403m000)
 5     |Print Bills of Lading (tdsls4421m000)
 6     |Print Sales Invoices (tdsls4404m000)
 8     |Generate Outbound Advice (tdilc4201m000)
```

SOURCE OF DATA

```
 BAAN Common            :
 Maintain Order Steps (tcmcs0139m000)
```
1.165 Order Types (tcedi200)
DEFINITION
Order types determine the character or function of an order and consequently, of the
meBaange.
  Examples:
  Normal order versus return order
  Invoice   versus credit note

APPLICATION OF DATA
Order types are used in:
•   recording supported meBaanges by relation in the b-object "EDI Master Data".
1.166 Order Types (tcmcs042)
DEFINITION
Order types are predefined procedures for processing orders. Order types determine which
order steps will be subsequently run in order to process a purchase or sales order.
The following pre-defined order types are available:

```
Order Type                 : PC1
Description                : Collect Order                    1
Purchase/Sales               Purchase
Cost Order                 : No
Return Order               : No
Collect Order [TFtcmcs042.coun: Yes
Subcontracting Order [TFtcmcs0:2No
Procedure                  :
- Print Purchase Invoices (tdpur4404m000)
- Process Delivered Purchase Orders (tdpur4223m000)

Order Type                 : PC2
Description                : Collect Order                    2
Purchase/Sales               Purchase
Cost Order                 : No
Return Order               : No
Collect Order [TFtcmcs042.coun: Yes
Subcontracting Order [TFtcmcs0:2No
Procedure                  :
- Print Goods Received Notes (tdpur4410m000)
- Print Purchase Invoices (tdpur4404m000)
- Process Delivered Purchase Orders (tdpur4223m000)

Order Type                 : PCS
Description                : Cost Order
Purchase/Sales               Purchase
Cost Order                 : Yes
Return Order               : No
Collect Order [TFtcmcs042.coun: No
Subcontracting Order [TFtcmcs0:2No
Procedure                  :
- Print Purchase Invoices (tdpur4404m000)
- Process Delivered Purchase Orders (tdpur4223m000)

Order Type                 : PN1
Description                : Warehouse Order                  1
Purchase/Sales               Purchase
Cost Order                 : No
Return Order               : No
Collect Order [TFtcmcs042.coun: No
Subcontracting Order [TFtcmcs0:2No
Procedure                  :
- Print Purchase Orders (tdpur4401m000)
- Print Goods Received Notes (tdpur4410m000)
- Maintain Receipts (tdpur4120m000)
- Print Claims (tdpur4420m000)
- Maintain Approvals (tdpur4121m000)
- Print Return Notes (tdpur4411m000)
- Print Purchase Invoices (tdpur4404m000)
- Process Delivered Purchase Orders (tdpur4223m000)

Order Type                 : PN2
Description                : Warehouse Order                  2
Purchase/Sales               Purchase
Cost Order                 : No
Return Order               : No
Collect Order [TFtcmcs042.coun: No
Subcontracting Order [TFtcmcs0:2No
Procedure                  :
- Print Purchase Orders (tdpur4401m000)
- Maintain Receipts (tdpur4120m000)
```

```
- Print Claims (tdpur4420m000)
- Maintain Approvals (tdpur4121m000)
- Print Storage Lists (tdpur4421m000)
- Print Return Notes (tdpur4411m000)
- Print Purchase Invoices (tdpur4404m000)
- Process Delivered Purchase Orders (tdpur4223m000)

Order Type               : PN3
Description              : Warehouse Order                    3
Purchase/Sales            Purchase
Cost Order               : No
Return Order             : No
Collect Order [TFtcmcs042.coun: No
Subcontracting Order [TFtcmcs0:2No
Procedure                :
- Maintain Receipts (tdpur4120m000)
- Print Claims (tdpur4420m000)
- Maintain Approvals (tdpur4121m000)
- Print Storage Lists (tdpur4421m000)
- Print Return Notes (tdpur4411m000)
- Print Purchase Invoices (tdpur4404m000)
- Process Delivered Purchase Orders (tdpur4223m000)

Order Type               : PN4
Description              : Warehouse Order                    4
Purchase/Sales            Purchase
Cost Order               : No
Return Order             : No
Collect Order [TFtcmcs042.coun: No
Subcontracting Order [TFtcmcs0:2No
Procedure                :
- Maintain Receipts (tdpur4120m000)
- Print Claims (tdpur4420m000)
- Maintain Approvals (tdpur4121m000)
- Print Return Notes (tdpur4411m000)
- Print Picking Lists (tdsls4402m000)
- Print Purchase Invoices (tdpur4404m000)
- Process Delivered Purchase Orders (tdpur4223m000)

Order Type               : PR1
Description              : Return Order
Purchase/Sales            Purchase
Cost Order               : No
Return Order             : Yes
Collect Order [TFtcmcs042.coun: Yes
Subcontracting Order [TFtcmcs0:2No
Procedure                :
- Print Purchase Invoices (tdpur4404m000)
- Process Delivered Purchase Orders (tdpur4223m000)

Order Type               : PS1
Description              : Subcontracting Order
Purchase/Sales            Purchase
Cost Order               : No
Return Order             : No
Collect Order [TFtcmcs042.coun: No
Subcontracting Order [TFtcmcs0:2Yes
Procedure                :
- Print Purchase Orders (tdpur4401m000)
- Print Goods Received Notes (tdpur4410m000)
- Maintain Receipts (tdpur4120m000)
- Print Claims (tdpur4420m000)
- Maintain Approvals (tdpur4121m000)
- Print Storage Lists (tdpur4421m000)
- Print Return Notes (tdpur4411m000)
- Print Purchase Invoices (tdpur4404m000)
- Process Delivered Purchase Orders (tdpur4223m000)

Order Type               : SC1
Description              : Collect Order                      1
```

```
Purchase/Sales              Sales
Cost Order                : No
Return Order              : No
Collect Order [TFtcmcs042.coun: Yes
Subcontracting Order [TFtcmcs0:2No
Procedure                 :
- Print Sales Invoices (tdsls4404m000)
- Process Delivered Sales Orders (tdsls4223m000)


Order Type                : SC2
Description               : Collect Order              2
Purchase/Sales              Sales
Cost Order                : No
Return Order              : No
Collect Order [TFtcmcs042.coun: Yes
Subcontracting Order [TFtcmcs0:2No
Procedure                 :
- Print Packing Slips (tdsls4403m000)
- Print Sales Invoices (tdsls4404m000)
- Process Delivered Sales Orders (tdsls4223m000)


Order Type                : SC3
Description               : Collect Order              3
Purchase/Sales              Sales
Cost Order                : No
Return Order              : No
Collect Order [TFtcmcs042.coun: Yes
Subcontracting Order [TFtcmcs0:2No
Procedure                 :
- Print Picking Lists (tdsls4402m000)
- Print Packing Slips (tdsls4403m000)
- Print Sales Invoices (tdsls4404m000)
- Process Delivered Sales Orders (tdsls4223m000)


Order Type                : SCS
Description               : Cost Order
Purchase/Sales              Sales
Cost Order                : Yes
Return Order              : No
Collect Order [TFtcmcs042.coun: No
Subcontracting Order [TFtcmcs0:2No
Procedure                 :
- Maintain Deliveries (tdsls4120m000)
- Print Sales Invoices (tdsls4404m000)
- Process Delivered Sales Orders (tdsls4223m000)


Order Type                : SN1
Description               : Warehouse Order            1
Purchase/Sales              Sales
Cost Order                : No
Return Order              : No
Collect Order [TFtcmcs042.coun: No
Subcontracting Order [TFtcmcs0:2No
Procedure                 :
- Print Order Acknowledgements (tdsls4401m000)
- Print Picking Lists (tdsls4402m000)
- Maintain Deliveries (tdsls4120m000)
- Print Packing Slips (tdsls4403m000)
- Print Bills of Lading (tdsls4421m000)
- Print Sales Invoices (tdsls4404m000)
- Process Delivered Sales Orders (tdsls4223m000)


Order Type                : SN2
Description               : Warehouse Order            2
Purchase/Sales              Sales
Cost Order                : No
Return Order              : No
Collect Order [TFtcmcs042.coun: No
Subcontracting Order [TFtcmcs0:2No
Procedure                 :
```

```
        - Print Picking Lists (tdsls4402m000)
        - Maintain Deliveries (tdsls4120m000)
        - Print Packing Slips (tdsls4403m000)
        - Print Bills of Lading (tdsls4421m000)
        - Print Sales Invoices (tdsls4404m000)
        - Process Delivered Sales Orders (tdsls4223m000)

        Order Type              : SN3
        Description             : Warehouse Order              3
        Purchase/Sales            Sales
        Cost Order              : No
        Return Order            : No
        Collect Order [TFtcmcs042.coun: No
        Subcontracting Order [TFtcmcs0:2No
        Procedure               :
        - Print Picking Lists (tdsls4402m000)
        - Maintain Deliveries (tdsls4120m000)
        - Print Packing Slips (tdsls4403m000)
        - Print Sales Invoices (tdsls4404m000)
        - Process Delivered Sales Orders (tdsls4223m000)

        Order Type              : SN4
        Description             : Warehouse Order              4
        Purchase/Sales            Sales
        Cost Order              : No
        Return Order            : No
        Collect Order [TFtcmcs042.coun: No
        Subcontracting Order [TFtcmcs0:2No
        Procedure               :
        - Print Picking Lists (tdsls4402m000)
        - Maintain Deliveries (tdsls4120m000)
        - Print Sales Invoices (tdsls4404m000)
        - Process Delivered Sales Orders (tdsls4223m000)

        Order Type              : SR1
        Description             : Return Order
        Purchase/Sales            Sales
        Cost Order              : No
        Return Order            : Yes
        Collect Order [TFtcmcs042.coun: Yes
        Subcontracting Order [TFtcmcs0:2No
        Procedure               :
        - Print Sales Invoices (tdsls4404m000)


SOURCE OF DATA

BAAN Common            :
Maintain Order Types (tcmcs0142m000)


APPLICATION OF DATA

BAAN Common            :
Maintain EDI MeBaanges Supported by Relations (tcedi0111m000)
Maintain Conversion of Order Types (out) (tcedi4132m000)


BAAN Distribution        :
Maintain Inquiries (tdpur1101m000)
Maintain Expiry Date for Returned Inquiry (tdpur1800s000)
Enter Specific Inquiry Numbers (tdpur1820s000)
Maintain Purchase Orders (tdpur4101m000)
Maintain Defaults by User (Purchase) (tdpur4123m000)
Enter Specific Purchase Order Numbers (tdpur4820s000)
Print Purchase Order Header History (tdpur5403m000)
Maintain Margin Control Parameters (tdsls0120m000)
Maintain Quotations (tdsls1101m000)
Delete Sales Quotation (tdsls1803s000)
Maintain Delivery Date in Order Lines (tdsls1809s000)
Enter Specific Quotation Numbers (tdsls1820s000)
Maintain Sales Orders (tdsls4101m000)
Maintain Defaults by User (Sales) (tdsls4123m000)
```

```
Delete Sales Order (tdsls4803s000)
Copy Bill of Material to Order (tdsls4812s000)
Enter Specific Sales Order Numbers (tdsls4820s000)
```

```
BAAN Service                    :
Maintain Order Types (tssma3103m000)
```

1.167 Order-Specific Inspection Data (Header) (tcqms050)

DEFINITION

Order-specific inspection data refers to customized master data. The use of order-specific data is optional.

1. These inspections are based on the master data and can be
                   customized for a particular order.
2. The customized data cannot be influenced by changes in the
                   master data. This is useful when there are, for example, a
                   number of samples over a period of time.

```
  The structure of order-specific inspections:

  - Order-Specific Inspection 1
    General Data of Order Origin
       - Header 1
         Sample Data
         (Test Groups by Quality ID            Data)
            - Line 1
              Characteristic 1
              (Characteristics by Quality ID           Data)
            - Line 2
              Characteristic 2
     - Header 2
       Sample Data
       (Test Groups by Quality ID            Data)
            - Line 1
              Characteristic 1
            - Line 2
              Characteristic 2
  - Order-Specific Inspection 2
    ...
     etc.
```

Header The header data of order-specific inspections consists of the sample data. For one order from the various origins, more than one set of sample data may exist.

Lines The line of an inspection is a combination of an aspect and a characteristic which will be tested on each sample.

SOURCE OF DATA

Order-specific inspection data can be maintained in the following sessions:

Header & Lines
•   Maintain Order-Specific Inspections (tcqms0149m000)
•   Maintain Order-Specific Inspection Data (Header) (tcqms0150s000)
•   Maintain Order-Specific Inspection Data (Lines) (tcqms0151s000)

Order-specific inspection date can be updated collectively by means of session "Global Update of Order-Specific Inspection Data (tcqms0250m000)".

Order-specific inspection data may originate from different origins, namely:

BAAN Distribution
•   Maintain Purchase Orders (Direct Delivery) (tdpur4102m000)
•   Maintain Purchase Order Lines (tdpur4102s000)
•   Maintain Sales Orders (Wholesale) (tdsls4102m000)
•   Maintain Sales Order Lines (tdsls4102s000)

BAAN Manufacturing
•   Maintain Production Orders (tisfc0101m000)
•   Maintain Estimated Materials (tisfc0110m000)
•   Enter Material Issue for Production Orders (ticst0101m000)
•   Maintain Production Planning (tisfc1101m000)

BAAN Process
•   Maintain Production Batches (pspmg0101m000)
•   Maintain Estimated Materials (pspmg0110m000)
•   Enter Material Issue for Production Batches (pspmg0111m000)
•   Maintain Estimated End Items (pspmg0113m000)
•   Maintain Estimated Co- and By-Products (pspmg0112m000)
•   Maintain Estimated Batch Planning (pspmg2100m000)

APPLICATION OF DATA

Based on this data, standard inspection orders can be generated.
1.168 Order-Specific Inspection Data (Lines) (tcqms051)
DEFINITION
Order-specific inspection data refers to customized master data. The use of order-specific data is optional.
1. These inspections are based on the master data and can be
                    customized for a particular order.
2. The customized data cannot be influenced by changes in the
                    master data. This is useful when there are, for example, a
                    number of samples over a period of time.

   The structure of order-specific inspections:

   - Order-Specific Inspection 1
     General Data of Order Origin
         - Header 1
           Sample Data
           (Test Groups by Quality ID   Data)
               - Line 1
                 Characteristic 1
                 (Characteristics by Quality ID   Data)
               - Line 2
                 Characteristic 2
         - Header 2
           Sample Data
           (Test Groups by Quality ID   Data)
               - Line 1
                 Characteristic 1
               - Line 2
                 Characteristic 2
   - Order-Specific Inspection 2
     ...
     etc.

Header The header data of order-specific inspections consists of the sample data. For one order from the various origins, more than one set of sample data may exist.
Lines The line of an inspection is a combination of an aspect and a characteristic which will be tested on each sample.
SOURCE OF DATA
Order-specific inspection data can be maintained in the following sessions:
Header & Lines
•   Maintain Order-Specific Inspections (tcqms0149m000)
•   Maintain Order-Specific Inspection Data (Header) (tcqms0150s000)
•   Maintain Order-Specific Inspection Data (Lines) (tcqms0151s000)
Order-specific inspection date can be updated collectively by means of session "Global Update of Order-Specific Inspection Data (tcqms0250m000)".
Order-specific inspection data may originate from different origins, namely:
BAAN Distribution
•   Maintain Purchase Orders (Direct Delivery) (tdpur4102m000)
•   Maintain Purchase Order Lines (tdpur4102s000)
•   Maintain Sales Orders (Wholesale) (tdsls4102m000)
•   Maintain Sales Order Lines (tdsls4102s000)
BAAN Manufacturing
•   Maintain Production Orders (tisfc0101m000)
•   Maintain Estimated Materials (tisfc0110m000)
•   Enter Material Issue for Production Orders (ticst0101m000)
•   Maintain Production Planning (tisfc1101m000)
BAAN Process
•   Maintain Production Batches (pspmg0101m000)
•   Maintain Estimated Materials (pspmg0110m000)
•   Enter Material Issue for Production Batches (pspmg0111m000)
•   Maintain Estimated End Items (pspmg0113m000)
•   Maintain Estimated Co- and By-Products (pspmg0112m000)
•   Maintain Estimated Batch Planning (pspmg2100m000)
APPLICATION OF DATA
Based on this data, standard inspection orders can be generated.
1.169 Order-Specific Inspections (tcqms049)
DEFINITION
Order-specific inspection data refers to customized master data. The use of order-specific data is optional.

1. These inspections are based on the master data and can be
                         customized for a particular order.
2. The customized data cannot be influenced by changes in the
                         master data. This is useful when there are, for example, a
                         number of samples over a period of time.

   The structure of order-specific inspections:

   - Order-Specific Inspection 1
     General Data of Order Origin
         - Header 1
           Sample Data
           (Test Groups by Quality ID   Data)
               - Line 1
                 Characteristic 1
                 (Characteristics by Quality ID   Data)
               - Line 2
                 Characteristic 2
         - Header 2
           Sample Data
           (Test Groups by Quality ID   Data)
               - Line 1
                 Characteristic 1
               - Line 2
                 Characteristic 2
   - Order-Specific Inspection 2
     ...
       etc.

Header The header data of order-specific inspections consists of the sample data. For one
order from the various origins, more than one set of sample data may exist.
Lines The line of an inspection is a combination of an aspect and a characteristic which
will be tested on each sample.
SOURCE OF DATA
Order-specific inspection data can be maintained in the following sessions:
Header & Lines
•   Maintain Order-Specific Inspections (tcqms0149m000)
•   Maintain Order-Specific Inspection Data (Header) (tcqms0150s000)
•   Maintain Order-Specific Inspection Data (Lines) (tcqms0151s000)
Order-specific inspection date can be updated collectively by means of session "Global
Update of Order-Specific Inspection Data (tcqms0250m000)".
Order-specific inspection data may originate from different origins, namely:
BAAN Distribution
•   Maintain Purchase Orders (Direct Delivery) (tdpur4102m000)
•   Maintain Purchase Order Lines (tdpur4102s000)
•   Maintain Sales Orders (Wholesale) (tdsls4102m000)
•   Maintain Sales Order Lines (tdsls4102s000)
BAAN Manufacturing
•   Maintain Production Orders (tisfc0101m000)
•   Maintain Estimated Materials (tisfc0110m000)
•   Enter Material Issue for Production Orders (ticst0101m000)
•   Maintain Production Planning (tisfc1101m000)
BAAN Process
•   Maintain Production Batches (pspmg0101m000)
•   Maintain Estimated Materials (pspmg0110m000)
•   Enter Material Issue for Production Batches (pspmg0111m000)
•   Maintain Estimated End Items (pspmg0113m000)
•   Maintain Estimated Co- and By-Products (pspmg0112m000)
•   Maintain Estimated Batch Planning (pspmg2100m000)
APPLICATION OF DATA
Based on this data, standard inspection orders can be generated.
1.170 Organizations (tcedi003)
DEFINITION
Organizations represent a set of standards used in communication through EDI.
SOURCE OF DATA
The data result from input or import in the session "Import EDI Data (tcedi6220m000)".
APPLICATION OF DATA
Organizations are used in:
•   maintaining meBaanges supported by your own application and by your trade relations
in the b-object "EDI Master Data";

- maintaining outgoing meBaanges by session in the b-object "EDI Master Data";
- maintaining (additional) code tables and conversion tables in the b-object "Coding and Conversion Data";
- printing and maintaining additional code tables in the b-object "Coding and Conversion Data";
- deleting item code conversion data by relation the b-object "Coding and Conversion Data";
- maintaining and printing conversion setups in the b-object "Coding and Conversion Data".
- printing mapping information in the b-object "Coding and Conversion Data";
- printing and displaying generated meBaanges (history) in the b-object "EDI History".

1.171 Outgoing MeBaanges by Session (tcedi015)

DEFINITION

Outgoing meBaanges by session are those (outgoing) meBaanges, with the associated organizations, which are produced by specific BAAN IV sessions.

SOURCE OF DATA

The data result from input or import in the session "Import EDI Data (tcedi6220m000)".

APPLICATION OF DATA

Outgoing meBaanges by session are produced in the modules:
- Purchase Control (PUR)
- Sales Control (SLS)
- Transport Order Control (TOC)
- Accounts Payable (ACP)

1.172 Packing Code IDs (tcedi214)

DEFINITION

Packing code IDs record (by organization) packing codes and the associated descriptions, e.g.:
- box
- pallet
- etc.

SOURCE OF DATA

The data result from input or import in the session "Import EDI Data (tcedi6220m000)".

APPLICATION OF DATA

Packing code IDs are used in:
- processing received meBaanges in the b-object "Communication".

1.173 Parameters (tcmcs095)

DEFINITION

Parameters are variables which are assigned a constant value. Changing parameter values will change the way in which the module operates, allowing you to adapt the module to the specific requirements of your company.

SOURCE OF DATA

First, running session "Initialize Parameters (tcmcs0295m000)" will assign default values to the parameters, which can subsequently be modified in the parameter sessions.

SOURCE OF DATA

BAAN Distribution (tdtd-20010):

Maintain ILC Parameters (tdilc0100m000) Maintain LTC Parameters (tdltc0100m000) Maintain Inquiry Parameters (tdpur1100m000) Maintain Purchase Contract Parameters (tdpur3100m000) Maintain Purchase Order Parameters (tdpur4100m000) Maintain Purchase Orders (tdpur4110m000) Maintain Purchase Order History Parameters (tdpur5100m000) Maintain Financial Integration Parameters (tdpur6100m000) Maintain Replenishment Orders (tdrpl0105m000) Maintain Quotation Parameters (tdsls1100m000) Maintain Sales Contract Parameters (tdsls3100m000) Maintain Sales Order Parameters (tdsls4100m000) Maintain Sales Orders (tdsls4110m000) Maintain Sales Order History Parameters (tdsls5100m000)

1.174 Payer's 1099 Details (tccom937)

DEFINITION

Payer's 1099 Details include various pieces of information required by the IRS for printing of 1099-MISC paper forms and generation of 1099-MISC magnetic/electronic filing.

1.175 Payment Schedules (tcmcs014)

DEFINITION

Payment schedules are agreements about the amounts to be paid by payment period. They are part of the terms of payment.

Example:
1st period: 20% of invoice to be paid in 30 days
2nd period: 35% of invoice to be paid in 90 days
3rd period: 45% of invoice to be paid within 105 days

SOURCE OF DATA

BAAN Common   :
Maintain Payment Schedules (tcmcs0114m000)
1.176 Periods (tcedi236)
DEFINITION
Periods record period codes and the associated descriptions (by organization) - e.g.:
days, weeks, quarters, etc.
SOURCE OF DATA
The data result from input or import in the session "Import EDI Data (tcedi6220m000)".
APPLICATION OF DATA
Periods are used in:
•   processing received meBaanges in the b-object "Communication".
1.177 Planning Board Groups 1 (tccom500)
DEFINITION
Planning board groups are used to define the layout, colors and font of the graphical
planning board.
SOURCE OF DATA
BAAN Common (tctc-20010): Maintain Planning Board Groups (tccom5101m000) Maintain
Planning Board Groups (tccom5105m000)
APPLICATION OF DATA
Maintain PSS Parameters (tppss0100m000)
BAAN Project (tptp-20010): Maintain Plans (tppss0110m000)
1.178 Plus/Minus Indicators (tcedi272)
DEFINITION
Plus/minus indicators add a plus or minus sign to a value.
SOURCE OF DATA
The data result from input or import in the session "Import EDI Data (tcedi6220m000)".
APPLICATION OF DATA
Plus/minus indicators are used in:
•   processing received meBaanges in the b-object "Communication".
1.179 Positions, Sequence numbers to be Generated (tcedi708)
This table stores the position numbers for "Positions, Sequence numbers to be Generated",
corresponding to the line items to be generated.
1.180 Price Groups (tcmcs024)
DEFINITION
Price groups are groups of items which have the same prices/discounts. These price groups
can be linked to customers and suppliers.
SOURCE OF DATA
BAAN Common (tctc-20010): Maintain Price Groups (tcmcs0124m000)
APPLICATION OF DATA
BAAN Distribution (tdtd-20010): Maintain Discounts by Supplier and Price Group
(tdpur0102m000) Maintain Discounts by Supplier (tdpur0103m000) Maintain Discounts by
Price List and Price Group (tdpur0105m000) Maintain Discounts by Price List
(tdpur0106m000) Maintain Discount Parameters by Supplier and Price Group (tdpur01 07s000)
Maintain Discount Parameters by Price List and Price Group (tdpur 0108s000) Maintain
Discount Parameters by Supplier (tdpur0110s000) Maintain Discount Parameters by Price
List (tdpur0112s000) Maintain Purchase Contract Lines (tdpur3102s000) Maintain Discounts
by Customer and Price Group (tdsls0102m000) Maintain Discounts by Customer
(tdsls0103m000) Maintain Discounts by Price List and Price Group (tdsls0105m000) Maintain
Discounts by Price List (tdsls0106m000) Maintain Discount Parameters by Customer and
Price Group (tdsls01 07s000) Maintain Discount Parameters by Price List and Price Group
(tdsls 0108s000) Maintain Discount Parameters by Customer (tdsls0110s000) Maintain
Discount Parameters by Price List (tdsls0112s000) [SE@td
sls0112s000] Copy BOM Components to Quotation (tdsls1812s000) Maintain Sales Contract
Lines (tdsls3102s000)
BAAN Manufacturing (titi-20010): Maintain Item Data (GRT) (tigrt1180s000) Maintain Item
Data (tiitm0101m000) Maintain Item Data (in BOM) (tiitm0108s000) Maintain Item Default
Data (tiitm0110m000)
BAAN Project (tptp-20010): Maintain Suppliers by Estimate Price Group (tpbop4120m000)
Maintain Item Default Data (tppdm0109m000) Maintain Standard Items (tppdm0110m000)
Maintain Standard Equipment (tppdm0112m000) Maintain Standard Subcontracting
(tppdm0113m000) Maintain Price Group Contracts by Estimate (tppdm4121m000) Maintain Price
Group Contracts by Project (tppdm6121m000)
BAAN Transportation (trtr-20010): Maintain General Items (trtcd1110m000) Maintain General
Items (Fast Input) (trtcd1111s000) Maintain Cost Sets by Price Group (trtco0120m000)
Maintain Transport Means Groups (trtfm1100m000)
Maintain Third-Party Items (trtpi1100m000) Maintain Blocking of Third-Party Items
(trtpi1101m000) Maintain Transport Rate Codes by Price Group (trtrc1120m000) Maintain
Locations (trwic1100m000) Maintain Blocking Statuses of Locations (trwic1101m000)
Maintain Storage Orders (trwoc1100m000) Maintain Storage Orders (Invoicing Data)

(trwoc1106m000) Maintain Storage Orders (General Data) (trwoc1107m000) Maintain
Warehousing Rate Codes by Price Group (trwrc1130m000)

1.181 Price Lists (tcmcs034)

DEFINITION

Price lists serve to identify groups of customers. Price lists are just one of the levels
at which prices and discounts are recorded in the system.

SOURCE OF DATA

BAAN Common (tctc-20010): Maintain Price Lists (tcmcs0134m000)

APPLICATION OF DATA

BAAN Common (tctc-20010): Maintain Customers (tccom1101m000) Maintain Prospects
(tccom1110m000) Maintain Suppliers (tccom2101m000)

BAAN Distribution (tdtd-20010): Maintain Prices by Price List and Item (tdpur0104m000)
Maintain Discounts by Price List and Price Group (tdpur0105m000) Maintain Discounts by
Price List (tdpur0106m000) Maintain Discount Parameters by Supplier and Price Group
(tdpur01 07s000) Maintain Discount Parameters by Price List and Price Group (tdpur
0108s000) Maintain Discount Parameters by Supplier (tdpur0110s000) Maintain Discount
Parameters by Price List (tdpur0112s000) Maintain Prices by Item (tdpur0113m000) Maintain
Inquiries (tdpur1101m000) Maintain Expiry Date for Returned Inquiry (tdpur1800s000) Enter
Specific Inquiry Numbers (tdpur1820s000) Maintain Purchase Orders (tdpur4101m000)
Maintain Costs Set by Purchase Price List by Supplier (tdpur4127m 000) Print Cost Sets by
Purchase Price List and Supplier (tdpur4427m00 0) Enter Specific Purchase Order Numbers
(tdpur4820s000) Print Purchase Order Header History (tdpur5403m000) Maintain Prices by
Price List and Item (tdsls0104m000) Maintain Discounts by Price List and Price Group
(tdsls0105m000) Maintain Discounts by Price List (tdsls0106m000) Maintain Discount
Parameters by Customer and Price Group (tdsls01 07s000) Maintain Discount Parameters by
Price List and Price Group (tdsls 0108s000) Maintain Discount Parameters by Customer
(tdsls0110s000) Maintain Discount Parameters by Price List (tdsls0112s000) Maintain
Prices by Item (tdsls0113m000) Maintain Quotations (tdsls1101m000) Delete Sales Quotation
(tdsls1803s000) Maintain Delivery Date in Order Lines (tdsls1809s000) Enter Specific
Quotation Numbers (tdsls1820s000) Maintain Sales Orders (tdsls4101m000) Maintain Costs
Set by Sales Price List and Customer (tdsls4127m00 0) Delete Sales Order (tdsls4803s000)
Copy Bill of Material to Order (tdsls4812s000) Enter Specific Sales Order Numbers
(tdsls4820s000)

BAAN Transportation (trtr-20010): Maintain Cost Sets by Price List (trtco0130m000)
Compare Subcontracting Costs (trtco1190m000) Compare Subcontracting Costs (trtco1191s000)
Maintain Transport Rate Codes by Price List (trtrc1130m000) Maintain Rate Codes by
Subcontractor Price List (trtrc1180m000) Maintain Warehousing Rate Codes by Price List
(trwrc1120m000)

BAAN Service (tsts-20010): Maintain Contracts (tssma2120m000)

1.182 Product Category (tccom938)

DEFINITION

Product categories enable the tax provider to compute tax based on the type of products
which are bought or sold. For example, it is common within the United States for
materials to be taxable and labor to be non-taxable. The product categories defined
should match the product categories defined within the external tax provider.

APPLICATION OF DATA

The above data is relevant for the following packages/modules:

BAAN Common
- Common Data (COM)
- Tables (MCS)

BAAN Distribution
- Location Control (ILC)
- Purchase Control (PUR)
- Sales Control (SLS)

BAAN Finance
- Accounts Payable (ACP)
- Accounts Receivable (ACR)
- Cash Management (CMG)
- General Ledger (GLD)

BAAN Manufacturing
- Product Configuration (PCF)
- Project Control (PCS)

BAAN Service
- BAAN Service Master Data (tssma10010)
- Service Contract Control (tssma10030)

1.183 Product Category Tax Matrix (tccom939)

DEFINITION

A product category tax matrix is used to associate a specific product category with a
range of items, item groups, contract types, GL accounts, and effectivity dates.

For tax calculations, the product category is determined based upon the item bought or sold, the contract type for service contracts, and the GL account specified for Finance transactions. For item-based transactions a series of lookups is performed. The product category tax matrix is searched by effectivity date and item code. If no product category is specified for the item and date, the product category is searched again using the item group associated to the item. For Vertex users, if no product category is found for either the item or the item's item group and effectivity date, the item code itself is passed to the tax provider as the product category. Otherwise, the product category is set to blanks.

APPLICATION OF DATA

The above data is relevant for the following packages/modules:

BAAN Common
*   Common Data (COM)
*   Tables (MCS)

BAAN Distribution
*   Location Control (ILC)
*   Purchase Control (PUR)
*   Sales Control (SLS)

BAAN Finance
*   Accounts Payable (ACP)
*   Accounts Receivable (ACR)
*   Cash Management (CMG)
*   General Ledger (GLD)

BAAN Manufacturing
*   Product Configuration (PCF)
*   Project Control (PCS)

BAAN Service
*   BAAN Service Master Data (tssma10010)
*   Service Contract Control (tssma10030)

1.184 Product Types (tcmcs015)

DEFINITION

Product types are a sorting and selecting criterion for items.

SOURCE OF DATA

BAAN Common (tctc-20010): Maintain Product Types (tcmcs0115m000)

APPLICATION OF DATA

BAAN Distribution (tdtd-20010): Copy BOM Components to Quotation (tdsls1812s000)

BAAN Manufacturing (titi-20010): Maintain Engineering Items (tiedm0110m000) Maintain Item Data (GRT) (tigrt1180s000) Maintain Item Data (tiitm0101m000) Maintain Item Data (in BOM) (tiitm0108s000) Maintain Item Default Data (tiitm0110m000)

BAAN Project (tptp-20010): Maintain Item Default Data (tppdm0109m000) Maintain Standard Items (tppdm0110m000)

1.185 Production Schedule Types (tcedi212)

1.186 QMS Parameters (tcqms000)

DEFINITION

Parameters are used to control the general features within QMS and the integrations with other modules and packages.

SOURCE OF DATA

*   Maintain QMS Parameters (tcqms0100m000)

APPLICATION OF DATA

Parameters are used to control "Quality Management System (QMS)".

1.187 Quality Combinations (tcqms011)

DEFINITION

Quality combinations indicate the relationships between items in specific situations (i.e. the origin) and the quality requirements by means of a quality ID.

Quality combinations consist, generally speaking, of three parts:
*   the module from which the inspection originates;
*   the item(s) which apply to the combination;
*   the quality ID which applies to the combination.

Defining the desired quality for an item can be done at several levels.

  Example:
  It is possible to define a combination of:

  a "Quality Group" and a "Quality ID"
 (general); a "Customer" and a "Quality ID"
 (specific); an "Item" and a "Quality ID"
 (specific).

Consequently, all customized items are included when a combination is made of that project, an origin, and a certain quality ID.

SOURCE OF DATA

- Maintain Quality Combinations (tcqms0111m000)

APPLICATION OF DATA

Quality combinations are used in several modules of BAAN IV", namely:
- Purchase Control (PUR)
- Sales Control (SLS)
- Shop Floor Control (SFC)
- Production Management (PMG)

1.188 Quality Groups (tcmcs029)

DEFINITION

Quality groups are groups of items with common quality characteristics. The data defined for the quality group are used as defaults for all items of that quality group.

SOURCE OF DATA

BAAN Common (tctc-20010):
- Maintain Quality Groups (tcmcs0129m000)

APPLICATION OF DATA

BAAN Common (tctc-20010):
- Maintain Quality Combinations (tcqms0111m000)
- Maintain Items by Quality Group (tcqms0120m000) [SE@tcqms0120m0 00]
- Copy Item Range to Quality Group (tcqms0220s000) [SE@tcqms0220s 000]

1.189 Quality IDs (tcqms010)

DEFINITION

Quality IDs are used to indicate certain quality requirements. All data neceBaanry to check these quality requirements is attached to a quality ID. The final link to the item(s) is made by means of quality combinations.

    Example:

    Quality ID
    - High quality
    - ID4500.1

SOURCE OF DATA
- Maintain Quality IDs (tcqms0110m000)

APPLICATION OF DATA
- Maintain Quality Combinations (tcqms0111m000)
- Maintain Characteristics by Quality ID (tcqms0115m000)
- Maintain Tests by Quality ID (tcqms0117m000)
- Maintain Test Groups by Quality ID (tcqms0136m000)
- Maintain Characteristics by Test Group (tcqms0137m000)
- Maintain Inspection Orders (tcqms1100s000)

1.190 Reasons for Rejection (tcmcs005)

DEFINITION

Reasons for rejection are the potential reasons for rejecting goods received from suppliers.

SOURCE OF DATA

BAAN Common (tctc-20010): Maintain Reasons for Rejection (tcmcs0105m000)

APPLICATION OF DATA

BAAN Distribution (tdtd-20010): Maintain Receipts (tdpur4120m000) Maintain Approvals (tdpur4121m000) Change Prices/Discounts after 'Maintain Receipts' (tdpur4122m000) Select Receipts (tdpur4131s000)

BAAN Finance (tftf-20010): Match Receipts (tfacp1131s000)

BAAN Common (tctc-20010): Maintain Standard Inspections by Origin (tcqms1120m000) Maintain Storage Inspections (tcqms2120m000)

1.191 Reasons for Tax Exemptions (tcmcs941)

DEFINITION

Some customers may be exempt from sales tax in certain jurisdictions. Reason codes are used to group these exemptions into like categories for reporting purposes.

1.192 Received Batch Reference (tcedi760)

DEFINITION

Incoming EDI meBaanges that are stored within the system are assigned a unique identifier (batch reference number). This batch reference number is associated with a particular network for traceability and for historical analysis.

SOURCE OF DATA

Batch references are created when running the session "Common Session for Incoming MeBaanges (tcedi7220s000)".

1.193 Received MeBaange Errors (tcedi751)

DEFINITION

This table contains the errors/warnings that resulted from the processing of incoming EDI meBaanges.

SOURCE OF DATA

These meBaanges were generated by the session "Common Session for Incoming MeBaanges (tcedi7220s000)".

APPLICATION OF DATA

The erroneous data can be viewed or maintained using the session "Maintain Saved MeBaanges to be Received (tcedi7150m000)". From that session, the meBaange data as well as the associated errors/warnings can be viewed by zooming to the session "Display Received MeBaange Errors (tcedi7551s000)". MeBaange data can be modified in the session "Maintain Saved MeBaange Data to be Received (tcedi7151s000)".

After approving the meBaange in the session "Approve Saved MeBaanges to be Received (tcedi7250m000)", the saved EDI meBaange can be re-processed by means of the session "Process Saved MeBaanges to be Received (tcedi7252m000)".

1.194 Received MeBaanges (tcedi702)

DEFINITION

The received meBaanges comprise the most important header data of meBaanges that have been sent by relations, and successfully processed and updated into the Baan application for which they were destined.

SOURCE OF DATA

These meBaanges result from executing the session "Common Session for Incoming MeBaanges (tcedi7220s000)".

1.195 Reference Multi-Company MeBaanges (tcedi712)

DEFINITION

This table holds the options that are available to zoom from the field "New Contents" in the session "Maintain Errors Saved MeBaanges (tcedi7104s000)" to the session or menu defined here.

1.196 Reference Number Types (tcedi220)

DEFINITION

Reference number types indicate the document associated with a particular number, for instance:
- "ON" Order Number
- "WB" Waybill Number

SOURCE OF DATA

The data result from input or import in the session "Import EDI Data (tcedi6220m000)".

APPLICATION OF DATA

Reference number types are used in:
- defining conversion data in the b-object "Coding and Conversion Data".

1.197 Reference Order Line Numbers (tcedi705)

1.198 Relation Structure for Outgoing MeBaanges (tcedi030)

DEFINITION

Relation structures for outgoing meBaanges are used to collect meBaanges for different relations and send them to a parent relation.

1.199 Relations (tcedi010)

DEFINITION

Relations are business relations with whom you exchange electronic data. A relation may be linked to a customer and/or a supplier.

APPLICATION OF DATA

Relations are used in:
- indicating which meBaanges are supported by specific relations in in the b-object "EDI Master Data";
- maintaining and printing relation identifications by network in the b-object "Networks";
- defining relation-specific conversions (for instance of item codes, addresses, warehouses, sales contract codes, etc) in the b-object "Coding and Conversion Data".

1.200 Relations by Network (tcedi028)

DEFINITION

Network identifications are the codes/network addresses by which relations can be identified by network.

APPLICATION OF DATA

In case of incoming meBaanges, network addresses are used to find out which relation is involved.

In case of outgoing meBaanges, the right network address for the relation is inserted in the meBaange. For outgoing meBaanges you can state when a new reference number must be generated.

1.201 Rounding Codes (tcmcs053)

DEFINITION

Rounding codes identify different ways to round off quantities and amounts.

SOURCE OF DATA

BAAN Common (tctc-20010): Maintain Rounding Codes (tcmcs0153m000)

APPLICATION OF DATA

Maintain Estimate Data (tppdm4100m000)

1.202 Routes (tcmcs004)
DEFINITION
Routes are pathways leading from one trade relation to another. Routes allow you to group trade relations based within the same area or along one convenient route.
Arranging addresses in routes enables picking lists and shipping notes to be printed sorted by route.
SOURCE OF DATA
BAAN Common (tctc-20010): Maintain Routes (tcmcs0104m000)
APPLICATION OF DATA
BAAN Common (tctc-20010): Maintain Customers (tccom1101m000) Maintain Delivery Addresses (tccom1102m000) Maintain Prospects (tccom1110m000)
BAAN Distribution (tdtd-20010): Maintain Quotations (tdsls1101m000) Maintain Specific Delivery Address (Quotations) (tdsls1103s000) Maintain Specific Postal Address (Quotations) (tdsls1104s000) Delete Sales Quotation (tdsls1803s000) Maintain Delivery Date in Order Lines (tdsls1809s000) Enter Specific Quotation Numbers (tdsls1820s000) Maintain Specific Delivery Address (Sales Contract) (tdsls3103s00 0) Maintain Specific Postal Address (Sales Contract) (tdsls3104s000)
Maintain Sales Orders (tdsls4101m000) Maintain Specific Delivery Address (Sales Order) (tdsls4103s000) Maintain Specific Postal Address (Sales Order) (tdsls4104s000) Delete Sales Order (tdsls4803s000) Copy Bill of Material to Order (tdsls4812s000) Enter Specific Sales Order Numbers (tdsls4820s000)
BAAN Transportation (trtr-20010): Maintain Standard Routes (trtop2100m000)
1.203 Sales Listing Data (tccom700)
DEFINITION
Sales Listings are lists with information about the nature, origin, value etc. of invoices. Companies established in EU-countries are obliged to use this document to make a tax declaration for their goods transactions within the EU.
SOURCE OF DATA
BAAN Common (tctc-20010): Maintain Sales Listing (tccom7170m000)
1.204 Samples (tcqms110)
DEFINITION
Samples are small quantities which are drawn from the total (order) quantity and are intended to show the quality of the entire order quantity.

    Example:
    Inspection Order   : 1000000001
    Sample Unit   :   pcs Piece
    Sample Size   :   100

    Sample   Date   Quantity [TF@tcqmssqua]
    ----
    1   22/11/1995   11:23:00   20 pcs
    2   24/11/1995   09:12:05   30 pcs
    3   28/11/1995   09:01:30   50 pcs

                                      Total   : 100 pcs

SOURCE OF DATA
•   Maintain Samples (tcqms1110m000)
•   Maintain Samples (Storage Inspections) (tcqms2110m000)
APPLICATION OF DATA
•   Enter Test Data (tcqms1115m000)
1.205 Samples History (tcqms310)
DEFINITION
The history of the samples drawn for inspection orders which are written to the inspection order history.
1.206 Saved MeBaanges to be Received (tcedi750)
DEFINITION
This table contains the saved EDI meBaange data that is read when processing incoming EDI meBaanges.
SOURCE OF DATA
The EDI meBaange data was saved by the session "Common Session for Incoming MeBaanges (tcedi7220s000)", instead of being updated into the BAAN IV application for which the meBaange is destined, for one of the following reasons:
1. Errors
                    Errors occurred during the validation process. The erred data
                    must be corrected prior to re-processing the meBaange.

2. Interactive Review

The meBaange for the relation is setup for interactive review, in which case the data must be approved prior to validating and processing the meBaange.

APPLICATION OF DATA
The data can be viewed and maintained by means of the session "Maintain Saved MeBaanges to be Received (tcedi7150m000)". After approval in the session "Approve Saved MeBaanges to be Received (tcedi7250m000)", the saved EDI meBaange can be re-processed by means of the session "Process Saved MeBaanges to be Received (tcedi7252m000)".
Once the saved meBaange is successfully processed and updated into the BAAN IV application for which it is destined, the saved meBaange is deleted from this file. If you desire to never process the meBaange, you may delete the meBaange by means of the session "Print and/or Delete Saved MeBaanges to be Received (tcedi7251m000)".

1.207 Schedule Release Categories (tcedi208)
DEFINITION
Schedule release categories indicate if a schedule must be regarded as an adaptation of or substitute for a previous schedule.
There are two possibilities:
*   replace the previous instruction as from the date and time indicated
*   adjust the previous instruction before the date and time indicated
During conversion, schedule release categories can be recorded in text fields.
SOURCE OF DATA
The data result from input or import in the session "Import EDI Data (tcedi6220m000)".
APPLICATION OF DATA
Schedule release categories are used in:
*   processing received meBaanges in the b-object
                "Communication".

1.208 Schedule Release Frequencies (tcedi202)
DEFINITION
Schedule release frequencies are schedules indicating the frequency with which the goods will be delivered. During conversion, these schedules can be recorded in text fields.
SOURCE OF DATA
The data result from input or import in the session "Import EDI Data (tcedi6220m000)".
APPLICATION OF DATA
Schedule release frequency codes are used in:
*   processing received meBaanges in the b-object "Communication".

1.209 Schedule Status Indicators (tcedi206)
DEFINITION
Schedule statuses inform the supplier about the degree to which the customer commits himself and hence, add an instruction to an order.
*   Firm order   : means that the supplier may deliver
*   Fabrication   : means that the supplier may start production
*   Raw material : means that the supplier may buy raw materials
During conversion, schedule statuses may be recorded in text fields.
SOURCE OF DATA
The data result from input or import in the session "Import EDI Data (tcedi6220m000)".
APPLICATION OF DATA
Schedule status indicators are used in:
*   processing received meBaanges in the b-object "Communication".

1.210 Seasonal Patterns (tcmcs016)
DEFINITION
Seasonal patterns define the fluctuation of certain values in the course of a year. They serve as parameters in forecast and advice functions.
SOURCE OF DATA
BAAN Common (tctc-20010): Maintain Seasonal Patterns (tcmcs0116m000)
APPLICATION OF DATA
BAAN Distribution (tdtd-20010): Maintain Items by Warehouse (tdinv0101m000) Copy BOM Components to Quotation (tdsls1812s000)
BAAN Manufacturing (titi-20010): Maintain Item Data (GRT) (tigrt1180s000) Maintain Item Data (tiitm0101m000) Maintain Item Data (in BOM) (tiitm0108s000) Maintain Item Default Data (tiitm0110m000) Maintain Plan Items (timps2101m000)
BAAN Project (tptp-20010): Maintain Item Default Data (tppdm0109m000) Maintain Standard Items (tppdm0110m000)

1.211 Select Tax Jurisdiction/ Temporary File (tccom900)

1.212 Selection Codes (tcmcs022)
DEFINITION
Selection codes are a selection criterion for items - in this way they can be selected by color, diameter, product expiry date, etc. They are merely informative in character.
SOURCE OF DATA
BAAN Common (tctc-20010): Maintain Selection Codes (tcmcs0122m000)

APPLICATION OF DATA

BAAN Distribution (tdtd-20010): Copy BOM Components to Quotation (tdsls1812s000)

BAAN Manufacturing (titi-20010): Maintain Engineering Items (tiedm0110m000) Maintain Item Data (GRT) (tigrt1180s000) Maintain Customized Item Data (GRT) (tigrt2180s000) Maintain Item Data (tiitm0101m000) Maintain Item Data (in BOM) (tiitm0108s000) Maintain Item Default Data (tiitm0110m000) Maintain Calculation Parts (tipcs0110m000) Maintain Customized Item Data (tipcs2121m000)

BAAN Project (tptp-20010): Maintain Item Default Data (tppdm0109m000) Maintain Standard Items (tppdm0110m000) Maintain Standard Equipment (tppdm0112m000) Maintain Standard Subcontracting (tppdm0113m000) Maintain Project Items (tppdm6110m000) Maintain Project Equipment (tppdm6112m000) Maintain Project Subcontracting (tppdm6113m000)

1.213 Shipment/Order Discrepancies (tcedi296)

DEFINITION

Shipment/order discrepancies explain the difference between ordered and delivered quantities, for instance:
- partial delivery with backorder
- partial delivery without backorder

The table states the possibilities for each organization by means of a code and a description.

SOURCE OF DATA

Data may result from:
- manual input of data
- importing data in the session "Import EDI Data (tcedi6220m000)"

APPLICATION OF DATA

Shipment/order discrepancy codes are used in:
- creating conversion tables for terms of payment in the b-object "Coding and Conversion Data"

1.214 Shipper-Supplied Equipment Indicators (tcedi282)

DEFINITION

The shipper-supplied equipment indicator indicates if the equipment is or is not provided by the shipper (principal).

SOURCE OF DATA

The data result from input or import in the session "Import EDI Data (tcedi6220m000)".

APPLICATION OF DATA

Shipper-supplied equipment indicator are used in:
- processing received meBaanges in the b-object "Communication".

1.215 Signals (tcmcs018)

DEFINITION

Signals are meBaanges appearing on the screen when you enter an item to which a signal code is linked. Signals can also be used to block the issue and/or requisition of goods.

SOURCE OF DATA

BAAN Common (tctc-20010): Maintain Signal Codes (tcmcs0118m000)

APPLICATION OF DATA

BAAN Distribution (tdtd-20010): Copy BOM Components to Quotation (tdsls1812s000)

BAAN Manufacturing (titi-20010): Maintain Engineering Items (tiedm0110m000) Maintain Item Data (GRT) (tigrt1180s000) Maintain Item Data (tiitm0101m000) Maintain Item Data (in BOM) (tiitm0108s000) Maintain Item Default Data (tiitm0110m000)

BAAN Project (tptp-20010): Maintain Item Default Data (tppdm0109m000) Maintain Standard Items (tppdm0110m000) Maintain Standard Equipment (tppdm0112m000) Maintain Standard Subcontracting (tppdm0113m000)

1.216 Single Tax Rates (tcmcs032)

DEFINITION

The tax rate consists of a single, flat percentage.

SOURCE OF DATA

BAAN Common (tctc-20010): Maintain Single Tax Rates (tcmcs0132s000)

1.217 Skills (tcmcs030)

DEFINITION

The special abilities of employees.

SOURCE OF DATA

BAAN Common (tctc-20010): Maintain Skills (tcmcs0130m000)

APPLICATION OF DATA

BAAN Common (tctc-20010): Maintain Characteristics (tcqms0101m000) Maintain Tests by Characteristic (tcqms0105m000) Maintain Test Instruments (tcqms0108m000) Maintain Tests by Quality ID (tcqms0117m000) Maintain Order-Specific Inspection Data (Lines) (tcqms0151s000) Maintain Inspection Order Lines (tcqms1101s000) Enter Calibration Dates (tcqms3202m000)

1.218 States (tcmcs943)

DEFINITION

Countries are the national states where your suppliers and customers are based. For each country, such data is available as the international dialing, telex and fax codes. Countries are used to compile statistical turnover surveys and in financial data reporting.

SOURCE OF DATA

BAAN Common (tctc-20010): Maintain Countries (tcmcs0110m000)

APPLICATION OF DATA

BAAN Common (tctc-20010): Maintain Company Data (tccom0100m000) Maintain Customers (tccom1101m000) Maintain Delivery Addresses (tccom1102m000) Maintain Customer Postal Addresses (tccom1103m000) Maintain Prospects (tccom1110m000) Maintain Suppliers (tccom2101m000) Maintain Supplier Postal Addresses (tccom2103m000) Maintain Import/Export Statistics (tccom7171m000) Maintain Conversion of Country Codes (in) (tcedi3102m000) Maintain Conversion of Tax Codes (in) (tcedi3108m000) Maintain Conversion of Country Codes (out) (tcedi4140m000) Maintain Conversion of Tax Codes (out) (tcedi4146m000) Maintain Warehouses (tcmcs0103m000) Maintain Credit Insurance Companies (tcmcs0109m000) Maintain Bank Addresses (tcmcs0120m000) Maintain Factoring Companies (tcmcs0125m000) Maintain Single Tax Rates (tcmcs0132s000) Maintain Multiple Tax Rates (tcmcs0133s000) Maintain Tax Rates by Tax Code (tcmcs0135s000) Maintain Tax Codes by Country (tcmcs0136m000)

BAAN Distribution (tdtd-20010): Maintain Inquiries (tdpur1101m000) Maintain Inquiry Lines (tdpur1102s000) Enter Inquiry Results (tdpur1103m000) Copy Quoted Inquiry Lines to Purchase Order (tdpur1303s000) Process Quoted Inquiry Lines (tdpur1304s000) Maintain Expiry Date for Returned Inquiry (tdpur1800s000) Enter Specific Inquiry Numbers (tdpur1820s000) Maintain Purchase Contracts (tdpur3101m000) Maintain Purchase Contract Lines (tdpur3102s000) Maintain Specific Delivery Address (Purchase Contract) (tdpur3103 s000) Maintain Specific Postal Address (Purchase Contract) (tdpur3104s0 00) Maintain Purchase Contract Status (tdpur3110m000) Copy Purchase Contracts (tdpur3801m000) Enter Specific Purchase Contract Numbers (tdpur3820s000) Maintain Purchase Orders (tdpur4101m000) Maintain Purchase Orders (Direct Delivery) (tdpur4102m000) Maintain Specific Delivery Address (Purchase Order) (tdpur4103s00 0) Maintain Specific Postal Address (Purchase Order) (tdpur4104s000)

Maintain Purchase Order (Direct Line Entry) (tdpur4105m000) Maintain Purchase Order Lines (Fast Input) (tdpur4107m000) Maintain Back Orders (tdpur4130m000) Calculate Additional Costs (tdpur4260s000) Calculate Purchase Order Line Discounts (tdpur4802s000) Delete Purchase Order (tdpur4803s000) Recalculate Purchase Price and Discount (tdpur4810s000) Enter Specific Purchase Order Numbers (tdpur4820s000) Print Purchase Order Header History (tdpur5403m000) Maintain Quotations (tdsls1101m000) Maintain Quotation Lines (tdsls1102s000) Maintain Specific Delivery Address (Quotations) (tdsls1103s000) Maintain Specific Postal Address (Quotations) (tdsls1104s000) Maintain Quotation Lines (Wholesale) (tdsls1107s000) Delete Sales Quotation (tdsls1803s000) Display Gross Profit of Quotation Line (tdsls1808s000) Maintain Delivery Date in Order Lines (tdsls1809s000) Copy BOM Components to Quotation (tdsls1812s000) Enter Specific Quotation Numbers (tdsls1820s000) Maintain Sales Contracts (tdsls3101m000) Maintain Sales Contract Lines (tdsls3102s000) Maintain Specific Delivery Address (Sales Contract) (tdsls3103s00 0) Maintain Specific Postal Address (Sales Contract) (tdsls3104s000)

Maintain Sales Contract Status (tdsls3110m000) Copy Sales Contracts (tdsls3801m000) Enter Specific Sales Contract Numbers (tdsls3820s000) Maintain Sales Orders (tdsls4101m000) Maintain Specific Delivery Address (Sales Order) (tdsls4103s000) Maintain Specific Postal Address (Sales Order) (tdsls4104s000) Maintain Installment Data (tdsls4106s000) Delete Sales Order (tdsls4803s000) Copy Bill of Material to Order (tdsls4812s000) Enter Specific Sales Order Numbers (tdsls4820s000) Maintain Invoice Analysis Accounts (tdsls6101m000) Maintain Invoice Analysis Accounts by Tax Code (tdsls6103m000)

BAAN Finance (tftf-20010): Maintain One-Time Supplier Addresses (tfacp1102m000) Maintain Purchase Invoices (tfacp1110s000) Maintain Terms of Payment (tfacp1111s000) Maintain Tax Transactions (tfacp1112s000) Maintain Purchase Invoice Transactions (tfacp1120s000) Match/Approve Purchase Invoices with Orders (tfacp1130m000) Approve Purchase Invoices (tfacp1140s000) Approve Price Differences (tfacp1142m000) Maintain Purchase Invoice Details (tfacp2100m000) Maintain Purchase Invoice Corrections (tfacp2110s000) Assign Credit Notes to Invoices (tfacp2120s000)

Assign Invoices to Credit Notes (tfacp2121s000)

Maintain One-Time Customer Addresses (tfacr1102s000) Maintain Sales Invoices (tfacr1110s000) Maintain Sales Invoice Transactions (tfacr1111s000) Maintain Terms of Payment (tfacr1112s000) Maintain Sales Invoice Details (tfacr2100m000) Maintain Sales Invoice Corrections (tfacr2110s000) Assign Credit Notes to Invoices (tfacr2120s000) Assign Credit Notes to Invoices (tfacr2121s000)

Maintain Doubtful Sales Invoices (tfacr2140s000) Maintain Reminder Diary (tfacr3130m000) Maintain Sales Invoice Header (tfacr4100m000) Maintain Sales Invoice Lines (tfacr4101s000) Maintain Posting Data by Tax Code (tfcmg0150m000) Maintain One-Time Supplier Addresses (tfcmg1101m000) Maintain Standing Orders (tfcmg1110m000) Maintain Posting Data of Standing Orders/Stand Alone Paym. (tfcmg 1113m000) Maintain Bank

Transactions (tfcmg2100s000) Assign Unallocated/Advance Receipts to Invoices (tfcmg2105s000) Assign Unallocated/Advance Payments to Invoices (tfcmg2106s000) Maintain Anticipated Payments (Details) (tfcmg2116s000) Maintain Anticipated Receipts (Details) (tfcmg2117s000) Maintain Cash Management Transactions (tfcmg2120s000) Maintain Customer Invoice Cash Date (tfcmg3110m000) Maintain Supplier Invoice Cash Date (tfcmg3111m000) Maintain Posting Data of Electronic Bank Statements (tfcmg5106s00 0) Maintain Relations by Tax Position (tfgld0121m000) Assign Protocol Numbers to Documents (tfgld0235m000) [SE@tfgld023

5m000] Maintain Journal Vouchers (tfgld1103s000) Change Document Details (tfgld1104s000) Maintain Opening Balances (tfgld1105s000) Maintain Journal Vouchers (Summarized) (tfgld1114s000) Maintain Journal Vouchers (Multiple Lines) (tfgld1115s000)

BAAN Manufacturing (titi-20010): Maintain Item Data (GRT) (tigrt1180s000) Maintain Customized Item Data (GRT) (tigrt2180s000) Maintain Item Data (tiitm0101m000) Maintain Item Data (in BOM) (tiitm0108s000) Maintain Item Default Data (tiitm0110m000) Maintain Customized Item Data (tipcs2121m000)

BAAN Project (tptp-20010): Maintain Item Default Data (tppdm0109m000) Maintain Standard Items (tppdm0110m000) Maintain Third Parties (tppdm0132m000) Maintain Estimate Data (tppdm4100m000) Maintain Archived Estimates (tppdm5190m000) Maintain Projects (tppdm6100m000) Maintain Customers by Project (tppdm6101s000) Maintain Project Status (tppdm6107m000) Maintain Project Items (tppdm6110m000) Maintain Archived Projects (tppdm7190m000) Maintain Pro Forma Invoice (tppin4165m000) Maintain Specific Invoice Addresses (tppin4166m000)

BAAN Transportation (trtr-20010): Maintain Sequence of Printing Address Data (tracs0110m000) Maintain Number of ZIP Code Characters by Country (tracs0120m000) Maintain Defaults by ZIP Code (tracs0130m000) Maintain Addresses (tracs1100m000) Maintain Addresses (Fast Input) (tracs1101s000)

Maintain Distance Table by ZIP Code (tracs4110m000) Maintain Fuel Refills (trcde1120s000) Maintain Expenses (trcde1140s000) Maintain Employee Data (trecs1100m000) Maintain Daily Reports (Expenses) (trhec3120s000) Maintain Financial Parameters (Invoice Analysis) (trics0110m000) Maintain Countries of Establishment (trtcd0102m000) Maintain Fuel Intake (trtfc2100m000) Maintain Fuel Intake from FINANCE (trtfc2102s000) Check Fuel Intake Bills (trtfc2110m000) Maintain Finished Activities (trtfm4100m000) Maintain Finished Activities (from FINANCE) (trtfm4102s000) Split Order Lines (trtoc1103s000) Standard Session for Transport Order Lines (All Data) (trtoc1180m 000) Maintain Transport Order Lines (trtoc1181m000) Maintain Transport Order Lines (trtoc1182m000) Maintain Transport Order Lines (trtoc1183m000) Maintain Transport Order Lines (trtoc1184m000) Maintain Transport Order Lines (trtoc1185m000) Maintain Transport Order Lines (trtoc1186m000) Maintain Transport Order Lines (trtoc1187m000) Maintain Transport Order Lines (trtoc1188m000) Maintain Document Lines (trtoc1189s000) Maintain Transport Order Lines (trtoc1190m000) Maintain Transport Order Lines (trtoc1191m000)

Maintain Standard Order Lines (trtoc3101m000) Maintain ZIP Codes by Standard Route (trtop2110m000) Maintain Storage Orders (trwoc1100m000) Maintain Storage Orders (Invoicing Data) (trwoc1106m000) Maintain Storage Orders (General Data) (trwoc1107m000) Maintain Assembly Orders (trwoc5100m000) Maintain Assembly Orders (Invoicing Data) (trwoc5106m000) Maintain Assembly Orders (General Data) (trwoc5107m000)

BAAN Service (tsts-20010): Maintain Service Orders (tssma3101m000) Maintain Specific Postal Address (Service) (tssma3102s100) Maintain Actual Service Order Costs and Revenues (tssma3110m000) Maintain Service Orders (Telephone Screen) (tssma3140m000) Maintain Service Orders (Planning) (tssma3141m000) Report Service Orders Completed (tssma3142m000) Close Service Orders (tssma3144m000) Maintain Service Order Cost Estimate (tssma3170m000) Display Service Orders (tssma3502s000) Enter Specific Service Order Numbers (tssma3820s000) Maintain Accounts for Invoice Analyses (tssma6106m000)

1.219 Statistics Groups (tcmcs044)

DEFINITION

Statistics groups are groups of items for which statistical information is collected and represented, e.g. using the session "Print Purchase Statistics (tdpst0401m000)" or "Print Sales Statistics (tdsst0401m000)".

SOURCE OF DATA

BAAN Common (tctc-20010): Maintain Statistics Groups (tcmcs0144m000)

APPLICATION OF DATA

BAAN Distribution (tdtd-20010): Maintain Purchase Orders (Direct Delivery) (tdpur4102m000) Maintain Purchase Order (Direct Line Entry) (tdpur4105m000) Maintain Purchase Order Lines (Fast Input) (tdpur4107m000) Maintain Back Orders (tdpur4130m000) Calculate Additional Costs (tdpur4260s000) Calculate Purchase Order Line Discounts (tdpur4802s000) Delete Purchase Order (tdpur4803s000) Recalculate Purchase Price and Discount (tdpur4810s000) Copy BOM Components to Quotation (tdsls1812s000) Maintain Sales Orders (Wholesale) (tdsls4102m000) Maintain Sales Orders (Wholesale) (tdsls4105m000) Signal Inventory Shortages (tdsls4801s000) Calculate Sales Order Line Discounts (tdsls4802s000) Display Gross Profit of Sales Order Line (tdsls4808s000) Update Delivery

Date in Sales Order Lines (tdsls4809s000) Recalculate Sales Price and Discount
(tdsls4810s000)
BAAN Manufacturing (titi-20010): Maintain Item Data (GRT) (tigrt1180s000) Maintain
Customized Item Data (GRT) (tigrt2180s000) Maintain Item Data (tiitm0101m000) Maintain
Item Data (in BOM) (tiitm0108s000) Maintain Item Default Data (tiitm0110m000) Maintain
Customized Item Data (tipcs2121m000)
BAAN Project (tptp-20010): Maintain Item Default Data (tppdm0109m000) Maintain Standard
Items (tppdm0110m000) Maintain Standard Equipment (tppdm0112m000) Maintain Standard
Subcontracting (tppdm0113m000) Maintain Project Items (tppdm6110m000) Maintain Project
Equipment (tppdm6112m000) Maintain Project Subcontracting (tppdm6113m000)
1.220 Statuses (tcmcs096)
Auxiliary table.
1.221 Storage Inspection History (tcqms302)
DEFINITION
Contains data about inspections of origin "Storage Inspection" which are posted to
history.
APPLICATION OF DATA
Contains details of accepted and rejected inventory as well as the actuals.
For more information, see session:
• Display Sample History (Storage Inspections) (tcqms4510m000)
1.222 Supplier Balances by Company (tccom021)
1.223 Supplier Postal Addresses (tccom022)
DEFINITION
Postal addresses are the addresses that are used to send correspondence to.
SOURCE OF DATA
BAAN Common (tctc-20010): Maintain Customer Postal Addresses (tccom1103m000)
BAAN Common (tctc-20010): Maintain Customer Postal Addresses (tccom1103s000)
APPLICATION OF DATA
BAAN Common (tctc-20010): Maintain Customers (tccom1101m000) Maintain Prospects
(tccom1110m000) Maintain Conversion of Postal Address Codes by Customer (in) (tce
di3112m000) Maintain Conv. of Postal Address Codes by Customer (out) (tcedi41 50m000)
BAAN Distribution (tdtd-20010): Maintain Quotations (tdsls1101m000) Delete Sales
Quotation (tdsls1803s000) Maintain Delivery Date in Order Lines (tdsls1809s000) Enter
Specific Quotation Numbers (tdsls1820s000) Maintain Sales Contracts (tdsls3101m000)
Maintain Sales Contract Status (tdsls3110m000) Copy Sales Contracts (tdsls3801m000) Enter
Specific Sales Contract Numbers (tdsls3820s000) Maintain Sales Orders (tdsls4101m000)
Delete Sales Order (tdsls4803s000) Copy Bill of Material to Order (tdsls4812s000) Enter
Specific Sales Order Numbers (tdsls4820s000) Maintain Marketing Projects by Relation
(tdsmi1103m000) Maintain Contacts by Relation (tdsmi1105m000)
BAAN Finance (tftf-20010): Maintain Sales Invoices (tfacr1110s000) Maintain Terms of
Payment (tfacr1112s000) Maintain Sales Invoice Details (tfacr2100m000) Maintain Sales
Invoice Corrections (tfacr2110s000) Assign Credit Notes to Invoices (tfacr2120s000)
Assign Credit Notes to Invoices (tfacr2121s000)
Maintain Doubtful Sales Invoices (tfacr2140s000) Maintain Reminder Diary (tfacr3130m000)
Maintain Sales Invoice Header (tfacr4100m000) Assign Unallocated/Advance Receipts to
Invoices (tfcmg2105s000) Maintain Customer Invoice Cash Date (tfcmg3110m000)
BAAN Service (tsts-20010): Maintain Locations (tssma1110m000) Maintain Contracts
(tssma2120m000) Maintain Service Orders (tssma3101m000) Maintain Service Orders
(Telephone Screen) (tssma3140m000) Maintain Service Orders (Planning) (tssma3141m000)
Report Service Orders Completed (tssma3142m000)
Close Service Orders (tssma3144m000) Display Service Orders (tssma3502s000) Enter
Specific Service Order Numbers (tssma3820s000)
1.224 Supplier's 1099 Details (tccom936)
DEFINITION
Supplier's 1099 details include various pieces of information required by the IRS in
printing paper 1099-MISC forms and generation of 1099-MISC magnetic/electronic filing.
1.225 Suppliers (tccom020)
DEFINITION
Suppliers are the persons or companies supplying goods or providing services to your
company.
SOURCE OF DATA
BAAN Common (tctc-20010): Maintain Suppliers (tccom2101m000)
APPLICATION OF DATA
BAAN Common (tctc-20010): Maintain Customers (tccom1101m000) Maintain Prospects
(tccom1110m000) Maintain Suppliers (tccom2101m000) Maintain Supplier Postal Addresses
(tccom2103m000) Maintain Banks by Supplier (tccom2105m000) Maintain Concern Structure of
Trade Relations (tccom3101m000) Maintain Relations (tcedi0110m000) Maintain Conversion of
Postal Address Codes by Supplier (in) (tce di3113m000) Maintain Conv. of Postal Address
Codes by Supplier (out) (tcedi41 51m000) Maintain Forwarding Agents (tcmcs0180m000)

BAAN Distribution (tdtd-20010): Enter Receipts of Serial Number Items (Collect.) (tdilc4813s000) Maintain Planned INV Purchase Orders (tdinv3120m000) Maintain Lots (tdltc0101m000) Copy Ranges of Lots (tdltc0103s000) Maintain Blockings by Lot and Transaction (tdltc0120m000) Convert Non-Lot Item to Lot Item (tdltc0130m000) Convert Lot Item to Non-Lot Item (tdltc0131m000) Maintain Prices by Supplier and Item (tdpur0101m000) Maintain Discounts by Supplier and Price Group (tdpur0102s000) Maintain Discounts by Supplier (tdpur0103m000) Maintain Discount Parameters by Supplier and Price Group (tdpur01 07s000) Maintain Price Parameters by Supplier and Item (tdpur0109s000) Maintain Discount Parameters by Supplier (tdpur0110s000) Enter Inquiry Results (tdpur1103m000) Copy Quoted Inquiry Lines to Purchase Order (tdpur1303s000) Process Quoted Inquiry Lines (tdpur1304s000) Maintain Expiry Date for Returned Inquiry (tdpur1800s000) Enter Specific Inquiry Numbers (tdpur1820s000) Maintain Purchase Contracts (tdpur3101m000) Maintain Purchase Contract Lines (tdpur3102s000) Maintain Purchase Contract Status (tdpur3110m000) Copy Purchase Contracts (tdpur3801m000) Enter Specific Purchase Contract Numbers (tdpur3820s000) Maintain Purchase Orders (tdpur4101m000) Maintain Purchase Orders (Direct Delivery) (tdpur4102m000) Maintain Purchase Order (Direct Line Entry) (tdpur4105m000) Maintain Item Descriptions by Supplier (tdpur4106m000) Maintain Purchase Order Lines (Fast Input) (tdpur4107m000) Maintain Receipts (tdpur4120m000) Maintain Approvals (tdpur4121m000) Change Prices/Discounts after 'Maintain Receipts' (tdpur4122m000)
Maintain Costs Set by Purchase Price List by Supplier (tdpur4127m 000) Maintain Back Orders (tdpur4130m000) Select Receipts (tdpur4131s000) Maintain Alternative Suppliers by Item (tdpur4150m000) Calculate Additional Costs (tdpur4260s000) Print Cost Sets by Purchase Price List and Supplier (tdpur4427m00 0) Calculate Purchase Order Line Discounts (tdpur4802s000) Delete Purchase Order (tdpur4803s000) Recalculate Purchase Price and Discount (tdpur4810s000) Enter Specific Purchase Order Numbers (tdpur4820s000) Print Purchase Order Header History (tdpur5403m000) Copy BOM Components to Quotation (tdsls1812s000)
BAAN Finance (tftf-20010): Maintain Received Purchase Invoices (tfacp1100m000) Maintain Purchase Invoices (tfacp1110s000) Maintain Terms of Payment (tfacp1111s000) Match/Approve Purchase Invoices with Orders (tfacp1130m000) Match Receipts (tfacp1131s000) Maintain Matched Receipts (tfacp1132s000) Approve Purchase Invoices (tfacp1140s000) Approve Price Differences (tfacp1142m000) Maintain Purchase Invoice Details (tfacp2100m000) Maintain Purchase Invoice Corrections (tfacp2110s000) Assign Credit Notes to Invoices (tfacp2120s000)
Assign Invoices to Credit Notes (tfacp2121s000)
Maintain Subcontractors (tfacp3110m000) Maintain Remittance Agreements (tfacp3130m000) Maintain One-Time Supplier Addresses (tfcmg1101m000) Maintain Standing Orders (tfcmg1110m000) Maintain Standing Order Payment Schedules (tfcmg1111s000) Maintain Posting Data of Standing Orders/Stand Alone Paym. (tfcmg 1113m000) Maintain Payment Advice (tfcmg1120m000) Reconciliation of Anticipated Payments/Receipts (tfcmg2102s000) Reconciliation of Receipts/Payments (tfcmg2103s000) Reconciliation of Receipts/Payments (tfcmg2104s000) Assign Unallocated/Advance Payments to Invoices (tfcmg2106s000) Maintain Anticipated Payments (tfcmg2110s000) Maintain Anticipated Receipts (tfcmg2111s000) Maintain Anticipated Payment Status (tfcmg2112s000) Maintain Anticipated Receipt Status (tfcmg2113s000) Maintain Check Master (tfcmg2115m000) Maintain Anticipated Payments (Details) (tfcmg2116s000) Maintain Anticipated Receipts (Details) (tfcmg2117s000) Select for Automatic Customer Reconciliation (tfcmg2121s000) Select for Automatic Supplier Reconciliation (tfcmg2122s000) [SE@
tfcmg2122s000] Selection for Automatic Reconciliation (tfcmg2123s000) Maintain Supplier Invoice Cash Date (tfcmg3111m000) Send Trade Notes/Checks to Bank (tfcmg4130m000) Maintain Converted Electronic Bank Statements (tfcmg5102m000) Maintain Electronic Bank Statements (tfcmg5103m000) Maintain Fixed Asset Master Data (tffas0106m000) Maintain Investments (tffas1101s000) Maintain Maintenance Costs (tffas1103s000) Maintain Fixed Asset Master Data (Simulation) (tffas4106m000) Maintain Fixed Asset Investments (Simulation) (tffas4119m000) Maintain Insurance Master Data (tffas5100m000)
BAAN Manufacturing (titi-20010): Maintain Subcontracting Rates (ticpr1160m000) Maintain Item Data (GRT) (tigrt1180s000) Maintain Customized Item Data (GRT) (tigrt2180s000) Maintain Item Data (tiitm0101m000) Maintain Item Data (in BOM) (tiitm0108s000) Maintain Item Default Data (tiitm0110m000) Maintain Planned MPS Purchase Orders (timps5130m000) Maintain Planned MRP Purchase Orders (timrp1121m000) Maintain Calculation Parts (tipcs0110m000) Maintain Subcontracting Rates by Budget (tipcs1131m000) Maintain Customized Item Data (tipcs2121m000) Maintain Subcontracting Rates by Project (tipcs3110m000) Maintain Planned PRP Purchase Orders (tipcs5120m000) Maintain Work Centers (tirou0101m000) Report Operations Completed (tisfc0102m000) Maintain Production Planning (tisfc1101m000) Maintain Production Planning by Planning Board (tisfc1105m000) Maintain Work Center Planning by Planning Board (tisfc1106m000) Maintain Machine Planning by Planning Board (tisfc1107m000) Subcontract Operations (tisfc2101m000)
BAAN Project (tptp-20010): Maintain Suppliers by Estimate Price Group (tpbop4120m000) Maintain Suppliers by Estimate and Material (tpbop4125m000) Maintain Suppliers by

Estimate and Equipment (tpbop4126m000) Maintain Suppliers by Estimate and Subcontracting (tpbop4127m000)
Maintain Invoices by Equipment Conversion Order (tpism0113s000) Maintain Invoices by Investment (tpism1132s000)
Maintain Third Party Services Trans. by Job Order (tpism3124s000)
Maintain Estimate Lines by Element (tppbs1120m000) Maintain Estimate Lines by Subelement (tppbs1125m000) Maintain Item Default Data (tppdm0109m000) Maintain Standard Items (tppdm0110m000) Maintain Standard Equipment (tppdm0112m000) Maintain Standard Subcontracting (tppdm0113m000) Maintain Teams (tppdm0144m000) Maintain Project Items (tppdm6110m000) Maintain Project Equipment (tppdm6112m000) Maintain Project Subcontracting (tppdm6113m000)
Maintain Supplier's Item Codes (tppdm7150m000) Maintain Supplier Diskette Layout (tppdm7151m000) Maintain Discount Groups by Supplier (tppdm7152m000) Maintain Units by Supplier (tppdm7156m000) Maintain Items by Supplier Discount Group (tppdm7158m000)
Maintain Departments (tppdm8102m000) Maintain Material Transactions to be Invoiced (tppin4157m000) Maintain Labor Transactions to be Invoiced (tppin4158m000) Maintain Equipment Transactions to be Invoiced (tppin4159m000) Maintain Subcontracting Transactions to be Invoiced (tppin4160m00 0) Maintain Commitments (Material) (tpppc2110m000)
Maintain Material Costs (tpppc2111m000) Maintain Subcontracting Hours (tpppc2132m000) Maintain Commitments (Equipment) (tpppc2150m000) Maintain Equipment Cost (tpppc2151m000) Maintain Commitments (Subcontracting) (tpppc2170m000) Maintain Subcontracting Costs (tpppc2171m000) Confirm Commitments (Material) (tpppc4100m000) Confirm Material Cost Transactions (tpppc4101m000) Confirm Subcontracting Hours Accounting (tpppc4103m000) Confirm Commitments (Equipment) (tpppc4104m000)
Confirm Equipment Cost Transactions (tpppc4105m000) Confirm Commitments (Subcontracting) (tpppc4106m000) Confirm Subcontracting Cost Transactions (tpppc4107m000) Maintain Material Recommendations (tppss6110m000) Maintain Equipment Recommendations (tppss6111m000) Maintain Subcontracting Recommendations (tppss6112m000) Maintain Purchase Budget Detail Lines (tpptc4120m000)
BAAN Transportation (trtr-20010): Maintain Fuel Refills (trcde1120s000) Maintain Costs (trtco1100m000) Maintain Cost Lines (trtco1101s000) Maintain Costs (Subcontracting) (trtco1105s000)
Compare Subcontracting Costs (trtco1190m000) Compare Subcontracting Costs (trtco1191s000) Maintain Service Stations (trtfc1100m000) Maintain Deliveries to Own Service Station (trtfc1120m000) Maintain Fuel Intake (trtfc2100m000) Maintain Fuel Intake from FINANCE (trtfc2102s000) Check Fuel Intake Bills (trtfc2110m000) Maintain Means of Transport (trtfm1110m000) Maintain Finished Activities (trtfm4100m000) Maintain Finished Activities (from FINANCE) (trtfm4102s000) Maintain Subcontracting Data by Order Line (trtoc1105m000) Maintain Subcontracting Data by Standard Order Line (trtoc3105s00 0) Maintain Subcontracting Data by Trip (trtop4105m000) Maintain Transport Rate Codes by Subcontractor (trtrc1170m000)
BAAN Service (tsts-20010): Maintain Installations (tssma1102m000) Maintain Installations (tssma1103s000) Maintain Installations by Contract (tssma2182m000)

1.226 Supported EDI MeBaanges (tcedi001)

DEFINITION

Supported meBaanges are incoming and/or outgoing meBaanges that are supported by the application. Such meBaanges may be "active" i.e., actually used within the company, or not.

SOURCE OF DATA

The data result from input or import in the session "Import EDI Data (tcedi6220m000)".

APPLICATION OF DATA

Supported meBaanges are used in:
* maintain conversion setups in the b-object "Coding and Conversion Data"
* printing mapping information in the b-object "Conversion Parameters"
* generating EDI meBaanges in the b-object "Communication"

1.227 Table Boosters (tcmcs098)

DEFINITION

Table Boosters enable you to load a whole table or specified rows of a table into interal memory to have fast access to data. Please note that not all tables are suitable to be loaded.

SOURCE OF DATA

BAAN Common (tctc-20010): Maintain Table Boosters (tcmcs0198m000)

1.228 Tax Authority Codes (tcmcs937)

DEFINITION

TAx authority codes are used to identify specific jurisdictions for collection of sales tax. Examples of specific tax authorities include the state of California and the province of Ontario.

1.229 Tax Authority Groups (tcmcs940)

DEFINITION

Tax Autority Groups are used to combine like types of Tax Authority Codes for reporting purposes

1.230 Tax Code IDs (tcedi240)

DEFINITION

A Tax code ID gives information about the coding system that has produced the Tax code. In EDIFACT, for instance:
- "SA" denotes a code determined by the supplier
- "ZZ" denotes a code determined in mutual consultation
- "EN" denotes coding according to EANCOM

SOURCE OF DATA

The data result from input or import in the session "Import EDI Data (tcedi6220m000)".

APPLICATION OF DATA

Tax code IDs are used in:
- defining conversion data in the b-object "Coding and Conversion Data".

1.231 Tax Codes (tcedi242)

DEFINITION

Tax codes denote common Tax rates.

SOURCE OF DATA

The data result from input or import in the session "Import EDI Data (tcedi6220m000)".

APPLICATION OF DATA

Tax codes are used in:
- defining conversion data in the b-object "Coding and Conversion Data".

1.232 Tax Codes (tcmcs037)

DEFINITION

A tax code represents a common tax rate. Tax codes are used to group items which are taxed at the same rate. Tax codes enable you to use both national and foreign tax rates within BAAN IV.

SOURCE OF DATA

BAAN Common (tctc-20010): Maintain Tax Codes (tcmcs0137m000)

APPLICATION OF DATA

BAAN Common (tctc-20010): Maintain Single Tax Rates (tcmcs0132s000) Maintain Multiple Tax Rates (tcmcs0133s000) Maintain Tax Rates by Tax Code (tcmcs0135s000) Maintain Tax Codes by Country (tcmcs0136m000)

BAAN Distribution (tdtd-20010): Copy BOM Components to Quotation (tdsls1812s000) Maintain Invoice Analysis Accounts by Tax Code (tdsls6103m000)

BAAN Finance (tftf-20010): Maintain ACP Parameters (tfacp0100m000) Maintain Purchase Invoices (tfacp1110s000) Maintain Terms of Payment (tfacp1111s000) Match/Approve Purchase Invoices with Orders (tfacp1130m000) Approve Purchase Invoices (tfacp1140s000) Approve Price Differences (tfacp1142m000) Maintain Purchase Invoice Details (tfacp2100m000) Maintain Purchase Invoice Corrections (tfacp2110s000) Assign Credit Notes to Invoices (tfacp2120s000)

Assign Invoices to Credit Notes (tfacp2121s000) Maintain Subcontracting Parameters (tfacp3100m000) Maintain Sales Invoices (tfacr1110s000) Maintain Terms of Payment (tfacr1112s000) Maintain Sales Invoice Details (tfacr2100m000) Maintain Sales Invoice Corrections (tfacr2110s000) Assign Credit Notes to Invoices (tfacr2120s000)

Assign Credit Notes to Invoices (tfacr2121s000) Maintain Doubtful Sales Invoices (tfacr2140s000) Maintain Reminder Diary (tfacr3130m000) Maintain Sales Invoice Lines (tfacr4101s000) Maintain Interest Invoice Related Data (tfacr5101m000) Maintain Posting Data by Tax Code (tfcmg0150m000) Maintain Standing Orders (tfcmg1110m000) Maintain Posting Data of Standing Orders/Stand Alone Paym. (tfcmg1113m000) Maintain Bank Transactions (tfcmg2100s000) Assign Unallocated/Advance Receipts to Invoices (tfcmg2105s000) Assign Unallocated/Advance Payments to Invoices (tfcmg2106s000) Maintain Anticipated Payments (Details) (tfcmg2116s000) Maintain Anticipated Receipts (Details) (tfcmg2117s000) Maintain Customer Invoice Cash Date (tfcmg3110m000) Maintain Supplier Invoice Cash Date (tfcmg3111m000) Maintain Posting Data of Electronic Bank Statements (tfcmg5106s00 0) Maintain Chart of Accounts (tfgld0108m000) Maintain Transaction Schedule Details (tfgld0113s000) Maintain Relations by Tax Position (tfgld0121m000)

BAAN Manufacturing (titi-20010): Maintain Item Data (GRT) (tigrt1180s000) Maintain Customized Item Data (GRT) (tigrt2180s000) Maintain Item Data (tiitm0101m000) Maintain Item Data (in BOM) (tiitm0108s000) Maintain Item Default Data (tiitm0110m000) Maintain Calculation Parts (tipcs0110m000) Maintain Customized Item Data (tipcs2121m000)

BAAN Project (tptp-20010): Maintain Item Default Data (tppdm0109m000) Maintain Standard Items (tppdm0110m000) Maintain Standard Equipment (tppdm0112m000) Maintain Standard Subcontracting (tppdm0113m000) Maintain Project Items (tppdm6110m000) Maintain Project Equipment (tppdm6112m000) Maintain Project Subcontracting (tppdm6113m000)

Maintain Installments by Project (tppin4151m000) Maintain Installments to be Invoiced (tppin4156m000) Maintain Advance Invoice Lines (tppin4167s000) Maintain Installment Invoice Lines (tppin4168s000) Maintain Material Invoice Lines (tppin4169s000)

Maintain Invoice Lines (Cost Plus Labor) (tppin4170s000) Maintain Invoice Lines (Cost Plus Equipment) (tppin4171s000) Maintain Invoice Lines (Cost Plus Subcontracting) (tppin4172s000)
Maintain Invoice Lines (Cost Plus Sundry Cost) (tppin4173s000) Maintain Unit Rate Invoice Lines (tppin4174s000)
BAAN Transportation (trtr-20010): Maintain Fuel Refills (trcde1120s000) Maintain Expenses (trcde1140s000) Maintain Daily Reports (Expenses) (trhec3120s000) Maintain Revenue Codes (trics0120m000) Maintain Items and Inventories by Service Station (trtfc1110m000)
Maintain Fuel Intake (trtfc2100m000) Maintain Fuel Intake from FINANCE (trtfc2102s000) Check Fuel Intake Bills (trtfc2110m000) Maintain Finished Activities (trtfm4100m000) Maintain Finished Activities (from FINANCE) (trtfm4102s000) Maintain Bills of Material for Logistical Units (trtoc1120s000) Collect Logistic Units (trtoc1121m000) Maintain Bills of Material for Logistical Units (trtoc1122s000) Collect Logistic Units (TDPUR Order Step) (trtoc1123m000) Maintain Standard Order Lines (trtoc3101m000) Maintain WIC Parameters (trwic0100m000) Maintain WOC Parameters (trwoc0100m000) Maintain Storage Orders (trwoc1100m000) Maintain Storage Orders (Invoicing Data) (trwoc1106m000) Maintain Storage Orders (General Data) (trwoc1107m000) Maintain Transhipment Order Lines (trwoc4101m000) Maintain Transhipment Order Lines (Invoicing Data) (trwoc4106m000) Maintain Transhipment Order Lines (General Data) (trwoc4107m000) Maintain Assembly Orders (trwoc5100m000) Maintain Assembly Orders (Invoicing Data) (trwoc5106m000) Maintain Assembly Orders (General Data) (trwoc5107m000) [SE@trwoc 5107m000]
BAAN Service (tsts-20010): Maintain Contracts (tssma2120m000) Maintain Actual Service Order Costs and Revenues (tssma3110m000) Maintain Service Order Cost Estimate (tssma3170m000)
1.233 Tax Codes by Country (tcmcs036)
DEFINITION
Tax codes by country define the country-specific tax data, e.g. the ledger accounts linked to these rates.
SOURCE OF DATA
BAAN Common (tctc-20010): Maintain Tax Codes by Country (tcmcs0136m000)
BAAN Distribution (tdtd-20010): Maintain Invoice Analysis Accounts by Tax Code (tdsls6103m000)
APPLICATION OF DATA
BAAN Common (tctc-20010): Maintain Conversion of Tax Codes (in) (tcedi3108m000) Maintain Conversion of Tax Codes (out) (tcedi4146m000) Maintain Single Tax Rates (tcmcs0132s000) Maintain Tax Rates by Tax Code (tcmcs0135s000)
BAAN Distribution (tdtd-20010): Maintain Inquiry Lines (tdpur1102s000) Enter Inquiry Results (tdpur1103m000) Copy Quoted Inquiry Lines to Purchase Order (tdpur1303s000) Process Quoted Inquiry Lines (tdpur1304s000) Maintain Purchase Contract Lines (tdpur3102s000) Maintain Purchase Orders (Direct Delivery) (tdpur4102m000) Maintain Purchase Order (Direct Line Entry) (tdpur4105m000) Maintain Purchase Order Lines (Fast Input) (tdpur4107m000) Maintain Back Orders (tdpur4130m000) Calculate Additional Costs (tdpur4260s000) Calculate Purchase Order Line Discounts (tdpur4802s000) Delete Purchase Order (tdpur4803s000) Recalculate Purchase Price and Discount (tdpur4810s000) Maintain Quotation Lines (tdsls1102s000) Maintain Quotation Lines (Wholesale) (tdsls1107s000) Display Gross Profit of Quotation Line (tdsls1808s000) Maintain Sales Contract Lines (tdsls3102s000) Maintain Sales Orders (Wholesale) (tdsls4102m000) Maintain Sales Orders (Wholesale) (tdsls4105m000) Maintain Installment Data (tdsls4106s000)
Signal Inventory Shortages (tdsls4801s000) Calculate Sales Order Line Discounts (tdsls4802s000) Display Gross Profit of Sales Order Line (tdsls4808s000) Update Delivery Date in Sales Order Lines (tdsls4809s000) Recalculate Sales Price and Discount (tdsls4810s000)
BAAN Finance (tftf-20010): Maintain Purchase Invoices (tfacp1110s000) Maintain Terms of Payment (tfacp1111s000) Match/Approve Purchase Invoices with Orders (tfacp1130m000) Approve Purchase Invoices (tfacp1140s000) Approve Price Differences (tfacp1142m000) Maintain Purchase Invoice Details (tfacp2100m000) Maintain Purchase Invoice Corrections (tfacp2110s000) Assign Credit Notes to Invoices (tfacp2120s000)
Assign Invoices to Credit Notes (tfacp2121s000)
Maintain Sales Invoices (tfacr1110s000) Maintain Terms of Payment (tfacr1112s000) Maintain Sales Invoice Details (tfacr2100m000) Maintain Sales Invoice Corrections (tfacr2110s000) Assign Credit Notes to Invoices (tfacr2120s000)
Assign Credit Notes to Invoices (tfacr2121s000)
Maintain Doubtful Sales Invoices (tfacr2140s000) Maintain Reminder Diary (tfacr3130m000) Maintain Sales Invoice Lines (tfacr4101s000) Maintain Posting Data by Tax Code (tfcmg0150m000) Maintain Standing Orders (tfcmg1110m000) Maintain Posting Data of Standing Orders/Stand Alone Paym. (tfcmg 1113m000) Maintain Payment Advice (tfcmg1120m000) Maintain Bank Transactions (tfcmg2100s000) Assign Unallocated/Advance Receipts to Invoices (tfcmg2105s000) Assign Unallocated/Advance Payments to Invoices (tfcmg2106s000) Maintain Anticipated Payments (Details) (tfcmg2116s000) Maintain

Anticipated Receipts (Details) (tfcmg2117s000) Maintain Customer Invoice Cash Date
(tfcmg3110m000) Maintain Supplier Invoice Cash Date (tfcmg3111m000) Maintain Direct Debit
Advice (tfcmg4120m000) Maintain Relations by Tax Position (tfgld0121m000)
BAAN Transportation (trtr-20010): Maintain Fuel Refills (trcde1120s000) Maintain Expenses
(trcde1140s000) Maintain Daily Reports (Expenses) (trhec3120s000) Maintain Fuel Intake
(trtfc2100m000) Maintain Fuel Intake from FINANCE (trtfc2102s000) Check Fuel Intake Bills
(trtfc2110m000) Maintain Finished Activities (trtfm4100m000) Maintain Finished Activities
(from FINANCE) (trtfm4102s000) Split Order Lines (trtoc1103s000) Standard Session for
Transport Order Lines (All Data) (trtoc1180m 000) Maintain Transport Order Lines
(trtoc1181m000) Maintain Transport Order Lines (trtoc1182m000) Maintain Transport Order
Lines (trtoc1183m000) Maintain Transport Order Lines (trtoc1184m000) Maintain Transport
Order Lines (trtoc1185m000) Maintain Transport Order Lines (trtoc1186m000) Maintain
Transport Order Lines (trtoc1187m000) Maintain Transport Order Lines (trtoc1188m000)
Maintain Document Lines (trtoc1189s000) Maintain Transport Order Lines (trtoc1190m000)
Maintain Transport Order Lines (trtoc1191m000) Maintain Standard Order Lines
(trtoc3101m000) Maintain Storage Orders (trwoc1100m000) Maintain Storage Orders
(Invoicing Data) (trwoc1106m000) Maintain Storage Orders (General Data) (trwoc1107m000)
Maintain Inbound Order Lines (trwoc2101m000) Maintain Inbound Order Lines (Invoicing
Data) (trwoc2106m000) Maintain Inbound Order Lines (General Data) (trwoc2107m000)
Maintain Outbound Order Lines (trwoc3101m000) Maintain Outbound Order Lines (Invoicing
Data) (trwoc3106m000) Maintain Outbound Order Lines (General Data) (trwoc3107m000)
Maintain Transhipment Order Lines (trwoc4101m000) Maintain Transhipment Order Lines
(Invoicing Data) (trwoc4106m000) Maintain Transhipment Order Lines (General Data)
(trwoc4107m000) Maintain Assembly Orders (trwoc5100m000) Maintain Assembly Orders
(Invoicing Data) (trwoc5106m000) Maintain Assembly Orders (General Data) (trwoc5107m000)
1.234 Tax Codes by Postal Code (tcmcs936)
DEFINITION
Tax codes are assigned to ranges of destination postal codes to be used as a default in
processing of orders and invoices within the Distribution, Service, and Finance modules.
Tax codes specified here may be overridden by exceptions defined in the Exceptions by Tax
Location (tcmcs939) and Exceptions for Taxes - Sales (tcmcs938) tables
1.235 Tax Exemptions for Customer by Tax Authority (tcmcs942)
DEFINITION
Some customers are exempt from sales tax within the jurisdiction of certain tax
authorities. Exemption information is defined for these customers here. Sales to a
customer with an un-expired exemption will not be taxed.
In addition, the orders and invoices printed in Distribution and Service for the exempted
sales will reference the exemption number when the "Print Exemption" field is set to yes
for that customer's country in the Countries table.
1.236 Tax Rates by Tax Code (tcmcs035)
DEFINITION
Tax rates by tax code determine the total tax rate. The latter is calculated according to
one of two methods:
Parallel The tax rate is added to the previous tax rate for this tax code.
     Example:
     Rate 1: 40%   (method for 1st rate has no effect)
     Rate 2: 10%   (method is parallel)
     Resulting rate is 50%   (40 + 10)

Cumulative The tax rate is calculated over the previous Tax rate. The result of the
calculation plus the Tax rate are added to the previous Tax rate.
     Example:
     Rate 1: 40%   (method for 1st rate has no effect)
     Rate 2: 10%   (method is cumulative)
     Resulting rate is 54%   (40 + ((40/100)*10) + 10)

 SOURCE OF DATA

 BAAN Common   :
 Maintain Tax Rates by Tax Code (tcmcs0135s000)

 APPLICATION OF DATA

 BAAN Common   :
 Maintain Multiple Tax Rates (tcmcs0133s000)

 BAAN Finance   :
 Maintain Relations by Tax Position (tfgld0121m000)
1.237 Temperature Qualifiers (tcedi270)
DEFINITION

Temperature qualifiers indicate the type of temperature a specific value refers to:
- transport temperature
- storage temperature

SOURCE OF DATA

The data result from input or import in the session "Import EDI Data (tcedi6220m000)".

APPLICATION OF DATA

Temperature qualifiers are used in:
- processing received meBaanges in the b-object "Communication".

1.238 Terms of Delivery (tcedi228)

DEFINITION

Terms of delivery record the agreements made with respect to the delivery of goods (by organization).

SOURCE OF DATA

The data result from input or import in the session "Import EDI Data (tcedi6220m000)".

APPLICATION OF DATA

Terms of delivery are used in:
- defining conversion data in the b-object "Coding and Conversion Data".

1.239 Terms of Delivery (tcmcs041)

DEFINITION

Terms of delivery are agreements concerning the delivery of goods; they appear as information on external documents.

SOURCE OF DATA

BAAN Common (tctc-20010): Maintain Terms of Delivery (tcmcs0141m000)

APPLICATION OF DATA

BAAN Common (tctc-20010): Maintain Customers (tccom1101m000) Maintain Prospects (tccom1110m000) Maintain Suppliers (tccom2101m000) Maintain Import/Export Statistics (tccom7171m000) Maintain Conversion of Terms of Delivery Codes (in) (tcedi3100m00 0) Maintain Conversion of Terms of Delivery Codes (out) (tcedi4130m0 00)

BAAN Distribution (tdtd-20010): Maintain Inquiries (tdpur1101m000) Maintain Expiry Date for Returned Inquiry (tdpur1800s000) Enter Specific Inquiry Numbers (tdpur1820s000) Maintain Purchase Contracts (tdpur3101m000) Maintain Purchase Contract Status (tdpur3110m000) Copy Purchase Contracts (tdpur3801m000) Enter Specific Purchase Contract Numbers (tdpur3820s000) Maintain Purchase Orders (tdpur4101m000) Enter Specific Purchase Order Numbers (tdpur4820s000) Print Purchase Order Header History (tdpur5403m000) Maintain Quotations (tdsls1101m000) Delete Sales Quotation (tdsls1803s000) Maintain Delivery Date in Order Lines (tdsls1809s000) Enter Specific Quotation Numbers (tdsls1820s000) Maintain Sales Contracts (tdsls3101m000) Maintain Sales Contract Status (tdsls3110m000) Copy Sales Contracts (tdsls3801m000) Enter Specific Sales Contract Numbers (tdsls3820s000) Maintain Sales Orders (tdsls4101m000) Delete Sales Order (tdsls4803s000) Copy Bill of Material to Order (tdsls4812s000) Enter Specific Sales Order Numbers (tdsls4820s000)

BAAN Transportation (trtr-20010): Maintain Transport Orders (trtoc1100m000) Maintain Transport Orders (trtoc1102s000) Maintain Standard Orders (trtoc3100m000)

1.240 Terms of Delivery Functions (tcedi258)

DEFINITION

Terms of delivery functions may be terms of delivery or terms of transport.

SOURCE OF DATA

The data result from input or import in the session "Import EDI Data (tcedi6220m000)".

APPLICATION OF DATA

Terms of delivery function codes are used in:
- processing received meBaanges in the b-object "Communication".

1.241 Terms of Payment (tcedi294)

DEFINITION

Terms of payment are the conditions of payment between the partners to a transaction.

SOURCE OF DATA

The data result from input or import in the session "Import EDI Data (tcedi6220m000)".

APPLICATION OF DATA

Terms of payment codes are used in:
- defining conversion data in the b-object "Coding and Conversion Data".

1.242 Terms of Payment (tcmcs013)

DEFINITION

Terms of payment are agreements concerning the period within which invoices are to be paid and the discount granted if an invoice is paid within a given period.

SOURCE OF DATA

BAAN Common (tctc-20010): Maintain Terms of Payment (tcmcs0113m000)

APPLICATION OF DATA

BAAN Common (tctc-20010): Maintain Customers (tccom1101m000) Maintain Prospects (tccom1110m000) Maintain Suppliers (tccom2101m000) Maintain Conversion of Terms of Payment Codes (in) (tcedi3126m000) Maintain Conversion of Terms of Payment Codes (out) (tcedi4166m00 0) Maintain Payment Schedules (tcmcs0114m000)

BAAN Distribution (tdtd-20010): Maintain Inquiries (tdpur1101m000) Maintain Expiry Date for Returned Inquiry (tdpur1800s000) Enter Specific Inquiry Numbers (tdpur1820s000) Maintain Purchase Contracts (tdpur3101m000) Maintain Purchase Contract Status (tdpur3110m000) Copy Purchase Contracts (tdpur3801m000) Enter Specific Purchase Contract Numbers (tdpur3820s000) Maintain Purchase Orders (tdpur4101m000) Enter Specific Purchase Order Numbers (tdpur4820s000) Print Purchase Order Header History (tdpur5403m000) Maintain Quotations (tdsls1101m000) Delete Sales Quotation (tdsls1803s000) Maintain Delivery Date in Order Lines (tdsls1809s000) Enter Specific Quotation Numbers (tdsls1820s000) Maintain Sales Contracts (tdsls3101m000) Maintain Sales Contract Status (tdsls3110m000) Copy Sales Contracts (tdsls3801m000) Enter Specific Sales Contract Numbers (tdsls3820s000) Maintain Sales Orders (tdsls4101m000) Delete Sales Order (tdsls4803s000) Copy Bill of Material to Order (tdsls4812s000) Enter Specific Sales Order Numbers (tdsls4820s000)

BAAN Finance (tftf-20010): Maintain Received Purchase Invoices (tfacp1100m000) Maintain Purchase Invoices (tfacp1110s000) Maintain Terms of Payment (tfacp1111s000) Match/Approve Purchase Invoices with Orders (tfacp1130m000) Approve Purchase Invoices (tfacp1140s000) Approve Price Differences (tfacp1142m000) Maintain Purchase Invoice Details (tfacp2100m000) Maintain Purchase Invoice Corrections (tfacp2110s000) Assign Credit Notes to Invoices (tfacp2120s000)

Assign Invoices to Credit Notes (tfacp2121s000)

Maintain Sales Invoices (tfacr1110s000) Maintain Terms of Payment (tfacr1112s000) Maintain Sales Invoice Details (tfacr2100m000) Maintain Sales Invoice Corrections (tfacr2110s000) Assign Credit Notes to Invoices (tfacr2120s000)

Assign Credit Notes to Invoices (tfacr2121s000)

Maintain Doubtful Sales Invoices (tfacr2140s000) Maintain Reminder Diary (tfacr3130m000) Maintain Sales Invoice Header (tfacr4100m000) Maintain Interest Invoice Related Data (tfacr5101m000) Assign Unallocated/Advance Receipts to Invoices (tfcmg2105s000) Assign Unallocated/Advance Payments to Invoices (tfcmg2106s000) Maintain Customer Invoice Cash Date (tfcmg3110m000) Maintain Supplier Invoice Cash Date (tfcmg3111m000)

BAAN Project (tptp-20010): Maintain Customers by Project (tppdm6101s000) Maintain Pro Forma Invoice (tppin4165m000)

BAAN Transportation (trtr-20010): Maintain Transport Orders (trtoc1100m000) Maintain Transport Orders (trtoc1102s000) Maintain Standard Orders (trtoc3100m000) Maintain Storage Orders (trwoc1100m000) Maintain Storage Orders (Invoicing Data) (trwoc1106m000) Maintain Storage Orders (General Data) (trwoc1107m000) Maintain Inbound Orders (trwoc2100m000) Maintain Inbound Orders (trwoc2105s000) Maintain Outbound Orders (trwoc3100m000) Maintain Outbound Orders (trwoc3105s000) Maintain Transhipment Orders (trwoc4100m000) Maintain Transhipment Orders (trwoc4105s000) Maintain Assembly Orders (trwoc5100m000) Maintain Assembly Orders (Invoicing Data) (trwoc5106m000) Maintain Assembly Orders (General Data) (trwoc5107m000)

BAAN Service (tsts-20010): Maintain Contracts (tssma2120m000) Maintain Service Orders (tssma3101m000) Maintain Service Orders (Telephone Screen) (tssma3140m000) Maintain Service Orders (Planning) (tssma3141m000) Report Service Orders Completed (tssma3142m000) Close Service Orders (tssma3144m000) Display Service Orders (tssma3502s000) Enter Specific Service Order Numbers (tssma3820s000)

1.243 Test Areas (tcqms007)

DEFINITION

Test areas are the physical locations where tests take place.

SOURCE OF DATA

- Maintain Test Areas (tcqms0107m000)

APPLICATION OF DATA

- Maintain Characteristics (tcqms0101m000)
- Maintain Tests by Characteristic (tcqms0105m000)
- Maintain Test Instruments (tcqms0108m000)
- Enter Calibration Dates (tcqms3202m000)
- Maintain Tests by Quality ID (tcqms0117m000)
- Maintain Order-Specific Inspection Data (Lines) (tcqms0151s000)
- Maintain Inspection Order Lines (tcqms1101s000)
- Enter Test Data (tcqms1115m000)

1.244 Test Data History (tcqms315)

DEFINITION

The history of all test data (the inspection results) as stored in the inspection order history.

1.245 Test Groups by Quality ID (tcqms036)

DEFINITION

Test groups are definitions of how to draw samples from an order quantity for a specific quality ID. These test groups are assigned to groups of characteristics which must be tested in the same sample.

  Example:
  Quality ID   100

```
Test Group              A1
Test Type               Single Sampling
Sample Size             1 %
```

This means that, for quality ID 100, a single sample will be taken of 1% out of the order quantity to which the quality ID applies.

SOURCE OF DATA
•   Maintain Test Groups by Quality ID (tcqms0136m000)
APPLICATION OF DATA
Test groups are used when inspection orders are generated by the system. An inspection order is generated by test group for each test group which is defined for a particular quality ID.
Test groups are used in the following sessions:
•   Maintain Characteristics by Test Group (tcqms0137m000)
•   Maintain Order-Specific Inspection Data (Header) (tcqms0150s000)
•   Maintain Inspection Orders (tcqms1100s000)
All quality data is linked to item(s) by means of quality combinations.
1.246 Tests (tcqms006)
DEFINITION
Tests refer to the examination or check to which a characteristic is subjected. Each characteristic can be linked to several tests.
SOURCE OF DATA
•   Maintain Tests (tcqms0106m000)
APPLICATION OF DATA
•   Maintain Characteristics (tcqms0101m000)
•   Maintain Characteristics by Aspect (tcqms0103m000)
•   Maintain Tests by Characteristic (tcqms0105m000)
•   Maintain Characteristics by Quality ID (tcqms0115m000)
•   Maintain Tests by Quality ID (tcqms0117m000)
•   Maintain Order-Specific Inspection Data (Lines) (tcqms0151s000)
•   Maintain Inspection Order Lines (tcqms1101s000)
1.247 Tests by Characteristic (tcqms005)
DEFINITION
Tests by characteristic are tests which are done to check the quality for a particular characteristic. General tests for a characteristic may be customized for specific combinations of aspects and characteristics.
SOURCE OF DATA
•   Maintain Tests by Characteristic (tcqms0105m000)
1.248 Tests by Quality ID (tcqms017)
DEFINITION
Tests by quality ID are alternative tests which are used to inspect characteristics with a particular quality ID.
SOURCE OF DATA
•   Maintain Tests by Quality ID (tcqms0117m000)
APPLICATION OF DATA
All quality data is linked to item(s) by means of quality combinations.
1.249 Third Parties (tcedi248)
DEFINITION
Third parties are organizations and companies which are only indirectly involved in a transaction: customs, forwarding agent, importer, etc.
SOURCE OF DATA
The data result from input or import in the session "Import EDI Data (tcedi6220m000)".
APPLICATION OF DATA
Third parties are used in:
•   defining conversion data in the b-object "Coding and Conversion Data".
1.250 Time Zone Specifiers (tcedi252)
DEFINITION
A time zone specifier indicates the time zone applying to the specified date and time - e.g. the supplier's local time zone.
SOURCE OF DATA
The data result from input or import in the session "Import EDI Data (tcedi6220m000)".
APPLICATION OF DATA
Time zone specifiers are used in:
•   processing received meBaanges in the b-object "Communication".
1.251 Titles (tcmcs019)
DEFINITION
Titles are the ways in which persons/companies are addressed. They are printed on documents over the address data (e.g.: "To the board of directors of").
SOURCE OF DATA

BAAN Common (tctc-20010): Maintain Titles (tcmcs0119m000)
APPLICATION OF DATA
BAAN Common (tctc-20010): Maintain Customers (tccom1101m000) Maintain Prospects
(tccom1110m000) Maintain Suppliers (tccom2101m000)
BAAN Distribution (tdtd-20010): Maintain Contacts by Relation (tdsmi1105m000)

1.252 Transport Stages (tcedi278)

DEFINITION
Transport stages indicate the type of transportation used in, for instance: pre-carriage,
main carriage and post-carriage.
SOURCE OF DATA
The data result from input or import in the session "Import EDI Data (tcedi6220m000)".
APPLICATION OF DATA
Transport stage codes are used in:
• processing received meBaanges in the b-object "Communication".

1.253 Transport Types (tcedi234)

DEFINITION
Transport types record the codes for various (types of) means of transport and the
associated descriptions.
SOURCE OF DATA
The data result from input or import in the session "Import EDI Data (tcedi6220m000)".
APPLICATION OF DATA
Dates/times are used in:
• processing received meBaanges in the b-object "Communication".

1.254 Type of Delivery Specifier (tcedi204)

DEFINITION
Types of delivery specify a change in an order line (Transcom) or the reason for calling
off an order (Odette), e.g.:
• extra unplanned delivery
• delivery required for sample inspection
• backorder
• urgent delivery
• cancellation of previous order
• etc.
During conversion, types of delivery can be recorded in text fields.
SOURCE OF DATA
The data result from input or import in the session "Import EDI Data (tcedi6220m000)".
APPLICATION OF DATA
Type of delivery type specifiers are used in:
• processing received meBaanges in the b-object "Communication".

1.255 Types of Contract and Carriage Condition (tcedi262)

DEFINITION
Carriage conditions are the terms and conditions for:
• (Dutch) national bills of lading according to AVC (General Transportation
Conditions)
• international bills of lading according to CMR (Convention de Marchandises par
Route)
SOURCE OF DATA
The data result from input or import in the session "Import EDI Data (tcedi6220m000)".
APPLICATION OF DATA
Carriage condition codes are used in:
• processing received meBaanges in the b-object "Communication".

1.256 Types of Monetary Amount (tcedi264)

DEFINITION
Types of monetary amount determine the character of the amount in the meBaange:
• payable amount
• customs value
• invoice amount
• insured value
• sample value (value of (free) sample)
• goods value
SOURCE OF DATA
The data result from input or import in the session "Import EDI Data (tcedi6220m000)".
APPLICATION OF DATA
Type of monetary amount codes are used in:
• processing received meBaanges in the b-object "Communication".

1.257 Types of Packages (tcedi276)

DEFINITION
Packing types record macking methods such as bulk (liquid or solid), container,
palletized, box, drum/barrel.
SOURCE OF DATA

The data result from input or import in the session "Import EDI Data (tcedi6220m000)".
APPLICATION OF DATA
Packing type codes are used in:
• processing received meBaanges in the b-object "Communication".
1.258 Types of Supplementary Information (tcedi260)
DEFINITION
Types of supplementary information specify the type of information conveyed by the EDI meBaange (Bill of Lading Remarks, General Information, of Special Service Request).
SOURCE OF DATA
The data result from input or import in the session "Import EDI Data (tcedi6220m000)".
APPLICATION OF DATA
Types of supplementary information codes are used in:
• processing received meBaanges in the b-object "Communication".
1.259 Unit Sets (tcmcs006)
DEFINITION
Unit sets are used to group units. A unit set can be linked to an item. In a unit set you can indicate which units can be used for the item, in what modules and for which purposes.
SOURCE OF DATA
BAAN Common (tctc-20010): Maintain Unit Sets (tcmcs0106m000)
APPLICATION OF DATA
BAAN Common (tctc-20010): Maintain Units by Unit Set (tcmcs0112m000)
BAAN Distribution (tdtd-20010): Copy BOM Components to Quotation (tdsls1812s000)
BAAN Manufacturing (titi-20010): Maintain Engineering Items (tiedm0110m000) Maintain Item Data (GRT) (tigrt1180s000) Maintain Customized Item Data (GRT) (tigrt2180s000) Maintain Item Data (tiitm0101m000) Maintain Item Data (in BOM) (tiitm0108s000) Maintain Item Default Data (tiitm0110m000) Maintain Item Data by Item and Container (tiitm0130m000) Update Containerized Items (tiitm0230m000) Maintain Calculation Parts (tipcs0110m000) Maintain Customized Item Data (tipcs2121m000)
BAAN Project (tptp-20010): Maintain Item Default Data (tppdm0109m000) Maintain Standard Items (tppdm0110m000)
1.260 Units (tcedi230)
DEFINITION
Units indicate physical quantities (by organization).
SOURCE OF DATA
The data result from input or import in the session "Import EDI Data (tcedi6220m000)".
APPLICATION OF DATA
Units are used in:
• defining conversion data in the b-object "Coding and Conversion Data".
1.261 Units (tcmcs001)
DEFINITION
Units are used to specify physical quantities such as Weight, Piece, Length, Area, Volume or Time.
SOURCE OF DATA
BAAN Common (tctc-20010): Maintain Units (tcmcs0101m000)
BAAN Distribution (tdtd-20010): Maintain Item Dimensions (tdsls4811s000)
BAAN Service (tsts-20010): Maintain Item Dimensions (tssma3109s000)
APPLICATION OF DATA
BAAN Common (tctc-20010): Maintain Conversion of Unit Codes (in) (tcedi3104m000) Maintain Conversion of Unit Codes (out) (tcedi4142m000) Maintain Units by Language (tcmcs0107m000) Maintain Price Groups (tcmcs0124m000)
BAAN Distribution (tdtd-20010): Maintain Locations (tdilc0110m000) (Un)block Locations by Transaction (tdilc0111m000) Maintain Inventory Transactions by Lot and Location (tdilc1121s00 0) Maintain Inventory Transfers by Lot and Location (tdilc1122s000) (Un)block Inventory by Transaction (tdilc1140m000) Maintain Approvals (tdilc4123s000) Enter Location Cycle Counting Data (tdilc5110m000) Maintain Inquiry Lines (tdpur1102s000) Enter Inquiry Results (tdpur1103m000) Copy Quoted Inquiry Lines to Purchase Order (tdpur1303s000) Process Quoted Inquiry Lines (tdpur1304s000) Maintain Purchase Contract Lines (tdpur3102s000) Maintain Purchase Orders (Direct Delivery) (tdpur4102m000) Maintain Purchase Order (Direct Line Entry) (tdpur4105m000) Maintain Purchase Order Lines (Fast Input) (tdpur4107m000) Maintain Items by Cost Set (tdpur4128m000) Maintain Back Orders (tdpur4130m000) Calculate Additional Costs (tdpur4260s000) Calculate Purchase Order Line Discounts (tdpur4802s000) Delete Purchase Order (tdpur4803s000)
Recalculate Purchase Price and Discount (tdpur4810s000) Maintain Replenishment Order Lines (tdrpl0111s000) Maintain Replenishment Order Deliveries (tdrpl0114m000) Confirm Backorders (tdrpl0120m000) Maintain Replenishment Order Receipts (tdrpl0122m000) Enter Specific Replenishment Order Numbers (tdrpl0482s000) Enter Specific Bill of Lading Numbers (tdrpl0483s000) Link Bills of Lading to Replenishment Orders (tdrpl0518s000) Maintain Quotation Lines (tdsls1102s000) Maintain Quotation Lines (Wholesale) (tdsls1107s000) Display Gross Profit of Quotation Line (tdsls1808s000) Copy BOM

Components to Quotation (tdsls1812s000) Maintain Sales Contract Lines (tdsls3102s000) Maintain Sales Orders (Wholesale) (tdsls4102m000) Maintain Sales Orders (Wholesale) (tdsls4105m000) Maintain Items by Cost Set (tdsls4128m000) Signal Inventory Shortages (tdsls4801s000) Calculate Sales Order Line Discounts (tdsls4802s000) Display Gross Profit of Sales Order Line (tdsls4808s000) [SE@tdsl s4808s000] Update Delivery Date in Sales Order Lines (tdsls4809s000) Recalculate Sales Price and Discount (tdsls4810s000)

BAAN Finance (tftf-20010): Maintain Sales Invoice Lines (tfacr4101s000) Maintain Chart of Accounts (tfgld0108m000) Maintain Dimensions (tfgld0110m000)

BAAN Enterprise Modeler (tgtg-20010): Maintain Performance Indicators (tgeis0111m000) Maintain PI Data by Period (tgeis0112m000)

BAAN Manufacturing (titi-20010): Maintain BOM Parameters (tibom0100m000) Maintain Simulated Purchase Prices (ticpr1170m000) Maintain Engineering Items (tiedm0110m000) Maintain Item Data (GRT) (tigrt1180s000) Maintain Customized Item Data (GRT) (tigrt2180s000) Maintain Item Data (tiitm0101m000) Maintain Item Data (in BOM) (tiitm0108s000) Maintain Item Default Data (tiitm0110m000) Maintain Conversion Factors (tiitm0120m000) Maintain Plan Items (timps2101m000) Maintain Calculation Parts (tipcs0110m000) Maintain Customized Item Data (tipcs2121m000) Maintain Planned PRP Purchase Orders (tipcs5120m000)

BAAN Project (tptp-20010): Maintain Element Data of Estimate Template (tpbop2120m000) Configure Estimate (tpbop2140s000) Maintain General Element Data (tpbop3108s000) Maintain Index (tpbop3118m000) Maintain Column Definition (tpbop3156m000) Maintain ISM Parameters (tpism0100m000) Maintain Elements (tppbs1100m000) Maintain Elements (tppbs1102s000) Maintain Subelements (tppbs1103s000) Maintain Estimate Lines by Element (tppbs1120m000) Maintain Estimate Lines by Subelement (tppbs1125m000) Maintain Contract Data of Elements (tppbs1170m000) Display Elements (tppbs1500s000) Display Subelements (tppbs1501s000) Maintain General Parameters (tppdm0100m000) Maintain Item Default Data (tppdm0109m000) Maintain Standard Items (tppdm0110m000) Maintain Standard Labor (tppdm0111m000) Maintain Standard Equipment (tppdm0112m000) Maintain Standard Subcontracting (tppdm0113m000) Maintain Standard Sundry Costs (tppdm0114m000) Maintain Wage Rates (tppdm0142m000) Maintain Codes by Coding System (tppdm0161m000) Maintain Standard Elements (tppdm0180m000) Maintain Standard Activities (tppdm0190m000) Maintain Wage Rates by Estimate (tppdm4133m000) Maintain Alternative Units by Project Item (tppdm6104m000) Maintain Project Items (tppdm6110m000) Maintain Project Labor (tppdm6111m000) Maintain Project Equipment (tppdm6112m000) Maintain Project Subcontracting (tppdm6113m000) Maintain Project Sundry Costs (tppdm6114m000) Maintain Units by Supplier (tppdm7156m000) Maintain Element Contract Data (tppin1100m000) Maintain Installments by Project (tppin4151m000) Maintain Installments to be Invoiced (tppin4156m000) Maintain Material Transactions to be Invoiced (tppin4157m000) Maintain Equipment Transactions to be Invoiced (tppin4159m000) Maintain Subcontracting Transactions to be Invoiced (tppin4160m00 0) Maintain Sundry Cost Transactions to be Invoiced (tppin4161m000) Maintain Installment Invoice Lines (tppin4168s000) Maintain Material Invoice Lines (tppin4169s000) Maintain Invoice Lines (Cost Plus Equipment) (tppin4171s000) Maintain Invoice Lines (Cost Plus Subcontracting) (tppin4172s000) Maintain Invoice Lines (Cost Plus Sundry Cost) (tppin4173s000) Maintain Unit Rate Invoice Lines (tppin4174s000) Maintain Progress by Element / Material (tpppc1120m000) Maintain Progress by Activity / Material (tpppc1140m000) Maintain Progress by Extension / Material (tpppc1180m000) Generate Activity Progress (Planning) (tpppc1250m000) Maintain Commitments (Material) (tpppc2110m000) Maintain Material Costs (tpppc2111m000) Maintain Material Cost Forecast for Final Result (Elements) (tppp c2116m000) Maintain Mat. Cost Forecast for Final Result (Act.) (tpppc2117m00 0) Maintain Commitments (Equipment) (tpppc2150m000) Maintain Equipment Cost (tpppc2151m000) Maintain Eqt. Cost Forecast for Final Result (Elem.) (tpppc2156m0 00) Maintain Eqt. Cost Forecast for Final Result (Act.) (tpppc2157m00 0) Maintain Commitments (Subcontracting) (tpppc2170m000) Maintain Subcontracting Costs (tpppc2171m000) Maintain Subcnt. Cost Forecast for Final Result (Elements) (tpppc 2176m000) Maintain Subcnt. Cost Forecast for Final Result (Act.) (tpppc2177 m000) Maintain Commitments (Sundry Costs) (tpppc2190m000) Maintain Sundry Costs (tpppc2191m000) Maintain Sundry Cost Forecast for Final Result (Elements) (tpppc2 196m000) Maintain Sundry Cost Forecast for Final Result (Activities) (tppp c2197m000) Confirm Commitments (Material) (tpppc4100m000) Confirm Material Cost Transactions (tpppc4101m000) Confirm Commitments (Equipment) (tpppc4104m000) Confirm Equipment Cost Transactions (tpppc4105m000) Confirm Commitments (Subcontracting) (tpppc4106m000) Confirm Subcontracting Cost Transactions (tpppc4107m000) Confirm Commitments (Sundry Costs) (tpppc4108m000) Confirm Sundry Cost Transactions (tpppc4109m000) Maintain PSS Parameters (tppss0100m000) Maintain Plans (tppss0110m000) Maintain Activities (tppss2120m000) Maintain Milestones (tppss2121m000) Maintain Material

Actions (tppss4110m000) Maintain Labor Actions (tppss4111m000) Maintain Equipment Actions (tppss4112m000) Maintain Subcontracting Actions (tppss4113m000) Maintain Sundry Cost Actions (tppss4114m000) Maintain Material Recommendations (tppss6110m000) Maintain PTC Parameters (tpptc0100m000) Maintain Elements (tpptc1100m000) Maintain Layouts for Extra Elements (tpptc1101m000) Maintain Element Budget (Material) (tpptc1110m000) Maintain Element Budget (Labor) (tpptc1111m000) Maintain Element Budget (Equipment) (tpptc1112m000) Maintain Element Budget (Subcontracting) (tpptc1113m000) Maintain Element Budget (Sundry Costs) (tpptc1114m000) Maintain Activity Budget (Material Lines) (tpptc2110m000) Maintain Activity Budget (Labor Lines) (tpptc2111m000) Maintain Activity Budget (Equipment Lines) (tpptc2112m000) Maintain Activity Budget (Subcontracting Lines) (tpptc2113m000) Maintain Activity Budget (Sundry Cost Lines) (tpptc2114m000) Maintain Purchase Budget Detail Lines (tpptc4120m000) BAAN Transportation (trtr-20010): Maintain Distance Table by City (tracs4100m000) Maintain Distance Table by ZIP Code (tracs4110m000) Maintain Entry Lines (trcde1101s000) Maintain Fuel Refills (trcde1120s000) Maintain Packing Items by Unit (trpac1120m000) Maintain Packing Items by Item (trpac1140m000) Maintain TCD Parameters (trtcd0100m000) Maintain General Items (trtcd1110m000) Maintain General Items (Fast Input) (trtcd1111s000) Maintain Item Transport Defaults (trtcd1120m000) Maintain Defaults by Customer (trtcd2120m000) Maintain Cost Lines (trtco1101s000) Maintain Costs (Subcontracting) (trtco1105s000) Maintain Items and Inventories by Service Station (trtfc1110m000) Maintain Fuel Intake (trtfc2100m000) Maintain Fuel Intake from FINANCE (trtfc2102s000) Check Fuel Intake Bills (trtfc2110m000) Maintain Transport Means Groups (trtfm1100m000) Maintain Means of Transport (trtfm1110m000) Maintain Warnings (trtfm2100m000) Split Order Lines (trtoc1103s000) Maintain Bills of Material for Logistical Units (trtoc1120s000) Collect Logistic Units (trtoc1121m000) Maintain Bills of Material for Logistical Units (trtoc1122s000) Collect Logistic Units (TDPUR Order Step) (trtoc1123m000) Standard Session for Transport Order Lines (All Data) (trtoc1180m 000) Maintain Transport Order Lines (trtoc1181m000) Maintain Transport Order Lines (trtoc1182m000) Maintain Transport Order Lines (trtoc1183m000) Maintain Transport Order Lines (trtoc1184m000) Maintain Transport Order Lines (trtoc1185m000) Maintain Transport Order Lines (trtoc1186m000) Maintain Transport Order Lines (trtoc1187m000) Maintain Transport Order Lines (trtoc1188m000) Maintain Document Lines (trtoc1189s000) Maintain Transport Order Lines (trtoc1190m000) Maintain Transport Order Lines (trtoc1191m000) Maintain Standard Order Lines (trtoc3101m000) Maintain Stop Lines (trtop3101m000) Maintain Quantities by Stop Line (trtop3167s000) Maintain Third-Party Items (trtpi1100m000) Maintain Blocking of Third-Party Items (trtpi1101m000) Maintain Alternative Units by Third-Party Item (trtpi1110m000) Maintain Transport Rate Codes (trtrc1100m000) Maintain Transport Rate Codes by Price Group (trtrc1120m000) Maintain Transport Rate Codes by Price List (trtrc1130m000) Maintain Transport Rate Codes by Customer (trtrc1140m000) Maintain General Transport Rate Codes (trtrc1150m000) Maintain Transport Rate Codes by Subcontractor (trtrc1170m000) Maintain Rate Codes by Subcontractor Price List (trtrc1180m000) Maintain WIC Parameters (trwic0100m000) Maintain Locations (trwic1100m000) Maintain Blocking Statuses of Locations (trwic1101m000) Enter Item Inventory Adjustments (trwic2100m000) Maintain Blocking Statuses of Item Inventories (trwic2101m000) Maintain Inventory Remarks (trwic2105s000) Maintain Minimum Inventory of Items (trwic4100m000) Maintain Minimum Inventory of Items by Location (trwic4101m000) Maintain WOC Parameters (trwoc0100m000) Maintain Storage Orders (trwoc1100m000) Maintain Units by Storage Order (trwoc1102s000) Maintain Storage Orders (Invoicing Data) (trwoc1106m000) Maintain Storage Orders (General Data) (trwoc1107m000) Maintain Inbound Order Lines (trwoc2101m000) Maintain Inbound Order Lines (Invoicing Data) (trwoc2106m000) Maintain Inbound Order Lines (General Data) (trwoc2107m000) Maintain Outbound Order Lines (trwoc3101m000) Maintain Outbound Order Lines (Invoicing Data) (trwoc3106m000) Maintain Outbound Order Lines (General Data) (trwoc3107m000) Maintain Transhipment Order Lines (trwoc4101m000) Maintain Transhipment Order Lines (Invoicing Data) (trwoc4106m000) Maintain Transhipment Order Lines (General Data) (trwoc4107m000) Maintain Assembly Orders (trwoc5100m000) Maintain Assembly Order Lines (trwoc5101m000) Maintain Assembly Orders (Invoicing Data) (trwoc5106m000) Maintain Assembly Orders (General Data) (trwoc5107m000) Maintain Warehousing Rate Codes (trwrc1100m000) Maintain Warehousing Rate Codes by Order Type (trwrc1102s000) Maintain Warehousing Rate Codes by Price List (trwrc1120m000) Maintain Warehousing Rate Codes by Price Group (trwrc1130m000) Maintain Warehousing Rate Codes by Customer (trwrc1140m000) Maintain Warehousing Rate Codes by Item (trwrc1150m000) Maintain General Warehousing Rate Codes (trwrc1160m000) Maintain Warehousing Rate Codes by Warehouse (trwrc1170m000) BAAN Service (tsts-20010): Maintain System Configuration Parameters (tssma0000m000) Maintain Installation Control Parameters (tssma1100m000) Maintain Items by Installation Type (tssma1107m000) Maintain Items by Servicing (tssma1121m000) Maintain Service Order Control Parameters (tssma3100m000) Maintain Actual Service Order Costs and Revenues (tssma3110m000) Maintain Appointment Confirmation (tssma3161m000) Maintain Service Order Cost Estimate (tssma3170m000) Maintain Parameters for Link with Finance (tssma6100m000)

1.262 Units By Unit Set (tcmcs012)

DEFINITION

Unit sets are used to group units. A unit set can be linked to an item. In a unit set you can indicate which units can be used for the item, in what modules and for which purposes.

SOURCE OF DATA

BAAN Common (tctc-20010): Maintain Unit Sets (tcmcs0106m000)

APPLICATION OF DATA

BAAN Common (tctc-20010): Maintain Units by Unit Set (tcmcs0112m000)

BAAN Distribution (tdtd-20010): Copy BOM Components to Quotation (tdsls1812s000)

BAAN Manufacturing (titi-20010): Maintain Engineering Items (tiedm0110m000) Maintain Item Data (GRT) (tigrt1180s000) Maintain Customized Item Data (GRT) (tigrt2180s000) Maintain Item Data (tiitm0101m000) Maintain Item Data (in BOM) (tiitm0108s000) Maintain Item Default Data (tiitm0110m000) Maintain Item Data by Item and Container (tiitm0130m000) Update Containerized Items (tiitm0230m000) Maintain Calculation Parts (tipcs0110m000) Maintain Customized Item Data (tipcs2121m000)

BAAN Project (tptp-20010): Maintain Item Default Data (tppdm0109m000) Maintain Standard Items (tppdm0110m000)

1.263 Units by Language (tcmcs007)

DEFINITION

Units by language are short language-dependent unit descriptions required to print the proper unit description on external documents in different languages.

SOURCE OF DATA

BAAN Common (tctc-20010): Maintain Units by Language (tcmcs0107m000)

1.264 Use of Performance Boosters (tcmcs097)

DEFINITION

Performance boosters enable you to increase the performance (processing speed) of sessions. Please be aware of the fact that the use of performance boosters may in some situations have a negative effect. This will especially occur if less data has to be processed and still a number of servers has been defined for that session and/or user. The time the various bshells take to start up will delay the program in such cases.

SOURCE OF DATA

APPLICATION OF DATA

1.265 Variables by Algorithm (tcqms022)

DEFINITION

All variables for a specific algorithm. A variable may be a characteristic with method:
- Fixed
- Variable

SOURCE OF DATA
- Maintain Variables by Algorithm (tcqms0122s000)

APPLICATION OF DATA

Variables by algorithm are only used for specific algorithms.
- Maintain Algorithms (tcqms0121m000)

1.266 Warehouses (tcmcs003)

DEFINITION

Warehouses are places where goods are kept in store. For each warehouse you can enter address data and data relating to its type.

SOURCE OF DATA

BAAN Common (tctc-20010): Maintain Warehouses (tcmcs0103m000)

APPLICATION OF DATA

BAAN Common (tctc-20010): Maintain Suppliers (tccom2101m000) Maintain Conversion of Warehouse Addresses (out) (tcedi4162m000)

BAAN Distribution (tdtd-20010): Maintain Locations (tdilc0110m000) (Un)block Locations by Transaction (tdilc0111m000) (Un)block Locations for All Transactions (tdilc0120m000) Unblock Locations (tdilc0121m000) Maintain Locations by Item (tdilc0130m000) Maintain Storage Conditions by Warehouse and Location (tdilc0151m 000) Maintain Warehouses and Locations by Storage Condition (tdilc0152 m000) Enter Inventory Transactions (tdilc1120m000) Maintain Inventory Transactions by Lot and Location (tdilc1121s00 0) Maintain Inventory Transfers by Lot and Location (tdilc1122s000) (Un)block Inventory by Transaction (tdilc1140m000) (Un)block Stock Point for All Transactions (tdilc1141m000) Unblock Stock Point (tdilc1142m000) Maintain Outbound Data (tdilc4101m000) Maintain Outbound Data (tdilc4102s000) Maintain Inbound Data (tdilc4103m000) Maintain Inbound Data (tdilc4104s000) Maintain Receipts (ILC) (tdilc4113s000) Enter Location Cycle Counting Data (tdilc5110m000) Maintain Items by Warehouse (tdinv0101m000) Enter Inventory Transactions by Item (tdinv1101m000)

Enter Warehouse Cycle Counting Data (tdinv1120m000) Maintain Planned INV Production Orders (tdinv3110m000) Maintain Planned INV Purchase Orders (tdinv3120m000) Maintain Inventory and WIP Transaction Accounts (tdinv8150m000) Maintain Inquiry Lines (tdpur1102s000) Enter Inquiry Results (tdpur1103m000) Copy Quoted Inquiry Lines to Purchase Order (tdpur1303s000) Process Quoted Inquiry Lines (tdpur1304s000) Maintain Purchase Contracts (tdpur3101m000) Maintain Purchase Contract Lines (tdpur3102s000) Maintain Purchase Contract Status (tdpur3110m000) Copy Purchase Contracts (tdpur3801m000) Enter Specific Purchase Contract Numbers (tdpur3820s000) Maintain Purchase Orders (tdpur4101m000) Maintain Purchase Orders (Direct Delivery) (tdpur4102m000) Maintain Purchase Order (Direct Line Entry) (tdpur4105m000) Maintain Purchase Order Lines (Fast Input) (tdpur4107m000) Maintain Receipts (tdpur4120m000) Maintain Approvals (tdpur4121m000) Change Prices/Discounts after 'Maintain Receipts' (tdpur4122m000) Maintain Defaults by User (Purchase) (tdpur4123m000) Maintain Back Orders (tdpur4130m000) Select Receipts (tdpur4131s000) Calculate Additional Costs (tdpur4260s000) Calculate Purchase Order Line Discounts (tdpur4802s000) Delete Purchase Order (tdpur4803s000) Recalculate Purchase Price and Discount (tdpur4810s000) Enter Specific Purchase Order Numbers (tdpur4820s000) Print Purchase Order Header History (tdpur5403m000) Maintain Replenishment Orders (tdrpl0110m000) Maintain Replenishment Order Lines (tdrpl0111s000) Maintain Replenishment Order Deliveries (tdrpl0114m000) Confirm Backorders (tdrpl0120m000) Maintain Replenishment Order Receipts (tdrpl0122m000) Enter Specific Replenishment Order Numbers (tdrpl0482s000) Enter Specific Bill of Lading Numbers (tdrpl0483s000) Link Bills of Lading to Replenishment Orders (tdrpl0518s000) Maintain Margin Control Parameters (tdsls0120m000) Maintain Quotation Lines (tdsls1102s000) Maintain Quotation Lines (Wholesale) (tdsls1107s000) [SE@tdsls110 7s000] Display Gross Profit of Quotation Line (tdsls1808s000) Copy BOM Components to Quotation (tdsls1812s000) Maintain Sales Contract Lines (tdsls3102s000) Maintain Sales Orders (Wholesale) (tdsls4102m000) Maintain Sales Orders (Wholesale) (tdsls4105m000) Maintain Deliveries (tdsls4120m000) Change Prices and Discounts after `Maintain Deliveries' (tdsls412 2m000) Maintain Defaults by User (Sales) (tdsls4123m000) Maintain and Confirm Back Orders (tdsls4125m000) Link Delivery Lines (tdsls4144s000) Signal Inventory Shortages (tdsls4801s000) Calculate Sales Order Line Discounts (tdsls4802s000) Display Gross Profit of Sales Order Line (tdsls4808s000) Update Delivery Date in Sales Order Lines (tdsls4809s000) Recalculate Sales Price and Discount (tdsls4810s000) Maintain Invoice Details Accounts (tdsls6102m000)

BAAN Finance (tftf-20010): Match Receipts (tfacp1131s000)

BAAN Manufacturing (titi-20010): Maintain Production BOMs (tibom1110m000) Enter Material Issue for Production Orders (ticst0101m000) Post Purchase Receipts to Work-in-Process (ticst0105s000) Maintain Item Data (GRT) (tigrt1180s000) Maintain Customized Item Data (GRT) (tigrt2180s000) Maintain Item Data (tiitm0101m000) Maintain Item Data (in BOM) (tiitm0108s000) Maintain Item Default Data (tiitm0110m000) Maintain Planned MPS Interplant Orders (timps5110m000) Maintain Planned MPS Production Orders (timps5120m000) Maintain Planned MPS Purchase Orders (timps5130m000) Maintain Planned MRP Production Orders (timrp1120m000) Maintain Planned MRP Purchase Orders (timrp1121m000) Maintain Generic BOMs (tipcf3110m000) Maintain Material Sheets (tipcs1110m000) Maintain Customized Item Data (tipcs2121m000) Maintain Customized BOMs (tipcs2150m000) Maintain Planned PRP Warehouse Orders (Wrh to Project) (tipcs5130 m000) Maintain Work Centers (tirou0101m000) Maintain Production Orders (tisfc0101m000) Maintain Estimated Materials (tisfc0110m000)

BAAN Project (tptp-20010): Maintain Warehouse Orders (tpism3123m000) Maintain General Parameters (tppdm0100m000) Maintain Item Default Data (tppdm0109m000) Maintain Standard Items (tppdm0110m000) Maintain Projects (tppdm6100m000) Maintain Project Status (tppdm6107m000) Maintain Departments (tppdm8102m000) Maintain PSS Parameters (tppss0100m000) Maintain Planned Warehouse Orders (tppss6115m000)

BAAN Transportation (trtr-20010): Maintain Sales Forecast by Warehouse and Item (trdrp0101m000) Maintain Bill of Distribution (trdrp0110m000) Maintain Planned Replenishment Orders (trdrp0120m000) Maintain Locations (trwic1100m000) Maintain Blocking Statuses of Locations (trwic1101m000) Maintain Storage Conditions by Location (trwic1110m000) Maintain Locations by Storage Condition (trwic1111m000) Enter Item Inventory Adjustments (trwic2100m000) Maintain Blocking Statuses of Item Inventories (trwic2101m000) Maintain Inventory Remarks (trwic2105s000) Maintain Minimum Inventory of Items by Location (trwic4101m000) Maintain Storage Orders (trwoc1100m000) Maintain Locations by Storage Order (trwoc1101s000) Maintain Storage Orders (Invoicing Data) (trwoc1106m000) Maintain Storage Orders (General Data) (trwoc1107m000) Maintain Inbound Order Lines (trwoc2101m000) Maintain Inbound Data by Location/Lot (trwoc2102s000) Maintain Inbound Order Lines (Invoicing Data) (trwoc2106m000) Maintain Inbound Order Lines (General Data) (trwoc2107m000) Maintain Outbound Order Lines (trwoc3101m000) Maintain Outbound Data by Location/Lot (trwoc3102s000) Maintain Outbound Order Lines (Invoicing Data) (trwoc3106m000) Maintain Outbound Order Lines (General Data) (trwoc3107m000) Maintain Transhipment Orders (trwoc4100m000) Maintain Transhipment Order Lines (trwoc4101m000) Maintain Transhipment Orders (trwoc4105s000) Maintain Transhipment Order Lines (Invoicing Data) (trwoc4106m000) Maintain Transhipment Order Lines (General Data) (trwoc4107m000) Maintain Assembly Orders (trwoc5100m000) Maintain Assembly Order Lines (trwoc5101m000) Maintain Usage by Location/Lot (trwoc5102s000) Maintain Assembly Orders (Invoicing Data) (trwoc5106m000) Maintain Assembly Orders (General Data)

(trwoc5107m000) Maintain Warehousing Rate Codes by Price List (trwrc1120m000) Maintain Warehousing Rate Codes by Price Group (trwrc1130m000) Maintain Warehousing Rate Codes by Customer (trwrc1140m000) Maintain Warehousing Rate Codes by Item (trwrc1150m000) Maintain Warehousing Rate Codes by Warehouse (trwrc1170m000)
BAAN Service (tsts-20010): Maintain Component History (tssma1106m000) Maintain Items by Servicing (tssma1121m000) Maintain Service Cars (tssma3106m000) Maintain Actual Service Order Costs and Revenues (tssma3110m000) Maintain Service Order Cost Estimate (tssma3170m000)

Methods

1.1   Additional Coding Data Procedure (tccov00010-tr0010)
1.2   Additional Coding Data Procedure (tcedi00032-tr0010)

```
                    +--------------------+
                    | Maintain Schedule  |
                    | Release Frequencies|
                    | (tcedi2102m000)    |
                    |                    |
                    +--------------------+
                             |
                    +--------------------+
                    | Maintain Type of   |
                    | Delivery Specifier |
                    | (tcedi2104m000)    |
                    |                    |
                    +--------------------+
                             |
                    +--------------------+
                    | Maintain Schedule  |
                    | Status Indicators  |
                    | (tcedi2106m000)    |
                    |                    |
                    +--------------------+
                             |
                    +--------------------+
                    | Maintain Schedule  |
                    | Release Categories |
                    | (tcedi2108m000)    |
                    |                    |
                    +--------------------+
                             |
                    +--------------------+
                    | Maintain Item Status|
                    | Indicators         |
                    | (tcedi2110m000)    |
                    |                    |
                    +--------------------+
                             |
                    +--------------------+
                    | Maintain Production|
                    | Schedule Types     |
                    | (tcedi2112m000)    |
                    |                    |
                    +--------------------+
                             |
                    +--------------------+
                    | Maintain Packing   |
                    | Code IDs           |
                    | (tcedi2114m000)    |
                    |                    |
                    +--------------------+
                             |
                    +--------------------+
                    | Maintain Dates/Times|
```

```
|  (tcedi2122m000)      |
|                       |
+-----------------------+
            |
+-----------------------+
| Maintain Transport    |
| Types                 |
| (tcedi2134m000)       |
|                       |
+-----------------------+
            |
+-----------------------+
| Maintain Periods      |
| (tcedi2136m000)       |
|                       |
+-----------------------+
            |
+-----------------------+
| Maintain Discounts    |
| (tcedi2138m000)       |
|                       |
+-----------------------+
            |
+-----------------------+
| Maintain Discounts    |
| and Surcharges        |
| (tcedi2144m000)       |
|                       |
+-----------------------+
            |
+-----------------------+
| Maintain MeBaange     |
| Function              |
| (tcedi2150m000)       |
|                       |
+-----------------------+
            |
+-----------------------+
| Maintain Time Zone    |
| Specifier             |
| (tcedi2152m000)       |
|                       |
+-----------------------+
            |
+-----------------------+
| Maintain Contact      |
| Function              |
| (tcedi2154m000)       |
|                       |
+-----------------------+
            |
+-----------------------+
| Maintain              |
| Communication         |
| Channel               |
| (tcedi2156m000)       |
|                       |
+-----------------------+
            |
+-----------------------+
| Maintain Terms of     |
| Delivery Function     |
| (tcedi2158m000)       |
```

```
|                    |
+--------------------+
          |
+--------------------+
| Maintain Type of   |
| Supplementary      |
| Information        |
| (tcedi2160m000)    |
|                    |
+--------------------+
          |
+--------------------+
| Maintain Type of   |
| Contract and       |
| Carriage Condition |
| (tcedi2162m000)    |
|                    |
+--------------------+
          |
+--------------------+
| Maintain Type of   |
| Monetary Amount    |
| (tcedi2164m000)    |
|                    |
+--------------------+
          |
+--------------------+
| Maintain Charge    |
| Category           |
| (tcedi2166m000)    |
|                    |
+--------------------+
          |
+--------------------+
| Maintain Dimension |
| Qualifier          |
| (tcedi2168m000)    |
|                    |
+--------------------+
          |
+--------------------+
| Maintain Temperature|
| Qualifier          |
| (tcedi2170m000)    |
|                    |
+--------------------+
          |
+--------------------+
| Maintain Plus/Minus |
| Indicator          |
| (tcedi2172m000)    |
|                    |
+--------------------+
          |
+--------------------+
| Maintain Measurement|
| Qualifier          |
| (tcedi2174m000)    |
|                    |
+--------------------+
          |
+--------------------+
| Maintain Type of   |
```

```
                          |  Packages          |
                          |  (tcedi2176m000)   |
                          |                    |
                          +--------------------+
                                    |
                          +--------------------+
                          |  Maintain Transport|
                          |  Stage             |
                          |  (tcedi2178m000)   |
                          |                    |
                          +--------------------+
                                    |
                          +--------------------+
                          |  Maintain Equipment|
                          |  Qualifier         |
                          |  (tcedi2180m000)   |
                          |                    |
                          +--------------------+
                                    |
                          +--------------------+
                          |  Maintain          |
                          |  Shipper-Supplied  |
                          |  Equipment Indicator|
                          |  (tcedi2182m000)   |
                          |                    |
                          +--------------------+
                                    |
                          +--------------------+
                          |  Maintain Dangerous|
                          |  Goods Regulations |
                          |  (tcedi2184m000)   |
                          |                    |
                          +--------------------+
                                    |
                          +--------------------+
                          |  Maintain Government|
                          |  Involvement       |
                          |  Indicator         |
                          |  (tcedi2186m000)   |
                          |                    |
                          +--------------------+
                                    |
                          +--------------------+
                          |  Maintain Government|
                          |  Agencies          |
                          |  (tcedi2188m000)   |
                          |                    |
                          +--------------------+
                                    |
                          +--------------------+
                          |  Maintain Government|
                          |  Actions           |
                          |  (tcedi2190m000)   |
                          |                    |
                          +--------------------+
```

1.3   Additional Conversion Data Procedure (tcedi00031-tr0010)

```
                          +--------------------+
                          |  Maintain Conversion|
                          |  of Sales Contract |
                          |  Codes by Relation |
                          |  (in) (tcedi3114m000)|
                          |                    |
                          +--------------------+
```

```
                         |
            +--------------------+
            | Maintain Conv. of  |
            | Sales Contract Codes|
            | by Relation (out)  |
            | (tcedi4152m000)    |
            |                    |
            +--------------------+
                         |
            +--------------------+
            | Maintain Conversion |
            | of Project Codes by |
            | Relation           |
            | (tcedi3116m000)    |
            |                    |
            +--------------------+
                         |
            +--------------------+
            | Maintain Conversion |
            | of Project Codes by |
            | Relation (out)     |
            | (tcedi4154m000)    |
            |                    |
            +--------------------+
                         |
            +--------------------+
            | Maintain Conv. of  |
            | Forwarding Agent   |
            | Codes by Relation  |
            | (in) (tcedi3118m000)|
            |                    |
            +--------------------+
                         |
            +--------------------+
            | Maintain Conv. of  |
            | Forwarding Agent   |
            | Codes by Relation  |
            | (out)              |
            | (tcedi4156m000)    |
            |                    |
            +--------------------+
                         |
            +--------------------+
            | Maintain Conversion |
            | of Employee Codes by|
            | Relation           |
            | (tcedi3120m000)    |
            |                    |
            +--------------------+
                         |
            +--------------------+
            | Maintain Conversion |
            | of Employee Codes by|
            | Relation (out)     |
            | (tcedi4158m000)    |
            |                    |
            +--------------------+
```

1.4   Address Verification for Tax Provider (tcglob0020-1subglob1.03)
U.S. and Canadian addresses, determined based upon the country code, should be entered in
a predefined format to enable the tax provider to identify a taxing jurisdiction. The
city, state, and ZIP code for U.S. addresses and city, province and postal code for
Canadian addresses should be entered in the following format:

                         U.S.   Canada
                         ----   ------

```
Address Line 3:              City, ST      City, PR
Address Line 4:              ZipCode       PostalCode
```

The city and state or province is entered on the third address line and the ZIP or postal
code is entered on the fourth. The state or province should be entered in abbreviated
form. If the state is spelled out, the system automatically converts it to the
abbreviated form. For example if 'California' is entered, it is automatically converted
to 'CA'.

During the maintenance of address information, the city, state/ province, and ZIP/postal
code are verified to ensure that a valid combination was entered. The meBaange
'%MStcapis1116.1' or Invalid province/postal code combination (tccom99114.1) is displayed
if an invalid address combination is entered. Activate option [1] to invoke the
jurisdiction verification and selection process for existing addresses.

The tax provider assigns a GEO code to each address to uniquely identify a jurisdiction.
The tax provider determines the GEO code based upon the address information entered and
the county and city limits selected. The format of the GEO code varies by tax provider.
TAXWARE uses a two-digit GEO code; the GEO code together with the city, state, and ZIP
code, identifies the taxing jurisdiction. Quantum uses a nine-digit GEO code comprised
of a two-digit state code, three-digit county code, and a four-digit city code. A tenth
digit is used to identify if the jurisdiction is inside or outside of the city limits.

In some cases the city, state, and ZIP code combination does not uniquely identify a
jurisdiction. This may occur because the combination may reside in multiple counties or
may be either inside or outsdie of the city limits. If this situation occurs, the system
automatically zooms to the session "Select Tax Jurisdiction (tccoml900s000)" where you
can select the appropriate jurisdiction based on the county and city limits flag (TAXWARE
only) is displayed. For Quantum users, the jurisdiction may be selected based on the
county displayed; an additional field 'Inside City Limits (Y/N)' is used to indicate if
the address is inside or outside of the city limits.

1.5   Algorithm Procedure (tcqms00020-tr0010)

Some basic data must be defined prior to the algorithm procedure, namely:

- Characteristics
- Aspects (Optional)
- Characteristics by Aspects (Optional)

```
    +--------------------+
    | Maintain Algorithm |
    | Variables          |
    | (tcqms0123m000)    |
    |                    |
    +--------------------+
             |
    +--------------------+
    | Maintain Algorithms|
    | (tcqms0121m000)    |
    |                    |
    +--------------------+
             |
    +--------------------+
    | Maintain Variables |
    | by Algorithm       |
    | (tcqms0122s000)    |
    |                    |
    +--------------------+
```

1.6   Calibration Procedure (tcqms00040-tr0010)

```
                    +--------------------+
                    | Select Instruments |
                    | for Calibration    |
                    | (tcqms3201m000)    |
                    |                    |
                    +--------------------+
                             |
                    +--------------------+
                    | Enter Calibration  |
                    | Dates              |
                    | (tcqms3202m000)    |
                    |                    |
                    +--------------------+
```

1.7   Chart and Planning Board Data Procedure (tccom00070-tr0010)

```
              +--------------------+ +--------------------+
              | Maintain Planning  | | Maintain Default   |
              | Board Groups       | | Charts by User and |
              | (tccom5101m000)    | | Session            |
              |                    | | (tccom5110m000)    |
              |                    | |                    |
              +--------------------+ +--------------------+
                        |
              +--------------------+
              | Maintain Planning  |
              | Board Groups       |
              | (tccom5105m000)    |
              |                    |
              +--------------------+
```

1.8   Coding and Conversion Data Procedure (tcedi00030-tr0010)

```
              +--------------------+
              | Maintain Terms of  |
              | Delivery           |
              | (tcedi2128m000)    |
              |                    |
              +--------------------+
                        |
              +--------------------+
              | Maintain Conversion|
              | of Terms of Delivery|
              | Codes (in)         |
              | (tcedi3100m000)    |
              |                    |
              +--------------------+
                        |
              +--------------------+
              | Maintain Conversion|
              | of Terms of Delivery|
              | Codes (out)        |
              | (tcedi4130m000)    |
              |                    |
              +--------------------+
                        |
              +--------------------+
              | Maintain Countries |
              | (tcedi2126m000)    |
              |                    |
              +--------------------+
                        |
              +--------------------+
              | Maintain Conversion|
              | of Country Codes   |
              | (in) (tcedi3102m000)|
              |                    |
              +--------------------+
                        |
              +--------------------+
              | Maintain Conversion|
              | of Country Codes   |
              | (out)              |
              | (tcedi4140m000)    |
              |                    |
              +--------------------+
                        |
              +--------------------+
              | Maintain Units     |
              | (tcedi2130m000)    |
```

```
  |                      |
  +----------------------+
             |
  +----------------------+
  | Maintain Conversion  |
  | of Unit Codes (in)   |
  | (tcedi3104m000)      |
  |                      |
  +----------------------+
             |
  +----------------------+
  | Maintain Conversion  |
  | of Unit Codes (out)  |
  | (tcedi4142m000)      |
  |                      |
  +----------------------+
             |
  +----------------------+
  | Maintain Item Code   |
  | IDs (tcedi2132m000)  |
  |                      |
  +----------------------+
             |
  +----------------------+
  | Maintain Conversion  |
  | of Item Codes by     |
  | Relation (in)        |
  | (tcedi3106m000)      |
  |                      |
  +----------------------+
             |
  +----------------------+
  | Maintain Conversion  |
  | of Item Codes        |
  | (General) (in)       |
  | (tcedi3122m000)      |
  |                      |
  +----------------------+
             |
  +----------------------+
  | Maintain Conversion  |
  | of Item Codes by     |
  | Relation (out)       |
  | (tcedi4144m000)      |
  |                      |
  +----------------------+
             |
  +----------------------+
  | Maintain Conversion  |
  | of Item Codes (out)  |
  | (tcedi4160m000)      |
  |                      |
  +----------------------+
             |
  +----------------------+
  | Maintain Tax Code    |
  | IDs (tcedi2140m000)  |
  |                      |
  +----------------------+
             |
  +----------------------+
  | Maintain Tax Codes   |
  | (tcedi2142m000)      |
```

```
    |                   |
    +-------------------+
             |
    +-------------------+
    | Maintain Conversion |
    | of Tax Codes (in) |
    | (tcedi3108m000)   |
    |                   |
    +-------------------+
             |
    +-------------------+
    | Maintain Conversion |
    | of Tax Codes (out) |
    | (tcedi4146m000)   |
    |                   |
    +-------------------+
             |
    +-------------------+
    | Maintain Address  |
    | Code IDs          |
    | (tcedi2118m000)   |
    |                   |
    +-------------------+
             |
    +-------------------+
    | Maintain Conv. of |
    | Delivery Address  |
    | Codes by Customer |
    | (in) (tcedi3110m000)|
    |                   |
    +-------------------+
             |
    +-------------------+
    | Maintain Conversion |
    | of Postal Address |
    | Codes by Customer |
    | (in) (tcedi3112m000)|
    |                   |
    +-------------------+
             |
    +-------------------+
    | Maintain Conversion |
    | of Postal Address |
    | Codes by Supplier |
    | (in) (tcedi3113m000)|
    |                   |
    +-------------------+
             |
    +-------------------+
    | Maintain Conv. of |
    | Delivery Address  |
    | Codes by Customer |
    | (out)             |
    | (tcedi4148m000)   |
    |                   |
    +-------------------+
             |
    +-------------------+
    | Maintain Conv. of |
    | Postal Address Codes|
    | by Customer (out) |
    | (tcedi4150m000)   |
    |                   |
```

```
        +--------------------+
                 |
        +--------------------+
        | Maintain Conv. of  |
        | Postal Address Codes|
        | by Supplier (out)  |
        | (tcedi4151m000)    |
        |                    |
        +--------------------+
                 |
        +--------------------+
        | Maintain Currencies |
        | (tcedi2192m000)    |
        |                    |
        +--------------------+
                 |
        +--------------------+
        | Maintain Conversion |
        | of Currency Codes  |
        | (in) (tcedi3124m000)|
        |                    |
        +--------------------+
                 |
        +--------------------+
        | Maintain Conversion |
        | of Currency Codes  |
        | (out)              |
        | (tcedi4138m000)    |
        |                    |
        +--------------------+
                 |
        +--------------------+
        | Maintain Terms of  |
        | Payment / Late     |
        | Payment Surcharges |
        | (tcedi2194m000)    |
        |                    |
        +--------------------+
                 |
        +--------------------+
        | Maintain Conversion |
        | of Terms of Payment |
        | Codes (in)         |
        | (tcedi3126m000)    |
        |                    |
        +--------------------+
                 |
        +--------------------+
        | Maintain Conversion |
        | of Terms of Payment |
        | Codes (out)        |
        | (tcedi4166m000)    |
        |                    |
        +--------------------+
                 |
        +--------------------+
        | Maintain Conversion |
        | of Late Payment    |
        | Surcharges (in)    |
        | (tcedi3130m000)    |
        |                    |
        +--------------------+
                 |
```

```
+--------------------+
| Maintain Conversion |
| of Late Payment    |
| Surcharges (out)   |
| (tcedi4170m000)    |
|                    |
+--------------------+
          |
+--------------------+
| Maintain Third     |
| Parties            |
| (tcedi2148m000)    |
|                    |
|                    |
+--------------------+
          |
+--------------------+
| Maintain Conversion |
| of Third Party Codes|
| by Relation (in)   |
| (tcedi3128m000)    |
|                    |
+--------------------+
          |
+--------------------+
| Maintain Conversion |
| of Third Party Codes|
| by Relation (out)  |
| (tcedi4168m000)    |
|                    |
+--------------------+
          |
+--------------------+
| Maintain Order Types|
| (tcedi2100m000)    |
|                    |
+--------------------+
          |
+--------------------+
| Maintain Conversion |
| of Order Types (out)|
| (tcedi4132m000)    |
|                    |
+--------------------+
          |
+--------------------+
| Maintain Address   |
| Types              |
| (tcedi2124m000)    |
|                    |
+--------------------+
          |
+--------------------+
| Maintain Conversion |
| of Address Types   |
| (out)              |
| (tcedi4134m000)    |
|                    |
+--------------------+
          |
+--------------------+
| Maintain Reference |
| Number Types       |
| (tcedi2120m000)    |
|
```

```
                          |                       |
                          +-----------------------+
                                     |
                          +-----------------------+
                          | Maintain Conversion   |
                          | of Reference Number   |
                          | Types (out)           |
                          | (tcedi4136m000)       |
                          |                       |
                          +-----------------------+
                                     |
                          +-----------------------+
                          | Maintain Conversion   |
                          | of Warehouse          |
                          | Addresses (out)       |
                          | (tcedi4162m000)       |
                          |                       |
                          +-----------------------+
                                     |
                          +-----------------------+
                          | Maintain Character    |
                          | Conversion Codes      |
                          | (tcedi4108m000)       |
                          |                       |
                          +-----------------------+
                                     |
                          +-----------------------+
                          | Maintain Character    |
                          | Conversions (out)     |
                          | (tcedi4109m000)       |
                          |                       |
                          +-----------------------+

                          + --- --- --- --- --- +
                          | Check/Clear           |
                          | Conversion of Item    |
                          | Codes by Relation     |
                          | (in) (tcedi3200m000)  |
                          |                       |
                          + --- --- --- --- --- +
                                     |
                          + --- --- --- --- --- +
                          | Check/Clear           |
                          | Conversion of Item    |
                          | Codes by Relation     |
                          | (out)                 |
                          | (tcedi4200m000)       |
                          |                       |
                          + --- --- --- --- --- +
                                     |
                          + --- --- --- --- --- +
                          | Copy Conversion       |
                          | Tables                |
                          | (tcedi7200m000)       |
                          |                       |
                          + --- --- --- --- --- +
```

1.9   Communication Procedure (tcedi00060-tr0010)

```
                          +-----------------------+
                          | EDI Interchange       |
                          | Controller            |
                          | (tcedi7210m000)       |
                          |                       |
                          +-----------------------+
```

```
                          |
             +--------------------+
             | Terminate Front-End |
             | EDI Processor       |
             | (tcedi0249m000)     |
             |                     |
             +--------------------+
                          |
             +--------------------+
             | Process Saved       |
             | MeBaanges to be     |
             | Received            |
             | (tcedi7252m000)     |
             |                     |
             +--------------------+
                          |
             +- - - - - - - - - - -+
             | Delete Trace Files  |
             | (tcedi7230m000)     |
             |                     |
             +- - - - - - - - - - -+
                          |
             +--------------------+
             | Generate EDI        |
             | MeBaanges           |
             | (tcedi7201m000)     |
             |                     |
             +--------------------+
                          |
             +--------------------+
             | Restart Generated   |
             | MeBaanges           |
             | (tcedi7221m000)     |
             |                     |
             +--------------------+
                          |
             +- - - - - - - - - - -+
             | EDI Interchange     |
             | Monitor             |
             | (tcedi7505m000)     |
             |                     |
             +- - - - - - - - - - -+
```

1.10   Communication for Multi-Company Networks (tcedi00060-multicomp)
Communication via a multicompany network goes as follows: When an EDI meBaange is
generated from the session "EDI Interchange Controller (tcedi7210m000)" or "Direct
Network Communication (tcedi7205m000)", the EDI relation is used to determine the
internal company for which the meBaanges are meant.
    e.g.: - Current Company 450

        - 'EDIREL'   "Relation"
        - 'CUSTOID'   "Customer"
        - Yes [ENtcyesno."Affiliated Company"
        - 560   "Affiliated Company No."
The generated EDI meBaange is placed in the directory "/appl_comm/c560" of the
multicompany network. While the meBaange is being generated, the "/command" directory of
the multicompany network will contain the file "multicomp.560". As long as this file is
in the above directory, no EDI meBaanges will be saved or read in the directory
"/appl_comm/c560"; the file also holds information on the write action being performed at
that moment.
The trace file of the EDI meBaange is in the subdirectory of the company in which the
meBaange has been generated. This subdirectory is called "/trace/c450".
There are 3 ways to copy the generated meBaange in the receiving company:
1.   By letting the system perform an automatic batch in the receiving company via the
session "EDI Interchange Controller (tcedi7210m000)".

2.   By starting the session "Direct Network Communication (tcedi7205m000)" in the receiving company (once only)
3.   By setting the field "Start Read Batch after Generating" to "Yes" in the session "Maintain Networks (tcedi0120m000)" in the sending company. The batch for reading meBaanges will then be automatically started (once only) in the receiving company. This possibility is only available if the files of the receiving company can be accessed directly.
When the EDI meBaange is copied in the receiving company, the file "multicomp.560" is again generated in the "/command" directory of the multicompany network. As a result, it is not possible to write to the directory "/appl_comm/c560" from another directory. All other data that is saved when the EDI meBaange is copied is written in the subdirectories "../c560".
If the destination company for the meBaanges cannot be reached directly, the meBaanges must be transferred manually to a receipt directory (appl_comm or appl_to) of the network at the receiving company.

1.11   Conversion Considerations for Tax Provider (tcglob0020-1subglob1.06)

For those users currently running BAAN IV, the Tax Provider Interface should be implemented at month end after closing out your financial period and before processing begins for the current period. However, we do recommend implementing at quarter end to facilitate tax reporting. If you are unable to convert at quarter end, both BAAN IV and the tax provider tax registers must be consulted when filing your quarterly reports.

Pre-Conversion Steps

The following should occur prior to implementing the Tax Provider Interface:
---------- 1.   Define the countries for which U.S. and Canadian address verification is to be performed using Maintain Country Tax Provider Register (tccoml140m000).
---------- 2.   Convert existing address information to predefined format.
U.S. and Canadian addresses, determined based upon the country code, should be in a predefined format to enable the tax provider to identify geo codes to uniquely identify a taxing jurisdiction.
The city, state, and ZIP code for U.S. addresses and city, province and postal code for Canadian addresses should be in the following format:
U.S.

| Address Line 3 | City, ST | Menlo Park, CA |
| Address Line 4 | Zip Code | 94025 |

Canada

| Address Line 3 | City, PR | Montreal, QB |
| Address Line 4 | Postal Code | H1A1A1 |

The state or province should be in abbreviated form.

Run Address Format Conversion Utility tccoml911m000) [SEtccoml911m000] to convert existing address formats. An invalid address report will be generated for U.S. and Canadian addresses which cannot be converted. These addresses should be corrected using the appropriate BAAN IV session.
---------- 3.   Repeat the above step until all addresses are in the correct format.
---------- 4.   Install TAXWARE's Master Tax System or Vertex's Quantum for Sales and Use Tax using the instructions provided by the tax provider vendor.
---------- 5.   Close the Fiscal Period using the session Close Periods (tfgld1206m000).

Conversion Steps

The following steps should be taken to implement the tax provider interface prior to entering transactions for the current fiscal period:
---------- 1.   Set the parameter '%FFtccoml150m0001txpr' to Yes using Maintain Tax Provider Parameters (tccoml150m000).
---------- 2.   Define the tax provider, either TAXWARE's Master Tax System or Quantum for Sales/Use Tax using Maintain API Parameters (tcapil136m000).
---------- 3.   Define tax provider-specific environment variables. Refer to Technical Implementation Considerations (tcglob00201subglob1.07) for more information.
---------- 4.   Verify and assign GEO codes to existing address information using Address Jurisdiction Verification Utility (tccoml910m000). Choose option to update. This utility will automatically assign a GEO code based upon the most likely candidate for valid addresses. For Quantum users, the city limits flag assigned to each address is set to Yes for inside the city limits.

An invalid address report will be generated for invalid address combinations. These addresses should be corrected using the appropriate BAAN IV session.

---------- 5.   Repeat the above step until all addresses are correct and have been assigned a GEO code.

---------- 6.   Evaluate GEO codes and redefine if neceBaanry.

In some cases it may be neceBaanry to assign a GEO code or city limits (Quantum users only) other than the defaults assigned if the address qualifies for multiple taxing jurisdictions. Review the report generated in 4. above. To change the GEO code for an existing address run its associated maintenance session. Activate option [1] to invoke the jurisdiction verification and selection process and select the appropriate taxing jurisdiction from the list provided. The city limits flag may be entered directly using the address's associated maintenance session.

---------- 7.   Using the TAXWARE or Quantum systems, enter your company, customer, and product-related information.

---------- 8.   Define the valid product categories using Maintain Product Categories (tccoml138m000). The product categories defined should match the product categories defined within the tax provider for proper tax processing.

---------- 9.   Enter the matrix of Item Groups, Items, Contract Types, and Account Numbers by product category using Maintain Product Category Tax Matrix (tccoml139m000).

---------- 10.   Enter the Sales/Service/Rental Use Indicator for Contract Types (tssma224) using Maintain Contract Types (tssma2124m000). This field indicates the type of tax processing required for the contract type since services and rentals can be taxed differently.

---------- 11.   For TAXWARE users, enter the Point of Title PaBaange for each Terms of Delivery (tcmcs041), either "Point of Origin" or "Point of Destination" using Maintain Terms of Delivery (tcmcs0141m000).

The Point of Title PaBaange indicates the location at which legal title is transferred to the purchaser. TAXWARE uses the Point of Title PaBaange along with other information, to determine the taxing jurisdiction.

Post-Conversion Considerations

---------- 1.   Reevaluation of your current tax structure within BAAN Finance (tftf-20010) should be considered since the tax provider does not require the complex methodology needed by non-tax provider users. When interfacing with a tax provider, the tax codes sole purpose is to define the GL accounts for which to post. Rates and jurisdiction will be determined by the tax provider.

You may want to consider using separate tax codes for Finance transactions. See step 2. below for more information.

---------- 2.   Since tax impact for financial transactions will not be written to the tax provider tax register, manual adjustments must be made within the provider for the tax prior to filing your quarterly reports. To facilitate tracking of the tax for finance transactions, you may want to consider using separate tax codes for these transactions.

---------- 3.   For Service Contracts the location of the covered installations is assumed as the delivery address. For proper taxation, separate contracts should be maintained for each customer location.

1.12   Conversion Parameter Procedure (tcedi00040-tr0010)

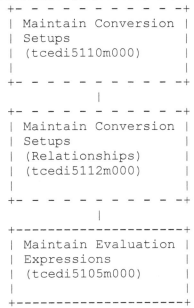

1.13   Currency Formats (tcmcs10010-sf0020)

In the application you can make use of flexible formats. Flexible formats allow the user to determine the exactness with which quantities, prices and amounts are presented. Quantities, prices and amounts can be presented to four decimal places. This degree of exactness can be adjusted through flexible formats. These are applied in two areas within the application:

• Currency formats (prices and amounts)
• Quantity formats (quantities)

Below, we describe the use of currency formats in detail. For a description of the use of quantity formats, you are referred to Quantity Formats (tcmcs10010sf0030).

Currency formats: The degree of exactness with which currencies are presented differs from one currency to the other. In practice, currencies of which the basic unit represents a relatively low value are generally presented as whole figures (e.g. Belgian frank or Italian lira). Currencies of which the basic unit represents a relatively high value are generally presented with one or more decimals (Dutch guilder, German mark). Several currencies can be used at the same time in one logistic/financial system. It is therefore desirable that each currency is rounded and presented in a manner that is characteristic for that currency.

You must first define the currency before setting up its format. This should be done in two places. First each currency must be made known to the system as generic unit in the session "Maintain Generic Units (ttaad1106m000)". (Most currencies have already been predefined in this session.) Subsequently, you must define the currency within the application in the session "Maintain Currencies (tcmcs0102m000)". The code of the currency defined in the session "Maintain Currencies (tcmcs0102m000)" should be equal to the code of the generic unit defined in session "Maintain Generic Units (ttaad1106m000)". The currency defined in the session "Maintain Currencies (tcmcs0102m000)" is then used in the application, on sales and purchase orders, etc.

Within the application, prices and amounts are arranged in a number of categories. Each category is identified by a format code. Format codes are available as predefined codes within the system. The table below lists all predefined format codes:

Format Code	Application
001	Rates (Manufacturing)
002	Rates (Transportation)
003	Prices
004	Cost Prices
005	Amounts
006	Cumulatives
007	Fuel Prices (Transportation)
008	Advances and Expenses
009	Amounts by Unit (Transportation)
010	Small Amounts
021	Small Amounts
095	Amounts (Finance)
096	Cumulatives (Finance)
400	Rates (Manufacturing and Project)

To each format code, you can link an unlimited number of generic units (= currencies), with the desired form of presentation. This is done in the session "Maintain Formats by Generic Unit (ttaad1107m000)". There are a great many different possibilities - it is possible, for instance, to present prices with a greater degree of exactness than amounts in the same currency.

Example: You wish prices in a specific currency to be registered with two decimal places, and amounts to be presented as whole numbers. Execute the following steps:

a)   Define the currency as generic unit in the session "Maintain Generic Units (ttaad1106m000)".

b)   Define the currency as application currency in the session "Maintain Currencies (tcmcs0102m000)".

c)   In the session "Maintain Formats by Generic Unit (ttaad1107m000)", select the format code for prices (003) and link a generic unit to it with a format allowing two decimal places to be specified. Execute the same steps for amounts; link formats without decimals to the format codes for amounts (a.o. 005 and 095).

Consequences: Within the application this will have the following consequences. It will be possible to enter amounts in whole numbers only. Decimals will not be accepted. In calculations, amounts will be rounded to whole numbers. Prices can be entered with up to two decimals. Prices will be calculated to two decimal places.

Note: The currency format system is subject to various limitations. As these are NOT tested by the application, users should be careful to comply with them:

• The currency in the session "Maintain Currencies (tcmcs0102m000)" must have the same code as the generic unit in the session "Maintain Generic Units (ttaad1106m000)".

•   When creating a new currency, you should check if the currency is present as a generic unit. You should furthermore check if a generic unit with the right format is available for all relevant format codes.

•   In the session "Maintain Currencies (tcmcs0102m000)" you can link a rounding factor to each currency (in the field "Rounding Factor"). This will allow you, for instance, to round amounts to multiples of 0.05. This rounding factor is not related to the format (and the degree of rounding resulting from it) recorded in the session "Maintain Formats by Generic Unit (ttaad1107m000)". Hence, it hardly makes sense to define a rounding factor of 0.01 in the session "Maintain Currencies (tcmcs0102m000)" if currency formats without decimals have been linked to the currency concerned in the session "Maintain Formats by Generic Unit (ttaad1107m000)". This rounding factor is only used to round amounts (not prices).

1.14   Defining Quality Combinations (tcqms00030-sf0011)

These are guidelines for the definition of new quality combinations in session "Maintain Quality Combinations (tcqms0111m000)".

Note:

There may be certain restrictions on these fields. In other cases, the available choices are indicated in between brackets '[]'.

Select "Origin":

Certain modules or packages may not be implemented.

Sales (SLS)

Enter the marked fields:

Quality Group * Project *

Only projects with status "Active".

Item *

Only if field "Quality Group" was skipped. Mandatory, if field "Project" was specified. The Item Type may be [Purchased/ Manufactured/ Cost/ Service/ Subcontracting

Container *

Customer *

Supplier

Position

Standard/Customized

Sub-Item

Container

Routing

Operation

Task

Only Recommended *

Blocking Method for Inspections *

[Block

[Continue Only if field "Only Recommended" is set to "Yes".

Quality ID *

Purchase (PUR)

Enter the marked fields:

Quality Group *

Project *

Only projects with status "Active".

Item *

Only if field "Quality Group" was skipped.Mandatory if field "Project" was specified.The Item Type may be [Purchased/Manufactured/ Subcontracting.

Container *

Customer

Supplier *

Position

Standard/Customized

Sub-Item

Container

Routing

Operation

Task

Only Recommended *

Blocking Method for Inspections *

[Block

[Continue Only if field "Only Recommended" is set to "Yes".

Quality ID *

Production (SFC)

Enter the marked fields:

Quality Group *

Project *

Only projects with status "Active".

Item *
Only if field "Quality Group" was skipped. Mandatory if field "Project" was specified.
The Item Type must be Manufactured and the item cannot be a Process Item.
Container
Customer
Supplier
Position
Standard/Customized
Sub-Item
Container
Routing
Operation
Task
Only Recommended *
Blocking Method for Inspections *
[Block before Posting/ Block after Posting [Continue Only if field "Only Recommended" is set to "Yes".
Quality ID *
Material (BOM)
Enter the marked fields:
Quality Group Project *
Only projects with status "Active".
Item *
The Item Type must be "Manufactured" and the item cannot be a Process Item.
Container
Customer
Supplier
Position *
Standard/Customized *
Only if the main item is Customized Item.
Sub-Item *
Enter a component or material:
Container
Routing
Operation
Task
Only Recommended *
Blocking Method for Inspections *
[Block
[Continue Only if field "Only Recommended" is set to "Yes".
Quality ID *
Routing (TI)
Enter the marked fields:
Quality Group Project *
Only projects with status "Active".
Item *
The Item Type must be Manufactured and the item cannot be a Process Item.
Container
Customer
Supplier
Position
Standard/Customized
Sub-Item
Container
Routing *
Operation *
Task *
Only Recommended *
Blocking Method for Inspections *
[Block on Operation/ Block on Compl. Operation [Continue Only if field "Only Recommended" is set to "Yes".
Quality ID *
Production (PMG)
Enter the marked fields:
Quality Group * Project Item *
Only if field "Quality Group" was skipped.
The item must be a process item.
Container *
Only if the item is Containerized.
Customer

Supplier
Position
Standard/Customized
Sub-Item
Container
Routing
Operation
Task
Only Recommended *
Blocking Method for Inspections *
[Block before Posting/ Block after Posting [Continue Only if field "Only Recommended" is set to "Yes"
Quality ID *
Material (FRM)
Enter the marked fields:
Quality Group
Project
Item *
The item must be a Process Item.
Container *
Specified   - the main item formula
Not specified - the end item formula
Customer
Supplier
Position *
Standard/Customized
Sub-Item *
Automatically filled by the position number in the formula.
Container *
Only if the sub-item is Containerized.
Routing
Operation
Task
Only Recommended *
Blocking Method for Inspections *
[Block
[Continue Only if field "Only Recommended" is set to "Yes".
Quality ID *
Routing (PS)
Enter the marked fields:
Quality Group
Project
Item *
The item must be a Process Item.
Container *
Only if the item is Containerized.
Customer
Supplier
Position
Standard/Customized
Sub-Item
Container
Routing *
Operation *
Task *
Only Recommended *
Blocking Method for Inspections *
[Block on Operation/ Block on Compl. Operation [Continue Only if field "Only Recommended" is set to "Yes".
Quality ID *
Storage Inspection
Storage inspections cover all the items in the inventory used in the following modules:
•   Inventory Control (INV)
•   Location Control (ILC)
Enter the marked fields:
Quality Group *
Project *
Only projects with status "Active".
Item *

Only if field "Quality Group" was skipped. Mandatory if field "Project" was specified.
The Item Type may be [Purchased/ Manufactured/ Cost/ Service/ Subcontracting
Container *
Only if the item is Containerized.
Customer
Supplier
Position
Standard/Customized
Sub-Item
Container
Routing
Operation
Task
Only Recommended *
Blocking Method for Inspections *
[Block
Quality ID *

1.15 EDI History Procedure (tcedi00070-tr0010)

```
                        +- - - - - - - - - -+
                        | Print History of  |
                        | Generated MeBaanges  |
                        | (tcedi7401m000)   |
                        |                   |
                        +- - - - - - - - - -+
                                 |
                        + --- --- --- --- ---
                        | Delete History of |
                        | Generated MeBaanges  |
                        | (tcedi7801m000)   |
                        |                   |
                        + --- --- --- --- ---
                                 |
                        +- - - - - - - - - -
                        | Print History of  |
                        | Received MeBaanges   |
                        | (tcedi7402m000)   |
                        |                   |
                        +- - - - - - - - - -+
                                 |
                        + --- --- --- --- ---
                        | Delete History of |
                        | Received MeBaanges   |
                        | (tcedi7802m000)   |
                        |                   |
                        + --- --- --- --- --- +
```

1.16 EDI Master Data Procedure (tcedi00010-tr0010)

```
                        +--------------------+
                        | Maintain          |
                        | Organizations     |
                        | (tcedi0103m000)   |
                        |                   |
                        +--------------------+
                                 |
                        +--------------------+
                        | Maintain EDI      |
                        | MeBaanges         |
                        | (tcedi0105m000)   |
                        |                   |
                        +--------------------+
                                 |
                        +--------------------+
                        | Maintain Supported |
                        | EDI MeBaanges     |
                        | (tcedi0101m000)   |
                        |                   |
```

```
                            +--------------------+
                            |                    |
                            +--------------------+
                            | Maintain Relations |
                            | (tcedi0110m000)    |
                            |                    |
                            +--------------------+
                                      |
                            +--------------------+
                            | Maintain EDI       |
                            | MeBaanges Supported|
                            | by Relations       |
                            | (tcedi0111m000)    |
                            |                    |
                            +--------------------+
                                      |
                            +--------------------+
                            | Maintain Relation  |
                            | Structure for      |
                            | Outgoing MeBaanges |
                            | (tcedi0130m000)    |
                            |                    |
                            +--------------------+
                                      |
                            +--------------------+
                            | Maintain Outgoing  |
                            | MeBaanges by Session|
                            | (tcedi0115m000)    |
                            |                    |
                            +--------------------+
```

100 % Sampling
Test Group (may be changed in the inspection order).
Test Type   : 100 %
Actual Data
Order Quantity [TFtcqms120.oqua: 10000 pieces
Sample Size   : 10000 pieces

Sample	est Quantity	uantity
1	500	1000
2	2500	5000
3	500	2000
4	1000	2000
		-----+
		10000

Single Sampling
Test Group (may be changed in the inspection order).
Test Type   : Single Sampling
Sample Size [TFtcqms036.sa[%] :   20 %
Actual Data
Order Quantity [TFtcqms120.oqua: 10000 pieces
Sample Size   : 2000 pieces

Sample	est Quantity	uantity
1	500	1000
2	100	1000
		----+
		2000

Continuous Sampling
Test Group (may be changed in the inspection order).
Test Type   : Continuous Sampling
Sample Size   : 100 pieces
Frequency   : 300 pieces
Consequently, a sample must be drawn for each 300 pieces produced.
Actual Data
Order Quantity   : 1300 pieces

Sample	est Quantity	uantity
1	50	100
2	100	100
```
```

```
3                        25                      100
4                        50                      100
```

4 samples x 300 pieces = 1200. The remaining 100 pieces will not be taken for sampling.

Test Data

```
Sample                   est Quantity                    uantity
1                        500                     1000
```

```
Characteristic                      : Length
Serial Number                       alue
1              13.4  cm                          Bad
2              15.8  cm                          Good
```

```
Characteristic                      : Diameter
1              2.1   cm                          Good
2              2.5   cm                          Good
```

The overall result of the first test quantity (Serial Number = 1) is bad whereas the overall result for the second test quantity is good. Depending on the "Acceptable Quality Level   ", the order quantity is either accepted or not. If, for example, the "Acceptable Quality Level   " is defined as 90%, the total order quantity is rejected.

1.18   Generating Standard Inspections (tcqms00050-sf0010)

Standard inspection orders are generated by the system when quality combinations or order-specific data exist and when the following sessions are used, sorted by origin:
•   Purchase (PUR) Maintain Receipts (tdpur4120m000) For this origin, field "Inspection" must be set to "Yes". See also session "Maintain Purchase Order Lines (tdpur4102s000)", screen 2.
•   Sales (SLS) AND module "Location Control (ILC)" Generate Outbound Advice (tdilc4201m000) Maintain Outbound Data (tdilc4101m000)
•   Sales (SLS) AND business object "Hard Allocations" Generate Hard Allocations (tdinv2201m000) Maintain Hard Allocations (tdinv2101m000)
•   Production (SFC), Material (BOM), Routing (TI) WITHOUT module "Location Control (ILC)" Release Production Orders (tisfc0204m000)
•   Material (BOM) AND module "Location Control (ILC)" Generate Outbound Advice (tdilc4201m000)
•   Production (PMG), Routing (PS) Release Production Batches (pspmg0204m000)
•   Material (FRM) Release Outbound Data (tdilc4202m000)

Finally, for all sales orders, purchase orders, production orders, and production batches, it is possible to maintain the inspection orders by origin, the order headers, and the order lines in the following sessions:
•   Maintain Standard Inspections by Origin (tcqms1120m000)
•   Maintain Inspection Orders (tcqms1100s000)
•   Maintain Inspection Order Lines (tcqms1101s000)

1.19   IRS 1099-MISC Reporting (tcglob0010-lsubglobl.04)

1.20   Import/Export Reporting (tccom00060-sf0010)

Import and export reporting comprises two elements: the sales listing and the statistics report. The Sales Listing is based on financial transactions resulting from export transactions, registered and processed at the invoice level. The statistics report is based on financial transactions, including some additional information, registered at the item level.

The transactions are supplied from various corners of the system; it is also possible to manually add, delete or modify transactions.

Periodically, all this data is processed and written to a a sequential file or printed on paper. The file or printed paper can then be sent to the proper authorities.

1.21   Incoming MeBaange Data (tcedi00080-tr0010)

```
                    +- - - - - - - - - -+
                    | Direct Network    |
                    | Communication     |
                    | (tcedi7205m000)   |
                    |                   |
                    +-------------------+
                              |
                    +- - - - - - - - - -+
                    | Print Saved MeBaanges|
                    | to be Received    |
                    | (tcedi7450m000)   |
```

```
|                    |
+--------------------+
         |
+- - - - - - - - - -+
| Print Received    |
| MeBaange Errors   |
| (tcedi7451m000)   |
|                    |
+--------------------+
         |
+- - - - - - - - - -+
| Display Saved     |
| MeBaanges to be   |
| Received          |
| (tcedi7550m000)   |
|                    |
+--------------------+
         |
+- - - - - - - - - -+
| Display Received  |
| MeBaange Errors   |
| (tcedi7551m000)   |
|                    |
+--------------------+
         |
+- - - - - - - - - -+
| Display Received  |
| Batch Reference   |
| (tcedi7560m000)   |
|                    |
+--------------------+
         |
+--------------------+
| Maintain Saved    |
| MeBaanges to be   |
| Received          |
| (tcedi7150m000)   |
|                    |
+--------------------+
         |
+- - - - - - - - - -+
| Maintain Selection|
| Criteria          |
| (tcedi7299s000)   |
|                    |
+--------------------+
         |
+--------------------+
| Maintain Saved    |
| MeBaange Data to be|
| Received          |
| (tcedi7151s000)   |
|                    |
+--------------------+
         |
+--------------------+
| Approve Saved     |
| MeBaanges to be   |
| Received          |
| (tcedi7250m000)   |
|                    |
+--------------------+
         |
```

```
                +--------------------+
                | Print and/or Delete|
                | Saved MeBaanges to be|
                | Received           |
                | (tcedi7251m000)    |
                |                    |
                +--------------------+
                          |
                +--------------------+
                | Process Saved      |
                | MeBaanges to be    |
                | Received           |
                | (tcedi7252m000)    |
                |                    |
                +--------------------+
```

1.22   Inspection Order and Order Line Status (tcqms00050-sf0020)

CONTENTS
1.   Inspection Order Status
2.   Inspection Order Line Status
3.   The Relationship between Order Status and Order Line Status

1.   INSPECTION ORDER STATUS

Field "Inspection Status" is used to indicate the current status of the inspection order.
The status can have the following values:

Free
If the inspection order is created and no action has been taken for the inspection order.

Active
If one of the order lines has status "Active".

Completed
If all order lines have status "Completed".

Processed
If the inspection order is processed by means of session "Process Inspection Orders
(tcqms1204m000)".

Closed
If the following session was used:
•   Check and Close Standard Inspections (tcqms1205m000)

2.   INSPECTION ORDER LINE STATUS

This field "Order Line Status" is used to indicate the current status of the inspection
order line. This status can have the following values:

Free
If the inspection order line is created and no action has been taken for the inspection
order line.

Printed
If the inspection order and its lines are printed by means of session "Print Inspection
Orders (tcqms1400m000)". Depending on the value of field "Mandatory Printing of
Inspection Order Documents", this step is either mandatory or optional.

Active
If test results are entered for an order line.

Completed
If all test results were entered for the line and for all related samples.

3.   THE RELATIONSHIP BETWEEN ORDER STATUS AND ORDER LINE STATUS

```
+-----------------------------------------------------------------------+
| Inspection Status               | Order Line Status                   |
|                                 |                                     |
|---------------------------------+-------------------------------------|
| Free                         -> |                                     |
|                                 | Free                                |
|                                 | Printed [ENtcqms.osta.(optional)    |
|                                 | Active                              |
| Active                          | <-                                  |
| If one line is "Active"         |                                     |
|                                 | Completed                           |
| Completed                       | <-                                  |
|                                 |                                     |
| If all lines are "Completed"    |                                     |
|                                 |                                     |
| Processed                       |                                     |
```

```
|                                    |                                                              |
| Closed                             |                                                              |
 +------------------------------------------------------------------------------------------------------+
1.23  Inspection Procedure (tcqms00050-tr0010)
                              +-------------------+
                              | Maintain Standard |
                              | Inspections by    |
                              | Origin            |
                              |  (tcqms1120m000)  |
                              |                   |
                              +-------------------+
                                        |
                              +-------------------+
                              | Maintain Inspection|
                              | Orders            |
                              |  (tcqms1100s000)  |
                              |                   |
                              +-------------------+
                                        |
                              +-------------------+
                              | Maintain Inspection|
                              | Order Lines       |
                              |  (tcqms1101s000)  |
                              |                   |
                              +-------------------+
                                        |
                              + - - - - ----------+
                              | Print Inspection * |
                              | Orders            |
                              |  (tcqms1400m000)  |
                              |                   |
                              +---------- - - - - -+
                                        |
                              +-------------------+
                              | Maintain Samples  |
                              |  (tcqms1110m000)  |
                              |                   |
                              |                   |
                              +-------------------+
                                        |
                              +-------------------+
                              | Enter Test Data   |
                              |  (tcqms1115m000)  |
                              |                   |
                              |                   |
                              +-------------------+
                                        |
                              +-------------------+
                              | Complete Inspection|
                              | Orders Collectively|
                              |  (tcqms1202m000)  |
                              |                   |
                              +-------------------+
                                        |
                              +-------------------+
                              | Process Inspection |
                              | Orders            |
                              |  (tcqms1204m000)  |
                              |                   |
                              +-------------------+
```
*) This session is mandatory or optional, depending on parameter "Mandatory Printing of
Inspection Order Documents" in session "Maintain QMS Parameters (tcqms0100m000)".
1.24 Integrations (tcqms00090-sf0000)
SEE ALSO METHOD(S)
•   Using QMS for Manufacturing Operations

- Using QMS in Production (SFC)
- Using QMS for Materials of Production Orders
- Using QMS for Process Operations
- Using QMS in Production (PMG)
- Using QMS for Materials of Batches

1.25   Master Data Procedure (tcqms00010-tr0010)

CONTENTS

1.   Main Procedure
2.   Additional Procedure

1.   MAIN PROCEDURE

This procedure is used to define the basic data of characteristics.

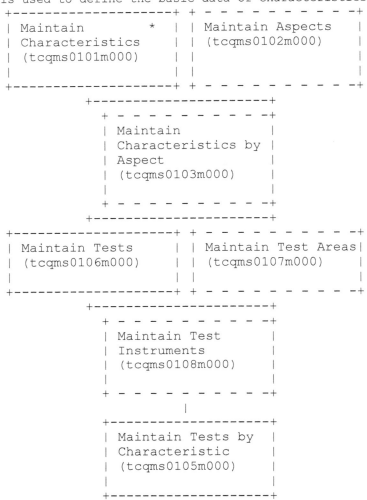

* Default fields may be empty since certain data is not yet entered, e.g. test area.

2.   ADDITIONAL PROCEDURES

For further information, see keyword(s)

- Option Sets
- Options

Characteristic:
 Characteristic Type   qms.ctyp.option]
 Method [TFtcqms001.mthd: Variable

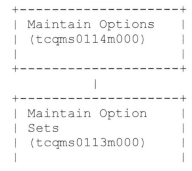

```
                     +-------------------+
```

1.26 Multi-Company Network (tcedi00020-multicomp)
EDI also allows you to exchange data between two or more local companies.
For each network you can indicate whether it is a multicompany network or not. This is
done via the field "Multicompany" in the session "Maintain Networks (tcedi0120m000)".
If you have indicated that it is, the system generates a directory structure that is
somewhat different from the normal structure.
•   A appl_comm directory is generated, instead of an appl_from or appl_to directory.
•   In the directories appl_comm, trace, appl_save, appl_text and store_recv the
subdirectory c999 is generated ('999' stands for the current company number)
SEE ALSO METHOD(S)
•   Network Directory Structure
In each company with which data is exchanged directly, the same multicompany network is
generated. The field "Path" must be the same. For each company a subdirectory will be
generated in the directory structure.
The easiest way to set up such a multicompany network is to use the sessions "Export EDI
Data (tcedi6221m000)" and "Import EDI Data (tcedi6220m000)". In the company of your
choice you create the multicompany network and the required EDI meBaanges and conversion
setups only once. This data can then be copied to the other companies.
When network data is being imported, the above subdirectory will be generated, where
needed.
If the company for which the EDI meBaanges are intended cannot be accessed directly,
generating a multicompany network at the receiving side is unneceBaanry.
For each company the network identifications must be entered (the session "Maintain
Relation Data by Network (tcedi0128m000)") and the required incoming and/or outgoing EDI
meBaanges specified (the session "Maintain EDI MeBaanges Supported by Relations
(tcedi0111m000)").
SEE ALSO METHOD(S)
•   Communication for Multi-Company Networks
1.27 Network Directory Structure (tcedi00020-structure)
The directory structure of a EDI network has the following subdirectories:
•   appl_from   (not included in a multicompany network)
Contains files with meBaanges generated by the system for an external relation.
•   appl_to   (not included in a multicompany network)
Contains files with external EDI meBaanges which are read in by the system.
•   appl_comm   (only included in a multicompany network)
Contains the generated meBaanges that must be read in by an internal company. The
meBaanges are in the subdirectory "/c999"; '999' stands for the company number under
which the meBaanges must be read in.
•   appl_save
Contains files in which the system has found errors while reading them in.
•   appl_text
Texts stored as ASCII files are included in this directory.
•   command
Contains semaphore files for:
•   the communication with the Front-end EDI-processor
•   the mutual communication between internal companies
•   trace
Contains ASCII files in which the processing sequence for EDI meBaanges that are read in
and generated is logged.
•   store_recv
If the parameter "Store All Received MeBaanges" is on "Yes", all the meBaanges received
will be logged here.
•   store_sent
If the parameter "Store All Sent MeBaanges" is on "Yes", all the meBaanges sent will be
logged here. In the case of a multicompany network, only the meBaanges received will be
logged.
   For example, the basic directory "/usr1/edi" will contain the
   following subdirectories:

```
                 /usr1/edi/appl_from ----------> or /usr1/edi/appl_comm
                 /usr1/edi/appl_to ------+
                 /usr1/edi/appl_save
                 /usr1/edi/appl_text
                 /usr1/edi/command
                 /usr1/edi/store_recv
                 /usr1/edi/store_sent
                 /usr1/edi/trace
```
1.28 Networking Procedure (tcedi00020-tr0010)

```
          +-------------------+
          | Maintain Networks |
          | (tcedi0120m000)   |
          |                   |
          +-------------------+
                    |
          +-------------------+
          | Maintain Connect  |
          | Frequencies by    |
          | Network           |
          | (tcedi0122m000)   |
          |                   |
          +-------------------+
                    |
          +-------------------+
          | Maintain Connect  |
          | Times by Network  |
          | (tcedi0125m000)   |
          |                   |
          +-------------------+
                    |
          +-------------------+
          | Generate Connect  |
          | Times by Network  |
          | (tcedi0225m000)   |
          |                   |
          +-------------------+
                    |
          +-------------------+
          | Maintain Relation |
          | Data by Network   |
          | (tcedi0128m000)   |
          |                   |
          +-------------------+
```

1.29   Order-Specific Inspection Procedure (tcqms00070-tr0010)

```
          +-------------------+
          | Maintain          |
          | Order-Specific    |
          | Inspections       |
          | (tcqms0149m000)   |
          |                   |
          +-------------------+
                    |
          +-------------------+
          | Maintain          |
          | Order-Specific    |
          | Inspection Data   |
          | (Header)          |
          | (tcqms0150s000)   |
          |                   |
          +-------------------+
                    |
          +-------------------+
          | Maintain          |
          | Order-Specific    |
          | Inspection Data   |
          | (Lines)           |
          | (tcqms0151s000)   |
          |                   |
          +-------------------+
```

This procedure is optional. If inspection orders are automatically generated, these orders are based on the master data or the order- specific inspection data.

In session "Maintain Order-Specific Inspections (tcqms0149m000)", all orders of the implemented origins are shown by means of their order number.
In session "Maintain QMS Parameters (tcqms0100m000)", the integrated modules are shown.
1.30   Outgoing MeBaange Data (tcedi00080-tr0020)

```
                              +- - - - - - - - - -+
                              | Display MeBaanges to |
                              | be Generated         |
                              | (tcedi7500m000)      |
                              |                      |
                              +- - - - - - - - - -+
                                        |
                              + --- --- --- --- ---
                              | Maintain MeBaanges to|
                              | be Generated         |
                              | (tcedi7100m000)      |
                              |                      |
                              + --- --- --- --- ---
```

1.31   Parameters for Tax Provider (tcglob0020-lsubglob1.01)
Parameters are used to indicate if the tax provider interface is used and the processing required.
Maintain API Parameters (tcapil136m000)
*   API type
*   Interface Provider
*   Interface Used
Maintain Tax Provider Parameters (tccoml150m000)
*   Tax Provider
*   Point of Title PaBaange
*   Warn if Tax on ACP invoices
1.32   Procedure Intra EU Transactions (tccom00060-tr0010)

```
                              +--------------------+
                              | Maintain Additional |
                              | Statistical         |
                              | Information Sets    |
                              | (tccom7105m000)     |
                              |                     |
                              +--------------------+
                                        |
                              +--------------------+
                              | Maintain Sales      |
                              | Listing             |
                              | (tccom7170m000)     |
                              |                     |
                              +--------------------+
                                        |
                              +--------------------+
                              | Process Sales       |
                              | Listing             |
                              | (tccom7270m000)     |
                              |                     |
                              +--------------------+
                                        |
                              +--------------------+
                              | Maintain            |
                              | Import/Export       |
                              | Statistics          |
                              | (tccom7171m000)     |
                              |                     |
                              +--------------------+
                                        |
                              +--------------------+
                              | Process             |
                              | Import/Export       |
                              | Statistics          |
                              | (tccom7271m000)     |
```

```
                   |                    |
         +--------------------+
```
1.33   Procedure TRITON Common Parameters (tcpar00010-tr0010)
1.34   Procedure for Deriving Default Tax Code (tcglob0010-lsubglobl.02)
The following procedure is used for deriving default tax codes in the destination sales
tax environment.
Part A: Derivation of Shipped to Postal Code
For SLS SMA WOC TOC
1. Postal Code from Delivery Address
2. Postal Code from Customer Address
For PUR TFC
1. Postal Code from Delivery Address
2. Postal Code from Own Warehouse Address
3. Postal Code from Own Address from com000
Part B: Exception for Taxes
Exceptions for Taxes can be defined for Country, Customer, Item, Item Group and Postal
Code
Exceptions can be defined by using the Maintain Exceptions for Taxes - Sales
(tcmcsl138m000) or Maintain Exceptions for Taxes - Purchase (tcmcsl146m000) sessions.
It is mandatory to enter the country code here. In addition to the country code, the
system will search other options in following order:
1.   Country, Customer/Supplier, Item, Item Group and Postal Code
2.   Country, Customer/Supplier, Item, Postal Code
3.   Country, Customer/Supplier, Item, Item Group
4.   Country, Customer/Supplier, Item
5.   Country, Customer/Supplier, Item Group, Postal Code
6.   Country, Customer/Supplier, Item Group,
7.   Country, Customer/Supplier, Postal Code,
8.   Country, Customer/Supplier
9.   Country, Item, Item Group, Postal Code
10.   Country, Item, Postal Code
11.   Country, Item, Item Group
12.   Country, Item
13.   Country, Item Group, Postal Code
14.   Country, Item Group
15.   Country, Postal Code
16.   Country
Part C: Exceptions by Locations
If no match is found in Part B, Part C is executed.
Exceptions by Locations can be defined using the Maintain Exceptions by Tax Location
(tcmcsl139m000) session.
Exceptions are define for Sales transactions only on the basis of the Ship to, Ship from
and point of Order Acceptance (Postal Address). This takes care of those exceptions where
the tax is derived based on the point of Origin or point of Order Acceptance with respect
to the point of Destination.
The Postal Code for Destination is derived as shown above
The Postal Code for Origin is derived as follows:
For SLS SMA WOC TOC

1. Postal Code from Own Warehouse or goods loading Address
2. Postal Code from Own Company Address

For PUR TFC

1. Postal Code from Supplier Address
The Postal Code for Order Acceptance is the postal code from the postal address of the
Order.
The priority of the search for exceptions is as follows:
1.   Country, Destination, Origin, Order Acceptance
2.   Country, Destination, Origin
3.   Country, Destination, Order Acceptance
4.   Country, Destination
5.   Country, Origin, Order Acceptance
6.   Country, Origin
7.   Country, Order Acceptance
8.   Country
Part D: Tax By Destination Postal Codes
If no match is found in Part B and Part C, the default tax code is derived from the
destination or the shipped to postal code.

Tax Codes by Destination Postal Code can be defined in the Maintain Tax Codes by Postal
Code (tcmcsl136m000) session.
The postal codes defined here are 'from' postal codes so the tax code will be the default
for the postal code where it is defined and all the postal codes between the current
postal code and the one defined in the next record for the same country.

1.35   Quality Control Procedure (tcqms00030-tr0010)

```
                                  Quality Side
                         +-------------------+
                         | Maintain Quality  |
                         | IDs (tcqms0110m000)|
                         |                   |
                         +-------------------+
                         +-------------------+
          +-------------------+ +-------------------+
          | Maintain          | | Maintain Tests by |
          | Characteristics by| | Quality ID        |
          | Quality ID        | | (tcqms0117m000)   |
          | (tcqms0115m000)   | |                   |
          |                   | |                   |
          +-------------------+ +-------------------+
                         +-------------------+
                         +-------------------+
                         | Maintain Test     |
                         | Groups by Quality |
                         | ID (tcqms0136m000)|
                         |                   |
                         +-------------------+
                                   |
                         +-------------------+
                         | Maintain          |
                         | Characteristics by|
                         | Test Group        |
                         | (tcqms0137m000)   |
                         |                   |
                         +-------------------+
       Logistic Side                 |
    +---------------------+          |
    || - Items          ||          |
    ||                  ||          |
    || - Items by Quality||          |
    ||   Group          ||          |
    ||                  ||          |
    || - Customers      ||+-------------------+
    ||                  |||                   |
    || - Suppliers      ||| Maintain Quality  |
    ||                  ||| Combinations      |
    ||                  ||| (tcqms0111m000)   |
    ||                  |||                   |
    || - Projects       ||+-------------------+
    ||                  ||
    || - Routings       ||
    || - Operations     ||
    +---------------------+
```

1.36   Quantity Formats (tcmcs10010-sf0030)
Flexible formats allow the user (within certain limits) to determine the exactness with
which quantities, prices and amounts are presented. Quantities, prices and amounts can be
presented with up to four decimal places. This degree of exactness can be adjusted
through flexible formats. These are applied in two areas within the application:
•   Quantity formats (quantities)
•   Currency formats (prices and amounts)
SEE ALSO METHOD(S)
•   Currency Formats
Quantity formats: The degree of exactness of quantities and the form in which they are
presented differs from one application area to the other. Quantities are arranged in

categories, each of which is identified by a format code. Format codes are recorded in the system. The predefined quantity format codes are listed in the table below:

Format Code	Application
Q03	BOM Unit
Q04	Net Quantity in BOM
Q05	Routing Unit
Q06	Production Rate
Q07	Component Quantity
Q08	Outbound Quantity
Q09	Finished Product Quantity
Q10	Quantity (MPS Data)
Q11	Number of Units
Q12	Ordered Quantity (PRP)
Q13	Ordered Quantity (PUR)
Q14	Quantity Planned (CRP)
Q20	Inventory Quantity
Q21	Warehouse Order Data 1
Q22	Warehouse Order Data 2
Q23	Cumulative Usage Quantity 1
Q24	Cumulative Usage Quantity 2
Q25	Ordered Quantity (SLS)
Q30	Formula Size
Q31	Net Quantity (FRM Components)
Q32	Routing Unit (Process)
Q33	Production Rate (Process)
Q34	Finished Product Quantity (Process)
Q35	Container Quantities
Q36	Component Quantities (Process)
Q37	Co/By Product Quantities (Process)
Q38	Quantity (QMS)
Q40	Quantity (SMA)
Q45	Installed Quantity (SMA)

To each format code, a generic unit must be linked with the right presentation form (in the session "Maintain Formats by Generic Unit (ttaad1107m000)").

Example: You wish inventory data to be registered with four decimals in your system and purchase and sales data with two.

Execute the following steps: a) In the session "Maintain Formats by Generic Unit (ttaad1107m000)", select the format code for inventory applications (Q20) and define a format with four decimal places. b) In the same session, select the format code for purchase and sales quantities (Q13 and Q25 respectively) and define a format with two decimals.

Consequences: Inventories are registered and presented in (rounded to) four decimals. Wherever inventory levels are maintained directly (e.g. inventory adjustments), quantities can be entered with up to four decimals. Amounts in purchase and sales control always have two decimal places. For example, order quantities are registered and presented in or rounded to two decimals, and ordered, delivered and backorder quantities can be entered with a precision of two decimals.

Note: The quantity format system is subject to the following limitations. As these are NOT tested by the application, users should be careful to comply with them:
•   Processes like order processing cannot be conducted with a higher precision than that of registering inventory.
•   In the session "Maintain Units (tcmcs0101m000)" you can link a rounding factor to each unit. In this way you can have the system round quantities to a specific multiple whenever a specific unit is involved.

1.37   Storage Inspection Procedure (tcqms00060-tr0010)

```
| Inspections        |
| (tcqms2120m000)    |
|                    |
+--------------------+
         |
+--------------------+
| Maintain Storage   |
| Inspection         |
| Inventory          |
| (tcqms2120s000)    |
|                    |
+--------------------+
+----------------------+
|+------------------+|  Part of the
|| Maintain Inspection||  Standard Procedure
|| Orders           ||
|| (tcqms1100s000)  ||
||                  ||
|+------------------+|
|         |          |
|+------------------+|
|| Maintain Inspection||
|| Order Lines      ||
|| (tcqms1101s000)  ||
||                  ||
|+------------------+|
|         |          |
|+ - - - - ----------+|
|| Print Inspection * ||
|| Orders           ||
|| (tcqms1400m000)  ||
||                  ||
|+--------- - - - - -+|
+----------------------+
+--------------------+
| Maintain Samples   |
| (Storage           |
| Inspections)       |
| (tcqms2110m000)    |
|                    |
+--------------------+
+----------------------+
|+--------------------+|  Part of the
|| Enter Test Data    ||  Standard Procedure
|| (tcqms1115m000)    ||
||                    ||
|+--------------------+|
|          |           |
|+--------------------+|
|| Complete Inspection||
|| Orders Collectively||
|| (tcqms1202m000)    ||
||                    ||
|+--------------------+|
|          |           |
|+--------------------+|
|| Process Inspection ||
|| Orders             ||
|| (tcqms1204m000)    ||
||                    ||
|+--------------------+|
+----------------------+
  +--------------------+
```

```
                    | Print and Close     |
                    | Storage Inspections |
                    | (tcqms2221m000)     |
                    |                     |
                    +---------------------+
```

*) This session is mandatory or optional, depending on parameter "Mandatory Printing of Inspection Order Documents" in session "Maintain QMS Parameters (tcqms0100m000)".

1.38 Storage Inspections (tcqms00060-sf0010)

Storage inspections are inspections on items in inventory. These items may need regular check-ups. To be able to do these check-ups or inspections, the items as well as the reason for inspection must be defined. For this purpose, session "Generate Storage Inspections (tcqms2220m000)" is used. The items selected by means of this session are blocked in inventory after which inspection orders are generated.

Next,the inventory must be assigned to a specific order. This means that there can be more than one order for all inventory of the same item. After this, the storage inspection order lines can be generated and the sample(s) can be drawn. Based on the test results that are entered, inventory is accepted or rejected.

All inventory is put on-hand (unblocked) by means of session "Print and Close Storage Inspections (tcqms2221m000)" . Rejected quantities can be taken from inventory by means of an inventory transfer.

1.39 Syntax for Expressions (tcqms00020-sf0030)

SYNTAX FOR EXPRESSIONS

VARIABLES

Variables are defined in session "Maintain Algorithm Variables (tcqms0123m000)" and can be linked to characteristics in session "Maintain Variables by Algorithm (tcqms0122s000)".

Variables are case sensitive and must be entered in uppercase to be regarded as proper variables.

  Example:
  Correct   : 1D, TA, V1, etc.
  Incorrect : 1d, Ta, ta, v1, etc.

OPERATORS

Arithmetic Operators:
  * / + - : multiplication/division/addition/subtraction
  \   : remainder after division
  &   : linking strings (alphanumeric arrays)

Logical Operators:
 or, and, not
Logical operators are used in Boolean expressions. These expressions are either 'true' or 'not true'. The logical value 'true' corresponds to value '1' and the logical value 'not true' to '0'.

Relational Operators:
  = : equal to
  <> : unequal to
  > : greater than
  >= : greater than or equal to
  < : less than
  <= : less than or equal to
Assignment commands are recorded by means of ":=".

Priority in Expressions:
Arithmetic operators have priority over relational operators. Relational operators have priority over logical operators. The priority sequence for arithmetic operators is: * / \ + -. The priority sequence for logical operators is: not, and, or. These sequences can be modified by means of round brackets.

  Example:
   3 + 4 * 5 = 23
   (3 + 4) * 5 = 35

FUNCTIONS

Arithmetic Functions:
 round(X,Y,Z): round off X value;
               Y the number of decimals
               Z rounding method (down = 0, normal = 1, up = 2)

 val(A)   : numeric value of string A   (val("8.7") = 8.7)
 abs(X)   : absolute value of X   (abs(-10.3) = 10.3)
 int(X)   : full value of X   (int(11.6) = 11   )
 pow(X,Y)   : involution   (pow(10,2) = 100   )
 sqrt(X)   : root of X   (sqrt(16) =   4   )
 min(X,Y)   : smallest values of X and Y   (min(6,10) =   6   )

```
 max(X,Y)    : largest values of X and Y          (max(6,10) =  10  )
 pi          : constant with PI value             (3.1415926...     )
Goniometric Functions:
  sin(X),  cos(X),  tan(X) : sine, cosine, or tangent of X (radials)
  asin(X), acos(X), atan(X): arcsine, arccosine, or arctangent of X
  hsin(X), hcos(X), htan(X): sine-, cosine-, or tangent-hyperbolicus of X
Logarithmic Functions:
  exp(X)  : e-power of X
  log(X)  : natural logarithm of X with base e
  log10(X): logarithmic value of X with base 10
Date Functions:
  time       : current time
  date       : current date
  date(d,m,y): date as day, month, and year
               e.g. date(1,5,1991) = May 1 1991
Numeric Intervals:
  Example:
   5 IN [12,30] = 0
  15 IN [12,30] = 1
EXAMPLE
       +---------------+
       | 1D + TA - BS  |
       +---------------+
```

Explanation:
 1D is aspect/characteristic DIAMETER/HEAD
 TA is aspect/characteristic TAIL/LENGTH
 BS is aspect/characteristic PITCH/WIDTH
 The results of these characteristics are used to evaluate the
 algorithm.

1.40   TRITON Common Parameters Relationships (tcpar00010-tr0020)

1.41   Table Coding (tcmcs10010-sf0010)

Tables are filled by defining codes and recording a quantity of data. The codes are defined only once, which enhances consistency within BAAN IV.

This approach precludes errors; moreover, it simplifies the maintenance of tables with codes. Codes may have up to three positions and are alphanumeric. If they consist of less than three positions, they will be right-aligned; this is important for sorting.

To coding methods are possible:
•   sequence number, for instance: 001, 002, 003, 004 etc.
•   self-explanatory codes, for instance: NED, ENG, GER, FRA etc.

If you select the first method, you are recommended to create parallel coding systems for countries, languages and currencies; the second method is to be preferred as only the code will appear on many reports and screen displays.

1.42   Tables for Destination Sales Tax (tcglob0010-lsubglobl.01)

In North America, sales tax is generally charged only to the final consumer. The tax rates are determined by the local authorities in the jurisdiction where the goods are received/consumed. In many cases there are multiple jurisdictions with authority over the same location. For example: the city, county, and state/province may each charge their own taxes and each set their own rules for what is taxable and whether there are exceptions or maximums.

In order to satisfy the requirement of "Destination Sales Tax" in BAAN IV, the delivery address is used to determine the appropriate tax code. The postal code field of the address is used to define the link from the delevery address to the tax code. Exceptions can be defined by customer, item, etc or by combination of origin and destination location.

Tax authority codes and groups are used to identify the jurisdiction applicable to a specific tax code or tax code level. Tax analysis report data can be selected and sorted based on the tax authority codes and tax authority groups.

1.43   Tables for Tax Provider (tcglob0020-lsubglob1.02)

Information such as registered countries, product categories, Point of Title PaBaange, and Sales/Service/Rental Use Indicator is maintained within BAAN IV to provide flexibility when interfacing to a tax provider.

SEE ALSO KEYWORD(S)
•   Country Tax Provider Register
•   Product Category
•   Product Category Tax Matrix

1.44   Tax Calculations (tcglob0010-lsubglobl.03)

Tax Calculations for Exception Cases

There are three new fields Defined along with the tax tables
"Maximum Tax Amount"
"Tax Base Amount"

"Rate for Excess Amount"
1.45   Tax Calculations for Tax Provider (tcglob0020-1subglob1.04)
BAAN IV computes tax on a line basis when interfaced to a tax provider. This is
neceBaanry to accommodate product taxability. The tax provider will compute the
applicable tax amount based upon the taxing jurisdiction, taxable amount, order type such
as sales or service and the type of product being sold or purchased. The tax provider
determines the taxing jurisdiction based upon the ship-from, ship-to, point of order
acceptance, and point of order origin (TAXWARE only) addresses which apply for the
transaction.
The following table indicates by order type, for BAAN Service (tsts-20010) and BAAN
Distribution (tdtd-20010), the hierarchy process used to identify the ship-from, ship-to,
point of order acceptance, and point of origin addresses:

Type of Order	Ship-from	Ship-to	Point of Ord. Accept.	Point of Ord. Origin
SLS order SLS quot. SRV order	SHIPPABLE ITEM - Warehouse NON-SHIP. ITEM - Company	- Specific delivery address - Delivery address - Customer	Company	Company
SLS instal.	Company	- Specific delivery address - Delivery code - Customer	Company	Company
PUR order	Supplier	- Specific delivery address - Warehouse - Company	- Specific postal address - Postal code - Supplier	- Specific postal address - Postal code - Supplier
SRV contr.	Company	- Specific del (loc) - Delivery code (location) - Customer	Company	Company

The following table indicates, by Finance session, for BAAN Finance (tftf-
20010), the hierarchy process used to identify the ship-from, ship-to, point of
order acceptance, and point of origin addresses:

Finance Session	Ship-from	Ship-to	Point of Ord. Accept.	Point of Ord. Origin
tfacp1110s000 tfacp1112s000 tfacp1120s000 tfacp2110s000	- One-time address - Supplier	Company	- One-time address - Supplier	- One-time address - Supplier
tfacr1110s000 tfacr1111s000 tfacr2110s000	Company	- One-time address - Customer	Company	Company
tfacr4100m000 tfacr4101s000	Company	- One-time address - Customer	Company	Company

tfacr5420m000	Company	- One-time address - Customer	Company	Company
tfcmg1113m000 tfcmg1113s000 tfcmg1120m000 tfcmg1220m000	- One-time address - Supplier	Company	- One-time address - Supplier	- One-time address - Supplier
tfcmg2100s000 tfcmg2108s000	ADV RECEIPT Company ADV PAYMENT - One-time address - Supplier	ADV RECEIPT - One-time address - Customer ADV PAYMENT Company	ADV RECEIPT Company ADV PAYMENT - One-time address - Supplier	ADV RECEIPT Company ADV PAYMENT - One-time address - Supplier
tfcmg2116s000	Supplier	Company	Supplier	Supplier
tfcmg2117s000	Company	Customer	Company	Company
tfcmg2140s000	Company ADV PAYMENT - Supplier	Customer ADV PAYMENT - Company	Company ADV PAYMENT - Supplier	Company ADV PAYMENT - Supplier
tfcmg4120m000	Company PUR INVOICE PUR CREDIT - Cust's Supplier	Customer PUR INVOICE PUR CREDIT Company	Company PUR INVOICE PUR CREDIT - Cust's Supplier	Company PUR INVOICE PUR CREDIT - Cust's Supplier
tfcmg2120s000 tfgld1103s000 tfgld1104s000 tfgld1105s000 tfgld1114s000 tfgld1115s000 tfgldl201m000 tfgld1204s000	Company	Company	Company	Company

The following table shows the values or hierarchy process used to determine the value, by order type or transaction type, of additional input information used by the tax provider for tax calculations.

Transaction Type	Sales/Service/ Rental/Purchase Indicator	Product Category	Point of Title PaBaange
SLS order	'Sales'	- Item code - Item group - Item code itself (VERTEX)	Terms of delivery
SLS install	'Sales'	- Installment item code - Item group - Item code	Terms of delivery

			itself (VERTEX)	
SRV order	'Service'	- Item code	Default
		- Item group	parameter
		- Item code	
		itself (VERTEX)	
SRV contract	Contract type	Contract type	Default
			parameter
PUR order	'Sales'	- Item code	Terms of
		- Item group	delivery
		- Item code	
		itself (VERTEX)	
Finance transactions	'Sales'	Ledger Account (if available)	Default parameter

When interfacing to a tax provider the tax code is used to determine the GL accounts for which to cost the tax. In addition the tax code indicates if the transaction is taxable -- a transaction with a blank tax code is considered non-taxable.

Tax information is stored for tracking and reporting purposes within the tax provider registers. The register stores information such as the type of transaction, document or invoice number, invoice date, and the amount of tax withheld by taxing jurisdiction. The tax provider tax register is updated automatically when invoicing definitively within BAAN Distribution and BAAN Service. Audit reports and tax reporting is available from the tax provider vendors.

1.46 Tax Impact on Sales Installments for Tax Provider (tcglob0020-1subglob1.05)

When interfacing with a tax provider, the tax withheld on sales installments is considered 'Estimated' tax. The estimated tax is considered as a part of the payment terms. The BAAN IV tax register and tax provider tax registers will not be updated for estimated tax. The actual tax is recognized when the order is settled. For Direct orders this occurs as shipments are made and invoices are generated. For Indirect orders, the tax is recognized when the order is closed and a final invoice is generated. The correction entry generated when closing an order in Maintain Installment Data (tdsls4106s000) will include the amount of tax and late payment surcharge due. The tax and late payment surcharge due will be included in the amount of the correction entry created and the tax code will be blank.

1.47 Technical Implementation Considerations (tcglob0020-1subglob1.07)

The Tax Provider interface requires several set up steps to create the link with the third party software. This process involves modification of both the system and application environment.

UNIX system maintenance and configuration

The tax provide interface uses UNIX meBaange queues to communicate with the BAAN IV product. The UNIX kernel must be configured to provide enough meBaange queues and a large enough buffer for passing meBaanges. The following kernel parameters should be examined and modified, if neceBaanry. (Please note that the specific parameter name(s) might vary slightly for different UNIX operating systems. If the parameter listed in the table does not exist, please find the parameter in your UNIX version with the same purpose.)

Parameter	Purpose	Recommended value
MSGMAX	This parameter specifies the maximum size of a meBaange	2048 or greater
MSGMNB	This parameter specifies the maximum number of bytes on meBaange queues system wide	System maximum
MSGTQL	This parameter specifies the maximum number of open meBaanges system wide	System maximum or (2 * BAAN IV users)
MSGMNI	This parameter specifies the maximum number of meBaange queues that can be used system wide	System maximum or (5 * BAAN IV users)

The interface is designed to allocate and deallocate meBaange queues at the start and close of the API. In the event of non-standard exit of the BAAN IV application, it is possible that meBaange queues could fail to be properly released. It is recommended that the UNIX system manager monitor the meBaange queues defined in the UNIX environment periodically. MeBaange queues that are currently allocated can be shown on most UNIX systems by issuing the following command, ipcs.

MeBaange queues that are owned by user root should never by removed, but meBaange queues owned by non active users can be deallocated by executing the following command (on most UNIX systems), ipcrm -q <meBaange queue number>.

Pre-installation steps

Please verify that there is an ANSI C compiler on the UNIX host system. The C compiler is required. Install the tax provider software and create the provider databases.

TAXWARE

The BAAN IV   Tax API requires
Verazip, Sales and Use Tax System, and the STEP
system from TAXWARE. The tax API will not work if
all of these products are not installed and
configured correctly. The TAXWARE products must be
configured to work together when TAXWARE is
installed. (See TAXWARE documentation for more
detail.)

Vertex

The BAAN IV   Tax API requires the
complete Quantum system, including the GeoCoder
and Sales Tax system. Put the tax provider
environmental variables in the /etc/profile or
.profile of each '%LBtcgen.p.aa' user.

TAXWARE

Variable	Purpose	Req./Opt.
AVPIN	Defines input directory for tax data files	Req.
AVPOUT	Defines output directory for tax data files	Req.
AVPAUDIT	Defines directory for tax audit files	Req.
AVPTEMP	Defines directory for temporary use by tax system	Req.
STEPIN	Defines input directory for step data files	Req.
STEPOUT	Defines output directory for step data files	Req.
STEPAUDIT	Defines directory for step audit files	Req.
STEPTEMP	Defines directory for temporary use by STEP	Req.
ZIPIN	Defines input directory for Verazip data files	Req.
ZIPOUT	Defines output directory for Verazip data files	Req.
ZIPTEMP	Defines directory for temporary use by Verazip	Req.

Vertex

Variable	Purpose	Req./Opt.
VERTEXGEO	Defines directory where geocode database resides	Req.
VERTEXRATE	Defines directory where rate database resides	Req.
VERTEXREG	Defines directory where register database resides	Req.
VERTEXTDM	Defines directory where TDM	Opt.*

```
                database resides
VERTEXPWD       Defines the working directory to   Opt.
                be used by the TDM
VERTEXUSER      Defines the user information when Opt.
                using a relational database
                system
VERTEXSERVER    Defines database information when Opt.
                using a relational database
                system
```

        *VERTEXTDM must be defined when using the TDM

Preparing the temporary directory

Create a temporary directory
Copy the proper library from $BSE/api/lib to the temporary directory libtavp.a for
TAXWARE
     libtvtx.a for Vertex
     libtaxb.a when TAXWARE and Vertex will both be used on the
     same system
Copy the proper makefile from $BSE/api/lib to the temporary directory Makefile.avp for
TAXWARE
     Makefile.vertex for Vertex
     Makefile.both when TAXWARE and Vertex will be used

Customizing the Makefile

Copy the Makefile (Makefile.vertex, Makefile.avp, or Makefile.both) to makefile Edit
makefile using an editor Make the following modifications to the file

TAXWARE

Set CC equal to the executable for the ANSI C compiler
Set CCOPTIONS equal to any compile options need for an
ANSI compilation
Set AVPDIR equal to the directory above the Btree library
Set AVPTAXDIR equal to the directory where the tax objects
and headers are found
Set AVPZIPDIR equal to the directory where the ZIP objects
and headers are found
Set AVPSTEPDIR equal to the directory where the step
objects and headers are found

Vertex

Set CC equal to the executable for the ANSI C compiler
Set CCOPTIONS equal to any compile options need for an
ANSI compilation
Set VERTEXDIR equal to the directory above the Vertex
product directories

Both

Follow the steps for editing the TAXWARE and Vertex
makefiles above

Create executable

Type make in the temporary directory Copy api6.1 from the temporary directory to $BSE/bin
Change the group of $BSE/bin/api6.1 to group bsp Change the owner of $BSE/bin/api6.1 to
user bsp Change permissions to 550 for $BSE/bin/api6.1

Configure BAAN IV shared memory

The tax provider frequently uses three utility programs to retrieve tax rates and
geocodes from the tax provider. Placing these objects into shared memory will greatly
enhance the speed of the tax provider api.
Enter the BAAN IV application as user bsp Execute the Maintain Shared Memory Data session
(ttaad4150m000) Insert a record, under package tc 4.0L b glo0, for the following program
objects

tcapil000m000
tcapidll1001
tcapidll1002
tccomdll0020
Convert to runtime Data dictionary
Troubleshooting / Error solving

There are several classes of errors that may occur due to problems with the third party software or incorrect data passed to the interface. These errors should occur very infrequently and in most cases will never appear.

Error range	Error information	Description
0-99	General communication failure errors	Communication
1100-1199	TAXWARE Verazip product error	TAXWARE product problem or data issue
1200-1299	TAXWARE Sales and Use Tax problem or error in tax calculation	TAXWARE product data issue
1300-1399	TAXWARE Sales and Use Tax problem or error in jurisdiction	TAXWARE product data issue
1400-1499	Vertex Geocoder product error problem or data issue	Vertex product
1500-1599	Vertex Quantum system tax problem calculation error calculation error	Vertex product or
1600-1699	Vertex Quantum system problem jurisdiction determination issue error	Vertex product or data

There are two UNIX environment variables that allow a longer "wait" time to be specified for API informations. These parameters will only need to be set on extremely heavily loaded systems or as an added safeguard against "spikes" in the system load. The default values for these parameters are reasonably high and will not generally need to be set. The APISTART variable specifies the number of second the 4GL session will wait for the API process to start. The API process will generally take less than a second to start. The APIWAIT variable specifies the amount of time the 4GL session will wait for an expected meBaange from the API. For example, if a request is made to calculate tax for a sales order, the 4GL session will wait no longer than twenty seconds for a response from the API. The API process will normally send information back to the 4GL session in less than a second.

Variable	Purpose	Tunes
APISTART	Defines maximum number of seconds BAAN IV will wait for api process to start. Default setting is 20, but if an error 12 occurs set APISTART to greater than 20 in the UNIX environment for each user.	API timeout
APIWAIT	Defines the maximum number of seconds MeBaange timeout BAAN IV will wait for a response from the api. The default setting is 20, if error 11 occurs, set APIWAIT to greater than 20 in the UNIX environment for each user.	

1.48   Units and Quantities in QMS (tcqms10010-sf0050)
CONTENTS
1.   Units
2.   Quantities
2a   Order Quantity
2b   Sample Size
2c   Sample Quantity
2d   Test Quantity
3.   Example
1.   UNITS
An important rule in QMS is that the following units must have the same physical quantity, e.g. "Length":
•   Characteristic Unit
•   Test Unit
•   Least Measurable Unit (of the instrument used to test the characteristic)

Example:

The quality of item "Tube" is determined by checking the following
characteristics:
- Length
- Diameter
- Volume

Characteristic   Length
Characteristic Unit [TFmt(meter).chun]

Tests by Characteristic
Test Unit [TF@tcqms005.cmn(centimeter)

2.   QUANTITIES
2a.   ORDER QUANTITY
The quantity for which the inspection is required. Consequently, the result of the
inspection order decides the quality of this quantity.
Depending on the origin of the order, the applicable quantity is:
•   Sales order quantity
•   Purchase order quantity (the delivered quantity)
•   Production order quantity (BAAN Manufacturing)
•   Production batch quantity (BAAN Process)
2b.   SAMPLE SIZE
The sample size is the total quantity of samples that are to be tested of the order
quantity, expressed in the unit of the sample size.
The sample size can be entered as a figure or as a percentage of either the order
quantity or the frequency.
2c.   SAMPLE QUANTITY
The actual quantity which is drawn from the total quantity. Each sample quantity can be
spit up into smaller parts or test quantities.
2d.   TEST QUANTITY
The test quantity is a part, an exact factor of the sample size, which is tested each
time, and is expressed in the same unit as the sample size. For each test quantity, the
result of the test can be entered in session "Enter Test Data (tcqms1115m000)".
For further information, see keyword(s)
•   Samples
3.   EXAMPLE
 Inspection Order Quantity : 1000 pieces
 Test Type   Single Sampling
 Percentage [TF@tcqms100.ps:s50%
 Sample Size [TF@tcqms100.s:m500 pieces
 (1000 * 50% = 500)

For this sample size, 3 samples are drawn:

Sample	Quantity	Quantity
1	50 pieces	200 pieces
2	50 pieces	200 pieces
3	50 pieces	100 pieces
		+

	Total	500 pieces

Test Results:

Sample	Serial Number	Result
1	1	Good
1	2	Bad
1	3	Good
1	4	Good
2	1	Good

```
|        |        |        |                    |
|   2    |   2    | Bad    |                    |
|        |        |        |                    |
|   2    |   3    | Good   |                    |
|        |        |        |                    |
|   2    |   4    | Good   |                    |
|        |        |        |                    |
|   3    |   5    | Good   |                    |
|        |        |        |                    |
|   3    |   6    | Bad    |                    |
|        |        |        |                    |
+-----------------------------------------------+
```

The sample quantity is 200 and the test quantity is 50. The test is
performed 4 times on the sample and the test data is entered for 4
results.

1.49 Using Algorithms (tcqms00020-sf0010)

CONTENTS

1.   Defining Algorithms
1a.   Characteristics
1b.   Variables
1c.   Algorithms
1d.   Units
2.   Using Algorithm Characteristics
2a.   Inspection Orders
2b.   Evaluating Algorithms

1.   DEFINING ALGORITHMS
1a.   CHARACTERISTICS
In session "Maintain Characteristics (tcqms0101m000)", the characteristics which are used
in algorithms are defined.
A characteristic can have the following methods:
•   Fixed
•   Variable
Obviously, a characteristic of type "Option" cannot be used in algorithms. All other
characteristics can be used as a fixed or variable figure in the algorithm.

1b. VARIABLES
In session "Maintain Algorithm Variables (tcqms0123m000)", all variable codes are
defined. These short codes are used in the expression of the algorithms. Variables can
be:
•   a fixed characteristic
•   a variable characteristic
The codes entered in this session can be used for different variables in algorithms.

1c. ALGORITMHS
The definition of algorithms comprises the following steps:
•   Create and/or modify the general data of an algorithm;
•   Use session "Maintain Variables by Algorithm (tcqms0122s000)" to assign
characteristics to the variables for this algorithm;
•   Enter the expression for this algorithm, using the defined variables. For the
syntax of expressions, see field "Expression".

1d. UNITS
When an algorithm is inserted, the units of the algorithm and the related characteristics
are checked since both units must have the same physical quantity. The system will not
check whether the correct conversion factors are used.
For further information, see method(s) •   "Units and Quantities in QMS".

2.   USING ALGORITHM CHARACTERISTICS
2a. INSPECTION ORDERS
When an inspection order line is added in "Maintain Inspection Order Lines
(tcqms1101s000)", the algorithm is also inserted for algorithm characteristics.

2b. EVALUATING ALGORITHMS
Test results are entered by means of the sessions:
•   Enter Test Data (tcqms1115m000)
•   Complete Inspection Orders Collectively (tcqms1202m000)
The result of the calculation of the expression of the algorithm depends on the value of
the variables measured. If all the variables of the sample that are used in the
expression are known, the system can calculate the expression.

1.50 Using Destructive Tests (tcqms00030-sf0010)
Using destructive tests for different test types:

A quality ID is invalid if the quality ID has a destructive test and QMS is not "Only recommended". Only one "Test Type" can have destructive tests. Each "Test Group" can have more than one destructive test. If a "Test Group" has a destructive test, it is mandatory to specify the sample percentage.

Single Sampling If a "Test Group" with "Single Sampling" has a destructive test, another "Test Group" with "Single Sampling" can only have a destructive test if the total sample percentage does not exceed 100%.

Continuous Sampling Per quality ID, it is allowed to have only one "Test Group" with "Continuous Sampling". This "Test Group" can only have destructive tests if there are no other test groups with destructive tests.

100 % Per quality ID, it is allowed to have only one Test Group with "100 %". This "Test Group" can only have destructive tests if there are no other test groups with destructive tests.

1.51 Using Destructive Tests (tcqms00050-sf0030)

Using destructive tests for different test types:

If an inspection order is not "Only Recommended", it is not allowed to have a destructive test for the inspection order. Only one "Test Type" can have destructive tests. Each inspection order can have more destructive tests. If an inspection order has a destructive test, it is mandatory to specify the sample percentage.

The destroyed quantity does not have any impact on the accepted or rejected quantities. The system only calculates the quantity which is destroyed according to the test.

Single Sampling If an inspection order with "Single Sampling" has a destructive test, another inspection order with "Single Sampling" can only have a destructive test if the total sample percentage does not exceed 100%.

Continuous Sampling Per quality ID, it is only allowed to have one inspection order with "Continuous Sampling". This inspection order can have destructive tests if there are no other inspection orders with destructive tests.

100 % Per quality ID, it is only allowed to have one inspection order with "100 %". This inspection order can have destructive tests if there are no other inspection orders with destructive tests.

1.52 Using Destructive Tests (tcqms00070-sf0010)

Using destructive tests for different test types:

If QMS is not "Only Recommended" for this order, it is not allowed to have a destructive test. Only one "Test Type" can have destructive tests. Each "Sequence" can have more than one destructive test. If a Sequence has a destructive test, it is mandatory to specify the sample percentage.

Single Sampling If a "Sequence" with "Single Sampling" has a destructive test, another "Sequence" with "Single Sampling" can only have a destructive test if the total sample percentage does not exceed 100%.

Continuous Sampling Per quality ID, it is only allowed to have one "Sequence" with "Continuous Sampling". This "Sequence" can only have destructive tests if there are no other sequences with destructive tests.

100 % Per quality ID, it is only allowed to have one "Sequence" with "100 %". This "Sequence" can only have destructive tests if there are no other sequences with destructive tests.

www.ingramcontent.com/pod-product-compliance
Lightning Source LLC
Chambersburg PA
CBHW082107070326
40689CB00052B/3734